W9-AOE-741

THE
CAMBRIDGE EDITION OF
THE LETTERS AND WORKS OF
D. H. LAWRENCE

THE WORKS OF D. H. LAWRENCE

LATE ESSAYS AND ARTICLES

D. H. LAWRENCE

EDITED BY
JAMES T. BOULTON

PUBLISHED BY THE PRESS SYNDICATE OF THE UNIVERSITY OF CAMBRIDGE
The Pitt Building, Trumpington Street, Cambridge, United Kingdom

CAMBRIDGE UNIVERSITY PRESS
The Edinburgh Building, Cambridge CB2 2RU, UK
40 West 20th Street, New York, NY 10011-4211, USA
477 Williamstown Road, Port Melbourne, VIC 3207, Australia
Ruiz de Alarcón 13, 28014 Madrid, Spain
Dock House, The Waterfront, Cape Town 8001, South Africa

http://www.cambridge.org

First published 2004

Printed in the United Kingdom at the University Press, Cambridge

Typeface Ehrhardt 10/12 pt *System* LaTeX 2ε [TB]

A catalogue record for this book is available from the British Library

ISBN 0 521 58431 0 hardback

CONTENTS

General editor's preface *page* vii
Acknowledgements ix
Prefatory note x
Chronology xi
Cue-titles xvi
Introduction xix
Lawrence: journalist and essayist xix
Reception xxxiv

LATE ESSAYS AND ARTICLES 1

Note on the texts 3
Mercury 7
[Return to Bestwood] 13
Getting On 25
Which Class I Belong To 33
Making Love to Music 41
[Autobiographical Fragment] ('[Newthorpe in 2927]') 49
The "Jeune Fille" Wants to Know (When She Asks 'Why?') 69
Laura Philippine 75
That Women Know Best (Women Always Know Best) 81
All There 86
Thinking about Oneself 90
Insouciance (Over-Earnest Ladies) 94
Master in his Own House (Deserted Battlefields) 98
Matriarchy (— And If Women *Were* Supreme. . .) 102
Ownership 107
Autobiography 111
Women Are So Cocksure 115
Why I don't Like Living in London (Dull London!) 119
Cocksure Women and Hen-sure Men 123

Hymns in a Man's Life 128
Red Trousers (Oh! for a New Crusade) 135
Is England Still a Man's Country 139
Sex Appeal (Sex Locked Out) 143
Do Women Change (Women Don't Change) 149
Enslaved by Civilisation (The Manufacture of Good Little Boys) 155
Give Her a Pattern (Woman in Man's Image) 160
Introduction to Pictures 166
Myself Revealed (Autobiographical Sketch) 175
Introduction to These Paintings 182
The State of Funk 218
Making Pictures 225
Pornography and Obscenity 233
Pictures on the Wall (dead pictures on the walls) 254
The Risen Lord 265
Men Must Work and Women as Well (Men and Women) 274
Nottingham and the Mining Countryside 285
We Need One Another 295
The Real Thing 303
Nobody Loves Me 311

Appendixes 321
I Early draft of 'The "Jeune Fille" Wants to Know' 321
II *Vanity Fair* version of 'Do Women Change' 327
III 'Mushrooms': an autobiographical fragment 333

Explanatory notes 337

Textual apparatus 377
Line-end hyphenation 424

A note on pounds, shillings and pence 425

GENERAL EDITOR'S PREFACE

D. H. Lawrence is one of the great writers of the twentieth century – yet the texts of his writings, whether published during his lifetime or since, are, for the most part, textually corrupt. The extent of the corruption is remarkable; it can derive from every stage of composition and publication. We know from study of his MSS that Lawrence was a careful writer, though not rigidly consistent in matters of minor convention. We know also that he revised at every possible stage. Yet he rarely if ever compared one stage with the previous one, and overlooked the errors of typists or copyists. He was forced to accept, as most authors are, the often stringent house-styling of his printers, which overrode his punctuation and even his sentence-structure and paragraphing. He sometimes overlooked plausible printing errors. More important, as a professional author living by his pen, he had to accept, with more or less good will, stringent editing by a publisher's reader in his early days, and at all times the results of his publishers' timidity. So the fear of Grundyish disapproval, or actual legal action, led to bowdlerisation or censorship from the very beginning of his career. Threats of libel suits produced other changes. Sometimes a publisher made more changes than he admitted to Lawrence. On a number of occasions in dealing with American and British publishers Lawrence produced texts for both which were not identical. Then there were extraordinary lapses like the occasion when a typist turned over two pages of MS at once, and the result happened to make sense. This whole story can be reconstructed from the introductions to the volumes in this edition; cumulatively they will form a history of Lawrence's writing career.

The Cambridge edition aims to provide texts which are as close as can now be determined to those he would have wished to see printed. They have been established by a rigorous collation of extant manuscripts and typescripts, proofs and early printed versions; they restore the words, sentences, even whole pages omitted or falsified by editors or compositors; they are freed from printing-house conventions which were imposed on Lawrence's style; and interference on the part of frightened publishers has been eliminated. Far from doing violence to the texts Lawrence would have wished to see published, editorial intervention is essential to recover them. Though we have to accept that some cannot now be recovered in their entirety because early states have not survived, we must be glad that so much evidence remains. Paradoxical as it may seem, the outcome of this recension will be texts which differ, often radically and certainly frequently, from those seen by the author himself.

Editors have adopted the principle that the most authoritative form of the text is to be followed, even if this leads sometimes to a 'spoken' or a 'manuscript' rather than a 'printed' style. We have not wanted to strip off one house-styling in order to impose another. Editorial discretion has been allowed in order to regularise Lawrence's sometimes wayward spelling and punctuation in accordance with his most frequent practice in a particular text. A detailed record of these and other decisions on textual matters, together with the evidence on which they are based, will be found in the textual apparatus which records variant readings in manuscripts, typescripts and proofs; and printed variants in forms of the text published in Lawrence's lifetime. We do not record posthumous corruptions, except where first publication was posthumous. Significant MS readings may be found in the occasional explanatory note.

In each volume, the editor's introduction relates the contents to Lawrence's life and to his other writings; it gives the history of composition of the text in some detail, for its intrinsic interest, and because this history is essential to the statement of editorial principles followed. It provides an account of publication and reception which will be found to contain a good deal of hitherto unknown information. Where appropriate, appendixes make available extended draft manuscript readings of significance, or important material, sometimes unpublished, associated with a particular work.

Though Lawrence is a twentieth-century writer and in many respects remains our contemporary, the idiom of his day is not invariably intelligible now, especially to the many readers who are not native speakers of British English. His use of dialect is another difficulty, and further barriers to full understanding are created by now obscure literary, historical, political or other references and allusions. On these occasions explanatory notes are supplied by the editor; it is assumed that the reader has access to a good general dictionary and that the editor need not gloss words or expressions that may be found in it. Where Lawrence's letters are quoted in editorial matter, the reader should assume that his manuscript is alone the source of eccentricities of phrase or spelling.

ACKNOWLEDGEMENTS

The editor of diverse material such as is collected in this volume incurs many debts to generous individuals and university libraries for copies of manuscripts, typescripts and publications, information and general or particularised guidance. The names of institutions will be found in the list of cue-titles below. Individuals to whom I am indebted include: Harry Barnwell, Anthony Bliss, Derek Britton, Michael Butler, the staff of the Eastwood Public Library, David Ellis, Gillian M. Evans, Ron Faulkes, Meraud Grant Ferguson, J. E. A. Field, Michel Fuchs, Vincent Giroud, James Hamilton, Cathy Henderson, Rosemary Howard, Christa Jansohn, Dorothy Johnston, David Kessler, David Kohl, Joan Leake, Ian Ledsham, John Martin, Dieter Mehl, Bernadette Paton, Emma Peers, Gerald Pollinger, Paul Poplawski, Barbara Smith-Laborde, Aidan Turner-Bishop, Richard Verdi, Richard Watson, the Wilcox family, the late David Wishart, Frances Young. I am grateful to Leigh Mueller for her rigorous sub-editing of my text. Andrew Brown and Linda Bree at Cambridge University Press have been an unfailing source of support and encouragement; Michael Black, the late Warren Roberts, Lindeth Vasey and John Worthen deserve special gratitude for sustained friendship and scholarly assistance during the preparation of this volume in particular and throughout the Lawrentian enterprise.

PREFATORY NOTE

The purpose of *Late Essays and Articles* is to bring together Lawrence's major essays such as the 'Introduction to These Paintings', *Pornography and Obscenity*, and his autobiographical pieces (two of which were hitherto unpublished) with the contents of the posthumous volume, *Assorted Articles* (except for 'On Being a Man' and 'On Human Destiny' collected elsewhere). The essays and articles – written during the period 1926–9 – are ordered chronologically according to the dates of composition which are either confidently known or reliably conjectured. Each is preceded by an account of the circumstances in which it was written and published.

Many of the articles which were published in newspapers or magazines appeared under titles manufactured by editors invariably without reference to Lawrence himself. The titles used here are exclusively those found on his manuscripts or implicitly accepted by him at a later (usually typescript or proof) stage. The alternative title invented editorially is shown in round brackets after Lawrence's own, in the list of 'Contents'; when an article was published under more than one alternative title, the one first used is given. Where Lawrence provided no title, the one generally accepted appears in square brackets.

J. T. B.

CHRONOLOGY

11 September 1885	DHL born in Eastwood, Nottinghamshire
September 1898–July 1901	Pupil at Nottingham High School
1902–1908	Pupil teacher; student at University College, Nottingham
7 December 1907	First publication: 'A Prelude', in *Nottinghamshire Guardian*
October 1908	Appointed as teacher at Davidson Road School, Croydon
November 1909	Publishes five poems in *English Review*
3 December 1910	Engagement to Louie Burrows; broken off on 4 February 1912
9 December 1910	Death of his mother, Lydia Lawrence
19 January 1911	*The White Peacock* published in New York (20 January in London)
19 November 1911	DHL ill with pneumonia; resigns his teaching post on 28 February 1912
March 1912	Meets Frieda Weekley; they leave for Germany on 3 May
23 May 1912	*The Trespasser*
September 1912–March 1913	At Gargnano, Lago di Garda, Italy
February 1913	*Love Poems and Others*
29 May 1913	*Sons and Lovers*
June–August 1913	DHL in England
August 1913–June 1914	In Germany, Switzerland and Italy
July 1914–December 1915	In London, Buckinghamshire and Sussex
13 July 1914	Marries Frieda Weekley in London
26 November 1914	*The Prussian Officer and Other Stories*
30 September 1915	*The Rainbow*; suppressed by court order on 13 November
June 1916	*Twilight in Italy*
July 1916	*Amores*
15 October 1917	After twenty-one months' residence in Cornwall, DHL ordered to leave by military authorities
October 1917–November 1919	In London, Berkshire and Derbyshire
26 November 1917	*Look! We Have Come Through!*
October 1918	*New Poems*

November 1919–February 1922	To Italy, then Capri and Sicily
20 November 1919	*Bay*
9 November 1920	Private publication of *Women in Love* (New York)
25 November 1920	*The Lost Girl*
10 May 1921	*Psychoanalysis and the Unconscious* (New York)
12 December 1921	*Sea and Sardinia* (New York)
March–August 1922	DHL in Ceylon and Australia
14 April 1922	*Aaron's Rod* (New York)
September 1922–March 1923	In New Mexico
23 October 1922	*Fantasia of the Unconscious* (New York)
24 October 1922	*England, My England* (New York)
March 1923	*The Ladybird, The Fox, The Captain's Doll*
March–November 1923	In Mexico and USA
27 August 1923	*Studies in Classic American Literature* (New York)
September 1923	*Kangaroo*
9 October 1923	*Birds, Beasts and Flowers* (New York)
December 1923–March 1924	DHL in England, France and Germany
March 1924–September 1925	In New Mexico and Mexico
28 August 1924	*The Boy in the Bush* (with Mollie Skinner)
10 September 1924	Death of his father, Arthur John Lawrence
14 May 1925	*St. Mawr together with The Princess*
September 1925–April 1926	DHL in England and, mainly, in Italy
7 December 1925	*Reflections on the Death of a Porcupine* (Philadelphia)
21 January 1926	*The Plumed Serpent*
30 April 1926	Coal strike begins
6 May 1926–10 June 1928	The Lawrences' home is Villa Mirenda, San Paolo, near Florence
13–29 July 1926	DHL visits Frieda's mother in Baden-Baden
c. 29 July 1926	Writes 'Mercury'
14–16 September 1926	Stays with sister Ada in Ripley, Derbyshire, and makes final visit to Eastwood
mid-late October 1926	Writes '[Return to Bestwood]'
19 November 1926	Coal strike ends
25–30 November 1926	DHL finishes first version of *Lady Chatterley's Lover*
c. 1 December 1926–25 February 1927	Writing second version of *Lady Chatterley's Lover*
c. 5–8 January 1927	Writes 'Getting On'
mid-April 1927	Writes 'Which Class I Belong To'
26 April 1927	Sends 'Making Love to Music' to Nancy Pearn
June 1927	*Mornings in Mexico* published by Secker in London (5 August in USA)

8 June 1927	DHL visits the Uffizi with Christine and Mary Christine Hughes
5–30 August 1927	In Villach, Austria
31 August–4 October 1927	At Villa Jaffe, Irschenhausen
ante 26 September 1927	Nancy Pearn and friend stay two days at Villa Mirenda
4–18 October 1927	DHL at Baden-Baden, Milan and Mirenda
c. 26–30 October 1927	Writes '[Autobiographical Fragment]' probably intended for Guiseppe Orioli's *Intimate Series*
8 December 1927–January 1928	Writing third version of *Lady Chatterley's Lover*
20 January–6 March 1928	At Chateau Beau Site, Les Diablerets, Switzerland
February 1928	*Cavalleria Rusticana and Other Stories* published in England; *The Escaped Cock* in *Forum* (USA)
27 March 1928	Negotiations begin with Dorothy Warren which lead to exhibition of paintings in 1929
25 April 1928	DHL invited to write for London *Evening News*
8 May 1928	'The "Jeune Fille" Wants to Know' in *Evening News* as 'When She Asks Why'
24 May 1928	*The Woman Who Rode Away* published by Secker (on 25 May in USA)
June? 1928	Writes 'Thinking About Oneself'
11–15 June 1928	DHL in France
17 June–6 July 1928	At Grand Hotel, Chexbres, Switzerland
July 1928	*Lady Chatterley's Lover* published by Orioli in Florence
7 July 1928	'Laura Philippine' in *T. P.'s and Cassell's Weekly*
9 July–18 September 1928	DHL in chalet, Kesselmatte, near Gsteig, Switzerland
ante 12 July 1928	Writes 'Ownership'
12 July 1928	'Insouciance' in *Evening News*, entitled 'Over-Earnest Ladies'
18 July 1928	DHL writes 'Autobiography' for French publisher
2 August 1928	'Master in his Own House' in *Evening News*
c. 11–16 August 1928	DHL writes 'Women Are So Cocksure'
September 1928	*Collected Poems* (London; July 1929 in USA)
3 September 1928	'Why I don't Like Living in London' in *Evening News* as 'Dull London!'
18 September–1 October 1928	DHL in Lichtental, Baden-Baden

27 September 1928	'Red Trousers' in *Evening News* as 'Oh! for a New Crusade'
2–15 October 1928	DHL at Grand Hotel, Le Lavandou, France
5 October 1928	'Matriarchy' in *Evening News* as '—And If Women *Were* Supreme . . . '
13 October 1928	'Hymns in a Man's Life' in *Evening News*
15 October–17 November 1928	DHL at Le Vigie, Ile de Port-Cros
17 November 1928–11 March 1929	At Hotel Beau Rivage, Bandol
25 November 1928	'Sex Appeal' in *Sunday Dispatch* as 'Sex Locked Out'
29 November 1928	'Is England Still *A Man's* Country?' in *Daily Express*; 'That Women Know Best' in *Daily Chronicle* as 'Women Always Know Best'
14–21 December 1928	DHL writes 'Introduction to Pictures'
January 1929	'Cocksure Women and Hen-sure Men' in *Forum*
18 January 1929	Police seize copies of *Lady Chatterley's Lover*; *Pansies* typescript seized on 23 January
17 February 1929	'Myself Revealed' in *Sunday Dispatch*
ante 23 February 1929	DHL writes 'The State of Funk'
12 March–7 April 1929	In Paris and environs
7–13? April 1929	Travels to Barcelona
17 April–18 June 1929	In Mallorca
28 April 1929	'Do Women Change' in *Sunday Dispatch* as 'Women Don't Change'
May 1929	'Give Her a Pattern' in *Vanity Fair* (New York) as 'Woman in Man's Image'
June 1929	*The Paintings of D. H. Lawrence* published with 'Introduction to These Paintings'
22 June 1929	DHL at Forte dei Marmi, Italy; then to Florence, 6–16 July
July 1929	'Making Pictures' in *Studio,* and in *Creative Art* (USA); Secker publishes *Pansies*
5 July 1929	Police raid Warren Gallery exhibition of DHL's paintings
16 July–25 August 1929	DHL in Baden-Baden and nearby
11 August 1929	Celebration of Frieda's fiftieth birthday
26 August–18 September 1929	DHL at Rottach in Austria
23 September 1929–6 February 1930	At Hotel Beau Rivage, then Villa Beau Soleil, in Bandol
September 1929	'Pornography and Obscenity' in July–September issue of *This Quarter* (Paris); 'Enslaved by Civilisation' in *Vanity Fair* (New York) as 'The Manufacture of Good Little Boys'

3 October 1929	'The Risen Lord' in *Everyman*
November 1929	'Men Must Work and Women as Well' in *Star Review* as 'Men and Women'
14 November 1929	*Pornography and Obscenity* in *Criterion Miscellany*
December 1929	'Pictures on the Wall' as 'dead pictures on the walls' in *Vanity Fair* (New York)
c. 28 December 1929	DHL sends text for *Assorted Articles* to Pollinger
6 February–1 March 1930	In sanatorium, 'Ad Astra', Vence
2 March 1930	Lawrence dies in Villa Robermond, Vence
April 1930	*Assorted Articles* published in London (11 April in USA)
May 1930	'We Need One Another' in *Scribner's Magazine* (USA)
June 1930	'The Real Thing' in *Scribner's Magazine*
June–August 1930	'Nottingham and the Mining Countryside' in *New Adelphi*
July 1930	'Nobody Loves Me' in *Life and Letters*
19 October 1936	*Phoenix* published in USA (November 1936 in England)

CUE-TITLES

A. Manuscript and typescript locations

HU	Harvard University
StaU	Stanford University
UCB	University of California at Berkeley
UCin	University of Cincinnati
UCLA	University of California at Los Angeles
UN	University of Nottingham
UT	University of Texas at Austin
YU	Yale University, Beinecke Rare Book and Manuscript Library

B. Printed Works

(The place of publication, here and throughout, is London unless otherwise stated.)

Brewster	Earl and Achsah Brewster. *D. H. Lawrence: Reminiscences and Correspondence.* Secker, 1934.
Draper	R. P. Draper, ed. *D. H. Lawrence: The Critical Heritage.* Routledge & Kegan Paul, 1970.
Early Years	John Worthen. *D. H. Lawrence: The Early Years*, 1885–1912. Cambridge: Cambridge University Press, 1991.
Letters, ii.	George J. Zytaruk and James T. Boulton, eds. *The Letters of D. H. Lawrence*. Volume II, June 1913–October 1916. Cambridge: Cambridge University Press, 1981.
Letters, v.	James T. Boulton and Lindeth Vasey, eds. *The Letters of D. H. Lawrence*. Volume V, March 1924–March 1927. Cambridge: Cambridge University Press, 1989.
Letters, vi.	James T. Boulton and Margaret H. Boulton, with Gerald M. Lacy, eds. *The Letters of D. H. Lawrence*. Volume VI, March 1927–November 1928. Cambridge: Cambridge University Press, 1991.

Letters, vii.	Keith Sagar and James T. Boulton, eds. *The Letters of D. H. Lawrence*. Volume VII, November 1928–February 1930. Cambridge: Cambridge University Press, 1993.
Letters, viii.	James T. Boulton, ed. *The Letters of D. H. Lawrence*. Volume VIII, Uncollected Letters and General Index. Cambridge: Cambridge University Press, 2000.
Nehls	Edward Nehls, ed. *D. H. Lawrence: A Composite Biography*. 3 volumes. Madison: University of Wisconsin Press, 1957–9.
OED2	J. A. Simpson and E. S. C. Weiner, eds. *The Oxford English Dictionary*. 2nd edn. Oxford: Clarendon Press, 1989.
Paintings	*The Paintings of D. H. Lawrence*. Mandrake Press, 1929.
Phoenix	Edward McDonald, ed. *Phoenix: The Posthumous Papers of D. H. Lawrence*. Heinemann, 1936.
Phoenix II	Warren Roberts and Harry T. Moore, eds. *Phoenix II: Uncollected, Unpublished and Other Prose Works by D. H. Lawrence*. Heinemann, 1968.
Powell	*The Manuscripts of D. H. Lawrence*. Los Angeles: The Public Library, 1937.
Roberts	Warren Roberts and Paul Poplawski. *A Bibliography of D. H. Lawrence*. 3rd edn. Cambridge: Cambridge University Press, 2001.
Sons and Lovers	D. H. Lawrence. *Sons and Lovers*. Ed. Helen Baron and Carl Baron. Cambridge: Cambridge University Press, 1992.
Tedlock	E. W. Tedlock. *The Frieda Lawrence Collection of D. H. Lawrence Manuscripts: A Descriptive Bibliography*. Albuquerque: University of New Mexico, 1948.

INTRODUCTION

Lawrence: journalist and essayist

Lawrence's relationship with 'journalism' was always problematic. In 1916 he had insisted that Hardy 'is our last great writer. Bennett is only a journalist in comparison . . . he is really a journalist, a time-server' (*Letters*, viii. 18–19). Though Lawrence was repeatedly censorious about the novelist Arnold Bennett, despising what he regarded as his 'resignation' in the face of human misery (i. 459), describing him as a 'pig in clover' (vi. 342) and 'a cad' (viii. 41), the derogatory application of the words 'journalist' and 'journalism' to indicate a non-creative form of literary activity was not confined to Bennett. Lawrence dismissed Gilbert Cannan's novel *Mendel*, for example, as 'journalism: statement without creation', 'a piece of journalism, absolutely without spark of creative fire' (iii. 35, 50). A fledgeling American novelist, Kyle Crichton, was told in 1925 that he was 'too journalistic, too much concerned with facts' and failing to explore 'the *human inside*' of his characters (v. 293). Furthermore Lawrence attacked Crichton's native land as generally responsible for what had gone wrong:

> it sees no value in the really creative effort, whereas it esteems, more highly than any other country, the journalistic effort: it loves a thrill or a sensation, but loathes to be in any way *moved*, inwardly affected so that a new vital adjustment is necessary . . . it seems to me impossible almost, to be a purely creative writer in America: everybody compromises with journalism and commerce. (v. 307–8)

So – uncreative, concerned almost exclusively with facts and the external appearance of diurnal existence, devoted to arousing a transient superficial excitement but no permanent enlargement of the human consciousness, and having a close association with financial reward: these presumptions about journalism habitually underpinned Lawrence's observations about other writers. As he embarked on his own late career as a writer for the public press he may have remembered his envy in 1916 of the ease with which John Middleton Murry seemed to 'make quite a lot by his journalism' when, in 1928, he told Martin Secker that writing 'little articles for the newspapers . . . seems *far* the best way of making money' (ii. 539, vii. 41). And, in view of the opening quotation, perhaps the final irony is to find Arnold Bennett reviewing Lawrence's posthumous *Assorted Articles* in April 1930 and declaring that 'Despite a certain occasional roughness in the writing of them, the articles might well serve as models for young journalists – also for old journalists . . . Lawrence was a first-rate journalist.'[1]

Lawrence had always been a keen reader of the press but his principal means of publishing in it during the last four years of his life was through the London office of his literary agent, Curtis Brown. There, the person responsible for periodical publications was Nancy Pearn, the 'golden . . . magazine girl' as Lawrence described her (vi. 459). It was she who handled the placing of all his articles, negotiating his fees with editors – applying pressure to obtain higher payment whenever possible – and either warning or flattering Lawrence himself in order to improve or sustain contacts with influential editors. She was not invariably successful. On 12 April 1927, for example, when Lawrence appeared to despair of making an adequate income from writing novels, he told her hopefully: 'I could probably live by little things. I mean in magazines' (vi. 29). Two weeks later he sent her 'a little thing post haste' with the instruction: 'If you don't like it, don't bother about it' (vi. 40). Whether or not Nancy Pearn liked it, 'Making Love to Music' failed to find a publisher in Lawrence's lifetime: living from 'little things' was not perhaps as easy as he imagined. The warning she gave on 25 April 1927 in response to his request for advice about the wisdom of publishing *Lady Chatterley's Lover* – that it could be 'dangerous financially speaking' to the magazine market (vi. 29 n. 5) – would have extra piquancy. Thus, when he disregarded her advice and, a year later, told her that he would publish his ' "shocking" novel [of which] everybody will disapprove – you certainly will' (vi. 347), Nancy Pearn's reaction on 13 April 1928 was predictable: 'let's hope the news of it won't reach any of the recently converted editors whose allegiance would thereby be made to tremble!'[2]

Among those most likely 'converted' at least partly by her influence, was Arthur E. Olley, literary editor of the London *Evening News*, a daily paper aimed at a wide readership and carrying some amusing general articles. As if to confirm Nancy Pearn's sense of the importance of journalism to a writer who, a few months earlier, had complained about poverty – managing 'to scramble through, but no more' (vi. 90) – Olley wrote to Lawrence (through Nancy Pearn) on 25 April 1928, inviting him to contribute an article to the *News*. At once, the very next day, she seized the opportunity to emphasise the

[1] Draper 340.

[2] In the Introduction and elsewhere, quotations from the letters to DHL from Nancy Pearn (1892–1950) and Laurence Pollinger (1898–1976) – both writing from the London office of DHL's literary agent, Curtis Brown – are taken from typed carbon copies held at UT.

significance of Olley's initiative:

Will you, if you can only make out what the editor really wants, write the article he suggests ... the publicity secured through the 'Evening News' is far from negligible, sometimes having immediate results in the way of increasing book sales. For this reason I have been looking forward to the opening up of some of these new newspaper markets for you – if only you can *bear* to tackle just those sorts of subjects which the Press adores.

Lawrence responded with alacrity and on 8 May the *Evening News* published his article, but under the title 'When She Asks "Why?"' whereas the typescript submitted to Olley was entitled 'The Bogey Between the Generations'.[3] There had been no consultation between writer and editor about the change, but Lawrence seemed quite unmoved. When, having seen the piece in print, he wrote to Nancy Pearn, he made no protest – not even a comment – about the new title (vi. 400–1). Reflected here is the difference he maintained between 'journalism' and 'creative writing': whereas he resisted – often strenuously – editorial interference in the latter, for the most part he accepted it without demur in the former. When, for example, in 1924 an editor wanted to shorten the novella 'The Woman Who Rode Away', Lawrence told Nancy Pearn: 'I don't quite fancy having my stories cut: they aren't like articles' (v. 109). The distinction invoked here was consistently upheld. Yet it would be wrong to infer from this that he was cavalier about style and language when he wrote as an essayist or journalist. His manuscripts frequently reveal considerable rewriting, interlinear additions, the weeding out of repeated words or phrases, and a conscious (usually successful) attempt to meet an editor's request for a specific number of words. Indeed, responding to the special requirements of his rôle, Lawrence was as meticulous in 'journalism' as in 'creative writing'.[4]

Nancy Pearn was understandably elated by Olley's enthusiasm for his new contributor: 'You've gone and been and hit it – meaning the journalistic market – for Mr Olley says he thinks "THE BOGEY BETWEEN THE GENERATIONS" quite suitable for his stupendous paper.' She added: 'If this does result in your finding that flashes of insight produce suggestions for similar articles you have only to let me know and I shall seek where to plant them to best advantage. Just jot them down with a few words as to the proposed line of development.'

Lawrence rejected the proposal for 'jotting down' titles or suggestions – 'it's a sure way of making me *not* write 'em' (vi. 401); he preferred to receive

3 DHL's adopted title was 'The "Jeune Fille" Wants to Know'.

4 Substantial passages of revision in DHL's manuscripts, to be found in the Explanatory Notes, provide evidence of his search for precision and accuracy; it was not feasible to record the innumerable small-scale examples of the same characteristic.

specified topics. Nevertheless by 13 May he had written his article, 'Laura Philippine', which, he told Nancy Pearn, 'if it won't do for the Olley man, it may for somebody else' (vi. 400–1). Most likely she trusted her own judgement and offered it to the 'middlebrow' periodical *T. P.'s & Cassell's Weekly*, where it appeared on 7 July. This interpretation seems borne out by her next letter to Lawrence, on 17 May:

Your appearance in the 'Evening News' raises terrific questions for discussion: the editor having been keen enough on the first one to suggest the possibility of arranging with you for four or six in the near future on agreed subjects, during which time he would not want you to write for any other paper. His conditions seem to call for a rise in fee, especially as I have been having other enquiries about you from newspaper editors – but it is not certain that he will be willing to go higher than the Ten Guineas just at present.

Nancy Pearn considered this 'quite a good price' though her estimate of Lawrence's worth became clear as she went on:

Then we have the 'Daily Chronicle' which is (and this is confidential, oh most confidential, for the moment in case some other paper should bag the idea!) planning a series by men under the magnificent title 'WHAT WOMEN HAVE TAUGHT ME'. Would you do them about a thousand words – we could probably get Fifteen Guineas – remembering, as you so cleverly did in the E[vening] N[ews] article, that you were writing for the G[reat] B[ritish] P[ublic] on this occasion.

This all looks like quite a coming boom in D. H. L. articles.

Having been given a specific topic and with the possibility of a handsome fee from a national newspaper, Lawrence responded in four days to the *Daily Chronicle*'s proposal, sending his article 'That Women Know Best' to Nancy Pearn on 21 May. He felt that it might be 'too much tongue in the cheek' but urged her to 'try it on 'em. As you say, it's fun' (vi. 404). As for Olley's suggestion that Lawrence should write exclusively for him during a period to be agreed, this proved acceptable: 'I suppose it would be only for a short time', Lawrence told Nancy Pearn on 21 May. Indeed he was excited at the prospect of a ready sale for his writing: 'if we can make them go higher than their ten quid, good for us. Perhaps after all the public is not such a dull animal, and would prefer an occasional subtle suave stone to polish its wits against. Let us see!' (vi. 403). Lawrence contracted to produce four articles for the *Evening News*. It was doubtless at least partly for this reason that publication of the article in the *Chronicle* was delayed until 29 November.

Lawrence contemplated writing for Olley with pleasure – 'I find it really rather amusing to write these little articles' (vi. 403) – but in late May and most of June 1928 he was in the process of moving from the Villa Mirenda outside

Florence and travelling to France and Switzerland, as well as reading the proofs, and generally overseeing the production, of *Lady Chatterley's Lover*. Olley had to wait. He expected results from the contract, however. He wrote on 12 June (via Nancy Pearn): 'I am glad to know you will write four further articles for us . . . do you feel inclined to write upon:- 1) Man Must be Master Again and 2) I Do Not Like London Life (and Why).' A third topic was added: 'Women are Cocksure but Never Quite Sure'. Apparently he received no answer. By late June his patience had worn thin. On 27 June Lawrence wrote to Nancy Pearn from Chexbres: 'The Olley man wrote and said could he have one of the four articles this week for the *Evening News*? Naturally it's doubtful if he'll *get* it this week. But I enclose the MS of "Insouciance" – could you have it typed and sent to him at once?' (vi. 438). The article bore no relation to the topics Olley had suggested on 12 June; it originated from a situation Lawrence had witnessed in the Grand Hotel, Chexbres; nevertheless Olley accepted and published it on 12 July, under the title 'Over-Earnest Ladies'. In direct response to the first of Olley's suggestions, Lawrence sent off to Nancy Pearn, on 28 June, his article entitled 'Master in his Own House', published on 2 August. By now he owed two articles to honour his undertaking to Olley. He therefore wrote to Nancy Pearn on 12 July: 'I enclose the other two articles for the *Evening News*. If Mr Olley doesn't like them, let him not print them. One doesn't want to force him against his taste – the latter being a purely mysterious quality' (vi. 460). The manuscripts of 'Matriarchy' and 'Ownership' were enclosed; Olley published the first as '—And If Women *Were* Supreme . . . ' on 5 October but rejected the second which remained unpublished until its inclusion in the posthumous *Assorted Articles* (1930).

Olley remained determined to see the contract fulfilled and wrote again to Nancy Pearn on 11 August enquiring whether Lawrence would write on the second suggestion in his letter of 12 June, and repeating the subject 'Women are Cocksure but Never Quite Sure'. Perhaps stung by the implied reproof, and despite his uncertain health – 'I feel a bit feeble and a poor rag' (vi. 513) – Lawrence replied to Nancy Pearn on 20 August: 'If that Mr Olley would print articles half as fantastic as his own letters, he'd be a gem! – But damn them, they are so *afraid* of their public, they can only balk, balk, balk!// Now let him have "Why I don't like London": and if he's afraid of it, I'll write one, "Why I don't like him"!' (vi. 516). Olley did like it; it appeared in the *News* on 3 September entitled 'Dull London!'

Nancy Pearn added a reminder on 23 August: 'Are you going to do the other article on "Women Are Cocksure . . . " for the "*Evening News*"?' So, with some seeming exasperation, Lawrence replied the next day: 'Here's the article on the "Cocksure Woman". Since he wants a slap at the ladies, he'd better have a little one for the men at the same time . . . He can cut it if he likes – but do keep me a complete copy' (vi. 521). Nancy Pearn acknowledged the arrival of 'Cocksure Women and Hen-sure Men' on 5 September but she must have been embarrassed by Olley's explanation in his letter of the 27th regretting that he could not use it: 'one has to be very careful not to lay a newspaper open to the danger of being lampooned by the vulgar'. He gave Lawrence the opportunity of altering the text but eventually decided that it was not possible to see 'how it could be altered to suit them'. Nancy Pearn kept it (as she told Lawrence on 20 November) 'on the chance of finding another home for it'; she succeeded in placing it with the American periodical, *Forum*, where it appeared in January 1929.

Lawrence's penultimate appearance in the *Evening News* was as the author of a lightweight piece, 'Red Trousers', sent from Gsteig in Switzerland on 13 September (vi. 563). Olley printed it on 27 September under the title, 'Oh! for a New Crusade'.

Lawrence's final contribution to the *Evening News* was an article originally written for a volume in German honouring the physician, poet and novelist, Hans Carossa. Lawrence sent his text to Nancy Pearn on 2 September and suggested that 'somebody might like it in English . . . Do as you like with this English version. If anybody wants it they can cut it if they like – do what they darn well please' (vi. 541). She was delighted to inform him on 11 October that Olley was impressed by the piece and had paid 15 guineas for it. His judgement was sound: 'Hymns in a Man's Life', one of the most vivid and memorable of Lawrence's journalistic writings, was published on 13 October.

Prominence and success in one newspaper inevitably generated interest elsewhere. 'Several papers have been ringing up', Nancy Pearn told Lawrence on 5 September 1928. She assured him in the same letter that 'the BBC is still keen for you to broadcast: especially so since those articles appeared in the "*Evening News*". And with an eye to the main chance she added: 'We have found that broadcasting really is quite a useful and dignified bit of publicity.' Lawrence's reply was decisive: 'the thought of broadcasting makes my blood run cold' (vi. 552). The request from *Film Weekly* in September 1928 for an article 'on the sort of film [Lawrence] would write or produce if there were no censor' also fell on deaf ears: 'I doubt if I could write about my uncensored Film – feel I haven't got one' (vi. 601 and n. 4). Nancy Pearn reminded him on 28 November that 'the "*Film Weekly*" people are keen to get that article from you under some such title as MY UNCENSORED FILM'; she believed Lawrence had agreed to comply if he 'could find enough to say about it'; but he was unmoved and the article was never written.

His customary readiness to satisfy the multitudinous demands made on him as a professional writer is illustrated by Richard Aldington's description of life on the Ile de Port-Cros during the four weeks from mid-October 1928 which he spent with the Lawrences: 'he went tranquilly on with his writing although he was so ill, and was angry and bitter about the attacks on him in England [over *Lady Chatterley's Lover*]. Every morning he sat up in bed, wearing an old hat as protection against an imaginary draught, and produced a short story or one of the little essays of *Assorted Articles*.'[5]

One of these 'little essays' was written for the influential broadsheet owned by Lord Beaverbrook, the *Daily Express*, which sparkled with controversy and was soon to achieve the largest circulation in the world. According to Nancy Pearn on 22 October, its editor was 'aching to know whether England is still a man's country'. In his reply on the 30th Lawrence agreed to 'have a shot' at the topic (vi. 602); a mere four days later he sent the article (vi. 606) and it appeared on 29 November as 'Is England Still *A Man's* Country?'

Also in his letter of 30 October he undertook to contribute to a series on 'What is Sex Appeal?' at the invitation of Bernard Falk, editor of the right-wing *Sunday Dispatch* owned by Viscount Rothermere (vi. 602). Six days later the article entitled by Lawrence 'Sex Appeal' was sent to Nancy Pearn and it appeared on 25 November as 'Sex Locked Out'. With good commercial sense he had 'made it 2000 words so it would do for *Vanity Fair* if they want it' (vi. 606);[6] they did want it and published it in July 1929. For her part, Nancy Pearn was 'tremendously impressed' by the article but even more important – as she told Lawrence on 15 November 1928 – Falk was 'so impressed that he has enthusiastically responded to the hint given him that he should pay more for it' than he first offered, and the price was raised from 15 to 25 guineas. Moreover, he was prepared to consider 'a minimum of six further articles' at the same fee. Nancy Pearn obviously relished the opportunity to add: 'This is all most exciting news to pour into the ear of Mr Olley, the "*Evening News*" being one of the same group of papers as the "Sunday Dispatch".' What prompted this jubilation was probably that Olley had rejected the article 'Do Women Change', which Lawrence sent on 8 November 'for *Evening News* or anybody who wants it' (vi. 610); it was Falk who eventually published it in the *Sunday Dispatch* (in April 1929) with the more assertive title, 'Women Don't Change'.

[5] Nehls, iii. 254.

[6] DHL probably remembered Nancy Pearn's warning on 23 October 1928 that *Vanity Fair* would not consider an article 'that does not run from nineteen hundred to two thousand two hundred words'. This was too long for newspaper editors but he was urged to bear it in mind 'when writing with magazines in view'.

The invitation from Falk that Lawrence should write six further articles for him was apparently not acted upon. However, the *Sunday Dispatch* was the one newspaper in Lawrence's lifetime to publish an avowedly autobiographical article; other essays such as 'Hymns in a Man's Life' or 'Nottingham and the Mining Countryside' contain clear autobiographical elements; but 'Myself Revealed', published on 17 February 1929, was the only fully autobiographical piece to appear in the public press before 1930. It was accompanied by a drawing (based on a photograph of 1915) of the author, by the distinguished portraitist Joseph Simpson. Falk offered to give Lawrence the original of the 'sketch' but was refused in the most genial fashion: 'it will only worry me . . . But do thank Mr Simpson for not making me satanic for once. Even his tragic brow that he gave me was better than the smirking Satanismus I am so used to' (vii. 189).

The *Sunday Dispatch* published nothing more by Lawrence, but a suggestion by Falk for another article led in a different direction: to what Nancy Pearn called 'the magazine market'. In her letter of 15 November 1928 she conveyed Falk's idea that 'an interesting article might be evolved out of your experiences in various parts of the world, and your observations on WHY AND HOW MAN IS BECOMING ENSLAVED BY CIVILISATION'. 'Good-O for the *Sunday Despatch*' was Lawrence's reply on 24 November; his article on the topic was enclosed with the letter (vii. 29). But Falk delayed for over three months; not till 8 April 1929 did Nancy Pearn tell Lawrence that 'the "*Sunday Dispatch*" are glad to have "ENSLAVED BY CIVILISATION", at Twenty-Five Guineas, and intend to get Rebecca West to reply to it'. Nothing came of the idea and in any case Falk had been forestalled by the New York monthly magazine, *Vanity Fair* (later merged into *Vogue*). On 18 March Nancy Pearn took obvious pleasure in writing to Lawrence: '"*Vanity Fair*" are getting terribly attached to you! They have now bought "ENSLAVED BY CIVILISATION" at a Hundred dollars'; they published it in September under the title, 'The Manufacture of Good Little Boys'.

Vanity Fair had in fact been 'attached' to Lawrence for some time. In the past, however – with the sole exception of 'On Being a Man' of which they were the first publishers, in 1924 – they had been content to reprint articles which had first appeared elsewhere. In 1929 there was a seeming change of policy. The article 'Give Her a Pattern', written at the specific request of the *Daily Express* and sent to Nancy Pearn on 9 December 1928 appeared first in *Vanity Fair*: re-titled 'Woman in Man's Image' it was published in the American magazine in May 1929, a month before its appearance in the London newspaper. 'Enslaved by Civilisation' followed in September. Similarly, though the article 'Pictures on the Wall' was the result of a direct approach from the editor of the *Architectural Review*, Hubert de Cronin Hastings, for 'an article on artists and decoration' (vii. 269), it was *Vanity Fair* in which it first appeared (entitled 'dead pictures on the walls'); the American magazine published it in December 1929, the English in February 1930. Indeed, so determined was the American editor Frank Crowninshield, to establish a continuing relationship with Lawrence that – as Nancy Pearn wrote on 23 September 1929 – '"*Vanity Fair*" . . . are keen to discuss a contract for a year [entailing] the delivery of probably one article a month on subjects to be agreed upon, at a sum in the neighbourhood of £40'. Lawrence was prepared to write articles for the magazine but not on such a contractual basis; in October he protested that his 'health went down rather with a slump . . . am feeling feeble' (vii. 512). Crowninshield persisted and offered a contract which did not insist on any specified dates of delivery and guaranteed $150 per article; Lawrence began to waver, agreeing to write a monthly piece and leaving the editor free to refuse it if he so wished, but insisting on a $200 fee (roughly equal to £41). On 4 November he sent three articles – 'We Need One Another', 'The Real Thing' and 'Nobody Loves Me' – written 'with an eye to *Vanity Fair*' but leaving Nancy Pearn to decide whether they were appropriate for the magazine (vii. 554 and n. 2). Whether she submitted them or decided against doing so is not known, but none of them ever appeared in it.[7] Editorial enthusiasm for Lawrence continued, nevertheless. The magazine's managing editor, Donald Freeman, renewed the attempt to secure a contract; his letter, forwarded by Nancy Pearn on 22 November 1929, informed Lawrence that 'Pictures on the Wall' reminded him once again 'how ideal a writer you are for Vanity Fair'. Freeman continued: 'I have asked your agents to submit a contract in our behalf which, although formidable, contains no restrictions that tie and bind uncomfortably. I hope you will want to sign it'. As late as 1 January 1930 Nancy Pearn reported that *Vanity Fair* continued to invite Lawrence to propose titles for articles which might be associated with a contract, but the invitation was too late. He confessed three weeks later: 'I haven't done any more about *Vanity Fair* essays – my health is so tiresome: haven't done anything' (vii. 624).

A considerable amount of Lawrence's energy from December 1928 onwards was devoted to three essays associated with painting, ostensibly at least. The first – 'Introduction to Pictures' – is a curiosity in that he made no reference to it in his letters and it does not once refer to pictures. At the outset he raises – but later deletes – the question 'What is art?' and, in order to answer

7 All were published posthumously: 'We Need One Another' and 'The Real Thing' in *Scribner's Magazine*, May and June 1930 respectively; 'Nobody Loves Me' in *Life and Letters*, July 1930.

it, uses the rest of the essay trying to define the nature of man. Written and abandoned in mid-December 1928, it was probably a first attempt to provide prefatory matter for the volume of Lawrence's *Paintings* which, by that time, he knew would be published by P. R. Stephensen in 1929.[8] The prefatory essay – 'Introduction to These Paintings' – which actually opened the volume was written between late December 1928 and 11 January 1929. It is particularly memorable for Lawrence's strenuous, mocking assault on Roger Fry's doctrine of 'Significant Form' and its eloquent apologia for Cézanne – his realism, success in revealing 'the back of the presented appearance'[9] and unremitting commitment to his art. The essay has little direct relevance to the paintings which it 'introduces', but it is one of Lawrence's major statements on the art of painting; his characteristic energy and imagination give it added distinction. The third essay, 'Making Pictures', was written on hotel notepaper in Barcelona at the instigation of the art magazine, *Studio*. Nancy Pearn acknowledged its arrival on 17 April 1929 and, a week later, informed Lawrence that the 10-guinea fee she had extracted from the *Studio* was 'above their usual rate'. 'Making Pictures' was published in July 1929 and twice reprinted in America: by *Creative Art* in the same month and *Vanity Fair* in August. The sales of the *Paintings* volume doubtless benefited from the resulting publicity.

In mid and late January 1929 two events underlined the threat to a professional writer of exposure to public disapprobation: the seizures by the police of copies of *Lady Chatterley's Lover* and by Customs officials of the typescript of Lawrence's collection of poems, *Pansies*. Official surveillance had compounded the hostile reaction to the novel by many sections of readers and the press. Lawrence's response was to write 'The State of Funk' which opens provocatively: 'What is the matter with the English, that they are so scared of everything? . . . funniest of all, they are scared stiff of the printed word.' It was, he told Nancy Pearn on 23 February, 'more or less stating my position' and could be offered to Bernard Falk at the *Sunday Dispatch* (vii. 188). Her apprehension at the possibility of litigation which might follow is manifest from her reply three days later when she assured Lawrence that she was pondering the most effective way to use the article: 'It may be best to wait a week until the legal side is clarified' (vii. 188 n. 4). She consulted Lawrence's barrister friend, St John Hutchinson – the nature of his advice is unknown, but the article was not published in Lawrence's lifetime. It had to await the volume of *Assorted Articles*.

Nancy Pearn's anxiety and reluctance to take precipitate action seemed to be justified by the prominence given to the seizure of the *Pansies* typescript

[8] See vii. 48–50, 70ff. [9] See below, p. 212.

in the parliamentary debate on 28 February. Its focus was on the censorship of documents regarded by Customs and Home Office officials as 'obscene'. From Lawrence's viewpoint it was therefore propitious that an opportunity should soon occur to publicise his own views on the topic. Edward Titus, the publisher shortly to issue in Paris the unexpurgated 'Popular Edition' of *Lady Chatterley's Lover*, invited him to write an article for the first number of his new journal, *This Quarter*. Despite uncertain health when he arrived in Mallorca on 17 April, Lawrence wrote his 4,000-word article, 'Pornography and Obscenity', which boldly addressed the subject then uppermost in his mind, one also attracting a great deal of public attention. It went to Nancy Pearn for typing on 29 April, was forwarded by her direct to Titus and he published it in September.

Immediately the London publishers Faber & Faber recognised the commercial advantage offered them: they invited Lawrence to write on the same subject for their series of pamphlets with distinctive orange paper wrappers, *Criterion Miscellany*. He hesitated – 'I'm sick to death of the British Public, all publishers, and all magazines' (vii. 467), he wrote on 5 September – but by the 8th he had extended the original article by a further 6,000 words and sent it to Curtis Brown's London office. In its lengthened form, *Pornography and Obscenity* was published as No. 5 in the *Criterion Miscellany* on 14 November. What Lawrence did not know was that Faber & Faber had invited the Home Secretary responsible for seizing copies of *Lady Chatterley's Lover* and the manuscript of *Pansies*, Joynson Hicks (now Viscount Brentford), to write No. 6 in the same series. 'Jix' – as he was known – entitled his pamphlet *Do We Need A Censor?*; his purpose was to justify the arguments he had used in the parliamentary debate on 28 February; and No. 6 was published to coincide with No. 5. The publishers had cleverly engineered a confrontation between the two principal antagonists. For his part, Lawrence not only demolished the known views of his opponent, he also had the satisfaction of telling his friend Charles Lahr three weeks later that *Pornography and Obscenity* had 'sold over 6,000 – more than any of the others' (vii. 589).

'Jix', too, expressed satisfaction at the reception of his pamphlet and at the same time – in his article 'How the censorship works' – reflected with scarcely concealed contempt on Lawrence 'on pornography'. Jix's piece appeared on 28 November (see vii. 584 n. 1.) in *Everyman*, a magazine with which Lawrence had an uneasy relationship. The editorial management held him in high regard, sympathising with him over the Customs' seizure of *Pansies*, and printing an intelligent 'appreciation' of him in April 1929, yet being inexplicably described by Lawrence as 'a cringing mongrel' (vii. 334 and n. 1). On 2 August he reiterated his 'rather poor opinion of *Everyman*' and his belief that 'they can pay nothing', but he did not hesitate to respond positively to their invitation 'to write for their series – "A Religion for the Young".' The piece he sent to Nancy Pearn conveyed his 'idea of a religion for the young . . . a nice article, much too good for them'; it was published on 3 October, entitled 'The Risen Lord'. In it the challenging emphasis on Christ's corporeal resurrection 'with hands and feet . . . with lips and stomach and genitals of a man'[10] recalls Lawrence's story *The Escaped Cock*, which would be published in Paris within a month. Indeed, he told Charles Lahr that the story had the 'same idea as in "The Risen Lord" ' (vii. 516). He may have been 'surprised they printed it' (vii. 532) but was presumably pleased with the £20 fee.[11]

Emily Lutyens, editor of the monthly magazine *Star Review*, wrote on 10 July 1929 offering Lawrence £20 for an article on 'Men and Women' which would form part of a series on aspects of modern life (vii. 405 n. 1). He accepted the invitation and sent his contribution, with the title as suggested, to Nancy Pearn on 5 August; he added: 'they may say my article isn't their line – I don't care' (vii. 405). However, it was readily accepted; Lawrence read the proof in early October; publication followed in November. It appears that he looked over the text in mid-December with a view to its inclusion in *Assorted Articles*, and decided to change the title from 'Men and Women' to 'Men Must Work and Women as Well' (which is adopted in this volume).

In the article Lawrence laments the momentum in modern living towards abstraction and thus to 'physical repulsion . . . we don't *want* the physical contact, we want to get away from it'.[12] With what enthusiasm, then, did he welcome the opportunity – in the essay 'Nottingham and the Mining Countryside' – not only to excoriate the ugliness of the English industrial landscape and the living conditions of its inhabitants, but also to celebrate what he could recreate from his youth: the highly developed 'physical, instinctive and intuitional contact' characteristic of miners like his father: 'the miners worked underground as a sort of intimate community, they knew each other practically naked, and with curious close intimacy . . . a contact almost as close as touch . . . the curious dark intimacy of the mine, the naked sort of contact'. Such 'intimate *togetherness*' had been discredited and defeated by the relentless drive for 'material prosperity above all things'. But, Lawrence insisted, 'the human soul needs actual beauty even more than bread'.[13]

The essay, one of the most admired among Lawrence's shorter writings, was triggered by a request from the editor of the *Architectural Review*, Hubert de Cronin Hastings, for him to consider the impact of industrialisation on the

[10] See below, p. 270.
[11] Nancy Pearn's secretary confirmed the amount on 3 September 1929.
[12] See below, p. 283. [13] See below, pp. 289, 292.

mining countryside. Hastings published it after Lawrence's death, in August 1930, but Murry had secured it for his highbrow quarterly journal *New Adelphi* two months earlier.

There are seven essays in the present volume not published in Lawrence's lifetime. 'Making Love to Music' is a light-hearted *jeu d'esprit* written in early April 1927 and coloured by his recent visit to Etruscan sites. It was sent to Nancy Pearn but Lawrence's throwaway remark – 'If you don't like it, don't bother about it' (vi. 40) – is a fair indication of his lack of serious expectation that she would ensure its publication. She did not; it was included in *Phoenix* in 1936.

The remaining five essays printed here are autobiographical; two of them are published for the first time. The first to be written – most likely in mid-to-late October 1926 – is '[Return to Bestwood]' which is a moving reflection on his return visit to Eastwood the month before, during the prolonged miners' strike, when he discovered in the local people 'an underneath ache and heaviness very much like my own . . . They are the only people who move me strongly, and with whom I feel myself connected in deeper destiny.'[14]

This essay was followed, chronologically, by the two hitherto unpublished: 'Getting On' and 'Which Class I Belong To'. The total absence from 'Getting On' of any reference to the ruinous strike which had so obviously distressed Lawrence points to a date of composition after the strike ended on 19 November 1926. This, together with the clear presumption in the essay that the deacon of the Congregational church, Lydia Lawrence's 'golden calf', Henry Saxton, was dead – he died on 1 January 1927 – suggests that it was the 'more or less personal article' requested but not published by the German publishers, Insel Verlag, a duplicate of which went to Nancy Pearn on 9 January (v. 620). For obvious reasons, it was 'the article on "Becoming a Success"' to which she later referred (v. 620 n. 1).

As for 'Which Class I Belong To', it was unquestionably the 'parent' of the essay entitled 'Myself Revealed', published in February 1929 by the *Sunday Dispatch*. The textual parallels between the two are too close for any other conclusion to be drawn.[15] In the text of 'Which Class . . . ' Lawrence implies that he wrote it 'Here, in Italy', thus prompting the conjecture that the essay was written in mid-April 1927 after his return from exploring the Etruscan sites. The editor of the *Dispatch* approached Nancy Pearn in December 1928 for an autobiographical piece and it is confidently assumed that 'Myself Revealed' was quarried from the earlier, unpublished essay probably written for but not used by a German publisher.

[14] See below, p. 22. [15] For further details, see below, p. 356.

Lawrence himself provides the date for the untitled '[Autobiographical Fragment]': October 1927. It is virtually certain that the story, much of it set a thousand years in the future (and entitled by Keith Sagar, 'A Dream of Life'),[16] originated as Lawrence's intended contribution to the series of books his friend Koteliansky hoped to publish. Thematically close to 'Making Love to Music', it presents Lawrence's 'home place' inhabited by men who had been tamed by their mothers and wives – 'good sons . . . good, steady husbands who would live for their wives and families' – so different from the men of his father's generation, a place indeed 'more depressing to me than death'.[17] This landscape is, in the dream-world imagined by the story's narrator, transformed into the kind of place Lawrence's birthplace might have been. Unfinished though it was, this 'Fragment' stands in sharp contrast to the factual, sketchy 'Autobiography' which Lawrence reluctantly provided in mid-July 1928 for the French publishing house, Kra. It was purely for publicity, about which he felt 'rather cold' (vi. 465).

Lawrence's brief fragment entitled 'Mushrooms' offers a not wholly inappropriate coda to the writing of his autobiographical pieces:

> It is perhaps absurd for any man to write his own autobiography. The one person I find it impossible to "know", is myself. I have dozens of little pictures of what purports to be myself, and which is me? None of them. The little animal is now become a bigger animal. But what sort of animal it is, I do not know, and do not vastly care.[18]

When Lawrence faced the task of assembling material for the volume which would be called *Assorted Articles* it is not surprising, then, that he included no more than a single autobiographical essay; it was the only one to have appeared in a newspaper: 'Myself Revealed' (entitled in the book, 'Autobiographical Sketch'). The choice was logical; as the prefatory note to the book explains: 'Most of the articles were written for newspapers and have appeared in newspapers, chiefly the *Evening News* and the *Sunday Dispatch*'.

Initially the prospect of publishing 'a book of small prose pieces' was somewhat disagreeable, as Lawrence told Laurence Pollinger on 7 January 1929 (Pollinger being responsible in Curtis Brown's agency for Lawrence's books as distinct from his periodical publications which were Nancy Pearn's domain). 'Surely it's not necessary!', he protested (vii. 122). However, Pollinger had sown the seed and doubtless continued to stimulate its growth because

16 In his edition of *The Princess and Other Stories* (1971).

17 See below, pp. 52, 54.

18 From the manuscript in UCin, first published as an epigraph in *Early Years* [vii]. For the full text see Appendix III.

on 2 August Lawrence wrote to him: 'I have been thinking if Secker wants a book of "articles" and short pieces for the late summer or spring, I'm sure there are plenty' (vii. 400). On the same day he reminded Nancy Pearn of his *Adelphi* articles 'a few years ago' which 'would come in handy for a book' (vii. 402).[19] And with increasing enthusiasm, in a third letter on 2 August, Lawrence assured his English publisher, Martin Secker, that 'there are plenty of articles to make a book, if we cared to hunt them all together – and a good many of them are, or were pretty popular when they appeared . . . I really think people are more interested in my articles than in my stories' (vii. 403). But the enthusiasm showed signs of waning. Possibly because, more and more, he felt unwell – 'feeling pretty rotten . . . miserable about my health' (vii. 530) – and, facing the prospect of treatment in a sanatorium, Lawrence told Pollinger on 1 November: 'About a Spring book of newspaper articles, if it was left to me, I should say don't do it. I've got a real revulsion from the thought of things coming out before the public – the nausea of it. But if you think I ought to have this book out, then do as you like, I don't care' (vii. 549). Lawrence did care, nevertheless: he went on to suggest several candidates for inclusion but hesitated about 'Making Pictures' and 'Pictures on the Wall' which he thought less 'newspapery' than others; they 'don't quite seem to fit the rest'. Furthermore he offered to 'think of a title' (invariably a problem for him). Negotiations continued during November and on the 30th he instructed Pollinger: 'I should like to see the complete MS of the suggested book of newspaper articles as soon as it is ready. Shall we call it "Orts and Slarts"! It means the beaux restes – pieces left over from a meal, etc. It's dialect – but Orts is in the dictionary' (vii. 584). 'Chips and Faggots' was another jocular suggestion (vii. 607). Finally, on 28 December, Lawrence told Secker: 'I have sent back the MSS of the book of articles to Pollinger. I put the title *Assorted Articles* as that seemed to me just what they are . . . Would you please send me galley proofs of the *Articles*, so that I can make alterations or stick bits in if I want to – to keep the book in harmony' (vii. 611). The publisher was reminded about galley proofs on 9 January 1930; it is presumed that Lawrence read them before the 21st since on that day he told his American admirer, Maria Chambers: 'All the essays are collected and are going to appear with Knopf in a volume of *Assorted Articles* at the end of April' (vii. 623–4). Lawrence died on 2 March. Secker published the volume in early April (it was reviewed in *The Times Literary Supplement* and the *Evening Standard* on the 10th), and Knopf in New York on 11 April.

[19] Only two *Adelphi* articles were included in the volume, 'On Being a Man' and 'On Human Destiny'. Both are found in *Reflections on the Death of a Porcupine and Other Essays*, ed. Michael Herbert (Cambridge, 1988).

Reception

As would be expected, almost the only evidence of public response to the essays and articles collected here lies in reviews of *The Paintings of D. H. Lawrence*, some of which included observations on the 'Introduction'; then of *Pornography and Obscenity*, especially in view of the clash with the former Home Secretary; and finally, of *Assorted Articles*. Lawrence's newspaper articles attracted private reactions from editors and, where they are known, these have been cited above. Otherwise, like most journalism both then and now, his articles doubtless met with approval, rejection or indifference, even perhaps a temporary *frisson*, but secured no permanent record.[20]

Reviews of the *Paintings*, whose publication coincided with the exhibition of Lawrence's pictures, inevitably fell foul of the indignation felt among most journalists when they visited the Warren Gallery. The *Daily Express* on 17 June 1929, for example, headlined its review of the exhibition one day after it was opened to the public: 'D. H. Lawrence as Painter / Censored Novelist's Pictures / Intimate Nudes'. A balanced appraisal of the book and its introductory essay was unlikely to follow; and it did not. Lawrence was quoted as merely dismissing leading English artists as 'bourgeoisie', disparaging the Northern races' alleged fear of the body and regarding English landscape painting as escapist: 'The glorification of the spirit, the mental consciousness which distinguishes us from beasts mean nothing to Mr Lawrence.' Paul Konody, art critic for the *Observer*, had described the paintings on 16 June as 'frankly disgusting' and 'an outrage on decency'; in the *Daily Telegraph* on 27 June they were 'gross and obscene' and 'lacking all sort of restraint'.[21] With such flagrant incitement of public hostility it was hardly likely that measured criticism of Lawrence's 'Introduction' would be found in the daily press.

Ostensibly, attempts were made in magazine reviews to produce serious criticism, but the results were much the same. Herbert Furst in *Apollo* for July 1929 conceded that the 'Introduction' was 'brilliantly written' but he felt bound to add: 'in an infinitely better style than his pictures are painted'. He continued:

> Both introduction and paintings, however, contain passages which are usually suppressed in polite society. Unfortunately one cannot help feeling that it is these passages which are the *raison d'être* of book and pictures . . . there is a good deal of prudery and hypocrisy in matters of sex, and all efforts to bring us to a more rational attitude towards its problems are to be welcomed. Only Mr Lawrence's is not one of them.[22]

[20] For one exception to this generalisation, see details of Paul Nash's rejoinder to 'Pictures on the Wall' below, pp. 255–6.

[21] For these reviews see Nehls, iii. 336, 338–9. Paul Konody (1872–1933) was a prolific writer on art, the author of biographies of several leading painters.

[22] Herbert Ernest Augustus Furst (1874–1945), art critic; wrote *Frank Brangwyn* (1918), etc.

In the *New Statesman* on 17 August (shortly after the magistrate's judgement on the paintings) Thomas Earp[23] admitted that Lawrence's views on painting 'are worthy of consideration' but added the barb: 'what is of value in his pronouncement is embedded in a large amount of dross'. He can be 'pertinent and illuminating'; his 'eulogy' of Cézanne is 'noble and moving'; but it is because Lawrence is 'so good a novelist we are interested in his views on painting' and his thesis about the decline in England of artistic creation and appreciation is nonsense. For this Lawrence castigated him privately in a letter which doubtless delighted Charles Lahr:

> I heard a little chicken chirp:
> My name is Thomas, Thomas Earp,
> and I can neither paint nor write,
> I can only put other people right . . . (vii. 447)

Many years after Lawrence's death Philip Trotter lamented that the 'Introduction' had not been replaced in the *Paintings* by Lawrence's essay, 'Making Pictures'. That, in Trotter's view, is 'at once the strangest and most convincing apologia ever written by a genuine but wholly unorthodox artist.'[24] It was entirely eclipsed by the 'Introduction' which attracted little but journalistic opprobrium in varying degrees.

In view of the widespread hostility which greeted his *Paintings* and its 'Introduction', Lawrence would take great pleasure in telling his sister, Emily King, on 30 November 1929: 'I saw the *New Statesman* standing up for me boldly this week' (vii. 582). The occasion was R. A. Barclay's highly favourable review of *Pornography and Obscenity* which he considered alongside Jix's *Do We Need A Censor?*[25] He found Lawrence's pamphlet 'profound and original in a very high degree', whereas Brentford's views were outdated. *Pornography and Obscenity*

> is far more interesting and important . . . genuinely profound . . . a real masterpiece of fundamental analysis written by a man of genius from the very bottom of his heart . . . he writes with a freedom which very few of us would venture, as well as with a veracious insight which very few of us possess . . . for all its vehemence and extravagances it is one of the most powerful and sane and penetrating pieces of writing that we have read for very many years . . . the work of a profound thinker.

In contrast Brentford talks the language of 'the temporary jack-in-office – honest but without thought' and would have been better advised not to have

[23] Thomas Wade Earp (1892–1958), critic and translator.
[24] See Nehls, iii. 190. Philip Coutts Trotter was the husband of Dorothy Warren in whose gallery DHL's paintings were exhibited.
[25] *New Statesman*, xxxiv (23 November 1929), 219–20. Reprinted in Draper 314–17.

attempted an answer to Lawrence. However, taken together the two publications represent 'a very interesting and important revival' of pamphleteering.

Barclay's enthusiasm was shared in large measure by E. M. Forster whose review appeared in the *Nation & Athenæum* on 11 January 1930.[26] He applauded 'the importance and novelty' of Lawrence's attack on Brentford's position: 'He has dealt a blow at reformers who are obsessed by purity and cannot see that their obsession is impure.' Forster sums up 'the conflict by saying that Lord Brentford wants to suppress everything except marriage, and Mr Lawrence to suppress nothing except suppression'. Characteristically he finds the solution 'not in the ringing clarion calls of either camp, but in the dull drone of tolerance, tolerance, tolerance'.

The essay excited little interest in America. The *Nation* (New York) alone granted it a brief review[27] and – somewhat like Forster – offered a solution to the conflict between Lawrence and his opponent: Lawrence should tolerate the censor's attitude to sex, the censor should accept Lawrence's conviction that the public should be frank about sex. The anonymous reviewer believed that, in the long run, Lawrence's argument would prevail.

Much more attention was inevitably paid to *Assorted Articles* published, on both sides of the Atlantic, in the month following Lawrence's death. The reviewer in *The Times Literary Supplement*, Philip Tomlinson, discovered in it 'a most refreshing Lawrence': 'none of the dark brooding . . . but calmness, a charming playfulness, an irony without anger . . . a sensible, good-humoured view of the world, expressed with the poetic animation that was the mark of Lawrence's finest work'.[28] Tomlinson went on to make the important claim that 'Lawrence thought in images'. He admitted that Lawrence's 'faults' are exhibited in *Assorted Articles* but insists that they prove to be 'quite irrelevant matters after all'.

The article 'Sex Appeal' was selected by Tomlinson as worthy of special commendation: 'simplicity itself . . . no ghost even of obsession'. The same article was picked out by Arnold Bennett in his review of the book (already cited above) in the *Evening Standard*, also on 10 April. For Bennett it illustrated his general thesis about Lawrence's journalistic skills: 'He chose his subjects well – clearly, succinctly, picturesquely, beautifully. He didn't flourish his pen before beginning, and when he had finished he knew he had finished, and

26 Reprinted in Draper 318–21.

27 'Who's Obscene?' *Nation* (New York), cxxx (26 February 1930), 236.

28 *TLS*, 10 April 1930, p. 315. Philip Tomlinson, journalist and translator, had collaborated with DHL's friend Samuel Solomonovich Koteliansky (1880–1955) on the edition of *The Life and Letters of Anton Tchekhov* (1925).

stopped. Not a word wasted. The subjects chosen were important, elemental, fundamental, and he struck at once deep down into the core of them.'

For 'P. M.', too, in the *Nation & Athenæum*, the same article – 'one of the most charming and sympathetic in the book' – was significant because it revealed Lawrence's 'true sentiments' on a subject concerning which he had been denounced as a 'morbid sex-maniac'. 'P. M.' continued: 'Few men, indeed, have written of the fundamental problems of life and death more bravely than he did. Sometimes he scolded and hectored and moralized; his style was often rough and careless – though how beautifully he could write when he wished to! – but fundamentally he was always a poet and an artist.'[29]

Reviews in America were numerous and began soon after the book appeared. Margery Latimer in *New York World*, on 27 April 1930, regarded *Assorted Articles* as an important work in which Lawrence 'speaks the words earned from his life and the risks he took' and guaranteed his readers 'immediacy of experience'. The *New York Herald Tribune* carried a review by Lorine Pruette on the same day. For her, Lawrence is revealed as 'a perplexed, sensitive person groping his way through life, secure in little more than the conviction that beauty may reside in the living flame between men and women, men and men'. A slightly unsympathetic note is evident here; it soon became more pronounced. Henry Hazlitt in the *Nation* three days later tended to dismiss the book as repeating what Lawrence had said before but here in essays that showed more passion than clear reasoning.[30] On 11 May the *New York Times Book Review* declared *Assorted Articles* to be negligible. Arthur Colton writing in the *Saturday Review of Literature* on 17 May commended the autobiographical pieces but found Lawrence elsewhere bitter and peevish.[31] It is, then, pleasing to conclude with the memorable observation from the best-known among the American reviewers, Sherwood Anderson, in *New Republic* on 21 May, that the essays in *Assorted Articles* are 'like a covey of quail at the edge of a field, little-feathered, trembling bundles of light'.[32]

[29] *Nation & Athenæum*, 3 May 1930, p. 148. On the same day the *Spectator* (cxliv. 743) found little more to say than that *Assorted Articles* was valuable for its presentation of DHL at his best and his worst.

[30] *Nation*, cxxx. 519. The same judgement was later expressed by Nicola Chiarcomonte in *L'Italia Letteraria* (Rome), iii (12 July 1931), 6. See *D. H. Lawrence: An Annotated Bibliography of Writings About Him*, ed. James C. Cowan (De Kalb, Ill.: Northern Illinois University Press, 1982), i. 143.

[31] *Saturday Review of Literature*, vi. 1043.

[32] *New Republic*, lxiii. 22–3. Anderson (1876–1941), novelist, particularly noted for his collection of stories, *Winesburg, Ohio* (1919).

LATE ESSAYS AND ARTICLES

NOTE ON THE TEXTS

The base-texts for the essays and articles in this volume are as follows:

'Mercury': autograph manuscript, 9 pp. (MS), UCB; collated with two identical carbon copy typescripts, 8 pp. (TS), UT and UCB; *Atlantic Monthly*, February 1927 (Per); and *Phoenix* (A1).

'[Return to Bestwood]': autograph untitled manuscript, 20 pp. (MS), UCin; collated with *Phoenix II* (E1).

'Getting On': autograph manuscript, 8 pp. (MS), UCin.

'Which Class I Belong To': autograph manuscript, 10 pp. (MS), UCin.

'Making Love to Music': autograph manuscript, 13 pp. (MS), YU; collated with carbon copy typescript, 11 pp. (TS), UCB and *Phoenix* (A1).

'[Autobiographical Fragment]': autograph untitled manuscript, 42 pp. (MS), UCB; collated with carbon copy typescript, 34 pp. (TS), UCB and *Phoenix* (A1).

'The "Jeune Fille" Wants to Know': *Assorted Articles* (E1); collated with *Evening News*, 8 May 1928 (Per1) and *Virginia Quarterly Review*, January 1929 (Per2).

'Laura Philippine': typescript, 7 pp. (TS), UCB; collated with *T. P.'s and Cassell's Weekly*, 7 July 1928 (Per) and *Assorted Articles* (E1).

'That Women Know Best': autograph manuscript, 5 pp. (MS), UCB; collated with *Daily Chronicle*, 29 November 1928 (Per) and *That Women Know Best*, ed. Roy Spencer, Santa Rosa, Black Sparrow Press, 1994 (A1).

'All There': autograph manuscript, 4 pp. (MS), UCB; collated with typescript 4 pp. (TS), UCB, and *Phoenix* (A1).

'Thinking About Oneself': autograph manuscript, 4 pp. (MS), UT; collated with carbon typescript, 4 pp. (TS1), UCB and UT; carbon typescript, 4 pp. (TS2), UCB; and *Phoenix* (A1).

'Insouciance': autograph manuscript, 4 pp. (MS), UT; collated with carbon typescript, 5 pp. (TS), UT; *Evening News*, 12 July 1928 (Per); and *Assorted Articles* (E1).

'Master in his Own House': autograph manuscript, 4 pp. (MS), UT; collated with carbon typescript, 5 pp. (TS), UT; *Evening News*, 2 August 1928 (Per1); *Vanity Fair*, November 1928 (Per2); and *Assorted Articles* (E1).

'Matriarchy': autograph manuscript, 6 pp. (MS), UT; collated with two typescripts, 7 pp. (TS1) UT and (TS2) HU; *Evening News*, 5 October 1928 (Per); and *Assorted Articles* (E1).

'Ownership': autograph manuscript, 4 pp. (MS), UCB; collated with typescript, 5 pp. (TS1), UT; carbon typescript, 5 pp. (TS2), UCB; and *Assorted Articles* (E1).

'Autobiography': autograph manuscript, 4 pp. (MS), UT; collated with typescript copy, 3 pp. (TS), Insel-Verlag, and Nehls, iii. 232–4 (A1).

'Women Are So Cocksure': autograph manuscript, 4 pp. (MS), UCB; collated with carbon typescript, 4 pp. (TS), UT, and *Phoenix* (A1).

'Why I don't Like Living in London': autograph manuscript, 4 pp. (MS), UT; collated with carbon typescript, 4 pp. (TS), UT; *Evening News*, 3 September 1928 (Per); and *Assorted Articles* (E1).

'Cocksure Women and Hen-sure Men': autograph manuscript, 3 pp. (MS), UCB; collated with carbon typescript, 5 pp. (TS), UT; *Forum*, January 1929 (Per); and *Assorted Articles* (E1).

'Hymns in a Man's Life': autograph manuscript, 6 pp. (MS), UN; collated with *Evening News*, 13 October 1928 (Per) and *Assorted Articles* (E1).

'Red Trousers': autograph manuscript, 4 pp. (MS), Forster; collated with carbon typescript, 5 pp. (TS), UT; *Evening News*, 27 September 1928 (Per); and *Assorted Articles* (E1).

'Is England Still a Man's Country': autograph manuscript, 6 pp. (MS), UT; collated with carbon typescript, 4 pp. (TS), UCB; *Daily Express*, 29 November 1928 (Per); and *Assorted Articles* (E1).

'Sex Appeal': autograph manuscript, 10 pp. (MS), UT; collated with *Sunday Dispatch*, 25 November 1928 (Per1); *Vanity Fair*, July 1929 (Per2); and *Assorted Articles* (E1).

'Do Women Change': autograph manuscript, 4 pp. (MS), UT, together with autograph extension to typescript of MS, 2 pp., UT, combining to give TSR; collated with typescript, revised authorially, 4 pp. (TS), UT; and *Assorted Articles* (E1).

'Enslaved by Civilisation': autograph manuscript, 4 pp. (MS), UT; collated with carbon typescript, 8 pp. (TS), UT; *Vanity Fair*, September 1929 (Per); and *Assorted Articles* (E1).

'Give Her a Pattern': autograph manuscript entitled 'Oh! These Women!', 6 pp. (MS), UCB; collated with carbon typescript bearing the authorial change which introduced the title, 'Give Her a Pattern', 7 pp. (TS), UT; *Vanity Fair*, May 1929 (Per1); *Daily Express*, 19 June 1929 (Per2); and *Assorted Articles* (E1).

'Introduction to Pictures': autograph manuscript, 17 pp. (MS), UT; collated with carbon typescript, 13 pp. (TS), UCB and *Phoenix* (A1).

'Myself Revealed': *Sunday Dispatch*, 17 February 1929 (Per); collated with *Assorted Articles* (E1).

'Introduction to These Paintings': autograph manuscript, 37 pp. (MS), UT; collated with carbon typescript, 58 pp. (TS1), UT; carbon typescript, 58 pp. (TS2), UCB; *The Paintings of D. H. Lawrence*, Mandrake Press, 1929 (E1); and *Phoenix* (A1).

'The State of Funk': autograph manuscript, 6 pp. (MS), UT; collated with carbon typescript, 9 pp. (TS), UT and *Assorted Articles* (E1).

'Making Pictures': autograph manuscript, 6 pp. (MS), UT; collated with carbon typescript, 9 pp. (TS), UT; *Studio*, July 1929 (Per1); *Vanity Fair*, August 1929 (Per2); and *Assorted Articles* (E1).

Pornography and Obscenity: autograph manuscript, 32 pp. (MS), UT; collated with typescript, 38 pp. (TS1), UCB; carbon typescript, 19 pp. (TS2), UCB; *This Quarter*, July–September 1929 (Per); *Criterion Miscellany, No. 5*, January 1930 (E1); and *Pornography and So On*, September 1936 (E2).

'Pictures on the Wall': carbon typescript, 14 pp. (TS), UT; collated with *Vanity Fair*, December 1929 (Per1); *Architectural Review*, February 1930 (Per2); *Assorted Articles* (E1).
'The Risen Lord': autograph manuscript, 6 pp. (MS), UCB; collated with carbon typescript, 12 pp. (TS), UCB; *Everyman*, 3 October 1929 (Per); and *Assorted Articles* (E1).
'Men Must Work and Women as Well': autograph manuscript entitled 'Men and Women', 12 pp. (MS), UT; collated with carbon typescript, 18 pp., authorially entitled 'Men Must Work and Women as Well' (TS), UT; *Star Review*, November 1929 (Per); and *Assorted Articles* (E1).
'Nottingham and the Mining Countryside': autograph manuscript, 9 pp. (MS), UCB; collated with carbon typescript, 13 pp. (TS), UCB; *New Adelphi*, June 1930 (Per1); *Architectural Review*, August 1930 (Per); and *Phoenix* (A1).
'We Need One Another': autograph manuscript, 11 pp. (MS), YU; collated with *Scribner's Magazine*, May 1930 (Per), and *Phoenix* (A1).
'The Real Thing': autograph manuscript, 10 pp. (MS), YU; collated with carbon typescript, 12 pp. (TS), UCB; *Scribner's Magazine*, June 1930 (Per); and *Phoenix* (A1).
'Nobody Loves Me': autograph manuscript, 12 pp. (MS), YU; collated with typescript, 13 pp. (TS), UT; *Life and Letters*, July 1930 (Per1); *Virginia Quarterly*, July 1930 (Per2); and *Phoenix* (A1).

Appendix I. Early draft for 'The "Jeune Fille" Wants to Know', autograph manuscript, 4 pp. (MS), UT.
Appendix II. 'Do Women Change' in *Vanity Fair* (New York), April 1929; collated with *Sunday Dispatch*, 28 April 1929.
Appendix III. 'Mushrooms': autograph manuscript, 1 p. (MS), UCin.

The apparatus records all textual variants, except for the following silent emendations:

1. Clearly inadvertent errors have been corrected; errors in intermediate typescripts that were corrected before the text appeared in print, have not been recorded.
2. DHL's normal placing of punctuation inside closing inverted commas has been followed since most of the volume is based on autograph manuscript originals; printed variants have not been recorded.
3. DHL's spelling of 'today', 'tonight', 'tomorrow' has been adopted and the hyphenated forms not recorded; similarly his spelling of 'connection' rather than 'connexion', his use of 'ise' endings in such words as 'realise' and derivative forms, his use of contractions such as 'don't', 'he's' or 'isn't' and his use of lower case for pronouns relating to Jesus Christ have been followed and variants are not recorded.
4. DHL normally expected titles of publications to be italicised; variants from his practice have not been recorded.
5. Ampersands in DHL's manuscripts have been silently expanded except where they occur while recording another variant.
6. The use of asterisks to separate paragraphs in newspaper articles has not been recorded, nor has the journalistic practice of creating subsidiary headings for blocks of text.

MERCURY

The Lawrences spent the second half of July 1926 with Frieda's mother in Baden-Baden; from the 19th onwards, in several letters written from there, Lawrence spoke of the extremes of weather they experienced: 'very hot, with constant threat of thunder which doesn't come'; 'very hot – then we had a storm and torrents of rain'; 'torrents and thunder . . . The woods steam' (*Letters*, v. 498–9, 502).[1] In view of the prominence of heat, thunder and a violent storm in the sketch, it is virtually certain that 'Mercury' was written at this time. While writing it Lawrence was particularly aware of 'the Sunday crowd' making its way to the summit of Merkur, the highest point in the district (668 m, $2\frac{1}{2}$ km east of Baden); it is conceivable that he made the ascent himself by funicular on Sunday 25 July, during the stormy period which seems to have followed 19–20 July (see v. 499).

On 2 September 1926, a month after leaving Baden for England, Lawrence wrote to Nancy Pearn, sending her an unnamed essay – 'this one, which I did in Baden and forgot' (v. 521) – which was most probably 'Mercury'. He mentioned it only once more, also in a letter to Nancy Pearn, in March 1927: 'good about "Mercury"' (v. 657), presumably with reference to its publication in *Atlantic Monthly* and/or in *Nation and Athenæum*, both a month earlier.

Lawrence visited Merkur again – but not to make the ascent – with his American friends, Earl and Achsah Brewster, in September 1928. The Brewsters were keen to see it because of 'the beautiful allegory' Lawrence had written about it. He remained at the foot of the funicular, while his companions went to 'the commanding height where man has felt the presence of gods known and unknown during the centuries – testifying to this are the Christian shrine, and the altar to Mercury above, another perhaps to Thor the thunderer, as Lawrence has chosen in his profound allegory'.[2]

[1] The *Badener Tagblatt* on 21 July 1926 reported a catastrophic storm during the night of 19–20 July which caused widespread destruction of buildings and crops; two men were seriously injured by a falling crane in nearby Karlsruhe (see David Ellis, *D. H. Lawrence: Dying Game, 1922–1930*, Cambridge, 1998, p. 309).

[2] Brewster 296–7.

MERCURY*

It was Sunday, and very hot. The holiday-makers flocked to the hill of Mercury, to rise two-thousand feet above the steamy haze of the valleys. For the summer had been very wet, and the sudden heat covered the land in hot steam.

Every time it made its ascent, the funicular was crowded. It hauled itself up the steep incline, that towards the top looked almost perpendicular, the steel thread of the rails in the gulf of pine-trees hanging like an iron rope against a wall. The women held their breath, and didn't look. Or they looked back towards the sinking levels of the river, steamed and dim, far-stretching over the frontier.

When you arrived at the top, there was nothing to do. The hill was a pine-covered cone, paths wound between the high tree-trunks, and you could walk round and see the glimpses of the world all round, all round: the dim far river-plain, with a dull glint of the great stream, to westwards; southwards the black, forest-covered, agile-looking hills, with emerald-green clearings and a white house or two; east the inner valley, with two villages, factory chimneys, pointed churches, and hills beyond; and north the steep hills of forest, with reddish crags and reddish castle-ruins. The hot sun burned overhead, and all was in steam.

Only on the very summit of the hill there was a tower, an outlook tower; a long restaurant with its beer-garden, all the little yellow tables standing their round discs under the horse-chestnut trees; then a bit of a rock-garden on the slope. But the great trees began again in wilderness, a few yards off.

The Sunday crowd came up in waves from the funicular. In waves they ebbed through the beer-garden. But not many sat down to drink. Nobody was spending any money. Some paid to go up the outlook tower, to look down on a world of vapours and black, agile-crouching hills, and half-cooked towns. Then everybody dispersed along the paths, to sit among the trees in the cool air.

There was not a breath of wind. Lying and looking upwards at the shaggy, barbaric middle-world of the pine-trees, it was difficult to decide whether the pure high trunks supported the upper thicket of darkness, or whether they descended from it like great cords stretched downwards. Anyhow, in between the tree-top world and the earth-world went the wonderful clean cords of innumerable proud tree-trunks, clear as rain. And as you watched, you saw that the upper world was faintly moving, faintly, most faintly swaying, with a circular movement, though the lower trunks were utterly motionless and monolithic.

There was nothing to do. In all the world, there was nothing to do, and nothing to be done. Why have we all come to the top of the Merkur?—there is nothing for us to do.

What matter! We have come a stride beyond the world. Let it steam and cook its half-baked reality below there. On the hill of Mercury we take no notice. Even we do not trouble to wander and pick the fat, blue, sourish bilberries. Just lie and see the rain-pure tree-trunks like chords of music between two worlds.

The hours pass by, people wander and disappear and re-appear. All is hot and quiet. Humanity is rarely boisterous any more. You go for a drink: finches run among the few people at the tables: everybody glances at everybody, but with remoteness.

There is nothing to do but to return and lie down under the pine-trees. Nothing to do. But why do anything, anyhow? The desire to do anything has gone. The tree-trunks, living like rain, they are quite active enough.

At the foot of the outlook tower there is an old tablet-stone with a very much battered Mercury, in relief. There is also an altar, or votive stone, both from the Roman times. The Romans are supposed to have worshipped Mercury on this summit. The battered god, with his round sun-head, looks very hollow-eyed and unimpressive in the purplish red sandstone of the district. And no-one any more will throw grains of offering in the hollow of the votive stone: also common, purplish-red sandstone, very local and un-Roman.

The Sunday people do not even look. Why should they? They keep passing on into the pine-trees. And many sit on the benches, many lie upon the long chairs. It is very hot, in the afternoon, and very still.

Till there seems a faint whistling in the tops of the pine-trees, and out of the universal semi-consciousness of the afternoon arouses a bristling uneasiness. The crowd is astir, looking at the sky. And sure enough, there is a great flat blackness reared up in the western sky, curled with white wisps and loose breast-feathers. It looks very sinister, as only the elements still can look. Under the sudden weird whistling of the upper pine-trees, there is a subdued babble and calling of frightened voices.

They want to get down, the crowd want to get down off the hill of Mercury, before the storm comes. At any price to get off this hill! They stream towards the funicular, while the sky blackens with incredible rapidity. And as the crowd presses down towards the little station, the first blaze of lightning opens out, followed immediately by a crash of thunder, and great darkness. In one strange movement, the crowd takes refuge in the deep verandah of the restaurant, pressing among the little tables in silence. There is no rain, and no definite wind, only a sudden coldness which makes the crowd press closer.

They press closer, in the darkness and the suspense. They have become curiously unified, the crowd, as if they had fused into one body. As the air sends a chill waft under the verandah, the voices murmur plaintively, like birds under leaves, the bodies press closer together, seeking shelter in contact.

The gloom, dark as night, seems to continue a long time. Then suddenly the lightning dances white on the floor, dances and shakes upon the ground, up and down, and lights up the white striding of a man, lights him up only to the hips, white and naked and striding, with fire on his heels. He seems to be hurrying, this fiery man whose upper half is invisible, and at his naked heels white little flames seem to flutter. His flat, powerful thighs, his legs white as fire stride rapidly across the open, in front of the verandah, dragging little white flames at the ankles, with the movement. He is going somewhere, swiftly.

In the great bang of the thunder, the apparition disappears, the earth moves, and the house jumps in complete darkness. A faint whimpering of terror comes from the crowd, as the cold air swirls in. But still, upon the darkness, there is no rain. There is no relief: a long wait.

Brilliant and blinding, the lightning falls again, a strange bruising thud comes from the forest, as all the little tables and the secret tree-trunks stand for one unnatural second exposed. Then the blow of the thunder, under which the house and the crowd reel as under an explosion. The storm is playing directly upon the Merkur. A belated sound of tearing branches comes out of the forest.

And again the white splash of the lightning on the ground: but nothing moves. And again the long, rattling, instantaneous volleying of the thunder, in the darkness. The crowd is panting with fear, as the lightning again strikes white, and something again seems to burst, in the forest, as the thunder crashes.

At last, into the motionlessness of the storm, in rushes the wind, with the fiery flying of bits of ice, and the sudden sea-like roaring of the pine-trees. The crowd winces and draws back, as the bits of ice hit in the face like fire. The roar of the trees is so great, it becomes like another silence. And through it is heard the crashing and splintering of timber, as the hurricane concentrates upon the hill.

Down comes the hail, in a roar that covers every other sound, threshing ponderously upon the ground and the roofs and the trees. And as the crowd surges irresistibly into the interior of the building, from the crushing of this ice-fall, still amid the sombre hoarseness sounds the tinkle and crackle of things breaking.

After an eternity of dread, it ends suddenly. Outside is a faint gleam of yellow light, over the snow and the endless débris of twigs and things broken. It is very cold, with the atmosphere of ice and deep winter. The forest looks wan, above the white earth, where the ice-balls lie in their myriads, six inches deep, littered with all the twigs and things they have broken.

"Yes! Yes!" say the men, taking sudden courage as the yellow light comes into the air. "Now we can go!"

The first brave ones emerge, picking up the big hail-stones, pointing to the overthrown tables. Some, however, do not linger. They hurry to the funicular station, to see if the apparatus is still working.

The funicular station is on the north side of the hill. The men come back, saying there is no-one there. The crowd begins to emerge upon the wet, crunching whiteness of the hail, spreading around in curiosity, waiting for the men who operate the funicular.

On the south side of the outlook tower two bodies lay in the cold but thawing hail. The dark blue of the uniforms showed blackish. Both men were dead. But the lightning had completely removed the clothing from the legs of one man, so that he was naked from the hips down. There he lay, his face sideways on the snow, and two drops of blood running from his nose into his big, blonde, military moustache. He lay there near the votive stone of the Mercury. His companion, a young man, lay face downwards, a few yards behind him.

The sun began to emerge. The crowd gazed in dread, afraid to touch the bodies of the men. Why had they, the dead funicular men, come round to this side of the hill, anyhow?

The funicular would not work. Something had happened to it in the storm. The crowd began to wind down the bare hill, on the sloppy ice. Everywhere the earth bristled with broken pine boughs and twigs. But the bushes and the leafy trees were stripped absolutely bare, to a miracle. The lower earth was leafless and naked as in winter.

"Absolute winter!" murmured the crowd, as they hurried, frightened, down the steep, winding descent, extricating themselves from the fallen pine-branches.

Meanwhile the sun began to steam in great heat.

[RETURN TO BESTWOOD]

This essay, to which Lawrence gave no title, was first published posthumously in *Phoenix II* (1968) where it received the title by which it has become generally known. The date of its composition, however, has not been generally agreed.

It is clear from his letters that Lawrence was staying with his younger sister Ada Clarke, in Ripley, 14–16 September 1926. This was shortly after his forty-first birthday (on 11 September) to which he alludes in the essay. His distress at the misery endured by the mining community in Eastwood ('Bestwood') as the result of the coal strike, then over four months old, is evident in his letters and in the essay; the acute shortage of food, for example, mentioned in the essay, is exactly duplicated in a letter to Koteliansky of 15 September (see Explanatory note to 16:17). Lawrence was particularly struck by the change in the attitude of women – they 'have turned into fierce communists', he told Koteliansky; and in the essay he vividly presents the behaviour of 'the little gang of women' in the market-place 'waving red flags . . . laughing loudly and using occasional bad language' (17:15–16). Derek Britton dates the incident described by Lawrence as occurring in Ripley market-place on 14 September, the day on which he arrived at his sister's home and on which he set out from Ripley for Eastwood.[1]

The use of the continuous present tense in the essay gives the impression of great immediacy, as if the writing were virtually concurrent with the events and the vigorous reactions they provoked in the author. Relying on this line of thinking would lead to the conclusion that '[Return to Bestwood]' was written in mid-to-late September 1926. An examination of the manuscript, however, leads to a different conclusion. It reveals that on no fewer than ten occasions Lawrence changed the past tense first used to the present, thus accentuating the dramatic immediacy. The most significant among all the alterations, however, occurs when Lawrence writes of his mother's hope that her children would 'get on' and makes his less-than-solemn boast that he lives in an old Italian villa,

[1] Derek Britton, *Lady Chatterley: The Making of the Novel* (1988), p. 136.

even if he rents only half of it. The essay as published reads: 'Myself, a snotty-nosed little collier's lad, I call myself at home when I sit in a heavy old Cinque-cento Italian villa' (18:24). But before Lawrence revised it, the manuscript originally read: 'Myself, a snotty-nosed little collier's lad, sitting here in this heavy old Cinque-cento Italian villa'. This undoubtedly establishes the composition of the essay as taking place later than the events described in it, in fact at the Villa Mirenda to which Lawrence returned on 4 October 1926. Moreover, two textual details suggest a close relationship between the date of the essay and the composition of the first version of *Lady Chatterley's Lover*, the opening 41 pages of which had been written at the Mirenda by 26 October (and the whole completed between 25 and 30 November).[2] Early in both the essay (19:17) and the novel (63:39–40) Lawrence uses the term 'Plutonic' and refers to Persephone; and in both – early enough in the novel (85:21–2) not to date it much beyond 26 October – are references to the 'ownership of property' having become 'a religious problem' (23:6). It is, of course, impossible to determine whether this assertion came first in the essay or in the novel. Nevertheless the combined evidence places the composition of '[Return to Bestwood]' in mid-to-late October 1926.[3]

[2] See *The First and Second Lady Chatterley Novels*, ed. Dieter Mehl and Christa Jansohn (Cambridge, 1999), p. xxiii.

[3] See also the introduction to 'Getting On' (p. 25).

[RETURN TO BESTWOOD]

I came home to the Midlands for a few days, at the end of September.* Not that there is any home, for my parents are dead. But there are my sisters, and the district one calls home; that mining district between Nottingham and Derby.

It always depresses me to come to my native district. Now I am turned forty, and have been more or less a wanderer for nearly twenty years, I feel more alien, perhaps, in my home place than anywhere else in the world. I can feel at ease in Canal Street, New Orleans, or in the Avenue Madero, in Mexico City, or in George Street, Sydney, in Trincomalee Street, Kandy, or in Rome or Paris or Munich or even London. But in Nottingham Road, Bestwood, I feel at once a devouring nostalgia and an infinite repulsion. Partly, I want to get back to the place as it was when I was a boy, and I waited so long to be served in the Co-op—I remember our Co-op number, 1553 A. L.* better than the date of my birth—and when I came out lugging a string net of groceries. There was a little hedge across the road from the Co-op then, and I used to pick the green buds which we called bread-and-cheese. And there were no houses in Gabes Lane. And at the corner of Queen Street, Butcher Bob* was huge and fat and taciturn.

Butcher Bob is long dead, and the place is all built up, I am never quite sure where I am, in Nottingham Rd. Walker Street* is not very much changed though—because the ash tree* was cut down when I was sixteen, when I was ill. The houses are still only on one side the street, the fields on the other. And still one looks across at the amphitheatre of hills which I still find beautiful, though there are new patches of reddish houses, and a darkening of smoke. Crich is still on the sky line to the west, and the woods of Annesley to the north, and Coney Grey Farm still lies in front. And there is still a certain glamour about the country-side. Curiously enough, the more motor-cars and tram-cars and omnibuses there are rampaging down the roads, the more the country retreats into its own isolation, and becomes more mysteriously inaccessible.

When I was a boy, the whole population lived very much more *with* the country. Now, they rush and tear along the roads, and have joy-rides and outings, but they never seem to touch the reality of the countryside. There are many more people, for one thing: and all these new contrivances, for another.

The country seems, somehow, fogged over with people, and yet not really touched. It seems to lie back, away, unreached and asleep. The roads are hard and metalled and worn with everlasting rush. The very field-paths seem wider and more trodden and squalid. Wherever you go, there is the sordid sense of humanity.

And yet the fields and the woods in between the roads and paths sleep as in a heavy, weary dream, disconnected from the modern world.

This visit, this September, depresses me peculiarly. The weather is soft and mild, mildly sunny in that hazed, dazed, uncanny sunless sunniness which makes the Midlands peculiarly fearsome to me. I cannot, cannot accept as sunshine this thin luminous vapourousness which passes as a fine day in the place of my birth. Oh Phœbus Apollo!* Surely you have turned your face aside!

But the special depression this time is the great coal strike,* still going on. In house after house, the families are now living on bread and margarine and potatoes. The colliers get up before dawn, and are away into the last recesses of the countryside, scouring the country for blackberries, as if there were a famine. But they will sell the blackberries at fourpence a pound, and so they'll be fourpence in pocket.

But when I was a boy, it was utterly *infra dig.* for a miner to be picking blackberries. He would never have demeaned himself to such an unmanly occupation. And as to walking home with a little basket—he would almost rather have committed murder. The children might do it,* or the women, or even the half-grown youths. But a married, manly collier!

But nowadays, their pride is in their pocket, and the pocket has a hole in it.

It is another world. There are policemen everywhere, great, big strange policemen with faces like a leg of mutton. Where they come from, heaven only knows: Ireland or Scotland, presumably, for they are no Englishmen. And they exist, along the countryside, in thousands. The people call them "blue-bottles,"* and "meat-flies." And you can hear a woman call across the street to another: "Seen any blow-flies about?"—Then they turn to look at the alien policemen, and laugh shrilly.

And this in my native place! Truly, one no longer knows the palm of his own hand. When I was a boy, we had our own police-sergeant, and two young constables. And the women would as leave have thought of calling Sergeant Mellor* a blue-bottle as calling Queen Victoria one. The Sergeant was a quiet, patient man, who spent his life trying to keep people out of trouble. He was another sort of shepherd, and the miners and their children were a flock to him. The women had the utmost respect for him.

But the women seem to have changed most in this, that they have no respect for anything. There was a scene in the market-place yesterday, a Mrs Hafton and a Mrs Rowley being taken off to court to be tried for insulting and obstructing the police.* The police had been escorting the black-legs from the mines, after a so-called day's work, and the women had made the usual row. They were two women from decent homes. In the past they would have died of shame, at having to go to court. But now, not at all.

They had a little gang of women with them in the market-place, waving red flags and laughing loudly and using occasional bad language. There was one, the decent wife of the post-man. I had known her and played with her as a girl. But she was waving her red flag, and cheering as the motor-bus rolled up.

The two culprits got up, hilariously, into the bus.

"Good luck, old girl! Let 'em have it! Give it the blue-bottles in the neck! Tell me what for! Three cheers for Bestwood! Strike while the iron's hot, girls!"

"So long! So long, girls! See you soon! Merry home-coming, what, eh?"

"Have a good time, now! Have a good time! Stick a pin in their fat backsides, if you can't move 'em any other road. We s'll be thinking of you!"

"So long! So long! See you soon! Who says Walker!"

"E-eh! E-eh!—"

The bus rolled heavily off, with the shouting women, amid the strange hoarse cheering of the women in the little market-place. The draughty little market-place where my mother shopped on Friday evenings, in her rusty little black bonnet, and where now a group of decent women waved little red flags and hoarsely cheered two women going to court!

O mamma mia!—as the Italians say. My dear mother, your little black bonnet would fly off your head in horrified astonishment, if you saw it now. You were so keen on progress: a decent working man, and a good wage! you paid my father's union pay for him, for so many years! you believed so firmly in the Co-op! you were at your Women's Guild* when they brought you word your father, the old tyrannus,* was dead! At the same time, you believed so absolutely in the ultimate benevolence of all the masters, of all the upper classes. One had to be grateful to them, after all!

Grateful! You can have your cake and eat it, while the cake lasts. When the cake comes to an end, you can hand on your indigestion. Oh my dear and virtuous mother, who believed in a Utopia of goodness, so that your own people were never quite good enough for you—not even the spoiled delicate boy, myself!—oh my dear and virtuous mother, behold the indigestion we have inherited, from the cake of perfect goodness you baked too often! Nothing was good enough! We must all rise into the upper classes! Upper! Upper! Upper!

Till at last the boots are all uppers, the sole is worn out, and we yell as we walk on stones.

My dear, dear mother, you were so tragic, because you had nothing to be tragic about! We, on the other side, having a moral and social indigestion that would raise the wind for a thousand explosive tragedies, let off a mild crepitus ventris* and shout: Have a good time, old girl! Enjoy yourself, old lass!

Never-the-less, we have all of us "got on." The reward of goodness, in my mother's far-off days, less than twenty years ago, was that you should "get on." *Be good, and you'll get on in life.*

Myself, a snotty-nosed little collier's lad, I call myself at home when I sit in a heavy old Cinque-cento Italian villa,* of which I rent only half, even then—surely I can be considered to have "got on." When I wrote my first book, and it was going to be published—sixteen years ago—and my mother was dying, a fairly well-known editor* wrote to my mother and said, of me: "By the time he is forty, he will be riding in his carriage!"

To which my mother is supposed to have said, sighing: "Ay, if he lives to be forty!"

Well, I am forty-one,* so there's one in the eye for that sighing remark. I was always weak in health, but my life was strong. Why had they all made up their minds that I was to die? Perhaps they thought I was too good to live. Well, in that case they were had!

And when I was forty, I was not even in my own motor-car. But I *did* drive my own two horses in a light buggy (my own) on a little ranch* (also my own, or my wife's, through me) away on the western slope of the Rocky Mountains. And sitting in my corduroy trousers and blue shirt, calling: "Get up Aaron! *Ambrose*!" then I thought of Austin

Harrison's prophecy. Oh Oracle of Delphos! Oracle of Dodona!* "Get up, Ambrose!" Bump! went the buggy over a rock, and the pine-needles slashed my face! See him driving in his carriage, at forty!—driving it pretty badly too! Put the brake on!

So I suppose I've got on, snotty-nosed little collier's lad, of whom most of the women said: "He's a *nice* little lad!" They don't say it now: if ever they say anything, which is doubtful. They've forgotten me entirely.

But my sister's "getting on" is much more concrete than mine. She is almost on the spot. Within six miles of that end dwelling in The Breach, which is the house I first remember—an end house of hideous rows of miners' dwellings, though I loved it, too—stands my sister's new house, "a lovely house!"—and her garden: "I wish mother could see my garden in June!"

And if my mother did see it, what then? It is wonderful the flowers that bloom in these Midlands, in June. A northern Persephone seems to steal out from the Plutonic,* coal-mining depths and give a real hoot of blossoms. But if my mother *did* return from the dead, and see that garden in full bloom, and the glass doors open from the hall of the new house, what then? Would she then say: It is reached! Consummatum est!

When Jesus gave up the ghost, he cried: It is finished!* Consummatum est! But was it? And if so, what? What was it that was consummate?

Likewise, before the war, in Germany I used to see advertised in the newspapers a moustache-lifter, which you tied on at night and it would make your moustache stay turned up, like the immortal moustache of Kaiser Wilhelm II,* whose moustache alone is immortal. This moustache-lifter was called: Es ist erreicht! In other words: It is reached! Consummatum est!

Was it? Was it reached? With the moustache lifter?

So the ghost of my mother, in my sister's garden. I see it each time I am there, bending over the violas, or looking up at the almond tree. Actually an almond tree! And I always ask, of the grey-haired, good little ghost: "Well what of it, my dear? What is the verdict?"

But she never answers, though I press her:

"Do look at the house, my dear! Do look at the tiled hall, and the rug from Mexico, and the brass from Venice, seen through the open doors, beyond the lilies and the carnations of the lawn beds! Do look! And do look at me, and see if I'm not a gentleman! Do say that I'm almost upper class!"

But the dear little ghost says never a word.

"Do say we've got on! Do say, we've arrived. Do say, it is reached, es ist erreicht, consummatum est!"

But the little ghost turns aside, she knows I am teasing her. She gives me one look, which is a look I know, and which says: "I shan't tell you, so you can't laugh at me. You must find out for yourself." And she steals away, to her place, wherever it may be.—"In my father's house are many mansions. If it were not so, I would have told you."*

The black slate roofs beyond the wind-worn young trees at the end of the garden are the same thick layers of black roofs of blackened brick houses, as ever. There is the same smell of sulphur from the burning pit bank.* Smuts fly on the white violas. There is a harsh sound of machinery. Persephone couldn't quite get out of hell, so she let spring fall from her lap along the upper workings.

But no! There are no smuts, there is even no smell of the burning pit bank. They cut the bank, and the pits are not working. The strike has been going on for months. It is September, but there are lots of roses on the lawn beds.

"Where shall we go this afternoon? Shall we go to Hardwick?"*

Let us go to Hardwick. I have not been for twenty years. Let us go to Hardwick.

"Hardwick Hall
More window than wall."

Built in the days of good Queen Bess, by that other Bess, termagant and tartar, Countess of Shrewsbury.

Butterley, Alfreton, Tibshelf*—what was once the Hardwick district is now the Notts-Derby coal area. The country is the same, but scarred and splashed all over with mines and mining settlements. Great houses loom from hill-brows, old villages are smothered in rows of miners' dwellings, Bolsover Castle* rises from the mass of the colliery village of Bolsover.—Böwser, we called it, when I was a boy.

Hardwick is shut. On the gates, near the old inn, where the atmosphere of the old world lingers perfect, is a notice: "This park is closed to the public and to all traffic until further notice. No admittance."

Of course! The strike! They are afraid of Vandalism.

Where shall we go? Back into Derbyshire, or to Sherwood Forest.

Turn the car. We'll go on through Chesterfield.* If I can't ride in my own carriage, I can ride in my sister's motor-car.

It is a still September afternoon. By the ponds in the old park, we see colliers slowly loafing, fishing, poaching, in spite of all notices.

And at every lane-end there is a bunch of three or four policemen, blue-bottles, big, big-faced, stranger policeman. Every field path, every stile seems to be guarded. There are great pits, coal mines, in the fields. And at the end of the paths coming out of the field from the colliery, along the high-road, the colliers are squatted on their heels, on the wayside grass, silent and watchful. Their faces are clean, white, and all the months of the strike have given them no colour and no tan. They are pit-bleached. They squat in silent remoteness, as if in the upper galleries of hell. And the policemen, alien, stand in a group near the stile. Each lot pretends not to be aware of the others.

It is past three. Down the path from the pit come straggling what my little nephew* calls "the dirty ones." They are the men who have broken strike, and gone back to work. They are not many: their faces are black, they are in their pit-dirt. They linger till they have collected, a group of a dozen or so "dirty ones", near the stile, then they trail off down the road, the policemen, the alien blue-bottles, escorting them. And the "clean ones", the colliers still on strike, squat by the wayside and watch without looking. They say nothing. They neither laugh nor stare. But there they are, a picket, and with their bleached faces they see without looking, and they register with the silence of doom, squatted down in rows by the road-side.

The "dirty ones" straggle off in the lurching, almost slinking walk of colliers, swinging their heavy feet and going as if the mine-roof were still over their heads. The big blue policemen follow at a little distance. No voice is raised: nobody seems aware of anybody else. But there is the silent, hellish registering in the consciousness of all three groups, clean ones, dirty ones, and blue-bottles.

So it is now all the way into Chesterfield, whose crooked spire lies below. The men who have gone back to work—they seem few, indeed—are lurching and slinking in quiet groups, home down the high-road, the police at their heels. And the pickets, with bleached faces, squat and lean and stand, in silent groups, with a certain pale fatality, like Hell, upon them.

And I, who remember the homeward-trooping of the colliers when I was a boy, the ringing of the feet, the red mouths and the quick whites of the eyes, the swinging pit-bottles, and the strange voices of men from the underworld calling back and forth, strong and, it seemed to me, gay with the queer, absolved gaiety of miners—I shiver, and feel I turn into a ghost myself. The colliers were noisy, lively, with strong underworld voices such as I have never heard in any other men, when I was a boy. And after all, it is not so long ago. I am only forty-one.

But after the war, the colliers went silent: after 1920. Till 1920 there was a strange power of life in them, something wild and urgent, that one could hear in their voices. They were always excited, in the afternoon, to come up above-ground: and excited, in the morning, at going down. And they called in the darkness with strong, strangely evocative voices. And at the little local foot-ball matches, on the damp, dusky Saturday afternoons of winter, great, full-throated cries came howling from the football field, in the zest and the wildness of life.

But now, the miners go by to the football match in silence like ghosts, and from the field comes a poor, ragged shouting. These are the men of my own generation, who went to the board school with me. And they are almost voiceless. They go to the welfare clubs, and drink with a sort of hopelessness.

I feel I hardly know any more the people I come from, the colliers of the Erewash Valley district.* They are changed, and I suppose I am changed. I find it so much easier to live in Italy. And they have got a new kind of shallow consciousness, all newspaper and cinema, which I am not in touch with. At the same time, they have, I think an underneath ache and heaviness very much like my own. It must be so, because when I see them, I feel it so strongly.

They are the only people who move me strongly, and with whom I feel myself connected in deeper destiny. It is they who are, in some peculiar way, "home" to me. I shrink away from them, and I have an acute nostalgia for them.

And now, this last time, I feel a doom over the country, and a shadow of despair over the hearts of the men, which leaves me no rest. Because the same doom is over me, wherever I go, and the same despair touches my heart.

Yet it is madness to despair, while we still have the course of destiny open to us.

One is driven back to search one's own soul, for a way out into a new destiny.

A few things I know, with inner knowledge.

I know that what I am struggling for is life, more life ahead, for myself and the men who will come after me: struggling against fixations and corruptions.

I know that the miners at home are men very much like me, and I am very much like them: ultimately, we want the same thing. I know they are, in the life sense of the word, good.

I know that there is ahead the mortal struggle for property.

I know that the ownership of property has become, now, a problem, a religious problem.* But it is one we can solve.

I know I want to own a few things: my personal things. But I also know that I want to own no more than those. I don't want to own a house, nor land, nor a motor-car, nor shares in anything. I don't want a fortune—not even an assured income.

At the same time, I don't want poverty and hardship. I know I need enough money to leave me free in my movements, and I want to be able to earn that money without humiliation.

I know that most decent people feel very much the same in this respect: and the indecent people must, in their indecency, be subordinated to the decent.

I know that we could, if we would, establish little by little a true democracy in England: we could nationalise the land and industries and means of transport, and make the whole thing work infinitely better than at present, *if we would*. It all depends on the spirit in which the thing is done.

I know we are on the brink of a class war.

I know we had all better hang ourselves at once, than enter on a struggle which shall be a fight for the ownership or non-ownership of property, pure and simple, and nothing beyond.

I know the ownership of property is a problem that may have to be fought out. But beyond the fight must lie a new hope, a new beginning.

I know our vision of life is all wrong. We must be prepared to have a new conception of what it means, *to live*. And everybody should try to help to build up this new conception, and everybody should be prepared to destroy, bit by bit, our old conception.

I know that man cannot live by his own will alone.* With his soul, he must search for the sources of the power of life. It is life we want.

I know that where there is life, there is essential beauty. Genuine beauty, which fills the soul, is an indication of life, and genuine ugliness, which blasts the soul, is an indication of morbidity.—But prettiness is opposed to beauty.

I know that, first and foremost, we must be sensitive to life and to its movements. If there is power, it must be sensitive power.

I know that we must look after the quality of life, not the quantity. Hopeless life should be put to sleep, the idiots and the hopeless sick and the true criminal. And the birth-rate should be controlled.*

I know we must take up the responsibility for the future, now. A great change is coming, and must come. What we need is some glimmer of a vision of a world that shall be, beyond the change. Otherwise we shall be in for a great débâcle.

What is alive, and open, and active, is good. All that makes for inertia, lifelessness, dreariness, is bad. This is the essence of morality.

What we should live for is life and the beauty of aliveness, imagination, awareness, and contact. To be perfectly alive is to be immortal.

I know these things, along with other things. And it is nothing very new to know these things. The only new thing would be to act on them.

And what is the good of saying these things, to men whose whole education consists in the fact that twice two are four?—which, being interpreted, means that twice tuppence is fourpence. All our education, the whole of it, is formed upon this little speck of dust.

GETTING ON

The dating of this essay, hitherto unpublished, relies on circumstantial evidence. In several respects its contents replicate those of '[Return to Bestwood]', therefore bringing them into chronological proximity: both refer to Lawrence's visit to his birthplace in September 1926; both include Austin Harrison's prediction for Lawrence's future and the observations on it by Lydia Lawrence and by Lawrence himself; both refer to 'getting on'; and in both the writer describes himself as 'snotty-nosed' or 'dirty-nosed' when young. There are, however, very important differences. There is no reference whatsoever to the strike which features so prominently in '[Return to Bestwood]'. Lawrence's distress and shock at the profound effects of the strike were so intense that it is difficult to believe that 'Getting On' was written when the strike was still current. It ended on 19 November 1926.

There are two further notable differences between the essays: the constant emphasis on 'success' in 'Getting On' and the prominence given in it to a person not mentioned at all in '[Return to Bestwood]': Henry Saxton, Lawrence's *bête noir* but admired by Lydia Lawrence.

In the second version of *Lady Chatterley's Lover* – written *c.* 1 December 1926 to 25 February 1927 – 'Paxton', for whom Saxton undoubtedly provided the model, is presented as still alive: 'he was over eighty now, and paralysed, but still a tyrant . . . at the age of eighty-four'.[1] The remarks occur in Chapter VI of the novel and were probably written before the end of 1926 when Saxton was 84 and, as the result of a stroke suffered six years before, 'paralysed' to some degree. He died on 1 January 1927. In 'Getting On', however, Lawrence writes of Saxton in the past tense. It is extremely improbable that Lawrence's family would have delayed sending news of the death to him; his views – as well as those of his mother – on Saxton would be well known. Though his first recorded mention of the death occurs in a letter to Ada Clarke over three weeks later (*Letters*, v. 631), this is very unlikely to indicate his first knowledge of it.

[1] *The First and Second Lady Chatterley Novels*, ed. Mehl and Jansohn, pp. 318–19.

The central theme is of further significance for dating. That the theme is 'success' can scarcely be doubted: there is Lydia Lawrence's humiliation at her husband's lack of success, her passionate desire for her children's financial success and her deference to the demonstrably successful (and now recently deceased) Henry Saxton; her hope – buoyed up by Austin Harrison's memorable commendation – for Lawrence's literary success in particular; but, despite the many favourable omens, there is also what he called his signal 'lack of "real" success' such as was conspicuous in the wealth achieved by the novelist Michael Arlen.

The cumulative weight of evidence leads to the conclusion that 'Getting On' was the 'more or less personal article' Lawrence wrote for the German publishing house, Insel-Verlag; he sent what is presumed to have been the ribbon copy direct to the publishers; and a duplicate went to Nancy Pearn on 9 January 1927 (v. 620). She acknowledged its arrival on 27 January, mildly lamenting the absence from it of 'rather more details as to just when and why and how and so on you came to write this and that', and entitling it for obvious thematic reasons as 'BECOMING A SUCCESS'. This was later echoed by Lawrence himself when he instructed Nancy Pearn: 'don't send out that autobiographical sketch of mine – "On being a Success" – please' (v. 648). Allowing time for the news of Saxton's death to reach Lawrence in Italy, the likelihood is that the piece was written certainly after 19 November 1926 and probably *c*. 5–8 January 1927.

It did not appear in the Insel-Verlag *Almanach* and has remained unpublished until the present edition.

GETTING ON

They talk about home, but what is home? I went this autumn once more to the place of my birth, a little mining town eight miles out of Nottingham. And once more I was on hot bricks, to get away. I find I can be at home anywhere, except at home. I feel perfectly calm in London or Paris or Rome or Munich or Sydney or San Francisco. The one place where I feel absolutely not at home, is my home place, where I lived for the first twenty-one years of my life.

"I remember, I remember
The house where I was born—"* very vaguely that is, because we left it when I was a year old. It was at a corner of the ugly streets of miners dwellings known as The Buildings, and it was stuck on to Henry Saxton's shop.* Henry Saxton was a burly bullying fellow with fair curly hair, and though he never pronounced an 'h' in the right place, he had a great opinion of Henry. I knew him well enough, because he was the afternoon Sunday-school superintendent for many years, and he kept us in order. And without knowing him, I disliked him, the loud and vulgar way he spoke.

My mother seemed, however, to have a respect for him. She, after all, was only a collier's wife, and at that, wife of a collier who drank, who never went to church, who spoke broad dialect, and was altogether one of the common colliers. My mother, of course, spoke good English and was not of the colliery class. She came from Nottingham, was a city girl, had been a sort of clerk to a lace manufacturer* whom she probably adored.

A queer woman, my mother. Why, in heaven's name, did she have such a respect for a man like Henry Saxton? She was far more intelligent than he, better educated, in that he wasn't educated at all, and infinitely better bred. Yet she spoke of him with an absolute, almost a tender, respect. And this puzzled my earliest childhood. As a tiny child, I had no instinctive respect for him, and no liking. He was loud-mouthed, aggressive, a pusher, a man who wore his gold watch and chain on his full stomach as if it gave off royal rays. My mother was a shrewd and ironical woman. Yet she looked up to Henry Saxton with tender respect.

And, since I was foreordained to accept all her values, I had to look up to Henry Saxton too.

He was, of course, terribly respectable. He was Sunday School Superintendent, he was a deacon at the Congregational Chapel, where he managed to make the life of each succeeding minister a misery, with his hectoring impudence. He criticised the sermons, he who hardly knew A from B: and if the congregation fell off a little, so that the collection on Sundays went down a few shillings, then he sacked the clergyman. The Chapel was another sort of shop to Henry, and the minister was his hired shopman. I remember only two ministers,* both good, honest men, whose memory I respect. And each of them was humiliated to the quick by Henry.

And my mother knew it all, yet she admired him. She thought him an infinitely more wonderful man than my father. Why, in heaven's name? Because he was a chapel man, and far more than that, because he was successful.* I can see now, that my mother found it so bitter to be very poor, with a husband who came home drunk and who was by no means "respected" in the village, and a dreary family of young children to bring up, that she had really just one idol, success. She felt herself humiliated beyond endurance by her conditions. Successful men succeeded in making money and passing beyond such conditions. Then let us have success at any price.

Now I am forty,* I realise that my mother deceived me. She stood for all that was lofty and noble and delicate and sensitive and pure, in my life. And all the time, she was worshipping success, because she hadn't got it. She was worshipping a golden calf* of a Henry Saxton.

I must say, it was not her *nature* to worship Henry Saxton. She could say very cutting things about him, very jeering. She would pull the tail of the golden calf very shrewdly. For instance, she would tell of people who came to his shop for sugar. Sugar in those days was very cheap. "What else do yer want besides sugar?" said Henry.—"Nothing."—"Then you can go. I shan't serve sugar to them as buys nothing else."—And off went the unfortunate collier's wife. Henry lost a tiny bit on sugar.

I think my mother admired even that in him. She thought it "strength." I remember the story from my very small childhood. Even then *I* thought it rudeness. But it is what makes success.

My mother was all the time sitting down between two stools: My father had charm and a certain warm, uncurbed vitality that made a glow in the house, when he was not in an evil temper. He loved my mother, in his own way, and thought her a much higher being than himself. She loved him physically, felt his charm always, and hated him for being false and mean in money matters. There was so little money. And he kept so much for himself, selfishly. He made "conditions" so wretched. So she despised him, and fought him tooth and nail.

She even fought her love for him, and hated him for his charm. At the same time, she had five children by him. And when she was well over forty, and he must have been forty-seven or more, and came back home at last from a convalescent home, after his leg had been smashed in a bad mining accident, she was in love with him like any girl, and he sat ruddy and resplendent on the sofa, being made much of: though this state of things didn't last, unfortunately. I was about fourteen, and for the first time my eyes were opened a little. I had thought he made her life an agony pure and simple. For years I prayed that he might either be converted into a chapel man, or die. They were not my own prayers. They were a child's prayers for his mother, who has captured him and in whom he believes implicitly.

My mother fought with deadly hostility against my father, all her life. He was not hostile, till provoked, then he too was a devil. But my mother began it. She seemed to begrudge his very existence. She begrudged and hated her own love for him, she fought against his natural charm, vindictively. And by the time she died, at the age of fifty-five, she neither loved him nor hated him any more. She had got over her feeling for him, and was "free." So she died of cancer.

Her feeling for us, also, was divided. We were her own, therefore she loved us. But we were "his," so she despised us a little.—I was the most delicate: a pale-faced, dirty-nosed frail boy. So she devoted a great love to me. And she also despised me. I was one of the inferior brats her love for my father—or her disastrous marriage with him—had thrust upon her. She loved me tenderly. And for me, of course, she was the one being on earth: or so I *thought*, anyhow. But now, in the after-years, I realise that she had decided I was going to die, and that was a great deal to her. Also, from many little things I remember, and from things my sisters tell me she said, I realise that she also despised the delicate brat with a chest catarrh and an abnormal love for her. She looked on us all as her lower class inferiors.

She admired me when I won a scholarship and went to the High school in Nottingham, and knew the swells. I was going to be a little gentleman!—But I made no friends among the little gentlemen, and went on quite aimiably, quite pleasantly at school, without making the slightest connection with the middle-class boys.* I never felt any connection, so it never occurred to me there might be any, We just lived with different outlooks.

It was Miriam* who gave me my first incentive to write—when I was about eighteen or nineteen. She was a poor girl on a little farm. Her people were poorer even than we. But it was they who roused me to consciousness. And it was for her, Miriam, I wrote scraps of poems and bits of a novel. I wrote them furtively, at home, pretending it was study: writing in the kitchen where all the household affairs were going on. My father hated study and books—he hated to see us poring. My mother liked to see us submissively studying, to "get on." She wanted to be proud of us. And of course, I know she twigged when I was writing poems or bits of a novel. She was so shrewd. I wrote in a college exercise book, and pushed the book in the shelf among the others. But she knew, and she read the things when I wasn't there. Never did she say anything to me. Nor did I say anything to her. She knew also I always took the scraps of writing to Miriam. Poor Miriam, she always thought them wonderful: otherwise I should never have gone on. But for her, I should probably never have written—I never thought of myself as a writer, or of anything special at all. I thought myself rather clever, after I had passed examinations, but because I was not strong, I thought myself of rather less account than most people: the weakling in health! And if I had never written, I probably should have died soon. The being able to express one's soul keeps one alive.

At last, when I was twenty-two, and going to college in Nottingham, one sunny warm day, half-day at college, when my mother loved me to come home and we were two together and alone, she took the exercise-book in which I had re-written the scene in the *White Peacock* where the bride runs up the church path. She put on her spectacles, and read with an amused look on her face.

"But my boy," she said, amused and a bit mocking, as she put down the book and took off her spectacles, "how do you *know* it was like that?"*

How did I know? My heart stood still. She treated it as if it were a school essay and she were the teacher: kindly and sceptical. And then I saw in her the slight contempt she had for me: nay, even more, the slight hostility to my presumptuousness. I might "get on" in the ordinary rut, and even become a school-master at three pounds a week. Which would be a great rise above my father. But that I should presume to "know" things off my own bat!—things I had not learned at school!—well, it was presumption in me.

So I became a school-teacher, and went down to Croydon, London, to teach boys in an elementary school, at ninety pounds a year. I hated it: I am no teacher. I wrote in the evenings, but never looked on myself as a writer. There was a burning sort of pleasure in writing: and Miriam loved everything I wrote. I never showed anything to my mother. She would have had an amused feeling about it all, and have felt sceptical. To this day, my family is annoyed that I write unpleasant books that nobody really wants to read: certainly *they* don't, although they work through them, I suppose, because they still "love" me so dearly: me, the brother Bertie, not the embarrassing D. H. Lawrence.

It was Miriam who first sent poems of mine to the English Review: when I was twenty-three. It was she who got back the answer, accepting them. And she was still at home in Underwood, I was in London, far away. Ford Madox Hueffer, who had just begun to edit the English Review—and he did it so well—immediately told me I was a genius: which was a mere phrase to me. Among the working classes, geniuses don't enter. Hueffer was very kind to me, so was Edward Garnett.* They were the first literary men I ever met—and the first men *really* outside my own class. They were very kind, very generous. Hueffer read the Manuscript of the *White Peacock*. I had by now finished the novel, having struggled for five years to get it out of the utterly unformed chaos of my consciousness, having written some of it eleven times, and all of it four times. I hewed it out with infinitely more labour than my father hewed out coal. But once it was done, I knew more or less what I had to do.

Hueffer said the *White Peacock* had every fault that an English novel can have—"but you are a genius." That is how they have always been with me. I have every fault that a writer can have—but I have genius. I used to say: For God's sake, don't insult me by calling me a genius. Now I let them talk.

Heinemann the publisher accepted *The White Peacock* at once, and gave me fifty pounds. My mother was dying of cancer: I was twenty-five. Heinemann's kindly sent me an advance copy of my novel. My mother held it in her hands, opened it—then it was enough. She died two days later. Perhaps she thought it spelled success. Perhaps she thought it helped to justify her life. Perhaps she only felt terribly, terribly bitter that she was dying, just as the great adventure was opening before her. Anyhow she died.

A few months before she died, Austin Harrison, who had taken over the English Review, which published all my early things, wrote to her: "By the time he is forty, he will be riding in his own carriage—" And my mother is supposed to have said: "Ay! if he lives to be forty!"—She was so sure of my not living, it seems! I might even ride in my carriage, if I lived! But I was not to live.—I don't know why. I always had more vitality than all the rest put together. My very vitality wore me thin. But vitality doesn't kill a man till it is dammed up.

Well, I am forty-one, and am not dead, neither have I yet ridden in my own carriage, not even in my own motor-car: only in my own buggy, driving my own two horses down the rocky trail of my own little ranch in New Mexico. That is all. Whether it justifies the oracle, who knows.

And what my mother would say to it all, I don't know. She would have hated my "sexual" writing, and have felt I had brought deep shame on her, when the "Rainbow" was suppressed. Or perhaps not. Perhaps she would have decided I was worth her backing. But she would have been chagrined at my lack of "real" success: that I don't make more money; that I am not *really* popular, like *Michael Arlen*, or *really* genteel, like Mr Galsworthy:* that I have a bad reputation as an improper writer, so that she couldn't discuss me complacently with my aunts: that I don't make any "real" friends among the upper classes: that I don't *really* rise in the world, only drift about without any *real* status. All this would have been a chagrin to her. It is perhaps as well she did not live to take part in the adventure.

WHICH CLASS I BELONG TO

To provide a date for this essay it is necessary to acknowledge its close relationship with 'Myself Revealed' which appeared in the *Sunday Dispatch* on 17 February 1929. There can be no doubt that the first was the 'parent' of the second. From the description of Lawrence's mother with her inability to speak even a sentence of dialect accurately, and her command of a 'fine Italian hand', to her 'little black bonnet [and] . . . shrewd, "different" face', through the account of Lawrence's education and meeting with the *littérateur*, Ford Madox Hueffer (1873–1939), to his own lack of intimacy with the Italian peasantry yet his recognition that they formed his '*ambiente*' – 'Which Class I Belong To' was patently the source of 'Myself Revealed'. It must therefore have been written before February 1929. Uncertainty remains, however, over the exact date of its composition and the circumstances which led to its existence.

When she acknowledged the receipt of 'Getting On' on 27 January 1927, Nancy Pearn said that she would keep her copy and 'ponder over the situation' about publishing it.[1] On 2 March she reiterated her intention to delay trying to place the essay 'for the time being'. As has been made clear above (see p. 26), the essay was not published. But over 20 months later, on 12 December 1928, Nancy Pearn wrote to Lawrence:

> And now how about the suggestion from the '*Sunday Dispatch*' that they be allowed to extract an article from that autobiographical sketch of yours I have been holding until just such an opportunity as the present occurred. You remember it – the one you wrote a few years ago for some German publication. The editor says he could use about a third of it, and if allowed to cut it in such a way as to make the fifteen hundred words or so article they envisage, will pay Twenty-five Guineas.

To conclude that the 'autobiographical sketch' to which Nancy Pearn was referring was 'Getting On' would be wrong. The article which

[1] In her letter of 27 January Nancy Pearn retitled the essay 'BECOMING A SUCCESS'; Lawrence echoed this on 25 February referring to it as 'On being a Success'; while these alternative titles were appropriate to 'Getting On', they were not applicable to 'Which Class I Belong To'.

appeared in the *Sunday Dispatch* – 'Myself Revealed' – could not conceivably have been extracted from 'Getting On'; its source was 'Which Class I Belong To'.

We must therefore accept that there had been a request from an unidentified German publication for an autobiographical sketch; that the request prompted Lawrence to write 'Which Class I Belong To'; and that it was this to which Nancy Pearn was referring in her letter of December 1928. She in turn had been approached by the *Dispatch* editor and had shown him the essay she had been 'holding' for a suitable 'opportunity'; he had asked for a shorter version and was provided with 'Myself Revealed'. Her remark about a sketch written 'a few years ago' is presumed to have amounted to no more than a colloquial inexactitude.

Internal evidence suggests that the article was written 'Here, in Italy' (39:35). Taking account of Lawrence's absences from the Villa Mirenda and making allowance for Nancy Pearn's imprecise reference to time past, the date of composition was *c*. mid-April 1927.

'Which Class I Belong To' is previously unpublished.

WHICH CLASS I BELONG TO

It seems to me now, that the gulf between the classes of society, in all the white world, is infinitely deeper than the gulf between nations. As a matter of fact, consciousness is above all things international, and any man of culture, no matter what nation he belongs to, has a permanent contact with any other conscious individual of the white race. One must stick to the white race, and not include the Hindus, even, because with them the European culture is super-imposed, as a sort of mimicry of the ruling races. But among the white race, educated people are very much alike, and can understand one another at once, even though their language be different. There are national idiosyncrasies and national biases. But the dynamic ideas and the conventional emotions and the behaviour are almost identical in the middle-class individuals of any European nation, or of America. There is no true upper class left.

The point is that the content of the consciousness is almost homogeneous in all people of the European culture: and in them all, the consciousness functions in very much the same way. In great things as in small, domestic politics or international finance, internal commerce or a world war, each nation behaves in almost the same way as each other nation: and what is more, thinks the same thoughts, says the same things, re-acts to the same stimuli.

This is, we repeat, the oneness of middle-class Europe. And in all the world there are today only two classes: middle-class and working class.

The cleavage is not vertical: it is horizontal. And there is one line of cleavage only. The middle-class has absorbed the upper class entirely. Kings now belong to the "best" bourgeoisie. The line of cleavage is horizontal. And it cuts through the whole civilised world, horizontally, dividing mankind into two layers, the upper and the lower.

It may be argued that the working classes today are only lower-middle-class. All are striving towards the same goal, to become richer and to have the disposing of riches. Seen from the outside, this is true. Seen from the inside, it is a great fallacy.

Myself, I was born among the working class. My father was a collier, and only a collier. He went down into the pit at twelve years old, and down the pit he went till he was nearly seventy. He could with great difficulty write a few words for a letter, and he could spell down the columns of the local newspaper. But though he always read some bit of the newspaper, he very rarely knew what it meant, the bit he had read. It never occurred to me that it was strange, that he should almost invariably say to my mother: "Lass, what's meanin' o' this 'ere about Canada?" Even when it was explained, a little impatiently, he knew no more. Canada, to him, was somewhere in America, and America was merely somewhere where you went when you were discontented at home. It was all words, and "talk." But he liked to appear to know something about it, because the colliers talked in the public-house, politics and newspaper-stuff, garbled into a sort of fairy-tale.

My father earned, I suppose, on an average, from thirty to thirty-five shillings a week. In summer, however, there were bad times, when the pits were not turning, and the wages would go down to twenty-five, twenty, even fifteen shillings. But though there was a family of children, my father always kept his own share. He never gave my mother more than thirty-shillings: in bad times, when he earned thirty shillings, he kept five for himself: out of twenty-five, he kept the same—or perhaps four shillings. He *had* to have money in his pocket, to go the public-house.

My mother belonged potentially to the middle-classes. She spoke kings English, never could speak a sentence of the dialect correctly, wrote a fine Italian hand and an amusing, clever letter, and preferred the novels of the two discrepant Georges, George Eliot and George Meredith.*

Nevertheless, ours was an absolutely working class home. My mother, in a shabby little black bonnet, was a working-man's wife, in spite of her shrewd, "different" face. And we were brought up as working-class children, pure and simple.

Till I was twelve, when I got a County Council scholarship, and went to Nottingham High School. This richly endowed school is supposed to be one of the best day schools in England. It was then under, Dr Gow, later of Westminster.*

Well, there was I suddenly figuring as a clever boy, and a pride to my mother. I suppose she was as surprised as I was.—We were a tiny batch of scholarship boys—"common" boys—among the rest of the truly middle-class lads, whose fathers were professors or lace-manufacturers or shop-keepers: anyhow, rich enough to pay the fees. But there was no very marked snobbishness. In Nottingham High School, I never had any sense of being looked down on, because I was a scholarship boy, of the working people. And yet there was a difference. There was a gap. It was nothing voluntary. I remember the better-class boys as having been kindly, almost always, and always ordinarily respectful. But there was a peculiar, indefinable difference. It was as if, boys of the same race, the same locality, the same everything, still we were, in some way, different *animals*.

After the High School, and a brief spell in an office, I became a school teacher, responsible for a class of boys, at half-a-crown a week for the first year.* Then, as a school-teacher, I went to Nottingham University to take the normal course. We who had matriculated were allowed to take the degree course, along with the paying students. And the first year, I took the Arts work.*

But it was the same again. The "normal" youths kept together, the paying students were apart. We met, we talked, we exchanged a modicum of ideas. But there was the indefinable gulf between the two sets. It was not snobbism, exactly. It was something deeper. It was something in the very way the heart beat. I remember I sent two poems to the college paper, *On dit*!*—and they refused them in exactly the same way the middle-class monthlies still would refuse them.

The mysterious difference in vibration between the working-class nature and that of the middle-class I never analysed, just accepting it as a fact. But there it was. Even one had no real pleasure listening to the professors. They had that other peculiar vibration which caused them to be uninteresting, and in some curious way, *outside* one's own life. By the end of the first year I was bored by the university,* dropped the degree work, went on with the normal course, did no work at all, and wrote bits of the White Peacock or read novels during lectures.

Again, no one was unfriendly. The professors were lenient, even made slight advances, very kindly. But it was no good. Unless one were by nature a climber, one could not respond in kind. The middle-class seemed quite open, quite willing for one to climb into it. And one turned away, ungratefully.

It was the same with the rest of the normal students. Only one climbed in among the other class, and he was a Jew. The cleverest man of my own year—also a normal student, and a cleverer fellow than myself, by far—was expelled, went loose, drank, and died.* So it was.

After college, I went down to Croydon, near London, to teach—at a hundred pounds a year. It was a new school,* and hard work. The actual teaching I didn't mind, and the boys, on the whole, I liked very much—they were of all sorts—but the so-called school discipline, the bossiness, the false sort of power one was obliged to assume, all that I hated.

It was when I was at Croydon, when I was twenty-three, that a girl-friend* sent some poems of mine to the English Review. Ford Madox Hueffer was then editor, for a brief, brilliant while. He wrote to me, and asked me to come and see him. And he was most kind. He got Heinemann's to publish "The White Peacock" at once. Hueffer said to me "Your book has got every fault that the English novel can have, but you have genius."—They never seemed to grudge me genius, because, perhaps, it is something that can be legitimately patronised. But published I was, and always have been, without any effort on my part. They always allowed me "genius", and every other fault the English novelist can have.

Hueffer introduced me to Edward Garnett, and no-one could have been kinder than he was, helping, advising, asking me down for the week-end to his house in Kent. In those school-teaching days, it was an adventure. And London was an adventure. Ezra Pound* was another adventure, and the Bayswater world he introduced me to. And then Austin Harrison,* who took over the English Review, would ask me to dinner or to a theatre, and I met all kinds of people.

And that I have not got a thousand friends, and a place in England among the esteemed, is entirely my own fault. The door to "success" has been held open to me. The social ladder has been put ready for me to climb. I have known all kinds of people, and been treated quite well by everyone, practically, whom I have known personally.

Yet here I am, nowhere, as it were, and infinitely an outsider. And of my own choice.

It is only this year, since coming back to Europe from America that I have asked myself why. Why, why, why could I never go through the open door, into the other world? Why am I forever on the outskirts?

And it seems to me the answer is banal enough: class! I cannot go into the middle-class world. I have, as far as circumstances go left the working-class world. So I have no world at all, and am content.

What is it, then, that prevents so many capable men from moving on in the apparently natural order of progress from the lower class into the upper class? Why can I not follow in the footsteps of Barrie, who is a son of the working-class?—or of Wells?*—and become well-to-do middle-class?

What is the peculiar repugnance one feels, towards entering the middle-class world? It is not that there is anything very difficult about it, it seems to me. On the contrary, nothing is so easy as to be a middle-class man among middle-class men: or call it upper-class, if you like. For one who can bring himself to it.

What is the obstacle? I have looked for it in myself, as a clue to this dangerous cleavage between the classes. And I find it is a very deep obstacle. It is in the manner of contact. The contact, among the lower classes—as perhaps, in the past, among the aristocracy—is much more immediate, more physical, between man and man, than it ever is among the middle classes. The middle class can be far more *intimate*, yet never so *near* to one another. It is the difference between the animal, physical affinity that can govern the lives of men, and the other, the affinity of culture and purpose, which actually does govern the mass today.

But the affinity of culture and purpose that holds the vast middle-class world together seems to me to be an intensification today, of the acquisitive and possessive instinct. The dominant instinct of the middle-class world, that is, of the whole world to day, is the possessive instinct, which in its active form is the acquisitive instinct.

It may be said that the working people are *more* acquisitive and more possessive by instinct, than the other class. This may be true of many. But any individual of the lower class who has the dominant acquisitive instinct will automatically pass into the middle or upper class.

The essential working man, like my father, for example, is far too vague to be really acquisitive. He will take sixpence, never thinking that he might have had a pound. And why? Because he wants the sixpence to go to the public-house, to be with the other men, in that queer physical contact which is the affinity of the blood, and is, in the long run, more deeply necessary to men than the affinity of the mind, but which, none the less, can be a prison either to man or woman who is confined to it. So that I myself could never go back into the working class, to the blindness, the obtuseness, the prejudice, the mass-emotions. But neither can I adapt myself to the middle-class, to sacrifice the old, deep blood-affinity between myself and my fellows.

Here, in Italy, my environment, my *ambiente* is formed by the peasants who work the *podere*.* I am not intimate with them, hardly say anything to them beyond Good-day!—yet they are there, they are present for me, and I for them. If I had to live with them in their cottage, it would be a prison to me. And yet, if I had to choose between two evils, I should choose that, rather than to be imprisoned in the circle of the *intelligentsia* and the middle-class.

Because, it seems to me, one *could* have both affinities, the physical affinity with one's fellow-men, and the mental or spiritual or "conscious" affinity. Yet you can't have them equally. One or the other must predominate. And the mental affinity, in its insistence on predominating, insists on the destruction and the sacrifice of the physical affinity. Even here in Italy, it is bad form to make gestures with your hands when you speak: and an Italian has to murder a good part of himself before he can suppress his gestures. But the middle class insists on it, and so it is done.

To enter the middle class, a man has to sacrifice something that is very deep and necessary to him, his natural physical affinity with other men and women. That is, *if he's got it*. If he hasn't got it, he is bastard middle-class already.

But it is the loss of the old, deep physical affinity between man and man, and man and woman, which causes the great gulf between the classes. And it is down this gulf that our civilisation will collapse: is already rapidly collapsing.

MAKING LOVE TO MUSIC

On 12 April 1927 – in a quandary about whether and how to publish his new novel, *Lady Chatterley's Lover*, and just returned from his tour of Etruscan sites preparatory to writing *Sketches of Etruscan Places* – Lawrence promised soon to send Nancy Pearn 'some small things' (*Letters*, vi. 29). A fortnight later, on 26 April, he sent her 'a little thing post haste' with the instruction: 'If you don't like it, don't bother about it – just give it to Barmby' (vi. 40). The 'little thing' was the essay 'Making Love to Music'; his letter was written on the last page of the manuscript. Whether Nancy Pearn forwarded it to A. W. Barmby, the manager of Curtis Brown's New York office, as Lawrence proposed, is not known. The piece remained unpublished until its inclusion in *Phoenix*.

MAKING LOVE TO MUSIC

"To me, dancing," said Romeo, "is just making love to music."

"That's why you never will dance with me, I suppose," replied Juliet.

"Well, you know, you are a bit too much of an individualist—"

It is a curious thing, but the ideas of one generation become the instincts of the next. We are all of us, largely, the embodied ideas of our grandmothers, and without knowing it, we behave as such. It is odd that the grafting works so quickly, but it seems to. Let the ideas change rapidly, and there follows a correspondingly rapid change in humanity. We become what we think. Worse still, we have become what our grandmothers thought. And our children's children will become the lamentable things that we are thinking. Which is the psychological visiting of the sins of the fathers upon the children.* For we do not become just the lofty or beautiful thoughts of our grandmothers. Alas no! We are the embodiment of the most potent ideas of our progenitors, and these ideas were mostly private ones, not to be admitted in public, but to be transmitted as instincts and as the dynamics of behaviour to the third and fourth generation. Alas for the thing that our grandmothers brooded over in secret, and wished and willed in private. That thing are we.

What did they wish and will? One thing is certain: they wished to be made love to, to music. They wished man were not a coarse creature, jumping to his goal, and finished. They wanted heavenly strains to resound, while he held their hand, and a new musical movement to burst forth, as he put his arm round their waist. With infinite variations the music was to soar on, from level to level of love-making, in a delicious dance, the two things inextricable, the two persons likewise.

To end, of course, before the so-called consummation of love-making, which, to our grandmothers in their dream, and therefore to us in actuality, is the grand anti-climax. Not a consummation, but a humiliating anti-climax.

This is the so-called act of love itself, the actual knuckle of the whole bone of contention: a humiliating anti-climax. The bone of contention, of course, is sex. Sex is very charming and very delightful, so long as you make love to music, and you tread the clouds with Shelley, in a two-step.* But to come at last to the grotesque bathos of copulation: no Sir! Nay-nay!

Even a man like Maupassant, an apparent devotee of sex, says the same thing:* and Maupassant is grandfather, or great-grandfather, to very many of us. Surely, he says, the act of copulation is the Creator's cynical joke against us. To have created in us all these beautiful and noble sentiments of love, to set the nightingale and all the heavenly spheres singing, merely to throw us into this grotesque posture, to perform this humiliating act, is a piece of cynicism worthy, not of a benevolent Creator, but of a mocking demon.

Poor Maupassant, there is the clue to his own catastrophe! He wanted to make love to music. And he realised, with rage, that copulate to music you cannot. So he divided himself against himself, and damned his eyes in disgust, then copulated all the more.

We, however, his grandchildren, are shrewder. Men *must* make love to music, and woman *must* be made love to, to a string and saxophone accompaniment. It is our inner necessity. Because our grandfathers, and especially our great-grandfathers, left the music most severely out of their copulations. So now we leave the copulation most severely out of our musical love-making. We *must* make love to music: it is our grandmothers' dream, become an inward necessity in us, an unconscious motive force. Copulate you cannot, to music. So cut out that part, and solve the problem.

The popular modern dances, far from being "sexual," are distinctly anti-sexual. But there again, we must make a distinction. We should say, the modern jazz and tango and Charleston, far from being an incitement to copulation, are in direct antagonism to copulation. Therefore it is all nonsense for the churches to raise their voice against dancing, against "making love to music." Because the Church, and society at large, has no particular antagonism to sex. It would be ridiculous, for sex is so large and all-embracing, that the religious passion itself is largely sexual. But, as they say, "sublimated." This is the great recipe for sex: only sublimate it! Imagine the quicksilver heated and passing off in weird, slightly poisonous vapour, instead of heavily rolling together and fusing: and there you have the process: sublimation: making love to music! Morality has really no quarrel at all with "sublimated" sex. Most "nice" things are "sublimated sex." What morality hates, what the Church hates, what modern *mankind* hates—for what, after all, is "morality" except the instinctive revulsion of the majority?—is just copulation. The modern youth especially just have an instinctive aversion from copulation. They love sex. But they inwardly loathe copulation, even when they play at it. As for playing at it, what else are they to do, given the toys? But they don't like it. They do it in a sort of self-spite. And they turn away, with disgust and relief, from this bedridden act, to make love once more to music.

And really, surely this is all to the good. If the young don't really *like* copulation, then they are safe. As for marriage, they will marry, according to their grandmothers' dream, for quite other reasons. Our grandfathers, or great-grandfathers, married crudely and unmusically, for copulation. That was the actuality—So the dream was all of music. The dream was the mating of two souls, to the faint chiming of the Seraphim.—We, the third and fourth generation, we are the dream made flesh.* They dreamed of a marriage with all things gross—meaning especially copulation—left out, and only the pure harmony of equality and intimate companionship remaining. And the young live out the dream. They marry: they copulate in a perfunctory and half-disgusted fashion, merely to show they can do it—And so they have children. But the marriage is made to music, the gramophone and the wireless orchestrate each small domestic act, and keep up the jazzing jig of connubial felicity, a felicity of companionship, equality, forbearance, and mutual sharing of everything the married couple have in common. Marriage set to music! The worn-out old serpent in this musical Eden of domesticity is the last, feeble instinct for copulation, which drives the married couple to clash upon the boring organic differences in one another, and prevents from being twin souls in almost identical bodies.—But we are wise, and soon learn to leave the humiliating act out altogether. It is the only wisdom.

We are such stuff as our Grandmothers' dreams were made on, and our little life is rounded by a band.*

The thing you wonder, as you watch the modern dancers making love to music in a dance-hall, is what kind of dances will our children's children dance? Our mothers' mothers danced quadrilles and sets of Lancers, and the waltz was almost an indecent thing to them. Our mothers' mothers' mothers danced minuets and Roger de Coverleys,* and smart and bouncing country dances which worked up the blood and danced a man nearer and nearer to copulation.

But Lo! even while she was being whirled round in the dance, our great-grandmother was dreaming of soft and throbbing music, and the arms of "one person," and the throbbing and sliding unison of this one, more elevated person, who would never coarsely bounce her towards bed and copulation, but would slide on with her forever, down the dim and sonorous vistas, making love without end to music without end, and leaving out entirely that disastrous, music-less full-stop of copulation, the end of ends.

So she dreamed, our great-grandmother, as she crossed hands and was flung around, and buffeted and busked towards bed, and the bouncing of the *bête à deux dos*.* She dreamed of men that were only embodied souls, not tiresome and gross males, lords and masters. She dreamed of "one person" who was all men in one, universal, and beyond narrow individualism.

So that now, the great-granddaughter is made love to by all men—to music—as if it were one man. To music, all men, as if it were one man, make love to her, and she sways in the arms, not of an individual, but of the modern species. It is wonderful. And the modern man makes love, to music, to all women, as if she were one woman. All woman, as if she were one woman! It is almost like Baudelaire making love to the vast thighs of Dame Nature herself:* except that that dream of our great-grandfather is still too copulative, though all-embracing.

But what is the dream that is simmering at the bottom of the soul of the modern young woman, as she slides to music across the floor, in the arms of the species, or as she waggles opposite the species, in the Charleston? If she is content, there is no dream. But woman is never content. If she were content, the Charleston and the Black Bottom* would not oust the tango.

She is not content. She is even less content, in the morning after the night before, than was her great-grandmother, who had been bounced by copulatory attentions. She is even less content, therefore her dream, though not risen yet to consciousness, is even more devouring and more rapidly subversive.

What is her dream, this slender, tender lady just out of her teens, who is varying the two-step with the Black Bottom? What can her dream be? Because what her dream is, that her children, and my children, or children's children, will become. It is the very ovum of the future soul, as my dream is the sperm.

There is not much left for her to dream of, because whatever she wants she can have. All men or no men, this man or that, she has the choice, for she has no lord and master. Sliding down the endless avenues of music, having an endless love endlessly made to her: she has this too. If she wants to be bounced into copulation, at a dead end, she can have that too: just to prove how monkeyish it is, and what a fumbling in the *cul de sac.*

Nothing is denied her, so there is nothing to want. And without desire, even dreams are lame. Lame dreams! Perhaps she has lame dreams, and wishes, last wish of all, she had no dreams at all.

But while life lasts, and is an affair of sleeping and waking, this is the one wish that will never be granted. From dreams no man escapeth, no woman either. Even the little blonde who is preferred by gentlemen* has a dream somewhere, if she, and we, and he, did but know it. Even a dream beyond emeralds and dollars.

What is it? What is the lame and smothered dream of the lady?—Whatever it is, she will never know: not till somebody has told it her, and then gradually, and after a great deal of spiteful repudiation, she will recognise it, and it will pass into her womb.

Myself, I do not know what the frail lady's dream may be. But depend upon one thing, it will be something very different from the present business. The dream and the business! - an eternal antipathy. So the dream, whatever it may be, will *not* be "making love to music." It will be something else.

Perhaps it will be the re-capturing of a dream that started in mankind, and never finished, was never fully unfolded. The thought occurred to me suddenly when I was looking at the remains of paintings on the walls of Etruscan tombs at Tarquinia.* There the painted women dance, in their transparent linen with heavier, coloured borders, opposite the naked-limbed men, in a splendour and an abandon which is not at all abandoned. There is a great beauty in them, as of life which has not finished. The dance is Greek, if you like, but not finished off like the Greek dancing. The beauty is not so pure, if you will, as the Greek beauty; but also it is more ample, not so narrowed. And there is not the slight element of abstraction, of inhumanity, which underlies all Greek expression, the tragic will.

The Etruscans, at least before the Romans smashed them, do not seem to have been tangled up with tragedy, as the Greeks were from the first. There seems to have been a peculiar-large carelessness about them, very human and non-moral. As far as one can judge, they never said: certain acts are immoral, just because we say so! They seem to have had a strong feeling for taking life sincerely as a pleasant thing. Even death was a gay and lively affair.

Moralists will say: Divine law wiped them out.—The answer to that is, divine law wipes everything out in time, even itself. And if the smashing power of the all-trampling Roman is to be identified with divine law, then all I can do is to look up another divinity.

No, I do believe that the unborn dream at the bottom of the soul of the shingled, modern young lady is this Etruscan young woman of mine, dancing with such abandon opposite her naked-limbed, strongly-dancing young man, to the sound of the double flute. They are wild with a dance that is heavy and light at the same time, and not a bit anti-copulative, yet not bouncingly copulative either.

That was another nice thing about the Etruscans: there was a phallic symbol everywhere, so everybody was used to it, and they no doubt all offered it small offerings, as the source of inspiration. Being part of the everyday life, there was no need to get it on the brain, as we tend to do.

And apparently the men, the men slaves at least, went gaily and jauntily round with no clothes on at all, and being therefore of a good brown colour, wore their skin for livery. And the Etruscan ladies thought nothing of it. Why should they? We think nothing of a naked cow, and we still refrain from putting our pet dogs into pants or petticoats: marvellous to relate: but then our ideal is Liberty, after all! So if the slave was stark naked, who gaily piped to the lady as she danced, and if her partner was three parts naked, and herself nothing but a transparency, well, nobody thought anything about it, there was nothing to shy off from, and all the fun was in the dance.

There it is, the delightful quality of the Etruscan dance. They are neither making love to music, to avoid copulation, nor are they bouncing towards copulation with a brass band accompaniment. They are just dancing a dance with the elixir of life. And if they have made a little offering to the stone phallus at the door, it is because when one is full of life one is full of possibilities, and the phallus gives life. And if they have made an offering also to the queer ark of the female symbol, at the door of a woman's tomb, it is because the womb too is the source of life, and a great fountain of dance-movements.

It is we who have narrowed the dance down to two movements: either bouncing towards copulation, or sliding and shaking and waggling, to elude it. Surely it is ridiculous to make love to music, and to music to be made love to! Surely the music is to dance to! And surely the modern young woman feels this, somewhere deep inside.

To the music one should dance, and dancing, dance. The Etruscan young woman is going gaily at it, after two-thousand five hundred years. She is not making love to music, nor is the dark-limbed youth, her partner. She is just dancing her very soul into existence, having made an offering on one hand to the lively phallus of man, on the other hand, to the shut womb-symbol of woman, and put herself on real good terms with both of them. So she is quite serene, and dancing herself as a very fountain of motion and of life, the young man opposite her dancing himself the same, in contrast and balance, with just the double flute to whistle round their naked heels.

And I believe this is, or will be, the dream of our pathetic music-stunned young girl of today, and the substance of her children's children, unto the third and fourth generation.

[AUTOBIOGRAPHICAL FRAGMENT]

Lawrence gave no title to his manuscript. Various names have been offered: Edward McDonald, in *Phoenix*, entitled the text '[Autobiographical Fragment]'; in 1937 Lawrence Clark Powell offered '[Newthorpe in 2927]'; both Tedlock in 1948 and Roberts in 1962 followed McDonald;[1] Keith Sagar reprinted the text in *The Princess and Other Stories* (1971) under the title 'A Dream of Life'. Sagar's is the most attractive suggestion; nevertheless, to avoid 'confusion worse confounded', it has seemed appropriate to follow the bibliographers' lead and entitle the story '[Autobiographical Fragment]'.

There can be little doubt at least about the approximate date of composition. Within the text Lawrence refers to it several times: 'it is late October' (56:16); 'the October afternoon' (61:19); 'This afternoon . . . in October, 1927' (67:20). Confirmation is apparently supplied in a letter of 26 October 1927 in which he tells Norman Douglas of the aspiration of his friend, Koteliansky, to become a publisher and to issue 'a series of little books, 8,000 to 10,000 words each – called *The Intimate Series* . . . something a little more "intimate" than you'd do for a magazine' (*Letters*, vi. 198). Lawrence adds: 'I'm trying to do a sort of story', a remark which he echoes when writing to his sister-in-law Else Jaffe a couple of days later (vi. 198). Though Kot never published it – Lawrence left his story unfinished – it is highly likely that the '[Autobiographical Fragment]' was intended to be his contribution to the projected series. Composition can therefore be dated *c*. 26–30 October 1927.

The text was first published in *Phoenix*.

[1] Powell 28; Tedlock 64–5; Roberts E30.

[AUTOBIOGRAPHICAL FRAGMENT]

Nothing depresses me more than to come home to the place where I was born, and where I lived my first twenty years, here, at Newthorpe, this coal-mining village on the Nottingham-Derby border.* The place has grown, but not very much, the pits are poor. Only it has changed. There is a tram-line from Nottingham through the one street, and buses to Nottingham and Derby. The shops are bigger, more plate-glassy: there are two picture palaces,* and one palais de danse.

But nothing can save the place from the poor, grimy, mean effect of the Midlands, the little grimy brick houses with slate roofs, the general effect of paltriness, smallness, meanness, fathomless ugliness, combined with a sort of chapel-going respectability. It is the same as when I was a boy, only more so.

Now, it is all tame. It was bad enough, thirty years ago, when it was still on the upward grade, economically. But then the old race of miners were not immensely respectable. They filled the pubs with smoke and bad language, and they went with dogs at their heels. There was a sense of latent wildness and unbrokenness, a weird sense of thrill and adventure in the pitch-dark Midland nights, and roaring, footballing Saturday afternoons. The country in between the colliery regions had a lonely sort of fierceness and beauty half-abandoned, and threaded with poaching colliers and whippet dogs. Only thirty years ago!

Now it seems so different. The colliers of today are the men of my generation, lads I went to school with. I find it hard to believe. They were rough, wild lads. They are not rough, wild man. The board school, the Sunday school, the Band of Hope,* and above all, their mothers got them under. Got them under, made them tame. Made them sober, conscientious, and decent. Made them good husbands. When I was a boy, a collier who was a good husband was an exception to the rule, and while the women with bad husbands pointed him out as a shining example, they also despised him a little, as a petticoat man.

But nearly all the men of my generation are good husbands. There they stand, at the street corners, pale, shrunken, well-dressed, decent, and *under*. The drunken colliers of my father's generation were not got under. The decent colliers of my generation are got under entirely. They are so patient, so forbearing, so willing to listen to reason, so ready to put themselves aside. And there they stand, at the street corners and the entry-ends,* the rough lads I went to school with, men now, with smart daughters and bossy wives and cigarette-smoking lads of their own. There they stand, thin, and white as cheap wax candles, spectral, as if they had no selves any more: decent, patient, self-effacing sort of men, who have seen the war and the high-water-mark wages, and now are down again, under, completely under, with not a tuppence to rattle in their pockets. There they are, poor as their fathers before them, but poor with a hopeless outlook and a new and expensive world around them.

When I was a boy, the men still used to sing: "There's a good time coming, boys, there's a good time coming!"* Well, it has come, and gone. If anybody sang now, they'd sing: "It's a bad time now, and a worse time coming." But the men of my generation are dumb, they have been got under and made good.

As for the next generation, that is something different. As soon as mothers become self-conscious, sons become what their mothers make them. My mother's generation was the first generation of working-class mothers to become really self-conscious. Our grandmothers were still too much under our grandfathers' thumb, and there was still too much masculine kick against petticoat rule. But with the next generation, the woman freed herself at least mentally and spiritually from the husband's domination, and then she became that great institution, that character-forming power, the mother of my generation. I am sure the character of nine-tenths of the men of my generation was formed by the mother: the character of the daughters too.

And what sort of characters? Well, the woman of my mother's generation was in reaction against the ordinary high-handed, obstinate husband who went off to the pub. to enjoy himself and to waste the bit of money that was so precious to the family. The woman felt herself the higher moral being: and justly, as far as economic morality goes. She therefore assumed the major responsibility for the family, and the husband let her. So she proceeded to mould a generation.

Mould it to the shape of her own unfulfilled desire, of course. What had she wanted, all her life?—a "good" husband, gentle and understanding and moral, one who did not go to pubs and drink and waste the bit of wages, but who lived for his wife and his children.

Millions of mothers in Great Britain, in the latter half of Victoria's reign, unconsciously proceeded to produce sons to pattern. And they produced them, by the million: good sons, who would make good, steady husbands who would live for their wives and families. And there they are! we've got 'em now! the men of my generation, men between forty and fifty, men who almost all had Mothers with a big m.

And then the daughters! Because the mothers who produced so many "good sons" and future "good husbands" were at the same time producing daughters, perhaps without taking so much thought or exercising so much will-power over it, but producing them just as inevitably.

What sort of daughters came from these morally-responsible mothers? As we should expect, daughters morally-confident. The mothers had known some little hesitancy in their moral supremacy. But the daughters were quite assured. The daughters were always right. They were born with a sense of self-rightness that sometimes was hoity-toity,* and sometimes was seemingly wistful: but there it was, the inevitable sense that I-am-right. This the women of my generation drew in with their mothers' milk, this feeling that they were "right" and must be "right" and nobody must gainsay them. It is like being born with one eye, you can't help it.

We are such stuff as our grandmothers' dreams are made on.* This terrible truth should never be forgotten. Our grandmothers dreamed of wonderful "free" womanhood in a "pure" world, surrounded by "adoring, humble, high-minded" men. Our mothers started to put the dream into practice. And we are the fulfilment. We are such stuff as our grandmothers' dreams were made on.

For I think it cannot be denied that ours is the generation of "free" womanhood, and a helplessly "pure" world, and of pathetic "adoring, humble, high-minded" men.

We are more or less such stuff as our grandmothers' dreams are made on. But the dream changes with every new generation of grandmothers. Already my mother, while having a definite ideal for her sons, of "humble, adoring, high-minded" men, began to have secret dreams of her own: dreams of some Don Juan sort of person whose influence would make the vine of Dionysus* grow and coil over the pulpit of our Congregational Chapel. I myself, her son, could see this dream peeping out, thrusting little tendrils through her paved intention of having "good sons." It was my turn to be the "good son." It would be my son's turn to fulfil the other dream, or dreams: the secret ones.

Thank God I have no son to undertake the onerous burden. Oh, if only every father could say to his boy: Look here, my son! These are your grandmother's dreams of a man. Now you look out!—My dear old grandmother, my mother's mother, I'm sure she dreamed me almost to a 't': except for a few details.

But the daughter starts, husbandly speaking, where the mother leaves off. The daughters of my mother, and of the mothers of my generation, start, as a rule, with "good husbands", husbands who never fundamentally contradict them, whose lifelong attitude is: All right, dear! I know I'm wrong, as usual.—This is the attitude of the husband of my generation.

It alters the position of the wife entirely. It is a fight for the woman to get the reins into her own hands, but once she's got them, there she is! the reins have got her. She's got to drive somewhere, to steer the matrimonial cart in some direction. "All right, dear! I'll let you decide it, since you know better than I do!" says the husband, in every family matter. So she must keep on deciding. Or, if the husband balks her occasionally, she must keep up the pressure till he gives in.

Now driving the matrimonial cart is quite an adventure for a time, while the children are little, and all that. But later, the woman begins to think to herself: "Oh damn the cart! Where do *I* come in?" She begins to feel she's getting nothing out of it. It's not good enough. Whether you're the horse or whether you're the driver doesn't make many odds. So long as you're both harnessed to the cart.

Then the woman of my generation begins to have ideas about her sons. They'd better not be so all-forsaken "good" as their father has been. They'd better be more sporting, and give a woman a bit more "life." After all, what's a family! It swallows a woman up, until she's fifty, and then puts the remains of her aside. Not good enough! No! My sons must be more manly, make plenty of money for a woman and give her a "life", and not be such a muff about "goodness" and being "right." What is being "right," after all? Better enjoy yourself while you've got the chance.

So the sons of the younger generation emerge into the world—my sons, if I'd got any—with the intrinsic maternal charge ringing in their ears: "Make some money and give yourself a good time—and all of us. Enjoy yourself!"

The young men of the younger generation begin to fulfil the hidden dreams of my mother. They are jazzy—but not coarse. They are a bit Don-Juanish, but, let us hope, entirely without brutality or vulgarity. They are more elegant, and not much more moral. But they are still humble before a woman, especially *the* woman!

It is the secret dream of my mother, coming true.

And if you want to know what the next generation will be like, you must fathom the secret dreams of your wife: the woman of forty or so. There you will find the clue. And if you want to be more precise, then find out what is the young woman of twenty's ideal of a man.

The poor young woman of twenty, she is rather stumped for an ideal of a man. So perhaps the next generation but one won't be anything at all.

We are such stuff as our grandmothers' dreams are made on. Even colliers are such stuff as their grandmothers' dreams are made on. And if Queen Victoria's dream was King George, then Queen Alexandra's was the Prince of Wales, and Queen Mary's will be*—what?

But all this doesn't take away from the fact that my home place is more depressing to me than death, and I wish my grandmother and all her generation had been better dreamers. "Those maids, thank God, are 'neath the sod,"* but their dreams we have still with us. It is a terrible thing to dream dreams that shall become flesh.

And when I see the young colliers dressed up like the Prince of Wales, dropping in to the Miners' Welfare for another drink, or into the "Pally" for a dance—in evening suit* to beat the band—or scooting down the black roads on a motor-bike, a leggy damsel behind—then I wish the mothers of my own generation, my own mother included, had been a little less *frivolous* as a dreamer. In life, so deadly earnest! But oh, what frivolous dreams our mothers must have had, as they sat in the pews of the Congregational Chapel with faces like saints. They must unconsciously have been dreaming jazz and short skirts, the Palais de Danse, the Film, and the motor-bike. It is enough to embitter one's most sacred memories, "Lead Kindly Light"*—unto the "Pally."—The eleventh commandment: "Enjoy yourselves!"

"Well, well! Even grandmothers' dreams don't always come true—that is, they aren't allowed to. They'd come true right enough otherwise. But sometimes fate, and that long dragon, the concatenation of circumstance, intervene. I am sure my mother never dreamed a dream that wasn't well-off. My poor old grandmother might still dream noble poverty—myself, to wit! But my mother? impossible! In her secret dreams, the sleeve-links were solid gold, and the socks were silk.

And now fate, the monster, frustrates. The pits don't work. There's reduced wages and short pay. The young colliers will have a hard time buying another pair of silk socks for the "Pally", when these are worn out. They'll have to go in wool. As for the young lady's fur coat—well, well! let's hope it is seal, or some other hard-wearing skin, and not that evanescent chinchilla or squirrel that moults in a season.

For the young lady won't get another fur coat in a hurry, if she has to wait for her collier father to buy it her. Not that he would refuse it her. What is a man for, except to provide for his wife and daughters? But you can't get blood out of a stone, nor cash out of a collier, not any more.

It is a soft, hazy October day, with the dark green Midlands fields looking somewhat sunken, and the oak-trees brownish, the mean houses shabby and scaly, and the whole countryside somewhat dead, expunged, faintly blackened under the haze. It is a queer thing that countries die along with their inhabitants. This countryside is dead: or so inert, it is as good as dead. The old sheep-bridge where I used to swing as a boy is now an iron affair. The brook where we caught minnows now runs on a concrete bed. The old sheep-dip, the dipping-hole, as we called it, where we bathed, has somehow disappeared, so has the mill-dam and the little water-fall. It is all a concrete arrangement now, like a sewer. And the people's lives are the same, all running in concrete channels like a vast cloaca.

At Engine Lane Crossing,* where I used to sit as a tiny child and watch the trucks shunting with a huge grey horse and a man with a pole, there are now no trucks. It is October, and there should be hundreds. But there are no orders. The pits are turning half time. Today they are not turning at all. The men are all at home: no orders, no work.

And the pit is fuming silently, there is no rattle of screens; and the head-stock wheels are still. That was always an ominous sign, except on Sundays: even when I was a small child. The head-stock wheels twinkling against the sky, that meant work and life, men "earning a living." if living can be earned.

But the pit is foreign to me anyhow, so many new big buildings round it, electric plant and all the rest. It's a wonder even the shafts are the same. But they must be: the shafts where we used to watch the cage-loads of colliers coming up suddenly, with a start: then the man streaming out to turn in their lamps, then trailing off, all grey, along the lane home: while the screens still rattled, and the pony on the sky-line still pulled along the tub of "dirt," to tip over the edge of the pit-bank.

It is different now: all so much more impersonal and mechanical and abstract. I don't suppose the children of today drop "nuts" of coal down the shaft, on Sunday afternoons, to hear them hit, hit with an awful resonance against the sides far down, before there comes the last final plump into the endlessly far-off sump. My father was always so angry if he knew we dropped coals down the shaft: If there was a man at t'bottom, it'd kill 'im straight off. How should you like that?—We didn't quite know how we should have liked it.

But anyhow Moorgreen is no more what it was: or it is too much more. Even the rose-bay willow-herb, which seems to love collieries, no longer showed its hairy autumn thickets and its last few spikes of rose around the pit-pond and on the banks. Only the yellow snapdragon, toad-flax, still was there.

Up from Moorgreen goes a footpath past the quarry and up the fields, out to Renshaw's farm.* This was always a favorite walk of mine. Beside the path lies the old quarry, part of it very old and deep and filled in with oak-trees and guelder-rose and tangle of briars, the other part open, with square wall neatly built-up with dry-stone on the side under the plough-fields, and the bed still fairly level and open. This open part of the quarry was blue with dog-violets in spring, and on the smallish brambles, the first handsome blackberries came in autumn. Thank heaven, it is late October, and too late for blackberries, or there would still be here some wretched men with baskets, ignominiously combing the brambles for the last berry. When I was a boy, how a man, a full-grown miner, would have been despised for going with a little basket lousing the hedges for a blackberry or two. But the men of my generation put their pride in their pocket, and now their pockets are empty.

The quarry was a haunt of mine, as a boy. I loved it because, in the open part, it seemed so sunny and dry and warm, the pale stone, the pale, slightly sandy bed, the dog-violets and the early daisies. And then the old part, the deep part, was such a fearsome place. It was always dark—you had to crawl under bushes. And you came upon honeysuckle and nightshade, that no-one ever looked upon. And at the dark sides were little, awful rocky caves, in which I imagined the adders lived.

There was a legend that these little caves or niches in the rocks were "everlasting wells," like the everlasting wells at Matlock.* At Matlock the water drips in caves, and if you put an apple in there, or a bunch of grapes, or even if you cut your hand off and put it in, it won't decay, it will turn everlasting. Even if you put a bunch of violets in, they won't die, they'll turn everlasting.

Later, when I grew up and went to Matlock—only sixteen miles away—and saw the infamous everlasting wells, that the water only made a hoary nasty crust of stone on everything, and the stone hand was only a glove stuffed with sand, being "petrified," I was disgusted. But still, when I see the stone fruits that people have in bowls for decoration, purple, semi-translucent stone grapes, and lemons. I think: *these* are the real fruits from the everlasting wells.

In the soft, still afternoon I found the quarry not very much changed. The red berries shone quietly on the briars. And in this still, warm, secret place of the earth I felt my old childish longing to pass through a gate, into a deeper, sunnier, more silent world.

The sun shone in, but the shadows already were deep. Yet I had to creep away into the darkness of bushes, into the lower hollow of the tree-filled quarry. I felt, as I had always felt, there was something there. And as I wound my way, stooping, through the unpleasant tangle, I started, hearing a sudden rush and clatter of falling earth. Some part of the quarry must be giving way.

I found the place, away at the depth under the trees and bushes, a new place where yellow earth and whitish earth and pale rock had slid down new in a heap. And at the top of the heap was a crack, a little slantingly-upright slit or orifice in the rock.

I looked at the new place curiously, the pallid new earth and rock among the jungle of vegetation, the little opening above, into the earth. A touch of sunlight came through the oak-leaves and fell on the new place and the aperture, and the place flashed and twinkled. I had to climb up to look at it.

It was a little crystalline cavity in the rock, all crystal, a little pocket or womb of quartz, among the common stone. It was pale and colourless, the stuff we call spar, from which they make little bowls and mementoes, in Matlock. But through the flat-edged, colourless crystal of the spar ran a broad vein of purplish crystal, wavering inwards as if it were arterial. And that was a vein of the Blue John spar, that is rather precious.

The place fascinated me, especially the vein of purple, and I had to clamber into the tiny cave, which would just hold me. It seemed warm in there, as if the shiny rock were warm and alive and it seemed to me there was a strange perfume, of rock, of living rock like hard, bright flesh, faintly perfumed with phlox. It was a subtle yet most fascinating secret perfume, an inward perfume. I crept right into the little cavity, into the narrow inner end where the vein of purple ran, and I curled up there, like an animal in its hole. "Now," I thought, "for a little while I am safe and sound, and the vulgar world doesn't exist for me."—I curled together with soft, curious voluptuousness. The scent of inwardness and of life, a queer scent like phlox, with a faint narcotic inner quality like opium or like truffles, became very vivid to me, then faded. I suppose I must have gone to sleep.

Later, I don't know how much later, it may have been a minute, or an eternity, I was wakened by feeling something lifting me, lifting me with a queer, half-sickening motion, curiously exciting, in a slow little rhythmic heave that was at once soft and powerful, gentle and violent, grateful and violating. I could do nothing, not even wake up: yet I was not really terrified, only utterly wonder-struck.

Then the lifting and heaving ceased, and I was cold. Something harsh passed over me: I realised it was my face: I realised I had a face. Then immediately a sharpness and bitingness flew into me, flew right into me, through what must have been my nostrils, into my body, what must have been my breast. Roused by a terrific shock of amazement, suddenly a new thing rushed into me, right into me, with a sweep that swept me away, and at the same time I felt that first thing moving somewhere in me, there was a movement that came aloud.

There were some dizzy moments when my I, my consciousness wheeled and swooped like an eagle that is going to wheel away into the sky and be gone. Yet I felt her, my I, my life, wheeling closer, closer, my consciousness. And suddenly she closed with me, and I knew, I came awake.

I knew. I knew I was alive. I even heard a voice say: "He's alive!" These were the first words I heard.

And I opened my eyes again and blinked with terror, knowing the light of day. I shut them again, and felt sensations out in space, somewhere, and yet upon *me*. Again my eyes were opened, and I even saw objects, great things that were here and were there and than were not there. And the sensations out in space drew nearer, as it were, to me, the middle me.

So consciousness swooped and swerved, returning in great swoops. I realised that I was I, and that this I was also a body that ended abruptly in feet and hands. Feet! yes, feet! I remembered even the word. Feet!

I roused a little, and saw a greyish pale nearness that I recognised was my body, and something terrible moving upon it and making sensations in it. Why was it grey, my own nearness? Then I felt that other sensation, that I call aloudness, and I knew it. It was "Dust of ages!"* That was the aloudness: "Dust of ages!"

In another instant I knew that violent movingness that was making sensations away out upon me. It was somebody. In terror and wonder the realisation came to me: it was somebody, another one, a man. A man, making sensations on me! A man, who made the aloudness: "Dust of ages." A man! Still I could not grasp it. The conception would not return whole to me.

Yet once it had lodged within me, my consciousness established itself. I moved, I even moved my legs, my far-off feet. Yes! And an aloudness came out of me, even of me. I knew. I even knew now that I had a throat. And in another moment I should know something else.

It came all of a sudden. I saw the man's face. I saw it, a ruddy sort of face with a nose and a trimmed beard. I even knew more. I said: "Why—?"

And the face quickly looked at me, with blue eyes into my eyes, and I struggled as if to get up.

"Art awake?" it said.

And somewhere, I knew there was the word Yes! But it had not yet come to me.

But I knew, I knew! Dimly I came to know that I was lying in sun on new earth that was spilled before my little, opened cave. I remembered my cave. But why I should be lying grey and stark-naked on earth in the sun outside I did not know; nor what the face was, nor whose.

Then there was more aloudness, and there was another one. I realised there could be more than one other one. More than one! More than one! I felt a new sudden something that made all of me move at once, in many directions, it seemed, and I became once more aware of the extent of me, and an aloudness came from my throat. And I remembered even that new something that was upon me. Many sensations galloping in all directions! But it was one dominant, drowning. It was water. Water! I even remembered water, or I knew I knew it. They were washing me. I even looked down and saw the whiteness; me, myself, white, a body.

And I remembered, that when all of me had moved to the touch of water, and I had made an aloudness in my throat, the men had laughed. Laughed! I remembered laughter.

So as they washed me. I came to myself. I even sat up. And I saw earth and rock, and a sky that I knew was afternoon. And I was stark naked, and there were two men washing me, and they too were stark naked. But I was white, pure white, and thin, and they were ruddy, and not thin.

They lifted me, and I leaned on one, standing, while the other washed me. The one I leaned on was warm, and his life softly warmed me. The other one rubbed me gently. I was alive. I saw my white feet like two curious flowers, and I lifted them one after another, remembering walking.

The one held me, and the other put a woollen shirt or smock over me. It was pale grey and red. Then they fastened shoes on my feet. Then the free one went to the cave, peering, and he came back with things in his hands, buttons, some discoloured yet unwasted coins, a dull but not-rusted pocket-knife, a waist-coat buckle, and a discoloured watch, whose very face was dark. Yet I know these things were mine.

"Where are my clothes?" I said.

I felt eyes looking at me, two blue eyes, two brown eyes, full of strange life.

"My clothes!" I said.

They looked at one another, and made strange speech. Then the blue-eyed said to me:

"Gone! Dust of ages!"

They were strange men to me, with their formal, peaceful faces and trimmed beards, like old Egyptians. The one on whom I was unconsciously leaning stood quite still, and he was warmer than the afternoon sunshine. He seemed to give off life to me, I felt a warmth suffusing into me, an inflooding of strength. My heart began to lift with strange, exultant strength. I turned to look at the man I was resting on, and met the blue, quiet shimmer of his eyes. He said something to me, in the quiet, full voice, and I nearly understood, because it was like the dialect. He said it again, softly and calmly, speaking to the inside of me, so that I understood as a dog understands, from the voice, not from the words.

"Can ta goo, o shollt be carried?"*

It sounded to me like that, like the dialect.

"I think I can walk," said I, in a voice that sounded harsh, after the soft, deep modulation of the other.

He went slowly down the heap of loose earth and stones, which I remembered had fallen. But it was different. There were no trees in an old quarry hollow. This place was bare, like a new working. And when we came out, it was another place altogether. Below was a hollow of trees, and a bare, grassy hillside swept away, with clumps of trees, like park land. There was no colliery, no railway, no hedges, no square, shut-in fields. And yet the land looked tended.

We stood on a little path of paved stone, only about a yard wide. Then the other man came up from the quarry, carrying tools, and wearing a grey shirt or smock with a red cord. He spoke with that curious soft inwardness, and we turned down the path, myself still leaning on the shoulder of the first man. I felt myself quivering with a new strength, and yet ghostlike. I had a curious sensation of lightness, not touching the ground as I walked as if my hand that rested on the man's shoulder buoyed me up. I wanted to know whether I was really buoyant, as in a dream.

I took my hand suddenly from the man's shoulder, and stood still. He turned and looked at me.

"I can walk alone," I said, and as in a dream I took a few paces forward. It was true, I was filled with a curious rushing strength that made me almost buoyant, scarcely needing to touch the ground. I was curiously, quiveringly strong, and at the same time buoyant.

"I can go alone!" I said to the man.

They seemed to understand, and to smile, the blue-eyed one showing his teeth when he smiled. I had a sudden idea: How beautiful they are, like plants in flower! But still, it was something I felt, rather than saw.

The blue-eyed one went in front, and I walked on the narrow path with my rushing buoyancy, terribly elated and proud, forgetting everything, the other man following silently behind. Then I was aware that the path had turned, and ran beside a road in a hollow where a stream was, and a cart was clanking slowly ahead, drawn by two oxen, and led by a man who was entirely naked.

I stood still, on the raised, paved path, trying to think, trying, as it were, to come awake. I was aware that the sun was sinking behind me, golden in the October afternoon. I was aware that the man in front of me also had no clothes on whatsoever, and he would soon be cold.

Then I made an effort, and looked round. On the slopes to the left were big, rectangular patches of dark plough-land. And men were ploughing still. On the right were hollow meadows, beyond the stream, with tufts of trees and many speckled cattle being slowly driven forwards. And in front the road swerved on, past a mill-pond and a mill, and a few little houses, and then swerved up a rather steep hill. And at the top of the hill was a town, all yellow in the late afternoon light, with yellow, curved walls rising massive from the yellow-leaved orchards, and above, buildings swerving in a long, oval curve, and round, faintly-conical towers rearing up. It had something at once soft and majestical about it, with its soft yet powerful curves, and no sharp angles or edges, the whole substance seeming soft and golden like the golden flesh of a city.

And I knew, even while I looked at it, that it was the place where I was born, the ugly colliery townlet of dirty red brick. Even as a child, coming home from Moorgreen, I had looked up and seen the squares of miners' dwellings, built by the Company, rising from the hill-top in the afternoon light like the walls of Jerusalem, and I had wished it were a golden city, as in the hymns we sang in the Congregational Chapel.*

Now it had come true. But the very realisation, and the very intensity of my *looking*, had made me lose my strength and my buoyancy. I turned forlorn to the men who were with me. The blue-eyed one came and took my arm, and laid it across his shoulder, laying his left hand round my waist, on my hip.

And almost immediately the soft, warm rhythm of his life pervaded me again, and the memory in me which was my old self went to sleep. I was like a wound, and the touch of these man healed me at once. We went on again, along the raised pavement.

Three horsemen came cantering up, from behind. All the world was turning home towards the town, at sunset. The horsemen slackened pace as they came abreast. They were men in soft, yellow sleeveless tunics, with the same still, formal Egyptian faces and trimmed beards as my companions. Their arms and legs were bare, and they rode without stirrups. But they had curious hats of beach-leaves on their heads. They glanced at us sharply, and my companions saluted respectfully. Then the riders cantered ahead again, the yellow tunics softly fluttering. No one spoke at all. There was a great stillness in all the world, and yet a magic of close-interwoven life.

The road now began to be full of people, slowly passing up the hill towards the town. Most were bare-headed, wearing the sleeveless woollen shirt of grey and red, with a red girdle, but some were clean-shaven, and dressed in grey shirts, and some carried tools, some fodder. There were women too, in blue or lilac smocks, and some men in scarlet smocks. But among the rest, here and there were men like my guide, quite naked, and some young women, laughing together as they went, had their blue smocks folded to a pad on their heads, as they carried their bundles, and their slender, rosy-tanned bodies were quite naked, save for a little girdle of white and green and purple cord-fringe that hung round their hips and swung as they walked. Only they had soft shoes on their feet.

They all glanced at me, and some spoke a word of salute to my companions, but no-one asked questions. The naked girls went very stately, with bundles on their heads, yet they laughed more than the men. And they were comely as berries on a bush. That was what they reminded me of: rose-berries on a bush. That was the quality of all the people: an inner stillness and ease, like plants that come to flower and fruit. The individual was like a whole fruit, body and mind and spirit, without split. It made me feel a curious, sad sort of envy, because I was not so whole, and at the same time, I was wildly elated, my rushing sort of energy seemed to come upon me again. I felt as if I were just going to plunge into the deeps of life, for the first time: belated, and yet a pioneer of pioneers.

I saw ahead the great rampart-walls of the town—then the road suddenly curved to gateway, all the people flowing in, in two slow streams, through the narrow side entrances.

It was a big gateway of yellow stone, and inside was a clear space, paved mostly with whitish stones, and around it stood buildings in the yellow stone, golden-looking, with pavement arcades supported on yellow pillars. My guides turned into a chamber where men in green stood on guard, and several peasants were waiting. They made way, and I was taken before a man who reclined on a dark-yellow couch, himself wearing a yellow tunic. He was blond, with the trimmed beard and hair worn long, cut round like the hair of a Florentine page. Though he was not handsome, he had a curious quality of beauty, that came from within. But this time, it was the beauty of a flower rather than of a berry.

My guides saluted him and explained briefly and quietly, in words I could only catch a drift of. Then the man looked at me, quietly, gently, yet I should have been afraid, if I had been his enemy. He spoke to me, and I thought he asked if I wanted to stay in their town.

"Did you ask me if I want to stay here?" I replied. "You see, I don't even know where I am."

"You are in this town of Nethrupp," he said, in slow English, like a foreigner. "Will you stay some time with us?"

"Why thank you, if I may," I said, too helplessly bewildered to know what I was saying.

We were dismissed, with one of the guards in green. The people were all streaming down the side street, between the yellow-coloured houses, some going under the pillared porticoes, some in the open road. Somewhere ahead a wild music began to ring out, like three bagpipes squealing and droning. The people pressed forward, and we came to a great oval space on the ramparts, facing due west. The sun, a red ball, was near the horizon.

We turned into a wide entrance and went up a flight of stairs. The man in green opened a door and ushered me in.

"All is thine!" he said.

My naked guide followed me into the room, which opened on to the oval and the west. He took a linen shirt and a woollen tunic from a small cupboard, and smilingly offered them to me. I realised he wanted his own shirt back, and quickly gave it him, and his shoes. He put my hand quickly between his two hands, then slipped into his shirt and shoes, and was gone.

I dressed myself in the clothes he had laid out, a blue-and-white striped tunic, and white stockings, and blue cloth shoes, and went to the window. The red sun was almost torching the tips of the tree-covered hills away in the west. Sherwood Forest* grown dense again. It was the landscape I knew best on earth, and still I knew it, from the shapes.

There was a curious stillness in the square. I stepped out of my window on to the terrace, and looked down. The crowd had gathered in order, a cluster of men on the left, in grey, grey-and-scarlet, and pure scarlet, and a cluster of women on the right, in tunics of all shades of blue and crocus lilac. In the vaulted porticoes were more people. And the red sun shone on all, till the square glowed again.

When the ball of fire touched the tree-tops, there was a queer squeal of bagpipes, and the square suddenly started into life. The men were stamping softly, like bulls, the women were softly swaying, and softly clapping their hands, with a strange noise, like leaves. And from under the vaulted porticoes, at opposite ends of the egg-shaped oval, came the soft booming and trilling of women and men singing against one another in the strangest pattern of sound.

It was all kept very soft, soft-breathing. Yet the dance swept into swifter and swifter rhythm, with the most extraordinary incalculable unison. I do not believe there was any outside control of the dance. The thing happened by instinct, like the wheeling and flashing of a shoal of fish or of a flock of birds dipping and spreading in the sky. Suddenly, in one amazing wing-movement, the arms of all the men would flash up into the air, naked and glowing, and with the soft, rushing sound of pigeons alighting the men ebbed in a spiral, grey and sparkled with scarlet, bright arms slowly leaning, upon the women, who rustled all crocus blue, rustled like an aspen, then in one movement scattered like lilac sparks, in every direction, from under the enclosing, sinking arms of the men, and suddenly formed slender rays of lilac branching out from red and grey knot of the men.

All the time the sun was slowly sinking, shadow was falling and the dance was moving slower, the women wheeling blue around the obliterated sun. They were dancing the sun down, and dancing as birds wheel and dance, and fishes in shoals, controlled by some strange unanimous instinct. It was at once terrifying and magnificent, I wanted to die, so as not to see it, and I wanted to rush down, to be one of them. To be a drop in that wave of life.

The sun had gone, the dance unfolded and faced inwards to the town, the men softly stamping, the women rustling and softly clapping, the voices of the singers drifting on like a twining wind. And slowly, in one slow wing-movement, the arms of the men rose up unanimous, in a sort of salute, and as the arms of the men were sinking, the arms of the women softly rose. It gave the most marvellous impression of soft, slow flight of two many-pinioned wings, lifting and sinking like the slow drift of an owl. Then suddenly everything ceased. The people scattered silently.

And two men came into the oval, the one with glowing lamps hung on a pole he carried across his shoulder, while the other quickly hung up the lamps within the porticoes, to light the town. It was night.

Some-one brought me a lighted lamp, and was gone. It was evening, and I was alone in a smallish room with a small bed, a lamp on the floor, and an unlighted fire of wood on the small hearth. It was very simple and natural. There was a small outfit of clothing in the cupboard, with a thick blue cloak. And there were a few plates and dishes. But in the room there were no chairs, but a long, folded piece of dark felt, on which one could recline. The light shone upwards from below, lighting the walls of creamy smoothness, like a chalk enamel. And I was alone, utterly alone, within a couple of hundred yards of the very spot where I was born.

I was afraid: afraid for myself. These people, it seemed to me, were not people, not human beings in my sense of the word. They had the stillness and the completeness of plants. And see how they could melt into one amazing instinctive thing, a human flock of motion.

I sat on the ground on the dark-blue felt, wrapped in the blue mantle, because I was cold and had no means of lighting the fire. Someone tapped at the door, and a man of the green guard entered. He had the same quiet, fruit-like glow of the men who had found me, a quality of beauty that came from inside, in some queer physical way. It was a quality I loved, yet it made me angry. It made me feel like a green apple, as if they had had all the real sun.

He took me out, and showed me lavatories and baths, with two lust* men standing under the douches. Then he took me down to a big, circular room with a raised hearth in the centre, and a blazing wood fire whose flame and smoke rose to a beautiful funnel-shaped canopy or chimney of stone. The hearth spread out beyond the canopy, and here some men reclined on the folded felts, with little white cloths before them, eating an evening meal of stiff porridge and milk, with liquid-butter, fresh lettuce, and apples. They had taken off their clothes, and lay with the firelight flickering on their healthy, fruit-like bodies, the skin glistening faintly with oil. Around the circular wall ran a broad dais where other men reclined, either eating or resting. And from time to time a man came in with his food, or departed with his dishes.

My guide took me out, to peep in a steaming room where each man washed his plate and spoon and hung them in his own little rack. Then my guide gave me a cloth and tray and dishes, and we went to a simple kitchen, where the porridge stood in great bowls over a slow fire, the melted butter was in a deep silver pan, the milk and the lettuce and fruit stood near the door. Three cooks guarded the kitchen, but the men from outside came quietly and took what they needed or what they wanted, helping themselves then returning to the great round room, or going away to their own little rooms. There was an instinctive cleanliness and decency everywhere, in every movement, in every act. It was as if the deepest instinct had been cultivated in the people, to be comely. The soft, quiet comeliness was like a dream, a dream of life at last come true.

I took a little porridge, though I had little desire to eat. I felt a curious surge of force in me: yet I was like a ghost, among these people. My guide asked me, would I eat in the round hall, or go up to my room. I understood, and chose the round hall. So I hung my cloak in the curving lobby, and entered the men's hall. There I lay on a felt against the wall, and watched the men, and listened.

They seemed to slip out of their clothing as soon as they were warm, as if clothes were a burden or a slight humiliation. And they lay and talked softly, intermittently, with low laughter, and some played games with draughtsmen and chessmen, but mostly they were still. The room was lit by hanging lamps, and it had no furniture at all. I was alone, and I was ashamed to take off my white sleeveless shirt. I felt, somehow, these men had no right to be so unashamed and self-possessed.

The green guard came again, and asked me, would I go to see somebody whose name I did not make out. So I took my mantle, and we went into the softly lighted street, under the porticoes. People were passing, some in cloaks, some only in tunics, and women were tripping along.

We climbed up towards the top of the town, and I felt I must be passing the very place where I was born, near where the Wesleyan Chapel stood. But now it was all softly-lighted, golden-coloured porticoes, with people passing in green or blue or grey-and-scarlet cloaks.

We came out on top into a circular space, it must have been where our congregational Chapel stood, and in the centre of the circle rose a tower shaped tapering rather like a lighthouse, and rosy-coloured in the lamplight. Away in the sky, at the club-shaped tip of the tower, glowed one big ball of light.

We crossed, and mounted the steps of another building, through the great hall where people were passing, on to a door at the end of a corridor, where a green guard was seated. The guard rose and entered to announce us, then I followed through an ante-chamber to an inner room with a central hearth and a fire of clear-burning wood.

A man came forward to meet me, wearing a thin, carmine-coloured tunic. He had brown hair and a stiff, reddish-brown beard, and an extraordinary glimmering kind of beauty. Instead of the Egyptian calmness and fruited impassivity of the ordinary people, or the steady, flower-like radiance of the chieftain in yellow, at the city gates, this man had a quavering glimmer like light coming through water. He took my cloak from me; and I felt at once he understood.

"It is perhaps cruel to awaken," he said, in slow, conscious English, "even at a good moment."

"Tell me where I am!" I said.

"We call it Nethrupp—but was it not Newthorpe?—Tell me, when did you go to sleep?"

"This afternoon, it seems,—in October, 1927."

"October, nineteen-twenty-seven!" he repeated the words curiously, smiling.

"Did I really sleep? Am I really awake?"

"Are you not awake?" he said smiling. "Will you recline upon the cushions? Or would you rather sit? See!"—He showed me a solid oak arm-chair, of the modern furniture-revival sort,* standing alone in the room. But it was black with age, and shrunken-seeming. I shivered.

"How old is that chair?" I said.

"It is just about a thousand years! a case of special preservation," he said.

I could not help it. I just sat on the rugs and burst into tears, weeping my soul away.

The man sat perfectly still for a long time. Then he came and put my hand between his two.

"Don't cry!" he said. "Don't cry! Man was a perfect child so long. Now we try to be men, not fretful children. Don't cry! Is not this better?"

"When is it? What year is this?" I asked.

"What year? We call it the year of the acorn. But you mean its arithmetic? You would call it the year two thousand nine hundred and twenty-seven."

"It cannot be," I said.

"Yet still it is."

"Then I am a thousand and forty-two years old!"

"And why not?"

"But how can I be?"

"How? You went to sleep, like a chrysalis: in one of the earth's little chrysalis wombs: and your clothes turned to dust, yet they left the buttons: and you woke up like a butterfly. But why not? Why are you afraid to be a butterfly that wakes up out of the dark for a little while, beautiful? Be beautiful, then, like a white butterfly. Take off your clothes and let the firelight fall on you. What is given, accept then—"

"How long shall I live now, do you think?" I asked him.

"Why will you always measure? Life is not a clock."

"It is true. I am like a butterfly, and I shall only live a little while. That is why I don't want to eat—

THE "JEUNE FILLE" WANTS TO KNOW

In April 1928 Lawrence was invited by Arthur Olley, Literary Editor of the *Evening News*, to contribute articles to the paper. Nancy Pearn, to whom the invitation had been sent, wrote to Lawrence – then at Villa Mirenda near Florence – on 26 April, urging him to respond positively and assuring him that the resulting publicity might well increase the sale of his books. This article was his first response; it must have been written quickly since it appeared in the *Evening News* on 8 May. Nancy Pearn wrote on the same day to congratulate Lawrence, to encourage him to write further articles and to send him a copy of the day's issue which also included a jocular piece by the novelist, Gladys Bronwyn Stern. Lawrence replied on 13 May, sending another article and commenting: 'I must say, I had gooseflesh when I saw that page with me in the *Evening News*, next the lady who knows why she couldn't marry a foreigner, because never a one asked her!' (*Letters*, vi. 401).

He would have noticed, but was apparently undisturbed by the fact, that his contribution had been entitled by Olley, 'When She Asks "Why?"' whereas Nancy Pearn's letter of 8 May makes it clear that the title given by Lawrence was 'The Bogey Between the Generations'. These must have been the words used as the heading of a typescript produced in Nancy Pearn's office and sent both to the *Evening News* and, later, to the *Virginia Quarterly Review* which published it in January 1929 under Lawrence's original title. This typescript would be the source not only for the newspaper and journal versions – which are textually very close – but also for most of the text in *Assorted Articles* where the article was first collected. The only surviving manuscript appears to be an early draft; it is printed below as Appendix 1.[1]

[1] The manuscript is crudely headed in pencil, seemingly by two persons, one of whom, though not Lawrence, may have been Frieda, judging by the handwriting. The heading does not include a title for the article but appears to record its publishing 'history' by some person(s) categorising the manuscript rather than preparing it for publication. It reads:

E. News Wants to Know Assorted Articles Jeune Fille fille

The claim that the missing typescript derived from a later manuscript is reinforced by the existence of a fragment from the proofs of *Assorted Articles* on which Lawrence wrote the final paragraph of the version published in the volume; it did not appear in either of the earlier printed texts. Not only, then, did Lawrence see and extend the text in *Assorted Articles*, he presumably accepted it as deriving from his own later manuscript, thus authorising its use as the base-text in this edition. Also, even if only tacitly, he accepted the title it bore in the printed volume. That title is the one used here. (We do not know whether it was devised by someone else or created by Lawrence himself.)

THE "JEUNE FILLE" WANTS TO KNOW

If you are a writer, nothing is more confusing than the difference between the things you have to say and the things you are allowed to print. Talking to an intelligent girl, the famous "*jeune fille*" who is the excuse for the great Hush! Hush! in print, you find, not that you have to winnow your words and leave out all the essentials, but that she, the innocent girl in question, is flinging all sorts of fierce questions at your head, in all sorts of shameless language, demanding all sorts of impossible answers. You think to yourself: "My heaven, *this* is the innocent young thing on whose behalf books are suppressed!" And you wonder "How on earth am I to answer her?"

You decide the only way to answer her is straight-forward. She smells an evasion in an instant, and despises you for it. She is no fool, this innocent maiden. Far from it. And she loathes an evasion. Talking to her father in the sanctum of his study, you have to winnow your words and watch your step, the old boy is so nervous, so tremulous lest anything be said that should hurt his feelings. But once away in the drawing-room or the garden, the innocent maiden looks at you anxiously, and it is all you can do to prevent her saying crudely, "Please don't be annoyed with daddy. You see, he *is* like that, and we have to put up with him"—or else from blurting out, "Daddy's an old fool, but he *is* a dear, isn't he?"

It is a queer reversal of the Victorian order. Father winces and bridles and trembles in his study or his library, and the innocent maiden knocks you flat with her outspokenness in the conservatory. And you have to admit that she is the man of the two; of the three, maybe. Especially when she says, rather sternly, "I hope you didn't let daddy see what you thought of him!" "But what *do* I think of him?" I gasp. "Oh, it's fairly obvious!" she replies coolly, and dismisses the point.

I admit the young are a little younger than I am; or a little older, which is it? I really haven't spent my years cultivating prunes and prisms,* yet, confronted with a young thing of twenty-two, I often find myself with a prune-stone in my mouth, and I don't know what to do with it.

"Why *is* daddy like that?" she says, and there is genuine pain in the question. "Like what?" you ask. "Oh, you know what I mean! Like a baby ostrich with its head in the sand! It only makes his rear so much the more conspicuous. And it's a pity, because he's awfully intelligent in other ways."

Now, what is a man to answer? "*Why* are they like that?" she insists. "Who?" say I. "Men!" she says; "men like daddy!" "I suppose it's a sort of funk," say I. "*Exactly*!" she pounces on me like a panther. "But what is there to be in a funk about?"

I have to confess I don't know. "Of course not!" she says. "There's nothing at all to be in a funk about. So why can't we make him see it?"

When the younger generation, usually the feminine half of it in her early twenties, starts firing off Whys? at me, I give in. Anything crosses her in the least —and she takes aim at it with the deadly little pistol of her inquiring spirit, and says "*Why?*" She is a deadly shot: Billy the Kid* is nothing to her; she hits the nail on the head every time. "Now, why can't I talk like a sensible human being to daddy?" "I suppose he thinks it is a little early for you to be quite so sensible," say I mildly. "Cheek! What *cheek* of him to think he can measure out the amount of sense I ought to have!" she cries. "Why does he think it?"

Why indeed? But once you start whying, there's no end to it. A hundred years ago, a few reformers piped up timorously, "Why is man so infinitely superior to woman?" And on the slow years came the whisper "He isn't!" Then the poor padded young of those days roused up. "Why are fathers *always* in the right?" And the end of the century confessed that they weren't. Since then, the innocent maiden has ceased to be anæmic; all maidens were more or less anæmic thirty years ago; and though she is no less innocent, but probably more so, than her stuffy grandmother or mother before her, there isn't a thing she hasn't shot her Why? at, or her Wherefore?—the innocent maiden of to-day. And digging implements are called by their bare, their barest names.* "Why should daddy put his foot down upon love? He's been a prize muff at it himself, judging from mother."

It's terrible, if all the sanctifications have to sit there like celluloid Aunt Sallies, while the young take pot shots at them. A real straight Why? aimed by sweet-and-twenty goes clean through them. Nothing but celluloid! and looking so important! Really, *why* . . . ?

The answer seems to be, bogey! The elderly to-day seem to be ridden by a bogey, they grovel before the fetish of human wickedness. Every young man is out to "ruin" every young maiden. Bogey! The young maiden knows a thing or two about that. She's not quite the raw egg she's supposed to be, in the first place. And as for most young men, they're only too nice, and it would grieve them bitterly to "ruin" any young maid, even if they knew exactly how to set about it. Of which the young maiden is perfectly aware, and "Why can't daddy see it?" He can, really. But he is so wedded to his bogey, that once the young man's back is turned, the old boy can see in the young boy nothing but a danger, a danger to my daughter! Wickedness in other people is an *idée fixe* of the elderly. "Ah, my boy, you will find that in life every man's hand is against you!" As a matter of fact, my boy finds nothing of the sort. Every man has to struggle for himself, true. But most people are willing to give a bit of help where they can. The world may really be a bogey. But that isn't because individuals are wicked villains. At least ninety-nine per cent. of individuals in this country, and in any other country as far as we have ever seen, are perfectly decent people who have a certain amount of struggle to get along, but who don't want to do anybody any harm, if they can help it.

This seems to be the general experience of the young, and so they can't appreciate the bogey of human wickedness which seems to dominate the minds of the old, in their relation to the succeeding generation. The young ask "What, exactly, is this bogey, this wickedness we are to be shielded from?" And the old only reply, "Of course, there is no danger to *us*. But to you, who are young and inexperienced . . . !"

And the young, naturally, see nothing but pure hypocrisy. They have no desire to be shielded. If the bogey exists, they would like to set eyes on him, to take the measure of this famous "wickedness." But since they never come across it, since they find meanness and emptiness the worst crimes, they decide that the bogey doesn't and never did exist, that he is an invention of the elderly spirit, the last stupid stick with which the old can beat the young and feel self-justified. "Of course, it's perfectly hopeless with mother and daddy, one has to treat them like mental infants," say the young. But the mother sententiously reiterates, "I don't mind, as far as I am concerned. But I have to protect my children."

Protect, that is, some artificial children that only exist in parental imagination, from a bogey that likewise has no existence outside that imagination, and thereby derive a great sense of parental authority, importance and justification.

The danger for the young is that they will question everything out of existence, so that nothing is left. But that is no reason to stop questioning. The old lies must be questioned out of existence, even at a certain loss of things worth having. When everything is questioned out of existence, then the real fun will begin putting the right things back. But nothing is any good till the old lies are got rid of.

LAURA PHILIPPINE

T. P.'s and Cassell's Weekly appears to have invited Lawrence to name the short story he considered supreme in the genre; his reply to the paper is missing but he reported to Nancy Pearn on 13 May 1928: 'I told *T. P.'s* I thought the best story in the world a certain one of Boccaccio's improper but charming tales from the *Decameron*. How's that for *T. P.*? If only he'll reprint the tale, I'll translate it for him gratis' (*Letters*, vi. 401). Coincidentally, with the same letter he enclosed his 'article "Laura-Philippine"'. Hesitantly he mentioned that the *Evening News* might accept it but 'if it won't do for the Olley man, it may for somebody else.' Nancy Pearn seems not to have kept Lawrence informed of its fate because, five weeks later, he was quite ignorant about it (vi. 438). Indeed the first news he received came after its publication in *T. P.'s* on 7 July: on 12 July he thanked her for '*T. P.'s* with "Laura Philippine".'[1]

He was rather dismissive of the publication – 'What a rag of a paper, *T. P.'s*' – and somewhat slighting about Aldous Huxley whose piece, 'What To Teach Our Boys', opened the issue of 7 July: 'How solemn Aldous, on the first page!' In fact, *T. P.'s* was not an appropriate target for such mockery. A 'middlebrow' literary weekly it maintained a commendable level of quality, publishing, for example, an article 'New Writers and their Novels' by Hugh Walpole on 30 June; 'The Place of Sex in Life' by Rose Macaulay on 14 July; and the first instalment of Quiller-Couch's Cambridge lectures on 'The Art of Writing' on 21 July. Most issues of *T. P.'s* – though not that of 7 July – also included a column entitled 'Congress of Words', conducted by none other than Frieda Lawrence's former husband, 'Prof. Ernest Weekley'.

The eponymous character in 'Laura Philippine' was undoubtedly modelled on a young American (about twenty years old), Mary Christine Hughes; the Lawrences had met her – with her mother Christine – in New Mexico in 1924 (v. 158). Lawrence's view of her was always of an amiable but shallow and lazy-minded coquette; when, for instance,

[1] Vi. 460–1. He suggested in the same letter that 'the Americans should have had a look at "Laura Philippine" – it's the kind of thing they like – *Vanity Fair* might have done it.' No American publication has been recorded.

in 1926 she was expected with her mother in Rome, he told Willard Johnson: 'Mary C. has changed the limited flirtation company of Santa Fe for the much more unlimited one of Rome, the eternal city at the game' (v. 600). The experiences which most vividly confirmed her (and, to a lesser extent, her mother's) philistinism and intellectual stupor were recounted to Earl Brewster on 7 June 1927:

> I was in the Uffizi . . . with them yesterday – 'my – look what awful hands she's got!' is all that comes out of Mary Christine for Lippo Lippi – they've never even *heard* of Botticelli – call him Bo'acelli with the stopped breath instead of the 't' – they don't know what the Renaissance was – . Standing in the Piazza Signoria I say – There's that Michelangelo *David* – and they reply: Which one is it then? – that one at the end? – meaning the Bandinelli. Then Mary C. discovers that – 'that guy's got a stone in his hand, so I guess he's the nut.' – It's partly affectation, but it's such a complete one that it's effectual . . . They're stone blind, culturally. All they can do is to call a man 'that guy' or a woman 'that skirt.' . . . Mary C. frankly loathes anything that wants to be looked at – except herself, other girls, clothes and shops . . . They've negated and negated and negated till there's *nothing* – and they themselves are empty vessels with a squirming mass of nerves. God, how loathsome! (vi. 79)

That was the young woman Lawrence recalled when, nearly a year later, he wrote 'Laura Philippine'.

The manuscript is unlocated; the typescript has provided the base-text.

LAURA PHILIPPINE

When you find two almonds in one shell, that's a Philippine. So when Philippa Homes had twins, she called them Laura Philippine, and Philip Joseph. And she went on calling them Laura Philippine and Philip Joseph, till it fixed, and they are it to this day, and Laura Philippine is twenty.

She is quite a lovely girl, tall and white-skinned, but except when she is dancing or driving a car or riding a horse, she's languid. Having had what is called a good education, she drawls in slang. She has rather wonderful blue eyes, asleep rather than sleepy, with the oddest red-gold lashes coming down over them; close, red-gold lashes. You notice the lashes because most of the daytime she doesn't trouble to raise them.

At about half-past eleven in the morning you suddenly come across her reclining on a lounge in the drawing-room, smoking a cigarette, showing several yards of good leg, and turning over a periodical without looking at it.

"Hello Laura Philippine, just got up?"

"This minute."

"How are you?"

"Same."

And she's nothing more to say. She turns over the periodical without looking at it, lights another cigarette, and time, since it can't help it, passes. At half-past twelve you find her in the hall in an elegant wrap, and a nut of a* little blue hat, looking as if she might possibly be drifting out of doors to commit suicide in some half-delicious fashion.

"Where are you going, Laura Philippine?"

"Out."

"Where's that?"

"Oh, meet some of the boys—"

"Well lunch is half-past one—"

But she is gone, with a completeness that makes it seem impossible she will ever come back. Yet back she comes, about two, when we are peeling our apple. She is the image of freshness in her bit of a putty-coloured frock, her reddish petals of hair clinging down over her ears, her cheeks pink by nature, till she almost powders them out of spite, her long white limbs almost too languid to move, and her queer fiery eyelashes down over her dark blue eyes.

"I told her not to serve me soup till I came."

"And I told her to serve it when she served us. Lunch is half-past one."

Laura Philippine sits down in front of her soup, which Philippa always had for lunch, out of spite. The parlour-maid comes in again.

"I won't have soup," says Laura Philippine. "What else is there?" And when she is told, she replies: "I won't take that either. I'll just take salad, and will you find me something to eat with it?"

The parlour-maid looks at Philippa, and Philippa says:

"I suppose you'd better bring the galantine."

So Laura Philippine, with pure indifference, eats galantine and salad, and drinks burgundy, which almost shows ruddy as it goes down her white throat.

"Did you find the boys?" I ask.

"Oh, quite."

"Did you drink cocktails?"

"Not before lunch. Gin and bitters."

I got no more out of her. But we went out in the afternoon, in the car. As we went through Windsor Park, I said:

"It is rather lovely, isn't it?"

"Oh quite!"

"But you don't look at it."

"What am I to look at it for?"

"Pleasure."

"No pleasure to me."

She looked at nothing—unless it might be at a well-dressed woman. She was interested in nothing: unless it were the boys, just at meal-times.

So she came with Philippa to Rome.

"Doing the sights of Italy with your mother, are you?" said I.

"Mother'll have a swell time taking me to see sights."

Mother did. Laura Philippine just smoked cigarettes and lowered her reddish-gold lashes over her dark-blue eyes, and said languidly: Is that so? We drove down to Ostia over the Campagna.—Oh look, Laura Philippine, there are still a few buffaloes!—Laura Philippine knocked cigarette-ash over the other side of the car in order not to look, and said yes!—Look at the old fortifications of Ostia, Laura Philippine!—Yes, I've seen 'em!—We came to the sea, got out of the car, and walked on to the shingle shore.—Call that the sea? said Laura Philippine. I said I did: the Mediterranean, at least.—Is it always that way? Why it must have something the matter with it!—And Laura Philippine reclined on the shingle, lit another cigarette, and was gone into a special void of her own, leaving the sea to take care of itself.—Where shall we have tea, Laura Philippine?—Oh, anywhere!—At the Castle of the Caesars?—Suit me all right!—If one had said in the cemetery, she would have answered the same.

She appeared at dinner looking very very modern.

"Where are you going tonight, Laura Philippine?"

"There's a dance at the Hotel de Russie."

"But you're not going alone."

"Oh, I shan't be alone. I know a whole crowd of 'em."

"But does your mother let you go off like that?"

"My mother! Imagine if she had to come along!—" Laura Philippine was animated. Her red-gold lashes lifted, her dark-blue eyes flashed.

"Do you Charleston?" she said. It was the day before yesterday, when people still said it. And she started wiggling in the middle of the drawing-room. She was flushed, animated, flashing, a weird sort of Bacchanal on the hills of Rome, wiggling there, and her white teeth showing in an odd little smile.

She was gone for good again. But next day about lunch time, there she was, lying down, faintly haunted by the last vestiges of life, otherwise quite passed out.—Have a good time?—Yes!—What time did you get home?—About four!—Dance all night?—Yes!—Isn't it too much for you?—Not a bit. If I could dance all day as well, I might keep going. It's this leaving off that does me in.—And she lapsed out.

One day Philippa said to her: Show him your poems. Yes, let him see them. He won't think you a fool.

They were really nice poems, like little sighs. They were poems to yellow leaves, then to a grey kitten, then to a certain boy. They were ghostly wisps of verse, somehow touching and wistful—you should care for somebody, Laura Philippine, said I.—Oh come! Not that old bait! she replied.—But you've got to live, said I.—I know It! said she. Why mention it?—But you're only twenty. Think of your future. The only single thing you care about it is jazz.—Exactly! But what are boys for, 'xcept to jazz with—Quite! But what about when you're thirty, and forty?—and fifty?—I suppose they'll invent new dances all the time, she said mildly. I see old birds trotting like old foxes, so why shouldn't I if I'm ninety? But you'll wear out, said I.—Not if anybody's a good dancer, and will wind me up, she said.—But are you happy? said I—Mother's always saying that. Why should anybody on earth want to be happy? I say to mother: show me somebody happy, then! And she shows me some guy, or some bright young thing, and gets mad when I say: See the pretty monkey! I'm not happy, thank God, because I'm not anything. Why should I be?

THAT WOMEN KNOW BEST

Perhaps as a result of Lawrence's first article in the *Evening News* on 8 May 1928, he was invited to contribute to a projected series in the *Daily Chronicle*. Nancy Pearn informed him on 17 May, that the *Daily Chronicle* planned to run a series of articles by men on the general subject of 'WHAT WOMEN HAVE TAUGHT ME' and offered to publish about 1,000 words on the subject by Lawrence. He would probably earn 15 guineas but had to remember that he was addressing 'the G[reat] B[ritish] P[ublic]' (*Letters*, vi. 403 n. 3). She added that there seemed to be 'quite a coming boom in D. H. L. articles'.

Lawrence set to work at once. He wrote quickly; the manuscript shows signs of haste; he was clearly not content until the theme had been effectively explored within the permitted compass. Eventually he achieved his goal of 1,000 words with remarkable accuracy. He opens with the memory of a conversation between his parents – first used in *Sons and Lovers* – and, to a considerable extent, the article is grounded in family experience, with his mother particularly in mind. Having completed his task to his own satisfaction, Lawrence was able to respond to Nancy Pearn's enquiry a mere four days after she made it: 'I send a little article for the *What Women Have Taught Me* series. Maybe they won't like it. Maybe too much tongue in the cheek. But try it on 'em. As you say, it's fun' (vi. 403–4). On 15 June she assured him that the article had been accepted.

Lawrence had, however, accepted a condition from the editor of the *Evening News* that he would not publish with 'any other paper' until he had completed five articles for the *News*. Nancy Pearn would, therefore, have to ensure that the *Chronicle* did not print the new essay before at least 27 September 1928 when the fifth article for Olley appeared. Indeed the *Chronicle* may have agreed to await the publication of Lawrence's seventh and final piece in the *News* on 13 October.

On 23 November the *Chronicle* announced that, beginning three days later, there would be a 'unique series of Confessions by writers famous for their acute presentation of the character of women', all giving an account of 'What Women Have Taught Me'. Six contributors were named:

Compton Mackenzie, André Maurois, Francis Brett Young, William Gerhardie and Archibald Marshall,[1] as well as Lawrence himself. The theme proposed by each writer was briefly indicated in the preliminary announcement; of Lawrence it was said: '"That woman knows best" is the gist of Mr D. H. Lawrence's penetrating analysis of woman and the sex relationship. "The only vivid and lively power which is left on earth – the power of earnest women," is his tribute.' When his contribution, fourth in the series, was printed on 29 November 1928, under the title 'Women Always Know Best', it was prefaced: 'Mr D. H. Lawrence, the brilliant novelist and short story writer, answers the question, "What have women taught me?" by recounting a personal experience and leaving readers to draw their own conclusions.' The text was accompanied by a photograph of Lawrence and a facsimile of his signature.

The essay was not collected in *Assorted Articles* or *Phoenix*. Edited by Roy Spencer, the texts of the manuscript and *Daily Chronicle* were published by the Black Sparrow Press (Santa Rosa, Calif.) in 1994. The present is the first collected edition.

[1] (Sir) Edward Morgan Compton Mackenzie (1883–1972), prolific writer of novels, essays, etc., who had been highly displeased by DHL's portrait of him in the story 'The Man Who Loved Islands' (1927); André Maurois (1885–1967), French biographer and novelist; Francis Brett Young (1884–1954), novelist, short-story writer and medical doctor; William Gerhardie (1895–1977), novelist and critic; Archibald Marshall (1866–1934), novelist and short-story writer.

THAT WOMEN KNOW BEST

When I was a small boy, I remember my father shouting at my mother: I'll make you tremble at the sound of my footstep!*—To me it seemed a very terrible, but *still* perfectly legitimate thing to say, and though I'm sure I wept, I secretly felt it rather splendid and right. Women and very small children should by nature tremble at the sound of the approaching wrath of the lord and master.

But alas! My mother, even though she was furious, only gave one of her peculiar amused little laughs and replied: Which boots will you wear?

It was done. No use my father storming: Never you mind which boots I shall wear!—Away flew one of the pigeons of illusion that fill the dovecot of a child's fancy. Supposing he wore his rubber-heeled shoes! or worse, his house-slippers, which always shuffled! No, it was no good. She wasn't going to tremble. What a pity! The lordly male could no longer make the dependent female tremble at the sound of his footstep. What a pity!

At a very tender age, I realised with regret that *that* particular game was up. A man was not lord and master any more; and why? because he no longer dictated what was right and what was wrong. He left that to the women: and that is the big stick. From my early childhood it puzzled me, between my two parents: Why does my mother care so much for what is right against what is wrong, and why doesn't my father care a bit?—For it was obvious he didn't care. If we broke the teapot or dodged Sunday School or said we'd been to Brinsley* when we hadn't, all my father would remark was: Ay, an' what will your mother say!—What indeed! Certainly all there was to be said, so my father was excused from saying anything.

Which perhaps was what he wanted. He put the big stick of right and wrong in my mother's hands, and said: Use it, you know best!—If, after that, he occasionally got a crack on the head himself, he might storm and rave, but he accepted it really. He knew she was right.

Which led me to wonder, as a small child, why God was a man, and not a woman. In heaven, God was the fount of right and wrong, and on earth, woman. Women knew best. Men didn't care. God knows best of all.—That was my childish arrangement of the moral scheme.

So naturally one listened to women. They knew best. My elder brothers both loved football and ruffling round.* One of them was by way of being a champion footballer. Also he was considered very clever, and learned French and Latin and worked at law, and the young women adored him. All of which was very manly and fine, and I was a little boy.

But nevertheless, he caved in in a minute before my mother.—My boy, there's been a young woman asking for you. Tell them not to come to the house, for I won't have it.—But mother, who was she?—I didn't enquire.—And my poor brother left on thorns. As a matter of fact the event had been thus: a very attractive (to me) young woman on the doorstep.—Is Mr Lawrence at home, please?—No, my husband is out.—Er—I meant the young Mr Lawrence.—I have three sons.—Oh—er—I meant Mr William.—My son William is not at home.—The door is shut firmly, and to me my mother, pink with indignation, says: The brazen huzzy!—To which I reply: But *why*, mother? She was nice.*—That's why! says my mother, and slams the question shut.

Clearly a question of right and wrong. Rather mysterious, but apparently very important. In fact, the real power lies in the hands of the one who really knows the difference between the two. My mother seemed a dead cert. In fact the knowing one seems to be always a woman. Clergymen pretend to be ministers and administers,* but they are in the hands of the women. No, the moral big stick is wielded by gentle woman, and red-faced men like my father, and footballing young champions like my brother knuckle under when she waves her moral sceptre.

So I started early to study the only vivid and lively power which is left on earth, the power of earnest women. Of course there is the power of money, mostly in the hands of men. But that is only materially, and not *vitally* interesting.*

It seemed to me that only in women could one find the grand uncanny courage of saying confidently what was right and what was wrong. And with that courage they seized the sceptre of the real power in life.

But did they really know? That was the burning point. Had they a mysterious gift, an inner voice, which infallibly told them? If so, that was the thing to learn from them. That was the secret of power.

Alas, after many years the truth comes out: they don't know. The courage is largely bravado. Even my mother, when she was older, realised that she didn't know. She had stood like a lighthouse for so many years. But when one put it to her: Are you quite sure you're showing the real way of life? she had to admit, she wasn't quite sure. The lighthouse wavered its beams and went out. It wasn't really sure of itself. It didn't absolutely know right from wrong.

Yet how splendid in the woman, that she put up such a superb bravado, while the men sat round on their hams* and said: Isn't she wonderful! We'll abide by what she says!

And how sad, that after all, the good earnest woman has been deceiving herself! There is no *absolute* right and wrong. But a decent, working right and wrong there has to be. And woman, who seemed so sure and exalted, didn't hit on the right sort after all. She's been hammering the wrong nail on the head, so the muddle is terrible. Perhaps the things that one can unlearn from women are more effective than the things one can learn. How not to be too sure of right and wrong, for example.

ALL THERE

Lawrence would be delighted by his journalistic success with the articles in the *Evening News* and *Daily Chronicle.* His pleasure would be reinforced by Nancy Pearn's enthusiastic reaction on 8 May 1928 – 'You've gone and been and hit it – meaning the journalistic market' – and by her encouragement for him to write further newspaper articles. One of the consequences may have been 'All There' but if Lawrence hoped that success would attend Nancy Pearn's efforts to place it with some editor, he was to be disappointed. She acknowledged its arrival in her London office on 4 June but no later reference to it is known. (See also 'Thinking about Oneself'.) It was first published in *Phoenix*.

ALL THERE

What you want to do, said Jimmy to Ciss, is to forget yourself.—So I can think of you all the time, I suppose, said Cecilia.—Well, not necessarily all the time. Now and then would do. But it'd do you a lot of good to forget yourself, persisted Jim.—I agree, snapped Cecilia. But why don't you make me? Why don't you give a girl a bit of a lift? You don't exactly sweep me off my feet, or lift me clean out of myself, I must say!—Dash it all, a fellow might as well try to sweep the Albert Memorial* off its feet. Seems to me you're cemented in! cried the exasperated Jim.—In what?—Eh?—What am I cemented in? demanded Cecilia.—Oh, how should I know? In your own idea of yourself! cried he, desperately.

Silence! One of those fatal and Egyptian silences* that can intervene between the fair sex and the unfair.

I should love to forget myself, if I were allowed, resumed Cecilia.—Who prevents you?—You do!—I wish I knew how.—You throw me back on myself, every time.—Throw you back on yourself! cried the mortified Jim. Why I've never seen you come an inch forward, away from yourself, yet.—I'm always coming forward to you, and you throw me back on myself, she declared.—Coming forward to me! he cried, in enraged astonishment. I wish you'd tell me when the movement begins.—You wouldn't see it, if I hooted like a bus.—I believe you, he groaned, giving up.

The gulf yawned between them. I, miserable ostrich, hid my head in the sands of the Times. The clock had the impertinence to tick extra-cheerfully.

Don't you think it's a boy's duty to make a girl forget herself? she asked of me, mercilessly.—If there's a good band, said I.—Precisely! cried Jim. The minute the saxophone lets on, she's as right as rain.—Of course! she said. Because then I don't have to forget myself, I'm all there. —We looked at her in some astonishment, and Jim, being a cub,* did the obvious.—Do you mean to say that the rest of the time you're not all there? he asked, with flat-footed humour.—Witty boy!, she said witheringly. No, naturally I leave my wits at home, when I go out with you.—Sounds like it! said Jim.

Now look here, said I. Do you mean to say you only feel quite yourself when you're dancing?—Not always then, she retorted.—And never any other time?—Never!—The word fell on top of us with a smack, and left us flat. Oh go on! cried Jimmy. What about the other day at Cromer?*—What about it? said she.—Ah! What were the wild waves saying!* cried he knowingly.—You may ask me, she replied. They hummed and hawed, but they never got a word out, as far as I'm concerned. —Do you mean to say you weren't happy! cried he, mortified.—I certainly never forgot myself, not for a moment, she replied. He made a gesture of despair.

But which do you mean? said I. Do you mean you were never all there, or that you were too much there? Which?—She became suddenly attentive, and Jimmy looked at her mockingly, with a sort of got-her-on-toast* look.—Why? she drawled languidly. I suppose when you can't forget yourself, it's because some of you's left out, and you feel it.—So you are only painfully aware of yourself when you're not altogether yourself—like a one-legged man trying to rub his missing toes, because they ache? said I. —She pondered a moment.—I suppose that's about the size of it, she admitted.—And nothing of you is left out in jazz? Jimmy demanded. —Not in good jazz—if the boy can dance, she replied.—Well I think you'll grant me that, said Jim. To which she did not reply.

So it takes a jazz band to get you all there? I asked.—Apparently! she replied.—Then why aren't you content to be only half there, till the band toots up?—Oh, I am. It's only friend James gets the wind up about the missing sections.—Hang it all! cried James—but I held up my hand like a high-church clergyman,* and hushed him off.—Then why don't you marry a boy who will prefer you only half there? I demanded of her.—What! marry one of those coat-hangers? You see me! she said, with cool contempt.

Then the point, said I, is that Jimmy leaves some of you out, and so he never sweeps you off your feet. And so you can't forget yourself, because part of you isn't embraced by Jimmy, and that part stands aside and gibbers.—Gibbers is the right word, like a lucky monkey! said Jim spitefully.—Better a whole monkey than half a man! said she.—So what's to be done about it? said I. Why not think about it? Which bit of the woman does Jimmy leave out of his manly embrace?—Oh, about nine-tenths of her! said she.—Nine-tenths of her being too conceited for nuts!* said Jimmy.

Look here! said I. This is vulgar altercation.—What do you expect, with a whipper-snapper like Jimmy? said she.—My stars! if that two-stepping Trissie says another word—! cried Jim.

Peace! said I. And give the last word to me, for I am the latter-day Aristotle, who has more to say even than a woman. Next time, Oh James, when you have your arms, both of them, around Cecilia—Which will be never! said Cecilia—then, I continued, you must say to yourself: I have here but one-tenth of my dear Ciss, the remaining nine-tenths being mysteriously elsewhere. Yet this one-tenth is a pretty good armful, not to say handful, and will do me very nicely; so forward the light brigade!* And you, Cecilia, under the same circumstance, will say to yourself: Alas, so little of me is concerned, that why should I concern myself? Jimmy gets his tenth. Let's see him make the most of it.

THINKING ABOUT ONESELF

From the evidence of the prominent watermark in the paper Lawrence used – a serpent and the letters 'CAB' – Tedlock (211) dates this essay as contemporary with a fragment of *The Escaped Cock* and 'All There', both written on the same paper. Since it is known that the latter was completed before 4 June 1928 and in view of some thematic and verbal echoes between the two short pieces, a date of ?June 1928 is proposed for 'Thinking about Oneself'. No reference is made to it in any of Lawrence's letters; it was first published in *Phoenix*.

THINKING ABOUT ONESELF

After all, we live most of our time alone, and the biggest part of our life is the silent yet busy stream of our private thoughts. We think about ourselves, and about the things that most nearly concern us, during the greater part of the day and night, all our life long. A comparatively small period is really spent in work or actual activity, where we say we "don't think." And a certain space is spent in sleep, where we don't know what we think, but where, in some sense, we keep on thinking. But the bulk of the time we think, or we muse or we dully brood about ourselves and the things that most nearly concern us.

Perhaps it is a burden, this consciousness. Perhaps we don't want to think. That is why people devote themselves to hobbies, why men drink and play golf, and women jazz and flirt, and everybody goes to the brainless cinema: all just to "get away from themselves" as they say. *Oh, forget it!* is the grand panacea. "You want to forget yourself," is the cry. The joy of all existence is supposed to be this "forgetting oneself."

Well perhaps it is! and perhaps it isn't. While a boy is getting "gloriously drunk" in the evening, in the process of forgetting himself, he knows perfectly well all the time that he'll remember himself next morning quite painfully. The same with the girls who jazz through the gay night. The same even with the crowd that comes out of the cinema. They've been forgetting themselves. But if you look at them, it doesn't seem to have been doing them much good. They look rather like the cat that has swallowed the stuffed canary, and feels the cotton-wool on its stomach.

You would think, to hear people talk, that the greatest bugbear you can possibly have is yourself. If you can't get away from yourself, if you can't forget yourself, you're doomed. The millstone is round your neck,* so you might as well jump in and drown yourself.

It seems curious. Why should I myself be the greatest bugbear to myself? Why should I be so terrified of being in my own company only, as if some skeleton clutched me in its horrid arms, the moment I am alone with myself?

It's all nonsense. It's perfectly natural for every man and every woman to think about himself or herself most of the time. What is there to be afraid of?—And yet people as a mass are afraid. You'd think everybody had a skeleton in the cupboard of their inside. Which of course they have. I've got a skeleton, and so have you. But what's wrong with him? He's quite a good solid wholesome skeleton. And what should I do without him? No no, I'm quite at home with my good and bony skeleton. So if he wants to have a chat with me, let him.

We all seem to be haunted by some spectre of ourselves, that we daren't face. "By Jove, that's me!"—And we bolt.—"Oh heaven, there's an escaped tiger in Piccadilly! Let's rush up Bond Street!"—"Look out! There's a tiger! Make for Maddox Street!"—"My God, there's a tiger here too! Let's get in the underground."—And underground we go, forgetting that we have to emerge somewhere, and whether it's Holland Park or the Bank, there'll be a tiger.

The only thing to do is: "All right! If there's a tiger, let's have a look at him."—As everybody knows, all you have to do with a tiger is to look him firmly in the eye. So with this alter ego, this spectral me that haunts my thoughts.

"I'm a poor young man and nobody loves me," says the spectre, the tiger. Look him firmly in the eye and reply: "Really! That's curious. In what way are you poor? Are you nothing *but* poor? Do you *want* to be loved? *How* do you want to be loved, and by whom, for example? And why *should* you be loved?"—Answering these questions is really amusing, far greater fun than running away from yourself and listening-in* and being inert.

If the tiger is a tigress, she mews wofully: "I'm such a nice person, and nobody appreciates me. I'm so unhappy!"—Then the really sporting girl looks her tigress in the eye and says: "Oh! What makes you so sure you're nice? *Where* are you nice? Are there no other ways of being nice but *your* way? Perhaps people are pining for a different sort of niceness from your sort. Better do something about it."

If it's a young married couple of tigers they wail: "We're so hard up, and there's no prospect."—Then the young he and she, if they've any spunk, fix their two tigers. "Prospect! What do you mean by prospect? Sufficient unto the day is the dinner thereof.* What is a prospect? Why should we need one? What sort of a one do we need? What's it all about?"

And answering these questions is fun, fun for a life-time. It's the essential fun of life, answering the tiger back. Thinking, thinking about oneself and the things that really concern one is the greatest fun of all, especially when, now and then, you feel you've really spoken to your skeleton.

INSOUCIANCE

Having published 'The "Jeune Fille" Wants to Know' in the *Evening News* on 8 May 1928, Arthur Olley pursued his new recruit and, on 17 May, asked Lawrence to contribute four more articles. Through Nancy Pearn, Lawrence responded positively on the 21st (*Letters*, vi. 403), inviting Olley to 'suggest the titles', thus prompting him, on 14 June, to offer 'Men Must be Master Again' as a possible topic for the first of the four articles.[1] At that very time the Lawrences were on the move; because of Lawrence's persistent coughing, they were asked to leave their hotel in Saint-Nizier, near Grenoble; they decided to head for Switzerland and – with the Brewsters – settled on the Grand Hotel overlooking Lake Geneva where they arrived on 17 June.

Olley pressed for the first of the promised articles, hoping to receive it in the week beginning 24 June. Lawrence felt unable to provide him with a piece on the topic proposed but, having already finished 'Insouciance', he sent the manuscript to Nancy Pearn on 27 June, asking for it to be typed and forwarded to Olley (vi. 438). The article was duly published in the *Evening News* on 12 July under the title – invented by the newspaper – 'Over-Earnest Ladies'. Three months later, on 25 September, Nancy Pearn told Lawrence that *Atlantic Monthly* had bought the piece for $50; it appeared under the authorised title in the pages of the magazine's 'Contributors' Club' in November 1928; as was not uncommon, the author's name was not given. The only other direct reference to it by Lawrence occurs in a letter to Achsah Brewster telling her of the *Atlantic Monthly* publication (vii. 28). Subsequently 'Insouciance' was collected in *Assorted Articles*.

[1] See introduction to 'Master in his Own House', p. 98.

INSOUCIANCE

My balcony is on the east side of the hotel,* and my neighbours on the right are a Frenchman, white-haired, and his white-haired wife, my neighbours on the left are two little white-haired English ladies. And we are all mortally shy of one another. When I peep out of my room in the morning and see the matronly French lady in a purple silk wrapper standing like the captain on the bridge surveying the morning, I pop in again before she can see me. And whenever I emerge during the day, I am aware of the two little white-haired ladies popping back like two white rabbits, so that literally I only see the white of their skirt hems.

This afternoon being hot and thundery, I woke up suddenly and went out on the balcony barefoot. There I sat serenely contemplating the world, and ignoring the two bundles of feet of the two little ladies which protruded from their open doorways, upon the end of the two chaises longues. A hot, still afternoon! the lake shining rather glassy away below, the mountains rather sulky, the greenness very green, all a little silent and lurid, and two mowers mowing with scythes down-hill just near, slush! slush! sound the scythe-strokes.

The little ladies become aware of my presence. I become aware of a certain agitation in the two bundles of feet wrapped in two discreet steamer-rugs and protruding on the end of two chaises longues from the pair of doorways upon the balcony next me. One bundle of feet suddenly disappears: so does the other. Silence!

Then lo! with odd sliding suddenness a little white-haired lady in grey silk, with round blue eyes, emerges and looks straight at me, and remarks that it is pleasant now.—A little cooler! say I, with false aimiability. She quite agrees, and we speak of the men mowing: how plainly one hears the long breaths of the scythes!—By now, we are tête-à-tête. We speak of cherries, strawberries, and the promise of the vine crop. This somehow leads to Italy, and the Signor Mussolini.* Before I know where I am, the little white-haired lady has swept me off my balcony, away from the glassy lake, the veiled mountains, the two men mowing, and the cherry-trees, away into the troubled ether of international politics.

I am not allowed to sit like a dandelion on my own stem. The little lady in a breath blows me abroad. And I was so pleasantly musing over the two men mowing: the young one, with long legs in bright blue cotton trousers, and with bare black head, swinging so slightly downhill, and the other, in black trousers, rather stout in front, and wearing a new straw hat of the boater variety, coming rather stiffly after, crunching the end of his stroke with a certain violent effort. I was watching the curiously different motions of the two men, the young thin one in bright blue trousers, the elderly fat one in stubby black trousers that stick out in front, the different amount of effort in their mowing, the lack of grace in the elderly one, his jerky advance, the unpleasant effect of the new "boater" on his head—and I tried to interest the little lady.

But it meant nothing to her. The mowers, the mountains, the cherry-trees, the lake, all the things that were *actually there*, she didn't care about. They even seemed to scare her off the balcony. But she held her ground, and instead of herself being scared away, she snatched me up like some ogress, and swept me off into the empty desert spaces of right and wrong, politics, fascism and the rest.

The worst ogress couldn't have treated me more villainously. I don't care about right and wrong, politics, fascism, abstract liberty or anything else of the sort. I want to look at the mowers, and wonder why fatness, elderliness and black trousers should inevitably wear a new straw hat of the boater variety, move in stiff jerks, shove the end of the scythe-stroke with a certain violence, and win my hearty disapproval, as contrasted with young long thinness, bright blue cotton trousers, a bare black head, and a pretty, lifting movement at the end of the scythe-stroke.

Why do modern people almost invariably ignore the things that are actually present to them? Why, having come out from England to find mountains, lakes, scythe-mowers and cherry-trees, does the little blue-eyed lady resolutely close her blue eyes to them all, now she's got them, and gaze away to Signor Mussolini, whom she hasn't got, and to fascism which is invisible anyhow? Why isn't she content to be where she is? Why can't she be happy with what she's got? Why must she *care*?

I see now why her round blue eyes are so round, so noticeably round. It is because she "cares." She is haunted by that mysterious bugbear of "caring." For everything on earth that doesn't concern her, she "cares." She cares terribly because far-off, invisible hypothetical Italians wear black shirts, but she doesn't care a rap that the elderly mower whose stroke she can hear wears black trousers, instead of bright blue cotton ones. Now if she would descend from the balcony and climb the grassy slope and say to the fat mower: Cher monsieur, pourquoi portez-vous les pantalons noirs? Why oh why do you wear black trousers?—then I should say: What an on-the-spot little lady!—But since she only torments me with International politics, I can only remark: What a tiresome, off-the-spot old woman!

They care! They simply are eaten up with caring. They are so busy caring about fascism or League of Nations* or whether France is right, or whether marriage is threatened, that they never know where they are. They certainly never live on the spot where they are. They inhabit abstract space, the desert void of politics, principles, right and wrong and so forth. They are doomed to be abstract. Talking to them is like trying to have a human relationship with the letter x in algebra.

There simply is a deadly breach between actual living and this abstract caring. What is actual living? It is a question mostly of direct contact. There was a direct, sensuous contact between me, the lake, mountains, cherry-trees, mowers, and a certain invisible but noisy chaffinch in a clipped lime-tree. All this was cut off by the fatal shears of that abstract word, fascism, and the little old lady next door was the Atropos who cut the thread of my actual life this afternoon.* She beheaded me, and flung my head into abstract space—. Then we are supposed to love our neighbours!

When it comes to living, we live through our instincts and our intuitions. Instinct makes me run from little over-earnest ladies, instinct makes me sniff the lime-blossom and reach for the darkest cherry. But it is intuition which makes me feel the uncanny glassiness of the lake this afternoon, the sulkiness of the mountains, the vividness of near green in thunder-sun, the young man in bright-blue trousers lightly tossing the grass from his scythe, the elderly man in a boater stiffly shoving his scythe-stroke, both of them sweating in the silence of the intense light.

MASTER IN HIS OWN HOUSE

The sequence of events described in the introduction to 'Insouciance' led Lawrence, apparently with considerable haste, to satisfy Olley's request for an article on the topic, 'Men Must be Master Again'. He had told Nancy Pearn on 27 June 1928 that he was unable to meet the request and had sent 'Insouciance' to placate the newspaper editor, but on the very next day he wrote to her: 'Here's another article for the *Evening News*' (*Letters*, vi. 441). It was Lawrence's response to Olley's proposal; on his manuscript it was entitled 'Men Must Rule'. A typescript was produced in Curtis Brown's office; it must have been submitted for the author's approval because, on the typescript the title is changed, in Lawrence's hand, to 'Master in his Own House'. Olley published the article under that title in the *Evening News* on 2 August. Nancy Pearn informed Lawrence on 24 August that, for a fee of $75, *Vanity Fair* had bought the right to publish it in the USA where it appeared in November, entitled 'Deserted Battlefields: *A Polemic Against Mass Thinking and Men's Modern Indifference to the Ancient Rewards*'. It was collected in *Assorted Articles* under Lawrence's revised title.

MASTER IN HIS OWN HOUSE

We still are ruled too much by ready-made phrases. Take for example: A man must be master in his own house.* There's a good old maxim, we all believe it in theory. Every little boy sees himself a future master in his own house. He grows up with the idea well fixed. So naturally, when his time comes and he finds, which he does pretty often, that he's *not* master in his own house, his nose is conventionally out of joint. He says: These overbearing modern women, they insist on bossing the show, and they're absolutely in the wrong.

What we have to be aware of is mass thinking. The idea that a man must be master in his own house is just a mass idea. No man really thinks it for himself. He accepts it en bloc, as a member of the mass. He is born, so to speak, tightly swaddled up in it, like a lamb in its wool. In fact we are born so woolly and swaddled up in mass ideas, that we hardly get a chance to move, to make a real move of our own. We just bleat foolishly out of a mass of woolly cloud, our mass-ideas, and we get no further. A man must be master in his own house. Feed the brute. An Englishman's home is his castle.* Two servants are better than one. Happy is the bride who has her own little car in her own little garage. It is the duty of a husband to give his wife what she wants. It is the duty of a wife to say "Yes darling!" to her husband:—all these are mass ideas, often contradicting one another, but always effective. If you want to silence a man, or a woman, effectively, trot out a mass idea. The poor sheep is at once mum.

Now the thing to do with a mass idea is to individualise it. Instead of massively asserting: A man must be master in his own house, the gentleman in question should particularise and say: I, Jim, must be master in my own house, The Rosebud, or The Doves' Nest, over my wife, Julia.—And as soon as you make it personal, and drag it to earth, you will feel a qualm about it. You can storm over the breakfast coffee: A man must be master in his own house! But it takes much more courage to say: My name's Jim, and I must be master in this house, the Rosebud, over you, Julia, my spouse!—This is bringing things to an issue. And things are rarely so brought. The lord and master fumes with a mass idea, and the spouse and helpmeet fumes with a mass resentment, and their mingled fumings make a nice mess of The Rosebud.

As a matter of fact, when Jim begins to look into his own heart, and also to look The Rosebud, which is his own house, firmly in the eye—he finds—O shattering discovery!—that he has very little desire to be master in The Rosebud. On the contrary, the idea rather nauseates him. And when he looks at Julia calmly pouring the coffee, he finds, if he's the usual Jim, that his desire to be master over that young dame is curiously non-existent.

And there's the difference between a mass idea and real individual thinking. A man must be master in his own house. But Jim finds the idea of being master in The Rosebud rather feeble, and the idea of being master over the cool Julia somehow doesn't inspire him. He doesn't really care whether The Rosebud has pink bows on the curtains or not. And he doesn't care really what Julia does with her day, while he's away at his job. He wants her to amuse herself and not bother him.—That is, if he's the ordinary Jim.

So that man being master in his own house falls flat when the man is indifferent to his mastery. And that's the worst of mass ideas: they remain, like fossils, when the life that animated them is dead. The problem of a man being master in his own house is today no problem, really, because the man is helplessly indifferent about it. He feels mere indifference; only now and then he may spout up the mass idea, and make an unreal fume which does a lot of harm.

We may take it for granted, that wherever woman bosses the show, it is because man doesn't want to. It is not rapacity and pushing on the woman's part. It is indifference on the man's. Men don't really care. Wherever they *do* care, there is no question of the intrusion of women. Men really care still about engineering and mechanical pursuits, so there is very little intrusion of women there. But men are sadly indifferent to clerking pursuits, and journalistic pursuits, and even to parliamentary pursuits. So women flood in to fill the vacuum. If we get a House of Commons filled with women members, it will be purely and simply for the reason that men, energetic men, are indifferent, they don't care any more about being Members of Parliament and making laws.

Indifference is a strange thing. It lies there under all the mass thinking and the mass activity, like a gap in the foundations.—We still make a great fuss about Parliament—and underneath, most men are indifferent to Parliament. All the fuss about a home of your own and a wife of your own: and underneath, the men are only too often indifferent to the house and the wife both. They are only too willing for the wife to do the bossing and the caring, so that they need neither care nor boss.

Indifference is not the same as insouciance. Insouciance means not caring about things that don't concern you; it also means not being pinched by anxiety. But indifference is inability to care, it is the result of a certain deadness or numbness. And it is nearly always accompanied by the pinch of anxiety. Men who can't care any more feel anxious about it. They have no insouciance. They are thankful if the women will care. And at the same time they resent the women's caring and running the show.

The trouble is not in the women's bossiness, but in the men's indifference. This indifference is the real malady of the day. It is a deadness, an inability to care about anything. And it is always pinched by anxiety.

And whence does the indifference arise? It arises from having cared too much, from having cared about the wrong thing, in the immediate past. If there is a growing indifference to politics on the part of men, it is because men have cared far too much about politics. If Jim is really indifferent to his little home, The Rosebud, if he leaves it all to Julia, that is because his father and grandfather cared far too much about their little homes, made them a bit nauseating. If men don't care very vitally about their jobs, nowadays, and leave them to women, it is because our fathers and grandfathers considered the job sacrosanct—which it isn't—and so wore out the natural feeling for it, till it became repulsive.

Men leave the field to women, when men become inwardly indifferent to the field. What women take over is really an abandoned battle. They don't pick up the tools and weapons of men, till men let them drop.

And then men, gnawed by the anxiety of their own very indifference, blame women and start re-iterating like parrots such mass ideas as: "Man must be master in his own house."

MATRIARCHY

Lawrence had accepted Olley's invitation to submit four articles for publication in the *Evening News* (see 'Insouciance'); he sent the third and fourth – 'Matriarchy' and 'Ownership' – to Nancy Pearn for typing on 12 July 1928 (*Letters*, vi. 461). She acknowledged their arrival on 16 July. Nearly a month later – on 11 August – she wrote again to tell Lawrence that Olley was undecided whether or not to accept them. Eventually he decided in favour of 'Matriarchy' and published it on 5 October. Lawrence had originally entitled the article 'Rule of Women' but, on his manuscript, deleted that and substituted 'Matriarchy'; it appeared in the *Evening News* entitled: '—And If Women *Were* Supreme . . .'. Olley introduced the article with the blurb, alongside a photograph of the writer: 'Mr D. H. Lawrence, writing in the mood of delicate irony of which he is master, gives a hint of what a world might be in which Woman, socially, came first.'

'Matriarchy' was collected in *Assorted Articles*.

MATRIARCHY

Whether they are aware of it or not, the men of today are a little afraid of the women of today; and especially the younger men. They not only see themselves in the minority, overwhelmed by numbers, but they feel themselves swamped by the strange unloosed energy of the silk-legged hordes. Women, women everywhere, and all of them on the war-path! The poor young male keeps up a jaunty front, but his masculine soul quakes. Women, women everywhere, silk-legged hosts that are up and doing, and no gainsaying them. They settle like silky locusts on all the jobs, they occupy the offices and the playing fields like immensely active ants, they buzz round the coloured lights of pleasure in amazing bare-armed swarms, and the rather dazed young male is, naturally, a bit scared. Tommy may not be scared of his own individual Elsie. But when he sees her with her scores of female "pals", let him bluff as he may, he is frightened.

Being frightened, he begins to announce: Man must be master again!—The *must* is all very well. Tommy may be master of his own little Elsie in the stronghold of his own little home. But when she sets off in the morning to her job, and joins the hosts of her petticoatless silk-legged "pals", who is going to master her? Not Tommy!

It's not a question of petticoat-rule. Petticoats no longer exist. The unsheathed silky legs of the modern female are petticoatless, and the modern young woman is not going to spend her life managing some little husband. She is not interested. And as soon as a problem ceases to contain interest, it ceases to be a problem. So that petticoat rule, which was such a problem for our fathers and grandfathers, is for us nothing. Elsie is not interested.

No, the modern young man is not afraid of being petticoat-ruled. His fear lies deeper. He is afraid of being swamped, turned into a mere accessory of bare-limbed, swooping woman. Swamped by her numbers, swamped by her devouring energy. He talks rather bitterly about rule of women, monstrous regimen of women, and about matriarchy, and, rather feebly, about man being master again. He knows perfectly well that he will never be master again. John Knox could live to see the head of his monstrous regimen of women, the head of Mary of Scotland,* just chopped off. But you can't chop off the head of the modern woman. As leave try to chop the head off a swarm of locusts. Woman has emerged, and you can't put her back again. And she's not going back of her own accord, not if she knows it.

So we are in for the monstrous rule of women, and a matriarchy. A matriarchy! This seems the last word of horror to the shuddering male. What it means, exactly, is not defined. But it rings with the hollow sound of man's subordination to woman. Woman cracks the whip, and the poor trained dog of a man jumps through the hoop. Nightmare!

Matriarchy, according to the dictionary, means mother-rule, the mother the head of the family. The children inherit the mother's name. The property is bequeathed from mother to daughter, with a small allowance for the sons. The wife, no doubt, swears to love and cherish her husband, and the husband swears to honour and obey his spouse.*—It doesn't sound so very different from what already is: except that when Tommy Smith marries Elsie Jones, he becomes Mr Jones: quite right too, nine cases out of ten.

And this is the matriarchy we are drifting into. No good trying to stem the tide. Woman is in flood.

But in this matter of matriarchy, let us not be abstract. Men and women will always be men and women. There is nothing new under the sun,* not even matriarchy. Matriarchies have been and will be. And what about them, in living actuality?—It is said that in the ancient dawn of history there was nothing but matriarchy: children took the mother's name, belonged to the mother's clan, and the man was nameless. There is supposed to be a matriarchy today among the Berbers* of the Sahara, and in Southern India, and one or two other rather dim places.

Yet, if you look at photographs of Berbers, the men look most jaunty and cocky, with their spears, and the terrible matriarchal women look as if they did most of the work. It seems to have been so in the remote past. Under the matriarchal system that preceded the patriarchal system of Father Abraham, the men seem to have been lively sports, hunting and dancing and fighting, while the women did the drudging and minded the brats.

Courage! Perhaps a matriarchy isn't so bad after all. A woman deserves to possess her own children and have them called by her name. As for the household furniture and the bit of money in the bank, it seems naturally hers.

Far from being a thing to dread, matriarchy is a solution to our weary social problem. Take the pueblo Indians of the Arizona desert. They still have a sort of matriarchy. The man marries into the woman's clan, and passes into *her* family house. His corn supply goes to *her* tribe. His children are the children of *her* tribe, and take *her* name, so to speak. Everything that comes into the house is hers, *her* property. The man has no claim on the house, which belongs to her clan, nor to anything within the house. The Indian woman's home is *her* castle.

So! And what about the man, in this dread matriarchy? Is he the slave of the woman? By no means. Marriage, with him, is a secondary consideration, a minor event. His first duty is not to his wife and children—they belong to the clan. His first duty is to the tribe. The man is first and foremost an active, religious member of the tribe. Secondarily, he is son or husband and father.

The real life of the man is not spent in his own little home, Daddy in the bosom of the family, wheeling the perambulator on Sundays. His life is passed mainly in the khiva, the great underground religious meeting-house where only the males assemble, where the sacred practices of the tribe are carried on: then also he is away hunting, or performing the sacred rites on the mountains, or he works in the fields. But he spends only certain months of the year in his wife's house, sleeping there. The rest he spends chiefly in the great khiva, where he sleeps and lives, along with the men, under the tuition of the old men of the tribe.

The Indian is profoundly religious. To him, life itself is religion: whether planting corn or reaping it, scalping an enemy or begetting a child: even washing his long black hair is a religious act. And he believes that only by the whole united effort of the tribe, day in, day out, year in, year out, in sheer religious attention and practice, can the tribe be kept vitally alive. Of course the religion is pagan, savage, and to our idea unmoral. But religion it is, and it is his charge.

Then the children. When the boys reach the age of twelve or thirteen, they are taken from the mother, and given into the charge of the old men. They live now in the khiva, or they are taken to the sacred camps in the mountains, to be initiated into manhood. Now their home is the khiva, the great sacred meeting-house underground. They may go and eat in their mother's house. But they live and sleep with the men.

And this is ancient matriarchy. And this is the instinctive form that society takes, even now. It seems to be a social instinct to send boys away to school at the age of thirteen, to be initiated into manhood. It is a social instinct in a man, to leave his wife and children safe in the home, while he goes out and foregathers with other men, to fulfil his deeper social necessities. There is the club and the public-house, poor substitutes for the sacred khiva, no doubt, and yet absolutely necessary to most men. It is in the clubs and public-houses that men have really educated one another by immediate contact, discussed politics and ideas, and made history. It is in the clubs and public-houses that men have tried to satisfy their deeper social instincts and intuitions. To satisfy his deeper social instincts and intuitions, a man must be able to get away from his family, and from women altogether, and foregather in the communion of men.

Of late years, however, the family has got hold of a man, and begun to destroy him. When a man is clutched by his family, his deeper social instincts and intuitions are all thwarted, he becomes a negative thing. Then the woman, perforce, becomes positive, and breaks loose into the world.

Let us drift back to matriarchy. Let the woman take the children and give them her name—it's a wise child that knows its own father.* Let the women take the property—what has a man to do with inheriting or bequeathing a grandfather's clock! Let the women form themselves into a great clan, for the preservation of themselves and their children. It is nothing but just.

And so, let men get free again, free from the tight littleness of family and family possessions. Give woman her full independence, and with it, the full responsibility of her independence. That is the only way to satisfy women once more: give them their full independence and full self-responsibility as mothers and heads of the family. When the children take the mother's name, the mother will look after the name all right.

And give the men a new foregathering ground, where they can meet and satisfy their deep social needs, profound social cravings which can only be satisfied apart from women. It is absolutely necessary to find some way of satisfying these ultimate social cravings in men, which are deep as religion in a man. It is necessary for the life of society, to keep us organically vital, to save us from the mess of industrial chaos and industrial revolt.

OWNERSHIP

Lawrence sent 'Ownership' (in manuscript initially entitled 'Property') for typing on 12 July 1928 (*Letters*, vi. 461). It was the last of the four extra articles for Arthur Olley and Nancy Pearn was asked to send it 'over to the *Evening News*'. Acknowledged by her on the 16th, its fate was still uncertain when she wrote on 11 August; not until 11 October was she able to inform Lawrence that Olley had decided to reject the article. For his part, Lawrence was seemingly indifferent when he responded on 30 October: 'I don't mind the *Evening News* not printing "Ownership" if they don't want to' (vi. 602). It was unpublished until collected in *Assorted Articles*.

OWNERSHIP

The question of the possession of property, I read somewhere lately, has now become a religious question. On the other hand, the religious people assert that the possession of property can never be a religious question,* because in his religious soul a man is indifferent to property either way. I only care about property, money, possessions of any sort, when I have no religion in me. As soon as real religion enters, out goes my interest in the things of this world.

This, I consider, is hard lines on a man; since I must spend the best part of my day earning my living and acquiring a modicum of possessions, I must acknowledge myself a religionless wretch most of my time: or else I must be a possessionless beggar and a parasite on industrious men.

There is something wrong with the arrangement. Work is supposed to be sacred, wages are slightly contemptible and mundane, and a savings-bank account is distinctly irreligious, as far as pure religion goes. Where are we, quite?

No getting away from it, there is something rather mean about saving money. But still more fatal is the disaster of having no money at all, when you need it.

The trouble about this property business, money, possessions, is that we are most of us exceedingly and excruciatingly bored by it. Our fathers got a great thrill out of making money, building their own house, providing for their old age and laying by something for their children. Children inherit their father's leavings: they never inherit their father's and mother's thrill: never more than the tail end of it: a point to which parents are consistently blind. If my father was thrilled by saving up, I shall be thrilled by blowing my last shilling. If my father gave all he had to the poor,* I shall quite enjoy making things pleasant for my own little self. If my father wasted, I shall probably economise. Unless, of course, my father was a jolly waster.

But fathers for the last fifty years have been saving up, building their own houses, acquiring neat little properties, leaving small inheritances to their children, and preaching the sanctity of work. And they have pretty well worn it all out. The young don't believe in the sanctity of work, they are bored by the thought of saving up for their children. If they do build themselves a little house, they are tired of it in ten minutes. They want a car to run around in, and money to spend: but possessions, as possessions, are simply a bore to them. What's the fun owning things anyway, unless you can do something with them?

So that the young are approaching the religious indifference to property, out of sheer boredom.

But being bored by property doesn't solve the problem. Because, no matter how bored you may be, you've got to live, and to do so you have to earn a living, and you have to own a certain amount of property. If you have wife and children, the earning and the property are a serious matter. So, many young men today drive themselves along in work and business, feeling a distinct inner boredom with it all, and bemoaning a thankless existence.

What's to be done about it? Why nothing, all in a hurry. The thing to do is to face the situation. A young man today says to himself: I'm bored! I'm bored by making money slowly and meagrely, I'm bored at the thought of owning my own little bit. Why haven't I a maiden aunt who'll die and leave me a thousand a year? Why can't I marry a rich wife? Why doesn't somebody set me up for life? Why—?

This seems to be peculiarly the attitude of the young Englishman. He truly doesn't want much, it's not riches he's after. All he wants, he says, is independence. By which he means, not real independence at all, but freedom from the bore of having to make a living.

To make a living was to our fathers and grandfathers an adventure; to us it is no more an adventure, it is a bore. And the situation is serious. Because, after all, it is change in feelings which makes changes in the world.

When it says in the Times:* The question of the possession of property has now become a religious question—it does not mean that the question whether I shall own my little six-roomed house or not has become a religious question. It is a vague hint at national ownership. It is becoming a religious question with us now, whether the nation or whether private individuals shall own the land and the industries. This is what is hinted at.

And perhaps national or private ownership is indeed becoming a religious question. But if so, like the question of a man and his own little house, it is becoming religious not because of our passionate interest in it, but because of our deadly indifference. Religion must be indifferent to the question of ownership, and we are, *au fond*, indifferent. Most men are inwardly utterly bored by the problem of individual ownership or national ownership; and therefore, at this point, they are inwardly utterly religious.

Ownership altogether has lost its point, its vitality. We are bored by ownership, public or private, national or individual. Even though we may hang on like grim death to what we've got, if somebody wants to snatch it—and the instinct is perfectly normal and healthy—still, for all that, we are inwardly bored by the whole business of ownership. And the sooner we realise it, the better. It saves us from the bogey of bolshevism.

If we could come to a fair unanimity on this point—the point that ownership is boring, making money is boring, earning a living is a bore—then we could wriggle out of a lot of the boredom. Take the land, for example. Nobody really wants it, when it comes to the point. Neither does anybody really want the coal-mines. Even the nation doesn't want them. The men of the nation are fed stiff with mines and land and wages.

Why not hand it all over to the women? to the women of Britain! The modern excessive need of money is a female need. Why not hand over to the women the means of making the money which they, the women, mostly need? Men must admit themselves flummoxed. If we handed over to the women the means of making money, perhaps there might be a big drop in the feminine need of money. Which after all is the straight road to salvation.

AUTOBIOGRAPHY

In mid-June 1928 Philippe Soupault, the literary director of the French publishing house, Kra, passed to the London office of Curtis Brown a request for a short biography of Lawrence. The request was relayed to Lawrence by Jean Watson, the manager of Curtis Brown's Foreign Department. His first reaction was to hope that a biographical piece which his sister-in-law Else Jaffe had been asked to write for the *Frankfürter Zeitung* in May 1928 might be adapted for Soupault: 'I simply can't write biographies of myself'[1] (*Letters*, vi. 391, 429–30). This hope was dashed; after receiving only 'trois lignes de notice biographique', Soupault repeated his request with greater urgency and some asperity on 30 June; whereupon Jean Watson wrote to Lawrence:

> Our Paris representative points out that Kra makes a great feature of his introductions, and that a good one would be extremely valuable publicity for your work in France. I have collected all the information I can from 'WHO'S WHO' and various other reference books, but apparently they want something more detailed and personal. Neither Secker nor Miss Pearn have nothing which meets the case. (Nehls, iii. 232)

Lawrence complied; using the backs of Soupault's letter of 30 June to Jean Watson and hers to Lawrence of 16 July, with the addition of one small sheet of paper, he wrote his 'Autobiography' and sent it to her two days later. His covering letter conveyed his irritation: 'With great reluctance I have forced myself to write out a draft of an autobiography – Let the Kra – Kra – Kraa! read *Sons and Lovers* and *The Rainbow* and he's got all he wants – and be damned to him.' He asked that typed copies of his manuscript be made for himself, Nancy Pearn and Soupault: 'Then I hope we'll have provided against the future. – I feel rather cold about French publicity of me' (vi. 465).

'Autobiography' was first published in Nehls, iii. 232–4; it was reprinted as 'Autobiographical Sketch' in *Phoenix II*.

[1] Cf. 'Mushrooms' in Appendix III.

AUTOBIOGRAPHY

David Herbert Lawrence—born 11 Sept. 1885 in Eastwood, Nottingham, a small mining town in the Midlands—father a coal-miner, scarcely able to read or write—Mother from the bourgeoisie, the cultural element in the house (read *Sons and Lovers*, the first part is all autobiography).*—Fourth of five children—two brothers oldest—then a sister, then D. H.—then another sister—always delicate health but strong constitution—went to elementary school and was just like anybody else of the miners' children—at age of twelve won a scholarship for Nottingham High School, considered best day school in England—purely bourgeois school—quite happy there, but the scholarship boys were a class apart—D. H. made a couple of bourgeois friendships, but they were odd fish,*—he instinctively recoiled away from the bourgeoisie, regular sort—left school at 16—had a severe illness—made the acquaintance of Miriam and her family, who lived on a farm,* and who really roused him to critical and creative consciousness (see Sons and Lovers). Taught in a rough and fierce elementary school of mining boys:* salary, first year, £5. – second year £10—third year £15—(from age of 17 to 21)—Next two years in Nottingham University, at first quite happy, then utterly bored.—Again the same feeling of boredom with the middle-classes, and recoil away from them instead of moving towards them and rising in the world. Took B. A. course, but dropped it; used to write bits of poems and patches of *The White Peacock* during lectures. These he wrote for Miriam, the girl on the farm, who was herself becoming a school-teacher. She thought it all wonderful—else, probably, he would never have written—His own family strictly "natural" looked on such performance as writing as "affectation." Therefore wrote in secret at home. Mother came upon a chapter of *White Peacock* — read it quizzically, and was amused. "But my boy, how do you know it was like that? You don't know —"—She thought one ought to *know*—and she hoped her son, who was "clever", might one day be a professor or a clergyman or perhaps even a little Mr Gladstone.* That would have been rising in the world—on the ladder. Flights of genius were nonsense—you had to be clever and rise in the world, step by step.—D. H. however recoiled away from the world, hated its ladder, and refused to rise. He had proper bourgeois aunts with "library" and "drawing-room" to their houses—but didn't like that either—preferred the powerful life in a miners kitchen—and still more, the clatter of nailed boots in the little kitchen of Miriam's farm. Miriam was even poorer then he—but she loved poetry and consciousness and flights of fancy above all. So he wrote for her—still without any idea of becoming a literary man at all—looked on himself as just a school-teacher—and mostly hated school-teaching. Wrote *The White Peacock* in bits and snatches, between age of 19 and 24. Most of it written six or seven times.

At the age of twenty-three, left Nottingham college and went for the first time to London, to be a teacher in a boys school in Croydon, £90. a year.* Already the intense physical dissatisfaction with Miriam. Miriam read all his writings—she alone. His mother, whom he loved best on earth, he never spoke to, about his writing. It would have been a kind of "showing-off", or affectation.—It was Miriam who sent his poems to Ford Madox Hueffer, who had just taken over *The English Review*. This was when D. H. was 24. Hueffer accepted, wrote to Lawrence, and was most kind and most friendly—Got Heinemann to accept the MS., a ragged and bulky mass, of *The White Peacock*—invited the school-teacher to lunch—introduced him to Edward Garnett*—and Garnett became a generous and genuine friend. Hueffer and Garnett launched D. H. into the literary world. Garnett got Duckworth to accept the first book of poems: *Love Poems and Others*. When Lawrence was 25, *The White Peacock* appeared. But before the day of publication, his mother died*—she just looked once at the advance copy, held it in her hand—

The death of his mother wiped out everything else—books published, or stories in magazines. It was the great crash, and the end of his youth. He went back to Croydon to the hated teaching—the £50 for the *White Peacock* paid the doctor etc for his mother.

Then a weary and bitter year—broke with Miriam—and again fell dangerously ill with pneumonia. Got slowly better. Was making a little money with stories, Austin Harrison,* who had taken over the *English Review*, being a staunch supporter, and Garnett and Hueffer staunch backers. In May, 1912, went away suddenly with his present wife, of German birth, daughter of Baron Friedrich von Richthofen.* They went to Metz, then Bavaria, then Italy—and the new phase had begun. He was 26—his youth was over—there came a great gap between him and it.

Was in Italy and Germany the greater part of the time between 1912 and 1914. In England during the period of the war—pretty well isolated. In 1915 *The Rainbow* was suppressed for immorality*—and the sense of detachment from the bourgeois world, the world which controls press, publication and all, became almost complete. He had no interest in it, no desire to be at one with it. Anyhow the suppression of *The Rainbow* had proved it impossible. Henceforth he put away any idea of "success," of succeeding with the British bourgeois public, and stayed apart.

Left England in 1919, for Italy—had a house for two years in Taormina, Sicily. In 1920 was published in America *Women in Love*—which every publisher for four years had refused to accept, because of *The Rainbow* scandal. In Taormina wrote *The Lost Girl*, *Sea and Sardinia*, and most of *Aaron's Rod*. In 1922 sailed from Naples to Ceylon, and lived in Kandy for a while—then on to Australia for a time—in each case taking a house and settling down. Then sailed from Sydney to San Francisco, and went to Taos, in New Mexico, where he settled down again with his wife, near the Pueblo of the Indians. Next year he acquired a small ranch high up on the Rocky Mountains, looking west to Arizona. Here, and in Old Mexico, where he travelled and lived for about a year, he stayed till 1926, writing *St. Mawr* in New Mexico, and the final version of *The Plumed Serpent* down in Oaxaca in Old Mexico.

Came to England 1926—but cannot stand the climate. For the last two years has lived in a villa near Florence, where *Lady Chatterley's Lover* was written.

WOMEN ARE SO COCKSURE

The dating of this essay is wholly conjectural, depending solely on circumstantial evidence; there is no direct reference to it in Lawrence's letters or other documents. With some confidence, however, its composition can be placed in August 1928. By title and theme it is akin to the article 'Cocksure Women and Hen-sure Men', sent to Nancy Pearn on 24 August in response to her letter of the 11th; indeed the one may have been a trial run for the other.

Further conjecture is prompted by the persistently personal, family orientation of the essay, beginning with reminiscences about Lawrence's parents and ending with the moral fable of the 'three sisters' which must allude to Frieda and her two sisters. Moreover, the second half of the essay makes frequent reference to women in their fifties, insisting, 'Beware, oh modern woman, the age of fifty' and drawing attention to the emotional changes in women 'particularly in those women who are the moral force in the household'. Then it is perhaps significant that on 11 August Frieda had her forty-ninth birthday, celebrated in great style, as Lawrence told Earl Brewster, an absentee from the occasion: 'Frieda had such a grand birthday feast . . . such a pile of gifts, and she was so *moved*. I of course was the mocker at the festival' (*Letters*, vi. 507). Was his mockery directed in part at the fact that 'inevitably the age of fifty will come upon her' (as the essay states)? Possibly at least the second half, if not the whole, of 'Women Are So Cocksure' was reminiscent of Lawrence's teasing remarks, even a speech, made at the birthday festival and afterwards read – like other pieces written at this time – for Earl Brewster's delectation after his return to Gsteig. The cumulative weight of conjecture would place composition about 11 August 1928 or a few days thereafter.

There is no evidence that Lawrence offered the essay for publication; it first appeared in *Phoenix*.

WOMEN ARE SO COCKSURE

My destiny has been cast among cocksure women. Perhaps when man begins to doubt himself, woman, who should be nice and peacefully hen-sure, becomes instead insistently cocksure. She develops convictions, or she catches them. And then woe-betide everybody.

It began with my mother. She was convinced about some things: one of them being that a man ought not to drink beer. This conviction developed from the fact, naturally, that my father drank beer. He sometimes drank too much. He sometimes boozed away the money necessary for the young family. Therefore the drinking of beer became to my mother the cardinal sin. No other sin was so red, so red-hot. She was like a bull before this red sin. When my father came in tipsy, she saw scarlet.*

We dear children were trained never, *never* to fall into this sin. We were sent to the Band of Hope, and told harrowing stories of drunkenness; we wept bitterly over the heroic youth who had taken the pledge* and sworn never never to touch nor to taste, and who clenched his teeth when his cruel comrades tried to force beer down his throat: but alas, he had lost one of his front teeth, and through this narrow gap beer trickled even down his gullet. So he died of a broken heart.

My mother, though a woman with a real sense of humour, kept her face straight and stern while we recounted this fearsome episode. And we were rigidly sent to the Band of Hope.

Years passed. Children became young men. It was evident my mother's sons were not going to hell down the beer-mug: they didn't care enough about it. My mother relaxed. She would even watch with pleasure while I drank a glass of ale, the fearful enemy, at supper. There was no longer a serpent in the glass, dash it down, dash it down.*

"But mother, if you don't mind if I drink a little beer, why did you mind so much about my father?"

"You don't realise what I had to put up with."

"Yes I do. But you made it seem a sin, a horror. You terrified our lives with the bogey of strong drink. You were absolutely sure it was utter evil. —Why isn't it utter evil any more?"

"You're different from your father—"

But she was just a little shame-faced. Life changes our feelings. We may get mellower, or we may get harsher, as time goes on. But we change. What outrages our feelings in the twenties will probably not outrage them in the fifties, not at all. And the change is much more striking in women than in men. Particularly in those women who are the moral force in the household, as my mother was.

My mother spoilt her life with her moral frenzy against John Barleycorn.* To be sure she had occasion to detest the alcoholic stuff. But why the moral frenzy? It made a tragedy out of what was only a nuisance. And at fifty, when the best part of life was gone, she realised it. And then what would she not have given to have her life again, her young children, her tipsy husband, and a proper natural insouciance, to get the best out of it all. When woman tries to be too much mistress of fate, particularly of other people's fates, what a tragedy!

As sure as a woman has the whip-hand over her destiny and the destinies of those near her, so sure will she make a mess of her own destiny, and a muddle of the others'. And just as inevitably as the age of fifty will come upon her, so inevitably will come the realisation that she has got herself into a hole. *She ought not to have been so cocksure.*

Beware, oh modern woman, the age of fifty. It is then that the play is over, the theatre shuts, and you are turned out into the night. If you have been making a grand show of your life, all off your own bat, and being grand mistress of your destiny, all triumphant, the clock of years tolls fifty, and the play is over. You've had your turn on the stage. Now you must go, out into the common night, where you may or may not have a true place of shelter.

It is dangerous for any body to be cocksure. But it is peculiarly dangerous, for a woman. Being basically a creature of emotion, she will direct all her emotion force full on to what seems to her the grand aim of existence. For twenty, thirty years she may rush ahead to the grand goal of existence. And then—the age of fifty approaches—the speed slackens—the driving-force begins to fail—the grand goal is not only no nearer, it is all too near. It is all round about. It is a waste of unspeakable dreariness.

There were three sisters.* One started out to be learned and to give herself to social reform. She was absolutely cocksure about being able to bring the world nearer salvation. The second obstinately decided to live her own life and to be herself. "The aim of my life is to be myself." She was cocksure about what her self was and how to be it. The aim of the third was to gather roses, whilst she might.* She had real good times with her lovers, with her dress-makers, with her husband and her children. All three had everything life could offer.

The age of fifty draws near. All three are in the state of vital bankruptcy of the modern woman of that age. The one is quite cynical about reform, the other begins to realise that the "self" she was so cocksure about doesn't exist, and she wonders what does exist. To the third the world is a dangerous and dirty place, and she doesn't know where to put herself.

Of all things, the most fatal to a woman is to have an aim, and be cocksure about it.

WHY I DON'T LIKE LIVING IN LONDON

On 12 June 1928 Arthur Olley wrote asking if Lawrence would consider producing articles on 'Man Must be Master Again' and 'I Do Not Like London Life (and Why)?' Nancy Pearn forwarded his letter and a fortnight later Lawrence responded: 'You know Mr Olley wants me to write "Why I don't like London!" Why London doesn't like me is more to the point. I'll send you that in a day or two – little article, I mean' (*Letters*, vi. 438). More than six weeks elapsed before Nancy Pearn reminded him on 11 August that Olley wanted to know whether he was prepared to write on the topics proposed two months before: 'Why I Don't Like London' and 'Women are Cocksure but Never Quite Sure'. Lawrence's reply on 20 August was jocular but brusque: 'Now let him have "Why I don't like London": and if he's afraid of it, I'll write one, "Why I don't like him"!' (vi. 516). Olley was not afraid of it; he published the article in the *Evening News* on 3 September 1928, entitled 'Dull London!', a title entered in an unknown hand on the typescript. It was collected in *Assorted Articles* under the same title and reprinted in *Phoenix II*. Lawrence's own title is restored in this edition.

WHY I DON'T LIKE LIVING IN LONDON

It begins the moment you set foot ashore, the moment you step off the boat's gangway. The heart suddenly, yet vaguely sinks. It is no lurch of fear. Quite the contrary. It is as if the life-urge failed, and the heart dimly sank. You trail past the benevolent policemen and the inoffensive passport officials, through the fussy and somehow foolish customs—we don't *really* think it matters if somebody smuggles in two pairs of false-silk* stockings—and we get into the poky but inoffensive train, with poky but utterly inoffensive people, and we have a cup of inoffensive tea from a nice, inoffensive boy, and we run through small, poky, but nice and inoffensive country, till we are landed in the big but unexciting station of Victoria, when an inoffensive porter puts us into an inoffensive taxi and we are driven through the crowded yet strangely dull streets of London to the cosy yet strangely poky and dull place where we are going to stay. And the first half-hour in London, after some years abroad, is really a plunge of misery. The strange, the grey and uncanny, almost deathly sense of *dulness* is overwhelming. Of course you get over it after a while, and admit that you exaggerated. You get into the rhythm of London again, and you tell yourself that it is *not* dull. And yet you are haunted, all the time, sleeping or waking, with the uneasy feeling: It is dull! It is all dull! This life here is one vast complex of dulness! I am dull. I am being dulled. My spirit is being dulled! My life is dulling down to London dulness.

This is the nightmare that haunts you the first few weeks of London. No doubt if you stay longer you get over it, and find London as thrilling as Paris or Rome or New York. But the climate is against me. I cannot stay long enough. With pinched and wondering gaze, the morning of departure, I look out of the taxi upon the strange dulness of London's arousing, a sort of death, and hope and life only return when I get my seat in the boat-train, and I hear all the Good-byes! Goodbye! Goodbye! Thank God to say Goodbye!

Now to feel like this about one's native land is terrible. I am sure I am an exceptional, or at least an exaggerated case. Yet it seems to me most of my fellow-countrymen have the pinched, slightly pathetic look in their faces, the vague, wondering realisation: It is dull! It is always essentially dull! My life is dull!

Of course England is the easiest country in the world, easy, easy and nice. Everybody is nice, and everybody is easy. The English people on the whole are surely the *nicest* people in the world,* and everybody makes everything so easy for everybody else, that there is almost nothing to resist at all. But this very easiness and this very niceness become at last a nightmare. It is as if the whole air were impregnated with chloroform or some other pervasive anaesthetic, that makes everything easy and nice, and takes the edge off everything, whether nice or nasty. As you inhale the drug of easiness and niceness, your vitality begins to sink. Perhaps not your physical vitality, but something else: the vivid flame of your individual life. England can afford to be so free and individual because no individual flame of life is sharp and vivid. It is just mildly warm and safe. You couldn't burn your fingers at it. Nice, safe, easy: the whole ideal. And yet under all the easiness is a gnawing uneasiness, as in a drug-taker.

It used not to be so. Twenty years ago, London was to me thrilling, thrilling, thrilling, the vast and roaring heart of all adventure. It was not only the heart of the world, it was the heart of the world's living adventure. How wonderful the Strand, the Bank, Charing Cross at night, Hyde Park in the morning!

True, I am now twenty years older. Yet I have not lost my sense of adventure. But now all the adventure seems to me crushed out of London. The traffic is too heavy. It used to be going somewhere, on an adventure. Now it only rolls massively and overwhelmingly, going nowhere, only dully and enormously *going*. There is no adventure at the end of the buses' journey. The bus lapses into an inertia of dulness, then dully starts again. The traffic of London used to roar with the mystery of man's adventure on the seas of life, like a vast sea-shell, murmuring a thrilling, half-comprehensible story. Now it booms like monotonous, far-off guns, in a monotony* of crushing something, crushing the earth, crushing out life, crushing everything dead.

And what does one do, in London? I, not having a job to attend to, lounge round and gaze in bleak wonder on the ceaseless dulness. Or I have luncheons and dinners with friends, and talk. Now my deepest private dread of London is my dread of this talk. I spend most of my days abroad saying little, or with a bit of chatter and a silence again. But in London I feel like a spider whose thread has been caught by somebody, and is being drawn out of him, so he must spin, spin, spin, and all to no purpose. He is not even spinning his own web, for his own reasons.

So it is in London, at luncheon, dinner, or tea. I don't want to talk. I don't mean to talk. Yet the talk is drawn out of me, endlessly. And the others talk, endlessly also. It is ceaseless, it is intoxicating, it is the only real occupation of us who do not jazz.* And it is purely futile. It is quite as bad as ever the Russians were: talk for talk's sake, without the very faintest intention of a result in action. Utter inaction, and storms of talk. That again is London to me. And the sense of abject futility in it all only deepens the sense of abject dulness, so all there is to do is to go away.

COCKSURE WOMEN AND HEN-SURE MEN

Arthur Olley had suggested on 12 June 1928 that Lawrence might consider writing an article for the *Evening News* on 'Women are Cocksure but Never Quite Sure' (see the introduction to 'Why I don't Like Living in London'). His invitation went unanswered so long that, eventually, on 23 August Nancy Pearn almost pleaded with Lawrence to respond: 'Are you going to do the . . . article on WOMEN ARE COCKSURE, BUT NEVER QUITE SURE for the "*Evening News*"?'

At this time the Lawrences were staying in a chalet, Kesselmatte, near Gsteig; Earl and Achsah Brewster were in a hotel nearby. Lawrence had not been idle. Achsah Brewster reported that he 'was writing articles during those days for newspapers . . . Almost every day there would be a new one to read to us' (Brewster 288). On one occasion the Brewsters' Indian friend, Boshi Sen, was present at the reading of 'Cocksure Women and Hen-sure Men'; he was particularly pleased by it and 'maintained that every woman in India ought to read it. Lawrence shook his head – "But they won't publish it even though they have asked for it!" – which incredible as it seems, proved to be true' (Brewster 289).

On 24 August, Lawrence sent Nancy Pearn what he called 'the article on the "Cocksure Woman"', with the added instruction that, whether or not Olley decided to cut it for publication, she was to keep 'a complete copy' (*Letters*, vi. 521). On this occasion she was slow to respond; Lawrence jogged her memory on 2 September and was assured on the 5th that the manuscript had arrived (vi. 541). Then Olley in turn delayed a decision; only on 27 September was Nancy Pearn able to convey his regrets that he could not use 'the one about sureness'. Lawrence was puzzled; a month later he told her that, since he had not seen Olley's letter of refusal, he could not decide 'how or why he wants me to alter "Cocksure Women": Can't he alter it himself?' (vi. 601). Almost another month passed before, on 20 November, Lawrence heard from Nancy Pearn that the *Evening News*, confirming their refusal of the article, declared that they did not see 'how it could be altered to suit them' (vi. 601 n. 3).

Lawrence's prediction had proved true: England refused the essay; but America, in the *Forum*, accepted it and paid a fee of $100. It appeared in 'Forum Table Talk' in January 1929, accompanied by a 'Scissor cut' of a cocksure cockerel by Hunt Diederich. It was collected in *Assorted Articles*.

COCKSURE WOMEN AND HEN-SURE MEN

It seems to me there are two aspects to women. There is the demure, and the dauntless. Men have loved to dwell, in fiction at least, on the demure maiden whose inevitable reply is: Oh yes if you please, kind sir! The demure maiden, the demure spouse, the demure mother—this is still the ideal. A few maidens, mistresses and mothers *are* demure. A few pretend to be. But the vast majority are not. We don't expect a girl skilfully driving her car to be demure, we expect her to be dauntless. What good would demure and maidenly members of Parliament be, inevitably responding: Oh yes if you please, kind sir!—Though of course there are masculine members of that kidney.—And a demure telephone girl? or even a demure stenographer? Demureness, to be sure, is outwardly becoming, it is an outward mark of femininity, like bobbed hair.* But it goes with inward dauntlessness. The girl who has to make her way in life has got to be dauntless, and if she has a pretty demure manner with it, then lucky girl. She kills two birds with two stones.

With the two kinds of femininity go two kinds of confidence: there are the women who are cocksure, and the women who are hensure. A really up-to-date woman is a cocksure woman. She doesn't have a doubt nor a qualm. She is the modern type. Whereas the old-fashioned demure woman was sure as a hen is sure, that is, without knowing anything about it. She went quietly and busily clucking around, laying her eggs and mothering her chickens in a kind of anxious dream that still was full of sureness. But not mental sureness. Her sureness was a physical condition, very soothing, but a condition out of which she could easily be startled or frightened.

It is quite amusing to see the two kinds of sureness in chickens. The cockerel is, naturally, cocksure. He crows because he is *certain* it is day. Then the hen peeps out from under her wing. He marches to the door of the hen-house and pokes out his head assertively: *Ah-ha! daylight of course, just as I said*!—And he majestically steps down the chicken-ladder towards *terra firma*, knowing that the hens will step cautiously after him, drawn by his confidence. So after him, cautiously, step the hens. He crows again: *Ha-ha! here we are*!—It is indisputable, and the hens accept it entirely. He marches towards the house. From the house a person ought to appear, scattering corn. Why does the person not appear? The cock will see to it. He is cocksure. He gives a loud crow in the doorway, and the person appears. The hens are suitably impressed, but immediately devote all their henny consciousness to the scattered corn, pecking absorbedly, while the cock runs and fusses, cocksure that he is responsible for it all.

So the day goes on. The cock finds a tit-bit, and loudly calls the hens. They scuffle up in henny surety, and gobble the tit-bit. But when they find a juicy morsel for themselves, they devour it in silence, hen-sure. Unless, of course, there are little chicks, when they most anxiously call the brood. But in her own dim surety, the hen is really much surer than the cock, in a different way. She marches off to lay her egg, she secures obstinately the nest she wants, she lays her egg at last, then steps forth again with prancing confidence, and gives that most assured of all sounds, the hen-sure cackle of a bird who has laid her egg. The cock, who is never so sure about anything as the hen is about the egg she has laid, immediately starts to cackle like the female of his species. He is pining to be hen-sure, for hen-sure is so much surer than cock-sure.

Nevertheless, cocksure is boss. When the chicken-hawk appears in the sky, loud are the cockerel's calls of alarm. Then the hens scuffle under the verandah, the cock ruffles his feathers on guard. The hens are numb with fear, they say: Alas, there is no health in us!* How wonderful to be a cock so bold! And they huddle numbed. But their very numbness is hen-surety.

Just as the cock can cackle, however, as if he had laid the egg, so can the hen-bird crow. She can more-or-less assume his cocksureness. And yet, she is never so easy, cocksure, as she used to be when she was hen-sure. Cocksure she is cocksure, but uneasy. Hensure, she trembles, but is easy.

It seems to me just the same in the vast human farmyard. Only nowadays all the cocks are cackling and pretending to lay eggs, and all the hens are crowing and pretending to call the sun out of bed. If women today are cocksure, men are hensure. Men are timid, tremulous, rather soft and submissive, easy in their very hen-like tremulousness. They only want to be spoken to gently. So the women step forth with a good loud *cock-a-doodle-do*!

The tragedy about cocksure women is that they are more cocky, in their assurance, than the cock himself. They never realise that when the cock gives his loud crow in the morning, he listens acutely afterward, to hear if some other wretch of a cock dares crow defiance: challenge. To the cock, there is always defiance, challenge, danger and death on the clear air: or the possibility thereof.

But alas, when the hen crows, she listens for no defiance or challenge. When she says *cock-a-doodle-do*! then it is unanswerable. The cock listens for an answer, alert. But the hen knows she is unanswerable. *Cock-a-doodle-do!* and there it is, take it or leave it!

And it is this that makes the cocksureness of women so dangerous, so devastating. It is really out of scheme,* it is not in relation to the rest of things. So we have the tragedy of cocksure women. They find, so often, that instead of having laid an egg, they have laid a vote, or an empty ink-bottle, or some other absolutely unhatchable object, which means nothing to them.

It is the tragedy of the modern woman. She becomes cocksure, she puts all her passion and energy and years of her life into some effort or assertion, without ever listening for the denial which she ought to take into account. She is cocksure, but she is a hen all the time. Frightened of her own henny self, she rushes to mad lengths about votes, or welfare, or sports, or business, she is marvellous, out-manning the man. But alas, it is all fundamentally disconnected. It is all an attitude, and one day the attitude will become a weird cramp, a pain, and then it will collapse. And when it has collapsed, and she looks at the eggs she has laid, votes, or miles of type-writing, years of business-efficiency, suddenly, because she is a hen and not a cock, all she has done will turn into pure nothingness to her. Suddenly it all falls out of relation to her basic henny self, and she realises she has lost her life. The lovely henny surety, the hen-sureness which is the real bliss of every female, has been denied her, she has never had it. Having lived her life with such utmost strenuousness and cocksureness, she has missed her life altogether. Nothingness!

HYMNS IN A MAN'S LIFE

About 15 September 1927, when the Lawrences were staying in Irschenhausen, near Munich, with Frieda's sister Else Jaffe, Lawrence met Franz Schoenberner, editor of the Munich periodical *Jugend*. One consequence was that Lawrence was invited to offer a story for publication in *Jugend*; he chose one written in 1919, his 'little "dog" story' (*Letters*, vi. 153), 'Rex'; *Jugend* published it in October 1928, translated into German by Else Jaffe.

More important for the present purpose was his introduction by Schoenberner to Hans Carossa, the poet and novelist who was also a physician specialising in tuberculosis. Lawrence was eager to meet him: 'if a poet who is a doctor can't tell me what to do with myself, then who can?' (vi. 156). Carossa visited Irschenhausen with Schoenberner, probably on 29 September 1927; having examined Lawrence he told his companion: 'An average man with those lungs would have died long ago . . . Maybe Lawrence can live two or even three years more. But no medical treatment can really save him.'[1] For his part, Lawrence was flattered by his visitors' knowledge of his writings (vi. 167); he liked Carossa personally – 'a nice man, mild as mashed potatoes' (vi. 172); so that when, in late August 1928, he was asked by Dr Anton Kippenberg, head of the Leipzig publishing house, Insel-Verlag, to contribute 'a short sketch' to a book of essays in honour of Carossa, he agreed at once (vi. 524). The 'sketch' proved to be 'Hymns in a Man's Life'.

It must have been written almost immediately after Lawrence received Kippenberg's invitation since, on 2 September 1928, he sent Frieda's German translation of it to Schoenberner and the English version to Nancy Pearn (vi. 540–1). To both correspondents he gave permission for the piece to be adjusted at their discretion: to the first he said, 'Shorten it or alter it as you like'; to the second, 'If anybody wants it they can cut it if they like – do what they darn well please.' To Schoenberner Lawrence added the genial remark: 'I don't know though

[1] Nehls, iii. 160.

why Hans Carossa makes me think of childhood and hymns; perhaps because he is so delicate.'

Lawrence's manuscript of the article went to Nancy Pearn for typing;[1] on 8 September 1928 he asked her to 'send a typescript copy' to Schoenberner (vi. 551). The German version was published first: 'Kirchenlieder im Leben Eines Mannes' in *Buch des Dankes für Hans Carossa* (*c.* September 1928). On 11 October Nancy Pearn told Lawrence with obvious pleasure that the *Evening News* staff were very impressed by 'Hymns in a Man's Life' and that she had been able to extract 15 guineas for it 'despite a little squeal on their part'. Their enthusiasm was reflected in an editorial puff – boxed and italicised – set alongside Lawrence's opening paragraph when the article appeared in the *News* on 13 October 1928:

Which of us can recall or weigh the things that deeply impressed his mind in childhood, ere knowledge had brought sophistication and dimmed the starlight of wonder to a mere chart of the heavens? In an article which he has chosen to call 'Hymns in a Man's Life', that brilliant novelist Mr. D. H. Lawrence tries to tell us what the hymns of his childhood meant to him, what a glamour and an inspiration lay in word and phrase and rhythm, what visions they conjured up in the golden haze of a child's half-formed imagination. The sounds meant so much and the sense was what the child mind chose to make of it.

It is clear that orthodoxy was never Mr Lawrence's strong point. The great and tragic facts of Christian history never stirred him deeply. But the hymns stirred him to pleasant wonder; there were phrases and place names that were the very stuff of what a child's dreams can be made.

Now he is older and the fruit of knowledge has banished him from the Eden of wonder; but the old hymns still carry with them the old thrill. Few who read Mr Lawrence's article but will eagerly compare it with their own spiritual experiences, experiences that so many are familiar with and so few can explain or express in words.

[1] Lawrence gave the manuscript to his niece, Emily King, who in turn presented it to the University of Nottingham. See V. de S. Pinto, 'Lawrence and the Nonconformist Hymns', in *A D. H. Lawrence Miscellany*, ed. Harry T. Moore (Carbondale, 1959), p. 104. Pinto included an edited text of the MS in his article.

HYMNS IN A MAN'S LIFE

Nothing is more difficult than to determine what a child takes in and does not take in, of its environment and its teaching.* This fact is brought home to me by the hymns which I learned as a child, and never forget. They mean to me almost more than the finest poetry, and they have for me a more permanent value, somehow or other. It is almost shameful to confess that the poems which have meant most to me, like Wordsworth's *Ode to Immortality* and Keats' Odes and pieces of *Macbeth* or *As You Like It* or *Midsummer Night's Dream*, and Goethe's lyrics such as "Über allen Gipfeln ist Ruh," and Verlaine "Ayant poussé la porte qui chancelle"*—all these lovely poems which after all give the ultimate shape to one's life; all these lovely poems, woven deep into a man's consciousness, are still not woven so deep in me as the rather banal nonconformist hymns that penetrated through and through my childhood.

"Each gentle dove
And sighing bough
That makes the eve
So fair to me
Has something far
Diviner now
It draws me back
To Galilee.—
O Galilee, sweet Galilee
Where Jesus loved so much to be,
O Galilee, sweet Galilee
Come sing thy songs again to me!"*

To me, the word Galilee has a wonderful sound. The Lake of Galilee! I don't want to know where it is. I never want to go to Palestine:* Galilee is one of those lovely glamorous worlds, not places, that exist in the golden haze of a child's half-formed imagination. And in my man's imagination it is just the same. It has been left untouched. With regard to the hymns which had such a profound influence on my childish consciousness, there has been no crystallising out, no dwindling into actuality, no hardening into the commonplace. They are the same to my man's experience as they were to me nearly forty years ago.

The moon, perhaps, has shrunken a little. One has been forced to learn about orbits, eclipses, relative distances, dead worlds, craters of the moon, and so on. The crescent at evening still startles the soul with its delicate flashing. But the mind works automatically, and says: "Ah, she is in her first quarter. She is all there, in spite of the fact that we see only this slim blade. The earth's shadow is over her."—And willy-nilly, the intrusion of the mental processes dims the brilliance, the magic of the first apperception.

It is the same with all things. The sheer delight of a child's apperception is based on *wonder*: and deny it as we may, knowledge and wonder counteract one another. So that as knowledge increases, wonder decreases. We say again: Familiarity breeds contempt. So that as we grow older, and become more familiar with phenomena, we become more contemptuous of them.—But that is only partly true. It has taken some races of men thousands of years to become contemptuous of the moon, and to the Hindu the cow is still wondrous. It is not familiarity that breeds contempt, it is the assumption of knowledge. Anybody who looks at the moon and says: "I know all about that poor orb," is, of course, bored by the moon.

Now the great and fatal fruit of our civilisation, which is a civilisation based on knowledge, and hostile to experience, is boredom. All our wonderful education and learning is producing a grand sum-total of boredom. Modern people are inwardly thoroughly bored. Do as they may, they are bored.

They are bored because they experience nothing. And they experience nothing because the wonder has gone out of them. And when the wonder has gone out of a man, he is dead. He is henceforth only an insect.

When all comes to all, the most precious element in life is wonder. Love is a great emotion, and power is power. But both love and power are based on wonder. Love without wonder is a sensational affair, and power without wonder is mere force and compulsion. The one universal element in consciousness which is fundamental to life, is the element of wonder. You cannot help feeling it in a bean as it starts to grow and pulls itself out of its jacket. You cannot help feeling it in the glisten of the nucleus of the amœba. You recognise it, willy nilly, in an ant busily tugging at a straw, in a rook, as it walks the frosty grass. They all have their own obstinate will. But also, they all live with a sense of wonder. Plant consciousness, insect consciousness, fish consciousness, animal consciousness, all are related by one permanent element, which we may call the religious element inherent in all life, even in a flea: the sense of wonder. That is our sixth sense. And it is the *natural* religious sense.

Somebody says that mystery is nothing, because mystery is something you don't know, and what you don't know is nothing to you.* But there are two ways of knowing. We admit there are two ways of knowing a woman—"Oh I know her very well, we've had many a long talk together:"—"And as he went, a strange woman sat by the road. And he went in unto her and knew her—"*

Even the real scientist works in the sense of wonder. The pity is, when he comes out of his laboratory he puts aside his wonder along with his apparatus, and tries to make it all perfectly didactic. Science in its true condition of wonder is as religious as any religion. But didactic science is as dead and boring as dogmatic religion. Both are wonderless and productive of boredom, endless boredom.

Now we come back to the hymns. They live and glisten in the depths of the man's consciousness in undimmed wonder, because they have not been subjected to any criticism or analysis. By the time I was sixteen I had criticised and got over the christian dogma. It was quite easy for me, my immediate forbears had already done it for me. Salvation, heaven, virgin birth, miracles, even the christian dogmas of right and wrong—one soon got them adjusted. I never could really worry about them. Heaven is one of the instinctive dreams. Right and wrong is something you can't dogmatise about, it's not so easy. As for my soul, I simply don't and never did understand how I could "save" it. One can save one's pennies. But how can one save one's soul? One can only *live* one's soul. The business is to live, really alive. And this needs wonder.

So that the miracle of the loaves and fishes* is just as good to me now as when I was a child. I don't care whether it is historically a fact or not. What does it matter? It is part of the genuine wonder. The same with all the religious teaching I had as a child, *apart* from the didacticism and sentimentalism. I am eternally grateful for the wonder with which it filled my childhood.

"Sun of my soul, thou Saviour dear
It is not night if thou be near—"

That was the last hymn at the Board School.* It did not mean to me any christian dogma, or any salvation. Just the words "Sun of my soul, thou

Saviour dear," penetrated me with wonder, and the mystery of twilight. At another time the last hymn was:

"Fair waved the golden corn
In Canaan's pleasant land—"*

And again I loved "Canaan's pleasant land." The wonder of "Canaan," which could never be localised.

I think it was good to be brought up a protestant: and among protestants, a nonconformist: and among nonconformists, a Congregationalist. Which sounds pharisaic. But I should have missed bitterly a direct knowledge of the Bible, and a direct relation to Galilee and Canaan, Moab and Kedron, those places that never existed on earth. And in the Church of England one would hardly have escaped those snobbish hierarchies of class, which spoil so much for a child.* And the Primitive Methodists,* when I was a boy, were always having "revivals" and being "saved." And I always had a horror of being saved.

So altogether, I am grateful to my "congregational" upbringing. The congregationalists are the oldest nonconformists, descendants of the Oliver Cromwell Independents.* They still had the Puritan tradition of no ritual. But they avoided the personal emotionalism which one found among the Methodists, when I was a boy.

I liked our chapel, which was tall and full of light, and yet still: and colourwashed pale green and blue, with a bit of lotus pattern. And over the Organ-loft: "O worship the Lord in the beauty of Holiness," in big letters.

That was a favourite hymn too.

"O Worship the Lord, in the beauty of holiness.
Bow down before him, his glory proclaim
With gold of obedience and incense of lowliness
Kneel and adore him, the Lord is his name—"*

I don't know what the "beauty of holiness" is, exactly. It easily becomes cant, or nonsense. But if you don't think about it,—and why should you?—it has a magic. The same with the whole verse. It is rather bad, really: "gold of obedience" and "incense of lowliness." But in me, to the music, it still produces a sense of splendour.

I am always glad we had the Bristol hymn-book, not Moody and Sankey.* And I am glad our Scotch minister* on the whole avoided sentimental messes such as "Lead Kindly Light," or even "Abide with me."* He had a healthy preference for healthy hymns.

"At even ere the sun was set
The sick oh Lord around thee lay.
Oh in what divers pains they met!
Oh in what joy they went away!"*

And often we had: "Fight the good fight with all thy might."*

In Sunday School I am eternally grateful to old Mr Remington* with his round white beard and his ferocity. He made us sing! And he loved the martial hymns.

"Sound the battle-cry
See the foe is nigh
Raise the standard high
For the Lord—"*

The ghastly sentimentalism that came like a leprosy over religion had not yet got hold of our colliery village. I remember when I was in Class II in the Sunday School, when I was about seven, a woman-teacher trying to harrow us about the Crucifixion. And she kept saying: "And aren't you sorry for Jesus? Aren't you sorry?" And most of the children wept. I believe I shed a crocodile tear or two, but very vivid is my memory of saying to myself: "I don't *really* care a bit."—And I could never go back on it. I never *cared* about the crucifixion, one way or another. Yet the *wonder* of it penetrated very deep in me.

Thirty-six years ago, men, even Sunday-school teachers, still believed in the fight for life, and the fun of it. "Hold the fort, for I am coming—"* It was far, far from any militarism or gun-fighting. But it was the battle-cry of a stout soul, and a fine thing too.

"Stand up, stand up for Jesus
Ye soldiers of the Lord—"*

Here is the clue to the ordinary Englishman—in the nonconformist hymns.

RED TROUSERS

Writing from Gsteig in Switzerland to Nancy Pearn, on 13 September 1928, Lawrence said, on the last page of the manuscript of 'Red Trousers': 'Article for the *Evening News*, if they want it' (*Letters*, vi. 563). It appeared there a fortnight later, on 27 September, but entitled: 'Oh! for a New Crusade'; there is no evidence that Lawrence was responsible for the revised title. The article was collected in *Assorted Articles* under his original title; that is also used here.

RED TROUSERS

A man wrote to me, in answer to my article in which I complained of London dulness:* Dear Sir, Have you ever paused to consider that the cause of our dulness is the cigarette? This is the tubular white ant which is sapping our civilisation.—

Now this man, at least, is not entirely dull. He is out on a crusade, a crusade against the "tubular white ant", from which he wants to rescue our holy civilisation. And whatever else a crusader may be, he is not, to himself at least, dull. He is inspired with a mission, and on the march. Which, perhaps, is better than sitting still and being inert.

But after all, a crusade may turn out ultimately dull: like the crusade of Votes for Women,* or teetotalism, or even the Salvation Army. When you've got the vote, it is dull. When people are merely teetotal, it is merely dull. When the Salvation Army has saved you, you may really feel duller than when you weren't saved. Or of course, you may not.

So that there are two sides to a crusade. The good side is the activity. There was a thrill in the Votes for Women processions, even in the sight of suffragettes being marched off by stout and semi-indignant policemen.* When I hear the tambourine clashing, and see the poke bonnets of the Salvation Army lasses and the funny scarlet of the men, and hear the piercing music of Marching to Zion, or Throw Out the Lifeline,* then I am invariably thrilled. Here is a crusade, of a sort, here is spunk! And even in the denunciative "tubular white ants" of my correspondent, there is a certain pep, a certain "go."

But the bad side of these crusades is the disillusion when the mission is fulfilled. Take the cigarette and dulness. Which causes which? Does dulness cause the cigarette, or the cigarette the dulness? Apparently it is a vicious circle: each causes the other. But at the very beginning, dulness causes the cigarette, after which the cigarette may cause more dulness, or may not, as the case may be. Anyhow that is not my crusade, because it isn't really interesting.

What is really the point is that a crusade is a sovereign remedy against dulness, but you'd better watch out that the end of the crusade isn't a greater dulness still. Nothing is such fun as a crusade, it is the adventure of adventures. But it is no good setting out grandly to rescue some Zion from the clutch of the infidel, if you're not going to care a button about the Zion when you've rescued it.

That's the trouble with most of our modern crusades, like Votes or Socialism or politics, freedom of little nations, and the rest. In the flush of youth, I believed in Socialism, because I thought it would be thrilling and delightful. Now I no longer believe very deeply in Socialism, because I am afraid it might be dull, duller even than what we've got now. In the past, it seemed wildly thrilling to think of a free Poland, or a free Bohemia. Now, we have a painful suspicion that free Cecho-Slovakia* is possibly duller than when it was an Austrian province.

What we want is life, first and foremost: to live, and to know that we are living. And you can't have life without adventure of some sort. There are two sorts of adventure: the hairs-breadth escape sort, and the more inward sort. The hairs-breadth escape sort is nearly used up, though of course small boys still climb trees, and there is speeding on the roads, the traffic danger, aeroplanes, and the North Pole. But this is meagre, compared to the wild old days when the Turk held Jerusalem, and the world was flat.

What remains is the vast field of social adventure. In the ancient recipe, the three antidotes for dulness, or boredom are sleep, drink, and travel. It is rather feeble. From sleep you wake up, from drink you become sober, and from travel you come home again. And then where are you? No, the two sovereign remedies for dulness are love, or a crusade.

But love is a thing you can do nothing about. It's like the weather. Whereas a crusade can be carefully considered. When the Salvation Army march out with drum and brass to pitch a stand at the street corner, they are on a crusade, and full of adventure, though they run no risk except that of ridicule. Probably they get more out of life than those who ridicule them: and that's the chief point.

Yet still, we can't all join the Salvation Army: there'd be nobody to save. And we sadly need a crusade. What are we going to do about it? Politics, Socialism, preaching of any sort: we feel there's not much in it. It is going to make greater dulness in the end. There is money, that is an adventure to a certain degree. But it is an adventure within definite limits, very definite limits. Besides, it is for his leisure that man needs a crusade.

Women, of course, are still thrilling in the last stages of their emancipation crusade. Votes, short skirts, unlimited leg, Eton crop,* the cigarette, and see-you-damned-first, these are the citadels captured by women: along with endless "jobs." Women, for a little while longer, have enough to thrill them in the triumphs of the emancipation crusade.

But the men, what are they going to do? The world of adventure is pretty well used up, especially for a man who has a wage to earn. He gets a little tired of being spoon-fed on wireless, cinema, and newspaper, sitting an inert lump while entertainment or information is poured into him. He wants to *do* something.

And what is there to be done? Thousands of things—and nothing. Golf, jazz, motoring—hobbies. But what we want is a crusade.

Find us a crusade. It is apparently impossible. There is no formula.

The thing to do is to decide that there is no crusade or holy war feasible at this moment, and to treat life more as a joke, but a good joke, a jolly joke. That would freshen us up a lot. Our flippant world takes life with a stupid seriousness. Witness the serious mock-morality of the film and the wireless, the spurious earnestness poured out. What a bore!

It is time we treated life as a joke again, as they did in the really great periods like the Renaissance. Then the young men swaggered down the street with one leg bright red, one leg bright yellow, doublet of puce velvet, and yellow feather in silk cap.

Now that is the line to take. Start with externals, and proceed to internals, and treat life as a good joke. If a dozen men would stroll down the Strand and Piccadilly tomorrow, wearing tight scarlet trousers fitting the leg, gay little orange-brown jackets and bright green hats, then the revolution against dulness which we need so much would have begun.* And, of course, those dozen men would be considerably braver, really, than Captain Nobile* or the other arctic venturers. It is not particularly brave to do something the public wants you to do. But it takes a lot of courage to sail gaily, in brave feathers, right in the teeth of a dreary convention.

IS ENGLAND STILL A MAN'S COUNTRY

There is no extant record of the approach by the editor of the *Daily Express* which must have preceded Lawrence's letter to Nancy Pearn on 30 October 1928, from the Ile de Port-Cros, assuring her that he would 'have a shot at "England as a man's country"' for the paper (*Letters*, vi. 602). The article was swiftly written; it was sent to her on 3 November (vi. 606) and she acknowledged its arrival on the 8th. At the end of the month, on the 29th, it appeared in the *Express*. Lawrence is described in the heading to the article as '*Famous Novelist, Poet and Critic*'; he is also honoured with a brief biographical note at the end which underscores his distinction as 'one of the most discussed novelists' and, quoting from an anonymous critic, adds that he is 'intolerable at his worst, at his best one of the greatest writers alive'.

IS ENGLAND STILL A MAN'S COUNTRY

They, that is men, Englishmen, get up and ask if England is still a man's country. The only answer is, it would be if there were any men in it. For what makes a man's country, do you imagine? Is it the landscape, or the number of pubs, or the rate of wages, or the size of boots? Is it the fact that the women say: I obey you, my lord?—If the men of England *feel* that England is no longer a man's country—for apparently it was so not very long ago—then it isn't. And if it isn't a man's country, then what in heaven's name is it?

The men will say, it's a woman's country. The women will immediately reply: I *don't* think!—And so it's nobody's country. Poor England! The men say it's no longer a man's country, it has fallen into the hands of the women. The women give a shout of scorn, and say Not half!—and proceed to demonstrate that England would be a very different place if it *were* a woman's country—my word, a changed shop altogether. And between the two of them, men and women, Old England rubs her eyes and says: Where am I? What am I? Am I at all? In short, do I exist?—And there's never a man nor a woman takes the trouble to answer, they're all so busy blaming one another.

If England is not a man's country, it isn't a woman's country either. That's obvious. Women didn't make England. And women don't run England today, in spite of the fact that nine-tenths of the voices on the telephone are female voices. Women today, wherever they are, show up. And they pipe up. They are heard and they are seen. No denying it. And it seems to get on the men's nerves. Quite! But that doesn't prove that the women own England and run England. They don't. They occupy, on the whole, rather inferior jobs, which they embellish with flowered voile and chiffon stockings and a number of airs and graces, and they are apt to be a drain on a man's cigarettes. What then? Is this the cormorant devouring England, gobbling it up under the eyes of the squeaking herring-gulls of men? Do the men envy the women these rather inferior jobs? Or do they envy them the flowered voile and chiffon stockings which decorate the jobs? Or is it the airs and graces they begrudge them, or the cigarettes?—that England is no more a man's country!

"When my father and my mother forsake me, then the Lord will take me up."* I suppose that's how poor old England feels today. The men have certainly forsaken her. They pretend the women have usurped the land, so the men need do no more about it. Which is very comfortable for the men. Very soft and nice and comfortable. Which is what the men of today want. No responsibility.

Soft and nice and comfortable! Soft jobs, nice wives, comfortable homes—that is supposed to be England today. And Englishmen are quite startled if you suggest that it might require more to make a real England.—What more *could* England be, they say, than soft and nice and comfortable?—And then they blame the women for being hard and unkind and uncomfortable, and usurping England.

England, we are told, has always been a fighting country, though never a military country. That is a cliché. But it seems true. The Englishman hated being bossed or bullied. So he hated being a soldier or a marine, because as such he was bossed and bullied. And when he felt anything or anybody coming to boss him and bully him, he got up prepared to plant his fist in the eye of the boss and bully. Which is a real man's spirit, and the only spirit that makes a country a man's country.

Nowadays, alas, a change has come over all that. The Englishman only wants to be soft and nice and comfortable, and to have no real responsibility, not even for his own freedom and independence. He's got all the political freedom he can manage, and so he cares nothing about it. He even won't mind if it's taken from him again, after his forefathers fought so hard for it. He's got political freedom, so he cares nothing about it. Which is a bit despicable, after all.

He's got political freedom, but he hasn't got economical freedom. There's the rub.* And the modern man feels it's not right. He feels he *ought* to have an income. A man's parents *ought* to leave him a sufficient independent income, and if they don't, he bears them a lifelong grudge. And worse still, he has to do a job.

Now this is the disaster that has happened to almost every Englishman—he's got to do a job. All day long and every day, all his life, he is condemned to a job. There's no getting away from it. Very few men can inherit a fortune or marry a fortune. A job!—that is the great inevitable. That is the boss and the bully. That is the tread-mill. The job! Men secretly and silently hate the job, today. They push it over to the women. Then they loudly and openly abuse the women for having taken it. And they ask, Is England a man's country? Or is it nothing but a dog-gone* women's show?

The answer is obvious. When a man wants a plum off a plum-tree, he climbs up and gets it. But if he won't face the climb, and stands under the tree with his mouth open, waiting for the plum to fall into it: and if while he stands waiting he sees a woman picking up a few plums that he wasn't smart enough even to pick up: and if he then begins to yell that the women have snatched away all the plum-trees from the impoverished men: then what are we to think of him?

If men find they've got political freedom only to realise* most disastrously their economic enslavement,* they'd better do something about it. It's no good despising their political freedom—that is ridiculous, for political freedom is a supremely valuable thing. And it's no good blaming the women. Women, poor things, have to live, just as much as men do. It's no good whining that England is no more a man's country.

It will be a man's country the instant there are men in it. And men will be men the instant they tackle their insuperable difficulty. The insuperable difficulty, the unsolvable problem are only insuperable and unsolvable because men can't make up their minds to tackle them. The insuperable difficulty to modern man is economic bondage. Slavery! Well, history is the long account of the abolishing of endless forms of slavery, none of which we ever want back again. Now we've got a new form of slavery. If every man who feels the burden of it determined ultimately to abolish it, using all his wits and powers and accepting no ready-made formula—then England would be a man's country, sure as eggs.*

SEX APPEAL

On the initiative of the editor of the *Sunday Dispatch* Lawrence was invited to contribute to a series of articles entitled 'What is Sex Appeal?' He heard of the proposal in a letter from Nancy Pearn, 11 October 1928; at the end of the month he accepted the invitation (*Letters*, vi. 602 and n. 1); on 5 November he sent the article to her: 'Here is the article on "Sex Appeal". I made it 2000 words so it would do for *Vanity Fair* if they want it. And if the *Sunday Dispatch* or whatever it is wants it at 1500 words, they can cut it down to please themselves' (vi. 606). A collation of the manuscript with the *Dispatch* text — entitled 'SEX LOCKED OUT', published on 25 November — shows that they cut it by no more than a few words here and there. Indeed the newspaper editor's pleasure at what Lawrence had submitted is clear from an italicised blurb which prefaces the text:

"Sex and beauty are one thing, like flame and fire. If you hate sex you hate beauty. If you love living *beauty you have a reverence for sex."*

In this passage sounds the keynote of the brilliant article from the pen of Mr D. H. Lawrence, the famous novelist and poet, which we print below. Unquestionably it is the finest analysis of that elusive quality sex-appeal made so far by any modern writer.

The article was appropriately illustrated with pictures of Lilian Gish, Charlie Chaplin, Rudolph Valentino and Diane de Poitiers who are named in it. Without the illustrations, the text was privately reprinted from the newspaper as a booklet for Christmas 1928; whether Lawrence sanctioned the publication is not known.

In a letter of 6 June 1929 he learned from Nancy Pearn that 'Vanity Fair is taking that "SEX APPEAL" article at Seventy-Five dollars'. The magazine published it in July, having inserted beneath the title: 'An Enlightening Essay Concerning a Phrase Which Everybody Knows and Nobody Understands'. In December 1929, under the title 'Men and Peacocks', it was published in the New York *Golden Book Magazine*. Finally it was collected in *Assorted Articles* as 'Sex *Versus* Loveliness'. The title on Lawrence's manuscript is used here.

SEX APPEAL

It is a pity that *sex* is such an ugly little word. An ugly little word, and really almost incomprehensible. What *is* sex, after all? The more we think about it, the less we know.

Science says it is an instinct: but what is an instinct? Apparently an instinct is an old, old habit that has become ingrained. But a habit, however old, has to have a beginning. And there is really no beginning to sex. Where life is, there it is. So sex is no "habit" that has been formed. Again, they talk of sex as an appetite, like hunger. An appetite: but for what? An appetite for propagation? It is rather absurd. They say a peacock puts on all his fine feathers to dazzle the pea-hen into letting him satisfy his appetite for propagation. But why should the pea-hen not put on fine feathers, to dazzle the peacock, and satisfy *her* desire for propagation? She has surely quite as great a desire for eggs and chickens as he has. We cannot believe that her sex-urge is so weak that she needs all that blue splendour of feathers to rouse her. Not at all. As for me, I never even saw a pea-hen so much as look at her lord's bronze and blue glory. I don't believe she ever sees it. I don't believe for a moment that she knows the difference between bronze, blue, brown or green. If I had ever seen a pea-hen gazing with rapt attention on her lord's flamboyancy, I might believe that he had put on all those feathers just to "attract" her. But she just never looks at him. Only she seems to get a little perky when he shudders all his quills at her, like a storm in the trees. Then she does seem to notice, just casually, his presence.

These theories of sex are amazing. A peacock puts on his glory for the sake of a wall-eyed pea-hen who never looks at him. Imagine a scientist being so naïve as to credit the pea-hen with a profound, dynamic appreciation of a peacock's colour and pattern. Oh highly-aesthetic peahen!

And a nightingale sings to attract his female. Which is mighty curious, seeing he sings his best when courtship and honeymoon are over, and the female is no longer concerned with him at all, but with her young.—Well then, if he doesn't sing to attract her, he must sing to distract her, or amuse her while she's sitting.

How delightful, how naïve theories are. But there is a hidden will behind them all. There is a hidden will behind all theories of sex, implacable. And that, strangely enough, is the will to deny, to wipe out the mystery of beauty. Because beauty is a mystery. You can neither eat it nor make flannel out of it.—Well then, says science, it is just a trick to catch the female and induce her to propagate. How naïve. As if the female needed inducing. She will propagate in the dark, even—so where then is the beauty trick.

Science has a mysterious hatred of beauty, because it doesn't fit in the cause-and-effect chain. And society has a mysterious hatred of sex, because it perpetually interferes with the nice money-making schemes of social man. So the two hatreds made a combine, and sex and beauty are mere propagation-appetite.

Now sex and beauty are one thing, like flame and fire. If you hate sex you hate beauty. If you love *living* beauty, you have a reverence for sex. Of course you can love old dead beauty and hate sex. But to love living beauty you must have a reverence for sex.

Sex and beauty are inseparable, like life and consciousness. And the intelligence which goes with sex and beauty, and arises out of sex and beauty, is intuition. The great disaster of our civilisation is the morbid hatred of sex—what, for example, could show a more poisoned hatred of sex than Freudian psycho-analysis?—which carries with it a morbid fear of beauty, "alive" beauty, and which causes the atrophy of our intuitive faculty and our intuitive self. The deep psychic disease of modern men and women is the diseased condition of the atrophied intuitive faculties. There is a whole world of life that we might know and enjoy by intuition, and by intuition alone. This is denied us, because we deny sex and beauty, the source of the intuitive life and of the insouciance which is so lovely in free animals and in plants.

Sex is the root of which intuition is the foliage and beauty is the flower. Why is a woman lovely, if ever, in her twenties? It is the time when sex rises softly to her face, as a rose to the top of a rose-bush.

And the appeal is the appeal of beauty. We deny it wherever we can. We try to make the beauty as shallow and trashy as possible. But first and foremost, sex appeal is the appeal of beauty.

Now beauty is a thing about which we are so uneducated, we can hardly speak of it. We try to pretend it is a fixed arrangement: straight nose, large eyes, etc. We think a lovely woman must look like Lilian Gish, a handsome man must look like Rudolf Valentino.* So we *think*. In actual life, we behave quite differently. We say: She's quite beautiful, but I don't care for her.—Which shows we are using the word *beautiful* all wrong. We should say: She has the stereotyped attributes of beauty, but she is not beautiful to me.

Beauty is an *experience*, nothing else. It is not a fixed pattern or an arrangement of features. It is something *felt*, a glow, or a communicated sense of fineness. What ails us is that our sense of beauty is so bruised and blunted, we miss all the best. But to stick to the film—there is a greater essential beauty in Charlie Chaplin's* odd face, than ever there was in Valentino's. There is a bit of true beauty in Chaplin's brows and eyes, a gleam of something pure. But our sense of beauty is so bruised and clumsy, we don't see it, and don't know it when we do see it. We can only see the blatantly obvious, like the so-called beauty of Rudolf Valentino, which only pleases because it satisfies some ready-made notion of handsomeness.

But the plainest person can look beautiful, can *be* beautiful. It only needs the fire of sex to rise delicately, to change an ugly face to a lovely one. That is really sex appeal: the communicating of a sense of beauty. And in the reverse way, no-one can be quite so repellant as a really pretty woman. That is, since beauty is a question of experience, not of concrete form, no-one can be as acutely ugly as a really pretty woman. When the sex-glow is missing, and she moves in ugly coldness, how hideous she seems, all the worse for her externals of prettiness.

What sex is, we don't know, but it must be some sort of fire. For it always communicates a sense of warmth, of glow. And when this glow becomes a pure shine, then we feel the sense of beauty.

But the communicating of the warmth, the glow of sex is true sex appeal. We all have the fire of sex slumbering or burning inside us. If we live to be ninety, it is still there. Or, if it dies, we become one of those ghastly living corpses which unfortunately are becoming more numerous in the world. Nothing is more ugly than a human being in whom the fire of sex has gone out. You get a nasty clayey creature whom everybody wants to avoid.

But while we are fully alive, the fire of sex smoulders or burns in us. In youth it flickers and shines, in age it glows softer and stiller, but there it is. We have some control over it; but only partial control. That is why society hates it. While ever it lives, the fire of sex, which is the source of beauty and anger, burns in us beyond our understanding. Like actual fire, while it lives it will burn our fingers if we touch it carelessly. And so social man, who only wants to be "safe", hates the fire of sex.

Luckily not many men succeed in being merely social men. The fire of the old Adam smoulders. And one of the qualities of fire is that it calls to fire. Sex-fire here kindles sex-fire there. It may only rouse the smoulder into a soft glow. It may call up a sharp flicker. Or it may rouse a flame: and then flame leans to flame, and starts a blaze.

Whenever the sex fire glows through, it will kindle an answer somewhere or other. It may only kindle a sense of warmth and optimism. Then you say: I like that girl, she's a real good sort. It may kindle a glow, that makes the world look kindlier, and life feel better. Then you say: She's an attractive woman, by Jove, I like her—. Or she may rouse a flame that lights up her own face first, before it lights up the universe. Then you say: She's a lovely woman. She looks lovely to me. Let's say no more—

It takes rather a rare woman to rouse a real sense of loveliness. It is not that a woman is born beautiful. We say that to escape our own poor, bruised, clumsy understanding of beauty. There have been thousands and thousands of women quite as good-looking as Diane de Poictiers or Mrs Langtry* or any of the famous ones. There are today thousands and thousands of superbly good-looking women. But oh, how few *lovely* women!

And why? Because of the failure of their sex-appeal. A good-looking woman only becomes lovely when the fire of sex rouses pure and fine in her, and flickers through her face and touches the fire in me. *Then* she becomes a lovely woman to me, then she is in the living flesh a lovely woman: not a mere photograph of one. And how lovely, a lovely woman! But alas, how rare! How bitterly rare, in a world full of unusually handsome girls and women.

Handsome, good-looking, but not lovely, not beautiful. Handsome and good-looking women are the women with good features and the right hair. But a lovely woman is an experience. It is a question of communicated fire. It is a question of sex appeal, in our poor, delapidated* modern phraseology. Sex appeal!—applied to Diana de Poictiers!—or even, in the lovely hours, to one's own wife! Why it is a libel and a slander in itself.

Nowadays, however, instead of the fire of loveliness it is sex appeal. The two are the same thing, I suppose, but on vastly different levels. The business-man's pretty and devoted secretary is still chiefly valuable because of her sex appeal. Which does not imply "immoral relations" in the slightest. Even today, a girl with a bit of generosity likes to feel she is helping a man, if the man will take her help. And this desire that he shall take her help is her sex appeal. It is the genuine fire, if of a very mediocre heat. Still, it serves to keep the world of "business" alive. Probably, but for the introduction of the lady secretary into the business-man's office, the business-man would have collapsed entirely by now. She calls up the sacred fire in her, and she communicates it to her boss. He feels an added flow of energy and optimism, and—business flourishes. That is perhaps the best result of sex appeal today—business flourishes.

There is, of course, the other side of sex-appeal—it can be the destruction of the one appealed to. When a woman starts using her sex-appeal for her own advantage, it is usually a bad moment for some poor devil. But this side of sex appeal has been overworked lately, so it is not nearly so dangerous as it was. The sex-appealing courtesans who ruined so many men in Balzac* no longer find it smooth running. Men have grown canny. They fight shy even of the emotional vamp. In fact, men are inclined to think they smell a rat the moment they feel the touch of feminine sex appeal today.

Which is a pity, for sex appeal is only a dirty name for a bit of life-flame. No man works so well and so successfully, as when some woman has kindled a little fire in his veins. No woman does her housework with real joy unless she is in love—and of course, a woman may go on being quietly in love for fifty years, almost without knowing it. If only our civilisation had taught us how to let sex appeal flow properly and subtly, how to keep the fire of sex clear and alive, flickering or glowing or blazing in all its varying degrees of strength and communication, we might all of us have lived all our lives in love, which means kindled and full of zest, in all kinds of ways and for all kinds of things. Whereas what a lot of dead ash there is to life now!

DO WOMEN CHANGE

This article originated during the Lawrences' stay on Ile de Port-Cros with Richard Aldington, Arabella Yorke and Brigit Patmore in October–November 1928. Lawrence said later that Arabella Yorke was responsible for typing 'what bit' of work he did on the island (*Letters*, vii. 22), so it is reasonable to assume that she produced the first typescript for the three copies sent to Nancy Pearn on 8 November 1928 'for *Evening News* or anybody who wants it' (vi. 610); five days later Nancy Pearn posted one to the *Sunday Dispatch*. The next mention we have of the article is on 5 January 1929 when Lawrence agreed to lengthen it by 650 words, probably in manuscript on a copy of the typescript; he would then send it direct to the manager of Curtis Brown's New York office, Edwin Rich (vii. 117). Rich placed it with the American *Vanity Fair*. The extension earned Lawrence an extra $50 (vii. 188). On 18 February Nancy Pearn wrote: 'If you feel like elaborating your "DO WOMEN CHANGE" article to fill six typewritten pages, the "*Sunday Dispatch*" will take this at the Twenty-five guineas rate. The editor says he would naturally want to use it as a leading article, and for that purpose it is a bit short as it stands' (vii. 188n). Lawrence responded on 23 February from Bandol:

> Herewith the extended article 'Do Women Change'. The extension came a bit too poetical, a bit too lovely. I had already added a chunk, an even bigger chunk, to this same article, for *Vanity Fair*... So perhaps you would rather get the *Vanity Fair* version from Rich – though I found they'd bowdlerised some of my phrases in the first half... Anyhow do as you wish – use this version or get the American one, which is a good bit longer. (vii. 188)

Examination of 'Women Don't Change' in the *Sunday Dispatch* on 28 April 1929, and 'Do Women Change?' in *Vanity Fair* in the same month, confirms that Nancy Pearn took Lawrence's advice, and obtained a copy of the extension sent to Rich; she then forwarded it to Bernard Falk, editor of the London paper. Falk gave his version centre-page prominence; he also embellished it with an illustration showing ladies elaborately dressed for Ascot in 1929 who – as the caption put it – '*will not differ essentially from those of the Ascot of 1909 or those who watched Olympic Games in Greece and the gladiatorial contests in Rome two thousand years ago.*' Though Falk and the *Vanity Fair* editor both felt free to alter Lawrence's text according to taste, it is clear that they were drawing on the same source. Unfortunately no copy of the original 650 words sent to Rich has survived.

The only version which stems directly and indisputably from Lawrence himself comprises the heavily emended typed transcript of the first manuscript, combined with the autograph extension – 'a bit too poetical, a bit too lovely' – sent to Nancy Pearn in February 1929. This combination provides the base-text used here; it was also the source of the text collected in *Assorted Articles* (and retitled 'Do Women Change?'). The substantially different text printed in *Vanity Fair* can be found in Appendix II; variants between it and the *Sunday Dispatch* version are recorded in the textual apparatus.

DO WOMEN CHANGE

They tell of all the things that are going to happen in the future—babies bred in bottles, all the love-nonsense cut out, women indistinguishable from men. But it seems to me bosh. We like to imagine we are something very new on the face of the earth. But it seems to me we flatter ourselves. Motor-cars and aeroplanes are something novel, if not something new—one could draw a distinction. But the people in them are merely people, and not many steps up, if any, it seems to me, from the people who went in litters or palanquins or chariots, or who walked on foot from Egypt to Jordan, in the days of Moses. Humanity seems to have an infinite capacity for remaining the same: that is, human.

Of course there are all kinds of ways of being human; but I expect almost every possible kind is alive and kicking today. There are little Cleopatras and Zenobias and Semiramises and Judiths and Ruths and even Mother Eves,* today just the same as in all the endless yesterdays. Circumstances make them little Cleopatras and Semiramises instead of big ones, because our age goes in for quantity regardless of quality. But sophisticated people are sophisticated people, no matter whether it is Egypt or Atlantis. And sophisticated people are pretty well all alike. All that varies is the proportion of "modern" people to all the other unmodern sorts, the sophisticated to the unsophisticated. And today there is a huge majority of sophisticated people. And they are probably very little different from all the other sophisticated people of all the other civilisations, since man was man.

And women are just part of the human show. They aren't something apart. They aren't something new on the face of the earth, like the loganberry* or artificial silk. Women are as sophisticated as men, anyhow, and they were never anything but women, and they are nothing but women today, whatever they may think of themselves. They say the modern woman is a new type. But is she? I expect, in fact I am sure there have been lots of women like ours in the past, and if you'd been married to one of them, you wouldn't have found her any different from your present wife. Women are women. They only have phases. In Rome, in Syracuse, in Athens, in Thebes, more than two or three thousand years ago, there was the bobbed-haired, painted, perfumed Miss and Mrs of today, and she inspired almost exactly the feelings that our painted and perfumed Misses and Mrses inspire, in the men.

I saw a joke in a German paper—a modern young man and a modern young woman leaning on an hotel-balcony at night, overlooking the sea: *He*: See the stars sinking down over the dark, restless ocean—! *She*: Cut it out! My room-number is 32!—

That is supposed to be very modern: the very modern woman. But I believe women in Capri under Tiberias said: *Cut it out*! to their Roman and Campanian* lovers, in just the same way. And women in Alexandria in Cleopatra's time. Certain phases of history are "modern." As the wheel of history goes round, women become "modern," then they become unmodern again. The Roman women of the late Empire were most decidedly "modern"—so were the women of Ptolemaic Egypt. True, modern cut-it-out women. Only the hotels were run differently.

Modernity, or modernness isn't something we've just invented. It's something that comes at the end of civilisations. Just as leaves in autumn are yellow, so the women at the end of every known civilisation—Roman, Greek, Egyptian etc—have been modern. They were smart, they were chic, they said cut-it-out, and they did as they jolly well pleased.

And then, after all, how deep does modernness go? Even in a woman? You give her a run for her money: and if you don't give it her, she takes it. The sign of modernness in a woman is that she says: Oh, cut it out, boy!—So the boy cuts it out—all the stars and ocean stuff.—My room-number's thirty-two!—Come to the point!

But the point, when you come to it, is a very bare little place, a very meagre little affair. It's extraordinary how meagre the point is once you've come to it. It's not much better than a full stop. So the modern girl comes to the point brutally and repeatedly, to find that her life is a series of full stops, then a mere string of dots. Cut it out, boy! .. .. .. When she comes to dot number one-thousand, she's getting about tired of dots, and of the plain point she's come to. The point is all too plain, and too obvious. It is so pointed that it is pointless. Following the series of dots comes a blank—a dead blank. There's nothing left to cut out. Blank-eye!*

Then the thoroughly modern girl begins to moan: Oh boy, do put something *in* again!—And the thoroughly modern boy, having cut it out so thoroughly that it will never grow again, tunes up with: I can't give you anything but love, Baby*—And the thoroughly modern girl accepts it with unction. She knows it's nothing but a most crest-fallen echo from a sentimental past. But when you've cut everything out so that it will never grow again, you are thankful even for echoes from a sentimental past.

And so the game begins again. Having cut it out, and brought it down to brass tacks,* you find brass tacks are the last thing you want to lie down on.—Oh boy, aren't you going to do something about it?—And the boy, having cut it all out so that it won't grow again, has no other bright inspiration but to turn the brass tacks round, when lo! they become the brass-headed nails that go around Victorian plush furniture. And there they are, the hyper-modern two.

No, women don't change. They only go through a rather regular series of phases. They are first the slave: then the obedient helpmeet: then the respected spouse: then the noble matron: then the splendid woman and citizen, then the independent female, then the modern girl, Oh, cut-it-out, boy!—And when the boy has cut it all out, the mills of God grind on,* and having nothing else to grind, they grind the cut-it-out girl down, down, down—back to—we don't know where—but probably to the slave once more, and the whole cycle starts afresh, on and on, till in the course of a thousand years or two we come once more to the really "modern" girl.—Oh, cut it out, boy!

A lead-pencil* has a point, an argument may have a point, remarks may be pointed, and a man who wants to borrow five pounds from you only comes to the point when he asks you for the fiver. Lots of things have points: especially weapons. But where is the point to life? where is the point to love? where, if it comes to the point, is the point to a bunch of violets? There is no point. Life and love are life and love, a bunch of violets is a bunch of violets, and to drag in the idea of a point is to ruin everything. Live and let live, love and let love, flower and fade, and follow the natural curve, which flows on, pointless.

Now women used to understand this better than men. Men, who were keen on weapons, which all have points, used to insist on putting points to life and love. But women used to know better. They used to know that life is a flow, a soft curving flow, a flowing together and a flowing apart and a flowing together again, in a long subtle motion that has no full-stops and no points, even if there are rough places. Women used to see themselves as a softly-flowing stream of attraction and desire and beauty, soft quiet rivers of energy and peace. Then suddenly the idea changes. They see themselves as isolated things, independent females, instruments, instruments for love, instruments for work, instruments for politics, instruments for pleasure—this, that and the other. And as instruments they become pointed, and they want everything, even a small child, even love itself, to have a point. When women start coming to the point, they don't hesitate. They pick a daisy, and they say: There must be a point to this daisy, and I'm going to get at it.—So they start pulling off the white petals, till there are none left. Then they pull away the yellow bits of the centre, and come to a mere green pad, still without having come to the point. Then in disgust they tear the green base of the flower across, and say: I call that a fool flower. It had no point to it!—

Life is not a question of points, but a question of flow. It's the *flow* that matters. If you come to think of it, a daisy even is like a little river flowing, that never for an instant stops. From the time when the tiny knob of a bud appears down among the leaves, during the slow rising up a stem, the slow swelling and pushing out the white petal-tips from the green, to the full round daisy, white and gold and gay, that opens and shuts through a few dawns, a few nights, poised on the summit of her stem, then silently shrivels and mysteriously disappears, there is no stop, no halt, it is a perpetual little streaming of a gay little life out into full radiance and delicate shrivelling, like a perfect little fountain that flows and flows, and shoots away at last into the invisible, even then without any stop.

So it is with life, and especially with love. There is no point. There is nothing you can cut out, except falsity, which isn't love or life. But the love itself is a flow, two little streams of feeling, one from the woman, one from the man, that flow and flow and never stop, and sometimes they twinkle with stars, sometimes they chafe, but still they flow on, intermingling: and if they rise to a floweriness like a daisy, that is part of the flow; and they will inevitably die down again, which is also part of a flow. And one relationship may produce many flowerinesses, as a daisy plant produces many daisies; but they will all die down again as the summer passes, though the green plant itself need not die. If flowers didn't fade they wouldn't be flowers, they'd be artificial things. But there are roots to faded flowers. And in the root the flow continues and continues. And only the flow matters: live and let live, love and let love. There is no point to love and life.*

ENSLAVED BY CIVILISATION

In November 1928 Lawrence was invited by the editor of the *Sunday Dispatch* to write an article on 'why and how man is becoming enslaved by civilisation.' His answer, 'Enslaved by Civilisation', was sent to Nancy Pearn on 24 November with an accompanying note: 'Good-O! for the *Sunday Despatch*' (*Letters*, vii. 29). She acknowledged receipt of the article four days later when assuring Lawrence that it 'is being typed'. Negotiations for publication of the article seem to have been protracted because not until 18 March 1929 did Lawrence hear from Nancy Pearn that it had been bought by *Vanity Fair* for $100. Three weeks later, on 8 April, she wrote again to inform him that the *Sunday Dispatch* had accepted the article, offered 25 guineas for it and hoped to persuade Rebecca West to reply to it (vii. 251 n. 2). By mid-April Lawrence—then in Barcelona—confessed that he had 'utterly forgotten' what the piece was about, and, for her part, Nancy Pearn's hopes for its future were to be disappointed: publication in *Vanity Fair* was delayed until September 1929 when it was printed under the title, 'The Manufacture of Good Little Boys'; the editor of the *Sunday Dispatch* apparently failed to engage Rebecca West's interest and wholly abandoned Lawrence's article. It was collected under its original title in *Assorted Articles*.

ENSLAVED BY CIVILISATION

The one thing men have not learned to do is to stick up for their own instinctive feelings, against the things they are taught. The trouble is, we are all caught young. Little boys are trundled off to school at the age of five, and immediately the game begins, the game of enslaving the small chap. He is delivered over into the hands of schoolmistresses, young maids, middle-aged maids, and old maids,* and they pounce on him, and with absolute confidence in their own powers, their own *rightness*, and their own superiority, they begin to "form" the poor little devil. Nobody questions for a moment the powers of these women to mould the life of a young man. The Jesuits say: give me a child till he is seven, and I will answer for him for the rest of his life.—Well, schoolmistresses are not as clever as Jesuits, and certainly not as clear as to what they are about, but they do the trick, nevertheless. They make the little boy into an incipient man, the man of today.

Now I ask you, do you really think that schoolmistresses are qualified to form the foundations of a *man*? They are almost all excellent women, and filled with the best of motives. And they have all passed some little exam. or other. But what, in the name of heaven, qualifies them to be the makers of men? They are all maids: young maids, middling maids, or old maids. They none of them know anything about men: that is to say, they are not *supposed* to know anything about men. What knowledge they have must be surreptitious. They certainly know nothing about manhood. Manhood, in the eyes of the schoolmistress, and especially the elderly schoolmistress, is something uncalled-for and unpleasant. Men, in the pleasant opinions of schoolmistresses, are mostly grown-up babies. Haven't the babies all been through the mistress's hands, and aren't the men almost identically the same?

Well, it may be so! It may be that men nowadays are all grown-up babies. But if they are, it is because they were delivered over in their tenderest years, poor little devils, to absolute petticoat rule: mothers first, then schoolmistresses. But the mother very quickly yields to the schoolmistress. It is amazing what reverence ordinary women have for the excellent old-maid mistress of the infants school. What the mistress says is Gospel. Kings are no more kings by divine right, but queens are queens and mistresses mistresses straight from God. It is amazing. It is fetish-worship. And the fetish is goodness.

"Oh, but Miss Teachem is so *good*, she's awfully *good*," say the approving mothers, in luscious voices.—"Now Johnny, you must mind what Miss Teachem says, she knows what is best for you. You must always listen to her!"

Poor Johnny, poor little devil! On the very first day, it is: "Now Johnny dear, you must sit like a good little boy, like all the other good little boys." And when he can't stand it, it is: "Oh Johnny dear, I wouldn't cry if I were you. Look at all the other good little boys, they don't cry, do they dear? Be a good little boy, and teacher will give you a teddy-bear to play with. Would Johnny like a teddy-bear to play with? There, don't cry then! Look at all the other good little boys. They are learning to write—to write! Wouldn't Johnny like to be a good little boy, and learn to write?"

As a matter of fact, Johnny wouldn't. At the bottom of his heart, he doesn't in the least want to be a good little boy and learn to write. But she comes it over him. Dear Teacher, she starts him off in the way he must go, poor little slave. And once started, he goes on wheels, being a good little boy like all the other good little boys. School is a very elaborate railway-system where good little boys are taught to run upon good lines till they are shunted off into life, at the age of fourteen, sixteen or whatever it is. And by that age the running-on-lines habit is absolutely fixed. The good big boy merely turns off one set of rails on to another. And it is so easy, running on rails, he never realises that he is a slave to the rails he runs on. Good boy!

Now the funny thing is that nobody, not even the most conscientious father, ever questions the absolute rightness of these school-marms. It is all for dear little Johnny's own good. And these school-marms know absolutely what Johnny's own good is. It is being a good little boy like all the other good little boys.

But to be a good little boy like all the other good little boys is to be at last a slave, or at least an automaton, running on wheels. It means that dear little Johnny is going to have all his own individual manhood nipped out of him, carefully plucked out, every time it shows a little peep. Nothing is more insidiously clever than an old maid's fingers at picking off the little shoots of manhood as they sprout out from a growing boy, and turning him into that neutral object, a good little boy. It is a subtle, loving form of mutilation, and mothers absolutely believe in it. "Oh, but I *want* him to be a good boy!"—She fails to remember how bored she gets with her good-boy husband. Good boys are very nice to mothers and schoolmistresses. But as men, they make a wishy-washy nation.

Of course, nobody wants Johnny to be a bad little boy. One would like him to be just a boy, with no adjective at all. But that is impossible. At the very best schools, where there is most "freedom", the subtle, silent *compulsion* towards goodness is perhaps strongest. Children are all silently, steadily, relentlessly bullied into being good. They grow up good. And then they are no good.

For what does goodness mean? It means, in the end, being like everybody else, and not having a soul to call your own. Certainly you mustn't have a feeling to call your own. You must be good, and feel exactly what is expected of you, which is just what other people feel. Which means that in the end you feel nothing at all, all your feeling has been killed out of you. And all that is left is the artificial stock emotion which comes out with the morning papers.

I think I belong to the first generation of Englishmen that was really broken in. My father's generation, at least among the miners where I was brought up, was still wild. But then my father had never been to anything more serious than a dame's school, and the dame, Miss Hight,* had never succeeded in making him a good little boy. She had barely succeeded in making him able to write his name. As for his feelings, they had escaped her clutches entirely: as they escaped the clutches of his mother. The country was still open. He fled away from the women and rackapelted* with his own gang. And to the end of his days, his idea of life was to escape over the fringe of virtue and drink beer and perhaps poach an occasional rabbit.

But the boys of my generation were caught in time. We were sent at the ripe age of five to Board schools, British schools, national schools,* and though there was far less of the Johnny dear! business, and no teddy-bears, we were forced to knuckle under. We were forced on to the rails. I went to the Board school. Most of us, practically all, were miners' sons. The bulk were going to be miners themselves. And we all hated school.

I shall never forget the anguish with which I wept, the first day. I was captured. I was roped in. The other boys felt the same. They hated school because they felt captives there. They hated the masters because they felt them as jailers. They hated even learning to read and write. The endless refrain was: "When I go down pit you'll see what xxxxxx sums I s'll do." That was what they waited for: to go down pit, to escape, to be men. To escape into the wild warrens of the pit, to get off the narrow lines of school.

The school-master was an excellent irascible old man with a white beard.* My mother had the greatest respect for him. I remember he flew into a rage with me because I did not want to admit my first name, which is David. "David! David!" he raved. "David is the name of a great and good man.* You don't like the name of David! You don't like the name of David!"—He was purple with indignation. But I had an unreasonable dislike of the name David, and still have, and he couldn't force me into liking it. But he wanted to.

And there it was. David was the name of a great and good man, so I was to be *forced* to like it. If my first name had been Ananias or Ahab, I should have been excused. But David! no! My father, luckily, didn't know the difference between David and Davy of the safety-lamp.*

But the old school-master gradually got us under. There were occasional violent thrashings. But what really did the trick was not the thrashing, but the steady, persistent pressure of: Honest, decent lads behave in my way, and no other.—And he got the lads under. Because he was so absolutely sure he was right, and because mothers and fathers all agreed he was right, he managed pretty well to tame the uncouth colliery lads during the six or seven years he was responsible for them. They were the first generation to be really tamed.

With what result? They went down pit, but even pit was no more the happy subterranean warren it used to be. Down pit everything was made to run on lines, too, new lines, up-to-date lines; and the men became ever less men, more mere instruments. They married, and they made what the women of my mother's generation always prayed for, good husbands. But as soon as the men were good husbands, the women were a tiresome, difficult unsatisfied lot of wives, so there you are! Without knowing it, they missed the old wildness, and were bored.

The last time I was back in the Midlands was during the great coal strike.* The men of my age, the men just over forty, were there, standing derelict, pale, silent, with nothing to say, nothing to do, nothing to feel, and great hideous policemen from God-knows-where waiting in gangs to keep them on the lines. Alas, there was no need. The men of my generation were broken in: they'll stay on the lines and rust there. For wives, schoolmasters, and employers of labour it is perhaps very nice to have men well broken in. But for a nation, for England, it is a disaster.

GIVE HER A PATTERN

On 6 December 1928 Nancy Pearn forwarded to Lawrence a cutting – sent by the editor of the *Daily Express* – 'on AND WE MARRY THESE WOMEN! from one of the American magazines'; it was accompanied by an enquiry from the editor: 'whether you [DHL] are willing to write a special article conveying some of these comments in a manner to suit yourself'. A few days later, on 12 December, Nancy Pearn acknowledged the arrival of Lawrence's article initially entitled 'Oh these Women!' Subsequently, on the typescript presumably sent to him from Curtis Brown's office, Lawrence altered the title to: 'Give Her a Pattern'.

First to publish the article was the American *Vanity Fair* in May 1929, with the title: 'Woman in Man's Image Concerning the Modern Male's Motives in Creating a Satisfactory Rôle for Womankind'. Under the title 'WOMEN', the *Daily Express* printed it on 19 June, two days after the paper had called attention to the exhibition of Lawrence's paintings in the Warren Gallery with the observation that his technique was 'repellent enough, but the subjects of some of [the paintings] will compel most spectators to recoil with horror.'[1] The article was accompanied by a photograph of the author when young, and headlined:

Excuse D. H. LAWRENCE, but he wishes to write about
WOMEN – Once More

Mr D. H. Lawrence the famous novelist, is 'in the news' this week in connection with a much-discussed West End exhibition of paintings by him. The exhibition marks his first public appearance as an artist, but his novels have often evoked storms of criticism and comment.

Not content with that disingenuous introduction, the editor saw fit to break into Lawrence's text two lines before Lawrence's use of 'Because' (164:17), with a brief homily (typographically boxed) on that word, headed '*HOW IS YOUR ENGLISH?*: The word BECAUSE is often wrongly used . . . After opening with THE REASON WAS or THE

[1] Nehls, iii. 338.

REASON WHY, the clause stating the reason must begin with THAT.' For his own part the editor pedantically expanded Lawrence's contractions such as 'didn't' and 'doesn't', and – like the editor of *Vanity Fair* – prudishly omitted references to the womb, *filles de joie*, the 'lurid prostitute on black silk sheets' and the like.

The article was collected in *Assorted Articles*.

GIVE HER A PATTERN

The real trouble about women is that they must always go on trying to adapt themselves to men's theories of women, as they always have done. When a woman is thoroughly herself she is being what her type of man wants her to be. When a woman is hysterical it's because she doesn't quite know what to be, which pattern to follow, which man's picture of woman to live up to.

For of course, just as there are many men in the world, there are many masculine theories of what women should be. But men run to type, and it is the type, not the individual, that produces the theory, or "ideal" of woman. Those very grasping gentry, the Romans, produced a theory, or ideal of the matron, which fitted in very nicely with the Roman property lust. "Caesar's wife should be above suspicion."*—So Caesar's wife kindly proceeded to be above it, no matter how far below it the Caesar fell. Later gentlemen like Nero produced the "fast" theory of woman, and later ladies were fast enough for anybody. Dante arrived with a chaste and untouched Beatrice, and chaste and untouched Beatrices began to march self-importantly through the centuries. The Renaissances discovered the learned woman, and learned women buzzed mildly into verse and prose. Dickens invented the child-wife, so child-wives have swarmed ever since. He also fished out his version of the chaste Beatrice, a chaste but marriageable Agnes.* George Eliot imitated this pattern, and it became confirmed. The noble woman, the pure spouse, the devoted mother took the field, and was simply worked to death. Our own poor mothers were this sort. So we younger men, having been a bit frightened of our noble mothers, tended to revert to the child-wife. We weren't very inventive. Only the child-wife must be a boyish little thing—that was the new touch we added. Because young men are definitely frightened of the real female. She's too risky a quantity. She is too untidy, like David's Dora. No, let her be a boyish little thing, it's safer. So a boyish little thing she is.

There are of course other types. Capable men produce the capable woman ideal. Doctors produce the capable nurse. Business men produce the capable secretary. And so you get all sorts. You can produce the masculine sense of honour (whatever that highly mysterious quantity may be) in women, if you want to.

There is, also, the eternal secret ideal of men—the prostitute. Lots of women live up to this ideal: just because men want them to.

And so, poor woman, destiny makes away with her. It isn't that she hasn't got a mind—she has. She's got everything that man has. The only difference is that she asks for a pattern. Give me a pattern to follow!—That will always be woman's cry. Unless of course she has already chosen her pattern quite young, then she will declare she is herself absolutely, and no man's idea of women has any influence over her.

Now the real tragedy is not that women ask and must ask for a pattern of womanhood. The tragedy is not, even, that men give them such abominable patterns, child-wives, little-boy-baby-face girls, perfect secretaries, noble spouses, self-sacrificing mothers, pure women who bring forth children in virgin coldness, prostitutes who just make themselves low, to please the men: all the atrocious patterns of womanhood that men have supplied to woman: patterns all perverted from any real natural fulness of a human being. Man is willing to accept woman as an equal, as a man in skirts, as an angel, a devil, a baby-face, a machine, an instrument, a bosom, a womb, a pair of legs, a servant, an encyclopedia, an ideal or an obscenity: the one thing he won't accept her as, is a human being, a real human being of the feminine sex.

And of course women love living up to strange patterns, weird patterns, the more uncanny the better. What could be more uncanny than the present pattern of the Eton-boy girl* with flower-like artificial complexion? It is just weird. And for its very weirdness women like living up to it. What can be more gruesome than the little-boy-baby-face pattern? Yet the girls take it on with avidity.

But even that isn't the real root of the tragedy. The absurdity, and often, as in the Dante-Beatrice business, the inhuman nastiness of the pattern—for Beatrice had to go on being chaste-untouched all her life, according to Dante's pattern, while Dante had a cosy wife and kids at home—even that isn't the worst of it. The worst of it is, as soon as a woman has really lived up to the man's pattern, the man dislikes her for it. There is intense secret dislike for the Eton-young-man girl, among the boys, now that she is actually produced. Of course she's very nice to show in public: absolutely the thing—But the very young men who have brought about her production detest her in private and in their private hearts are appalled by her.

When it comes to marrying, the pattern goes all to pieces. The boy marries the Eton-boy girl, and instantly, he hates the *type*. Instantly his mind begins to play hysterically with all the other types, noble Agneses, chaste Beatrices, clinging Doras and lurid *filles de joie*.* He is in a wild welter of confusion. Whatever pattern the poor woman tries to live up to, he'll want another.—And that's the condition of modern marriage.

Modern woman isn't really a fool. But modern man is. That seems to me the only plain way of putting it. The modern man is a fool, and the modern young man a prize fool. He makes a greater mess of his woman than men have ever made. Because he absolutely doesn't know *what* he wants her to be. We shall see the changes in the woman-pattern follow one another fast and furious, now, because the young men hysterically don't know what they want. Two years hence women may be in crinolines—there was a pattern for you!—or a bead flap,* like naked negresses in mid-Africa—or they may be wearing brass armour, or the uniform of the Horse Guards. They may be anything. Because the young men are off their heads, and don't know what they want.

The women aren't fools, but they *must* live up to some pattern or other. They *know* the men are fools. They don't really respect the pattern. Yet a pattern they must have, or they can't exist.

Women are not fools. They have their own logic, even if it's not the masculine sort. Women have the logic of emotion, men have the logic of reason. The two are complementary, and mostly in opposition. But the woman's logic of emotion is no less real and inexorable than the man's logic of reason. It only works differently.

And the woman never really loses it. She may spend years living up to a masculine pattern. But in the end, the strange and terrible logic of emotion will work out the smashing of that pattern, if it has not been emotionally satisfactory. This is the partial explanation of the astonishing changes in women. For years they go on being chaste Beatrices or child wives. Then on a sudden—bash! The chaste Beatrice becomes something quite different, the child-wife becomes a roaring lioness! The pattern didn't suffice, emotionally.

Whereas men are fools. They are based on a logic of reason, or are supposed to be. And then they go and behave, especially with regard to women, in a more-than-feminine unreasonableness. They spend years training up the little-boy-baby-face type, till they've got her perfect. Then the moment they marry her, they want something else. Oh beware, young women, of the young men who adore you! The moment they've got you they'll want something utterly different. The moment they marry the little-boy-baby-face, instantly they begin to pine for the noble Agnes, pure and majestic, or the infinite mother with deep bosom of consolation, or the perfect business-woman, or the lurid prostitute on black silk sheets: or, most idiotic of all, a combination of all the lot of them at once. And that is the logic of reason! When it comes to women, modern men are idiots. They don't know what they want, and so they never want, permanently, what they get. They want a cream cake that is at the same time ham and eggs and at the same time porridge. They are fools. If only women weren't bound by fate to play up to them!

For the fact of life is that women *must* play up to man's pattern. And she only gives her best to a man when he gives her a satisfactory pattern to play up to. But today, with a stock of ready-made, worn-out, idiotic patterns to live up to, what can women give to men but the trashy side of their emotions! What could a woman possibly give to a man who wanted her to be a boy-baby-face? What could she possibly give him but the dribblings of an idiot?—And, because women aren't fools, and aren't fooled even for very long at a time, she gives him some nasty, cruel digs with her claws, and makes him cry for Mother-dear!—abruptly changing his pattern.

Bah! men are fools. If they want anything from women, let them give women a decent, satisfying idea of womanhood—not these trick patterns of washed-out idiots.

INTRODUCTION TO PICTURES

This piece is never mentioned in Lawrence's letters; it was not published until 1936 (in *Phoenix*); and though the title is indisputably in his own hand, the essay contains no reference whatever to pictures and no more than a single reference to art – and that in an opening paragraph which Lawrence firmly deleted in his manuscript. The deleted opening began, 'What is art?' and, in order to answer the question, Lawrence felt compelled first 'to say what man is'. His attempt to define the nature of man accounts for the thrust of the essay below.

Its date is established circumstantially. The manuscript is in a notebook following the Lasca translation which Lawrence reported as 'nearly done' on 1 November 1928 (*Letters*, vi. 605) and which was sent to Orioli from Ile de Port-Cros whence he departed on 17 November (vii. 21). The 'Introduction to Pictures' is, therefore, likely to have been written during Lawrence's stay at Hotel Beau Rivage in Bandol where he arrived on the same day. If, as Tedlock persuasively argues, it was 'an abandoned beginning of the introduction' to the volume of Lawrence's *Paintings* (Tedlock 173), then its composition would not have anticipated P. R. Stephensen's declaration of interest in publishing the book. The first known mention of a possible 'portfolio of [Lawrence's] pictures' by the Fanfrolico Press occurs in a letter to Giuseppe Orioli, the Florentine publisher of *Lady Chatterley's Lover*. This was on 9 December, by which date Lawrence had not heard directly from 'the Franfrolico people . . . Who are they?' (vii. 48). He was obviously excited by the idea and alerted friends to it (vii. 49–50), but he was 'not at all sure about it' when he wrote to his sister Emily on 10 December. It was only on 14 December that he broached the possibility to Stephensen's associate, Jack Lindsay, of 'a portfolio of reproductions of my pictures'; it was then that 'a little introductory essay on painting, modern painting' came into view (vii. 60). Stephensen's intention to publish the 'portfolio' was confirmed by Lawrence when writing to Dorothy Warren on 19 December (vii. 70). Significantly, two days later he asked Koteliansky to order for him a copy of Roger Fry's *Cézanne*, a request that heralded the onslaught on the theory of 'significant form' in the introduction which actually appeared in the *Paintings* volume. It is, therefore, reasonable to assume that by then he had abandoned his first shot at a 'foreword' and that the composition of the 'Introduction to Pictures', begun *c.* 14 December 1928, was given up *c.* 21st.

INTRODUCTION TO PICTURES

Man* is anything from a forked radish* to an immortal spirit. He is pretty well everything that ever was or will be, absolutely human and absolutely inhuman. If we did but know it, we have every imaginable and unimaginable feeling streaking somewhere through us. Even the most pot-headed American judge* who feels that his daughter will be lost forever if she hears the word *cunt*, has all the feelings of a satyr careering somewhere inside him, very much suppressed and distorted. And the reason that Puritans are so frightened of life is that they happen, unfortunately, to be alive in spite of themselves.

The trouble with poor, pig-headed man is that he makes a selection out of the vast welter of his feelings, and says: I *only* feel these excellent selected feelings, and you, moreover, are allowed only to feel these excellent select feelings too.—Which is all very well, till the pot boils over, or blows up.

When man fixes on a few select feelings and says that these feelings must be felt exclusively, the said feelings rapidly become repellant. Because we've *got* to love our wives, we make a point of loving somebody else. The moment the mind *fixes* a feeling, that feeling is repulsive. Take a greedy person, who falls right into his food. Why is he so distasteful? Is it because his stomach is asserting itself? Not at all! It is because his *mind*, having decided that food is good, or good for him, drives on his body to eat and eat and eat. The poor stomach is over-loaded in spite of itself. The appetites are violated. The natural appetite says: I've had enough!—But the fixed mind, fixed on feeding, forces the jaws, the gullet to go on working, the stomach to go on receiving. And this is greed. And no wonder it is repulsive.

The same is precisely true of drinking, smoking, drug-taking, or any of the vices. When did the *body* of a man ever like getting drunk? Never! Think how it reacts, how it vomits, how it tries to repudiate the excess of drink, how utterly wretched it feels when its sane balance is overthrown. But the mind or spirit of a man finds in intoxication some relief, some escape, some sense of licence, so the drunkenness is forced upon the unhappy stomach and bowels, which gradually get used to it, but which are slowly destroyed.

If only we would realise that, until perverted by the mind, the human body preserves itself continually in a delicate balance of sanity! That is what it is always striving to do, and always it is shoved over by the pernicious mental consciousness, called the spirit. As soon as even a baby finds something good, it howls for more, till it is sick. That is the nauseating side of the human consciousness. But it is not the body. It is the mind, the self aware of itself, which says: This is good, I will go on and on and on eating it!—The human spirit is the self aware of itself. This self-awareness *may* make us noble. More often it makes us worse than pigs. We need above all things a curb upon this spirit of ours, this self aware of itself, which is our spirituality and our vice.

As a matter of fact, we need to be a little more *radically* aware of ourselves. When a man starts drinking, and his stomach simply doesn't want any more, it is time he put a check on his independent spirit and obeyed his stomach. When a man's body has reached one of its periods of loneliness, and with a sure voice cries that it wants to be alone and intact, it is then, inevitably, that the accursed perversity of the spirit, the self aware of itself, is bound to whip the unhappy senses into excitement and to force them into fornication. It is then, when a man's body cries to be left alone and intact, that man forces himself to be a Don Juan.* The same with women. It is the price we have to pay for our precious spirit, our self aware of itself, which we don't yet know how to handle.

And when a man has forced himself to be a Don Juan, you may bet his children will force themselves to be Puritans, with a nasty, *greedy* abstinence, as greedy as the previous gluttony. Oh bitter inheritance, the human spirit, the self aware of itself! The self aware of itself, that says: I like it, so I will have it all the time!—and then, in revulsion, says: I don't like it, I will have *none* of it, and no man shall have any of it.—Either way, it is sordid, and makes one sick. Oh lofty human spirit, how sordid you have made us! What a viper Plato was, with his distinction into body and spirit, and the exaltation of the spirit,* the self aware of itself. The human spirit, the self aware of itself, is only tolerable when controlled by the divine, or demonish sanity which is greater than itself.

It is difficult to know what name to give to that most central and vital clue to the human being, which clinches him into integrity. The best is to call it his vital sanity. We then escape the rather nauseating emotional suggestions of words like soul and spirit and holy ghost.

We can escape from the trap of the human spirit, the self aware of itself, in which we are entrapped, by going quite, quite still and letting our whole sanity assert itself inside us, and set us into rhythm.

But first of all we must know we are entrapped. We most certainly are. You may call it intellectualism, self-consciousness, the self aware of itself, or what you will: you can even call it just human consciousness, if you like: but there it is. Perhaps it is simplest to stick to a common word like self-consciousness. In modern civilisation we are all self-conscious. All our emotions are mental, self-conscious. Our passions are self-conscious. Our feelings are self-conscious. We are an intensely elaborate and intricate clock-work of nerves and brain. Nerves and brain! but still, a clock-work. A mechanism, and hence incapable of experience.

The nerves and brain are the apparatus by which we signal and *register* consciousness. Consciousness, however, does not take rise in the nerves and brain. It takes rise elsewhere: in the blood, in the corpuscules,* somewhere very primitive and pre-nerve and pre-brain. Just as energy generates in the electron. Every speck of protoplasm, every living cell is *conscious*. All the cells of our body are conscious. And all the time, they give off a stream of consciousness which flows along the nerves and keeps us spontaneously alive. While the flow streams through us, from the blood to the heart, the bowels, the viscera, then along the sympathetic system of nerves into our spontaneous minds, making us breathe, and see, and move, and be aware, and *do* things spontaneously, while this flow streams as a flame streams ceaselessly, we are lit up, we glow, we live.

But there is another process. There is that strange switch-board of consciousness, the brain, with its power of transferring spontaneous energy into voluntary energy: or consciousness, as you please: the two are very closely connected. The brain can transfer spontaneous consciousness, which we are *unaware* of—into voluntary consciousness, which we *are* aware of, and which we call consciousness exclusively.

Now it is nonsense to say there cannot be a consciousness in us of which we are *always* unaware. We are never aware of sleep except when we awake. If we didn't sleep, we should never know we were awake. But we *are* very much aware of our "consciousness." We are aware that it is a state only. And we are aware that it displaces another state. The other state we may negatively call the unconscious. But it is a poor way of putting it. To say that a skylark sings unconsciously is feeble. The skylark of course sings consciously. But with the other, spontaneous or sympathetic consciousness, which flows up like a flame from the corpuscules of all the body to the gates of the body, through the muscles and nerves of the sympathetic system to the hands and eyes and all the organs of utterance. The skylark does *not* sing like the lady in the concert-hall, consciously, mentally, deliberately, with the voluntary consciousness.

Some very strange process takes place in the brain, the process of cognition. This process of cognition consists in the forming of ideas, which are units of transmuted consciousness. These ideas can then be stored in the memory, or wherever it is that the brain stores its ideas. And these ideas are alive: they are little batteries in which so much energy of consciousness is stored.

It is here that our secondary consciousness comes in, our mind, our mental consciousness, our cerebral consciousness. Our mind is made up of a vast number of live ideas, and a good number of dead ones. Ideas are like the little electric batteries of a flash-light, in which a certain amount of energy is stored, which expends itself and is not renewed. Then you throw the dead battery away.

But when the mind has a sufficient number of these little batteries of ideas in store, a new process of life starts in. The moment an idea forms in the mind, at that moment does the old integrity of the consciousness break. In the old myths, at that moment we lose our "innocence", we partake of the tree of knowledge, and we become "aware of our nakedness":* in short, self-conscious. The self becomes aware of itself, and then the fun begins, and then the trouble starts.

The first thing the self-aware-of-itself realises is that it is a derivative, not a primary entity. The second thing it realises is that the spontaneous self with its sympathetic consciousness and non-ideal reaction is the original reality, the old Adam, over which the self-aware-of-itself has no originative power. That is, the self-aware-of-itself knows it can frustrate the conscious flow of the old Adam, divert it, but it cannot stop it: it knows, moreover, that as the moon is a luminary because the sun shines, so it, the self-aware-of-itself, the mental consciousness, the spirit, is only a sort of reflection of the great primary consciousness of the old Adam.

Now the self-aware-of-itself has *always* the quality of egoism. The spirit is *always* egoistic. The greatest spiritual commands are *all* forms of egoism, usually inverted egoism, for deliberate humility, we are all well aware, is a rabid form of egoism. The Sermon on the Mount* is a long string of utterances from the self-aware-of-itself, the spirit, and all of them are rabid aphorisms of egoism, back-handed egoism.

The moment the self-aware-of-itself comes into being, it begins egoistically to assert itself. It cuts immediately at the wholeness of the pristine consciousness, the old Adam, and wounds it. And it goes on with the battle. The greatest enemy man has or ever can have is his own spirit, his own self-aware-of-itself.

This self-aware ego *knows* it is a derivative, a satellite. So it must assert itself. It knows it has no power over the original body, the old Adam, save the secondary power of the idea. So it begins to store up ideas, those little batteries which *always* have a moral, or good-and-bad implication.

For four thousand years man has been accumulating these little batteries of ideas, and using them on himself, against his pristine consciousness, his old Adam. The queen bee of all human ideas since 2000 B.C. has been the idea that the body, the pristine consciousness, the great sympathetic life-flow, the steady flame of the old Adam is *bad*, and must be conquered. Every religion taught the conquest: science took up the battle tooth and nail: culture fights in the same cause: and only art sometimes—or always—exhibits an internecine conflict and betrays its own battle-cry.

I believe that there was a great age, a great epoch when man did not make war: previous to 2000 B.C. Then the self had not really become aware of itself, it had not separated itself off, the spirit was not yet born, so there was no internal conflict, and hence no permanent external conflict. The external conflict of war, or of industrial competition is only a reflection of the war that goes on inside each human being, the war of the self-conscious ego against the spontaneous old Adam.

If the self-conscious ego once wins, you get immediate insanity, because our primary self is the old Adam, in which rests our sanity. And when man starts living from his self-conscious energy, women at once begin to go to pieces, all the "freedom" business sets in. Because women are only kept in equilibrium by the Old Adam. Nothing else can avail.

But the means which the spirit, the self-conscious ego, the personality, the self-aware-of-itself takes to conquer the vital self or Old Adam are curious. First it has an idea, a semi-truth in which some of the energy of the vital consciousness is transmuted and stored. This idea it projects down again on to the spontaneous affective body. The very first idea is the idea of shame. The spirit, the self-conscious ego looks at the body and says: You are shameful!—The body, for some mysterious reason (really, because it is so vulnerable) immediately feels ashamed. Ah-ha! Now the spirit has got a hold. It discovers a second idea. The second idea is work. The spirit says: Base body! you need all the time to eat food. Who is going to give you food? You must sweat for it, sweat for it, or you will starve.

Now before the spirit emerged white and tyrannous in the human consciousness, man had not concerned himself deeply about starving. Occasionally, no doubt, he starved: but no oftener than the birds do, and they don't often starve. Anyhow he cared no more about it than the birds do. But now he feared it, and fell to work.

And here we see the mysterious power of ideas, the power of raising emotion, primitive emotions of shame, fear, anger, and sometimes joy; but usually the specious joy over another defeat of the pristine self.

So the spirit, the self-aware-of-itself organised a grand battery of dynamic ideas, the pivotal idea being almost always the idea of self-sacrifice and the triumph of the self-aware-of-itself, that pale Galilean* simulacrum of a man.

But wait! Wait! There is a nemesis. It is great fun overcoming the Old Adam while the Old Adam is still lusty and kicking: like breaking in a bronco. But nemesis, strange nemesis. The old Adam isn't an animal that you can *permanently* domesticate. Domesticated, he goes deranged.

We are the sad results of a four-thousand-year effort to break the Old Adam, to domesticate him utterly. He is to a large extent broken and domesticated.

But then what? Then, as the flow of pristine or spontaneous consciousness gets weaker and weaker, the grand dynamic ideas go deader and deader. We have got a vast magazine of ideas, all of us. But they are practically all dead batteries, played out. They can't provoke any emotion or feeling or reaction in the spontaneous body, the old Adam. Love is a dead shell of an idea—we don't react—for love is only one of the great dynamic ideas, now played out. Self-sacrifice is another dead shell. Conquest is another. Success is another. Making good is another.

In fact, I don't know of one great idea or ideal—they are the same—which is still alive today. They are all dead. You can turn them on, but you get no kick. You turn on love, you fornicate till you are black in the face—you get no real thing out of it. The old Adam plays his last revenge on you, and refuses to respond *at all* to any of your ideal pokings. You have gone dead. You can't feel anything, and you may as well know it.

The mob, of course, will always deceive themselves that they are feeling things, even when they are not. To them, when they say: *I love you!* there will be a huge imaginary feeling, and they will act up according to schedule. All the love on the film, the close-up kisses and the rest, and all the response in buzzing emotion in the audience, is *all* acting up, all according to schedule. It is all just cerebral, and the body is just forced to go through the antics.

And this deranges the natural body-mind harmony on which our sanity rests. Our masses are rapidly going insane.

And in the horror of nullity—for the human being comes to have his own nullity in horror, he is terrified by his own incapacity to feel anything at all, he has a mad fear, at last, of his own self-consciousness—the modern man sets up the reverse process of katabolism, destructive sensation. He can no longer have any living productive feelings. Very well, he will have destructive sensations, produced by katabolism on his most intimate tissues.

Drink, drugs, jazz, speed, "petting", all modern forms of thrill, are just the production of sensation by the katabolism of the finest conscious cells of our living body. We explode our own cells and release a certain energy and accompanying sensation. It is, naturally, a process of suicide. And it is just the same process as ever: the self-conscious ego, the spirit, attacking the pristine body, the old Adam. But now the attack is direct. All the wildest bohemians and profligates are only doing directly what their puritanical grandfathers did indirectly: killing the body of the Old Adam. But now the lust is direct self-murder. It only needs take a few more strides, and it is promiscuous murder, like the war.

But we see this activity rampant today: the process of the sensational katabolism of the conscious body. It is perhaps even more pernicious than the old conservative attack on the old Adam, certainly it is swifter. But it is the same thing. There is no volta face.* There is no new spirit. It may be a *Life of Christ** or it may be a book on Relativity or a slim volume of lyrics or a novel like the telephone directory: it is still the same old attack on the living body. The body is still made disgusting. Only the moderns drag in all the excrementa* and the horrors and put them under your nose and say: Enjoy that horror!—Or they write about love as if it were a process of endless pissing—except that they write kissing instead of pissing—and they say: Isn't it lovely!

MYSELF REVEALED

Nancy Pearn wrote to Lawrence on 12 December 1928 telling him that the *Sunday Dispatch* wanted to extract an article of about 1,500 words from the autobiographical sketch he 'wrote a few years ago for some German publication' (*Letters*, vii. 65n.). Though the identity of the 'publication' remains a mystery, Lawrence's agreement to the proposal was immediate, in a letter of 15 December. As for the sketch from which the new article was to be taken, there is no doubt that it was 'Which Class I Belong To'.[1] The parallels between it and 'Myself Revealed' are frequent and exact; at one point in the latter Lawrence even says, 'I live in . . . this [Italian] villa' (180:29) which – though true when he wrote 'Which Class I Belong To' – was no longer so in December 1928: he left the Villa Mirenda the previous June and was then at the Hotel Beau Rivage in Bandol. This error might strengthen the suspicion that Lawrence may not have been wholly responsible for the printed text of 'Myself Revealed'. When he returned the proofs of the article to Nancy Pearn on 11 January 1929 he remarked: 'It seems all right – clever girl!' (vii. 123). Whether he was referring to her arranging for the *Sunday Dispatch* to re-use old material in a new form, or whether she was being congratulated on her skill in personally reducing – or perhaps helping Lawrence to reduce – the original to the length required, it is impossible now to determine. However, his approval of the text sent to and printed by the *Dispatch* is beyond dispute; it is this that appears below (no manuscript or typescript has survived).

'Myself Revealed' appeared in the *Dispatch*, alongside the editorial, on 17 February 1929. It was accompanied by a '*PORTRAIT STUDY OF MR D. H. LAWRENCE Specially drawn by Joseph Simpson*'. Simpson (1879–1939), a well-known artist – portraitist of Edward VII and Robert Louis Stevenson among others – portrayed a younger Lawrence, facially unlined and gentle but unsmiling and rather melancholy.[2] Below the title of the article the author was described as '*The Most-Discussed Novelist of*

[1] The tentative suggestion (vii. 198 n. 3) that the 'longer form' in which the article first existed may have been '[Return to Bestwood']' is erroneous.

[2] A photograph by Elliott and Fry in 1915 was the basis for Simpson's portrait.

the Day' and the text was prefaced as follows: '"*It all happened by itself and without any groans from me*", *confesses Mr D. H. Lawrence in this intensely personal account of how, after starting life as the son of a collier, he became one of our greatest living novelists.*'

In late February 1929, the radical publisher Charles Lahr (soon to be responsible for the unexpurgated *Pansies*) suggested that 'Myself Revealed' should be issued as a 'booklet'. He was dissuaded by Lawrence on the grounds that it 'is too small to print alone' (vii. 198). It was included in *Assorted Articles* under the title 'Autobiographical Sketch'.[1]

[1] It was translated by Kurt Fiedler in the *Insel Almanach*, 1930, as 'D. H. Lawrence: über sich selbst'.

MYSELF REVEALED

They ask me: "Did you find it very hard to get on and to become a success?" And I have to admit that if I can be said to have got on, and if I can be called a success, then I *did not* find it hard.

I never starved in a garret, nor waited in anguish for the post to bring me an answer from editor or publisher, nor did I struggle in sweat and blood to bring forth mighty works,* nor did I ever wake up and find myself famous.

I was a poor boy. I *ought* to have wrestled in the fell clutch of circumstance, and undergone the bludgeonings of chance* before I became a writer with a very modest income and a very questionable reputation. But I didn't. It all happened by itself and without any groans from me.

It seems a pity. Because I was undoubtedly a poor boy of the working classes, with no apparent future in front of me. But after all, what am I now?

I was born among the working classes and brought up among them. My father was a collier, and only a collier, nothing praiseworthy about him. He wasn't even respectable, in so far as he got drunk rather frequently, never went near a chapel, and was usually rather rude to his little immediate bosses at the pit.

He practically never had a good stall, all the time he was a butty,* because he was always saying tiresome and foolish things about the men just above him in control at the mine. He offended them all, almost on purpose, so how could he expect them to favour him? Yet he grumbled when they didn't.

My mother was, I suppose, superior. She came from town, and belonged really to the lower bourgeoisie. She spoke King's English, without an accent, and never in her life could even imitate a sentence of the dialect which my father spoke, and which we children spoke out of doors.

She wrote a fine Italian hand, and a clever and amusing letter when she felt like it. And as she grew older she read novels again, and got terribly impatient with "Diana of the Crossways" and terribly thrilled by "East Lynne."*

But she was a working man's wife, and nothing else, in her shabby little black bonnet, and her shrewd, clear, "different" face. And she was very much respected, just as my father was not respected. Her nature was quick and sensitive, and perhaps really superior. But she was down, right down in the working class, among the mass of poorer colliers' wives.

I was a delicate, pale brat with a snuffy nose, whom most people treated quite gently as just an ordinary delicate little lad. When I was twelve I got a county council scholarship, twelve pounds a year, and went to Nottingham High School.

After leaving school I was a clerk for three months, then had a very serious pneumonia illness, in my seventeenth year, that damaged my health for life.

A year later I became a school teacher and after three years' savage teaching of collier lads I went to take the "normal" course in Nottingham University.*

As I was glad to leave school, I was glad to leave college. It had meant mere disillusion, instead of the living contact of men. From college I went down to Croydon, near London, to teach in a new elementary school at a hundred pounds a year.

It was while I was at Croydon, when I was twenty-three, that the girl* who had been the chief friend of my youth, and who was herself a school teacher in a mining village at home, copied out some of my poems, and without telling me sent them to the "English Review," which had just had a glorious re-birth under Ford Madox Hueffer.*

Hueffer was most kind. He printed the poems, and asked me to come and see him. The girl had launched me, so easily, on my literary career, like a princess cutting a thread, launching a ship.*

I had been tussling away for four years, getting out "The White Peacock" in inchoate bits, from the underground of my consciousness. I must have written most of it five or six times, but only in intervals, never as a task or a divine labour, or in the groans of parturition.

I would dash at it, do a bit, show it to the girl; she always admired it; then realise afterwards it wasn't what I wanted, and have another dash. But at Croydon I had worked at it fairly steadily, in the evenings after school.

Anyhow, it was done, after four or five years' spasmodic effort. Hueffer asked at once to see the manuscript. He read it immediately, with the greatest cheery sort of kindness and bluff. And in his queer voice, when we were in an omnibus in London, he shouted in my ear: "It's got every fault that the English novel can have."

Just then the English novel was supposed to have so many faults, in comparison with the French, that it was hardly allowed to exist at all. "But," shouted Hueffer in the 'bus, "you've got GENIUS."

This made me want to laugh, it sounded so comical. In the early days, they were always telling me I had got genius, as if to console me for not having their own incomparable advantages.

But Hueffer didn't mean that. I always thought he had a bit of genius himself. Anyhow, he sent the MS. of "The White Peacock" to William Heinemann, who accepted it at once, and made me alter only four little lines whose omission would now make anybody smile.* I was to have £50 when the book was published.

Meanwhile Hueffer printed more poems and some stories of mine in the "English Review," and people read them and told me so, to my embarrassment and anger. I hated being an author, in people's eyes. Especially as I was a teacher.

When I was twenty-five my mother died, and two months later "The White Peacock" was published, but it meant nothing to me. I went on teaching for another year, and then again a bad pneumonia illness intervened. When I got better I did not go back to school. I lived henceforward on my scanty literary earnings.

It is 17 years since I gave up teaching and started to live an independent life of the pen. I have never starved, and never even felt poor, though my income for the first ten years was no better, and often worse, than it would have been if I had remained an elementary school-teacher.

But when one has been born poor a very little money can be enough. Now my father would think I am rich, if nobody else does. And my mother would think I have risen in the world, even if I don't think so.

But something is wrong, either with me or with the world, or with both of us. I have gone far and met many people, of all sorts and all conditions,* and many whom I have genuinely liked and esteemed.

People, *personally*, have nearly always been friendly. Of critics we will not speak, they are different fauna from people. And I have *wanted* to feel truly friends with some, at least, of my fellow-men.

Yet I have never quite succeeded. Whether I get on *in* the world is a question; but I certainly don't get on very well *with* the world. And whether I am a worldly success or not I don't really know. But I feel, somehow, not much of a human success.

By which I mean that I don't feel there is any very cordial or fundamental contact between me and society, or me and other people. There is a breach. And my contact is with something that is non-human, non-vocal.

I used to think it had something to do with the oldness and worn-outness of Europe. Having tried other places, I know that is not so. Europe is, perhaps, the least worn-out of the continents, because it is the most lived in. A place that is lived in lives.

It is since coming back from America that I ask myself seriously: Why is there so little contact between myself and the people whom I know? Why has the contact no vital meaning?

And if I write the question down, and try to write the answer down, it is because I feel it is a question that troubles many men.

The answer, as far as I can see, has something to do with class. Class makes a gulf, across which all the best human flow is lost. It is not exactly the triumph of the middle-classes that has made the deadness, but the triumph of the middle-class *thing*.

As a man from the working-class, I feel that the middle-class cut off some of my vital vibration when I am with them. I admit them charming and educated and good people often enough. *But they just stop some part of me from working*. Some part has to be left out.

Then why don't I live with my working people? Because their vibration is limited in another direction. They are narrow, but still fairly deep and passionate, whereas the middle-class is broad and shallow and passionless. Quite passionless. At the best they substitute affection, which is the great middle-class positive emotion.

But the working-class is narrow in outlook, in prejudice, and narrow in intelligence. This again makes a prison. One can belong absolutely to no class.

Yet I find, here in Italy, for example, that I live in a certain silent contact with the peasants who work the land of this villa. I am not intimate with them, hardly speak to them save to say good-day. And they are not working for me; I am not their *padrone*.

Yet it is they, really, who form my *ambiente*,* and it is from them that the human flow comes to me. I don't want to live with them in their cottages; that would be a sort of prison. But I want them to be there, about the place, their lives going along with mine, and in relation to mine.

I don't idealise them. Enough of that folly! It is worse than setting school-children to express themselves in self-conscious twaddle. I don't expect them to make any millennium here on earth, neither now nor in the future. But I want to live near them, because their life still flows.

And now I know, more or less, why I cannot follow in the footsteps even of Barrie or of Wells,* who both came from the common people also and are both such a success. Now I know why I cannot rise in the world and become even a little popular and rich.

I cannot make the transfer from my own class into the middle-class. I cannot, not for anything in the world, forfeit my passional consciousness and my old blood-affinity with my fellow-men and the animals and the land, for that other thin, spurious mental conceit which is all that is left of the mental consciousness once it has made itself exclusive.

INTRODUCTION TO THESE PAINTINGS

Lawrence was known as a painter for some time before the ill-fated exhibition at the Warren Gallery in London which opened on 14 June 1929. From April to November 1928 he was courted by gallery-owners in New York – Elizabeth Hare and Alfred Stieglitz – and in London – Ena Mathias (Claridge Gallery), Oliver Brown (Leicester Galleries) and Dorothy Warren at her own. Each of them was interested in mounting an exhibition of his paintings. Indeed, as early as August 1927 Dorothy Warren (whom Lawrence had known since 1915 as the niece of Lady Ottoline Morrell) had shown an interest in exhibiting them (*Letters*, vi. 127). Lawrence at first confidently expected that her Warren Gallery show would begin in May or June 1928; then he agreed to send her some pictures in April so that she could exhibit in October; but by July he had discovered that she was not to be trusted to keep her promises.[1] In August, irritated by her procrastination and total silence, Lawrence thought he might 'go and stop her' (vi. 506, 528); September saw his spirits rise again following an encouraging letter from her (vi. 535–6); and 5–26 October appeared to be the agreed period for the exhibition.[2] However, probably because of her forthcoming marriage to Philip Trotter in November, postponement proved inevitable. 'No news of the Warren' was a recurring message to a variety of friends (vi. 611). Angrily Lawrence complained to their mutual friend Dorothy Brett on 24 November: 'That bitch Dorothy Warren has my pictures hung all ready, but seems scared to open' (vii. 26–7). Stieglitz was told on 3 December 1928: 'As for my show, the scatterbrained Dorothy Warren has postponed it till New Year' (vii. 36).

It was also in December 1928 that the possibility of 'a portfolio of reproductions of [Lawrence's] paintings, which are in Dorothy Warrens gallery awaiting exhibition' (vii. 48) first occurs in his correspondence. Lawrence found the proposal, from the Fanfrolico Press under the management of Percy Reginald Stephensen, very appealing (vii. 50). In fact, Fanfrolico soon 'more or less dissolved' (vii. 253), and it was the

[1] See vi. 381, 383, 386, 402, 405, 445–8.

[2] See vi. 506, 528, 535–7, 542, 544–6, 551, 554.

Mandrake Press funded by the wealthy book dealer Edward Goldston, and directed by Stephensen, which assumed responsibility for the book of paintings.

Lawrence warmed to the task of writing his introduction. Koteliansky was pressed into service. Writing from Bandol on 21 December 1928, Lawrence urgently enquired:

> Could you ask any of the booksellers to send me *at once*, with the bill, a copy of Roger Fry's *Cézanne* book. It would make a good starting point for me to write a good peppery foreword *against* all that significant form piffle. And if you can easily lay hands on a cheap copy of Tolstoi's *What is Art?* send me that too, *with the bill*. (vii. 82)

Christmas celebrations notwithstanding, by 2 January 1929 he could report to Stephensen: 'I have done two-thirds of my painting introd. – one of the best things I've done – corpses in it like currants in cake, Mr Clive Bell etc.' (vii. 117).[1] By 11 January Lawrence had completed 'about 10,000 words'; three days later he sent his manuscript of what he then referred to as 'Introduction to the Paintings', to Pollinger at Curtis Brown's London office for typing, with the instruction: 'two copies, and please send me the typescript to revise' (vii. 125, 136, 150). Despite interference from the police (who had seized copies of *Lady Chatterley's Lover* and the *Pansies* typescript), the introduction was received by Pollinger (vii. 148 n. 1), typed, read by Lawrence and returned by him 'with a few corrections' (vii. 163) on 5 February. Two days later he told Stephensen that the typescript had gone back to Pollinger 'with a few corrections . . . not important' (vii. 168), but adds: 'Did you read it? and did you like it? Ask Jack Lindsay if he knows if my few facts are sound – about Elizabeth's eyebrows and James I's inherited pox-effects, etc. I read them somewhere. I think it's a good essay – ' The questions presuppose that Stephensen had had access to the text of the essay, presumably the second typescript from Curtis Brown's office since there was no other copy available. Collation of surviving typescripts suggests that Pollinger had the essay retyped, taking account of the 'few corrections'; the corrected version (TS2), which includes some compositor's instructions for ligatures, would then be submitted to Stephensen for type-setting at the Botolph Printing Works, Kingsway, London.

[1] Clive Bell (1881–1964), member of the Bloomsbury group and critic of literature and art; he set out to develop a complete theory of visual art in *Art* (1914) and in the course of it invented the term 'significant form' to which DHL took vigorous exception.

Lawrence corrected proofs as he told Kot on 1 March 1929: 'I am correcting the Foreword to my paintings – proofs' (vii. 197). They have not survived but collation of TS2 with the first published 'Introduction' reveals a considerable amount of rewriting at proof-stage. When, on 1 March, Lawrence returned the proofs to Stephensen he drew attention to one change only: 'I never intended the heading to be "Introduction to Painting" – Have made it now: "Introduction to These Paintings"' (vii. 198). Stephensen undoubtedly discovered more changes than Lawrence admitted; the substantive changes he included resulting from Lawrence's proof-reading are incorporated in the text here.

Subsequently, after the publication of *Paintings* in June 1929, there was some discussion of the possibility that the essay might be separately published; Lawrence wondered whether Random House might undertake it: 'It's a good essay for a limited edition, and they need only omit one sentence' (vii. 462). Discussion continued until within a month of his death (vii. 640) but came to nothing.[1] Earlier he had also proposed to Stephensen the publication of a cheaper edition of *Paintings*: 'for which, if you like, I can write a quite different introductory essay, more simple, more popular, and referring to the pictures themselves' (vii. 300). This proposal, too, was fruitless.

[1] The essay has been reprinted on several occasions either fully, as in *Phoenix*, or in extracts, as in *Art and Painting* (1951), *Selected Poetry and Prose*, ed. T. R. Barnes (1957) and *Selected Critical Writings*, ed. Michael Herbert (Oxford, 1998).

INTRODUCTION TO THESE PAINTINGS*

The reason the English produce so few painters is not that they are, as a nation, devoid of a genuine feeling for visual art: though to look at their productions, and to look at the mess which has been made of actual English landscape, one might really conclude that they were, and leave it at that. But it is not the fault of the God that made them. They are made with æsthetic sensibilities the same as anybody else. The fault lies in the English attitude to life.

The English, and the Americans following them, are paralysed by fear. That is what thwarts and distorts the Anglo-Saxon existence, this paralysis of fear. It thwarts life, it distorts vision, and it strangles impulse: this overmastering fear. And fear what of, in heaven's name? What is the Anglo-Saxon stock today so petrified with fear about? We have to answer that before we can understand the English failure in the visual arts: for on the whole, it is a failure.

It is an old fear, which seemed to dig in to the English soul at the time of the Renaissance. Nothing could be more lovely and fearless than Chaucer. But already Shakespeare is morbid with fear, fear of consequences. That is the strange phenomenon of the English Renaissance: this mystic terror of the consequences, the consequences of action. Italy too had her reaction, at the end of the Sixteenth century, and showed a similar fear. But not so profound, so overmastering. Aretino* was anything but timorous: he was bold as any Renaissance novelist, and went one better.

What appeared to take full grip on the northern consciousness at the end of the Sixteenth century was a terror, almost a horror of sexual life. The Elizabethans, grand as we think them, started it. The real "mortal coil"* in Hamlet is all sexual, the young man's horror of his mother's incest, sex carrying with it a wild and nameless terror which, it seems to me, it had never carried before. Œdipus and Hamlet are very different in this respect. In Œdipus there is no recoil in horror from sex itself: Greek drama never shows us that. The horror, when it is present in Greek tragedy, is against *destiny*, man caught in the toils of destiny. But with the Renaissance itself, particularly in England, the horror is sexual. Orestes* is dogged by destiny and driven mad by the Eumenides. But Hamlet is overpowered by horrible revulsion from his physical connection with his mother, which makes him recoil in similar revulsion from Ophelia, and almost from his father even as a ghost. He is horrified at the merest suggestion of physical connection, as if it were an unspeakable taint.

This no doubt is all in the course of the growth of the "spiritual-mental" consciousness, at the expense of the instinctive-intuitive consciousness. Man came to have his own body in horror, especially in its sexual implications: and so he began to suppress with all his might his instinctive-intuitive consciousness, which is so radical, so physical, so sexual. Cavalier poetry, love-poetry, is already devoid of body. Donne, after the exacerbated revulsion-attraction excitement of his earlier poetry, becomes a divine. "—Drink to me only with thine eyes," sings the cavalier: an expression incredible in Chaucer's poetry. "I could not love thee dear so well loved I not honour more,"* sings the cavalier lover. In Chaucer the "dear" and the "honour" would have been more or less identical.

But with the Elizabethans the grand rupture had started, in the human consciousness, the mental consciousness recoiling in violence away from the physical, instinctive-intuitive. To the Restoration dramatists sex is, on the whole, a dirty business, but they more or less glory in the dirt. Fielding tries in vain to defend the Old Adam. Richardson with his calico purity and his underclothing excitements sweeps all before him. Swift goes mad with sex and excrement revulsion. Sterne flings a bit of the same excrement humorously around. And physical consciousness gives a last song in Burns, then is dead. Wordsworth, Keats, Shelley, the Brontes, all are post-mortem poets. The essential instinctive-intuitive body is dead, and worshipped in death—all very unhealthy. Till Swinburne and Oscar Wilde try to start a revival from the mental field. Swinburne's "white thighs"* are purely mental.

Now in England—and following, in America—the physical self was not just fig-leafed over or suppressed in public, as was the case in Italy and on most of the Continent. In England it excited a strange horror and terror. And this extra morbidity came, I believe, from the great shock of syphilis and the realisation of the consequences of the disease. Wherever syphilis, or "pox" came from, it was fairly new in England at the end of the fifteenth century. But by the end of the sixteenth, its ravages were obvious, and the shock of them had just penetrated the thoughtful and the imaginative consciousness. The royal families of England and Scotland were syphilitic, Edward VI and Elizabeth born with the inherited consequences of the disease. Edward VI died of it while still a boy. Mary died childless and in utter depression. Elizabeth had no eyebrows, her teeth went rotten, she must have felt herself, somewhere, utterly unfit for marriage, poor thing. That was the grisly horror that lay behind the glory of Queen Bess. And so the Tudors died out: and another syphilitic-born unfortunate came to the throne, in the person of James I. Mary Queen of Scots had no more luck than the Tudors, apparently. Apparently Darnley was reeking with the pox, though probably at first she did not know it. But when the Archbishop of St. Andrews* was christening her baby James, afterwards James I of England, the old clergyman was so dripping with pox that she was terrified lest he should give it to the infant. And she need not have troubled, for the wretched infant had brought it into the world with him, from that fool Darnley. So James I of England slobbered and shambled, and was the wisest fool in Christendom,* and the Stuarts likewise died out, the stock enfeebled by the disease.

With the royal families of England and Scotland in this condition we can judge what the noble houses, the nobility of both nations, given to free living and promiscuous pleasure, must have been like. England traded with the East and with America, England, unknowing, had opened her doors to the disease. The English aristocracy travelled and had curious taste in loves. And pox entered the blood of the nation, particularly of the upper classes, who had more chance of infection. And after it had entered the blood, it entered the consciousness, and it hit the vital imagination.

It is possible that the effects of syphilis and the conscious realisation of its consequences gave a great blow also to the Spanish psyche, precisely at this period. And it is possible that Italian society, which was on the whole so untravelled, had no connection with America, and was so privately self-contained, suffered less from the disease. Some-one ought to make a thorough study of the effects of "pox" on the minds and the emotions and imagination of the various nations of Europe, at about the time of our Elizabethans.

The apparent effect on the Elizabethans and the Restoration wits is curious. They appear to take the whole thing as a joke. The common oath, "pox on you!" was almost funny. But how common the oath was! How the word "pox" was in every mind, and in every mouth. It is one of the words that haunt Elizabethan speech. Taken very manly, with a great deal of Falstaffian bluff, treated as a huge joke! Pox! why, he's got the pox! Ha-ha! what's he been after?

There is just the same attitude among the common run of men today, with regard to the minor sexual diseases. Syphilis is no longer regarded as a joke, according to my experience. The very word itself frightens men. You could joke with the word pox. You can't joke with the word syphilis. The change of word has killed the joke. But men still joke about *clap*! which is a minor sexual disease. They pretend to think it manly, even, to have the disease, or to have had it. "What! never had a shot of clap!" cries one gentleman to another. "Why where have you been all your life!" If we changed the word and insisted on "gonorrhœa," or whatever it is, in place of "clap," the joke would die. And anyhow I have had young men come to me green and quaking, afraid they've caught "a shot of clap."

Now in spite of all the Elizabethan jokes about pox, pox was no joke to them. A joke may be a very brave way of meeting a calamity, or it may be a very cowardly way. Myself, I consider the Elizabethan pox joke a purely cowardly attitude. They didn't think it funny, for by God it *wasn't* funny. Even poor Elizabeth's lack of eyebrows and her rotten teeth were not funny. And they all knew it. They may not have known it was the direct result of pox: though probably they did. This fact remains, that no man can contract syphilis, or any deadly sexual disease, without feeling the most shattering and profound terror go through him, through the very roots of his being. And no man can look without a sort of horror on the effects of a sexual disease in another person. We are so constituted, that we are all at once horrified and terrified. The fear and dread has been so great, that the pox joke was invented as an evasion, and following that, the great hush! hush! was imposed. Man was *too* frightened, that's the top and bottom of it.

But now, with remedies discovered, we need no longer be *too* frightened. We can begin, after all these years, to face the matter. After the most fearful damage has been done.

For an overmastering fear is poison to the human psyche. And this overmastering fear, like some horrible secret tumour, has been poisoning our consciousness ever since the Elizabethans, who first woke up with dread to the entry of the original syphilitic poison into the blood.

I know nothing about medicine and very little about diseases, and my facts are such as I have picked up in casual reading.* Nevertheless I am convinced that the secret awareness of syphilis, and the utter secret terror and horror of it, has had an enormous and incalculable effect on the English consciousness, and on the American. Even when the fear has never been formulated, there it has lain, potent and overmastering. I am convinced that *some* of Shakespeare's horror and despair, in his tragedies, arose from the shock of his consciousness of syphilis. I don't suggest for one moment Shakespeare ever contracted syphilis. I have never had syphilis myself. Yet I know and confess how profound is my fear of the disease, and more than fear, my horror. In fact, I don't think I am so very much afraid of it. I am more horrified, inwardly and deeply, at the idea of its existence.

All this sounds very far from the art of painting. But it is not so far as it sounds. The appearance of syphilis in our midst gave a fearful blow to our sexual life. The real natural innocence of Chaucer was impossible after that. The very sexual act of procreation might bring as one of its consequences a foul disease, and the unborn might be tainted from the moment of conception. Fearful thought! It is truly a fearful thought, and all the centuries of getting used to it won't help us. It remains a fearful thought, and to free ourselves from this fearful dread we should use all our wits and all our efforts, not stick our heads in the sand of some idiotic joke or still more idiotic don't-mention-it. The fearful thought of the consequences of syphilis, or of any sexual disease, upon the unborn, gives a shock to the impetus of fatherhood in any man, even the cleanest. Our consciousness is a strange thing, and the knowledge of a certain fact may wound it mortally, even if the fact does not touch us directly. And so I am certain that *some* of Shakespeare's father-murder complex, *some* of Hamlet's horror of his mother, of his uncle, of all old men came from the feeling that fathers may transmit syphilis, or syphilis-consequences, to children. I don't know even whether Shakespeare was actually aware of the consequences to a child born of a syphilitic father or mother. He may not have been, though most probably he was. But he certainly was aware of the effects of syphilis itself, especially on men. And this awareness struck at his deep sex imagination, at his instinct for fatherhood, and brought in an element of terror and abhorrence there where man should feel anything but terror and abhorrence, into the procreative act.

The terror-horror element which had entered the imagination with regard to the sexual and procreative act was at least partly responsible for the arise of Puritanism, the beheading of the king-father Charles, and the establishment of the New England colonies. If America really sent us syphilis, she got back the full recoil of the horror of it, in her puritanism.

But deeper even than this, the terror-horror element led to the crippling of the consciousness of man. Very elementary in man is his sexual and procreative being, and on his sexual and procreative being depend many of his deepest instincts and the flow of his intuition. A deep instinct of kinship joins men together, and the kinship of flesh and blood keeps the warm flow of intuitional awareness streaming between human beings. Our true awareness of one another is intuitional, not mental. Attraction between people is really instinctive and intuitional, not an affair of judgment. And in mutual attraction lies perhaps the deepest pleasure in life, mutual attraction which may make us "like" our travelling companion for the two or three hours we are together, then no more, or mutual attraction that may deepen to powerful love, and last a life-time.

The terror-horror element struck a blow at our feeling of physical communion. In fact it almost killed it. We have become ideal beings, creatures that exist in idea, to one another, rather than flesh-and-blood kin. And with the collapse of the feeling of physical, flesh-and-blood kinship, and the substitution of an ideal, social or political oneness, came the failing of our intuitive awareness, and the great unease, the *nervousness* of mankind. We are *afraid* of the instincts. We are *afraid* of the intuition within us. We suppress the instincts, and we cut off our intuitional awareness from one another and from the world. The reason being some great shock to the procreative self. Now we know one another only as ideal or social or political entities, fleshless, bloodless, and cold, like Bernard Shaw's creatures.* Intuitively we are dead to one another, we have all gone cold.

But by intuition alone can man *really* be aware of man, or of the living, substantial world. By intuition alone can man love and know either woman or world, and by intuition alone can he bring forth again images of magic awareness which we call art. In the past men brought forth images of magic awareness, and now it is the convention to admire these images. The convention says, for example, we must admire Botticelli or Giorgione, so Baedeker stars the pictures,* and we admire them. But it is all a fake. Even those that get a thrill, even when they call it ecstasy, from these old pictures, are only undergoing a cerebral excitation. Their deeper responses, down in the intuitive and instinctive body, are not touched. They cannot be, because they are dead. A dead intuitive body stands there and gazes at the corpse of beauty: and usually it is completely and honestly bored, sometimes it feels a mental coruscation which it calls an ecstasy or an aesthetic response.*

Modern people, but particularly English and Americans, *cannot* feel anything with the whole imagination.* They can see the living body of imagery as little as a blind man can see colour. The imaginative vision, which includes physical intuitional perception, they *have not got*. Poor things, it is dead in them. And they stand in front of a Botticelli Venus, which they know is conventionally "beautiful," much as a blind man might stand in front of a bunch of roses and pinks and monkey-musk saying: Oh, do tell me which is red, let me feel red! now let me feel white! oh, let me feel it! What is this I am feeling? monkey-musk? is it white? oh, do you say it is yellow blotched with orange-brown? oh, but I can't feel it! What *can* it be? is white velvetty, or just silky?—

So the poor blind man! Yet he may have an acute perception of alive beauty. Merely by touch and scent, his intuitions being alive, the blind man may have a genuine and soul-satisfying experience of images. But not pictorial images. These are forever beyond him.

So those poor English and Americans in front of the Botticelli Venus. They stare so hard, they do so *want* to see. And their eyesight is perfect. But all they can see is a sort of nude woman on a sort of shell on a sort of pretty greenish water. As a rule they rather dislike the "unnaturalness" or "affectation" of it. If they are high-brows they may get a little self-conscious thrill of æsthetic excitement. But real imaginative awareness, which is so largely physical, is denied them. *Ils n'ont pas de quoi*,* as the Frenchman said of the angels, when asked if they made love in heaven.

Ah the dear high-brows who gaze in a sort of ecstasy and get a correct mental thrill! Their poor high-brow bodies stand there as dead as dust-bins, and can no more feel the sway of complete imagery upon them than they can feel any other real sway. *Ils n'ont pas de quoi*. The instincts and the intuitions are so nearly dead in them, and they fear even the feeble remains. Their fear of the instincts and intuitions is even greater than that of the English Tommy* who calls: "Eh, Jack! come an' look at this girl standin' wi' no clothes on, an' two blokes spittin' at 'er"—That is his vision of Botticelli's Venus. It is, for him, complete, for he is void of image-seeing imagination. But at least he doesn't have to work up a cerebral excitation, as the highbrow does, who is really just as void.

All alike, cultured and uncultured, they are still dominated by that unnamed, yet overmastering dread and hate of the instincts deep in the body, dread of the strange intuitional awareness of the body, dread of anything but ideas, which *can't* contain bacteria. And the dread all works back to a dread of the procreative body, and is partly traceable to the shock of the awareness of syphilis.

The dread of the instincts included the dread of intuitional awareness. "Beauty is a snare"—"Beauty is but skin-deep"—"Handsome is as handsome does"—"Looks don't count"—"Don't judge by appearances"—if we only realised it, there are thousands of these vile proverbs which have been dinned in to us for over two hundred years. They are all of them false. Beauty is not a snare, nor is it skin-deep, since it always involves a certain loveliness of modelling, and handsome doers are often ugly and objectionable people, and if you ignore the look of the thing you plaster England with slums and produce at last a state of spiritual depression that is suicidal, and if you don't judge by appearances, that is, if you can't trust the *impression* which things make on you, you are a fool. But all these base-born proverbs, born in the cash-box, hit direct against the intuitional consciousness. Naturally, man gets a great deal of his life's satisfaction from beauty, from a certain sensuous pleasure in the look of the thing. The old Englishman built his hut of a cottage with a childish joy in its appearance, purely intuitional and direct. The modern Englishman has a few borrowed ideas, simply doesn't know *what* to feel, and makes a silly mess of it: though perhaps he is improving, hopefully, in this field of architecture and house-building. The intuitional faculty, which alone relates us in direct awareness to physical things and substantial presences, is atrophied and dead, and we don't know *what* to feel. We know we ought to feel something, but what?—oh tell us what! And this is true of all nations, the French and Italians as much as the English. Look at new French suburbs! Go through the crockery and furniture departments in the *Dames de France** or any big shop. The blood in the body stands still, before such crétin ugliness. One has to decide that the modern bourgeois is a crétin.

This movement against the instincts and the intuition took on a moral tone in all countries. It started in hatred. Let us never forget that. Modern morality has its roots in hatred, a deep, evil hate of the instinctive, intuitional, procreative body. This hatred is made more virulent by fear, and an extra poison is added to the fear by unconscious horror of syphilis. And so we come to modern bourgeois consciousness, which turns upon the secret pole of fear and hate. That is the real pivot of all bourgeois consciousness in all countries: fear and hate of the instinctive, intuitional, procreative body in man or woman. But of course this fear and hate had to take on a righteous appearance, so it became moral, said that the instincts, intuitions and all the activities of the procreative body were evil, and promised a *reward* for their suppression. That is the great clue to bourgeois psychology: the reward business. It is screamingly obvious in Maria Edgeworth's tales,* which must have done unspeakable damage to ordinary people.—Be good, and you'll have money. Be wicked, and you'll be utterly penniless at last, and the good ones will have to offer you a little charity.—This is sound working morality in the world. And it makes one realise that, even to Milton, the true hero of *Paradise Lost* must be Satan.* But by this baited morality the masses were caught and enslaved to industrialism before ever they knew it, the good ones got hold of the goods, and our modern "civilisation" of money, machines and wage-slaves was inaugurated. The very pivot of it, let us never forget, being fear and hate, the most intimate fear and hate, fear and hate of one's own instinctive, intuitive body, and fear and hate of every other man's and every other woman's warm, procreative body and imagination.

Now it is obvious what result this will have on the plastic arts, which depend entirely on the representation of substantial bodies, and on the intuitional perception of the *reality* of substantial bodies. The reality of substantial bodies can only be perceived by the imagination, and the imagination is a kindled state of consciousness in which intuitive awareness predominates. The plastic arts are all imagery, and imagery is the body of our imaginative life, and our imaginative life is a great joy and fulfilment to us, for the imagination is a more powerful and more comprehensive flow of consciousness than our ordinary flow. In the flow of true imagination we know in full, mentally and physically at once, in a greater, enkindled awareness. At the maximum of our imagination we are religious. And if we deny our imagination, and have no imaginative life, we are poor worms who have never lived.

In the seventeenth and eighteenth centuries we have the deliberate denial of intuitive awareness, and we see the results on the arts. Vision became more optical, less intuitive, and painting began to flourish. But what painting! Watteau, Ingres, Poussin, Chardin have some imaginative glow still. They are still somewhat free. The puritan and the intellectual has not yet struck them down with his fear and hate obsessions. But look at England! Hogarth, Reynolds, Gainsborough,* they all are already bourgeois.* The coat is really more important than the man. It is amazing how important clothes suddenly become, how they *cover* the subject. An old Reynolds colonel in a red uniform is much more a uniform than an individual, and as for Gainsborough, all one can say is: What a lovely dress and hat! what really expensive Italian silk!—This painting of garments continued in vogue, till pictures like Sargent's* seem to be nothing but yards and yards of satin from the most expensive shops, having some pretty head popped on at the top. The imagination is quite dead. The optical vision, a sort of flashy coloured photography of the eye, is rampant.

In Titian, in Velasquez, in Rembrandt* the people are there inside their clothes all right, and the clothes are imbued with the life of individual, the gleam of the warm procreative body comes through all the time, even if it be an old, half-blind woman or a weird, ironic little Spanish princess. But modern people are nothing inside their garments, and a head sticks out at the top and hands stick out of the sleeves, and it is a bore. Or, as in Lawrence or Raeburn,* you have something very pretty but almost a mere cliché, with very little instinctive or intuitional perception to it.

After this, and apart from landscape and water-colour, there is strictly no English painting that exists. As far as I am concerned, the Pre-Raphaelites don't exist, Watts* doesn't, Sargent doesn't, and none of the moderns.

There is the exception of Blake. Blake is the only painter of imaginative pictures, apart from landscape, that England has produced.* And unfortunately there is so little Blake, and even in that little the symbolism is often artificially imposed. Nevertheless Blake paints with real intuitional awareness and solid instinctive feeling. He dares handle the human body, even if he sometimes makes it a mere ideograph. And no other Englishman has even dared handle it with alive imagination. Painters of composition pictures in England, of whom perhaps the best is Watts, never quite get beyond the level of cliché, sentimentalism, and *funk*. Even Watts is a failure, though he made some sort of try: and Etty's nudes in York fail imaginatively, though they have some feeling for flesh. And the rest, the Leightons,* even the moderns, don't really do anything. They never get beyond studio models and clichés of the nude. The image never gets across to us, to seize us intuitively. It remains merely optical.

Landscape, however, is different. Here the English exist and hold their own. But, for me, personally, landscape is always waiting for something to occupy it. Landscape seems to me *meant* as a background to an intenser vision of life, so to my feeling painted landscape is background with the real subject left out.

Nevertheless, it can be very lovely, especially in water-colour, which is a more bodiless medium, and doesn't aspire to very substantial existence, and is so small that it doesn't try to make a very deep seizure on the consciousness. Water-colour will always be more of a statement than an experience.

And landscape, on the whole, is the same. It doesn't call up the more powerful responses of the human imagination, the sensual, passional responses. Hence it is the favourite modern form of expression in painting. There is no deep conflict. The instinctive and intuitional consciousness is called into play, but lightly, superficially. It is not confronted with any living, procreative body.

Hence the English have delighted in landscape, and have succeeded in it well. It is a form of escape for them, from the actual human body they so hate and fear, and it is an outlet for their perishing æsthetic desires. For more than a century we have produced delicious water-colours, and Wilson, Crome, Constable, Turner* are all great landscape painters. Some of Turner's landscape compositions are, to my feeling, among the finest that exist. They still satisfy me more even than Van Gogh's or Cézanne's* landscapes, which make a more violent assault on the emotions, and repel a little for that reason. Somehow I don't want landscape to make a violent assault on my feelings. Landscape is background with the figures left out or reduced to minimum, so let it stay back. Van Gogh's surging earth and Cézanne's explosive or rattling planes worry me. Not being profoundly interested in landscape, I prefer it to be rather quiet and unexplosive.

But of course the English delight in landscape is a delight in escape. It is always the same. The northern races are so innerly afraid of their own bodily existence, which they believe fantastically to be an evil thing—you could never find them feel anything but uneasy shame, or an equally shameful gloating, over the fact that a man was having intercourse with his wife, in his house next door—that all they cry for is an escape. And especially, art must provide that escape.

It is easy in literature. Shelley is pure escape: the body is sublimated into sublime gas. Keats is more difficult—the body can still be *felt* dissolving in waves of successive death—but the death-business is very satisfactory. The novelists have even a better time. You can get some of the lusciousness of Hetty Sorrell's "sin," and you can enjoy condemning her to penal servitude for life. You can thrill to Mr. Rochester's *passion*, and you can enjoy having his eyes burnt out.* So it is all the way: the novel of "passion"!

But in paint it is more difficult. You couldn't paint Hetty Sorrell's sin or Mr. Rochester's passion without being really shocking. And you *daren't* be shocking. It was this fact that unsaddled Watts and Millais. Both might have been painters, if they hadn't been Victorians. As it is, each of them is a wash-out.

Which is the poor feeble history of art in England, since we can lay no claim to the great Holbein.* And art on the Continent, in the last century? It is more interesting, and has a fuller story. An artist *can* only create what he really religiously *feels* is truth, religious truth really *felt*, in the blood and the bones. The English could never think anything connected with the body *religious*—unless it were the eyes. So they painted the social appearance of human beings, and hoped to give them wonderful eyes.—But they *could* think landscape religious, since it had no sensual reality. So they felt religious about it and painted it as well as it could be painted, maybe, from their point of view.

And in France? In France it was more or less the same, but with a difference. The French, being more rational, decided that the body had its place, but that it should be rationalised. The Frenchman of today has the most reasonable and rationalised body possible. His conception of sex is basically hygienic. A certain amount of copulation is good for you, just as a certain amount of wine, etc., is good for you. *Ça fait du bien au corps*!* sums up the physical side of a Frenchman's idea of love, marriage, food, sport and all the rest. Well, it is more sane, anyhow, than the Anglo-Saxon terrors. The Frenchman is afraid of syphilis and afraid of the procreative body, but not quite so deeply. He has known for a long time that you can take precautions. And he is not profoundly imaginative.

Therefore he has been able to paint. But his tendency, just like that of all the modern world, has been to get away from the body, while still paying attention to its hygiene, and still not violently quarrelling with it. Puvis de Chavannes is really as sloppy as all the other spiritual sentimentalisers. Renoir* is jolly: ça fait du bien au corps! is his attitude to the flesh. If a woman didn't have buttocks and breasts, she wouldn't be paintable, he said, and he was right. Ça fait du bien au corps. What do you paint with, Maître?—With my penis, and be damned!—Renoir didn't try to get away from the body. But he had to dodge it in some of its aspects, rob it of its natural terrors, its natural demonishness. He is delightful, but a trifle banal. Ça fait du bien au corps!—Yet how infinitely much better he is than any English equivalent.

Courbet, Daumier, Dégas,* they all painted the human body. But Daumier satirised it, Courbet saw it as a toiling thing, Dégas saw it as a wonderful instrument. They all of them deny it its finest qualities, its deepest instincts, its purest intuitions. They prefer, as it were, to industrialise it. They deny it the best imaginative existence.

And the real grand glamour of modern French art, the real outburst of delight came when the body was at last dissolved of its substance, and made part and parcel of the sunlight-and-shadow scheme. Let us say what we will, but the real grand thrill of modern French art was the discovery of light, the discovery of light, and all the subsequent discoveries of the impressionists, and of the post-impressionists, even Cézanne. No matter how Cézanne may have reacted from the impressionists, it was they, with their deliriously joyful discovery of light and "free" colour, who really opened his eyes. Probably the most joyous moment in the whole history of painting was the moment when the incipient impressionists discovered light, and with it, colour. Ah, then they made the grand, grand escape into freedom, into infinity, into light and delight. They escaped from the tyranny of solidity and the menace of mass-form. They escaped, they escaped from the dark procreative body which so haunts a man, they escaped into the open air, *plein air* and *plein soleil*:* light and almost ecstasy.

Like every other human escape, it meant being hauled back later with the tail between the legs. Back comes the truant, back to the old doom of matter, of corporate existence, of the body sullen and stubborn and obstinately refusing to be transmuted into pure light, pure colour, or pure anything. It is not concerned with purity. Life isn't. Chemistry and mathematics and ideal religion are, but these are only small bits of life, which is itself bodily, and hence neither pure nor impure.

After the grand escape into impressionism and pure light, pure colour, pure bodilessness—for what is the body but a shimmer of lights and colours!—poor art came home truant and sulky, with its tail between its legs. And it is this return which now interests us. We know the escape was illusion, illusion, illusion. The cat had to come back. So now we despise the "light" blighters* too much. We haven't a good word for them. Which is nonsense, for they too are wonderful, even if their escape was into le grand néant, the great nowhere.

But the cat came back. And it is the home-coming tom that now has our sympathy: Renoir, to a certain extent, but mostly Cézanne, the sublime little grimalkin, who is followed by Matisse and Gauguin and Derain and Vlaminck and Braque* and all the host of other defiant and howling cats that have come back, perforce, to form and substance and *thereness*, instead of delicious nowhereness.

Without wishing to labour the point, one cannot help being amused at the dodge by which the Impressionists made the grand escape from the body. They metamorphosed it into a pure assemblage of shifting lights and shadows, all coloured. A web of woven, luminous colour was a man, or a woman—and so they painted her, or him: a web of woven shadows and gleams. Delicious! and quite true as far as it goes. A purely optical, *visual* truth: which paint is supposed to be. And they painted delicious pictures: a little too delicious. They bore us, at the moment. They bore people like the very modern critics intensely. But very modern critics need not be so intensely bored. There is something very lovely about the good impressionist pictures. And ten years hence critics will be bored by the present run of post-impressionists, though not so passionately bored, for these post-impressionists don't move us as the impressionists moved our fathers. We have to persuade ourselves, and we have to persuade one another to be impressed by the post-impressionists, on the whole. On the whole, they rather depress us. Which is perhaps good for us.

But modern art criticism is in a curious hole. Art has suddenly gone into rebellion, against all the canons of accepted religion, accepted good form, accepted everything. When the cat came back from the delicious impressionist excursion, it came back rather tattered, but bristling and with its claws out. The glorious escape was all an illusion. There *was* substance still in the world, a thousand times be damned to it! There *was* the body, the great lumpy body. There it was, you had it shoved down your throat. What really existed was lumps, lumps. Then paint 'em. Or else paint the thin "spirit" with gaps in it and looking merely dishevelled and "found out." Paint had found the spirit out.

This is the sulky and rebellious mood of the post-impressionists. They still hate the body—hate it. But in a rage they admit its existence, and paint it as huge lumps, tubes, cubes, planes, volumes, spheres, cones, cylinders, all the "pure" or mathematical forms of substance. As for landscape, it comes in for some of the same rage. It has also suddenly gone lumpy. Instead of being nice and ethereal and non-sensual, it was discovered by Van Gogh to be heavily, overwhelmingly substantial and sensual. Van Gogh took up landscape in heavy spadefuls. And Cézanne had to admit it. Landscape too, after being, since Claude Lorraine,* a thing of pure luminosity and floating shadow, suddenly exploded, and came tumbling back on to the canvases of artists in lumps. With Cézanne landscape "crystallised," to use one of the favourite terms of the critics, and it has gone on crystallising into crystals, cubes, cones, pyramids and so-forth ever since.

The impressionists brought the world at length, after centuries of effort, into the delicious one-ness of light. At last, at last! Hail holy Light! the great natural One, the universal, the universaliser! We are not divided, all one body we*—one in Light, lovely light!—No sooner had this pæan gone up than the post-impressionists, like Judas, gave the show away. They exploded the illusion, which fell back to the canvas of art in a chaos of lumps.

This new chaos of course needed new apologists, who therefore rose up in hordes to apologise, almost, for the new chaos. They felt a little guilty about it, so they took on new notes of effrontery, defiant as any Primitive Methodists,* which indeed they are: the Primitive Methodists of art criticism. These evangelical gentlemen at once ran up their chapels, in a Romanesque or Byzantine shape, as was natural for a primitive and a methodist, and started to cry forth their doctrines in the decadent wilderness.* They discovered once more that the æsthetic experience was an ecstasy, an ecstasy granted only to the chosen few, the elect,* among whom said critics were, of course, the arch-elect. This was out-doing Ruskin. It was almost Calvin come to art.* But let scoffers scoff, the æsthetic ecstasy was vouchsafed only to the few, the elect, and even then, only when they had freed their minds of false doctrine. They had renounced the mammon of "subject" in pictures, they went whoring* no more after the Babylon of painted "interest," nor did they hanker after the flesh-pots of artistic "representation." Oh purify yourselves, ye who would know the æsthetic ecstasy, and be lifted up to the "white peaks of artistic inspiration." Purify yourselves of all base hankering for a tale that is told, and of all low lust for likenesses. Purify yourselves, and know the one supreme way, the way of Significant Form. I am the revelation and the way! I am Significant Form, and my unutterable name is Reality. Lo, I am Form and I am Pure, behold I am Pure Form. I am the revelation of Spiritual Life, moving behind the veil. I come forth and make myself known, and I am Pure Form, behold I am Significant Form.*

So the prophets of the new era in art cry aloud to the multitude, in exactly the jargon of the revivalists, for revivalists they are.* They will revive the Primitive Method-brethren, the Byzantines, the Ravennese, the early Italian and French primitives (which ones, in particular, we aren't told) these were Right, these were Pure, these were Spiritual, these were Real! And the builders of early Romanesque churches, Oh my brethren! these were holy men, before the world went a-whoring after Gothic. Oh return, my brethren, to the Primitive Method, lift up your eyes to Significant Form and be saved.—

Now myself, brought up a nonconformist as I was, I just was never able to understand the language of salvation.* I never knew what they were talking about, when they raved about being saved, and safe in the arms of Jesus, and Abraham's bosom, and seeing the great light, and entering into glory:* I just was puzzled, for what did it *mean*? It seemed to work out as a getting rather drunk on your own self-importance, and afterwards coming dismally sober again and being rather unpleasant. That was all I could see in actual experience, of the entering-into-glory business. The term itself, like something which ought to mean something but somehow doesn't, stuck on my mind like an irritating burr, till I decided that it was just an artificial stimulant to the individual self-conceit. How could I enter into glory, when glory is just an abstraction of a human state, and not a separate reality at all? If glory means anything at all, it means the thrill a man gets when a great many people look up to him with mixed awe, reverence, delight. Today, it means Rudolf Valentino.* So that the cant about entering into glory is just used fuzzily to enhance the individual's sense of self-importance—one of the rather cheap cocaine-phrases.

And I'm afraid "æsthetic ecstasy" sounds to me very much the same, especially when accompanied by exhortations. It sounds like another great uplift into self-importance, another apotheosis of personal conceit: especially when accompanied by a lot of jargon about the pure world of reality existing behind the veil of this vulgar world of accepted appearances, and of the entry of the elect through the doorway of visual art. Too evangelical altogether, too much chapel and Primitive Methodist, too obvious a trick for advertising one's own self-glorification. The ego, as an American says, shuts itself up and paints the inside of the walls sky-blue, and thinks it is in heaven.*

And then the great symbols of this salvation. When the evangelist says: Behold the lamb of God!*—what on earth does he want one to behold? Are we invited to look at a lamb, with woolly muttony appearance, frisking and making its little pills? Awfully nice, but what *has* it got to do with God or my soul? Or the cross! What *do* they expect us to see in the cross? a sort of gallows? or the mark we use to cancel a mistake?—cross it out! That the cross by itself was supposed to *mean* something always mystified me.—The same with the Blood of the Lamb.—Washed in the blood of the Lamb!* always seemed to me an extremely unpleasant suggestion. And when Jerome says: He who has once washed in the blood of Jesus need never wash again!*—I feel like taking a hot bath at once, to wash off even the suggestion.

And I find myself equally mystified by the cant phrases like Significant Form and Pure Form. They are as mysterious to me as the Cross and the Blood of the Lamb. They are just the magic jargon of invocation, nothing else. If you want to invoke an æsthetic ecstasy, stand in front of a Matisse and whisper fervently under your breath: "Significant Form! Significant Form!"—and it will come. It sounds to me like a form of masturbation, an attempt to make the body react to some cerebral formula.

No, I am afraid modern criticism has done altogether too much for modern art. If painting survives this outburst of ecstatic evangelicism, which it will, it is because people do come to their senses, even after the silliest vogue.

And so we can return to modern French painting, without having to quake before the bogey, or the Holy Ghost of Significant Form: a bogey which doesn't exist if we don't mind leaving aside our self-importance when we look at a picture.

The actual fact is that in Cézanne modern French art made its first tiny step back to real substance, to objective substance, if we may call it so. Van Gogh's earth was still subjective earth, himself projected into the earth. But Cézanne's apples* are a real attempt to let the apple exist in its own separate entity, without transfusing it with personal emotion. Cézanne's great effort was, as it were, to shove the apple away from him, and let it live of itself. It seems a small thing to do: yet it is the first real sign that man has made for several thousands of years that he is willing to admit that matter *actually* exists. Strange as it may seem, for thousands of years, in short, ever since the mythological "Fall," man has been pre-occupied with the constant pre-occupation of the denial of the existence of matter, and the proof that matter is only a form of spirit.—And then, the moment it is done, and we realise finally that matter is only a form of energy, whatever that may be, in the same instant matter rises up and hits us over the head and makes us realise that it exists absolutely, since it is compact energy itself.

Cézanne felt it in paint, when he felt for the apple. Suddenly he felt the tyranny of mind, the white, worn-out arrogance of the spirit, the mental consciousness, the enclosed ego in its sky-blue heaven self-painted. He felt the sky-blue prison. And a great conflict started inside him. He was dominated by his old mental consciousness, but he wanted terribly to escape the domination. He wanted to *express* what he suddenly, convulsedly knew: the existence of matter. He terribly wanted to paint the real existence of the body, to make it artistically palpable. But he couldn't. He hadn't got there yet. And it was the torture of his life. He wanted to be himself in his own procreative body—and he couldn't. He was, like all the rest of us, so intensely and exclusively a mental creature, or a spiritual creature, or an egoist, that he could no longer identify himself with his intuitive body. He wanted to, terribly. At first he determined to do it by sheer bravado and braggadocio. But no good, it couldn't be done that way. He had, as one critic says, to become humble.* But it wasn't a question of becoming humble. It was a question of abandoning his cerebral conceit and his "willed ambition," and coming down to brass tacks. Poor Cézanne, there he is in his self-portraits, even the early showy ones, peeping out like a mouse and saying: I *am* a man of flesh, am I not?—For he was not quite, as none of us are. The man of flesh has been slowly destroyed through centuries, to give place to the man of spirit, the mental man, the ego, the self-conscious I. And in his artistic soul, Cézanne knew it, and wanted to rise in the flesh. He couldn't do it, and it embittered him. Yet, with his apple, he did shove the stone from the door of the tomb.*

He wanted to be a man of flesh, a real man: to get out of the sky-blue prison into real air. He wanted to live, really live in the body, to know the world through his instincts and his intuitions, and to be himself in his procreative blood, not in his mere mind and spirit. He wanted it, he wanted it terribly. And whenever he tried, his mental consciousness, like a cheap fiend, interfered. If he wanted to paint a woman, his mental consciousness simply overpowered him and wouldn't let him paint the woman of flesh, the first Eve who lived before any of the fig-leaf nonsense.* He couldn't do it. If he wanted to paint people, intuitively and instinctively, he couldn't do it. His mental concepts shoved in front, and these he *wouldn't* paint—mere representations of what the *mind* accepts, not what the intuitions gather—and they, his mental concepts, wouldn't let him paint from intuition, they shoved in between all the time, so he painted his conflict and his failure, and the result is almost ridiculous.

Woman he was not allowed to know by intuition; his mental self, his ego, that bloodless fiend, forbade him. Man, other men he was likewise not allowed to know—except by a few, few touches. The earth likewise he was not allowed to know: his landscapes are mostly acts of rebellion against the mental concept of landscape. After a fight tooth and nail for forty years, he did succeed in knowing an apple, fully; and not quite so fully, a jug or two. That was all he achieved.

It seems little, and he died embittered. But it is the first step that counts, and Cézanne's apple is a great deal, more than Plato's Idea.* Cézanne's apple rolled the stone from the mouth of the tomb, and if poor Cézanne couldn't unwind himself from his cerements and mental winding-sheet, but had to lie still in the tomb, till he died,* still he gave us a chance.

The history of our era is the nauseating and repulsive history of the crucifixion of the procreative body for the glorification of the spirit, the mental consciousness. Plato was an arch-priest of this crucifixion. Art, that handmaid, humbly and honestly served the vile deed, through three thousand years at least. The Renaissance put the spear through the side of the already crucified body,* and syphilis put poison into the wound made by the imaginative spear. It took still three hundred years for the body to finish: but in the nineteenth century it became a corpse, a corpse with an abnormally active mind: and today it stinketh.

We, dear reader, you and I, we were born corpses and we are corpses. I doubt if there is even one of us who has even known so much as an apple, a whole apple. All we know is shadows, even of apples. Shadows of everything, of the whole world, shadows even of ourselves. We are inside the tomb, and the tomb is wide and shadowy like hell, even if sky-blue by optimistic paint, so we think it is all the world. But our world is a wide tomb full of ghosts, replicas. We are all spectres, we have not been able to touch even so much as an apple. Spectres we are to one another. Spectre you are to me, spectre I am to you. Shadow you are even to yourself.—And by shadow I mean idea, concept, the abstracted reality, the ego. We are not solid. We don't live in the flesh. Our instincts and intuitions are dead, we live wound round with the winding-sheet of abstraction. And the touch of anything solid hurts us. For our instincts and intuitions, which are our feelers of touch and knowing through touch, they are dead, amputated. We walk and talk and eat and copulate and laugh and piss and evacuate wrapped in our winding-sheets, all the time wrapped in our winding-sheets.

So that Cézanne's apple hurts. It made people shout with pain. And it was not till his followers had turned him again into an abstraction, that he was ever accepted. Then the critics stepped forth and abstracted his good apple into Significant Form, and henceforth Cézanne was saved. Saved for democracy. Put safely in the tomb again, and the stone rolled back. The resurrection was postponed once more.

As the resurrection will be postponed ad infinitum by the good bourgeois corpses in their cultured winding-sheets. They will run up a chapel to the risen body, even if it is only an apple, and kill it on the spot. They are wide awake, are the corpses, on the alert. And a poor mouse of a Cézanne is alone in the years. Who else shows a spark of awakening life, in our marvellously civilised cemetery? All is dead, and dead breath preaching with phosphorescent effulgence about æsthetic ecstasy and Significant Form. If only the dead would bury their dead.* But the dead are not dead for nothing. Who buries his own sort? The dead are cunning and alert to pounce on any spark of life and bury it, even as they have already buried Cézanne's apple and put up to it a white tombstone of Significant Form.

For who of Cézanne's followers does anything but follow at the triumphant funeral of Cézanne's achievement? They follow him in order to bury him, and they succeed. Cézanne is deeply buried under all the Matisses and Vlamincks of his following, while the critics read the funeral homily.

It is quite easy to accept Matisse and Vlaminck and Friesz* and all the rest. They are just Cézanne abstracted again. They are all just tricksters, even if clever ones. They are all mental, mental, mental, egoists, egoists, egoists. And therefore they are all acceptable now to the enlightened corpses of connoisseurs. You needn't be afraid of Matisse and Vlaminck and the rest. They will never give your corpse-anatomy a jar. They are just shadows, minds mountebanking and playing charades on canvas. They may be quite amusing charades, and I am all for the mountebank. But of course it is all games inside the cemetery, played by corpses and *hommes d'esprit*, even *femmes d'esprit*, like Mademoiselle Laurencin.*—As for l'esprit, said Cézanne, I don't give a fart for it.—Perhaps not! But the connoisseur will give large sums of money. Trust the dead to pay for their amusement, when the amusement is deadly!

The most interesting figure in modern art, and the only really interesting figure, is Cézanne: and that, not so much because of his achievement, as because of his struggle. Cézanne was born at Aix in Provence in 1839: small, timorous, yet sometimes bantam defiant, sensitive, full of grand ambition, yet ruled still deeper by a naïve, Mediterranean sense of truth or reality, imagination, call it what you will. He is not a big figure. Yet his struggle is truly heroic. He was a bourgeois, and one must never forget it. He had a moderate bourgeois income. But a bourgeois in Provence is much more real and human than a bourgeois in Normandy. He is much nearer the actual people, and the actual people are much less subdued by awe of his respectable bourgeois money.

Cézanne was naïf to a degree, but not a fool. He was rather insignificant, and grandeur impressed him terribly. Yet still stronger in him was the little flame of life where he *felt* things to be true. He didn't betray himself in order to get success, because he couldn't: to his nature it was impossible: he was too pure to be able to betray his own small real flame for immediate rewards. Perhaps that is the best one can say of a man, and it puts Cézanne, small and insignificant as he is, among the heroes. He would *not* abandon his own vital imagination.

He was terribly impressed by physical splendour and flamboyancy, as people usually are in the lands of the sun. He admired terribly the splendid virtuosity of Paul Veronese and Tintoretto,* and even of later and less good baroque painters. He wanted to be like that—terribly he wanted it. And he tried very, very hard, with bitter effort. And he always failed. It is a cant phrase with the critics to say "he couldn't draw." Mr. Fry says: "With all his rare endowments, he happened to lack the comparatively common gift of illustration, the gift that any draughtsman for the illustrated papers learns in a school of commercial art—"*

Now this sentence gives away at once the hollowness of modern criticism. In the first place, can one learn a "gift" in a school of commercial art, or anywhere else? A gift surely is given, we tacitly assume by God or Nature or whatever higher power we hold responsible for the things we have no choice in.

Was then Cézanne devoid of this gift? Was he simply incapable of drawing a cat so that it would look like a cat? Nonsense! Cézanne's work is full of accurate drawing. His more trivial pictures, suggesting copies from other masters, are perfectly well drawn—that is, conventionally: so are some of the landscapes, so even is that portrait of M. Geffroy and his books, which is, or was so famous.* Why these cant phrases about not being able to draw! Of course Cézanne could draw, as well as anybody else. And he had learned everything that was necessary in the art schools.

He *could* draw. And yet, in his terrifically earnest compositions in the late Renaissance or Baroque manner, he drew so badly. Why? Not because he couldn't. And not because he was sacrificing "significant form" to "insignificant form," or mere slick representation, which is apparently what artists themselves mean when they talk about drawing. Cézanne knew all about drawing: and he surely knew as much as his critics do about significant form. Yet he neither succeeded in drawing so that things looked right, nor combining his shapes so that he achieved real form. He just failed.

He failed, where one of his little slick successors would have succeeded with one eye shut. And why? Why did Cézanne fail in his early pictures? Answer that, and you'll know a little better what art is. He didn't fail because he understood nothing about drawing or significant form or æsthetic ecstasy. He knew about them all, and didn't give a spit for them.

Cézanne failed in his earlier pictures because he was trying with his mental consciousness to do something which his living provençal body didn't want to do, or couldn't do. He terribly wanted to do something grand and voluptuous and sensuously satisfying, in the Tintoretto manner. Mr. Fry calls that his "willed ambition," which is a good phrase, and says he had to learn humility, which is a bad phrase.*

The "willed ambition" was more than a mere willed ambition—it was a genuine desire. But it was a desire that thought it could be satisfied by ready-made baroque expressions, whereas it needed to achieve a whole new marriage of mind and matter. If we believed in re-incarnation, then we should have to believe that after a certain number of new incarnations into the body of an artist, the soul of Cézanne *would* produce grand and voluptuous and sensually rich pictures—but not at all in the baroque manner. Because the pictures he actually did produce with undeniable success are the first steps in that direction, sensual and rich with not the slightest hint of baroque, but new, the man's new grasp of substantial reality.

There was, then, a certain discrepancy between Cézanne's *notion* of what he wanted to produce, and his other, intuitive knowledge of what he *could* produce. For whereas the mind works in possibilities, the intuitions work in actualities, and what you *intuitively* desire, that is possible to you. Whereas what you mentally or "Consciously" desire is nine times out of ten impossible: hitch your wagon to a star,* and you'll just stay where you are—!

So the conflict, as usual, was not between the artist and his medium, but between the artist's *mind* and the artist's *intuition* and *instinct*. And what Cézanne had to learn was not humility—cant word!—but honesty: honesty with himself. It was not a question of any gift or significant form or æsthetic ecstasy: it was a question of Cézanne being himself, just Cézanne. And when Cézanne is himself he is not Tintoretto nor Veronese nor anything baroque at all. Yet he is something *physical*, and even sensual: qualities which he had identified with the masters of virtuosity.

In passing, if we think of Henri Matisse, a real virtuoso, and imagine him possessed with a "willed ambition" to paint grand and flamboyant baroque pictures, then we know at once that he would not have to "humble" himself at all, but that he would start in and paint with great success grand and flamboyant modern-baroque pictures. He would succeed because he has the gift of virtuosity. And the gift of virtuosity simply means that you don't have to humble yourself, or even be honest with yourself, because you are a clever mental creature who is capable at will of making the intuitions and instincts subserve some mental concept: in short, you can prostitute your body to your mind, your instincts and intuitions you can prostitute to your "willed ambition," in a sort of masturbation process, and you can produce the impotent glories of virtuosity.—But Veronese and Tintoretto are real painters, they are not mere *virtuosi*, as some of the later men are.—

The point is very important. Any creative act occupies the whole consciousness of a man. This is true of the great discoveries of science as well as of art. The truly great discoveries of science and real works of art are made by the whole consciousness of man working together in unison and oneness; instinct, intuition, mind, intellect all fused into one complete consciousness, and grasping what we may call a complete truth, or a complete vision, a complete revelation in sound. A discovery, artistic or otherwise, may be more or less intuitional, more or less mental: but intuition will have entered into it, and mind will have entered too. The whole consciousness is concerned, in every case.—And a painting requires the activity of the whole imagination, for it is made of imagery, and the imagination is that form of complete consciousness in which predominates the intuitive awareness of forms, images, a *physical* awareness.

And the same applies to the genuine *appreciation* of a work of art, or the *grasp* of a scientific law, as to the production of the same. The whole consciousness is occupied, not merely the mind alone, or merely the body. The mind and spirit alone can never really grasp a work of art, though they may, in a masturbating fashion, provoke the body into an ecstasised response. The ecstasy will die out into ash and more ash. And the reason we have so many trivial scientists promulgating fantastic "facts" is that so many modern scientists likewise work with the mind alone, and *force* the intuitions and instincts into a prostituted acquiescence. The very statement that water is H_2O is a mental *tour de force*. With our bodies, we know that water is *not* H_2O, our intuitions and instincts both know it is not so. But they are bullied by the impudent mind. Whereas if we said that water, under certain circumstances produces two volumes of hydrogen and one of oxygen, then the intuitions and instincts would agree entirely. But that water *is composed of* two volumes of hydrogen to one of oxygen we cannot physically believe. It needs something else. Something is missing.—Of course, alert science does not ask us to believe the commonplace assertion of: *water* is H_2O, but school-children have to believe it.

A parallel case is all this modern stuff about astronomy, stars, their distances and speeds and so on, talking of billions and trillions of miles and years and so forth: it is just occult. The mind is revelling in words, the intuitions and instincts are just left out, or prostituted into a sort of ecstasy. In fact the sort of ecstasy that lies in absurd figures such as 2,000,000,000,000,000,000,000,000 miles or years or tons, figures which abound in modern *scientific* books on astronomy, is just the sort of æsthetic ecstasy that the over-mental critics of art assert they experience today from Matisse's pictures. It is all poppy-cock. The body is either stunned to a corpse, or prostituted to ridiculous thrills, or stands coldly apart.

When I read how far off the suns are, and what they are made of, and so on, and so on, I believe all I am *able* to believe, with the true imagination. But when my intuition and instinct can grasp no more, then I call my mind to a halt. I am not going to accept mere mental asseverations. The mind can assert anything, and pretend it has proved it. My beliefs I test on my body, on my intuitional consciousness, and when I get a response there, then I accept. The same is true of great scientific "laws," like the law of evolution. After years of acceptance of the "laws" of evolution—rather desultory or "humble" acceptance—now I realise that my vital imagination makes great reservations. I find I can't, with the best will in the world, believe that the species have "evolved" from one common life-form. I just can't feel it, I have to violate my intuitive and instinctive awareness of something else, to make myself believe it. But since I know that my intuitions and instincts may still be held back by prejudice, I seek in the world for someone to make me intuitively and instinctively feel the truth of the "law"—and I don't find anybody. I find scientists, just like artists, asserting things they are *mentally* sure of, in fact cocksure, but about which they are much too egoistic and ranting to be *intuitively, instinctively* sure. When I find a man, or a woman, intuitively and instinctively sure of anything I am all respect. But for scientific or artistic braggarts how can one have respect! The intrusion of the egoistic element is a sure proof of intuitive uncertainty. No man who is sure by instinct and intuition *brags*, though he may fight tooth and nail for his beliefs.

Which brings us back to Cézanne, why he couldn't draw, and why he couldn't paint baroque masterpieces. It is just because he was real, and could only believe in his own expression when it expressed a moment of wholeness or completeness of consciousness in himself. He could not prostitute one part of himself to the other. He *could* not masturbate, in paint or words. And that is saying a very great deal, today; today, the great day of the masturbating consciousness, when the mind prostitutes the sensitive responsive body, and just forces the reactions. The masturbating consciousness produces all kinds of novelties, which thrill for the moment, then go very dead. It cannot produce a single genuinely new utterance.

What we have to thank Cézanne for is not his humility, but for his proud, high spirit that refused to accept the glib utterances of his facile mental self. He wasn't poor-spirited enough to be facile—nor humble enough to be satisfied with visual and emotional clichés. Thrilling as the baroque masters were to him in themselves, he realised that as soon as he reproduced them, he produced nothing but cliché. The mind is full of all sorts of memory, visual, tactile, emotional memory, memories, groups of memories, systems of memories. A cliché is just a worn-out memory that has no more emotional or intuitional root, and has become a habit. Whereas a novelty is just a new grouping of clichés, a new arrangement of accustomed memories. That is why a novelty is so easily accepted: it gives the little shock or thrill of surprise, but it does not *disturb* the emotional and intuitive self. It forces you to see nothing new. It is only a novel compound of clichés. The work of most of Cézanne's successors is just novel, just a new arrangement of clichés, soon growing stale. And the clichés are Cézanne-clichés, just as in Cézanne's own earlier pictures his clichés were all, or mostly baroque-clichés.

Cézanne's early history as a painter is a history of his fight with his own cliché. His consciousness wanted a new realisation. And his ready-made mind offered him all the time a ready-made expression. And Cézanne, far too inwardly proud and haughty to accept the ready-made clichés that came from his mental consciousness, stocked with memories, and which appeared mocking at him on his canvas, spent most of his time smashing his own forms to bits. To a true artist, and to the living imagination, the cliché is the deadly enemy. Cézanne had a bitter fight with it. He hammered it to pieces a thousand times. And still it re-appeared.

Now again we can see why Cézanne's drawing was so bad. It was bad because it represented a smashed, mauled cliché, terribly knocked about. If Cézanne had been willing to accept his own baroque cliché, his drawing would have been perfectly conventionally "all right," and not a critic would have had a word to say about it. But when his drawing was conventionally all right, to Cézanne himself it was mockingly all wrong, it was cliché. So he flew at it and knocked all the shape and stuffing out of it, and when it was so mauled that it was all wrong, and he was exhausted with it, he let it go; bitterly, because it still was not what he wanted. And here comes in the comic element in Cézanne's pictures. His rage with the cliché made him distort the cliché sometimes into parody, as we see in pictures like *The Pasha* and *La Femme*.* "You *will* be cliché, will you?" he gnashes. "Then *be* it!" And he shoves it in a frenzy of exasperation over into parody. And the sheer exasperation makes the parody still funny: but the laugh is a little on the wrong side of the face.

This smashing of the cliché lasted a long way into Cézanne's life: indeed, it went with him to the end. The way he worked over and over his forms was his nervous manner of laying the ghost of his cliché, burying it. Then when it disappeared perhaps from his forms themselves, it lingered in his composition, and he had to fight with the *edges* of his forms and contours, to bury the ghost there. Only his colour he knew was not cliché. He left it to his disciples to make it so.

In his very best pictures, the best of the still-life compositions, which seem to me Cézanne's greatest achievement, the fight with the cliché is still going on. But it was in the still-life pictures he learned his final method of *avoiding* the cliché: just leaving gaps through which it fell into nothingness. So he makes his landscape succeed.

In his art, all his life long Cézanne was tangled in a two-fold activity: he wanted to express something, and before he could do it, he had to fight the hydra-headed cliché, whose last head he could never lop off. The fight with the cliché is the most obvious thing in his pictures. The dust of battle rises thick, and the splinters fly wildly. And it is this dust of battle and flying of splinters which his imitators still so fervently imitate. If you give a chinese dress-maker a dress to copy, and the dress happens to have a darned rent in it, the dress-maker carefully tears a rent in the new dress, and darns it in exact replica. And this seems to be the chief occupation of Cézanne's disciples, in every land. They absorb themselves reproducing imitation mistakes. He let off various explosions, in order to blow up the stronghold of the cliché, and his followers make grand firework imitation of the explosions, without the faintest inkling of the true attack. They do, indeed, make an onslaught on representation, true-to-life representation: because the explosion in Cézanne's pictures blew this up. But I am convinced that what Cézanne himself wanted *was* representation. He *wanted* true-to-life representation. Only he wanted it *more* true to life. And once you have got photography, it is a very, very difficult thing to get representation *more* true-to-life: which it has to be.

Cézanne was a realist, and he wanted to be true to life. But he would not be content with the optical cliché. With the impressionists, purely optical vision perfected itself and fell *at once* into cliché, with a startling rapidity. Cézanne saw this. Artists like Courbet and Daumier were not purely optical, but the other element in these two painters, the intellectual element, was cliché. To the optical vision they added the concept of force-pressure, almost like a hydraulic brake, and this force-pressure concept is mechanical a cliché, though still popular. And Daumier added mental satire, and Courbet added a touch of a sort of socialism: both cliché and unimaginative.

Cézanne wanted something that was neither optical nor mechanical nor intellectual. And to introduce into our world of vision something which is neither optical nor mechanical nor intellectual-psychological requires a real revolution. It was a revolution Cézanne began, but which nobody, apparently, has been able to carry on.

He wanted to touch the world of substance once more with the intuitive touch, to be aware of it with the intuitive awareness, and to express it in intuitive terms. That is, he wished to displace our present mode of mental-visual consciousness, the consciousness of mental concepts, and substitute a mode of consciousness that was predominantly intuitive, the awareness of touch. In the past, the primitives painted intuitively, but *in the direction* of our present mental-visual, conceptual form of consciousness. They were working away from their own intuition. Mankind has never been able to trust the intuitive consciousness— and the decision to accept that trust marks a very great revolution in the course of human development.

Without knowing it, Cézanne, the timid little conventional man sheltering behind his wife and sister and the Jesuit father, was a pure revolutionary.* When he said to his models: Be an apple! Be an apple!—he was uttering the foreword to the fall not only of Jesuits and the Christian idealists altogether, but to the collapse of our whole way of consciousness, and the substitution of another way. If the human being is going to be primarily an Apple, as for Cézanne it was, then you are going to have a new world of men: a world which has very little to say, men that can sit still and just be physically there and be truly non-moral. That was what Cézanne meant with his: "Be an apple!" He knew perfectly well that the moment the model began to intrude her personality and her "mind," it would be cliché, and moral, and he would have to paint cliché. The only part of her that was not banal, known *ad nauseam*, living cliché, the only part of her that was not living cliché was her appleyness. Her body, even her very sex was known, nauseously: *connu! connu!** the endless chain of known cause-and-effect, the infinite web of the hated cliché which nets us all down in utter boredom. He knew it all, he hated it all, he refused it all, this timid and "humble" little man. He knew, as an artist, that the only bit of a woman which nowadays escapes being ready-made and ready-known cliché is the appley part of her.—Oh, be an apple, and leave out all your thoughts, all your feelings, all your mind and all your soul, which we know all about and find boring beyond endurance. Leave it all out—and be an apple!—It is the appleyness of the portrait of Cézanne's wife that makes it so permanently interesting: the appleyness, which carries with it also the feeling of knowing the other side as well, the side you don't see, the hidden side of the moon. For the intuitive apperception of the apple is so *tangibly* aware of the apple that it is aware of it *all round*, not only just of the front. The eye sees only fronts, and the mind, on the whole, is satisfied with fronts. But intuition needs all-aroundness, and instinct needs insideness. The true imagination is forever curving round to the other side, to the back of presented appearance.*

So to my feeling the portraits of Madame Cézanne, particularly the portrait in the red dress, are more interesting than the portrait of M. Geffroy, or the portraits of the housekeeper or the gardener. In the same way the *Card-players* with two figures please me more than those with four.*

But we have to remember, in his figure-paintings, that while he was painting the appleyness he was also deliberately painting *out* the so-called humanness, the personality, the "likeness," the physical cliché. He had deliberately to paint it out, deliberately to make the hands and face rudimentary, and so on, because if he had painted them in fully, they would have been cliché. He *never* got over the cliché domination, the intrusion and interference of the ready-made concept, when it came to people, to men and women. Especially to women he could only give a cliché response—and that maddened him. Try as he might, woman remained a known, ready-made cliché object to him, and he *could not* break through the conceptual obsession to get at the intuitive awareness of her. Except with his wife—and in his wife he did at least know the appleyness. But with his housekeeper he failed somewhat. She is a bit cliché, especially the face. So really is M. Geffroy.

With men Cézanne often dodged it by insisting on the clothes, those stiff cloth jackets bent into thick folds, those hats, those blouses, those curtains. Some of the *Card-players*, the big ones with four figures, seem just a trifle banal, so much occupied with painted *stuff*, painted clothing, and the humanness a bit cliché. Nor good colour nor clever composition, nor "planes" of colour nor anything else will save an emotional cliché from being an emotional cliché, though they may, of course, garnish it and make it more interesting.

Where Cézanne did sometimes escape the cliché altogether and really give a complete intuitive interpretation of actual objects is in some of the still-life compositions. To me, these good still-life scenes are purely representative and quite true-to-life. Here Cézanne did what he wanted to do: he made the things quite real, he didn't deliberately leave anything out, and yet he gave us a triumphant and rich intuitive vision of a few apples and kitchen pots. For once his intuitive consciousness triumphed, and broke into utterance. And here he is inimitable. His imitators imitate his accessories of table-cloths folded like tin, etc.—the unreal parts of his pictures—but they don't imitate the pots and apples, because they can't. It's the real appleyness, and you can't imitate it. Every man must create it new and different out of himself: new and different. The moment it looks "like" Cézanne, it is nothing.

But at the same time that Cézanne was triumphing with the apple and appleyness, he was still fighting with the cliché. When he makes Madame Cézanne most *still*, most appley, he starts making the universe slip uneasily about her. It was part of his desire: to make the human form, the *life* form, come to rest. Not static—on the contrary. Mobile but come to rest. And at the same time, he set the unmoving material world into motion. Walls twitch and slide, chairs bend or rear up a little, cloths curl like burning paper. Cézanne did this partly to satisfy his intuitive feeling that nothing is really *statically* at rest—a feeling he seems to have had strongly—as when he watched the lemons shrivel or go mildewed, in his still-life group, which he left lying there so long so that he *could* see that gradual flux of change: and partly to fight the cliché, which says that the inanimate world *is* static, and that walls *are* still. In his fight with the cliché, he denied that walls are still and chairs are static. In his intuitive self he *felt* for their changes.

And these two activities of his consciousness occupy his later landscapes. In the best landscapes, we are fascinated by the mysterious *shiftiness* of the scene under our eyes, it shifts about as we watch it. And we realise, with a sort of transport, how intuitively *true* this is of landscape. It is *not* still. It has its own weird anima, and to our wide-eyed perception it changes like a living animal under our gaze. This is a quality that Cézanne sometimes got marvellously.

Then again, in other pictures he seems to be saying: Landscape is not like this and not like this and not like this and not . . . etc.—and every *not* is a little blank space in the canvas, defined by the remains of an assertion. Sometimes Cézanne builds up a landscape essentially out of omissions. He puts fringes on the complicated vacuum of the cliché, so to speak, and offers us that. It is interesting in a *repudiative* fashion—but it is not the new thing. The appleyness, the intuition has gone. We have only a mental repudiation. This occupies many of the later pictures: and ecstasises the critics.

And Cézanne was bitter. He had never, as far as his *life* went, broken through the horrible glass screen of the mental concepts, to the actual *touch* of life. In his art, he had touched the apple, and that was a great deal. He had intuitively known the apple and intuitively brought it forth on the tree of his life, in paint. But when it came to anything beyond the apple, to landscape, to people, and above all to nude woman, the cliché had triumphed over him. The cliché had triumphed over him, and he was bitter, misanthropic. How not be misanthropic, when men and women are just clichés to you, and you hate the cliché! Most people, of course, love the cliché—because most people *are* the cliché. Still for all that there is perhaps more appleyness in man, and even in nude woman, than Cézanne was able to get at. The cliché obtruded, so he just abstracted away from it. Those last water-colour landscapes are just abstractions from the cliché. They are blanks, with a few pearly-coloured sort of edges. The blank is vacuum, which was Cézanne's last word against the cliché. It is a vacuum. And the edges are there to assert the vacuity.

And the very fact that we can re-construct almost instantly a whole landscape from the few indications Cézanne gives, shows what a cliché the landscape is, how it exists already, ready-made, in our minds, how it exists in a pigeon-hole of the consciousness, so to speak, and you need only be given its number to be able to get it out, complete. Cézanne's last water-colour landscapes, made up of a few touches on blank paper, are a satire on landscape altogether. *They leave so much to the imagination*!—that immortal cant phrase, which means they give you the clue to a cliché and the cliché comes. That's what the cliché exists for. And that sort of imagination is just a rag-bag memory stored with thousands and thousands of old and really worthless sketches, images, etc., clichés.

We can see what a fight it means, the escape from the domination of the ready-made mental concept, the mental consciousness stuffed full of clichés that intervene like a complete screen between us and life. It means a long, long fight, that will probably last for ever. But Cézanne did get as far as the apple—I can think of nobody else who has done anything.

When we put it in personal terms, it is a fight in man between his own ego, which is his ready-made mental self which inhabits either a sky-blue self-tinted heaven or a black, self-tinted hell, and his other free intuitive self. Cézanne never freed himself from his ego, in his life. He haunted the fringes of experience.—"I who am so feeble in life."* But at least he knew it. At least he had the greatness to feel bitter about it—not like the complacent bourgeois who now "appreciate" him!

So now perhaps it is the English turn. Perhaps this is where the English will come in. They have certainly stayed out very completely. It is as if they had received the death-blow to their instinctive and intuitive bodies in the Elizabethan age, and since then they have steadily died, till now they are complete corpses. As a young English painter, an intelligent and really modest young man said to me: But I do think we ought to begin to paint good pictures, now that we know pretty well all there is to know about how a picture should be made. You do agree, don't you, that technically we know almost all there is to know about painting?—

I looked at him in amazement. It was obvious that a new-born babe was as fit to paint pictures, as he was. He knew technically all there was to know about pictures: all about two-dimensional and three-dimensional composition, also the colour-dimension and the dimension of values in that view of composition which exists apart from form: all about the value of planes, the value of the angle in planes, the different values of the same colour on different planes: all about edges, visible edges, tangible edges, intangible edges: all about the nodality of form-groups, the constellating of mass-centres: all about the relativity of mass, the gravitation and the centrifugal force of masses, the resultant of the complex impinging of masses, the isolation of a mass in the line of vision: all about pattern, line pattern, edge pattern, tone pattern, colour pattern, and the pattern of moving planes: all about texture, impasto, surface, and what happens at the edge of the canvas: also which is the æsthetic centre of the canvas, the dynamic centre, the effulgent centre, the kinetic centre, the mathematical centre and the Chinese centre: also the points of departure in the foreground, and the points of disappearance in the background, together with the various routes between these points, namely, as the crow flies, as the cow walks, as the mind intoxicated with knowledge reels and gets there: all about spotting, what you spot, which spot, on the spot, how many spots, balance of spots, recedence of spots, spots on the explosive vision and spots on the co-ordinative vision: all about literary interest and how to hide it successfully from the policeman: all about photographic representation, and which heaven it belongs to, and which hell: all about the sex-appeal of a picture, and when you can be arrested for solicitation, when for indecency: all about the psychology of a picture, which section of the mind it appeals to, which mental state it is intended to represent, how to exclude the representation of all other states of mind from the one intended, or how, on the contrary, to give a hint of complementary states of mind fringing the state of mind portrayed: all about the chemistry of colours, when to use Windsor and Newton and when not, and the relative depth of contempt to display for Lefranc:* on the history of colour, past and future, whether cadmium will really stand the march of ages, whether viridian will go black, blue, or merely greasy, and the effect on our great-great-grandsons of the flake white and zinc white and white lead we have so lavishly used: on the merits and demerits of leaving patches of bare, prepared canvas, and which preparation will bleach, which blacken: on the mediums to be used, the vice of linseed oil, the treachery of turps,* the meanness of gums, the innocence or the unspeakable crime of varnish: on allowing your picture to be shiny, on insisting that it should be shiny, or weeping over the merest suspicion of gloss, and rubbing it with a raw potato: on brushes, and the conflicting length of the stem, the best of the hog, the length of bristle most to be desired on the many varying occasions, and whether to slash in one direction only: on the atmosphere of London, on the atmosphere of Glasgow, on the atmosphere of Rome, on the atmosphere of Paris, and the peculiar action of them all upon vermilion, cinnabar, pale cadmium yellow, mid-chrome, emerald green, veronese green, linseed oil, turps, and Lyalls' perfect medium:* on quality, and its relation to light, and its ability to hold its own in so radical a change of light as that from Rome to London:—All these things the young man knew—and out of it, God help him, he was going to make pictures.

Now such innocence and such naïveté, coupled with true modesty, must make us believe that we English have indeed, at least as far as paint goes, become again as little children:* very little children: tiny children: babes: nay, babes unborn. And if we have really got back to the state of the unborn babe, we are perhaps almost ready to be born. The English *may* be born again,* pictorially. Or, to tell the truth, they may begin for the first time to be born: since as painters of composition pictures they don't really exist. They have reached the stage where their innocent egos are entirely and totally enclosed in pale-blue glass bottles of insulated inexperience. Perhaps now they *must* hatch out!

"Do you think we may be on the brink of a Golden Age again, in England?" one of our most promising young writers asked me, with that same half-timorous innocence and naïveté of the young painter. I looked at him—he was a sad young man—and my eyes nearly fell out of my head. A golden age! He looked so ungolden, and though he was twenty years my junior, he felt also like my grandfather. A golden age! in England! a golden age! now, when even money is paper! when the enclosure in the ego is final, when they are hermetically sealed and insulated from all experience, from any *touch*, from anything *solid*.

"I suppose it's up to *you*," said I.

And he quietly accepted it.

But such innocence, such naïveté must be a prelude to something. It's a *ne plus ultra*.* So why shouldn't it be a prelude to a golden age? If the innocence and naïveté as regards artistic expression doesn't become merely idiotic, why shouldn't it become golden? The young might, out of a sheer sort of mental blankness, strike the oil of their live intuition, and get a gusher. Why not? A golden gush of artistic expression! "now we know pretty well everything that can be known about the technical side of pictures." A golden age! With the artists all in bottles! bottled up!

THE STATE OF FUNK

On 23 February 1929, when returning 'Do Women Change' – extended at the request of Bernard Falk, editor of the *Sunday Dispatch* – Lawrence remarked to Nancy Pearn: 'I enclose also another article, more or less stating my position, and you can offer it to the *Sunday Despatch*, but I don't mind a bit if they don't want it' (*Letters*, vii. 188). The article was 'The State of Funk'. The necessity he felt to state his 'position' was driven by recent events: the seizure, on 18 January, of six copies of *Lady Chatterley's Lover* by the police and their threat that further copies found entering the country from Florence would be seized and destroyed (vii. 146 n. 4); and the visit by Scotland Yard officers on 23 January to inform Pollinger that typescripts of *Pansies* had been impounded as 'obscene and indecent' (vii. 149 n. 1). Lawrence also knew that the seizure of *Pansies* in the mail was to be raised in the Commons through a question to the Home Secretary (vii. 172). In the light of the evolving situation he probably felt it desirable to make a preemptive strike through a newspaper article. A remark in his letter to Falk on 24 February suggests that this was his motive: 'I sent Miss Pearn an article yesterday, to show you, putting "very delicately" on tip-toe like Agag, my position with regards to my naughty book etc. If it's not suitable for the *Dispatch*, I don't mind at all' (vii. 189).

The onus was now on Nancy Pearn to decide the next move. Understandably apprehensive about the consequences, she did not immediately forward the article to Falk; she explained to Lawrence on 26 February: 'I am thinking over the way to use this, which will be to your greatest advantage. It may be best to wait a week until the legal side is clarified . . . As you may already have heard we are in close touch with Mr St John Hutchinson with a view to deciding on a course of action.' Hutchinson, both barrister and aspiring politician (he stood, unsuccessfully, for the Isle of Wight parliamentary constituency in 1929), probably advised against over-hasty publication. At any rate, Nancy Pearn delayed further action, reporting to Lawrence on 8 April: 'I am holding the "Funk" article, but I fancy something effective may be done with this if you don't mind the possible necessity for a bit of a cut here and there.' In the end, nothing 'effective' was done; 'The State of Funk' was first published in *Assorted Articles*.

THE STATE OF FUNK

What is the matter with the English, that they are so scared of everything? They are in a state of blue funk, and they behave like a lot of mice when somebody stamps on the floor. They are terrified about money, finance, about ships, about war, about work, about Labour, about Bolshevism, and funniest of all, they are scared stiff of the printed word. Now this is a very strange and humiliating state of mind, in a people which has always been so dauntless. And, for the nation, it is a very dangerous state of mind. When a people falls into a state of funk, then God help it. Because mass funk leads sometime or other to mass panic, and then—one can only repeat, God help us.

There is, of course, a certain excuse for fear. The time of change is upon us. The need for change has taken hold of us. We are changing, we have got to change, and we can no more help it than leaves can help going yellow and coming loose in autumn, or than bulbs can help shoving their little green spikes out of the ground in spring. We are changing, we are in the throes of change, and the change will be a great one. Instinctively, we feel it. Intuitively, we know it. And we are frightened. Because change hurts. And also, in the periods of serious transition, everything is uncertain, and living things are most vulnerable.

But what of it? Granted all the pains and dangers and uncertainties, there is no excuse for falling into a state of funk. If we come to think of it, every child that is begotten and born is a seed of change, a danger to its mother, at childbirth a great pain, and after birth, a new responsibility, a new change. If we fell into a state of funk about it, we should cease having children altogether. *If* we fall into a state of funk, indeed, the best thing is to have no children. But why fall into a state of funk?

Why not look things in the face like men, and like women? A woman who is going to have a child says to herself: Yes, I feel uncomfortable, sometimes I feel wretched, and I have a time of pain and danger ahead of me. But I have a good chance of coming through all right, especially if I am intelligent, and I bring a new life into the world. Somewhere I feel hopeful, even happy. So I must take the sour with the sweet. There is no birth without birth-pangs.—

It is the business of men, of course, to take the same attitude towards the birth of new conditions, new ideas, new emotions. And sorry to say, most modern men don't. They fall into a state of funk. We all of us know that ahead of us lies a great social change, a great social readjustment. A few men look it in the face and try to realise what will be best. We none of us *know* what will be best. There is no ready-made solution. Ready-made solutions are almost the greatest danger of all. A change is a slow flux, which must happen bit by bit. And it must *happen*. You can't drive it like a steam-engine. But all the time you can be alert and intelligent about it, and watch for the next step, and watch for the direction of the main trend. Patience, alertness, intelligence, and a human goodwill and fearlessness, that is what you want in a time of change. Not funk.

Now England is on the brink of great changes, radical changes. Within the next fifty years the whole framework of our social life will be altered, will be greatly modified. The old world of our grandfathers is disappearing like thawing snow, and is as likely to cause a flood. What the world of our grandchildren will be, fifty years hence, we don't know. But in its social form it will be very different from our world of today. We've got to change. And in our power to change, in our capacity to make new intelligent adaptations to new conditions, in our readiness to admit and fulfil new needs, to give expression to new desires and new feelings, lies our hope and our health. Courage is the great word. Funk spells sheer disaster.

There is a great change coming, bound to come. The whole money arrangement will undergo a change: what, I don't know. The whole industrial system will undergo a change. Work will be different and pay will be different. The owning of property will be different. Class will be different, and human relations will be modified and perhaps simplified. If we are intelligent, alert and undaunted, then life will be much better, more generous, more spontaneous, more vital, less basely materialistic. If we fall into a state of funk, impotence and persecution, then things may be very much worse than they are now. It is up to us. It is up to men to be men. While men are courageous and willing to change, nothing terribly bad can happen. But once men fall into a state of funk, with the inevitable accompaniment of bullying and repression, then only bad things can happen. To be firm is one thing. But bullying is another. And bullying of any sort whatsoever can have nothing but disastrous results. And when the mass falls into a state of funk, and you have mass-bullying, then catastrophe is near.

Change in the whole social system is inevitable not merely because conditions change—though partly for that reason—but because people themselves change. We change. You and I, we change and change vitally, as the years go on. New feelings arise in us, old values depreciate, new values arise. Things we thought we wanted most intensely we realise we don't care about. The things we built our lives on crumble and disappear, and the process is painful. But it is not tragic. A tadpole that has so gaily waved its tail in the water must feel very sick when the tail begins to drop off and little legs begin to sprout. The tail was its dearest, gayest, most active member, all its little life was in its tail. And now the tail must go. It seems rough on the tadpole: but the little green frog in the grass is a new gem, after all.

As a novelist, I feel it is the change inside the individual which is my real concern. The great social change interests me and troubles me, but it is not my field. I know a change is coming—but I know we must have a more generous, more human system, based on the life values and not on the money values. That I know. But what steps to take I don't know. Other men know better.

My field is to know the feelings inside a man, and to make new feelings conscious. What really torments civilised people is that they are full of feelings they know nothing about; they can't realise them, they can't fulfil them, they can't *live* them. And so they are tortured. It is like having energy you can't use—it destroys you. And feelings are a form of vital energy.

I am convinced that the majority of people today have good, generous feelings which they can never know, never experience, because of some fear, some repression. I do not believe that people would be villains, thieves, murderers and sexual criminals if they were freed from legal restraint. On the contrary, I think the vast majority would be much more generous, good-hearted and decent if they felt they dared be. I am convinced that people want to be more decent, more good-hearted than our social system of money and grab allows them to be. The awful fight for money, into which we are all forced, hurts our good-nature more than we can bear. I am sure this is true of a vast number of people.

And the same is true of our sexual feelings: only worse. There, we start all wrong. Consciously, there is supposed to be no such thing as sex in the human being. As far as possible, we never speak of it, never mention it, never, if we can help it, even think of it. It is disturbing. It is—somehow—wrong.

The whole trouble with sex is that we daren't speak of it and think of it naturally. We are not secretly sexual villains. We are not secretly sexually depraved. We are just human beings with living sex. We are all right, if we had not this unaccountable and disastrous *fear* of sex. I know, when I was a lad of eighteen, I used to remember with shame and rage, in the morning, the sexual thoughts and desires I had had the night before. Shame, and rage, and terror lest anybody else should have to know. And I *hated* the self that I had been, the night before.

Most boys are like that, and it is, of course, utterly wrong. The boy that had excited sexual thoughts and feelings was the living, warm-hearted, passionate me. The boy that in the morning remembered these feelings with such fear, shame and rage was the social, mental me: perhaps a little priggish, and certainly in a state of funk. But the two were divided against one another. A boy divided against himself: a girl divided against herself: a people divided against itself: it is a disastrous condition.

And it was a long time before I was able to say to myself: I am *not* going to be ashamed of my sexual thoughts and desires, they are me myself, they are part of my life. I am going to accept myself sexually as I accept myself mentally and spiritually, and know that I am one time one thing, one time another, but I am always myself. My sex is me as my mind is me, and nobody will make me feel shame about it.—

It is long since I came to that decision. But I remember, how much freer I felt, how much warmer and more sympathetic towards people. I had no longer anything to hide from them, no longer anything to be in a funk about, lest they should find it out. My sex was me, like my mind and my spirit. And the other man's sex was him, as his mind was him, and his spirit was him. And the woman's sex was her, as her mind and spirit were herself too. And once this quiet admission is made, it is wonderful how much deeper and more real the human sympathy flows. And it wonderful how difficult the admission is to make, for man or woman: the tacit, natural admission, that allows the natural warm flow of the blood-sympathy, without repression and holding back.

I remember when I was a very young man, I was enraged, when with a woman, if I was reminded of her sexual actuality. I only wanted to be aware of her personality, her mind and spirit. The other had to be fiercely shut out. Some part of the natural sympathy for a woman had to be shut away, cut off. There was a mutilation in the relationship all the time.

Now, in spite of the hostility of society, I have learned a little better. Now I know that a woman is her sexual self too, and I can feel the normal sex sympathy with her. And this silent sympathy is utterly different from desire or anything rampant or lurid. If I can really sympathise with a woman in her sexual self, it is just a form of warm-heartedness and compassionateness, the most natural life-flow in the world. And it may be a woman of seventy-five, or a child of two, it is the same. But our civilisation, with its horrible fear and funk and repression and bullying, has almost destroyed the natural flow of common sympathy, between men and men and men and women.

And it is this that I want to restore into life: just the natural warm flow of common sympathy between man and man, man and woman. Many people hate it, of course. Many men hate it that one should tacitly take them for sexual, physical men instead of mere social and mental personalities. Many women hate it the same. Some, the worst, are in a state of rabid funk. The papers call me "lurid", and a "dirty-minded fellow." One woman, evidently a woman of education and means, wrote to me out of the blue: "You, who are a mixture of the missing-link and the chimpanzee etc"—and told me my name stank in men's nostrils: though since she was Mrs Something or other, she might have said women's nostrils.—And these people think they are being perfectly well-bred and perfectly "right." They are safe inside the convention, which also agrees that we are sexless creatures and social beings merely, cold and bossy and assertive, cowards safe inside a convention.

Now I am one of the least lurid of mortals, and I don't at all mind being likened to a chimpanzee. If there is one thing I don't like it is cheap and promiscuous sex. If there is one thing I insist on it is that sex is a delicate, vulnerable, vital thing, that you mustn't fool with. If there is one thing I deplore it is heartless sex. Sex must be a real flow, a real flow of sympathy, generous and warm, and not a trick thing, or a moment's excitation, or a mere bit of bullying.

And if I write a book about the sex relations of a man and a woman, it is not because I want all men and women to begin having indiscriminate lovers and love-affairs, off the reel.* All this horrid scramble of love-affairs and prostitution is only part of the funk, bravado and *doing it on purpose*. And bravado and *doing it on purpose* is just as unpleasant and hurtful as repression, just as much a sign of secret fear.

What you have to do is to get out of the state of funk, sex funk. And to do so, you've got to be perfectly decent, and you have to accept sex fully in the consciousness. Accept sex in the consciousness, and let the normal physical awareness come back, between you and other people. Be tacitly and simply aware of the sexual being in every man and woman, child and animal: and unless the man or woman is a bully, be sympathetically aware. It is the most important thing just now, this gentle physical awareness. It keeps us tender and alive at a moment when the great danger is to go brittle, hard, and in some way dead.

Accept the sexual, physical being of your self, and of every other creature. Don't be afraid of it. Don't be afraid of the physical functions. Don't be afraid of the so-called obscene words. There is nothing wrong with the words. It is your fear that makes them bad, your endless fear. It is your fear which cuts you off physically even from your nearest and dearest. And when men and women are physically cut-off, they become at last dangerous, bullying, cruel. Conquer the fear of sex, and restore the natural flow. Restore even the so-called obscene words, which are part of the natural flow.* If you don't, if you don't put back a bit of the old warmth into life, there is savage disaster ahead.

MAKING PICTURES

On their way to Barcelona in April 1929, the Lawrences paused briefly in Carcassonne; while there Lawrence wrote to Nancy Pearn on 10 April: 'I heard that *The Studio* wanted me to do an article on my pictures – I'll do it as soon as I sit still – this week-end if possible' (*Letters*, vii. 249). As he later explained to Pollinger in October (vii. 536), he had heard of the request through the American publisher, Albert Boni. Lawrence did not know in April that Boni's interest stemmed from his ownership of *Creative Art*, a New York magazine 'of fine and applied art' which simply consisted of an issue of the *Studio* (published in London) with the addition of an American supplement.[1] During their conversations in Paris in April, when Boni tried to persuade Lawrence that he should become his American publisher, Boni asked Lawrence if he would 'write an article about the pictures for *The Studio*'; Lawrence, 'though a bit surprised', agreed to try (vii. 536). Boni knew that the volume of Lawrence's paintings was in the course of production by the Mandrake Press; he did not reveal the connection between *Studio* and *Creative Art*; indeed, not until the summer of 1929 was Lawrence aware – 'from an American friend' (vii. 536) – of the existence of the American magazine. However, Lawrence proceeded to honour the undertaking he had given.

On 15 April, only five days after his initial letter to Nancy Pearn, he wrote again, from Barcelona: 'I enclose article for the *Studio* on "Making Pictures." Hope you can make it out – and will you let them have it – and will you ask them to put in the name of the Japanese artist [Ito] who is in vogue in Paris and does pencilly nudes – I can't remember names' (vii. 251). The article was written on headed notepaper from the Hôtel de la Cité in Carcassonne which the Lawrences had left on 10 April. Nancy Pearn, having acknowledged receipt of the manuscript on the 17th, told Lawrence on the 25th that 'Ten guineas is as high as we could get the "*Studio*" to rise for your "MAKING PICTURES" article: this being above their usual rate.' Generous as usual towards specialist

[1] The art critic and author Lee Simonson (1888–1967) edited *Creative Art*, May 1928 – November 1929.

publications, he responded on 1 May: 'Just have yours about £10, for the *Studio* article. I suppose these little papers really can't pay more – and if they can't, I don't mind' (vii. 269 and n. 2). Instead of sending payment to his agent, the *Studio* directed the 10 guineas to Lawrence himself; business-like, Lawrence informed Pollinger and, characteristically methodical in financial matters, 'forwarded the cheque to the bank' (vii. 348).

In June 1929 the American magazine *Vanity Fair* showed interest in publishing 'Making Pictures'. Nancy Pearn informed Lawrence on 14 June that they 'are planning to use it in their July issue', and on 30 July she confirmed that $100 would be paid for permission.

The article appeared in *Studio* in July 1929; it was illustrated with Lawrence's oil painting, *Finding of Moses*, indifferently reproduced in black and white. *Creative Art* published the article in the same month. It appeared in the August issue of *Vanity Fair* with the explanatory headline: 'An English Novelist, Turned Painter, Discovers That Creative Art Is a Thing of the Spirit'. It was first collected in *Assorted Articles* despite Lawrence's own view that 'Making Pictures' did not 'quite seem to fit the rest' (vii. 549–60).

MAKING PICTURES

ONE has to eat one's own words. I remember I used to assert, perhaps I have even written it: Everything that can possibly be painted has been painted, every brush-stroke that can possibly be laid on canvas has been laid on. The visual arts are at a dead end.—Then suddenly, at the age of forty, I begin painting myself and am fascinated.

Still, going through the Paris picture-shops this year of grace,* and seeing the Dufys and Chiricos etc, and the Japanese Ito* with his wish-wash nudes with pearl-button eyes, the same weariness comes over one. They are all so would-be, they make such efforts. They at least have nothing to paint. In the midst of them, a graceful Friescz flower-piece, or a blotting-paper Laurencin* seems a masterpiece. At least here is a bit of *natural* expression in paint: trivial enough, when compared to the big painters, but still, as far as they go, real.

What about myself, then? What am I doing, bursting into paint? I am a writer, I ought to stick to ink. I have found my medium of expression: why, at the age of forty, should I suddenly want to try another?

Things happen, and we have no choice. If Maria Huxley hadn't come rolling up to our house near Florence with four rather large canvases,* one of which she had busted, and presented them to me because they had been abandoned in her house, I might never have started in on a real picture in my life. But those nice stretched canvases were too tempting. We had been painting doors and window-frames in the house, so there was a little stock of oil, turps, and colour in powder, such as one buys from an Italian drogheria. There were several brushes for house-painting. There was a canvas on which the unknown owner had made a start—mud-grey, with the beginnings of a red-haired man. It was a grimy and ugly beginning, and the young man who had made it had wisely gone no further. He certainly had had no inner compulsion: nothing in him, as far as paint was concerned; or if there was anything in him, it had stayed in, and only a bit of the mud-grey "group" had come out.

So for the sheer fun of covering a surface and obliterating that mud-grey, I sat on the floor with the canvas propped against a chair—and with my house-paint brushes and colours in little casseroles, I disappeared into that canvas. It is to me the most exciting moment—when you have a blank canvas and a big brush full of wet colour, and you plunge. It is just like diving in a pond—then you start frantically to swim. As far as I am concerned, it is like swimming in a baffling current and being rather frightened and very thrilled, gasping and striking out for all you're worth. The knowing eye watches sharp as a needle: but the picture comes clean out of instinct, intuition, and sheer physical action. Once the instinct and intuition get into the brush-tip, the picture *happens*, if it is to be a picture at all.

At least, so my first picture happened—the one I have called *A Holy Family*.* In a couple of hours there it all was, man, woman, child, blue shirt, red shawl, pale room—all in the rough, but, as far as I am concerned, a picture. The struggling comes later. But the picture itself comes in the first rush, or not at all. It is only when the picture has come into being that one can struggle and make it *grow* to completion.

Ours is an excessively conscious age. We *know* so much, we feel so little. I have lived enough among painters and around studios to have had all the theories—and how contradictory they are—rammed down my throat. A man has to have a gizzard like an ostrich to digest all the brass tacks and wire nails of modern art theories. Perhaps all the theories, the utterly indigestible theories, like nails in an ostrich's gizzard, do indeed help to grind small and make digestible all the emotional and aesthetic pabulum that lies in an artist's soul. But they can serve no other purpose. Not even corrective. The modern theories of art make real pictures impossible. You only get theses, expositions, critical ventures in paint, and fantastic negations. And the bit of fantasy that may lie in the negation—as in a Dufy or a Chirico—is just the bit that has escaped theory and perhaps saves the picture. Theorise, theorise all you like—but when you start to paint, shut your theoretic eyes and go for it with instinct and intuition.

Myself, I have always loved pictures, the pictorial art. I never went to an art-school, I have had only one real lesson in painting in all my life. But of course I was thoroughly drilled in "drawing," the solid-geometry sort, and the plaster-cast sort, and the pin-wire sort. I think the solid-geometry sort, with all the elementary laws of perspective, was valuable. But the pin-wire sort and the plaster-cast light-and-shade sort was harmful. Plaster casts and pin-wire outlines were always so repulsive to me, I quite early decided I "couldn't draw." I couldn't draw, so I could never do anything on my own. When I did paint jugs of flowers or bread and potatoes or cottages in a lane, copying from Nature, the result wasn't very thrilling. Nature was more or less of a plaster cast to me—those plaster-cast heads of Minerva* or figures of Dying Gladiators which so unnerved me as a youth. The "object," be it what it might, was always slightly repulsive to me once I sat down in front of it, to paint it. So of course I decided I couldn't really paint. Perhaps I can't. But I verily believe I can make pictures, which is to me all that matters in this respect. The art of painting consists in making pictures—and so many artists accomplish canvases without coming within miles of painting a picture.

I learnt to paint from copying other pictures—usually reproductions, sometimes even photographs. When I was a boy, how I concentrated over it! copying some perfectly worthless scene of an old bridge with a gipsy-van, at twilight: copying from a reproduction in some magazine. I worked with almost dry water-colour, stroke by stroke, covering half a square-inch at a time, each square-inch perfect and completed, proceeding in a kind of mosaic advance, with no idea at all of laying on a broad wash. Hours and hours of intense concentration, inch by inch progress, in a method entirely wrong—and yet those copies of mine managed, when they were finished, to have a certain something that delighted me: a certain glow of life, which was beauty to me. A picture lives with the life you put into it. If you put no *life* into it—no thrill, no concentration of delight or exaltation of visual discovery—then the picture is dead, like so many canvases, no matter how much thorough and scientific work is put into it. Even if you only copy a purely banal reproduction of an old bridge, some sort of keen, delighted awareness of the old bridge or of its atmosphere, or the image it has kindled inside you, can go over on to the paper and give a certain touch of life to a banal conception.

It needs a certain purity of spirit to be an artist, of any sort. The motto which should be written over every School of Art is: "Blessed are the pure in spirit, for theirs is the kingdom of heaven."* But by "pure in spirit" we mean pure in spirit. An artist may be a profligate and from the social point of view, a scoundrel. But if he can paint a nude woman, or a couple of apples, so that they are a living image, then he was pure in spirit, and, for the time being, his was the kingdom of heaven. This is the beginning of all art, visual or literary or musical: be pure in spirit. It isn't the same as goodness. It is much more difficult and nearer the divine. The divine isn't only good, it is all things.

One may see the divine in natural objects: I saw it today, in the frail, lovely little camellia flowers on long stems, here on the bushy and splendid flower-stalls of the Ramblas* in Barcelona. They were different from the usual fat camellias, more like gardenias, poised delicately, and I saw them like a vision. So now, I could paint them. But if I had bought a handful, and started in to paint them "from nature," then I should have lost them. By staring at them I should have lost them. I have learnt by experience. It is personal experience only. Some men can only get at a vision by staring themselves blind, as it were: like Cézanne. Staring kills my vision. That's why I could never "draw," at school. One was supposed to draw what one stared at.

The only thing one can look into, stare into, and see only vision, is the vision itself: the visionary image. That is why I am glad I never had any training but the self-imposed training of copying other men's pictures. As I grew more ambitious, I copied Leader's landscapes, and Frank Brangwyn's cartoon-like pictures, then Peter de Wint and Girtin water-colours.* I can never be sufficiently grateful for the series of English Water-Colour Painters, published by the Studio in eight parts, when I was a youth. I had only six of the eight parts, but they were invaluable to me. I copied them with the greatest joy, and found some of them extremely difficult. Surely I put as much labour into copying from those water-colour reproductions as most modern art-students put into all their years of study. And I had enormous profit from it. I not only acquired a considerable technical skill in handling water-colour—let any man try copying the English water-colour artists, from Paul Sandby* and Peter de Wint and Girtin up to Frank Brangwyn and the impressionists like Brabazon,* and he will see how much skill he requires—but also I developed my visionary awareness. And I believe one can only develop one's visionary awareness by close contact with the vision itself: that is, by knowing pictures, real vision-pictures, and by dwelling on them, and really, dwelling in them. It is a great delight, to dwell in a picture. But it needs a purity of spirit, a sloughing of vulgar sensation and vulgar interest, and above all, vulgar contact, that few people know how to perform. Oh, if art-schools only taught that! If, instead of saying: This drawing is wrong, incorrect, badly drawn, etc.—they would say: Isn't this in bad taste? isn't it insensitive? isn't that an insentient curve with none of the delicate awareness of life in it?—But art is treated all wrong. It is treated as if it were a science, which it is not. Art is a form of religion, minus the Ten Commandment business,* which is sociological. Art is a form of supremely delicate awareness and atonement—meaning at-oneness, the state of being at one with the object. Art is the great atonement in delight—for I can never look on art save as a form of delight.

All my life, I have from to time gone back to paint, because it gave me a form of delight that words can never give. Perhaps the joy in words goes deeper, and is for that reason more unconscious. The *conscious* delight is certainly stronger in paint. I have gone back to paint for real pleasure—and by paint I mean copying, copying either in oils or water. I think the greatest pleasure I ever got came from copying Fra Angelico's *Flight into Egypt* and Lorenzetti's big picture of the Thebaïd, in each case working from [a] photograph and putting in my own colour: or perhaps even more, a Carpaccio picture in Venice.* Then I *really* learned what life, what powerful life has been put into every curve, every motion of a great picture. Purity of spirit, sensitive awareness, intense eagerness to portray an inward vision, how it all comes back to you, from a great picture, particularly an Italian. The English water-colours are frail in comparison—and the French and the flemings are shallow—The great Rembrandt I never tried to copy, though I loved him intensely, even more than I do now: and Rubens I never tried,* though I always liked him so much. Only he seemed so spread out. But I have copied Peter de Hooch, and Vandyck,* and others that I forget. Yet none of them gave me the deep thrill of the Italians, Carpaccio, or the lovely *Death of Procris** in the National Gallery, or that *Wedding* with the scarlet legs, in the Uffizi, or a Giotto from Padua.* I must have made many copies in my day, and got endless joy out of them.

Then suddenly, by having a blank canvas, I discovered I could make a picture myself. That is the point, to make a picture on a blank canvas. And I was forty before I had the real courage to try. Then it became an orgy, making pictures.

I have learnt now not to work from objects, not to have models, not to have a technique. Sometimes, for a water-colour, I have worked direct from a model. But it always spoils the *picture*. I can only use a model when the picture is already made: then I can look at the model to get some detail which the vision failed me with, or to modify something which I *feel* is unsatisfactory and I don't know why. Then a model may give a suggestion. But at the beginning, a model only spoils the picture. The picture must all come out of the artist's inside awareness of forms and figures. We can call it memory, but it is more than memory. It is the image as it lives in the consciousness, alive like a vision, but unknown. I believe many people have in their consciousness living images that would give them the greatest joy to bring out. But they don't know how to go about it. And teaching only hinders them.

To me, a picture has delight in it, or it isn't a picture. The saddest pictures of Piero della Francesca or Sodoma or Goya* have still that indescribable delight that goes with the real picture. Modern critics talk a lot about ugliness, but I never saw a real picture that seemed to me ugly. The theme may be ugly, there may be a terrifying, distressing, almost repulsive quality, as in El Greco.* Yet it is all, in some strange way, swept up in the delight of a picture. No artist, even the gloomiest, ever painted a picture without the curious delight in image-making.

PORNOGRAPHY AND OBSCENITY

It is clear from a letter of 19 April 1929, written in Mallorca, that Lawrence had been invited to contribute an article to *This Quarter*, a new magazine soon to be launched in Paris by Edward Titus who, in the following month, would publish an 'Unabridged Popular Edition' of *Lady Chatterley's Lover*. The Lawrences had arrived in Mallorca only on 17 April, having left Paris on the 7th. Lawrence himself was exhausted from his four-week stay in Paris: he had been negotiating with Titus over *Lady Chatterley's Lover*, with the Crosbys over their edition of *The Escaped Cock*, with Albert Boni about his American publications and, in addition, satisfying the diverse social demands placed on a celebrated writer in the French capital. From Paris he and Frieda made their way to Mallorca via Orléans, Lyons, Carcassonne, Perpignan and Barcelona. So, writing to Titus on 19 April, Lawrence could reasonably plead that he was 'too unsettled for the moment' (*Letters*, vii. 259) but would not forget Titus's invitation. Nor did he. Ten days later he sent the manuscript of 'Pornography and Obscenity' to Nancy Pearn for typing. He also agreed to Titus's request that the article was not to be offered for publication by 'anybody else, either in England or America' (vii. 268). Lawrence knew that Titus would not 'be able to pay much' (vii. 269) but he regarded the article as a friendly gesture in return for Titus's willingness to bring out the Paris edition of 'Our Lady'. The article (of about 4,000 words) duly appeared in *This Quarter*, in the issue covering July–September 1929.

Titus had not been slow to recognise Lawrence's notoriety following police action over *Lady Chatterley's Lover* and *Pansies* typescripts, in January 1929, and the consequent Parliamentary debate on 28 February about the censorship of documents regarded by officialdom as 'obscene'. When to these events were added the police raid on the Warren Gallery and the confiscation of some Lawrence paintings in July, he became – from a publisher's viewpoint – irresistible as a person to give vent to his feelings on censorship. Faber & Faber seized the opportunity. In late August or early September they invited Lawrence to write on the subject for their *Criterion Miscellany*; unknown to him, they also invited the

Home Secretary responsible for the police actions in January, Joynson Hicks (now Viscount Brentford), to write on the same topic. As E. M. Forster was later to remark: 'It was a happy and indeed a witty thought of the publishers to induce the most remarkable of our novelists and our most notorious Home Secretary to write pamphlets on the subject of indecency.'[1] When the Faber invitation arrived, Lawrence hesitated; he told Laurence Pollinger at Curtis Brown's literary agency on 5 September:

I don't know if I'll do the Faber article – what's the good! I'm sick to death of the British Public, all publishers, and all magazines – and feel I never want to see a word of mine in public print again. But I'll read the 'Obscenity' article [written for Titus] over, and if it interests me in itself, I'll lengthen it. Random House might publish it as a pamphlet. As for Faber & Faber – I should get about £10– out of them and a batch of insults – What's the point! But I'll let you know finally about this, this week. (vii. 467–8)

A mere three days later he wrote again to Pollinger:

Here is the conclusion of the article on *Obscenity and Pornography*. It now makes about ten thousand words. You can give it to Faber & Faber if you like, for their monthly criterion and their rather silly little shilling books. They are almost sure to reject it: which will be perhaps just as well. If they accept, they may leave out small bits, if they want to, but they must tell me first. (vii. 470–1)

Somewhat to Lawrence's surprise, Fabers were prepared to 'risk the obscenity article' so long as he omitted the allegation that 'the books of Sir James Barrie and Mr Galsworthy . . . are far more pornographical than the liveliest story in the *Decameron*: because they tickle and excite to private masturbation, which the wholesome Boccaccio never does' (vii. 503 and n. 2).[2] Lawrence agreed to the deletion as he told Pollinger on 29 September and again on 3 October.

Matters then moved swiftly. Lawrence returned the signed contract to Pollinger on 11 October; he had read proofs by 1 November; and the paperback edition of *Pornography and Obscenity*, No. 5 of *Criterion Miscellany*, was published on the 14th (vii. 526, 549). Seemingly a review had appeared by the 18th; it has not been identified but it was sufficiently hostile to provoke Lawrence's remark to Pollinger: 'I'm glad *Obscenity* is biting through their skin, as I intended it should. Mr Lawrence not

[1] *Nation and Athenaeum*, 11 January 1930, xlvi. 508. Quoted in Draper 318.

[2] See 252:39–253:3. (Unfortunately the relevant file at Faber & Faber has not survived.) Textual collation suggests that other changes were introduced without DHL's knowledge: see, for example, 243:26, 244:6, 252:16–24.

only believes what he says, he knows it's true' (vii. 568). Similarly, while assuring Titus that the pamphlet had not provoked official displeasure in England, he was obviously pleased to report that 'the people hate it' (vii. 569). This view reappears in a letter to his elder sister, Emily King, who would receive a complimentary copy – 'Stirs them up a bit. That Jix [Joynson Hicks] is a mealy-mouthed worm' – a sentiment repeated to Pollinger also on 30 November: 'what a mealy-mouthed maggot that Jix is!' (vii. 582, 584 and n. 4). The explanation for these outbursts against 'Jix' lies in his article in *Everyman* on 28 November, entitled 'HOW THE CENSORSHIP WORKS', justifying his arguments in his own Faber pamphlet, *Do We Need a Censor?* He expressed satisfaction with the reception of the pamphlet except from 'a certain section of the community who prefer to put liberty before decency'. He went on to question what 'the average father of a family would say if he found his daughter reading Mr D. H. Lawrence's latest pamphlet on pornography'; he alluded to 'an exhibition of pictures . . . which it was alleged were indecent . . . and the exhibition was closed'; and he recalled how 'two poems by a well-known man were caught in the post, quite accidentally – not under the Home Secretary's warrant, but simply on the haphazard opening by the Customs authorities of a parcel to see whether it contained anything contraband. It was found to contain a most pernicious poem.' The opening of the Home Office file in 1999 on Lawrence's *Pansies* reveals the extent to which Jix was economical with the truth.[3]

Lawrence was overjoyed with the sales of his pamphlet: '1200 a week', he told his Italian friend and publisher, 'Pino' Orioli; 'over 6,000 – more than any of the others', Charles Lahr was told on the same day, 9 December 1929 (vii. 588–9). And in 'the others' he included H. G. Wells's *Imperialism and the Open Conspiracy* – No. 3 in the *Criterion Miscellany* – as well as No. 6, Jix's *Do We Need a Censor?*, both published, along with Lawrence's pamphlet, in November 1929.

Faber & Faber issued a hardback edition in January 1930; the first American edition was published by Alfred Knopf in New York on 28 February 1930; and the first collected edition came from Faber & Faber – *Pornography and So On* on 24 September 1936 (a month before the essay was included in *Phoenix*). The text in all these cases was expurgated as Faber & Faber had requested; the unexpurgated text printed here follows the manuscript of the expanded version.

[3] See James T. Boulton, 'D. H. Lawrence's *Pansies* and the State, 1929', *Journal of the D. H. Lawrence Society*, ed. Bethan Jones (Eastwood, Autumn 2000), pp. 5–16.

PORNOGRAPHY AND OBSCENITY

What they are depends, as usual, entirely on the individual. What is pornography to one man is the laughter of genius to another.

The word itself, we are told, means "pertaining to harlots"—the graph of the harlot.* But nowadays, what is a harlot? If she was a woman who took money from a man in return for going to bed with him—really, most wives sold themselves, in the past, and plenty of harlots gave themselves, when they felt like it, for nothing. If a woman hasn't got a tiny streak of a harlot in her, she's a dry stick as a rule. And probably most harlots had somewhere a streak of womanly generosity. Why be so cut and dried? The law is a dreary thing, and its judgments have nothing to do with life.

The same with the word *obscene*: nobody knows what it means.* Suppose it were derived from *obscena*: that which might not be represented on the stage,—how much further are you? None! What is obscene to Tom is not obscene to Lucy or Joe, and really, the meaning of a word has to wait for majorities to decide it. If a play shocks ten people in an audience, and doesn't shock the remaining five hundred, then it is obscene to ten and innocuous to five hundred: hence, the play is not obscene, by majority. But *Hamlet* shocked all the Cromwellian Puritans, and shocks nobody today, and some Aristophanes* shocks everybody today, and didn't galvanise the later Greeks at all, apparently. Man is a changeable beast, and words change their meanings with him, and things are not what they seemed, and what's what becomes what isn't, and if we think we know where we are it's only because we are so rapidly being translated to somewhere else. We have to leave everything to the majority, everything to the majority, everything to the mob, the mob, the mob. They know what is obscene and what isn't, they do. If the lower ten million doesn't know better than the upper ten men, then there's something wrong with mathematics. Take a vote on it! Show hands, and prove it by count! Vox populi, vox Dei. Odi profanum vulgum. Profanum vulgum! profanum vulgum.*

So it comes down to this: if you are talking to the mob, the meaning of your words is the mob-meaning, decided by majority. As somebody wrote to me: the American law on obscenity is very plain, and America is going to enforce the law.—Quite, my dear, quite, quite, quite! The mob knows all about obscenity. Mild little words that rhyme with spit or farce are the height of obscenity. Supposing a printer put "h" in the place of "p", by mistake, in that mere word spit? Then the great American public knows that this man has committed an obscenity, an indecency, that his act was lewd, and as a compositor he was pornographical. You can't tamper with the great public, British or American. *Vox populi, vox Dei*, don't you know. If you don't we'll let you know it.—At the same time, this *vox Dei* shouts with praise over movie-pictures and books and newspaper accounts that seem, to a sinful nature like mine, completely disgusting and obscene. Like a real prude and Puritan, I have to look the other way. When obscenity becomes mawkish, which is its palatable form for the public, and when the *Vox populi, vox Dei* is hoarse with sentimental indecency, then I have to steer away, like a Pharisee, afraid of being contaminated.* There is a certain kind of sticky universal pitch that I refuse to touch.

So again, it comes down to this: you accept the majority, the mob, and its decisions, or you don't. You bow down before the *Vox populi, vox Dei*, or you plug your ears not to hear its obscene howl. You perform your antics to please the vast public, *Deus ex machina*,* or you refuse to perform for the public at all, unless now and then to pull its elephantine and ignominious leg.

When it comes to the meaning of anything, even the simplest word, then you must pause. Because there are two great categories of meaning, forever separate. There is mob-meaning, and there is individual meaning. Take even the word *bread*. The mob-meaning is merely: stuff made with white flour into loaves, that you eat.—But take the individual meaning of the word *bread*: the white, the brown, the corn-pone, the home-made, the smell of bread just out of the oven, the crust, the crumb, the unleavened bread, the shew-bread, the staff of life, sourdough bread, cottage loaves, French bread, Viennese bread, black bread, a yesterday's loaf, rye, Graham, barley, rolls, Bretzeln, Kringeln, scones, damper, matsen—* there is no end to it all, and the word *bread* will take you to the ends of time and space, and far-off down avenues of memory. But this is individual. The word *bread* will take the individual off on his own journey, and its meaning will be his own meaning, based on his own genuine imaginative reactions. And when a word comes to us in its individual character, and starts in us the individual responses, it is a great pleasure to us. The American advertisers have discovered this, and some of the cunningest American literature is to be found in advertisements of soap-suds, for example. These advertisements are *almost* prose-poems. They give the word soap-suds a bubbly, shiny individual meaning which is very skilfully poetic, would, perhaps, be quite poetic to the mind which could forget that the poetry was bait on a hook.

Business is discovering the individual, dynamic meaning of words, and poetry is losing it. Poetry more and more tends to far-fetch its word-meanings, and this results once again in mob-meanings, which arouse only a mob-reaction in the individual. For every man has a mob self and an individual self, in varying proportions. Some men are almost all mob-self, incapable of imaginative individual responses. The worst specimens of mob-self are usually to be found in the professions, lawyers, professors, clergymen and so on. The business man, much maligned, has a tough outside mob-self, and a scared, floundering, yet still alive individual self. The public, which is feeble-minded like an idiot, will never be able to preserve its individual reactions from the tricks of the exploiter. The public is always exploited and always will be exploited. The methods of exploitation merely vary. Today the public is tickled into laying the golden egg. With imaginative words and individual meanings it is tricked into giving the great goose-cackle of mob-acquiescence. Vox populi, vox Dei. It has always been so, and will always be so. Why? Because the public has not enough wit to distinguish between mob-meanings and individual-meanings. The mass is forever vulgar, because it can't distinguish between its own original feelings and feelings which are diddled into existence by the exploiter. The public is always profane, because it is controlled from the outside, by the trickster, and never from the inside, by its own sincerity. The mob is always obscene, because it is always second-hand.

Which brings us back to our subject of pornography and obscenity. The reaction to any word may be, in any individual, either a mob-reaction or an individual reaction. It is up to the individual to ask himself: Is my reaction individual, or am I merely reacting from my mob self?—

When it comes to the so-called obscene words, I should say that hardly one person in a million escapes mob-reaction. The first reaction is almost sure to be mob-reaction, mob-indignation, mob-condemnation. And the mob gets no further. But the real individual has second thoughts, and says: Am I *really* shocked? Do I *really* feel outraged and indignant?—And the answer of any individual who has ever got so far as to ask himself the question, sincerely, is bound to be: No, I am not shocked, not outraged, nor indignant. I know the word, and take it for what it is, and

I am not going to be jockeyed into making a mountain out of a molehill, not for all the law in the world.—

Now if the use of a few so-called obscene words will startle man or woman out of a mob-habit into an individual state, well and good. And word-prudery is so universal a mob-habit that it is time we were startled out of it.

But still we have only tackled obscenity, and the problem of pornography goes even deeper. When a man is startled into his individual self, he still may not be able to know, inside himself, whether Rabelais is or is not pornographic: and over Aretino or even Boccaccio* he may perhaps puzzle in vain, torn between different emotions.

One essay on Pornography, I remember, comes to the conclusion that pornography in art is that which is calculated to arouse sexual desire, or sexual excitement. And stress is laid on the fact, whether the author or artist *intended* to arouse sexual feelings. It is the old vexed question of intention, become so dull today, when we know how strong and influential our unconscious intentions are. And why a man should be held guilty of his conscious intentions, and innocent of his unconscious intentions, I don't know, since every man is more made up of unconscious intentions than of conscious ones. I am what I am, not merely what I think I am.

However—!—We take it, I assume, that *pornography* is something base, something unpleasant. In short, we don't like it. And why don't we like it? Because it arouses sexual feelings?

I think not. No matter how hard we may pretend otherwise, most of us rather like a moderate rousing of our sex. It warms us, stimulates us like sunshine on a grey day. After a century or two of Puritanism, this is still true of most people. Only the mob-habit of condemning any form of sex is too strong to let us admit it naturally. —And there are, of course, many people who are genuinely repelled by the simplest and most natural stirring of sexual feeling. But these people are perverts, who have fallen into hatred of their fellow men: thwarted, disappointed, unfulfilled people, of whom, alas, our civilisation contains so many. And they nearly always enjoy some unsimple and unnatural form of sex excitement, secretly.

Even quite advanced art critics would try to make us believe that any picture or book which had "sex appeal" was ipso facto a bad book or picture. This is just canting hypocrisy. Half the great poems, pictures, music, stories of the whole world are great by virtue of the beauty of their sex appeal. Titian or Renoir, the Song of Solomon or *Jane Eyre*,

Mozart or *Annie Laurie*,* the loveliness is all interwoven with sex appeal, sex stimulus, call it what you will. Even Michael Angelo,* who rather hated sex, can't help filling the Cornucopia with phallic acorns. Sex is a very powerful, beneficial and necessary stimulus in human life, and we are all grateful when we feel its warm, natural flow through us, like a form of sunshine.

So we can dismiss the idea that sex appeal in art is pornography. It may be so to the grey Puritan, but the grey Puritan is a sick man, soul and body sick, so why should we bother about his hallucinations! Sex appeal, of course, varies enormously. There are endless different kinds, and endless degrees of each kind. Perhaps it may be argued that a mild degree of sex appeal is not pornographical, whereas a high degree is. But this is a fallacy. Boccaccio at his hottest seems to me less pornographical than *Pamela* or *Clarissa Harlowe** or even *Jane Eyre* or a host of modern books or films which pass uncensored. At the same time Wagner's *Tristan and Isolde** seems to me very near to pornography, and so, even, do some quite popular Christian hymns.

What is it, then? It isn't a question of sex appeal, merely: nor even a question of deliberate intention on the part of the author or artist to arouse sexual excitement. Rabelais sometimes had a deliberate intention, so, in a different way, did Boccaccio. And I'm sure poor Charlotte Bronte, or the authoress of *The Sheik** did *not* have any deliberate intention to stimulate sex feelings in the reader. Yet I find *Jane Eyre* verging towards pornography and Boccaccio seems to me always fresh and wholesome.

The British Home Secretary,* who prides himself on being a very sincere Puritan, grey, grey in every fibre, said with indignant sorrow in one of his outbursts on improper books: "—and these two young people, who had been perfectly pure up till that time, after reading this book went and had sexual intercourse together—!!!"—*One up to them*! is all we can answer. But the grey Guardian of British Morals seemed to think that if they had murdered one another, or worn each other to rags of nervous frustration, it would have been much better. The grey disease!

Then what is pornography, after all this? It isn't sex appeal or sex stimulus in art. It isn't even a deliberate intention on the part of the artist to arouse or excite sexual feelings. There's nothing wrong with sexual feelings in themselves, so long as they are straightforward and not sneaking or sly. The right sort of sex stimulus is invaluable to human daily life. Without it, the world grows grey. I would give everybody the gay Renaissance stories to read, they would help to shake off a lot of grey self-importance, which is our modern civilised disease.

But even I would censor genuine pornography, rigorously. It would not be very difficult. In the first place, genuine pornography is almost always underworld, it doesn't come into the open. In the second, you can recognise it by the insult it offers, invariably, to sex, and to the human spirit.

Pornography is the attempt to insult sex, to do dirt on it. This is unpardonable. Take the very lowest instances, the picture post-cards sold underhand, by the underworld, in most cities. What I have seen of them have been of an ugliness to make you cry. The insult to the human body, the insult to a vital human relationship! Ugly and cheap they make the human nudity, ugly and degraded they make the sexual act, trivial and cheap and nasty.

It is the same with the books they sell in the underworld. They are either so ugly they make you ill, or so fatuous you can't imagine anybody but a cretin or a moron reading them, or writing them.

It is the same with the dirty limericks that people tell after dinner, or the dirty stories one hears commercial travellers telling each other in a smoke-room. Occasionally there is a really funny one, that redeems a great deal. But usually they are just ugly, and repellant, and the so-called "humour" is just a trick of doing dirt on sex.

Now the human nudity of a great many modern people is just ugly and degraded, and the sexual act between modern people is too often the same, merely ugly and degrading. But this is nothing to be proud of. It is the catastrophe of our civilisation. I am sure no other civilisation, not even the Roman, has showed such a vast proportion of ignominious and degraded nudity, and ugly, squalid, dirty sex. Because no other civilisation has driven sex into the underworld, and nudity to the W. C.

The intelligent young, thank Heaven, seem determined to alter in these two respects. They are rescuing their young nudity from the stuffy, pornographical hole-and-corner underworld of their elders, and they refuse to be sneaking about the sexual relation. This is a change the elderly grey ones of course deplore, but it is in fact a very great change for the better, a real revolution.

But it is amazing how strong is the will in ordinary vulgar people, to do dirt on sex. It was one of my fond illusions, when I was young, that the ordinary healthy-seeming sort of men, in railway carriages or the smoke-room of an hotel or a pullman, were healthy in their feelings and had a wholesome rough devil-may-care attitude to sex. All wrong! All wrong! Experience teaches that common individuals of this sort have a disgusting attitude to sex, a disgusting contempt of it, a disgusting desire to insult it. If such fellows have intercourse with a woman, they triumphantly feel that they have done her dirt, and now she is lower, cheaper, more contemptible than she was before.

It is individuals of this sort that tell dirty stories, carry indecent picture post-cards, and know the indecent books. This is the great pornographical class—the really common men-in-the-street and women-in-the-street. They have as great a hate and contempt of sex as the greyest Puritan, and when an appeal is made to them, they are always on the side of the angels. They insist that a film-heroine shall be a neuter, a sexless thing of washed-out purity. They insist that real sex-feeling shall only be shown by the villain or villainess, low lust. They find a Titian nude or a Renoir really indecent, and they don't want their wives and daughters to see it.

Why? Because they have the grey disease of sex-hatred, coupled with the yellow disease of dirt-lust. The sex functions and the excrementary functions in the human body work so close together, yet they are, so to speak, utterly different in direction. Sex is a creative flow, the excrementary flow is towards dissolution, de-creation, if we may use such a word. In the really healthy human being the distinction between the two is instant, our profoundest instincts are perhaps our instincts of opposition between the two flows.

But in the degraded human being the deep instincts have gone dead, and then the two flows become identical. *This* is the secret of really vulgar people and of pornography: the sex flow and the excrement flow is the same thing to them. It happens when the psyche deteriorates, and the profound controlling instincts collapse. Then sex is dirt and dirt is sex, and sexual excitement becomes a playing with dirt, and any sign of sex in a woman becomes a show of her dirt. This is the condition of the common, vulgar human being whose name is legion, and who lifts his voice and it is the *Vox populi vox Dei*. And this is the source of all pornography.

And for this reason we must admit that *Jane Eyre* or Wagner's *Tristan* are much nearer to pornography than is Boccaccio. Wagner and Charlotte Bronte were both in the state where the strongest instincts have collapsed, and sex has become something slightly obscene, to be wallowed in, but despised. Mr. Rochester's sex passion is not "respectable" till Mr. Rochester is burnt, blinded, disfigured, and reduced to helpless dependence. Then, thoroughly humbled and humiliated, it may be merely admitted. All the previous titillations are slightly indecent, as in *Pamela* or *Mill on the Floss* or *Anna Karenin*.* As soon as there is sex excitement with a desire to spite the sexual feeling, to humiliate it and degrade it, the element of pornography enters.

For this reason, there is an element of pornography in nearly all nineteenth-century literature and very many so-called pure people have a nasty pornographical side to them, and never was the pornographical appetite stronger than it is today. It is a sign of a diseased condition of the body politic. But the way to treat the disease is not Puritanism and more Puritanism. That only covers up the tumour and makes it fester worse. The only way is to come out into the open with sex and sex stimulus. The real pornographer truly dislikes Boccaccio, because the fresh healthy naturalness of the Italian story-teller makes the modern pornographical shrimp feel the dirty worm he is. Today, Boccaccio should be given to everybody young or old, to read if they like. Only a natural fresh openness about sex will do us any good, now we are being swamped by secret or semi-secret pornography. And perhaps the Renaissance story-tellers, Boccaccio, Lasca* and the rest, are the best antidote we can find now, just as more plasters of Puritanism are the most harmful remedy we can resort to.

*The whole question of pornography seems to me a question of secrecy. Without secrecy there would be no pornography. But secrecy and modesty are two utterly different things. Secrecy has always an element of fear in it, amounting very often to hate. Modesty is gentle and reserved. Today, modesty is thrown to the winds even in the presence of the grey Home Secretaries. But secrecy is hugged, being a vice in itself. And the attitude of the grey ones is: Dear young ladies, you may abandon all modesty, so long as you hug your dirty little secret.—

This "dirty little secret" has become infinitely precious to the mob of people today. It is a kind of hidden sore or inflammation which, when rubbed or scratched, gives off sharp thrills that seem delicious. So the dirty little secret is rubbed and scratched more and more, till it becomes more and more secretly inflamed, and the nervous and psychic health of the individual is more and more impaired. One might easily say that half the love novels and half the love-films today depend entirely for their success on the secret rubbing of the dirty little secret. You can call this sex-excitement if you like, but it is sex-excitement of a secretive, furtive sort, quite special. The plain and simple sex excitement, quite open and wholesome, which you find in some Boccaccio stories is not for a minute to be confused with the furtive excitement aroused by rubbing the dirty little secret in all secrecy in modern best-sellers. This furtive, sneaking, cunning rubbing of an inflamed spot in the imagination is the very quick of modern pornography, and it is a beastly and very dangerous thing. You can't so easily expose it, because of its very furtiveness and its sneaking cunning. So the cheap and popular modern love-novel and love-film flourishes and is even praised by grey Home Secretaries and other moral guardians, because you get the sneaking thrill fumbling under all the purity of dainty underclothes, without one single gross word to let you know what is happening.

Without secrecy there would be no pornography. But if pornography is the result of sneaking secrecy, what is the result of pornography? What is the effect on the individual?

The effect on the individual is manifold, and always pernicious. But one effect is perhaps inevitable. The pornography of today, whether it be the pornography of the rubber-goods shop or the pornography of the popular novel, film, and play, is an invariable stimulant to the vice of self abuse, onanism, masturbation, call it what you will. In young or old, man or woman, boy or girl, modern pornography is a direct provocative of masturbation. It cannot be otherwise. When the grey ones wail that the young man and the young woman went and had sexual intercourse, they are bewailing the fact that the young man and the young woman didn't go separately and masturbate. Sex must go somewhere, especially in young people. So, in our glorious civilisation, it goes in masturbation. And the mass of our popular literature, the bulk of our popular amusements just exists to provoke masturbation. Masturbation is the one thoroughly secret act of the human being, more secret even than excrementation. It is the one functional result of sex-secrecy, and it is stimulated and provoked by our glorious popular literature of fretty pornography, which rubs on the dirty secret without letting you know what is happening.

Now I have heard men, teachers and clergymen, commend masturbation as the solution of an otherwise insoluble sex problem. This at least is honest. The sex problem is there, and you can't just will it away. There it is, and under the ban of secrecy and taboo in mother and father, teacher, friend and foe, it has found its own solution, the solution of masturbation.

But what about the solution? Do we accept it? Do all the grey ones of this world accept it? If so, they must now accept it openly. We can none of us pretend any longer to be blind to the fact of masturbation, in young and old, man and woman. The moral guardians who are prepared to censor all open and plain portrayal of sex must now be made to give their only justification: We prefer that the people shall masturbate.—If this preference is open and declared, then the existing forms of censorship are justified. If the moral guardians prefer that the people shall masturbate, then their present behaviour is correct, and popular amusements are as they should be. If sexual intercourse is deadly sin, and masturbation is comparatively pure and harmless, then all is well. Let things continue as they now are.

Is masturbation so harmless, though? Is it even comparatively pure and harmless? Not to my thinking. In the young, a certain amount of masturbation is inevitable, but not therefore natural. I think, there is no boy or girl who masturbates without feeling a sense of shame, anger and futility. Following the excitement comes the shame, anger, humiliation, and the sense of futility. This sense of futility and humiliation deepens as the years go on, into a suppressed rage, because of the impossibility of escape. The one thing that it seems impossible to escape from, once the habit is formed, is masturbation. It goes on and on, on into old age, in spite of marriage or love affairs or anything else. And it always carries this secret feeling of futility and humiliation, futility and humiliation. And this is, perhaps, the deepest and most dangerous cancer of our civilisation.

Instead of being a comparatively pure and harmless vice, masturbation is certainly the most dangerous sexual vice that a society can be afflicted with, in the long run. Comparatively pure it may be—purity being what it is. But harmless!!!

The great danger of masturbation lies in its merely exhaustive nature. In sexual intercourse, there is a give and take. A new stimulus enters as the native stimulus departs. Something quite new is added as the old surcharge is removed. And this is so in all sexual intercourse where two creatures are concerned, even in the homosexual intercourse. But in masturbation there is nothing but loss. There is no reciprocity. There is merely the spending away of a certain force and no return. The body remains, in a sense, a corpse, after the act of self-abuse. There is no change, only deadening. There is what we call dead loss. And this is not the case in any act of sexual intercourse between two people. Two people may destroy one another in sex. But they cannot just produce the null effect of masturbation.

The only positive effect of masturbation is that is seems to release certain mental energy, in some people. But it is mental energy which manifests itself always in the same way, in a vicious circle of analysis and impotent criticism, or else a vicious circle of false and easy sympathy, sentimentalism. The sentimentalism and the niggling analysis, often self-analysis, of most of our modern literature, is a sign of self-abuse. It is the manifestation of masturbation, the sort of conscious activity stimulated by masturbation, whether male or female. The outstanding feature of such consciousness is that there is no real object, there is only subject. This is just the same whether it be a novel or a work of science. The author never escapes from himself, he pads along within the vicious circle of himself. There is hardly a writer living who gets out of the vicious circle of himself—or a painter either. Hence the lack of creation, and the stupendous amount of production. It is a masturbation result, within the vicious circle of the self. It is self-absorption made public.

And of course the process is exhaustive. The real masturbation of Englishmen began only in Victoria's reign.* It has continued with an increasing emptying of the real vitality and the real *being* of men, till now people are little more than shells of people. Most of the responses are dead, most of the awareness is dead, nearly all the constructive activity is dead, and all that remains is a sort of shell, a half-empty creature fatally self-pre-occupied and incapable of either giving or taking. Incapable either of giving or taking, in the vital self. And this is masturbation result. Enclosed within the vicious circle of the self, with no vital contacts outside, the self becomes emptier and emptier, till it is almost a nullus, a nothingness.

But null or nothing as it may be, it still hangs on to the dirty little secret, which it must still secretly rub and inflame. Forever the vicious circle. And it has a weird, blind will of its own.

One of my most sympathetic critics wrote: If Mr. Lawrence's attitude to sex were adopted, then two things would disappear, the love lyric and the smoking room story.—* And this, I think, is true. But it depends which love-lyric he means. If it is the: Who is Sylvia, what is she?*—then it may just as well disappear. All that pure and noble and heaven-blessed stuff is only the counterpart to the smoking-room story. *Du bist wie eine Blume!* Jawohl!* One can see the elderly gentleman laying his hands on the head of the pure maiden and praying God to keep her forever so pure, so clean and beautiful. Very nice for him! Just pornography! tickling the dirty little secret and rolling his eyes to heaven! He knows perfectly well that if God keeps the maiden so clean and pure and beautiful—in his vulgar sense of clean and pure—for a few more years, then she'll be an unhappy old maid, and not pure nor beautiful at all, only stale or pathetic. Sentimentality is a sure sign of pornography. Why should "sadness strike through the heart" of the old gentleman, because the maid was pure and beautiful? Anybody but a masturbator would have been glad, and would have thought: What a lovely bride for some lucky man!—But no, not the self-enclosed, pornographic masturbator. Sadness has to strike into his beastly heart!—Away with such love-lyrics, we've had too much of their pornographic poison, tickling the dirty little secret and rolling the eyes to heaven.

But if it is a question of the sound love-lyric—"My love is like a red, red rose—!"* then we are on other ground. My love is like a red, red rose only when she's *not* like a pure, pure lily. And nowadays the pure, pure lilies are mostly festering,* anyhow. Away with them and their lyrics. Away with the pure, pure lily lyric, along with the smoking-room story. They are counterparts, and the one is as pornographic as the other. *Du bist wie eine Blume*—is really as pornographic as a dirty story: tickling the dirty little secret and rolling the eyes to heaven.—But oh, if only Robert Burns had been accepted for what he is, then love might still have been like a red, red rose?

The vicious circle, the vicious circle! The vicious circle of masturbation! The vicious circle of self-consciousness that is never *fully* self-conscious, never fully and openly conscious, but always harping on the dirty little secret. The vicious circle of secrecy, in parents, teachers, friends—everybody. The specially vicious circle of family. The vast conspiracy of secrecy in the press, and at the same time, the endless tickling of the dirty little secret. The endless masturbation! and the endless purity! The vicious circle!

How to get out of it? There is only one way: Away with the secret! No more secrecy! The only way to stop the terrible mental itch about sex is to come out quite simply and naturally into the open with it. It is terribly difficult, for the secret is cunning as a crab. Yet the thing to do is to make a beginning. The man who said to his exasperating daughter: My child, the only pleasure I ever had out of you was the pleasure I had in begetting you—has already done a great deal to release both himself and her from the dirty little secret.

How to get rid of the dirty little secret! It is, as a matter of fact, extremely difficult for us secretive moderns. You can't do it by being wise and scientific about it, like Dr. Marie Stopes:* though to be wise and scientific like Dr. Marie Stopes is better than to be utterly hypocritical, like the grey ones. But by being wise and scientific in the serious and earnest manner you only tend to disinfect the dirty little secret, and either kill sex altogether with too much seriousness and intellect, or else leave it a miserable disinfected secret. The unhappy "free and pure" love of so many people who have taken out the dirty little secret and thoroughly disinfected it with scientific words is apt to be more pathetic even than the common run of dirty-little-secret love. The danger is, that in killing the dirty little secret, you kill dynamic sex altogether, and leave only the scientific and deliberate mechanism.

This is what happens to many of those who become seriously "free" in their sex, free and pure. They have mentalised sex till it is nothing at all, nothing at all but a mental quantity. And the final result is disaster, every time.

The same is true, in an even greater proportion, of the emancipated bohemians: and very many of the young are bohemian today, whether they ever set foot in bohemia or not. But the bohemian is "sex free". The dirty little secret is no secret either to him or her. It is, indeed, a most blatantly open question. There is nothing they don't say: everything that can be revealed is revealed, And they do as they wish.

And then what? They have apparently killed the dirty little secret, but somehow, they have killed everything else too. Some of the dirt still sticks, perhaps; sex remains still dirty. But the thrill of secrecy is gone. Hence the terrible dreariness and depression of modern bohemia, and the inward dreariness and emptiness of so many young people of today. They have killed, they imagine, the dirty little secret. The thrill of secrecy is gone. Some of the dirt remains. And for the rest, depression, inertia, lack of life. For sex is the fountain-head of our energetic life, and now the fountain ceases to flow.

Why? For two reasons. The idealists along the Marie Stopes line, and the young bohemians of today have killed the dirty little secret as far as their personal self goes. But they are still under its dominion socially. In the social world, in the press, in literature, film, theatre, wireless, everywhere purity and the dirty little secret reign supreme. At home, at the dinner table, it is just the same. It is the same wherever you go. The young girl, and the young woman is by tacit assumption pure, virgin, sexless. *Du bist wie eine Blume.* She, poor thing, knows quite well that flowers, even lilies, have tippling yellow anthers and a sticky stigma, sex, rolling sex. But to the popular mind flowers are sexless things, and when a girl is told she is like a flower, it means she is sexless and ought to be sexless. She herself knows quite well she isn't sexless and she isn't merely like a flower. But how bear up against the great social lie forced on her? She can't! She succumbs, and the dirty little secret triumphs. She loses her interest in sex, as far as men are concerned, but the vicious circle of masturbation and self-consciousness encloses her even still faster.

This is one of the disasters of young life today. Personally, and among themselves, a great many, perhaps a majority of the young people of today have come out into the open with sex and laid salt on the tail of the dirty little secret. And this is a very good thing.—But in public, in the social world, the young are still entirely under the shadow of the grey elderly ones. The grey elderly ones belong to the last century, the eunuch century, the century of the mealy-mouthed lie,* the century that has tried to destroy humanity, the Nineteenth Century. All our grey ones are left over from this century. And they rule us. They rule us with the grey, mealy-mouthed, canting lie of that great century of lies which, thank God, we are drifting away from. But they rule us still with the lie, for the lie, in the name of the lie. And they are too heavy and too numerous, the grey ones. It doesn't matter what government it is. They are all grey ones, left over from the last century, the century of mealy-mouthed liars, the century of purity and the dirty little secret.

So there is one cause for the depression of the young: the public reign of the mealy-mouthed lie, purity and the dirty little secret, which they themselves have privately overthrown. Having killed a good deal of the lie in their own private lives, the young are still enclosed and imprisoned within the great public lie of the grey ones. Hence the excess, the extravagance, the hysteria, and then the weakness, the feebleness, the pathetic silliness of the modern youth. They are all in a sort of prison, the prison of a great lie and a society of elderly liars. And this is one of the reasons, perhaps the main reason why the sex-flow is dying out in the young, the real energy is dying away. They are enclosed within a lie, and the sex won't flow. For the length of a complete lie is never more than three generations; and the young are the fourth generation of the 19th century lie.

The second reason why the sex-flow is dying is, of course, that the young, in spite of their emancipation, are still enclosed within the vicious circle of self-conscious masturbation. They are thrown back into it, when they try to escape, by the enclosure of the vast public lie of purity and the dirty little secret. The most emancipated bohemians, who swank most about sex, are still utterly self-conscious and enclosed within the narcissus-masturbation circle. They have perhaps less sex even than the grey ones. The whole thing has been driven up into their heads. There isn't even the lurking hole of a dirty little secret. Their sex is more mental than their arithmetic; and as vital physical creatures they are more non-existent than ghosts. The modern bohemian is indeed a kind of ghost, not even Narcissus,* only the image of Narcissus reflected on the face of the audience.

The dirty little secret is most difficult to kill. You may put it to death publicly a thousand times, and still it re-appears, like a crab, stealthily from under the submerged rocks of the personality. The French, who are supposed to be so open about sex, will perhaps be the last to kill the dirty little secret. Perhaps they don't want to. Anyhow mere publicity won't do it.

You may parade sex abroad, but you will not kill the dirty little secret. You may read all the novels of Marcel Proust,* with everything there in all detail. Yet you will not kill the dirty little secret. You will perhaps only make it more cunning. You may even bring about a state of utter indifference and sex-inertia, still without killing the dirty little secret. Or you may be the most wispy and enamoured little Don Juan of modern days, and still the core of your spirit will merely be the dirty little secret. That is to say, you will still be in the narcissus-masturbation circle, the vicious circle of self-enclosure. For wherever the dirty little secret exists, it exists as the centre of the vicious circle of masturbation self-enclosure. And wherever you have the vicious circle of masturbation self-enclosure, you have at the core the dirty little secret. And the most high-flown sex-emancipated young people today are perhaps the most fatally and nervously enclosed within the masturbation self-enclosure. Nor do they want to get out of it, for there would be nothing left to come out.

But some people surely do want to come out of the awful self-enclosure. Today, practically everybody is self-conscious and imprisoned in self-consciousness. It is the joyful result of the dirty little secret. Vast numbers of people don't want to come out of the prison of their self-consciousness: they have so little left to come out with. But some people, surely, want to escape this doom of self-enclosure which is the doom of our civilisation. There is surely a proud minority that wants once and for all to be free of the dirty little secret.

And the way to do it is, first, to fight the sentimental lie of purity and the dirty little secret wherever you meet it, inside yourself or in the outside world. Fight the great lie of the 19th Century, which has soaked through our sex and our bones. It means fighting with almost every breath, for the lie is ubiquitous.

Then secondly, in his adventure of self-consciousness a man must come to the limits of himself and become aware of something beyond him. A man must be self-conscious enough to know his own limits, and to be aware of that which surpasses him. What surpasses me is the very urge of life that is within me, and this life urges me to forget myself and to yield to the stirring half-born impulse to smash up the vast lie of the world, and make a new world. If my life is merely to go on in a vicious circle of self-enclosure, masturbating self-consciousness, it is worth nothing to me. If my individual life is to be enclosed within the huge corrupt lie of society today, purity and the dirty little secret, then it is worth not much to me. Freedom is a very great reality. But it means, above all things, freedom from lies. It is first, freedom from myself, from the lie of myself, from the lie of my all-importance, even to myself; it is freedom from the self-conscious masturbating thing I am, self-enclosed. And second, freedom from the vast lie of the social world, the lie of purity and the dirty little secret. All the other monstrous lies lurk under the cloak of this one primary lie. The monstrous lie of money lurks under the cloak of purity. Kill the purity-lie, and the money-lie will be defenseless.

We have to be sufficiently conscious, and self-conscious, to know our own limits and to be aware of the greater urge within us and beyond us. Then we cease to be primarily interested in ourselves. Then we learn to leave ourselves alone, in all the affective centres: not to force our feelings in any way, and never to force our sex. Then we make the great onslaught on to the outside lie, the inside lie being settled. And that is freedom and the fight for freedom.

The greatest of all lies in the modern world is the lie of purity and the dirty little secret. The grey ones left over from the Nineteenth Century are the embodiment of this lie. They dominate in society, in the press, in literature, everywhere. And, naturally, they lead the vast mob of the general public along with them.

Which means, of course, perpetual censorship of anything that would militate against the lie of purity and the dirty little secret, and perpetual encouragement of what may be called permissible pornography, pure, but tickling the dirty little secret under the delicate underclothing. The grey ones will pass and will commend floods of evasive pornography, and will suppress every outspoken word.

The law is a mere figment. In his article on the '*censorship*' *of Books*, in the *Nineteenth Century*, the new Viscount Brentford, late Home Secretary, says: "Let it be remembered that the publishing of an obscene book, the issue of an obscene post-card or pornographic photograph—are all offences against the law of the land, and the Secretary of State who is the general authority for the maintenance of law and order most clearly and definitely cannot discriminate between one offence and another in discharge of his duty."

So he winds up, *ex cathedra* and infallible. But only ten lines above he has written: "I agree, that if the law were pushed to its logical conclusion, the printing and publication of such books as *The Decameron*, Benvenuto Cellini's *Life*, and Burton's *Arabian Nights** might form the subject of proceedings. But the ultimate sanction of all law is public opinion, and I do not believe for one moment that prosecution in respect of books that have been in circulation for many centuries would command public support."*

Ooray then for public opinion! It only needs that a few more years shall roll.—But now we see that the Secretary of State most clearly and definitely *does* discriminate between one offence and another in discharge of his duty. He discriminates for Benvenuto, and he discriminates against *The Well of Loneliness*.* Simple and admitted discrimination on his part! How do we know, at this moment, that public opinion would really support the suppression of *The Well of Loneliness*? Was public opinion ever really asked? Was it consulted? Or did the Secretary of State and a few of his grey ones decide for a moment that they *were* public opinion *in propria persona*?* And at this moment, are they really public opinion in allowing the *Decameron* to be publicly sold? If the public were forced to read the *Well of Loneliness* and the *Decameron*, and then a vote were taken, I'm afraid there would be ten votes for the suppression of the *Decameron* to one for suppression of the *Well of Loneliness*? What is this public opinion? Just more lies on the part of the grey ones. They would suppress Benvenuto tomorrow, if they dared. But they would make laughing-stocks of themselves, because *tradition* backs up Benvenuto. It isn't public opinion at all. It is the grey ones afraid of making still bigger fools of themselves.

But the case is simple. If the grey ones are going to be backed by a general public, then every new book that would smash the mealy-mouthed lie of the 19th century will be suppressed as it appears. Yet let the grey ones beware. The general public is nowadays a very unstable affair, and no longer loves its grey ones so dearly, with their old lie. And there is another public, the small public of the minority, which hates the lie and the grey ones that perpetuate the lie, and which has its own dynamic ideas about pornography and obscenity. You can't fool all the people all the time,* even with purity and a dirty little secret.

And this minority public knows well that the books of Sir James Barrie and Mr. Galsworthy, not to mention the mass of* lesser fry, are far more pornographical than the liveliest story in the *Decameron*: because they tickle the dirty little secret and excite to private masturbation, which the wholesome Boccaccio never does. And the minority public knows full well that the most obscene painting on a Greek vase—Thou still unravished bride of quietness*—is not as pornographical as the close-up kisses on the film, which excite men and women to secret and separate masturbation.

And perhaps one day even the general public will desire to look the thing in the face, and see for itself the difference between the sneaking masturbation-pornography of the press, the film, and present-day popular literature, and then the creative portrayals of the sexual impulse that we have in Boccaccio or the Greek vase-paintings or some Pompeian art, and which are necessary for the fulfilment of our consciousness.

As it is, the public mind is today bewildered, on this point, bewildered almost to idiocy. When the police raided my picture show,* they did not in the least know what to take. So they took every picture where the smallest bit of the sex organs of either man or woman showed. Quite regardless of subject or meaning or anything else: they would allow anything, these dainty policemen in a picture show, except the actual sight of a fragment of the human *pudenda*. This was the police test. The dabbing on of a postage stamp—especially a green one that could be called a leaf—would in most cases have been quite sufficient to satisfy this "public opinion".

It is, we can only repeat, a condition of idiocy. And if the purity-with-a-dirty-little-secret lie is kept up much longer, the mass of society will really be an idiot, and a dangerous idiot at that. For the public is made up of individuals. And each individual, even grey Home Secretaries,* has sex, and is pivoted on sex. And if, with purity and a dirty little secret you drive every individual into the masturbation self-enclosure, and keep him there, then you will produce a state of general idiocy. For the masturbation self-enclosure produces idiots. Perhaps, if we are all idiots, we shan't know it. But God preserve us!

PICTURES ON THE WALL

Lawrence wrote to Nancy Pearn on 1 May 1929:

The editor of the *Architectural Review*

H. de C. Hastings, 9 Queen Anne's Gate, Westminster S. W. 1. asked me for an article on artists and decoration, so will you let him see the enclosed. I don't know whether it is the kind of thing he wants – if not, no matter. – But if he doesn't want it, probably some other 'decorative' magazine would take it – and I should think America might like it, too. (*Letters*, vii. 269)[1]

Three weeks later, Hastings 'wrote that he likes the "Wall Pictures" article very much and will pay twenty guineas. Good for him' (vii. 295). According to a letter from Nancy Pearn to Lawrence on 30 July, *Vanity Fair* (New York) had also agreed to accept the article and would pay $125 for it.

Vanity Fair published it first, in December 1929, and entitled it 'dead pictures on the walls', adding the byline: 'BY D. H. LAWRENCE advocating the wholesale scrapping of stale art and the circulation of new and living paintings'. The *Architectural Review* published it in February 1930, as 'Pictures on the Walls', the same title as appeared in *Assorted Articles* two months later. There was, however, an important difference between the two texts. That in the *Review* is considerably longer; at the end it has three paragraphs which do not occur in any other state of the text. Moreover, this extra material is directed entirely to the major Italian Exhibition in London which opened on 1 January 1930. By then Lawrence was in Bandol, in his final illness; he could not have visited the exhibition in Burlington House, nor did he give any indication elsewhere that he knew of its existence. It is conceivable that – in correspondence now lost – Hastings sent a catalogue of the exhibition and invited him to comment on it: Hastings's obvious respect for Lawrence makes this a plausible suggestion. However, it is questionable whether Lawrence would have extended the article for Hastings and failed to make any corresponding adjustment to the text in *Assorted Articles*, the galley

[1] Both Powell (No. 115) and Tedlock (238) saw the manuscript which is now unlocated; both record the title in DHL's hand as: 'Pictures on the Wall'.

proofs of which he was still expecting to receive on 9 January (vii. 619). Therefore, in the absence of wholly reliable evidence that Lawrence was personally responsible for the additional paragraphs, it has seemed editorially more responsible to include them in the Explanatory notes. (For the text of the extra material see Explanatory note on 264:17.)

When Hastings invited Lawrence to write for his magazine – whose subtitle was 'A Magazine of Architecture and Decoration' – he doubtless had in view the series which would begin in January 1930 on 'Modern Decoration'. The painter Paul Nash contributed the first article in the series, focusing attention on 'the modern evolution of English furnishing'. His was the last article in the *Review* in January 1930. The second in the series, in February, was by Yoi Maraini on the work of the modern Italian school. Lawrence's article, though not formally in the same series, fell between the two, as the first in the February issue. Nash had been concerned to argue for the development of a distinctive 'national style' by 'designers and craftsmen working in England',[1] a theme which was developed by the editor as applied to literary style, in his 'Marginalia' in the February issue. Hastings proclaimed the 'absence of pretension [as] the very base of English style' and went on: 'Take as an apt example the writing method of a first-rate English stylist like D. H. Lawrence. When analysed his remarks seem to consist entirely of colloquialisms. But Mr Lawrence does more than try to express himself naturally – he tries to express himself in the most informal and unpretentious way possible.'[2]

The April issue of the *Review* contained a further article by Nash entitled: 'The Public and Art: Or a Brand from the Burning'. In it he makes clear that he regarded Lawrence's article as contributing to a wider debate on 'the public and art . . . how to bring the work of contemporary painters and sculptors, musicians and architects, designers and decorators into closer touch with the *general* public'.[3] He took serious issue, however, with Lawrence's

> naïve article about Pictures on Walls . . . Stated briefly, Mr Lawrence's opinion was that when you were tired of a picture it should be burnt – I confess I read this with some uneasiness. Such a creed, once it got hold on the public mind, would certainly clear off a lot of rubbish, but it would also inevitably destroy many works of art.[4]

Nevertheless, Nash expressed his 'sympathy with the wish that the public should become familiar – in the best sense of the word – with

[1] *Architectural Review*, lxvii (January–June 1930), 45.
[2] Ibid., lxvii. 108. [3] Ibid., lxvii. 167. [4] Ibid.

modern works of art of all kinds and that is what Mr Lawrence was really talking about when you stand clear of all his dead rags and bonfires.'[1]

In his 'Marginalia' in the May 1930 issue of the *Review*, the editor showed himself alert to the possible accusation that Nash's attack was 'disrespectful, and even callous, appearing as it did immediately following the tragic event of Lawrence's death'.[2] With obvious relief he conveyed the message from Nash that 'the article was written in Lawrence's lifetime' and no disrespect whatsoever was intended.

[1] Ibid., lxvii. 168. [2] Ibid., lxvii. 306.

PICTURES ON THE WALL

Whether wall-pictures are or are not an essential part of interior decoration in the home seems to be considered debateable. Yet since there is scarcely one house in a thousand which doesn't have them, we may easily conclude that they are, in spite of the snobbism which pretends to prefer blank walls. The human race loves pictures. Barbarians or civilised, we are all alike, we straightway go to look at a picture if there is a picture to look at. And there are very few of us who wouldn't love to have a perfectly fascinating work hanging in our room, that we could go on looking at, if we could afford it. Instead, unfortunately, as a rule, we have only some mediocre thing left over from the past, that hangs on the wall just because we've got it, and it must go somewhere. If only people would be firm about it, and rigorously burn *all* insignificant pictures, frames as well, how much more freely we should breathe indoors. If only people would go round their walls every ten years and say, Now what about that oil-painting, what about that reproduction, what about that photograph? What do they mean? What do we get from them? Have they any point? Are they worth keeping?—The answer would almost invariably be No. And then what? Shall we say, Oh, let them stay! They've been there ten years, we might as well leave them!—But that is sheer inertia and death to any freshness in the home. A woman might as well say: I've worn this hat for a year, so I may as well go on wearing it for a few more years.—A house, a home, is only a greater garment, and just as we feel we must renew our clothes and have fresh ones, so we should renew our homes and make them in keeping. Spring-cleaning isn't enough. Why do fashions in clothes change? Because, really, we ourselves change, in the slow metamorphosis of time. If we imagine ourselves now in the clothes we wore six years ago, we shall see that it is impossible. We are, in some way, different persons now, and our clothes express our different personality.

And so should the home. It should change with us, as we change. Not so quickly as our clothes change, because it is not so close in contact. More slowly, but just as inevitably, the home should change around us. And the change should be more rapid in the more decorative scheme of the room: pictures, curtains, cushions; and slower in the solid furniture. Some furniture may satisfy us for a life-time. Some may be quite unsuitable after ten years. But certain it is, that the cushions and curtains and pictures will begin to be stale after a couple of years. And staleness in the home is stifling and oppressive to the spirit. It is a woman's business to see to it. In England especially we live so much indoors that our interiors must live, must change, must have their seasons of fading and renewing, must come alive to fit the new moods, the new sensations, the new selves that come to pass in us with the changing years. Dead and dull permanency in the home, dreary sameness, is a form of inertia, and very harmful to the modern nature, which is in a state of flux, sensitive to its surroundings far more than we really know.

And, do as we may, the pictures in a room are in some way the key to the atmosphere of a room. Put up grey photogravures,* and a certain greyness will dominate in the air, no matter if your cushions be daffodils. Put up Baxter* prints, and for a time you will have charm, after that, a certain stuffiness will ensue. Pictures are strange things. Most of them die as sure as flowers die, and, once dead, they hang on the wall as stale as brown, withered bouquets. The reason lies in ourselves. When we buy a picture because we like it, then the picture responds fresh to some living feeling in us. But feelings change: quicker or slower. If our feeling for the picture was superficial, it wears away quickly—and quickly the picture is nothing but a dead rag hanging on the wall. On the other hand, if we can see a little deeper, we shall buy a picture that will at least last us a year or two, and give a certain fresh joy all the time, like a living flower. We may even find something that will last us a life-time. If we found a masterpiece, it would last many life-times. But there are not many masterpieces of any sort, in this world.

The fact remains, there are pictures of every sort, and people of every sort to be pleased by them; and there is, perhaps, a limit to the length of time that even a masterpiece will please mankind. Raphael now definitely bores us, after several centuries, and Michael Angelo* begins to.

But we needn't bother about Raphael or Michael Angelo, who keep up their fresh interest for centuries. Our concern is rather with pictures that may be dead rags in six months, all the fresh feeling for them gone. If we think of Landseer, or Alma Tadema,* we see how even traditional connoisseurs like Dukes of Devonshire* paid large sums for momentary masterpieces that now hang on the ducal walls as dead and ridiculous rags. Only a very uneducated person nowadays would want to put those two Landseer dogs: *Dignity and Impudence*, on the drawing-room wall. Yet they pleased immensely in their day. And the interest was sustained, perhaps, for twenty years. But after twenty years, it has become a humiliation to keep them hanging on the walls of Chatsworth or wherever they hang. They should be burnt, of course. They only make an intolerable stuffiness wherever they are, and remind us of the shallowness of our taste.

And if this is true of *Dignity and Impudence*, or Millais' *Bubbles*,* which have a great deal of technical skill in them, how much more true is it of cheap photogravures, which have none. Familiarity wears a picture out. Since Whistler's Portrait of his Mother* was used for advertisement, it has lost most of its appeal, and become for most people a worn-out picture, a dead rag. And once a picture has been really popular, and then died into staleness, it never revives again. It is dead forever. The only thing is to burn it.

Which applies very forcibly to photogravures and other such machine pictures. They may have fascinated the young bride, twenty years ago. They may even have gone on fascinating her for six months or two years. But at the end of that time they are almost certainly dead, and the bride's pleasure in them can only be a reminiscent sentimental pleasure, or that rather vulgar satisfaction in them as pieces of property. It is fatal to look on pictures as pieces of property. Pictures are like flowers, that fade away sooner or later, and die, and must be thrown in the dustbin and burnt. It is true of all pictures. Even the beloved Giorgione* will one day die to human interest—but he is still very lovely, after almost five centuries, still a fresh flower. But when at last he is dead, as so many pictures are that hang on honoured walls, let us hope he will be burnt. Let us hope he won't still be regarded as a piece of valuable property, worth huge sums, like lots of dead-as-doornails canvases today.

If only we could get rid of the idea of "property", in the arts! The arts exist to give us pleasure or joy. A yellow cushion gives us pleasure. The moment it ceases to do so, take it away, have done with it, give us another.—Which we do, and so cushions remain fresh and interesting, and the manufacturers manufacture continually new, fresh, fascinating fabrics. The natural demand causes a healthy supply.

In pictures it is just the opposite. A picture, instead of being regarded, like a flower or a cushion, as something that must be fresh and fragrant with attraction, is looked on as solid property. We may spend ten shillings on a bunch of roses, and throw away the dead stalks without thinking we have thrown away ten shillings. We may spend two guineas on the cover of a lovely cushion, and strip it off and discard it the moment it is stale, without for a moment lamenting the two guineas. We know where we are. We paid for aesthetic pleasure, and we have had it. Lucky for us that money can buy roses or lovely embroidery.—Yet if we pay two pounds for some picture, and are tired of it after a year, we can no more burn that picture than we can set the house on fire. It is uneducated folly on our part. We *ought* to burn the picture, so that we can have real fresh pleasure in a different one, as in fresh flowers and fresh cushions. In every school, it is taught: Never leave stale flowers in a vase. Throw them away!—so it should be taught: Never leave stale pictures on the wall. Burn them! The value of a picture lies in the aesthetic emotion it brings, exactly as if it were a flower. The aesthetic emotion dead, the picture is a piece of ugly litter.

Which belies the tedious dictum that a picture should be part of the architectural whole, built in to the room, as it were. This is fallacy. A picture is decoration, not architecture. The room exists to shelter us and house us, the picture exists only to please us, to give us certain emotions. Of course there can be harmony or disharmony between the pictures and the whole *ensemble* of a room. But in any room in the world you could carry out dozens of different schemes of decoration, at different times and to harmonise with each scheme of decoration there are hundreds of different pictures. The built-in theory is all wrong. A picture in a room is the gardenia in my buttonhole. If the tailor "built" a permanent and irremovable gardenia in my morning coat buttonhole, I should be done in.

Then there is the young school which thinks pictures should be kept in stacks like books in a library, and looked at for half-an-hour or so at a time, as we turn over the leaves of a book of reproductions. But this again entirely disregards the real psychology of pictures. It is true, the great trashy mass of pictures are exhausted in half-an-hour. But then why keep them in a stack, why keep them at all? On the other hand, if I had a Renoir nude, or a good Friesz flower-study, or even a Brabazon* water-colour, I should want to keep it at least a year or two, and hang it up in a chosen place, to live with it and get all the fragrance out of it. And if I had the Titian *Adam and Eve*,* from the Prado, I should want to have it hanging in my room all my life, to look at: because I know it would give me a subtle rejoicing all my life, and would make my life delightful. And if I had some Picassos, I should want to keep them about six months, and some Braque I should like to have for about a year: then, probably, I should be through with them. But I would not want a Romney* even for a day.

And so it varies, with the individual and with the picture, and so it should be allowed to vary. But at present, it is not allowed to vary. We all have to stare at the dead rags our fathers and mothers hung on the walls, just because they are *property*.

But let us change it. Let us refuse to have our vision filled with dust and nullity of dead pictures in the home. Let there be a grand conflagration of dead "art", immolation of canvas and paper, oil-colours, water-colours, photographs and all, a grand clearance.

Then what? Then ask Harrod's about it. Don't, for heaven's sake, go and spend twenty guineas on another picture that will have to hang on the wall till the end of time just because it cost twenty guineas. Go to Harrod's and ask them what about their Circulating Picture scheme? They have a circulating library—or other people have: huge circulating libraries. People hire books till they have assimilated their content. Why not the same with pictures?

Why should not Harrod's have a great "Library" of pictures? Why not have a great "pictuary",* where we can go and choose a picture? There would be men in charge who knew about pictures, just as librarians know about books. We subscribe, we pay a certain deposit, and our pictures are sent home to us: to keep for one year, for two, for ten, as we wish: at any rate, till we have got all the joy out of them, and want a change.

In the pictuary you can have everything except machine-made rubbish that is not worth having. You can have big supplies of modern art, fresh from the artists, etchings, engravings, drawings, paintings: you can have the lovely new colour-reproductions that most of us can't afford to buy: you can have frames to suit. And here you can choose, choose what will give you real joy, and will suit your home for the time being.

There are few, very few great artists in any age. But there are hundreds and hundreds of men and women with genuine artistic talent and beautiful artistic feeling, who produce quite lovely works that are never seen. They are lovely works—not immortal, not masterpieces, not "great": yet they are lovely, and will keep their loveliness a certain number of years: after which they will die, and the time will have come to destroy them.

Now it is a tragedy that all these pictures with their temporary loveliness should be condemned to a premature dust-heap. For that is what they are. Contemporary art belongs to contemporary society. Society at large *needs* the pictures of its contemporaries, just as it needs the books. Modern people read modern books. But they hang up pictures that belong to no age whatever, and have no life, and have no meaning, but are mere blotches of deadness on the walls.

The living moment is everything. And in pictures we never experience it. It is useless asking the public to "see" Matisse* or Picasso or Braque. They will never see more than an odd horrific canvas, anyhow. But does the modern public read James Joyce or Marcel Proust?* It does not. It reads the great host of more congenial and more intelligible contemporary writers. And so the modern public is more or less up-to-date and on the spot about the general run of modern books. It is conscious of the literature of its day, moderately awake and intelligent in that respect.

But of the pictures and drawings of its day it is blankly unaware. The general public feels itself a hopeless ignoramus when confronted with modern works of art. It has no clue to the whole unnatural business of modern art, and is just hostile. Even those who are tentatively attracted are uneasy, and they dare never *buy*. Prices are comparatively high, and you may so easily be let in for a dud. So the whole thing is a deadlock.

Now the only way to keep the public in touch with art is to let it get hold of works of art. It was just the same with books. In the old five-guinea and two-guinea days there was no public for literature, except the squire class. The great reading-public came into being with the lending library. And the great picture-loving public would come into being with the lending pictuary. The public *wants* pictures hard enough. But it simply can't get them.

And this will continue so long as a picture is regarded as a piece of property, and not as a source of aesthetic emotion, of sheer pleasure, as a flower is. The great public was utterly deprived of books, till books ceased to be looked on as lumps of real estate, and came to be regarded as something belonging to the mind and consciousness, a spiritual instead of a gross material property. Today, if I say: "Doughty's *Arabia Deserta** is a favourite book of mine," then the man I say it to won't reply: "Yes, I own a copy,"—he will say: "Yes, I have read it." In the eighteenth century he would probably have replied: "I have a fine example *in folio* in my library."—and the sense of "property" would have overwhelmed any sense of literary delight.

The cheapening of books freed them from the gross property valuation and released their true spiritual value. Something of the same must happen for pictures. The public wants and needs badly all the real aesthetic stimulus it can get. And it knows it. When books were made available, the vast reading public sprang into being almost at once. And a vast picture-loving public would arise, once the public could get at the pictures, personally.

There are thousands of quite lovely pictures, not masterpieces, of course, but with real beauty, *which belong to today*, and which remain, stacked dustily and hopelessly in corners of artists' studies, going stale. It is a great shame. The public wants them, but it never sees them: and if it does see an occasional few, it daren't buy, especially as "art" is high-priced, for it feels incompetent to judge. At the same time, the unhappy, work-glutted artists of today want above all things to let the public have their works. And these works are, we insist, an essential part of the education and emotional experience of the modern mind. It is necessary that adults should *know* them, as they know modern books. It is necessary that children should be familiar with them, in the constant stream of creation. Our aesthetic education is become immensely important, since it is so immensely neglected.

And there we are: the pictures going to dust, for they don't keep their freshness, any more than books or flowers or silks, beyond a certain time: yet their freshness now is the breath of life to us, since it means hours and days of delight. And the public is pining for the pictures, but daren't buy, because of the money-property complex. And the artist is pining to let the public have them, but daren't make himself cheap. And so the thing is an *impasse*, simple state of frustration.

Now for Messrs. Harrods and their lending library—or pictuary—of modern works of art. Or, better still, an Artists' Co-operative Society, to supply pictures on loan or purchase, to the great public. Today, nobody buys pictures, except as a speculation. If a man pays a hundred pounds for a canvas, he does it in the secret belief that that canvas will be worth a thousand pounds in a few years' time.

The whole attitude is disgusting. The reading public only asks of a book that it shall be entertaining, it doesn't give a hang as to whether the book will be considered a great book five years hence. The great public wants to be entertained and, sometimes, delighted, and literature exists to supply the demand. Now there is a great deal of delight in even a very minor picture, produced by an artist who has delicate artistic feeling and some skill, even if he be not wildly original. There are hundreds and hundreds of perfectly obscure pictures stuck away in corners of studios, which would, I know, give me a real delight if they were hung in my room for a year. After a while they would go stale: but not nearly as quickly as a bunch of lilac, which yet I love and set with pleasure on the table. As a tree puts beauty into a flower that will fade, so all the hosts of minor artists, one way and another, put beauty and delight into their pictures, that likewise will not last beyond their rhythmic season. But it is a wicked shame and waste that nearly all these pictures, with their modicum of beauty and their power of giving delight, should just be taken from the easel to be laid on the dust-heap, while a beauty-starved public doesn't even get a look at them. It is all very well saying the public should buy. A picture is cheap at twenty pounds, and very cheap at ten pounds, and "given away" at five pounds. And the public is not only shy, it has a complex about buying any picture that hasn't at least the chance of turning out a masterpiece of ultimate extraordinary value.

It is all nonsensical and futile. The only way now is for the hosts of small artists to club together and form an Artists' Co-operative Society, with proper business intelligence and business energy, to supply the public with pictures on the public's own terms. Or for the shrewd business-men of the world to take the matter up and make a profitable concern of it, as publishers have made a profitable concern of publishing books.*

THE RISEN LORD

On 2 August 1929 Lawrence told Nancy Pearn:

I am sending you the article which *Everyman* asked me to write for their series – 'A Religion for the Young'. This is my idea of a religion for the young – don't know if they'll print it – and don't care very much, for I have a rather poor opinion of *Everyman* – and I'm sure they can pay nothing. But it's a nice article, much too good for them, so take care of it for me. (*Letters*, vii. 401)

He then added an instruction, which was repeated on the manuscript itself, that she should 'read the beginning and correct my quotations [from the Apostles' Creed] where wrong'.[1] The editor of *Everyman*, Charles Benjamin Purdom, had chosen a most opportune moment to issue his invitation. On the very same day that Lawrence sent his article, he also wrote to Harry and Caresse Crosby, the American publishers of *de luxe* editions in Paris, to enquire about progress on the Black Sun edition of *The Escaped Cock*, the novella which he had earlier described as 'a story of the Resurrection' (vi. 50). Indeed later, in October 1929, Lawrence told Charles Lahr that the novella and the *Everyman* article shared the 'same idea' (vii. 516). He was very keen to have both pieces published: he told Caresse Crosby on 16 September, 'I am very anxious to see the book' (vii. 487); Nancy Pearn was reminded on 28 September to send a copy of the article to his American 'disciple', Maria Cristina Chambers, as soon as it appeared, and Nancy Pearn had to tell him that publication was not expected until November. In fact she had been wrongly informed because the article appeared in *Everyman* on 3 October; it was prefaced by the editorial statement: '*Mr D. H. Lawrence, one of the most distinguished and original of present day poets and novelists, has written this special contribution to our series*, "*A Religion for the Young*."' Another opportunity for publication (in America) seemingly presented itself in mid-October when the editor of a new 'Little Magazine', *Pagany*, sought a contribution from Lawrence. He offered 'The Risen Lord'; but the editor, Richard Johns – disappointed not to secure something 'fresh, exciting, and young in imagery' – rejected what he regarded as

[1] See Explanatory note to 267:10.

a 'Sunday Supplement sort of piece' despite the temptation to have the name of 'an established and honored author' on the cover of his first issue (vii. 524 and n. 3). Immediate efforts to find an American publisher for the article failed (vii. 551); it remained unpublished in the USA until its inclusion in a Knopf collection, *The Later D. H. Lawrence*, in 1952.

The first English book publication was in *Assorted Articles*.

THE RISEN LORD

"The risen lord, the risen lord
has risen in the flesh,
and treads the earth to feel the soil
though his feet are still nesh"*

The churches loudly assert: We preach Christ crucified!—But in so doing, they preach only half of the passion, and do only half their duty. The Creed says: "Was crucified, dead, and buried . . . the third day He rose again from the dead." And, again, "I believe in the resurrection of the body . . . "* So that to preach Christ Crucified is to preach half the truth. It is the business of the Church to preach Christ born among men—which is Christmas—; Christ crucified, which is Good Friday; and Christ Risen, which is Easter. And after Easter, till November and All Saints, and till Annunciation, the year belongs to the Risen Lord: that is, all the full-flowering spring, all summer, and the autumn of wheat and fruit, all belong to Christ Risen.

But the Churches insist on Christ crucified, and rob us of the blossom and fruit of the year. The Catholic Church, which has given us our images, has given us the Christ Child, in the lap of woman, and again, Christ Crucified: then the Mass, the mystery of atonement through sacrifice. Yet all this is really preparatory, these are the preparatory stages of the real living religion. The Christ Child, enthroned in the lap of the Mother, is obviously only a preparatory image, to prepare us for Christ the Man. Yet a vast mass of Christians stick there.

What we have to remember is that the great religious images are only images of our own experience, or of our own state of mind and soul. In the Catholic Countries, where the Madonna-and-Child image overwhelms everything else, the man visions himself all the time as a child, a Christ Child, standing on the lap of a virgin mother. Before the war, if an Italian hurt himself, or suddenly fell into distress, his immediate cry was: *O mamma mia! mamma mia!—Oh mother, mother!*—The same was true of many Englishmen. And what does this mean? It means that the man sees himself as the child, the innocent saviour-child, enthroned on the lap of the all-pitying virgin mother. He lives according to this image of himself—the image of the guileless "good" child sheltered in the arms of an all-sheltering mother—until the image breaks in his heart.

And during the war, this image broke in the hearts of most men, though not in the hearts of their women. During the war, the man who suffered most bitterly suffered beyond the help of wife or mother, and nor wife nor mother nor sister nor any beloved could save him from the guns. This fact went home in his heart, and broke the image of mother and Christ-child, and left in its place the image of Christ crucified.

It was not so, of course, for the woman. The image did not break for her. She visioned herself still as the all-pitying, all-sheltering Madonna, on whose lap the man was enthroned, as in the old pictures, like a Christ-child. And naturally the woman did not want to abandon this vision of herself. It gave her her greatest significance; and the greatest power. Break the image, and her significance and her power were gone. But the man came back from the war and denied the image—for him it was broken. So she fought to maintain it, the great vision of man, the Christ Child, enthroned in the lap of the all-pitying virginal woman. And she fought in vain, though not without disastrous result.

For the vision of the all-pitying and all-helpful Madonna was shattered in the hearts of men, during the war. The all-pitying and all-helpful Woman actually did not, whether she could or not, prevent the guns from blowing to pieces the men who called upon her. So her image collapsed, and with it, the image of the Christ Child. For the man who went through the war, the resultant image inevitably was Christ Crucified, Christ tortured on the Cross. And Christ Crucified is essentially womanless.

True, many of the elderly men who never went through the war still insist on the Christ-child business, and most of the elderly women insist on their benevolent Madonna supremacy. But it is in vain. The guns broke the image in the hearts of middle-aged men, and the young were born, or are come to real consciousness, after the image was already smashed.

So there we are! We have three great image-divisions among men and women today. We have the old and the elderly, who never were exposed to the guns, still fatuously maintaining that man is the Christ-child and woman the infallible safe-guard from all evil and all danger. It is fatuous, because it absolutely didn't work. Then we have the men of middle age, who were all tortured and virtually put to death by the war. They accept Christ crucified as their image, are essentially womanless, and take the great cry: *Consummatum est! – It is finished!** as their last word.—Thirdly we have the young, who never went through the war. They have no illusions about it, however, and the death-cry of their elder generation: *It is finished!* rings cold through their blood. They cannot answer. They cannot even scoff. It is no joke, and never will be a joke.

And yet, neither of the great images is *their* image. They cannot accept the child-and-mother position which the old buffers still pose in. They cannot accept the Christ Crucified finality of the generations immediately ahead. For they, the young, came into the field of life after the death-cry *Consummatum est!* had rung through the world, and while the body, so to speak, was being put into the tomb. By the time the young came on to the stage, Calvary* was empty, the tombs were closed, the women had lost forever the Christ-child and the virgin saviour, and it was altogether the day after, cold, bleak, empty, blank, meaningless, almost silly.

The young came into life, and found everything finished. Everywhere the empty crosses, everywhere the closed tombs, everywhere the manless, bitter or over-assertive women, everywhere the closed grey disillusion of Christ Crucified, dead, and buried, those grey empty days between Good Friday and Easter.

And the Churches, instead of preaching The Risen Lord, go on preaching the Christ Child and Christ crucified. Now man cannot live without some vision of himself. But still less can he live with a vision that is not true to his inner experience and inner feeling. And the vision of Christ Child and Christ crucified are both untrue to the inner experience and feeling of the young. They don't feel that way. They show the greatest forbearance and tolerance of their elders, for whom the two images *are* livingly true. But for the post-war young, neither the Christ Child nor Christ Crucified means much.

I doubt whether the Protestant Churches, which supported the war, will ever have the faith and the power of life to take the great step onwards, and preach Christ Risen. The Catholic Church might. In the countries of the Mediterranean, Easter has always been the greatest of the holy days, the gladdest and holiest, not Christmas, the birth of the Child. Easter, Christ Risen, the Risen Lord, this, to the old faith, is still the first day in the year. The Easter festivities are the most joyful, the Easter processions the finest, the Easter ceremonies the most splendid. In Sicily the women take into church the saucers of growing corn, the green blades rising tender and slim like green light, in little pools, filling round the altar. It is Adonis.* It is the re-born year. It is Christ Risen. It is the Risen Lord. And in the warm south still a great joy floods the hearts of the people on Easter Sunday. They feel it, they feel it everywhere. The Lord is risen. The Lord of the rising wheat and the plum-blossoms is warm and kind upon earth again, after having been done to death by the evil and the jealous ones.

The Roman Catholic Church may still unfold this part of the Passion fully, and make men happy again. For Resurrection is indeed the consummation of all the passion. Not even Atonement, the being at one with Christ through partaking in his sacrifice consummates the Passion finally. For even after Atonement men still must live, and must go forward with the vision. After we share in the body of Christ, we rise with him in the body. And that is the final vision that has been blurred to all the Churches.

Christ risen in the flesh! we must accept the image complete, if we accept it at all. We must take the mystery in its fulness and in fact. It is only the image of our own experience. Christ rises, when he rises from the dead, in the flesh, not merely as spirit. He rises with hands and feet, as Thomas knew for certain:* and if with hands and feet, then with lips and stomach and genitals of a man. Christ risen, and risen in the whole of his flesh, not with some left out.

Christ risen in the full flesh! What for? It is here the gospels are all vague and faltering, and the Churches leave us in the lurch. Christ risen in the flesh in order to lurk obscurely for six weeks on earth, then be taken vaguely up into heaven in cloud? Flesh, solid flesh, feet and bowels and teeth and eyes of man, taken up into heaven in a cloud, and never put down again?

It is the only part of the great mystery which is all wrong. The virgin birth, baptism, the temptation, the teaching, Gethsemane,* the betrayal, the crucifixion, the burial and the resurrection, these are all true according to our inward-experience. They are what men and women go through, in their different ways. But floated up into heaven as flesh and blood, and never set down again—this nothing in all our experience will ever confirm. If aeroplanes take us up, they bring us down, or let us down. Flesh and blood belong to the earth, and only to the earth. We know it.

And Jesus was risen flesh and blood. He rose a man on earth to live on earth. The greatest test was still before him: his life as a man on earth. Hitherto he had been a sacred child, a teacher, a messiah, but never a full man. Now, risen from the dead, he rises to be a man on earth, and live his life of the flesh, the great life, among other men. This is the image of our inward state, today.

This is the image of the young: the Risen Lord. The teaching is over, the crucifixion is over, the sacrifice is made, the salvation is accomplished. Now comes the true life, man living his full life on earth, as flowers live their full life, without rhyme or reason except the magnificence of coming forth into fulness.

If Jesus rose from the dead in triumph, a man on earth triumphant in renewed flesh, triumphant over the mechanical anti–life convention of Jewish priests, Roman despotism, and universal money-lust; triumphant above all over his own self–absorption, self-consciousness, self-importance; triumphant and free as a man in full flesh and full, final experience, even the accomplished acceptance of his own death; a man at last full and free in flesh and soul, a man at one with death: then he rose to become at one with life, to live the great life of the flesh and the soul together, as peonies or foxes do, in their lesser way. If Jesus rose as a full man, in full flesh and soul, then he rose to take a woman to himself, to live with her, and to know the tenderness and blossoming of the two–ness with her; he who had been hitherto so limited to his oneness, or his universality, which is the same thing. If Jesus rose in the full flesh, he rose to know the tenderness of a woman, and the great pleasure of her, and to have children by her. He rose to know the responsibility and the peculiar delight of children, and also the exasperation and nuisance of them. If Jesus rose as a full man, in the flesh, he rose to have friends, to have a man friend whom he would hold sometimes to his breast,* in strong affection, and who would be dearer to him than a brother, just out of the sheer mystery of sympathy. And how much more wonderful, this, than having disciples! If Jesus rose a full man in the flesh he rose to do his share in the world's work, something he really liked doing. And if he remembered his first life, it would neither be teaching nor preaching, but probably carpentering again, with joy, among the shavings. If Jesus rose a full man in the flesh, he rose to continue his fight with the hard-boiled conventionalists like Roman judges and Jewish priests and money-makers of every sort. But this time, it would no longer be the fight of self-sacrifice that would end in crucifixion. This time, it would be a freed man fighting to shelter the rose of life from being trampled on by the pigs. This time, if Satan attempted temptations in the wilderness,* the Risen Lord would answer: Satan, your silly temptations no longer tempt me. Luckily I have died to that sort of self-importance and self-conceit. But let me tell you something, old man! Your name's Satan, isn't it? and your name is Mammon?* You are the selfish hog that's got hold of all the world, aren't you? Well look here my boy, I'm going to take it all from you, so don't worry. The world and the power and the riches thereof, I'm going to take them all from you, Satan or Mammon or whatever your name is. Because you don't know how to use them. The earth is the Lord's, and the fulness thereof,* and it's going to be. Men have risen from the dead and learned not to be so greedy and self-important. We left most of that behind in the late tomb. Men have risen beyond you, Mammon, they are your risen lords. And so, you hook–nosed, glisten-eyed, ugly, money-smelling anachronism, you've got to get out. Men have not died and risen again for nothing. Whom do you think the earth belongs to, you stale old rat? The earth is the Lord's, and is given to the men who have died and had the power to rise again. The earth is given to the men who have risen from the dead, risen, you old grabber, and when did you ever rise? Never! So go you down to oblivion, and give your place to the risen men, and the women of the risen men. For man has been dispossessed of the full earth and the earth's fulness long enough. And the poor women, they have been shoved about manless and meaningless long enough. The earth is the Lord's and the fulness thereof, and I, the Risen Lord, am here to take possession. For now I am fully a man, and free above all from my own self-importance. I want life, and the pure contact with life. What are riches, and glory, and honour, and might, and power, to me who have died and lost my self-importance? That's why I am going to take them all from you, Mammon, because I care nothing about them. I am going to destroy all your values, Mammon: all your money values and conceit values, I am going to destroy them all.

Because only life is lovely, and you, Mammon, prevent life. I love to see a squirrel peep round a tree: and left to you, Mammon, there will soon be no squirrels to peep. I love to hear a man singing a song to himself, and if it is an old, improper song about the fun between lads and girls, I like it all the better. But you, beastly mealy-mouthed Mammon, you would arrest any lad that sings a gay song.* I love the movement of life, and the beauty of life, Oh Mammon, since I am risen, I love the beauty of life intensely; columbine flowers, for example, the way they dangle, or the delicate way a young girl sits and wonders, or the rage with which a man turns and kicks a fool dog that suddenly attacks him—beautiful that, the swift fierce turn and lunge of a kick, then the quivering pause for the next attack; or even the slightly silly glow that comes over some men as they are getting tipsy—it still is a glow, beautiful; or the swift look a woman fetches me, when she would *really* like me to go off with her, but she is troubled; or the real compassion I saw a woman express for a man who slipped and wrenched his foot: life, the beauty, the beauty of life! But that which is anti-life, Mammon, like you, and money, and machines, and prostitution, and all that tangled mass of self-importance and greediness and self-conscious conceit which adds up to Mammon, I hate it. I hate it, Mammon, I hate you and am going to push you off the face of the earth, Mammon, you great mob-thing, fatal to men—

MEN MUST WORK AND WOMEN AS WELL

Through Nancy Pearn, Lawrence heard that, on 10 July 1929, the editor of *Star Review*, (Lady) Emily Lutyens, had invited him to contribute an article 'of about four thousand words on the subject of Men and Women' which would form part of 'a series . . . dealing with various aspects of life under modern conditions' (*Letters*, vii. 405 n. 1). Lawrence accepted the invitation and, on 5 August, sent his piece to Nancy Pearn with the comment: 'they may say my article isn't their line – I don't care' (vii. 405). But Emily Lutyens did not hesitate to accept it and, on 19 September, enquired how many proof copies would be required;[1] Lawrence's own corrected proofs were returned to Nancy Pearn on 4 October (vii. 512). In his letter to Emily Lutyens, he requested that copies of the issue of *Star Review* in which the article would appear be sent to Maria Cristina Chambers and to his friend and publisher 'Pino' Orioli, as well as to himself in Bandol (vii. 499). The article appeared in the November issue, under the title 'Men and Women', which Lawrence had used in his manuscript.

On 30 November 1929, with reference to the book which would become *Assorted Articles*, he instructed Pollinger to send 'the complete MS [a term Lawrence often used to include typescripts] of the suggested book of newspaper articles as soon as it is ready' (vii. 584). Presumably the texts of the contents were being typed in Curtis Brown's office because on 28 December Lawrence told his publisher Martin Secker: 'I have sent back the MSS of the book of articles to Pollinger' (vii. 611). It was, therefore, in roughly mid-December that he had looked again at a typed copy of the piece recently published as 'Men and Women' and – though making no other changes – altered the title in his own hand to 'Men Must Work and Women as Well'; that was its title when it was republished in *Assorted Articles*. Since that was Lawrence's final choice, it is adopted here.

[1] Her original letter is at UT.

MEN MUST WORK AND WOMEN AS WELL

Supposing that circumstances go on pretty much in the same way they're going on in now, then men and women will go on pretty much in the same way they are now going on in. There is always an element of change, we know. But change is of two sorts: the next step, or a jump in another direction. The next step is called progress. If our society continues its course of gay progress along the given lines, then men and women will do the same: always along the given lines.

So what is important in that case is not so much men and women, but the given lines. The railway train doesn't matter particularly in itself. What matters is where it is going to. If I want to go to Crewe, then a train to Bedford is supremely uninteresting to me, no matter how full it may be. It will only arouse a secondary and temporal interest if it happens to have an accident.

And there you are with men and women today. They are not particularly interesting, and they are not, in themselves, particularly important. All the thousands and millions of bowler hats and neat hand-bags that go bobbing to business every day, may represent so many immortal souls, but somehow we feel that is not for us to say. The clergyman is paid to tickle our vanity in these matters. What all the bowler hats and neat handbags represent to you and me and to each other is business, my dear, and a job.

So that granted the present stream of progress towards better business and better jobs continues, the point is, not to consider the men and women bobbing in the stream, any more than you consider the drops of water in the Thames—but where the stream is flowing. Where is the stream flowing, indeed, the stream of progress? Everybody hopes, of course, it is flowing towards bigger business and better jobs. And what does that mean, again, to the man under the bowler hat and the woman who clutches the satchel?

It means, of course, more money, more congenial labours, and fewer hours. It means freedom from all irksome tasks. It means, apart from the few necessary hours of highly-paid and congenial labour, that men and women shall have nothing to do except enjoy themselves. No beastly housework for the women, no beastly homework for the men. Free! free to enjoy themselves. More films, more motor-cars, more dances, more golf, more tennis and more getting completely away from yourself. The great goal of enjoyment is to get away from yourself. And the goal of life is enjoyment.

Now if men and women want these things with sufficient intensity, they may really get them, and go on getting them. While the game is worth the candle, men and women will go on playing the game. And it seems today as if the motor-car, the film, the radio and the jazz were worth the candle. This being so, progress will continue from business to bigger business, and from job to better job. This is, in very simple terms, the plan of the universe laid down by the great magnates of industry like Mr. Ford.* And they know what they are talking about.

But—and the but is a very big one—it is not easy to turn business into bigger business, and it is sometimes *impossible* to turn uncongenial jobs into congenial ones. This is where science really leaves us in the lurch, and calculation collapses. Perhaps in Mr. Ford's super-factory of motor-cars all jobs may be made abstract and congenial. But the woman whose cook falls foul of the kitchen range, heated with coal, every day, hates that cool range herself even more darkly than the cook hates it. Yet many housewives can't afford electric cooking. And if every one could, it still doesn't make housework entirely congenial. All the inventions of modern science fail to make housework anything but uncongenial to the modern woman—be she mistress or servant-maid. Now the only decent way to get something done is to get it done by somebody who quite likes doing it. In the past, cooks really enjoyed cooking and housemaids enjoyed scrubbing. Those days are over: like master, like man, and still more so, like mistress, like maid. Mistress loathes scrubbing: in two generations, maid loathes scrubbing. But scrubbing must be done. At what price?—raise the price. The price is raised, the scrubbing goes a little better. But after a while, the loathing of scrubbing becomes again paramount in the kitchen-maid's breast, and then ensues a general state of tension, and a general outcry: *Is* it worth it? Is it really worth it?

What applies to scrubbing applies to all labour that cannot be mechanised or abstracted. A girl will slave over shorthand and typing for a pittance, because it is not muscular work. A girl will not do housework well, not for a good wage. Why? Because, for some mysterious or obvious reason, the modern woman and the modern man hate physical work. Ask your husband to peel the potatoes, and earn his deep resentment. Ask your wife to wash your socks, and earn the same. There is still a certain thrill about "mental" and purely mechanical work – like attending a machine. But actual labour has become to us, with our education, abhorrent.

And it is here that science has not kept pace with human demand. It is here that progress is fatally threatened. There is an enormous, insistent demand on the part of the human being that mere labour, such as scrubbing, hewing and loading coal, navvying, the crude work that is the basis of all labour, shall be done away with. Even washing dishes. Science hasn't even learned how to wash dishes for us yet. The mistress who feels so intensely bitter about her maid who will not wash the dishes properly does so because she herself so loathes washing them. Science has rather left us in the lurch in these humble but basic matters. Before babies are conveniently bred in bottles, let the scientist find a *hey presto!** trick for turning dirty tea-cups into clean ones: since it is upon science we depend for our continued progress.

Progress, then, which proceeds so smoothly, and depends on science, does not proceed as rapidly as human feelings change. Beef-steaks are beef-steaks still, though all except the eating is horrible to us. A great deal must be done about a beefsteak, besides the eating of it. And this great deal is done, we have to face the fact, unwillingly. When the mistress loathes trimming and grilling a beef-steak, or paring potatoes or wringing the washing, the maid will likewise loathe these things, and do them at last unwillingly, and with a certain amount of resentment.

The one thing we don't sufficiently consider, in considering the march of human progress, is also the very dangerous march of human feeling that goes on at the same time, and not always parallel. The change in human feeling! And one of the greatest changes that has ever taken place in man and woman is this revulsion from physical effort, physical labour and physical contact, which has taken place within the last thirty years. This change hits woman even harder than man, for she has always had to keep the immediate physical side going. And now it is repellant to her—just as nearly all physical activity is repellant to modern man. The film, the radio, the gramophone were all invented because physical effort and physical contact have become repulsive to man and woman alike. The aim is to abstract as far as possible. And science is our only help. And science still can't wash the dinner things or darn socks, or even mend the fire. Electric heaters or central heating, of course! But that's not all.

What then is the result? In the abstract we sail ahead to bigger business and better jobs and babies bred in bottles and food in tabloid* form. But meanwhile science hasn't rescued us from beef-steaks and dish-washing, heavy labour and howling babies. There is a great hitch. And owing to the great hitch, a great menace to progress. Because every day, mankind hates the business of beef-steaks and dish-washing, heavy labour and howling babies more bitterly.

The house-wife is full of resentment—she can't help it. The young husband is full of resentment—he can't help it—when he has to plant potatoes to eke out the family income. The housemaid is full of resentment, the navvy is full of resentment, the collier is full of resentment, and the collier's wife is full of resentment, because her man can't earn a proper wage. Resentment grows as the strange fastidiousness of modern men and women increases. Resentment, resentment, resentment—because the basis of life is still brutally physical, and that has become repulsive to us. Mr. Ford, being in his own way a genius, has realised that what the modern workman wants, just like the modern gentleman, is abstraction. The modern workman doesn't *want* to be "interested" in his job. He wants to be as little interested, as nearly perfectly mechanical as possible. This is the great will of the people, and there is no gainsaying it. It is precisely the same in woman as in man. Woman demands an electric cooker because it makes no call on her attention or her "interest" at all. It is almost a pure abstraction, a few switches, and no physical contact, no *dirt*, which is the inevitable result of physical contact, at all. If only we could make housework a real abstraction, a matter of turning switches and guiding a machine, the housewife would again be more or less content. But it can't quite be done, even in America.

And the resentment is enormous. The resentment against *eating*, in the breast of modern woman who has to prepare food, is profound. Why all this work and bother about *mere eating*? Why indeed? Because neither science nor evolution has kept up with the change in human feeling, and beefsteaks are beefsteaks still, no matter how detestable they may have become to the people who have to prepare them. The loathsome fuss of food continues and will continue, in spite of all talk about tabloids. The loathsome digging of coal out of the earth, by half-naked men, continues, deep underneath Mr. Ford's super-factories—There it is, and there it will be, and you can't get away from it. While men quite enjoyed hewing coal, which they did; and while women really enjoyed cooking, even with a coal range, which they did—then all was well. But suppose society *en bloc* comes to hate the thought of sweating cooking over a hot range, or sweating hacking at a coal seam, then what are you to do? You have to ask, or to demand that a large section of society shall do something they have come to hate doing, and which you would hate to do yourself. What then? Resentment and ill-feeling!

Social life means all classes of people living more or less harmoniously together. And private life means men and women, man and woman living together more or less congenially. If there is serious discord between the social classes, then society is threatened with confusion. If there is serious discord between man and woman, then the individual, and that means practically everybody, is threatened with internal confusion and unhappiness.

Now it is quite easy to keep the working-classes in harmonious working order, so long as you don't ask them to do work they simply do not want to do. The board-schools* however did the fatal deed. They said to the boys: Work is noble, but what you want is to *get on*, you don't want to stick down a coal-mine all your life. Rise up, and do *clean* work! become a school-teacher or a clerk, not a common collier.—

This is sound board-school education, and is in keeping with all the noblest social ideals of the last century. Unfortunately it entirely overlooks the unpleasant effect of such teaching on those who *cannot* get on, and who must perforce stick down a coal-mine all their lives. And these, in the board-school of a mining-district, are at least ninety percent of the boys: it must be so. So that ninety per cent of these board-school scholars are deliberately taught, at school, to be malcontents: taught to despise themselves for not having "got on," for not having "got out of the pit", for sticking down all their lives doing "dirty work" and being "common colliers." Naturally, every collier, doomed himself, wants to get his boys out of the pit, to be gentlemen. And since this again is *impossible* in ninety per-cent of the cases, the number of "gentlemen," or clerks and school-teachers, being strictly proportionate to the number of colliers, there comes again the sour disillusion. So that by the third generation you have exactly what you've got today, the young malcontent collier. He has been deliberately produced by modern education coupled with modern conditions, and is logically, inevitably and naturally what he is: a malcontent collier. According to all the accepted teaching, he ought to have risen and bettered himself: equal opportunity, you know. And he hasn't risen and bettered himself. Therefore he is more or less a failure in his own eyes even. He is doomed to do dirty work. He is a malcontent.

Now even Mr. Ford can't make coal-mines clean and shiny and abstract. Coal won't be abstracted. Even a Soviet can't do it. A coal-mine remains a hole in the black earth, where blackened men hew and shovel and sweat. You can't abstract it, or make it an affair of pulling levers. And what is even worse, you can't abandon it, you can't do away with it. There it is, and it has got to be. Mr. Ford forgets that his clean and pure and harmonious super-factory, where men only pull shining levers or turn bright handles, has all had to be grossly mined and smelted, before it could come into existence. Mr. Ford is one of the various heavens of industry. But these heavens rest on various hells of labour, always did and always will. Science rather leaves us in the lurch in these matters. Science is supposed to remove these hells for us. And—it doesn't. Not at all!

If you had never taught the blackened men down in the various hells that they *were* in hell, and made them despise themselves for being there—a *common* collier, a *low* laborer—the mischief could never have developed so rapidly. But now we have it, all society resting on a labour basis of smouldering resentment. And the collier's question: How would *you* like to be a collier?—is unanswerable. We know perfectly well we should dislike it intensely.—At the same time my father, who never went to a board-school, quite liked it. But he has been improved on. Progress! Human feeling has changed, changed rapidly and radically. And science has not changed conditions, to fit.

What is to be done? We all loathe brute physical labour. We all think it is horrible to have to do it. We consider those that actually do do it low and vile, and we have told them so, for fifty years, urging them to get away from it and "better themselves." Which would be very nice, if everybody *could* get on, and brute labour could be abandoned: as, scientifically, it ought to be. But actually, not at all. We are forced to go on forcing a very large proportion of society to remain "unbettered," "low and common," "common colliers, common laborers," since a very large portion of humanity must still spend its life labouring. Now and in the future, science having let us down in this respect. You can't teach mankind to "better himself" unless you'll better the gross earth to fit him. And the gross earth remains what it was, and man its slave. For neither science nor evolution shows any signs of saving us from our gross necessities. The labouring masses are and will be, even if all else is swept away: because they must be. They represent the gross necessity of man, which science has failed to save us from.

So then what? The only thing that remains to be done is to make labour as likeable as possible, and try to teach the labouring masses to like it. Which, given the trend of modern feeling, not only sounds but is fatuous: Mankind *en bloc* gets more fastidious and more "nice" every day. Every day it loathes dirty work more deeply. And every day, the whole pressure of social consciousness works towards making everybody more fastidious, more "nice," more refined, and more unfit for dirty work.—Before you make all humanity unfit for dirty work, you should first remove the necessity for dirty work.

But such being the condition of men and women with regard to work—a condition of repulsion in the breasts of men and women for the work that has got to be done—what about private life, the relation between man and woman? How does the new fastidiousness and nicety of mankind affect this?*

Profoundly! The revulsion from physical labour, physical effort, physical contact has struck a death-blow at marriage and home life. In the great trend of the times, a woman cannot save herself from the universal dislike of house-work, house-keeping, rearing children and keeping a home going. Women make the most unselfish efforts in this direction, because it is generally expected of them. But this cannot remove the *instinctive* dislike of preparing meals and scouring saucepans, cleaning baby's bottles or darning the man's underwear, which a large majority of women feel today. It is something which there is no denying, a real physical dislike of doing these things. Many women school themselves and are excellent house-wives, physically disliking it all the time. And this, though admirable, is wearing. It is an exhaustive process, with many ill results.

Can it be possible that women actually ever did like scouring saucepans and cleaning the range?—I believe some few women still do. I believe that twenty years ago, even, the majority of women enjoyed it. But what, then, has happened? Can human instincts really change?

They can, and in the most amazing fashion. And this is the great problem for the sociologist: the violent change in human instinct, especially in women. Woman's instinct used to be all for home, shelter, the protection of the man, and the happiness of running her own house. Now it is all against. Woman *thinks* she wants a lovely little home of her own—but her instinct is all against it, when it means matrimony. She *thinks* she wants a man of her own, but her instinct is dead against having him around all the time. She would like him on a long string, that she can let out or pull in, as she feels inclined. But she just doesn't want him inevitably and insidiously there all the time—not even every evening—not even for week-ends, if it's got to be a fixture. She wants him to be merely intermittent in her landscape, even if he is always present in her soul, and she writes him the most intimate letters every day. All well and good! But her *instinct* is against him, against his permanent and perpetual physical presence. She doesn't want to feel his presence as something material, unavoidable and permanent. It goes dead against her grain, it upsets her instinct. She loves him, she loves, even, being faithful to him. But she doesn't want him substantially around. She doesn't want his actual physical presence—except in snatches. What she *really* loves is the thought of him, the idea of him, the *distant* communion with him—varied with snatches of actually being together, like little festivals, which we are more or less glad when they are over.

Now a great many modern girls feel like this, even when they force themselves to behave in the conventional side-by-side fashion. And a great many men feel the same—though perhaps not so acutely as the woman. Young couples may force themselves to be conventional husbands-and-wives, but the strain is often cruel, and the result often disastrous.

Now then we see the trend of our civilisation, in terms of human feeling and human relation. It is, and there is no denying it, towards a greater and greater abstraction from the physical, towards a further and further physical separateness between men and women, and between individual and individual. Young men and women today are together all the time, it will be argued. Yes, but they are together as good sports, good chaps, in strange independence of one another, intimate one moment, strangers the next, hands-off! all the time, and as little connected as the bits in a kaleidoscope.

The young have the fastidiousness, the nicety, the revulsion from the physical intensified. To the girl of today, a man whose physical presence she is aware of, especially a bit *heavily* aware of, is or becomes really abhorrent. She wants to fly away from him to the uttermost ends of the earth. And as soon as women or girls get a bit female physical, young men's nerves go all to pieces. The sexes can't stand one another. They adore one another as spiritual or personal creatures, all talk and wit and back-chat, or jazz and motor-cars and machines, or tennis and swimming—even sitting in bathing-suits all day on a beach. But this is all peculiarly non-physical, a flaunting of the body in its non-physical, merely optical aspect. So much nudity, fifty years ago, would have made man and woman quiver through and through. Now, not at all! People flaunt their bodies to show how unphysical they are. The more the girls are not desired, the more they uncover themselves.

And this means, when we analyse it out, repulsion. The young are, in a subtle way, physically repulsive to one another, the girl to the man and the man to the girl. And they rather enjoy the feeling of repulsion, it is a sort of contest. It is as if the young girl said to the young man today: I rather like you, you know. You are so thrillingly repulsive to me.—And as if the young man replied: Same here!—There may be, of course an intense bodiless sort of affection between young men and women. But as soon as either becomes a positive physical presence to the other, immediately there is repulsion.

And marriages based on the thrill of physical repulsion, as so many are today, even when coupled with mental "adoring" or real wistful, bodiless affection, are in the long run—not so very long either—catastrophic. There you have it, the great "spirituality" of our age, potent now in every class, and in practically every individual. The great "spirituality", the great "betterment" or refinement: the great fastidiousness: the great "niceness" of feeling: when a girl must be a flat thin bodiless stick, and a boy a correct mannequin, each of them abstracted towards real caricature: what does it all amount to? What is its motive force?

What it amounts to, really, is physical repulsion. The great spirituality of our age means that we are all physically repulsive to one another. The great advance in refinement of feeling and squeamish fastidiousness means that we hate the *physical* existence of anybody and everybody, even ourselves. The amazing move into abstraction on the part of the whole of humanity—the film, the radio, the gramophone—means that we loathe the physical element in our amusements, we don't *want* the physical contact, we want to get away from it. We don't *want* to look at flesh-and-blood people—we want to watch their shadows on a screen. We don't *want* to hear their actual voices: only transmitted through a machine. We must get away from the physical.

The vast mass of the lower classes—and this is most extraordinary—are even more grossly abstracted, if we may use the term, than the educated classes. The uglier sort of working man, today, truly has no body and no real feelings at all. He eats the most wretched food, because taste has left him, he only *sees* his meal, he never *really* eats it. He drinks his beer by idea, he no longer tastes it at all. This must be so, or the food and the beer could not be as bad as they are. And as for his relation to his women—his poor women, they are pegs to hang showy clothes on, and there's the end of them. It is a horrible state of feelingless depravity, atrophy of the senses.

But under it all, as ever, as everywhere, vibrates the one great impulse of our civilisation, physical recoil from every other being and from every form of physical existence. Recoil, recoil, recoil. Revulsion,

revulsion, revulsion. Repulsion, repulsion, repulsion. This is the rhythm that underlies our social activity, everywhere, with regard to physical existence.

Now we are all basically and permanently physical. So is the earth, so even is the air. What then is going to be the result of all this recoil and repulsion, which our civilisation has deliberately fostered?

The result is really only one and the same: some form of collective social madness. Russia, being a very physical country, was in a frantic state of physical recoil and "spirituality", twenty years ago. We can look on the revolution, really, as nothing but a great outburst of anti-physical insanity. We can look on Soviet Russia as nothing but a logical state of society established in anti-physical insanity.—Physical and material are, of course, not the same; in fact they are subtly opposite. The machine is absolutely material, and absolutely anti-physical—as even our fingers know. And the Soviet is established on the image of the machine, "pure" materialism. The Soviet hates the real physical body far more deeply even than it hates Capital. It mixes it up with the bourgeois. But it sees very little danger in it, since all western civilisation is now mechanised, materialised, and ready for an outburst of insanity which shall throw us all into some purely machine-driven unity of lunatics.

What about it then? What about it, men and women? The only thing to do is to get your bodies back, men and women. A great part of society is irreparably lost: abstracted into non-physical, mechanical entities whose motive power is still recoil, revulsion, repulsion, hate, and ultimately, blind destruction. The driving force *underneath* our society remains the same: recoil, revulsion, hate. And let this force once run out of hand, and we know what to expect. It is not only in the working class. The well-to-do classes are just as full of the driving force of recoil, revulsion, which ultimately becomes hate. The force is universal in our spiritual civilisation. Let it once run out of hand, and then—

It only remains for some men and women, individuals, to try to get back their bodies and preserve the other flow of warmth, affection, and physical unison. There is nothing else to do.

NOTTINGHAM AND THE MINING COUNTRYSIDE

Evidence for the date of composition of this, one of Lawrence's most celebrated essays, rests principally on his opening words: 'I was born nearly forty-four years ago'. His forty-fourth birthday fell on 11 September 1929. It has also been conjectured that the reminiscent thrust of the essay was prompted by an account of a visit to Eastwood by his publisher and friend, P. R. Stephensen, to which Lawrence responded in his letter of 5 September (*Letters*, vii. 468 and n. 4). Though composition probably did occur in the early days of September 1929, it is now clear that the instigator was not Stephensen but the editor of the *Architectural Review*, Hubert de Cronin Hastings. In April–May 1929 he had commissioned Lawrence's article 'Pictures on the Wall' (see above); satisfied with that, and planning an issue which would explore the deleterious effects of industrialisation on the face of England, together with the contrasting example of Sweden, Hastings wrote again to Lawrence. Unfortunately the correspondence has not survived but its existence and its purpose are clear from the prefatory note to the essay when it appeared in the *Review*, in August 1930, under the provocative and ironic title (partly using Lawrence's own words):

Then Disaster Looms Ahead / Mining-Camp Civilization. / The English Contribution to Progress. / *By* D. H. Lawrence.

The note read:

This article, the last he wrote, was the product of correspondence between D. H. Lawrence and the Editor of THE ARCHITECTURAL REVIEW. *Lawrence had been asked to write something about his own mining countryside, and the result, apparently unfinished, was found in an MS book after his death.*

It is now published as it was found, a protest against the shapeless kind of industrialization, which we can point to with whatever vanity we feel, as the result of the English ideal of Muddling Through.

While not accepting Hastings's assertion that the article was the last Lawrence wrote, or that it remained unfinished, there is no reason to doubt his account of its origin. Lawrence's article was followed, in the same issue, by one entitled: 'Progress. / The Swedish Contribution'.

Though the article was commissioned by Hastings, he was not the first to publish it; that prize fell to Lawrence's erstwhile friend John Middleton Murry as editor of *New Adelphi*, in June 1930, where it was preceded by a poem (dated May 1919), 'TO D. H. LAWRENCE' by 'D. L. P.', most likely the wife of Murry's close friend Max Plowman: Dorothy Lloyd Plowman. The first collected publication of the essay was in *Phoenix*.

NOTTINGHAM AND THE MINING COUNTRYSIDE

I was born nearly forty-four years ago, in Eastwood, a mining village of some three thousand souls, about eight miles from Nottingham, and one mile from the small stream, the Erewash, which divides Nottinghamshire from Derbyshire. It is hilly country, looking west to Crich and towards Matlock, sixteen miles away, and east and north-east towards Mansfield and the Sherwood Forest district. To me it seemed, and still seems, an extremely beautiful countryside, just between the red sandstone and the oak-trees of Nottingham, and the cold limestone, the ash-trees, the stone fences of Derbyshire. To me, as a child and young man, it was still the old England of the forest and agricultural past; there were no motor-cars, the mines were, in a sense, an accident in the landscape, and Robin Hood and his merry men were not very far away.

The string of coal-mines of B.W. & Co.* had been opened some sixty years before I was born, and Eastwood had come into being as a consequence. It must have been a tiny village at the beginning of the nineteenth century, a small place of cottages and fragmentary rows of little four-roomed miners' dwellings, the homes of the old colliers of the eighteenth century, who worked in the bits of mines, foot-rill mines* with an opening in the hillside into which the miners walked, or windlass mines, where the men were wound up one at a time, in a bucket, by a donkey. The windlass mines were still working when my father* was a boy and the shafts of some were still there, when I was a boy.

But somewhere about 1820 the company must have sunk the first big shafts—not very deep—and installed the first machinery, or the real industrial colliery. Then came my grandfather,* a young man trained to be a tailor, drifting from the south of England, and got the job of company tailor for the Brinsley mine. In those days the Company supplied the men with the thick flannel vests, or singlets, and the mole-skin trousers lined at the top with flannel, in which the colliers worked. I remember the great rolls of coarse flannel and pit-cloth which stood in the corner of my grandfather's shop when I was a small boy, and the big, strange old sewing-machine, like nothing else on earth, which sewed the massive pit-trousers. But when I was only a child the company discontinued supplying the men with pit-clothes.

My grandfather settled in in an old cottage down in a quarry-bed, by the brook at Old Brinsley, near the pit. A mile away, up at Eastwood, the Company built the first miners' dwellings—it must be nearly a hundred years ago. Now Eastwood occupies a lovely position on a hill-top, with the steep slope towards Derbyshire and the long slope towards Nottingham. They put up a new church, which stands fine and commanding, even if it has no real form, looking across the awful Erewash Valley at the church of Heanor, similarly commanding, away on a hill beyond. What opportunities, what opportunities! These mining villages *might* have been like the lovely hill-towns of Italy, shapely and fascinating. And what happened?

Most of the little rows of dwellings of the old-style miners were pulled down, and dull little shops began to rise along the Nottingham Road, while on the down-slope of the north side, the Company erected what is still known as the New Buildings, or the Square. These New Buildings consist of two great hollow squares of dwellings planked down on the rough slope of the hill, little four-room houses with the "front" looking outward into the grim blank street, and the "back", with a tiny square brick yard, a low wall, and a W.C. and ash-pit, looking into the desert of the square, hard, uneven, jolting black earth tilting rather steeply down, with these little back yards all round, and openings at the corners. The squares were quite big, and absolutely desert save for the posts for clothes lines, and people passing, children playing on the hard earth. And they were shut in like a barracks enclosure, very strange.

Even fifty years ago the squares were unpopular. It was "common" to live in the Square. It was a little less common to live in The Breach, which consisted of six blocks of rather more pretentious dwellings erected by the Company in the valley below, two rows of three blocks, with an alley between. And it was most "common", most degraded of all to live in Dakins Row, two rows of the old dwellings, very old, black, four-roomed little places, that stood on the hill again, not far from the Squares.

So the place started. Down the steep street between the Squares, Scargill Street, the Wesleyan chapel was put up, and I was born in the little corner shop just above. Across the other side the square the miners themselves built the big barn-like Primitive Methodist Chapel. Along the hill-top ran the Nottingham Road, with its scrappy, ugly mid-Victorian shops. The little market-place, with a superb outlook, ended the village on the Derbyshire side, and was just left bare, with the Sun

Inn on one side, the chemist across, with the gilt pestle-and-mortar, and a shop at the other corner, the corner of Alfreton Road and Nottingham Road.

In this queer jumble of the old England and the new, I came into consciousness. As I remember, little local speculators already began to straggle dwellings in rows, always in rows, across the fields: nasty red-brick flat-faced dwellings with dark slate roofs. The bay-window period only began when I was a child. But most of the country was untouched.

There must be three or four hundred Company houses in the Squares and the streets that surround the Squares, like a great barracks wall. There must be sixty or eighty Company houses in The Breach. The old Dakins Row will have thirty to forty little holes. Then counting the old cottages and rows left with their old gardens down the lanes and along the twitchells,* and even in the midst of Nottingham Road itself, there were houses enough for the population, there was no need for much building. And not much building went on, when I was small.

We lived in the Breach, in a corner house. A field-path came down under a great hawthorn hedge. On the other side was the brook, with the old sheep-bridge going over into the meadows. The hawthorn hedge by the brook had grown tall as tall trees: and we used to bathe from there in the dipping-hole, where the sheep were dipped:* just near the fall from the old mill-dam, where the water rushed. The mill only ceased grinding the local corn when I was a child. And my father, who always worked in Brinsley pit, and who always got up at five oclock, if not at four, would set off in the dawn across the fields at Coney Grey, and hunt for mushrooms in the long grass, or perhaps pick up a skulking rabbit, which he would bring home at evening inside the lining of his pit-coat.

So that the life was a curious cross between industrialism and the old agricultural England of Shakespeare and Milton and Fielding and George Eliot.* The dialect was broad Derbyshire, and always "thee" and "thou". The people lived almost entirely by instinct, men of my father's age could not really read. And the pit did not mechanise men. On the contrary. Under the butty system, the miners worked underground as a sort of intimate community, they knew each other practically naked, and with curious close intimacy, and the darkness and the underground remoteness of the pit "stall",* and the continual presence of danger, made the physical, instinctive and intuitional contact between men very highly developed, a contact almost as close as touch, very real and very powerful. This physical awareness and intimate *togetherness* was at its strongest down pit. When the men came up into the light, they blinked.

They had, in a measure, to change their flow. Nevertheless they brought with them above-ground the curious dark intimacy of the mine, the naked sort of contact, and if I think of my childhood, it is always as if there was a lustrous sort of inner darkness, like the gloss of coal, in which we moved and had our real being.* My father loved the pit. He was hurt badly, more than once, but he would never stay away. He loved the contact, the intimacy, as men in the war loved the intense male comradeship of the dark days. They did not know what they had lost till they lost it. And I think it is the same with the young colliers of today.

Now the colliers had also an instinct of beauty. The colliers' wives had not. The colliers were deeply alive, instinctively. But they had no daytime ambition, and no daytime intellect. They avoided, really, the rational aspect of life. They preferred to take life instinctively and intuitively. They didn't even care very profoundly about wages. It was the women, naturally, who nagged on this score. There was a big discrepancy when I was a boy, between the collier who saw, at the best, only a brief few hours of daylight, often no daylight at all, during the winter weeks: and the collier's wife, who had all the day to herself, when the man was down pit.

The great fallacy is, to pity the man. He didn't dream of pitying himself, till agitators and sentimentalists taught him to. He was happy: or more than happy, he was fulfilled. Or he was fulfilled on the receptive side, not on the expressive. The collier went to the pub and drank, in order to continue his intimacy with his mates. They talked endlessly, but it was rather of wonders and marvels, even in politics, than of facts. It was hard facts, in the shape of wife, money, and nagging home necessities, which they fled away from, out of the house to the pub: and out of the house to the pit.

The collier fled out of the house as soon as he could, away from the nagging materialism of the woman. With the women, it was always: This is broken, now you've got to mend it!—or else: We want this, that and the other, and where is the money coming from?—The collier didn't know and didn't care very deeply—his life was otherwise. So he escaped. He roved the countryside, with his dog, prowling for a rabbit, for nests, for mushrooms, anything. He loved the countryside, just the indiscriminating feel of it. Or he loved just to sit on his heels and watch—anything or nothing. He was not intellectually interested. Life for him did not consist in facts, but in a flow. Very often, he loved his garden. And very often, he had a genuine love of the beauty of flowers. I have known it often and often, in colliers.

Now the love of flowers is a very misleading thing. Most women love flowers as possessions, and as trimmings. They can't look at a flower, and wonder a moment, and pass on. If they see a flower that arrests their attention, they must at once pick it, pluck it. Possession! A possession! Something added on to *me*!—And most of the so-called love of flowers today is merely this reaching out of possession and egoism: something I've *got*: something that embellishes *me*. Yet I've seen many a collier stand in his back garden looking down at a flower with that odd, remote sort of contemplation which shows a *real* awareness of the presence of beauty. It would not even be admiration, or joy, or delight, or any of those things which so often have a root in the possessive instinct. It would be a sort of contemplation: which shows the incipient artist.

The real tragedy of England, as I see it, is the tragedy of ugliness. The country is so lovely: the man-made England is so vile. I know that the ordinary collier, when I was a boy, had a peculiar sense of beauty, coming from his intuitive and instinctive consciousness, which was awakened down pit. And the fact that he met with just cold ugliness and raw materialism when he came up into daylight, and particularly when he came to the Square or the Breach, and to his own table, killed something in him and in a sense, spoiled him as a man. The woman almost invariably nagged about material things. She was taught to do it, she was encouraged to do it. It was a mother's business to see that her sons "got on", and it was the man's business to provide the money. In my father's generation, with the old wild England behind them, and the lack of education, the man was not beaten down. But in my generation, the boys I went to school with, colliers now, have all been beaten down, what with the din-din-dinning of Board Schools, books, cinemas, clergymen, the whole national and human consciousness hammering on the fact of material prosperity above all things.

The men are beaten down, there is prosperity for a time, in their defeat—and then disaster looms ahead. The root of all disaster is disheartenment. And men are disheartened. The men of England, the colliers in particular, are disheartened. They have been betrayed and beaten.

Now though perhaps nobody knew it, it was ugliness which really betrayed the spirit of man, in the nineteenth century. The great crime which the moneyed classes and promoters of industry committed in the palmy Victorian days was the condemning of the workers to ugliness, ugliness, ugliness: meanness and formless and ugly surroundings, ugly ideals, ugly religion ugly hope, ugly love, ugly clothes, ugly furniture, ugly houses, ugly relationship between workers and employers. The human soul needs actual beauty even more than bread. The middle classes jeer at the colliers for buying pianos—but what is the piano, often as not, but a blind reaching out for beauty. To the woman it is a possession and a piece of furniture and something to feel superior about. But see the elderly colliers trying to learn to play, see them listening with queer alert faces to their daughter's execution of *The Maiden's Prayer*,* and you will see a blind, unsatisfied craving for beauty. It is far more deep in the men than the women. The women want show. The men want beauty, and still want it.

If the Company, instead of building those sordid and hideous Squares, then, when they had that lovely site to play with, there on the hill top: if they had put a tall column in the middle of the small market-place, and run three parts of a circle of arcade round the pleasant space: where people could stroll or sit, and with handsome houses behind! If they had made big, substantial houses, in apartments of five or six rooms, and with handsome entrances. If above all, they had encouraged song and dancing—for the miners still sang and danced—and provided handsome space for these. If only they had encouraged some form of beauty in dress, some form of beauty in interior life—furniture, decoration. If they had given prizes for the handsomest chair or table, the loveliest scarf, the most charming room that the men or women could make! If only they had done this, there would never have been an industrial problem. The industrial problem arises from the base forcing of all human energy into a competition of mere acquisition.

You may say the working man would not have accepted such a form of life: the Englishman's home is his castle etc. etc.—"My own little home". But if you can hear every word the next-door people say, there's not much castle. And if you can see everybody in the square, if they go to the W.C.! And if your one desire is to get out of your "castle" and your "own little home"!—well, there's not much to be said for it. Anyhow it's only the woman who idolises "her own little home"—and it's always the woman at her worst, her most greedy, most possessive, most mean. There's nothing to be said for the "little home" any more: a great scrabble of ugly pettiness over the face of the land.

As a matter of fact, till 1800 the English people were strictly a rural people—very rural. England has had towns for centuries, but they have never been real towns, only clusters of village streets. Never the real *urbs*. The English character has failed to develop the real *urban* side of a man, the civic side. Siena is a bit of a place, but it is a real city, with citizens intimately connected with the city. Nottingham is a vast place sprawling towards a million,* and it is nothing more than an amorphous agglomeration. There *is* no Nottingham, in the sense that there is Siena. The Englishman is stupidly undeveloped as a citizen. And it is partly due to his "little home" stunt, and partly to his acceptance of hopeless paltriness in his surrounding. The new cities of America are much more genuine cities, in the Roman sense, than is London or Manchester. Even Edinburgh used to be more of a true city than any town England ever produced.

That silly little individualism of "the Englishman's home is his castle"—and "my own little home" is out of date. It would work almost up to 1800, when every Englishman was still a villager and a cottager. But the industrial system has brought a great change. The Englishman still likes to think of himself as a "cottager"—"my home, my garden." But it is puerile. Even the farm-laborer today is psychologically a town-bird. The English are town-birds through and through, today, as the inevitable result of their complete industrialisation. Yet they don't know how to build a city, how to think of one, or how to live in one. They are all suburban, pseudo-cottagey, and not one of them knows how to be truly urban—the citizen as the Romans were citizens—or the Athenians—or even the Parisians, till the war came.

And this is because we have frustrated that instinct of community which would make us unite in pride and dignity in the bigger gesture of the citizen, not the cottager. The great city means beauty, dignity, and a certain splendour. This is the side of the Englishman that has been thwarted and shockingly betrayed: England is a mean and petty scrabble of paltry dwellings called "homes." I believe in their heart of hearts all Englishmen loathe their little homes—but not the women. What we want is a bigger gesture, a greater scope, a certain splendour, a certain grandeur, and beauty, big beauty. The American does far better than we, in this.

And the promoter* of industry, a hundred years ago, dared to perpetrate the ugliness of my native village. And still more monstrous, promoters of industry today are scrabbling over the face of England with miles and square miles of red-brick "homes," like horrible scabs. And the men inside these little red rat-traps get more and more helpless, being more and more humiliated, more and more dissatisfied, like trapped rats. Only the meaner sort of women go on loving the little home which is no more than a rat-trap to her man.

Do away with it all, then. At no matter what cost, start in to alter it. Never mind about wages and industrial squabbling. Turn the attention elsewhere. Pull down my native village to the last brick. Plan a nucleus. Fix the focus. Make a handsome gesture of radiation from the focus. And then put up big buildings, handsome, that sweep to a civic centre. And furnish them with beauty. And make an absolute clean start. Do it place by place. Make a new England. Away with little homes! Away with scrabbling pettiness and paltriness. Look at the contours of the land, and build up from these, with a sufficient nobility. The English may be mentally or spiritually developed. But as citizens of splendid cities they are more ignominous than rabbits. And they nag, nag, nag all the time about politics and wages and all that, like mean narrow housewives.

WE NEED ONE ANOTHER

On 23 September 1929 Nancy Pearn passed the information to Lawrence: '"*Vanity Fair*", I hear, are keen to discuss a contract for a year. Such a contract would entail the delivery of probably one article a month on subjects to be agreed upon, at a sum in the neighbourhood of £40, and would leave us free to negotiate separately over here. Does the idea attract you?' (*Letters*, vii. 512 n. 2). In his reply on 4 October (vii. 512), Lawrence expressed interest in the proposal but, in view of his health, also hesitation about a commitment to supply an article every month for a year. Nevertheless it is perhaps significant that, on the very next day, he told Enid Hilton, the daughter of his old Eastwood friends, Willie and Sallie Hopkin, that he had written 'a newspaper article' (vii. 513); it may have been 'We Need One Another'. What is certain, however, is that a month later, on 4 November, he wrote to Nancy Pearn: 'I'm sending you three articles which I wrote with an eye to *Vanity Fair*, but I don't know if they are suitable. When they are typed, will you read them, and *don't* offer them to *Vanity Fair* if you think them unsuitable' (vii. 554). She replied on 7 November, acknowledging the arrival of the three articles and identifying them as 'Nobody Loves Me', 'We Need One Another' and 'The Real Thing' (vii. 554 n. 2).

Before the year's end, *Vanity Fair* had decided to reject all three, a decision Nancy Pearn conveyed to Lawrence on 1 January 1930. However she continued her efforts to place them and was able to tell Lawrence on 3 February that 'We Need One Another' had been accepted for *Scribner's Magazine*; the article appeared there in May 1930 and as an independent publication in 1933 (see Roberts A64). It was first collected in *Phoenix*.

WE NEED ONE ANOTHER*

We may as well admit it: men and women need one another. We may as well, after all our kicking against the pricks, our revolting and our sulking, give in and be graceful about it. We are all individualists: we are all egoists: we all believe intensely in freedom, our own at all events. We all want to be absolute, and sufficient unto ourselves. And it is a great blow to our self-esteem that we simply *need* another human being. We don't mind airily picking and choosing among women—or among men, if we are a woman. But to have to come down to the nasty, sharp-pointed brass tacks of admitting: My God, I can't live without that obstreperous woman of mine!—this is terribly humiliating to our isolated conceit.

And when I say: "without that woman of mine!", I do not mean a mistress, the sexual relation in the French sense. I mean the woman: my relationship to the woman herself. There is hardly a man living who can exist at all cheerfully without a relationship to some particular woman: unless, of course, he makes another man play the rôle of woman. And the same of woman. There is hardly a woman on earth who can live cheerfully without some intimate relationship to a man; unless she substitutes some other woman for the man.

So there it is!—Now for three thousand years men, and women, have been struggling against this fact. In Buddhism, particularly, a man could never possibly attain the supreme Nirvana if he so much as saw a woman out of the corner of his eye. "Alone I did it!" is the proud assertion of the gentleman who attains Nirvana. And "Alone I did it!" says the Christian whose soul is saved. They are the religions of overweening individualism, resulting, of course, in our disastrous modern egoism of the individual. Marriage, which on earth is a sacrament, is dissolved by the decree absolute of death. In heaven there is no giving and taking in marriage.* The soul in heaven is supremely individual, absolved from every relationship except that with the Most High. In heaven there is neither marriage nor love, nor friendship nor fatherhood nor motherhood, nor sister nor brother nor cousin: there is just me, in my perfected isolation, placed in perfect relation to the Supreme, the Most High.

When we talk of Heaven, we talk, really, of that which we would most like to attain, and most like to be here on earth. The condition of heaven is the condition to be longed for, striven for, now.

Now if I say to a woman, or to a man: "Would you like to be purely free of all human relationships, free from father and mother, brother and sister, husband, lover, friend, or child? free from all these human entanglements, and reduced purely to your own pure self, connected only with the Supreme Power, the Most High?"—then what would the answer be? What is the answer, I ask you? What is your own sincere answer?

I expect, in almost all cases, it is an emphatic "yes." In the past, most men would have said "yes," and most women "no." But today, I think, many men might hesitate, and nearly all women would unhesitatingly say "Yes."

Modern men, however, have so nearly achieved this Nirvana-like condition of having no real human relationships at all, that they are beginning to wonder what and where they are. What are you, when you've asserted your grand independence, broken all the ties, or "bonds," and reduced yourself to a "pure" individuality? What are you?

You may imagine you are something very grand, since few individuals even approximate to this independence without falling into deadly egoism and conceit: and emptiness. The real danger is, reduced to your own single merits and cut off from the most vital human contacts, the danger is that you are left just simply next to nothing. Reduce any individual, man or woman, to his elements, or her elements, and what is she? what is he? Extremely little! Take Napoleon, and stick him alone on a miserable island, and what is he? a peevish, puerile little fellow. Put Mary Stuart in a nasty stone castle of a prison, and she becomes merely a catty little person. Now Napoleon was not a peevish, puerile little fellow, even if he became such when isolated on St. Helena. And Mary Queen of Scots was only a catty little person when she was isolated in Fotheringay or some such hole.* This grand isolation, this reducing of ourselves to our very elemental selves, is the greatest fraud of all. It is like plucking the peacock naked of all his feathers, to try to get at the real bird. When you've plucked the peacock bare, what have you got? Not the peacock, but the naked corpse of a bird.

And so it is with us and our grand individualism. Reduce any of us to the *mere* individual that we are, and what do we become? Napoleon becomes a peevish, puerile little fellow, Mary Queen of Scots becomes a catty little person, St. Simeon Stylites, stuck up on his pillar,* becomes a conceited lunatic, and we, wonderful creatures as we are, become trashy conceited little modern egoists. The world today is full of silly impertinent egoists who have broken all the finer human ties, and base their claims to superiority on their own emptiness and nullity. But the empty ones are being found out. Emptiness, which makes a fine noise, deceives for a short time only.

The fact remains, that when you cut off a man and isolate him in his own pure and wonderful individuality, you haven't got the man at all, you've only got the dreary fag end of him. Isolate Napoleon, and he is nothing. Isolate Immanuel Kant,* and his grand ideas will still go on tick-tick-ticking inside his head, but unless he could write them down and communicate them, they might as well be the ticking of the death-watch beetle. Take even Buddha himself, if he'd been whisked off to some lonely place and planted cross-legged under a bhô-tree* and nobody had ever seen him or heard any of his Nirvana talk, then I doubt he wouldn't have got much fun out of Nirvana, and he'd have been just a crank. In absolute isolation, I doubt if any individual amounts to much: or if any soul is worth saving; or even having. "And I, if I be lifted up, will draw all men unto me."* But if there were no other men to be lifted, the whole show would be a fiasco.

So that everything, even individuality itself, depends on relationship. "God cannot do without me," said an eighteenth century Frenchman. What he meant was, that if there were no human beings, if Man did not exist, then God, the God of Man, would have no meaning. And it is true. If there were no men and women, Jesus would be meaningless. In the same way, Napoleon on St. Helena became meaningless, and the French nation lost a great part of its meaning without him. In connection with his army and the nation, a great power streamed out of Napoleon, and from* the French people there streamed back to him a great responsive power, and therein lay his greatness, and theirs. That is, in the relationship. The light shines only when the circuit is completed. The light does not shine with one half of the current. Every light is some sort of completed circuit. And so is every life, if it is going to be a life.

We have our very individuality in relationship. Let us swallow this important and prickly fact. Apart from our connections with other people we are barely individuals, we amount, all of us, to next to nothing. It is in the living touch between us and other people, other lives, other phenomena that we move and have our being.* Strip us of our human contacts and of our contact with the living earth and the sun, and we are almost bladders of emptiness. Our individuality means nothing.

A skylark that was alone on an island would be songless and meaningless, his individuality gone, running about like a mouse in the grass. But if there were one female with him, it would lift him singing into the air, and restore him his real individuality.*

And so with men and women. It is in relationship to one another that they have their true individuality and their distinct being: in contact, not out of contact. This is sex, if you like. But it is no more sex than sunshine on the grass is sex. It is a living contact, give and take: the great and subtle relationship of men and women, man and woman. In this and through this we *become* real individuals, without it, without the real contact, we remain more or less nonentities.*

But of course, it is necessary to have the contact alive and unfixed. It is not a question of: Marry the woman and have done with it.—That is only one of the stupid recipes for avoiding contact and killing contact. There are many popular dodges for killing* every possibility of true contact: like sticking a woman on a pedestal, or the reverse, sticking her beneath notice; or making a "model" housewife of her, or a "model" mother, or a "model" help-meet. All mere devices for avoiding any contact with her. A woman is not a "model" anything. She is not even a distinct and definite personality. It is time we got rid of these fixed notions. A woman is a living fountain whose spray falls delicately around her, on all that come near. A woman is a strange soft vibration on the air, going forth unknown and unconscious, and seeking a vibration of response.—Or else she is a discordant, jarring, painful vibration, going forth and hurting everyone within range. And a man the same. A man as he lives and moves and has being, is a fountain of life-vibration, quivering and flowing towards some-one, something that will receive his outflow and send back an inflow, so that a circuit is completed, and there is a sort of peace. Or else he is a source of irritation, discord, and pain, harming everyone near him.

But while we remain healthy and positive, we seek all the time to come into true human relationship with other human beings. Yet it has to happen, the relationship, almost unconsciously—we can't *deliberately* do much with a human connection, except smash it: and that is usually not difficult. On the positive side, we can only most carefully let* it take place, without interfering or forcing.

We are labouring under a false conception of ourselves. For centuries, man has been the conquering hero, and woman has been merely the string to his bow, part of his accoutrement. Then woman was allowed to have a soul of her own, a separate soul. So the separating business started, with all the clamour of freedom and independence. Now the freedom and independence have been rather overdone, they lead to an empty nowhere, the rubbish heap of all our dead feelings and waste illusions.

The conquering hero business is as obsolete as Marshal Hindenburg,* and about as effective. The world sees attempts at revival of this stunt, but they are usually silly, in the end. Man is no longer a conquering hero. Neither is he a supreme soul isolated and alone in the universe, facing the Unknown in the eternity of death. That stunt is also played out, though the pathetic boys of today keep on insisting on it: especially the pathetic boys who wrap themselves in the egoistic pathos of their sufferings during the late war.

But both stunts are played out, both the conquering hero and the pathetic hero clothed in suffering and facing Eternity in the soul's last isolation. The second stunt is, of course, more popular today, and still dangerous to the self-pitying, played-out specimens of the younger generation. But for all that, it is a dud stunt, finished.

What a man has to do today is to admit, at last, that all these fixed ideas are no good. As a fixed object, even as an individuality or a personality, no human being, man or woman, amounts to much. The great I AM* does not apply to human beings, so they may as well leave it alone. As soon as anybody, man or woman, becomes a great I AM, he becomes nothing. Man or woman, each is a flow, a flowing life. And without one another, we can't flow, just as a river cannot flow without banks. A woman is one bank of the river of my life, and the world is the other. Without the two shores, my life would be a marsh. It is the relationship to woman, and to my fellow-men, which makes me myself, a river of life.*

And* it is this, even, that gives me my soul. A man who has never had a vital relationship to any other human being doesn't really have a soul. We cannot feel that Immanuel Kant ever had a soul. A soul is something that forms and fulfils itself in my contacts, my living touch with people I have loved or hated or truly known. I am born with the clue to my soul. The wholeness of my soul I must achieve.—And by my soul I mean my wholeness. What we suffer from today is the lack of a sense of our own wholeness, or completeness, which is peace. What we lack, what the young lack, is a sense of being whole in themselves. They feel so scrappy, they have no peace. And by peace I don't mean inertia, but the full flowing of life, like a river.

We lack peace because we are not whole. And we are not whole because we have known only a tithe of the vital relationships we might have had.

We live in an age which believes in stripping away the relationships. Strip them away, like an onion, till you come to pure, or blank nothingness. Emptiness. That is where most men have come now: to a knowledge of their own complete emptiness. They wanted so badly to be "themselves" that they became nothing at all: or next to nothing.

It is not much fun, being next to nothing. And life ought to be fun, the greatest fun. Not merely "having a good time" in order to "get away from yourself." But real fun in being yourself. Now there are two great relationships possible to human beings: the relationship of man to woman, and the relationship of man to man. As regards both, we are in a hopeless mess.

But the relationship of man to woman is the central fact in actual human life. Next comes the relationship of man to man. And a long way after, all the other relationships, fatherhood, motherhood, sister, brother, friend.

A young man said to me the other day, rather sneeringly: "I'm afraid I can't believe in the regeneration of England by sex."—I said to him: "I'm sure you can't."—He was trying to inform me that he was above such trash as sex, and such commonplace as women. He was the usual vitally below par, a hollow and egoistic young man, infinitely wrapped up in himself, like a sort of mummy that will crumble if unwrapped.

But what is sex, after all, but the symbol of the relation of man to woman, woman to man? And the relation of man to woman is wide as all life. It consists in infinite different flows between the two beings, different, even apparently contrary. Chastity is part of the flow between man and woman, so is physical passion. And beyond these, an infinite range of subtle communication which we know nothing about. I should say that the relation between any two decently married people changes profoundly every few years, often without their knowing anything about it; though every change causes pain, even if it brings a certain joy. The long course of marriage is a long event of perpetual change, in which a man and a woman mutually build up their souls and make themselves whole. It is like rivers flowing on, through new country, always unknown.

But we are so foolish, and fixed by our limited ideas. A man says: "I don't love my wife any more, I no longer want to sleep with her."—But why should he always want to sleep with her? How does he know what other subtle and vital interchange is going on between him and her, making them both whole, in this period when he doesn't want to sleep with her? And she, instead of jibbing and saying that all is over and she must find another man and get a divorce, why doesn't she pause, and listen for a new rhythm in her soul, and look for the new movement in the man. With every change, a new being emerges, a new rhythm establishes itself, we renew our life as we grow older, and there is real peace. Why oh why do we want one another to be always the same, fixed, like a menu-card that is never changed.

If only we had more sense. But we are held by a few fixed ideas, like sex, money, what a person "ought" to be, and so forth, and we miss the whole of life. Sex is a changing thing, now alive, now quiescent, now fiery, now apparently quite gone, quite gone. But the ordinary man and woman haven't the gumption to take it in all its changes. They demand crass, crude sex-desire, they demand it always, and when it isn't forthcoming then—smash-bash! smash up the whole show. Divorce! Divorce!

I am so tired of being told that I want mankind to go back to the condition of savages. As if modern city people weren't about the crudest, rawest, most crassly savage monkeys that ever existed, when it comes to the relation of man and woman. All I see in our vaunted civilisation is men and women smashing each other emotionally and psychically to bits, and all I ask is that they should pause and consider.

For sex, to me, means the whole of the relationship between man and woman. Now this relationship is far greater than we know. We only know a few crude forms, mistress, wife, mother, sweet-heart. The woman is like an idol, or a marionette, always forced to play one rôle or another: sweet-heart, mistress, wife, mother. If only we could break up this fixity, and realise the unseizable quality of real womanhood: that a woman is a flow, a river of life quite different from a man's river of life: and that each river must flow in its own way, though without breaking its bounds: and that the relation of man to woman is the flowing of two rivers side by side, sometimes even mingling, then separating again, and travelling on. The relationship is a life-long change and a life-long travelling. And that is sex. At periods, sex-desire itself departs completely. Yet the great flow of the relationship goes on all the same, undying, and this is the flow of living sex, the relation between man and woman, that lasts a life-time, and of which sex-desire is only one vivid, most-vivid manifestation.*

THE REAL THING

For the circumstances which led to the writing of 'The Real Thing' see the introduction to 'We Need One Another'. Having been rejected by *Vanity Fair*, the article was accepted for *Scribner's Magazine* and published there in June 1930. It was collected in *Phoenix*.

THE REAL THING

Most revolutions are explosions: and most explosions blow up a great deal more than was intended. It is obvious, from later history, that the French didn't really want to blow up the whole monarchic and aristocratic system, in the 1790's. Yet they did it, and try as they might, they could never really put anything together again. The same with the Russians: they want to blow a gateway in a wall, and they blow the whole house down.

All fights for freedom, that succeed, go too far, and become in turn the infliction of a tyranny. Like Napoleon or a soviet.* And like the freedom of women. Perhaps the greatest revolution of modern times is the emancipation of women: and perhaps the deepest fight for two thousand years and more has been the fight for woman's independence, or freedom, call it what you will. The fight was deeply bitter: and, it seems to me, it is won. It is even going beyond, and becoming a tyranny of woman, of the individual woman in the house, and of the feminine ideas and ideals in the world. Say what we will, the world is swayed by feminine emotion today, and the triumph of the productive and domestic activities of man over all his previous military or adventurous or flaunting activities is a triumph of the woman in the home. The male is subservient to the female need, and outwardly, man is submissive to the demands of woman.

But inwardly, what has happened? It cannot be denied that there has been a fight. Woman has not won her freedom without fighting for it: and she still fights, fights hard, even when there is no longer any need. For man has fallen. It would be difficult to point to a man in the world today who is not subservient to the great woman-spirit that sways modern mankind. But still not peacefully. Still the sway of a struggle, the sway of conflict.

Woman in the mass has fought her fight politically. But woman the individual has fought her fight with individual man, with father, brother, and particularly with husband. All through the past, except for brief periods of revolt, woman has played a part of submission to man. Perhaps the inevitable nature of man and woman demands such submission.

But it must be an instinctive, unconscious submission, made in unconscious faith. At certain periods this blind faith of woman in man seems to weaken, then break. It always happens at the end of some great phase, before another phase sets in. It always seems to start, in man, an overwhelming worship of woman, and a glorification of queens. It always seems to bring a brief spell of glory, and a long spell of misery after. Man yields in glorifying the woman, the glory dies, the fight goes on.

It is not necessarily a sex struggle. The sexes are not by nature pitted against one another in hostility. It only happens so, in certain periods: when man loses his unconscious faith in himself, and woman loses her faith in him, unconsciously and then consciously. It is not biological sex struggle. Not at all. Sex is the great uniter, the great unifier. Only in periods of the collapse of instinctive life-assurance in men does sex become a great weapon and divider.

Man loses his faith in himself, and woman begins to fight him. Cleopatra really fought Anthony—that's why he killed himself.* But he had first lost faith in himself, and leaned on love, which is a sure sign of weakness and failure. And when woman once begins to fight her man, she fights and fights, as if for freedom. But it is not even freedom she wants. Freedom is a man's word: its meaning, to a woman, is really rather trivial. She fights to escape from a man who doesn't really believe in himself, she fights and fights, and there is no freedom from the fight. Woman is truly less free today than ever she has been since time began: in the womanly sense of freedom. Which means, she has less peace, less of that lovely womanly peace that flows like a river, less of the lovely, flower-like repose of a happy woman, less of the nameless joy in life, purely unconscious, which is the very breath of a woman's being, than ever she has had since she and man first set eyes on one another. Today, woman is always tense and strung up, alert, and bare-armed, not for love but for battle. In her shred of a dress and her little helmet of a hat, her cropped hair and her stark bearing she is a sort of soldier, and look at her as one may, one can see nothing else. It is not her fault. It is her doom. It happens when man loses his primary faith in himself and in his very life.

Now through the ages thousands of ties have formed between men and women. In the ages of discredit, these ties are felt as bonds, and must be fought loose. It is a great tearing and snapping of sympathies, and of unconscious sympathetic connections. It is a great rupture of unconscious tenderness and unconscious flow of strength between man and woman. Man and woman are not two separate and complete entities. In spite of all protestation, we must continue to assert it. Man and woman are not even two separate persons: not even two separate consciousnesses, or minds. In spite of vehement cries to the contrary, it is so. Man is connected with woman forever, in connections visible and invisible, in a complicated life-flow that can never be analysed. It is not only man and wife: the woman facing me in the train, the girl I buy cigarettes from, all send forth to me a stream, a spray, a vapour of female life that enters my blood and my soul, and makes me me. And back again, I send the stream of male life which soothes and satisfies and builds up the woman. So it still is, very often, in public contacts. The more general stream of life-flow between men and women is not so much broken and reversed as the private flow. Hence we all tend more and more to live in public. In public men and women are still kind to one another, very often.

But in private, the fight goes on. It had started in our great-grandmothers: it was going strong in our grandmothers: and in our mothers it was the dominant factor in life. The women *thought* it was a fight for righteousness. They *thought* they were fighting the man to make him "better," and to make life "better" for the children. We know now, the ethical excuse was only an excuse. We know now that our fathers were fought and beaten by our mothers, not because our mothers really knew what was "better," but because our fathers had lost their instinctive hold on the life-flow and the life-reality, and therefore the female had to fight them at any cost, blind, and doomed.

We saw it going on as tiny children: the battle. We believed the moral excuse. But we lived to be men, and to be fought in turn. And now we know there is no excuse, moral or immoral. It is just phenomenal. And our mothers, who asserted such a belief in "goodness," were tired of that self-same goodness even before their death.

No, the fight was, and is, for itself. And it is pitiless—except in spasms and pauses. A woman does not fight a man for his love—though she may say so a thousand times over. She fights him because she knows, instinctively he *cannot* love. He has lost his peculiar belief in himself, his instinctive faith in his own life-flow, and so he cannot love. He *cannot*. The more he protests, the more he asserts, the more he kneels, the more he worships, the less he loves. A woman who is worshipped, or even adored, knows perfectly well, in her instinctive depths, that she is not loved, that she is being swindled. She encourages the swindle, oh enormously, it flatters her vanity. But in the end comes Nemesis and the Furies,* pursuing the unfortunate pair. Love between man and woman is neither worship nor adoration, but something much deeper, much less showy and gaudy, part of the very breath, and as ordinary, if we may say so, as breathing. Almost as necessary. In fact, love between man and woman is really just a kind of breathing.

No woman ever got a man's love by fighting for it: at least, by fighting *him*. No man ever loved a woman until she left off fighting him. And when will she leave off fighting him? When he has, apparently, submitted to her? (for the submission is always, at least partly, false and a fraud) No, then least of all—When a man has submitted to a woman, she usually fights him worse than ever, more ruthlessly. Why doesn't she leave him? Often she does. But what then? She merely takes up with another man in order to resume the fight. The need to fight with man is upon her, inexorable. Why can't she live alone? She can't. Sometimes she can join with other women, and keep up the fight in a group. Sometimes she *must* live alone, for no man will come forward to fight with her. Yet, sooner or later, the need for contact with a man comes over a woman again. It is imperative. If she is rich, she hires a dancing partner, a gigolo, and humiliates him to the last dregs. The fight is not ended. When the great Hector is dead, it is not enough. He must be trailed naked and defiled; tied by the heels to the tail of a contemptuous chariot.*

When is the fight over? Ah when! Modern life seems to give no answer. Perhaps when a man finds his strength and his rooted belief in himself again. Perhaps when the man has died, and been painfully born again with a different breath, a different courage, and a different kind of care, or carelessness. But most men can't and daren't die in their old, fearful selves. They cling to their women in desperation, and come to hate them with cold and merciless hate, the hate of a child that is persistently ill-treated. Then even the hate dies, the man escapes into the final state of egoism, when he has no true feelings any more, and cannot be made to suffer.

That is where the young are now. The fight is more or less fizzling out, because both parties have become hollow. There is a perfect cynicism. The young men know that most of the "benevolence" and "motherly love" of their adoring mothers was simply egoism again, and an extension of self, and a love of having absolute power over another creature. Oh these women who secretly lust to have absolute power over their own children—for their own good!—do they think the children are deceived? Not for a moment! You can read in the eyes of the small modern child: "My mother is trying to bully me with every breath she draws, but though I am only six, I can really resist her."—It is the fight, the fight. It has degenerated into the mere fight to impose the will over some other creature: mostly, now, mother over her children. She fails again, abjectly. But she goes on.

For the great fight with the man has come almost to an end. Why? is it because man has found a new strength, has died the death in his old body and been born with a new strength and a new sureness? Alas, apparently not so at all. Man has dodged, side-tracked. Tortured and cynical and unbelieving, he has let all his feelings go out of him, and remains a shell of a man, very nice, very pleasant, in fact the best of modern men. Because nothing really moves him except one thing, a threat against his own safety. He is terrified of not feeling "safe." So he keeps his woman there, between him and the world of dangerous feelings and demands.

But he feels nothing. It is the great *counterfeit* liberation, the counterfeit of Nirvana and the peace that passeth all understanding.* It *is* a sort of Nirvana, and a sort of peace: in sheer nullity. At first, the woman cannot realise it. She rages, she goes mad. Woman after woman you can see smashing herself against the figure of a man who has achieved the state of false peace, false strength, false power: the egoist. The egoist, he who has no more spontaneous feelings, and can be made to suffer humanly no more. He who derives all his life henceforth at second-hand, and is animated by self-will and some sort of secret ambition to *impose* himself, either on the world or on other individuals. See a man, or a woman trying to impose herself, himself, and you have an egoist in natural action. But the true *pose* of the modern egoist is that of perfect suaveness and kindness and humility: oh, always—delicately humble!

When a man achieves this triumph of egoism: and many men have achieved it today, practically all the successful ones, certainly all the charming ones, and all the "artistic" ones: then the woman concerned is apt to go really a little mad. She gets no more responses. The fight has suddenly given out. She throws herself against a man, and he is not there, only the sort of glassy image of him receives her shocks and feels nothing. She becomes wild, outrageous. The explanation of the impossible behaviour of some women in their thirties lies here. Suddenly nothing comes back at them in the fight, and they go crazy, demented, as if they were on the brink of a fearful abyss. Which they are.

And then they either go to pieces: or else, with one of those sudden turns typical of women, they suddenly realise. And then, almost instantly, their whole behaviour changes. It is over. The fight is finished. The man has side-tracked. He becomes, in a sense, negligible, though the basic animosity is only rarified, made more subtle. And so you have the smart young woman in her twenties. She no longer fights her man—or men. She leaves him to his devices, and as far as possible invents her own. She may have a child to bully. But as a rule she pushes the child away as far as she can. No, she is now quite alone. If the man has no real feelings, she has none either. No matter how she feels about her husband, unless she is in a state of nervous rage she calls him angel of light, and winged messenger,* and loveliest man, and my beautiful pet boy. She flips it all over him, like eau de Cologne. And he takes it quite for granted, and suggests the next amusement. And their life is "one round of pleasure," to use the old banality: until the nerves collapse. Everything is counterfeit: counterfeit complexion, counterfeit jewels, counterfeit elegance, counterfeit charm, counterfeit endearment, counterfeit passion, counterfeit culture, counterfeit love of Blake, or of The Bridge of San Luis Rey, or Picasso,* or the latest film star. Counterfeit sorrows and counterfeit delights, counterfeit woes and moans, counterfeit ecstasies, and under all, a hard, hard realisation that we live by money, and money alone: and a terrible lurking fear of nervous collapse, collapse.

These are, of course, the extreme cases of the modern young. They are those who have got way beyond tragedy or real seriousness, that old-fashioned stuff. They are—they don't know where they are. And they don't care. But they are at the far end of the great fight between men and women.

Judging them as a result, the fight hardly seems to have been worth it. But we are looking on them still as fighters. Perhaps there is something else, positive, as a result.

In their own way, many of these young ones who have gone through everything and reached a stage of emptiness and disillusion unparalleled since the decadent Romans of Ravenna, in the Fifth century, they are now, in very fear and forlornness beginning to put out feelers towards some new way of trust. They begin to realise that, if they are not careful, they will have missed life altogether. Missed the bus! They, the smart young who are so swift at hopping on to a thing, to have missed life itself, not to have hopped on to it! Missed the bus! to use London slang! Let the great chance slip by, while they were fooling round! The young are just beginning uneasily to realise that this may be the case. They are just beginning uneasily to realise that all that "life" which they lead, rushing around and being so smart, perhaps isn't life after all, and they are missing the real thing.

What then? What *is* the real thing? Ah, there's the rub.* There are millions of ways of living, and it's all life. But what is the real thing in life? What is it that makes you *feel* right, makes life really feel good?

It is the great question. And the answers are old answers. But every generation must frame the answer in its own way. What makes life good to me is the sense that, even if I am sick and ill, I am alive, alive to the depths of my soul, and in touch, somewhere in touch with the vivid life of the cosmos. Somehow my life draws strength from the depths of the universe, from the depths among the stars, from the great "World." Out of the great World comes my strength, and my reassurance. One could say "God," but the word "God" is somehow tainted. But there *is* a flame or a Life Everlasting wreathing through the cosmos forever, and giving us our renewal, once we can get in touch with it.

It is when men lose their contact with this eternal life-flame, and become merely personal, things in themselves, instead of things kindled in the flame, that the fight between man and woman begins. It cannot be avoided, any more than nightfall or rain. The more conventional and correct a woman may be, the more inwardly devastating she is once she feels the loss of the greater control and the greater sustenance. She becomes emotionally destructive, she can no more help it than she can help being a woman, when the great connection is lost.

And then there is nothing for men to do but to turn back to life itself. Turn back to the life that flows invisibly in the cosmos, and will flow for ever, sustaining and renewing all living things. It is not a question of sins or morality, of being good or being bad. It is a question of renewal, of being renewed, vivified, made new and vividly alive and aware, instead of being exhausted and stale, as men are today. How to be renewed, re-born, re-vivified: that is the question men must ask themselves, and women too.*

And the answer will be difficult. Some trick with glands or secretions, or raw food, or drugs won't do it. Neither will some wonderful revelation or message. It is not a question of knowing something, but of doing something. It is a question of getting into contact again with the *living* centre of the cosmos. And how are we to do it?

NOBODY LOVES ME

From 9 July to 18 September 1928 the Lawrences lived in the chalet, Kesselmatte, near Gsteig; their friends the American painters Earl and Achsah Brewster, with their daughter Harwood, stayed in a nearby hotel. On 13 July Lawrence wrote to Maria Huxley: 'The [Brewsters] came to tea and [Achsah] as near being in a real temper as ever I've seen her. She said: I don't know how it (the place) makes you feel, but I've lost *all* my *cosmic consciousness* and *all* my *universal love*. I feel I don't care one bit about *humanity*. – I said: Good for you [Achsah]!' (*Letters*, vi. 462). There can be no doubt that the opening paragraph of 'Nobody Loves Me' refers directly not only to the general relationship between the Lawrences and the Brewsters, but specifically to the conversation reported to Maria Huxley and partly italicised in both the letter and the article. The reference to 'Ruth' as being 'fifty or so' confirms her identity with Achsah Brewster who was fifty in 1928.

The existence of Lawrence's letter has given rise to a dispute over the date of the article. There are two principal possibilities: on the one hand that the quotation in the article from his conversation with Achsah Brewster places the composition of the piece shortly after 13 July 1928; on the other, that the opening words – 'Last year we had a little house up in the Swiss mountains' – point to a date of composition at least a year later. The balance of probability rests with the second. Lawrence was not in the habit of deceiving his readers or disguising occasions to which he made unambiguous reference. Moreover, his remarkably retentive memory is one of his most notable characteristics. In 'That Women Know Best', for example, he quotes a remark by his father in precisely the same words as were used in *Sons and Lovers* published fifteen years earlier, and another conversation between his parents that closely follows the text in the same novel.[1] It seems, indeed, most likely that 'Nobody Loves Me' was written – like

[1] See Explanatory notes to 'That Women Know Best' 83:3 and 84:18.

'We Need One Another' and 'The Real Thing' – shortly before the letter to Nancy Pearn of 4 November 1929 which accompanied the three articles.

Rejected by *Vanity Fair*, 'Nobody Loves Me' was published in both *Life and Letters* and *Virginia Quarterly Review* in July 1930. It was collected in *Phoenix*.

NOBODY LOVES ME

Last year we had a little house up in the Swiss mountains, for the summer. A friend came to tea: a woman of fifty or so, with her daughter: old friends.—"And how are you all?" I asked, as she sat, flushed and rather exasperated after the climb up to the chalet, on a hot afternoon, wiping her face with a too-small handkerchief.—"Well!" she replied, glancing almost viciously out of the window at the immutable slopes and peaks opposite.—"I don't know how *you* feel about it—but—these mountains!—well!—I've lost *all* my *cosmic consciousness*, and *all* my *love* of *humanity*—"

She is, of course, New England of the old school—and usually transcendentalist calm.* So that her exasperated frenzy of the moment—it was really a frenzy—coupled with the New England language and slight accent, seemed to me really funny. I laughed in her face, poor dear, and said: "Never mind! Perhaps you can do with a rest from your cosmic consciousness and your love of humanity."

I have often thought of it since: of what she really meant. And every time, I have had a little pang, realising that I was a bit spiteful to her. I admit, her New England transcendental habit of loving the cosmos *en bloc* and humanity *en masse** did rather get on my nerves, always. But then she had been brought up that way. And the fact of loving the cosmos didn't prevent her from being fond of her own garden—though it did, a bit; and her love of humanity didn't prevent her from having a real affection for her friends: except that she felt she *ought* to love them in a selfless and general way, which was rather annoying. Nevertheless, that, to me, rather silly language about cosmic consciousness and love of humanity did stand for something that was not merely cerebral. It stood, and I realised it afterwards, for her peace, her inward peace with the universe and with man. And this she could *not* do without. One may be at war with society, and still keep one's deep peace with mankind. It is not pleasant to be at war with society, but sometimes it is the only way of preserving one's peace of soul, which is peace with the living, struggling, *real* mankind. And this latter one cannot afford to lose. So I had no right to tell my friend she could do with a rest from her love of humanity. She couldn't, and none of us can: if we interpret *love of humanity* as that feeling of being at one with the struggling soul, or spirit or whatever it is, of our fellow men.

Now the wonder to me is that the young do seem to manage to get on without any "cosmic consciousness" or "love of humanity." They have, on the whole, shed the cerebral husk of generalisation from their emotional state: the cosmic and humanity touch. But it seems to me they have also shed the flower that was inside the husk. Of course you can hear a girl exclaim: "*Really*, you know, the colliers are darlings, and it's a shame the way they're treated." She will even rush off and register a vote for her darlings. But she doesn't really care—and one can sympathise with her. This caring about the wrongs of unseen people has been rather overdone. Nevertheless, though the colliers or cotton-workers or whatever they be are a long way off and we can't do anything about it, still, away in some depth of us, we know that we are connected vitally, if remotely, with these colliers or cotton workers, we dimly realise that mankind is one, almost one flesh.* It is an abstraction, but it is also a physical fact. In some way or other, the cotton workers of Carolina, or the rice-growers of China are connected with me and, to a faint yet real degree, part of me. The vibration of life which they give off reaches me, touches me, and affects me all unknown to me. For we are all more or less connected, all more or less in touch: all humanity. That is, until we have killed the sensitive responses in ourselves, which happens today only too often.

Dimly, this is what my transcendentalist meant by her "love of humanity," though she tended to kill the real thing by labelling it so philanthropically and bossily. Dimly, she meant her sense of participating in the life of all humanity, which is a sense we all have, delicately and deeply, when we are at peace in ourselves. But let us lose our inward peace, and at once we are likely to substitute for this delicate inward sense of participating in the life of all mankind, another thing, a nasty pronounced benevolence, which wants to do good to all mankind, and is only a form of self-assertion and of bullying. From this sort of love of humanity, good Lord deliver us!* and deliver poor humanity. My friend was a tiny bit tainted with this form of self-importance, as all transcendentalists were. So if the mountains, in their brutality, took away the tainted love, good for them. But my dear Ruth—I shall call her Ruth—had more than this. She had, woman of fifty as she was, an almost girlish naïve sense of living at peace, real peace, with her fellow-men. And this she could not afford to lose. And save for that taint of generalisation and *will*, she would never have lost it, even for that half-hour in the Swiss mountains. But she meant the "cosmos" and "humanity" to fit her will and her feelings, and the mountains made her realise that the cosmos *wouldn't*. When you come up against the cosmos, your consciousness is likely to suffer a jolt. And humanity, when you come down to it, is likely to give your "love" a nasty jar. But there you are.

When we come to the younger generation, however, we realise that "cosmic consciousness" and "love of humanity" have really been left out of their composition. They are like a lot of brightly coloured bits of glass, and they only feel just what they bump against, when they're shaken. They make an accidental pattern with other people, and for the rest they know nothing and care nothing.

So that cosmic consciousness and love of humanity, to use the absurd New England terms, are really dead. They were tainted. Both the cosmos and humanity were too much manufactured in New England. They weren't the real thing. They were, very often, just noble phrases to cover up self-assertion, self-importance, and benevolent bullying. They were just activities of the ugly, self-willed ego, determined that humanity and the cosmos should exist as New England allowed them to exist, or not at all. They were tainted with bullying egoism, and the young, having fine noses for this sort of smell, would have none of them.

The way to kill any feeling is to insist on it, harp on it, exaggerate it. Insist on loving humanity, and sure as fate you'll come to hate everybody. Because of course, if you insist on loving humanity, then you insist that it shall be lovable: which half the time, it isn't. In the same way, insist on loving your husband, and you won't be able to help hating him secretly. Because of course nobody is *always* lovable. If you insist they shall be, this imposes a tyranny over them, and they become less lovable. And if you force yourself to love them—or pretend to—when they are not lovable, you falsify everything, and fall into hate. The result of forcing any feeling is the death of that feeling, and the substitution of some sort of opposite. Whitman insisted on sympathising with everything and everybody: so much so, that he came to believe in death only, not just his own death, but the death of all people. In the same way the slogan *Keep smiling*! produces at last a sort of savage rage in the breast of the smilers, and the famous "cheery morning greeting" makes the gall accumulate in all the cheery ones.

It is no good. Every time you force your feelings, you damage yourself and produce the opposite effect to the one you want. Try to force yourself to love somebody, and you are bound to end by detesting that same somebody. The only thing to do is to have the feelings you've really got, and not make up any of them. And that is the only way to leave the other person free. If you feel like murdering your husband, then don't say: "Oh, but I love him dearly. I'm *devoted* to him." That is not only bullying yourself, but bullying him. He doesn't want to be *forced*, even by love. Just say to yourself: "I could murder him, and that's a fact. But I suppose I'd better not."—And then your feelings will get their own balance.

The same is true of love of humanity. The last generation, and the one before that *insisted* on loving humanity. They cared terribly for the poor suffering Irish and Armenians and Congo Rubber negroes* and all that. And it was a great deal of it fake, self-conceit, self-importance. The bottom of it was the egoistic thought: "I'm so good, I'm so superior, I'm so benevolent, I care intensely about the poor suffering Irish and the martyred Armenians and the oppressed negroes, and I'm going to save them, even if I have to upset the English and the Turks and the Belgians severely —" This love of mankind was half self-importance and half a desire to interfere and put a spoke in other people's wheels. The younger generation, smelling the rat under the lamb's-wool of Christian Charity, said to themselves: No love of humanity for me!

They have, if the truth be told, a secret detestation of all oppressed or unhappy people who need "relief." They rather hate "the poor colliers," "the poor cotton workers," "the poor starving Russians," and all that. If there came another war, how they would loathe "the stricken Belgians"!—And so it is: the father eats the pear, and the son's teeth are set on edge.*

Having overdone the sympathy touch, especially the love of humanity, we have now got the recoil away from sympathy. The young don't sympathise, and they don't want to. They are egoists, and frankly so. They say quite honestly: "I don't give a hoot in hell for the poor oppressed this-that-and-the-other." And who can blame them? Their loving forbears brought on the Great War. If love of humanity brought on the Great War, let us see what frank and honest egoism will do. Nothing so horrible, we can bet.

The trouble about frank and accepted egoism is its unpleasant effect on the egoist himself. Honesty is very good, and it is good to cast off all the spurious sympathies and false emotions of the pre-war world. But casting off spurious sympathy and false emotion need not entail the death of all sympathy and all deep emotion, as it seems to do in the young. The young quite deliberately *play* at sympathy and emotion.

"Darling child, how lovely you look tonight! I *adore* to look at you!"—and in the next breath, a little arrow of spite. Or the young wife to her husband: "My beautiful love, I feel so precious when you hold me like that, my perfect dear!—But shake me a cocktail, angel, would you? I need a good kick—you *angel* of light!"—

The young, at the moment, have a perfectly good time strumming on the keyboard of emotion and sympathy, tinkling away at all the exaggerated phrases of rapture and tenderness, adoration and delight, while they feel—nothing, except a certain amusement at the childish game. It is so *chic* and charming to use all the most precious phrases of love and endearment amusingly, just amusingly, like the tinkling in a music box.

And they would be very indignant if told they had no love of humanity. The English ones profess the most amusing and histrionic love of England, for example. "There is only one thing I care about, except my beloved Philip, and that is England, our precious England. Philip and I are both prepared to die for England, at any moment."—At the moment, England does not seem to be in any danger of asking them, so they are quite safe. And if you gently enquire: "But what, in your imagination, is England?"—they reply fervently: "The great tradition of the English, the great idea of England."—Which seems comfortably elastic and non-committal.

And they cry: "I would give anything for the cause of freedom. Hope and I have wept tears, and saddened our precious marriage bed, thinking of the trespass on English liberty. But we are calmer now, and determined to fight calmly to the utmost." Which calm fight consists in taking another cocktail and sending out a wildly emotional letter to somebody perfectly irresponsible. Then all is over, and freedom is forgotten, and perhaps religion gets a turn, or a wild outburst over some phrase in the burial service.*

This is the advanced young of today. I confess it is amusing, while the coruscation lasts. The trying part is when the fireworks have finished—and they don't last very long, even with cocktails—and the grey stretches intervene. For with the advanced young, there is no warm daytime and silent night. It is all fireworks of excitement and stretches of grey emptiness, then more fireworks. And, let the grisly truth be owned, it is rather exhausting.

Now in the grey intervals in the life of the modern young one fact emerges in all its dreariness, and makes itself plain to the young themselves, as well as to the onlooker. The fact that they are empty: that they care about nothing and nobody: not even the amusement they seek so strenuously. Of course this skeleton is not to be taken out of the cupboard. "Darling angel man, don't start being a nasty white ant. Play the game, angel face, play the game, don't start saying unpleasant things and rattling a lot of dead man's bones! Tell us something nice, something amusing. Or let's be *really* serious, you know, and talk about bolshevism or *la haute finance*. Do be an angel of light, and cheer us up, you nicest precious pet! —"

As a matter of fact, the young are becoming afraid of their own emptiness. It's awful fun throwing things out of the window. But when you've thrown everything out, and you've spent two or three days sitting on the bare floor and sleeping on the bare floor and eating off the bare floor, your bones begin to ache, and you begin to wish for some of the old furniture back, even if it was the ugliest Victorian horse hair.

At least, that's how it seems to me the young women begin to feel. They are frightened at the emptiness of their house of life, now they've thrown everything out of the window. Their young Philips and Peters and so on don't seem to make the slightest move to put any new furniture in the house of the young generation. The only new piece they introduce is a cocktail-shaker and perhaps a wireless set. For the rest, it can stay blank.

And the young women begin to feel a little uneasy. Women don't like to feel empty. A woman hates to feel that she believes in nothing and stands for nothing. Let her be the silliest woman on earth, she will take something seriously: her appearance, her clothes, her house, something. And let her be not so very silly, and she wants more than that. She wants to feel, instinctively, that she amounts to something and that her life stands for something. Women, who so often are angry with men because men cannot "just live," but must always be wanting some purpose in life, are themselves, perhaps, the very root of the male necessity for a purpose in life. It seems to me that in a woman the need to feel that her life *means* something, stands for something, and amounts to something is much more imperative than in a man. The woman herself may deny it emphatically: because, of course, it is the man's business to supply her life with this "purpose." But a man can be a tramp, purposeless, and be happy. Not so a woman. It is a very, very rare woman who can be happy if she feels herself "outside" the great purpose of life. Whereas, I verily believe, vast numbers of men would gladly drift away as wasters, if there were anywhere to drift to.

A woman cannot bear to feel empty and purposeless. But a man may take a real pleasure in that feeling. A man can take real pride and satisfaction in pure negation: "I am quite empty of feeling, I don't care the slightest bit in the world for anybody or anything except myself. But I do care for myself, and I'm going to survive in spite of them all, and I'm going to have my own success without caring the least in the world how I get it. Because I'm cleverer than they are, I'm cunninger than they are, even if I'm weak. I must build myself proper protections, and entrench myself, and then I'm safe. I can sit inside my glass tower and feel nothing and be touched by nothing, and yet exert my power, my will, through the glass walls of my ego."

That, roughly, is the condition of a man who accepts the condition of true egoism, and emptiness, in himself. He has a certain pride in the condition, since in pure emptiness of real feeling he can still carry out his ambition, his will to egoistic success.

Now I doubt if any woman can feel like this. The most egoistic woman is always in a tangle of hate, if not of love. But the true male egoist neither hates nor loves. He is quite empty, at the middle of him. Only on the surface he has feelings: and these he is always trying to get away from. Inwardly, he feels nothing. And when he feels nothing, he exults in his ego and knows he is safe. Safe, within his fortifications, inside his glass tower.

But I doubt if women can even understand this condition in a man. They mistake the emptiness for depth. They think the false calm of the egoist who really feels nothing, is strength. And they imagine that all the defences which the confirmed egoist throws up, the glass tower of imperviousness, are screens to a real man, a positive being. And they throw themselves madly on the defences, to tear them down and come at the real man, little knowing that there *is* no real man, the defences are only there to protect a hollow emptiness, an egoism, not a human man.

But the young are beginning to suspect. The young women are beginning to respect the defences, for they are more afraid of coming upon the ultimate nothingness of the egoist, than of leaving him undiscovered. Hollowness, nothingness—it frightens the women. They cannot be *real* nihilists. But men can. Men can have a savage satisfaction in the annihilation of all feeling and all connection, in a resultant state of sheer negative emptiness, when there is nothing left to throw out of the window, and the window is sealed.

Women wanted freedom. The result is a hollowness, an emptiness which frightens the stoutest heart. Women then turn to women for love. But that doesn't last. It can't. Whereas the emptiness persists and persists.

The love of humanity is gone, leaving a great gap. The cosmic consciousness has collapsed upon a great void. The egoist sits grinning furtively in the triumph of his own emptiness. And now what is woman going to do? Now that the house of life is empty, now that she's thrown all the emotional furnishing out of the window, and the house of life, which is her eternal home, is empty as a tomb, now what is dear forlorn woman going to do?

APPENDIX I

EARLY DRAFT OF 'THE "JEUNE FILLE" WANTS TO KNOW'

NOTE ON THE TEXT

What appears to be an early draft for 'The "Jeune Fille" Wants to Know' is transcribed here from the untitled manuscript (UT). DHL's deletions and additions are shown.

If you are a writer, nothing is more <startling today> annoying than the difference between the things you are allowed to say, and the things you are allowed to print. Talking to an intelligent girl, the famous "jeune fille" who is the excuse for the great Hush! Hush! in print, you find, not that you have to winnow your words and leave out all the essentials, but that she, the innocent girl in question, is flinging all sorts of impossible questions at your head, in all sorts of crude and impossible language, demanding all sorts of terrible answers. You think to yourself: My heaven, this is the innocent young thing on whose behalf books are suppressed!—And you wonder: How on earth am I to answer her!

Then you decide: The only way to answer is quite simply and frankly, since the questions are simply and frankly put, and the innocent maiden is by no means a fool. No, far from it. When I talk to her father in the privacy of his study, I find myself forced to winnow my words and watch my step, the old boy is so nervous, so tremulous lest anything should ⌐be said to¬ hurt his feelings. But once I'm away in the drawing-room or the garden, the innocent maiden looks at me anxiously, as if to say: Please don't be annoyed by Daddy. You see he is like that, and we have to put up with him.—And it requires all one's silent command to prevent her from blurting out: Daddy's an old fool, but he *is* a dear, isn't he!

And that is the queer reversal of the old Victorian order. Father winces and bridles and trembles in his study or his library, and the innocent maiden knocks you flat with her outspokenness in the conservatory. And you have to admit that she is the man of the two: of the three, maybe. Especially when she says, rather sternly: I hope you didn't let Daddy see what you thought of him.—But what *do* you think of him? I gasp.—Oh, it's fairly obvious! she replies coolly, and dismisses the point.

I admit, the young are a little younger than I am: or a little older, which is it? I really haven't spent my years cultivating <my> prunes and prisms, yet, confronted with a young thing of twenty-two, I often find myself with a prune-stone in my mouth. And I don't quite know what to do with it.

"Why *is* Daddy like that?" she says, and there is real pain in the question.—"Like what?" you ask.—"Oh, you know what I mean! Like a baby ostrich with his head in the sand! It only makes his other end so *much* more conspicuous! And it's a pity, because he's awfully intelligent in other ways —"

What am I to answer?—*Why* are they like that? she insists.—Who? say I.—Men like Daddy!—Poor child, she sits really perplexed.—I suppose it's a sort of funk, say I.—*Exactly*! she pounces on me like a panther. But what is there to be in a funk about?

I have to confess I don't know.—Of course not! she says. There's nothing at all to be in a funk about. Then why can't we make him see it?

When the younger generation, usually the feminine half of it, in her early twenties, starts firing off her Whys? at me, I know I'm lost. Anything that crosses her in the least, she take aim at it with her little pistol of an enquiring spirit, and says: But *why*—? She is a deadly shot, and she hits the nail on the head every time.—Now *why* can't I talk like a sensible human being to Daddy?—I suppose he thinks you ought not to be quite so sensible, so early! say I mildly.—Cheek! she retorts. Why should *he* measure out what sense I ought to have?

Why indeed! But once you start whying, there's no end to it. A hundred years ago, a few reformers piped up timorously: Why is man so infinitely superior to woman? And on the slow years came the whisper: He isn't! Then the young roused up.—Why are fathers always in the right? And the end of the century confessed that they weren't. Since then, the innocent maiden has ceased to be anaemic—all maidens were anaemic, thirty years ago; and though she is just as innocent, probably more so, than her more stuffy grandmother or mother, there isn't a thing she hasn't <confess> discussed, and not a single thing she hasn't shot her Why? and Wherefore? at.—Why should Daddy put his foot down about love? He's been a prize muff at <?> it himself, judging from mother.

It is terrible, if all the <sanctified authorities of> sanctifications have to burst like celluloid Aunt-Sallies when a real true Why? hits them, aimed by sweet and twenty. One is forced to ask, why is it?

And the answer seems to be, Bogey! The elderly, today, seem to be real fetish-worshippers, worshipping the Bogey of human wickedness. Every young man is out to "ruin" every young maiden. Bogey! The young maiden knows a thing or two about that. She's not quite the raw egg she's <made out> supposed to be. And as for most young men, they're really very nice, and it would grieve them bitterly to "ruin" any young maiden ⌐, even if they knew how to do it.¬ Which the young maiden knows perfectly well, and: "Why can't Daddy see it?"—He can, really, but he loves his bogey: being a mild angel himself, he has to imagine a rampaging Satan somewhere, so he imagines it in other people.

"Ah my boy, you will find that in life every man's hand is against you!"—As a matter of fact, the boy finds nothing of the sort. Every man has to struggle for himself, true. But most people are willing to give a bit of help where they can. The world may really be a bogey, but that isn't because individuals are wicked villains. At least ninety-nine per-cent of individuals in our country and the countries we know by contact, are perfectly decent <wh> human beings who want to get on, but who don't want to do anybody any harm, if they can help it.

In short, the real figure that stands between the young and the old is the Bogey of human wickedness. The young don't believe in it at all. And the old say: Of course, there is no danger to *us*, but to the young—!!!! <It is a tale? of> Which is pure hypocrisy, and the young know it. It is the last stupid weapon of a stupid tyranny.—"Of course it's perfectly hopeless with Daddy and mother, one has to treat them like mental infants," say the young. And the <old> ⌐mother sententiously¬ says: "For myself, I don't mind. But I must protect my children."

Protect them, that is, from a bogey that doesn't exist, but which gives her a sense of maternal authority and justification.

APPENDIX II

VANITY FAIR *VERSION OF 'DO WOMEN CHANGE'*

NOTE ON THE TEXT

Vanity Fair (New York) published 'Do Women Change?', with the sub-title, 'Being the Opinions of a Famous English Novelist on the Mutations of Femininity', in April 1929. The text printed is so substantially different from what is confidently believed to have been DHL's intention that it warrants separate publication.

DO WOMEN CHANGE?

They tell of all the things that are going to happen in the future—babies bred in bottles, all the love-nonsense cut out, women indistinguishable from men. But it seems to me bosh. We like to imagine we are something very new on the face of the earth. But don't we flatter ourselves? Motor-cars and aeroplanes are something novel, if not something new—one could draw a distinction. But the people in them are merely people, and not many steps up, if any, from the people who went in litters or palanquins or chariots, or who walked on foot from Egypt to Jordan, in the days of Moses. Humanity seems to have an infinite capacity for remaining the same—that is, human.

Of course there are all kinds of ways of being human; but I expect almost every possible kind is alive and kicking today. There are little Cleopatras and Zenobias and Semiramises and Judiths and Ruths and even Mother Eves, today just as there were in all the endless yesterdays. Circumstances make them little Cleopatras and little Semiramises instead of big ones, because our age goes in for quantity regardless of quality. But sophisticated people are sophisticated people, no matter whether it is Egypt or Atlantis. And sophisticated people are pretty well all alike. All that varies is the proportion of "modern" people to all the other unmodern sorts, the sophisticated to the unsophisticated. And today there is a huge majority of sophisticated people. And they are probably very little different from all the other sophisticated people of all the other civilizations, since man was man.

And women are just part of the human show. They aren't something apart. They aren't something new on the face of the earth, like the loganberry or artificial silk. Women are as sophisticated as men, anyhow, and they were never anything but women, and they are nothing but women today, whatever they may think of themselves. They say the modern woman is a new type. But is she? I expect, in fact I am sure, there have been lots of women like ours in the past, and if you'd been married to one of them, you wouldn't have found her different from your present wife. Women are women. They only have phases. In Rome, in Syracuse, in Athens, in Thebes, more than two or three thousand years ago, there was the bob-haired, painted, perfumed Miss and Mrs. of today and she inspired almost exactly the feelings that our painted and perfumed Misses and Mrses. inspire in our men.

I saw a joke recently in a "modern" German weekly—a modern young man and a modern young woman were leaning on a hotel balcony at night, overlooking the sea:

HE: "See the stars sinking down over the dark, restless ocean!"

SHE: "Never mind that nonsense! My room-number is 32!—"

That is supposed to be very modern: the very modern woman. But I believe women in Capri under Tiberius said "Never mind that nonsense!" to their Roman and Campanian lovers, in just the same way. And women in Alexandria in Cleopatra's time. Certain phases of history are "modern". As the wheel of history goes round women become "modern", then they become unmodern again. The Roman women of the late Empire were most decidedly "modern"—so were the women of Ptolemaic Egypt. True modern never-mind-that-nonsense women. Only the hotels were run differently.

Modernity or modernism isn't something we've just invented. It's something that comes at the end of civilizations. Just as leaves in autumn are yellow, so the women at the end of every known civilization—Roman, Greek, Egyptian etc.—have been modern. They were smart, they were chic, they said "never mind that nonsense", and they did pretty much as they pleased.

And then, after all, how deep does modernness go? Even in a woman? You give her a run for her money: and if you don't give it her, she takes it. The sign of modernness in a woman is that she says: "Oh, never mind that nonsense, boy!"—So the boy never-minds it—never-minds the stars and ocean stuff.—"My room-number is 32!"—Come to the point!

But the point, when you come to it, is a very bare little place, a very meagre little affair. It's not much better than a full-stop. So the modern girl comes to the point brutally and repeatedly, to find that her life is a series of full-stops, then a mere series of dots. Never mind that nonsense, boy! . . . . . Then she comes to being tired of dots, and of the plain point she's come to. The point is all too plain and too obvious.

And so the game begins again. Having never-minded it, and brought it down to brass tacks, you find brass tacks are the last thing you want to lie down on.

No, women don't change. They only go through a rather regular series of phases. They are first the slave: then the obedient helpmeet: then the respected spouse: then the noble matron: then the splendid woman and citizen: then the independent female: then the modern never-mind-it girl. And when her edict has been obeyed, the mills of God grind on, and having nothing else to grind, they grind the never-mind-it girl down, down, down—back to—we don't know exactly where—but probably to the slave once more, and the whole cycle starts afresh, on and on, till, in the course of a thousand years or two, we come once more to the "modern" never-mind-it girl.

And the modern never-mind-it girl of today has just come to the point where the fun leaves off. Why? For the simple reason that the modern boy *doesn't* mind it. When men and women start cutting all the nonsense out of one another there's pretty soon nothing left. There is certainly very little left of the love business. So that when the boy begins leaving out all the stars and ocean nonsense, he begins leaving out the girl too. As the process continues, and he leaves out the moonlight and the solitude and even the occasional bouquet of flowers, the girl dwindles and dwindles in his feelings, till at last she does become a mere point in his Consciousness, next to nothing. And not until she is a blank, blank, blanketty nothing to him emotionally (except perhaps a residual irritant) does she wake up and realize that it has happened. In urging him to cut out all the nonsense she has cut herself out, completely. For in some strange way, she herself was the very nonsense she was so anxious to eliminate. When a woman gets into a critical mood, all a man's feelings about her will seem to her nonsense, sickening nonsense. She amputates herself from the boy's consciousness, and then stares at the blank where she ought to be. She stares at it helpless and paralysed, and has not the faintest idea what to do about it. She has reached the point where she is nothing, blank nothing to the man. The eliminating process has been so complete. And then, she begins to be nothing to herself.

For the bitter truth of a woman is, that if she is nothing, or as good as nothing, to any man, she soon becomes nothing to herself. She becomes nothing to herself, and turns into one of these bitter women who assert themselves all the time, with a hammering self-assertion because they are nothing; or she hitches on to a job, and hopes to justify her existence in work, or in a cause; or she repents, not in sack-cloth and ashes, but in the prettiest frock she can find, and sets out once more in the hope that some boy will feel a bit of nonsense about her. And this time, she is not going to cut out all the nonsense. She is pining now to be treated to a little stars and ocean stuff, to be mixed up with the moon, and given a bouquet of flowers.

For after all, there is a difference between sentiment and sentimentality. And if the boy is sufficiently moved by the presence of the girl really to feel an emotion at the sight of the stars sinking over the ocean, that's one to the girl. It's a piece of flattery. A woman has a hold over a man, in the long run, not by her power of brutally and pointedly coming to the point and cutting all the rest out, but by her power of calling up in him all kinds of emotions which to her are perhaps irrelevant and nonsensical—have nothing to do with *her*—but which in the boy are just the natural reaction to the presence of the woman who really touches him. The more associations a woman can evoke in a man—associations with stars, ocean, moon, violets, humanity, the future, and so on—the stronger is her hold.

But women are not fools for very long. They soon learn their lesson, and the moment they have learnt their lesson, they change. The girl who was so smart cutting out all the nonsense of stars and ocean, in the boy, will change like a shot, and be considerably more humble about stars and ocean, once she realizes that she has reduced herself to a nonentity. And the moment she realizes it, she will begin the cycle all over again.

APPENDIX III

'MUSHROOMS': AN AUTOBIOGRAPHICAL FRAGMENT

NOTE ON THE TEXT

'Mushrooms' (MS UCin) consists of a one-page fragment of an undated autobiographical sketch which Lawrence probably wrote in 1926–7.

MUSHROOMS

It is perhaps absurd for any man to write his own autobiography. The one person I find it impossible to "know", is myself. I have dozens of little pictures of what purports to be myself, and which is me? None of them. The little animal is now become a bigger animal. But what sort of animal it is, I do not know, and do not vastly care.

The little animal was a pasty-faced boy born to have bronchitis and a weak chest, but otherwise lively enough. A little animal that

EXPLANATORY NOTES

EXPLANATORY NOTES

Mercury

8:1 **Mercury** Merkur, surrounded at a distance by forest on three sides, with the Black Forest to the s. and the Hohenbaden (Altes Schloss) ruins – the 'reddish castle-ruins' (8:20) – to the n.e.

[Return to Bestwood]

15:2 **September.** DHL was at the home of his elder sister Emily King (1882–1962), in Nottingham on 13 September 1926; he stayed with his younger sister, Ada Clarke (1887–1948), at her home in Gee Street, Ripley (Derbyshire), 14–16 September, from where he made his final visit to his birthplace, Eastwood in Nottinghamshire.

15:15 **the Co-op . . . A. L.** The shop belonging to the local Co-operative Society which supplied moderately priced goods and distributed such profits as were made among the Society's members . . . Every member had a number for his/her account and presumably these initials were those of DHL's father, Arthur John Lawrence (1846–1924).

15:20 **Bob** Probably a reference to the Eastwood butcher, Gethin Hogg.

15:22 **Walker Street** In 1887 the Lawrence family moved from Victoria Street where DHL was born, to the 'end house' (see 19:11) in the Breach, and from there to 3 Walker Street four years later. For another description of the view from Walker Street to Crich and Annesley, see v. 592.

15:23 **the ash tree** The 'huge old ash-tree' is significant on two occasions in *Sons and Lovers*. Its 'shriek' and 'almost demoniacal noise' in the high wind reflect the 'anguish of the home discord' and the 'shrieks and cries' of Paul's parents in their furious altercation (84:23–85:1). Its 'monstrous and black' appearance in the late evening matches the family's desolation as the coffin of Paul's brother William is brought into the house (168:38–9).

16:15 **Phœbus Apollo!** God of the sun.

16:17 **coal strike,** DHL was shocked at the effects of the strike (running since 30 April 1926) on his native region. He wrote to his friend Koteliansky from Ripley, on 15 September 1926: 'This strike has done a lot of damage – and there is a lot of misery – families living on bread and margarine and potatoes – nothing more. The women have turned into fierce communists . . . It feels a different place' (v. 536). He later described the strike as 'an insanity' (v. 552) and 'one of the greatest disasters that has ever happened to England' (v. 565); the sight of miners, pickets and policemen was like 'a spear' pushed 'through the side of *my* England' (v. 592).

16:27 **children . . . it,** In *Sons and Lovers* Paul and his brother Arthur, knowing their mother's love of blackberries, would scour the surrounding countryside 'so long as a blackberry was to be found' (92:37–93:6).

16:35 **"blue-bottles,"** A term applied to the police since at least 1846 (*OED*).

17:2 **Mellor** Whether invented on this occasion or not, the name was common in the Eastwood locality; for example, the Mellor family were responsible for building the Walker Street houses; most famously the name was adapted for use in *Lady Chatterley's Lover*.

17:10 **scene . . . police.** Derek Britton believes that DHL was recalling a scene which took place in Ripley on 14 September 1926 when women were taken to court in Heanor charged with the intimidation of a miner who had returned to work (a 'black-leg', one of the 'dirty ones' at 21:12). See Britton, *Lady Chatterley: The Making of the Novel*, 102–3.

17:40 **Women's Guild** The Women's Co-operative Guild actively promoted the intellectual and political advancement of women; Lydia Lawrence was treasurer of the Eastwood branch for several years. See *Early Years* 21–2.

18:1 **tyrannus,** Lydia Lawrence's father, George Beardsall (1825–99), was recreated as George Coppard in *Sons and Lovers* where he is presented as proud, stern, 'rather bitter . . . harsh in government, and in familiarity ironic', and in theological matters sympathetic to St Paul (*Sons and Lovers* 18:6–9).

18:18 **crepitus ventris** A rumbling of the stomach, a belch (Latin).

18:24 **Italian villa,** DHL and Frieda moved into the Villa Mirenda, near Scandicci s.e. of Florence, on 6 May 1926. He told his devoted friend Dorothy Brett (1883–1977) on 15 May: 'We've taken the top half of this old villa . . . crowning a little hilltop in the Tuscan style' (v. 453).

18:27 **editor** See also 19:1. Austin Harrison (1873–1928), editor of the *English Review* 1909–23, published many of DHL's early poems, stories and reviews.

18:32 **forty-one,** DHL was 41 on 11 September 1926.

18:38 **ranch** Kiowa Ranch near Taos, New Mexico, given by the wealthy American Mabel Dodge Luhan (1879–1962) to Frieda Lawrence who later, in return, gave her the manuscript of *Sons and Lovers*.

19:1 **Delphos! . . . Dodona!** The sites of two famous oracles, the first (dedicated to Apollo) at the foot of Mount Parnassus, the second (dedicated to Zeus) in the Greek village of Epiros.

19:17 **Persephone . . . Plutonic,** Legend says that Pluto, ruler of Hades, seized Persephone and took her as his queen to the underworld; as she went she dropped lilies which turned into daffodils; she is said to return to earth for six months each year.

19:21 **Consummatum . . . finished!** Latin and English versions of Jesus' final words from the cross: see John xix. 30.

19:26 **Wilhelm II,** German emperor (1859–1941).

20:7 **"In . . . you."** John xiv. 2.

20:11 **pit bank.** The mound near the pit-head where the coal is sorted and screened.

20:18 **Hardwick?"** The late sixteenth-century Elizabethan mansion built by Elizabeth ('Bess') Talbot, dowager Countess of Shrewsbury (1518–1608), famous for its abundance of windows.

20:25 **Butterley, Alfreton, Tibshelf** Derbyshire mining communities.

20:29 **Bolsover Castle** Seventeenth-century castle in the village 6 miles from Chesterfield.

20:36 **Chesterfield.** Derbyshire town; the Church of St Mary and All Saints is renowned for a lead-covered wooden spire which suffered severe timber-warping leading in turn to its remarkably twisted appearance. (See 21:28.) Derek Britton believes that, having been refused entrance to Hardwick Hall, and though he did visit Chesterfield, DHL's 'real goal' on that afternoon was 'the home of the Sitwell family at Renishaw' (pp. 141–2), 6 miles east of Chesterfield, to which he had been invited by Sir George and Lady Ida when he saw them in Italy in June 1926 (v. 476).

21:12 **nephew** Probably William Herbert, then 3 years old, rather than John Lawrence Clarke, then 11.

22:18 **district.** The valley of the river Erewash contains the towns of Heanor and Ilkeston, and, in 1926, abounded in coal-mines.

23:6 **religious problem.** According to Derek Britton DHL had recently read in *The Times Literary Supplement* 'that in contemporary society the ownership of property had become a religious question' and he quoted it both in this essay and 'in all versions of *Lady Chatterley*' (pp. 163–4). See *The First and Second Lady Chatterley Novels*, ed. Dieter Mehl and Christa Jansohn (Cambridge, 1999), 85:20–2, 410:33–4; *Lady Chatterley's Lover*, ed. Michael Squires (Cambridge, 1993), 181:3.

23:32 **man . . . alone.** Cf. 'Man shall not live by bread alone', Matthew v. 4.

24:3 **Hopeless . . . controlled.** Such views were not uncommon in the 1920s. In his book, *Hereditary Genius* (1869), Francis Galton (1822–1911), a leading modern exponent of eugenics, had proposed both the need and the means for producing a gifted race. The American Eugenics Society (founded in 1926), aiming at the same objective, argued for the sterilisation of insane, retarded and epileptic citizens.

Getting On

27:10 **I remember . . . born—"** Thomas Hood (1799–1843), 'I remember' (1826), ll. 1–2.

27:13 **Buildings . . . shop.** 8a Victoria Street, Eastwood, where DHL was born, was one of the 'New Buildings' built for miners' families by the pit owners, Barber Walker & Co. in the 1870s . . . Henry Saxton (1843–1927), local councillor and prominent in the Congregational Church, owned the grocer's shop on the corner of Victoria Street and Scargill Street (see *Early Years* 31–3).

27:24 **clerk . . . manufacturer** It is more likely that her connection with the Nottingham lace industry was as a lace-drawer (see *Early Years* 14).

28:10 **ministers,** Revd J. Loosemoore and Revd Robert Reid, Congregational ministers.

28:16 **successful.** The inordinate respect with which Saxton was regarded in Eastwood is clear from the account of his death and funeral in the *Eastwood and Kimberley Advertiser*, 5 January 1927.

28:23 **forty,** When DHL wrote this essay he was already 41; see 32:4.

28:26 **golden calf** During Moses' absence on Mount Sinai, Aaron made a golden calf which the Israelites then worshipped: Exodus xxxii. 4ff.

29:40 **High school . . . boys.** DHL attended Nottingham High School as a scholarship boy, 1898–1901 . . . it is not wholly true that he made no 'connection' with middle-class boys: his closest friends at school – Ernest Woodford and Thomas Marsden – were both from the bourgeoisie (see *Early Years* 83–5).

30:3 **Miriam** I.e. Jessie Chambers (1887–1944), intimate friend of DHL's youth; the prototype for Miriam in *Sons and Lovers*.

30:31 **"But . . . that?"** On this incident see *Early Years* 141.

31:15 **Hueffer . . . Garnett.** Ford Madox Hueffer (later Ford) (1873–1939), novelist and editor, founded the *English Review* in 1908; for his remarks about *The White Peacock* and DHL as a 'genius' see 'Which Class I Belong To', p. 38:10, and viii. 3 . . . Edward Garnett (1868–1937), the very influential figure in literary London and, in 1911 when he first made contact with DHL, reader for the publisher, Duckworth.

32:14 *Arlen* . . . **Galsworthy**: Michael Arlen, originally Dikran Kouyoumdjian (1895–1956), author of the bestselling novel, *The Green Hat* (1924) . . . John Galsworthy (1867–1933), novelist, on whom DHL wrote a critical essay in February 1927, condemning his 'cheap cynicism smothered in sentimentalism' (*Phoenix* 550).

Which Class I Belong To

36:26 **Eliot . . . Meredith.** George Eliot (1819–80) . . . George Meredith (1828–1909); Lydia Lawrence 'got terribly impatient with [his] *Diana of the Crossways*' (see 'Myself Revealed' 177:33).

36:34 **Nottingham High School . . . Westminster.** DHL won a County Council Scholarship and moved from Beauvale Board School to Nottingham High School in September 1898 . . . Revd Dr James Gow (1854–1923) had been Headmaster of the High School since 1885; he became Headmaster of Westminster School in 1891.

37:10 **office . . . year.** From late September to December 1901 DHL was a clerk with J. H. Haywood Ltd, manufacturers of surgical, athletic and other appliances in Nottingham . . . In October 1902 DHL began as a pupil-teacher in the Albert Street School, Eastwood, at a salary of £12 p.a.

37:13 **Nottingham University . . . work.** Having passed the London Matriculation examination in mid-1905, DHL was qualified to enter the Day-Training Department of Nottingham University College to pursue the Normal (i.e. non-degree) course leading to a Teacher's Certificate . . . encouraged by his Head of Department and by his mother, DHL decided to follow (but subsequently abandoned) a degree course in Arts.

37:19 **paper, . . . *dit!*** In the Foreword to his *Collected Poems* (1928) DHL wrote: 'I had offered the little poem "Study" to the Nottingham University *Magazine* [*Gong*], but they returned it' (*Phoenix* 253). No reference is made to a second poem . . . Presumably DHL intended to be ironic: '*As they call it!*' (French).

37:26 **university,** Cf. 'college boredom became a disease . . . College disappointed me painfully', *Letters* (ed. James T. Boulton, Cambridge, 1979), i. 49, 72.

37:37 **Jew . . . died.** Neither the 'Jew' nor the very clever fellow-student has been identified.

37:39 **school,** Davidson Road School where DHL taught October 1908 – February 1912.

38:5 **girl-friend** I.e. Jessie Chambers.

38:18 **Pound** DHL met the American poet, Ezra Pound (1885–1972) at a literary party at the Reform Club in November 1909 and found him 'jolly nice' but 'his god is beauty, mine, life' (i. 145). DHL added: 'He is rather remarkable – a good bit of a genius, and with not the least self consciousness.'

38:20 **Hueffer . . . Garnett . . . Harrison,** See Explanatory notes to 'Getting On' 31:15 and '[Return to Bestwood]' 18:27.

38:38 **Barrie . . . Wells?** Sir James Barrie (1860–1937) was the son of a Scottish weaver . . . Herbert George Wells (1866–1946) was the son of an unsuccessful shop-keeper; both, in DHL's view, had declined into prosperous 'suburbanians' (v. 94).

39:36 ***podere*.** farm (Italian). DHL's detachment from the peasants was not as complete as he suggests; see, for example, accounts of Christmas parties for them at the Villa Mirenda: v. 619, vi. 234–5, 252–3, 256.

Making Love to Music

42:13 **sins of the fathers . . . children.** Cf. Exodus xx. 5: 'visiting the iniquity of the fathers upon the children unto the third and fourth generation'.

43:2 **Shelley, . . . two-step.** Cf. 'Ode to the West Wind' l. 44 . . . A round dance with gliding steps in duple rhythm.

43:5 **Maupassant . . . says the same thing:** In what follows DHL accurately summarises a long passage of conversation in the short story, 'L'Inutile Beauté' (1890) by Guy de Maupassant (1850–93): see *Contes et Nouvelles*, ed. L. Forestier (Paris, 1979), pp. 1216–17.

44:14 **made flesh.** Cf. John i. 14: 'And the Word was made flesh'.

44:30 **We are such . . . band.** Cf. Shakespeare, *The Tempest*, IV. i. 156–8: 'We are such stuff/As dreams are made on; and our little life/Is rounded with a sleep.'

44:35 **quadrilles . . . Lancers . . . waltz . . . Roger de Coverleys,** A square dance involving four couples . . . a species of quadrille . . . the waltz was regarded, in 1825, as 'a riotous and indecent German dance' (*OED*) . . . an English country-dance (the spelling of the name derives from Addison's *Spectator*, 1711–14, though the tune pre-dates that).

45:8 ***bête à deux dos.*** 'beast with two backs' (French): Shakespeare, *Othello* I. i. 117.

45:18 **Baudelaire . . . Dame Nature herself:** DHL was recalling sonnet XIX, 'La Géante' ('The Giantess') from *Les Fleurs du mal* (1857) by Charles Baudelaire (1821–67), in which the French poet imagines exploring Nature's 'magnifiques formes' ('magnificent limbs') and climbing the slopes of 'ses genoux énormes' ('her tremendous knees'). See *Mr Noon*, ed. Lindeth Vasey (Cambridge, 1984), p. 251:35–7, for another reference to this poem.

45:24 **the Charleston . . . Black Bottom** A lively ballroom dance, popular in the 1920s, involving shaking the leg in side kicks . . . a very popular dance in, and for a time after, 1926. The *Observer* remarked, 6 February 1927: 'The accounts of the new dances are discouraging. There is the Black Bottom, the very name of which spoils a spring morning' (*OED*).

46:8 **blonde . . . preferred by gentlemen** Cf. *Gentlemen Prefer Blondes* (1925), a bestseller of the 1920s, by Anita Loos (1893–1981). See v. 574 and n. 4.

46:23 **Etruscan tombs at Tarquinia.** See DHL's *Sketches of Etruscan Places*, ed. Simonetta de Filippis (Cambridge, 1992), 'The Painted Tombs of Tarquinia', pp. 41–133, especially pp. 47–56.

[Autobiographical Fragment]

50:4 **come home . . . border.** DHL was born on 11 September 1885 in Eastwood, a 'coal-mining village' on the border between Nottinghamshire and Derbyshire. The village of Newthorpe was 7 miles, Eastwood $8\frac{1}{2}$ miles n.w. of Nottingham; both were on the Great Northern railway line. Roy Spencer states that during his last two years in Eastwood DHL 'began to meet his friends at the Ram Inn in Newthorpe' (*D. H. Lawrence Country*, 1979, p. 42).

50:8 **picture palaces,** I.e. cinemas.

50:26 **board school . . . Band of Hope,** A Board School was managed by a school board as required by the Elementary Education Act, 1870 . . . the title originated in 1847, applied to groups of children organised for temperance work; members pledged themselves to abstain from alcohol. Paul Morel was a member of such a 'Band' (*Sons and Lovers* 83:15).

51:4 **entry-ends,** I.e. the open ends of a passage between or common to adjoining houses.

51:13 **"There's . . . coming!"** From the song, 'The Good Time Coming', by Charles Mackay (1814–89); it regained popularity during the First World War.

52:13 **hoity-toity,** I.e. haughty or superior.

52:19 **We . . . made on.** See 'Making Love to Music', Explanatory note to 44:30.

52:33 **vine of Dionysus** Dionysus in Greek mythology, or Bacchus in Roman, was the god of wine.

54:10 **Queen Victoria's . . . be** Victoria (1819–1901) was succeeded in 1901 by Edward VII (1841–1910) who was married to Alexandra (1844–1925); he in turn was succeeded in 1910 by the Prince of Wales who, as George V (1863–1936), was on the throne when DHL wrote this essay. The wife of George V was Princess Mary of Teck (1867–1953).

54:14 **"Those . . . sod,"** Unidentified.

54:18 **Prince of Wales . . . "Pally" . . . evening suit** In 1927 the Prince of Wales was George V's eldest son who became Edward VIII on 20 January 1936 and abdicated on 11 December . . . The 'Palais de Danse' . . . dinner jacket (or tuxedo).

54:26 **"Lead Kindly Light"** Popular hymn by John Henry Newman (1802–90). Cf. *Sons and Lovers* 31:12.

55:18 **Engine Lane Crossing,** DHL was recalling having watched coal-trucks going to and from Moorgreen Colliery. See *Early Years* 278.

56:9 **Renshaw's farm.** Though the name Renshaw had family connections – James Lawrence (1851–80) had married Mary Ellen Renshaw – DHL may have had in mind Haggs Farm occupied by the Chambers family with whom (especially Jessie Chambers) he had close associations. (Mary Renshaw is the girl in the fragment of the 'Burns novel'; see Nehls i. 184ff.)

56:31 **Matlock** The Derbyshire town of Matlock, n.w. of Eastwood, was known for its several petrifying wells and caverns, including the 'Blue John Cavern' (see 57:27).

58:33 **"Dust of ages!"** Perhaps echoing the title of the well-known hymn, 'Rock of Ages' (1775) by Augustus Toplady (1740–78).

60:21 **"Can . . . carried?"** In the local dialect of Eastwood: 'Can you walk or would you like to be carried?'

61:38 **squares . . . walls of Jerusalem, . . . Chapel.** The 'Squares' or 'New Buildings' – arranged in quadrangles – were miners' houses built in Eastwood by the colliery owners, Barber Walker & Co. Cf. 'Nottingham and the Mining Countryside', p. 288 . . . Cf. *Women in Love*, ed. David Farmer, Lindeth Vasey and John Worthen (Cambridge, 1987), p. 255:1–3 . . . the hymn, trans. J. M. Neale (1818–66), 'Jerusalem the golden, / With milk and honey blest'.

64:6 **Sherwood Forest** The forest which once covered a fifth of Nottinghamshire and was reputedly the home of the legendary Robin Hood.

65:33 **lust** The word clearly means 'sturdy' or 'well-built', but there can be no doubt that DHL wrote 'lust' and not 'lusty' though this is how it was rendered by his typist and in print by the editors of *Phoenix*. Adjectivally the word is not recognised in *OED* or in the *English Dialect Dictionary*; but *OED2* records a comparable use in Robert Graves's *They Hanged my Saintly Billy* (1957), p. 10: 'As a baby he was very lust and fat'.

67:26 **solid . . . sort,** DHL alludes to the Arts and Crafts movement and seems to have in mind a chair of the kind designed by such as Ambrose Heal (1872–1959) and Gordon Russell (1892–1980) who used modern methods to produce furniture based on English traditional styles.

The "Jeune Fille" Wants to Know

71:31 **prunes and prisms,** Cf. Dickens, *Little Dorrit* (1857), II. v: 'prunes and prism, are all very good words for the lips'.

72:16 **Billy the Kid** The nickname of William H. Bonney Jr (1859/60–81), one of the most notorious gunfighters of the American West; reputed to have killed twenty-seven men, he was himself gunned down by a sheriff in New Mexico.
72:31 **digging . . . names.** Cf. 'to call a spade a spade', colloquialism meaning to be straightforward or blunt.

Laura Philippine

77:24 **nut of a** I.e. smart, fashionable.

That Women Know Best

83:3 **I'll . . . footstep!** Exactly the same words are attributed to Paul Morel's father in *Sons and Lovers* 49:13.
83:25 **Brinsley** DHL's parents had their first home in Brinsley, 1 mile n. of Eastwood; Arthur Lawrence worked there as a miner, 1883–1912.
84:4 **My elder brothers . . . ruffling round.** DHL's elder brothers were George Arthur (1876–1967) and William Ernest (1878–1901). William was very talented; skilled in soccer he also had intellectual interests as DHL indicates; he died young and was hero-worshipped by the family . . . behaving rather wildly and mischievously.
84:18 **My boy** [84:9] . . . **nice.** A slightly longer version of the same exchange occurs in *Sons and Lovers* 74:1–75:28.
84:23 **ministers and administers,** I.e. they are both servants and directors of affairs.
84:30 **lively [84:27] . . .** ***vitally*** **interesting.** This brief passage replaced the original deleted in *MS* p. 4 (for an explanation of symbols used, see p. 379):

> <<unfinished book, the book which adds a new page to itself every day, that exists on earth: the book of living women. Wome<a>n ha<s>ve an uncanny courage, which nowadays looks to me often like bravado. <They> ⌐she¬ <stand> <s> ⌐It is in woman alone that we find the grand uncanny courage of life, the life-experience faced and weighted up. And nowadays her courage often looks like bravado. She stands up in the midst of the universe and says: This is right, this is wrong, and I know it!—¬ The storm of life sweeps round her, and men, having nothing else to go by, say: She is right! She is the light-house. She is the fog-horn. She is the siren of safety. We steer by her.
>
> To me, women are more interesting than men because they press on ⌐open-eyed and¬ so dauntlessly, into the dark seas of <right and wrong> ⌐experience¬ the exploration of the inner and emotional life, while the men sit and wait on the shore, saying: All right, darling, I'm sure you know best. <What> ⌐But what¬ I have learnt from women is that they *don't* know best. They don't *really* know right from wrong ⌐at all. They even begin to doubt themselves.¬ But that isn't the point. One doesn't go to women to learn the ten, or ten thousand commandments One goes to women to learn where they get that superb bravado of making men believe in them and their ten thousand commandments, which are after all no more than wild words on the wind.>>

85:5 **sat . . . hams** I.e. squatted.

All There

87:8 **Albert Memorial** In Kensington Gardens, London, designed by Sir Gilbert Scott and erected in 1872 to commemorate Prince Albert, Consort of Queen Victoria.

87:12 **Egyptian silences** I.e. total silences. (Cf. the complete darkness which Moses caused to envelop the whole of Egypt: Exodus x. 22–3.)

87:30 **cub,** Gauche youth.

88:4 **Cromer?** Resort on the Norfolk coast.

88:5 **What . . . saying!** From a song by Joseph Edwards Carpenter (1813–85), 'What are the wild waves saying?' composed in response to Paul Dombey's experiences in Dickens's *Dombey and Son* (1846–8). See ii. 62 and n. 2.

88:13 **got-her-on-toast** I.e. she appears to be at Jim's mercy.

88:26 **held up . . . clergyman,** Allusion to the exaggerated liturgical gestures allegedly beloved of Anglo-Catholic clergy.

88:38 **too . . . nuts!** I.e. too conceited to be tolerated.

89:7 **forward . . . brigade!** Tennyson's poem 'The Charge of the Light Brigade' (1854), l. 9.

Thinking about Oneself

91:30 **millstone . . . neck,** Cf. Luke xvii. 2 ('a millstone were hanged about his neck and he were thrown into the sea').

92:26 **listening-in** I.e. listening to the radio.

92:37 **Sufficient . . . thereof.** Cf. Matthew vi. 34 ('Sufficient . . . the evil thereof').

Insouciance

95:2 **the hotel,** DHL was staying in the Grand Hotel, Chexbres-sur-Vevey, Switzerland; from his 'little balcony' (*Letters*, vi. 429) he had a splendid view of the mountains and over Lake Geneva. When, in November 1928, he told the Brewsters that the *Atlantic Monthly* had published his essay involving 'our little old ladies of Chexbres' (vii. 28), DHL tacitly admitted the essay's – at least partly – factual basis. Earl Brewster declared unambiguously: '*Insouciance* describes an incident at this [Grand] hotel' (Brewster 171).

95:31 **Mussolini.** Benito Mussolini (1883–1945), Italy's Prime Minister and Fascist dictator (cf. vi. 307 and n. 3).

97:7 **League of Nations** Created by the victorious allies at the Paris Peace Conference of 1919.

97:19 **Atropos . . . afternoon.** The Greeks and Romans supposed that there were three controlling Fates: Clotho who held the distaff; Lachesis who spun the thread of life; and Atropos who arbitrarily cut the thread when life was ended. DHL may have alluded to Milton's lines in *Lycidas* (1637): 'Comes the blind Fury with th'abhorred shears / And slits the thin-spun life' (ll. 75–6).

Master in his Own House

99:3 **A man . . . house.** *The Oxford Dictionary of English Proverbs* (Oxford, 3rd edn, 1970) does not accord this proverbial status; however, it seems closely allied to the proverb, 'One master in an house is enough' (p. 517).

99:18 **Feed the brute . . . Englishman's . . . castle.** Advice offered in *Punch* (lxxxix. 206) in 1886 to a wife who feels neglected by her husband . . . Unchallenged as a proverb from 1581 until Mr Grummer in Dickens, *Pickwick Papers* (1837), dismissed it as 'gammon', or nonsense (ed. J. Kinsley, Oxford, 1986, p. 362).

Matriarchy

104:1 **monstrous regimen[103:32] . . . Knox . . . Mary of Scotland,** John Knox (1505–72), Scottish Calvinist and prominent anti-papal writer, published the *First Blast against the Monstrous Regiment of Women* (1558) in which he denounced both Mary of Guise (1515–60), the Regent of Scotland, and her daughter, Mary Queen of Scots (1542–87) who was executed in 1587. ('Regiment' or 'regimen' meant 'government' or 'rule'.)

104:15 **love and cherish . . . obey his spouse.** DHL reverses the duties of husband and wife; in the marriage service set out in the *Book of Common Prayer* the woman swears 'to love, cherish and obey' her husband.

104:23 **nothing new . . . sun,** Ecclesiastes i. 8 ('there is no new thing under the sun').

104:27 **Berbers** Indigenous, largely Muslim, peoples of North Africa, scattered in tribes across Morocco, Algeria, Tunisia, Libya and Egypt.

106:17 **it's . . . father.** Cf. 'It is a wise father that knows his own child' (Shakespeare, *The Merchant of Venice*, II. i. 83).

Ownership

108:5 **The question . . . religious question,** This passage replaced the original opening which DHL deleted in *MS*: 'What is property after all? Roughly, it is something which a man possesses of his own, that other people would like to possess, but they can't because the other man owns it.'

108:28 **gave . . . poor,** DHL's phrasing echoes Mark x. 21.

109:29 **the Times:** Unlocated.

Autobiography

112:5 **(read . . . autobiography).** In *MS* the whole parenthesis reads: '(let them read *Sons & Lovers*. the first part is all autobiography – you might send them a copy).' The first two words and the last six were roughly crossed out, perhaps by someone in Curtis Brown's office, and omitted in *TS*; in any case DHL would not have expected his remarks to be conveyed to Kra, still less to appear in print.

112:13 **a couple . . . fish,** Perhaps Ernest Woodford and Thomas Haynes Marsden (see *Early Years* 85–6).

112:15 **farm,** Haggs Farm, Underwood, near Eastwood, the home of Jessie Chambers and her family.

112:17 **Taught in . . . boys:** DHL was a pupil-teacher at the British School in Eastwood, October 1902 – July 1905.

112:32 **Mr Gladstone.** William Ewart Gladstone (1809–98), statesman and author, four times Prime Minister.

113:13 **teacher in . . . year.** DHL began teaching at Davidson Road School, Croydon, in October 1908; he resigned on 28 February 1912.

113:21 **Hueffer, [113:17] . . . Garnett** See Explanatory note to 'Getting On', 31:15.

113:26 **mother died** Lydia Lawrence died on 9 December 1910; *The White Peacock* was published (in London) on 20 January 1911.

113:34 **Austin Harrison,** Hueffer was dismissed as editor of the *English Review* in December 1909; he was replaced by Austin Harrison (see Explanatory note to '[Return to Bestwood]' 18:27).

113:37 **Friedrich von Richthofen.** Frieda Lawrence's father (1845–1915), a professional soldier, was the garrison administrative officer at Metz.

114:3 ***The Rainbow* . . . immorality** The Bow Street magistrate's warrant to seize all copies of *The Rainbow* was served on the publishers, Methuen & Co., on 3 November 1915; they pleaded guilty to the charge of obscenity at Bow Street on 13 November and the destruction of copies was ordered. See *The Rainbow*, ed. Mark Kinkead-Weekes (Cambridge, 1989), pp. xlv–li.

Women Are So Cocksure

116:12 **He sometimes [116:8] . . . scarlet.** Several early scenes in *Sons and Lovers* exemplify these remarks: e.g. Morel's exasperated comment, 'everything's the *beer*!'; Paul's 'private religion . . . Lord, let my father die'; and the scene following Morel's drunken return to his house (*Sons and Lovers* 48:13–15, 85:19–21, 86:15–87:19).

116:15 **Band of Hope . . . the pledge** See Explanatory note to '[Autobiographical Fragment]' 50:26.

116:27 **serpent . . . down.** DHL was alluding to a temperance song by the American evangelist and hymn-writer, Revd Robert Lowry (1826–99), entitled 'There's a serpent in the glass', which had as its refrain, 'Dash it down! Dash it down!' See *The Standard Book of Song for Temperance Meetings and Home Use*, ed. T. Bowick and J. A. Birch (1880), p. 142.

117:8 **John Barleycorn.** Personification of malt liquor, popularised by Robert Burns in his poem *Tam O'Shanter* (1791), ll. 105–6.

117:35 **three sisters.** There can be little doubt that DHL had the von Richthofen sisters in mind: Else (1874–1973) who 'served freedom and justice' and became Professor of Social Economics; Frieda (Lawrence) (1879–1956) 'determined to prove herself a significant being, a significant *woman*'; and Johanna (1882–1971) who, 'all her life long . . . had the attention of men, for she was the beauty of the family' (Martin Green, *The von Richthofen Sisters*, 1974, pp. 16, 17, 22).

117:40 **gather . . . might.** Cf. Robert Herrick (1591–1674), 'To Virgins, to Make Much of Time' (1684), l. 1: 'Gather ye rosebuds while ye may'.

Why I don't Like Living in London

120:8 **false-silk** This compound is not recorded in *OED*; DHL's meaning is perhaps 'imitation' rather than 'artificial' silk.

121:5 **English people . . . *nicest* people in the world,** Cf. DHL's poem collected in *More Pansies* (1932), 'The English are so Nice!': 'The English are so nice / so awfully nice / they are the nicest people in the world' (Vivian de Sola Pinto and Warren Roberts, eds., *The Complete Poems of D. H. Lawrence*, 1964, ii. 659–60).

121:32 **monotony** DHL wrote 'monoty' in *MS*; it is assumed that 'monotony' was intended; 'monody' is also a possibility.

122:6 **jazz.** I.e. to play or dance to jazz music; *OED*'s first recorded use of the word as a verb is in 1918.

Cocksure Women and Hen-sure Men

125:13 **bobbed hair.** This hair-style – short and even all the way round – had been fashionable for about ten years: in 1928 *Punch* reported the 'alarming spread of bobbing' (*OED*). Frieda Lawrence had her hair 'bobbed' in November 1925; 'I have short hair! "fancy" myself', she told Dorothy Brett (v. 335).

126:23 **there . . . us!** From the General Confession in the Order of Morning Prayer, *The Book of Common Prayer*.

127:9 **out of scheme,** I.e. abnormal, causing disjunction.

Hymns in a Man's Life

130:3 **Nothing . . . teaching.** *MS* originally began: <It is hard for a man who has had what is called a religious upbringing to get the viewpoint of a man who has not been brought up "religiously.">

130:11 **Goethe's . . . chancelle"** Goethe's 'Wandrers Nachtlied: Ein Gleiches'. ll. 1–2 ('Over all the mountain tops is peace'), written September 1780 and published in *Werke*, 1815 . . . 'Ayant poussé la porte étroite qui chancelle' ('Having pushed open the narrow wavering door'), the opening line of Verlaine's sonnet, 'Après Trois Ans', No. 3 in *Poèmes Saturniens* (1866).

130:27 **"Each [130:17] . . . me!"** From 'Evening', by Robert Morris (1818–88), in Ira David Sankey's *Sacred Songs and Solos* (1881).

130:29 **I never . . . Palestine:** DHL felt differently in 1919 when he urged Dr David Eder (then political head of the Zionist Executive in Jerusalem): 'do take me to Palestine . . . I seriously want to go to Palestine' (*Letters of D. H. Lawrence*, ed. James T. Boulton and Andrew Robertson, Cambridge, 1984, iii. 353–4).

132:7 **Somebody says . . . you.** Unidentified.

132:11 **But [132:7] . . . her—"** These sentences were reduced in *MS* (p. 3) in an unknown hand, to: 'But there is more than one way of knowing.' DHL's text is restored.

(The language of the last sentence is biblical, meaning that the man had sex with the woman.)

132:30 **miracle ... fishes** Matthew xiv. 15–21; Mark vi. 35–44.

132:38 **"Sun of ... School.** One of the most popular of English hymns was actually a cento from 'Evening' by John Keble (1792–1866) in *The Christian Year* (1827) ... DHL attended the Beauvale Board School, Eastwood, 1892–8.

133:4 **"Fair ... land—"** From 'Child's Hymn' by John Hampden Gurney (1802–62). DHL originally extended the quotation in *MS* (p. 4) to include the following two lines, subsequently deleted: <<When full of joy this shining morn / We viewed the <pleasant> ⌐ smiling¬land—">>

133:13 **one would ... child.** *MS* (p. 5) originally read: <it is hardly possible to escape the sense of class-division and snobbism.>

133:14 **Primitive Methodists,** They seceded from the Wesleyan Methodist Church in 1810 with the intention of recovering the original methods of teaching, preaching, etc., practised by the founders of Methodism; the two branches were reunited in 1932.

133:18 **congregationalists ... Independents.** Congregationalism developed out of the Puritan movement in western Christianity. Its adherents, holding firmly to the belief in the priesthood of all believers, were known as Independents in the mid seventeenth century; they gained great prestige and considerable political influence when Oliver Cromwell (1599–1658) aligned himself with their cause.

133:29 **"O Worship [133:26] ... name—"** From 'Epiphany; or, Divine Worship' by John Samuel Bewley Monsell (1811–75), in *Hymns of Love and Praise* (1863).

133:36 **Bristol ... Sankey.** DHL probably had in mind the popular *Collection of Hymns adapted to Public Worship* (Bristol, 1769; 9th edn, Norwich, 1814), commonly known as *The Bristol Hymn Book*, compiled by John Ash and Caleb Evans. (V. de S. Pinto was in error when he identified the hymn-book as *The Bristol Tune Book* (1863?); see *A D. H. Lawrence Miscellany*, pp. 111–12.) ... The renowned American evangelists, Dwight Lyman Moody (1837–99) and Ira David Sankey (1840–1908). Sankey was the principal compiler of the often-reissued *Gospel Hymns* to which Moody did not contribute; it came to be associated with both men because of their collaborative missionary work.

133:36 **Scotch minister** Revd Robert Reid (1868–1955), Congregational Minister in Eastwood, 1897–1911.

133:38 **"Lead ... me."** Two extremely popular hymns: 'Lead Kindly Light', written by John Henry Newman in 1833 and published in *Lyra Apostolica* (1836); and 'Abide with Me' by Henry Francis Lyte (1793–1847), published in his *Miscellaneous Poems* (1868). DHL had roundly condemned Newman's hymn in 'Morality and the Novel' (1925) (see *Study of Thomas Hardy and Other Essays*, ed. Bruce Steele, Cambridge, 1985, 176:1–4).

134:4 **"At even [134:1] ... away!"** From 'Evening' by Henry Twells (1823–1900), published in *Hymns Ancient and Modern* (1868) (' ... Oh, with what joy ... ').

134:5 **"Fight ... might."** Another hymn by J. S. B. Monsell (cf. note to 133:29).

134:6 **Mr Remington** His name was Rimmington (see *Early Years* 66).

134:12 **"Sound . . . Lord—"** From 'Christian Courage' by William Fisk Sherwin (1826–99), published in *Bright Jewels for the Sunday School* (New York, 1869).

134:23 **"Hold . . . coming—"** A Moravian missionary hymn; see John Julian, *A Dictionary of Hymnology* (1925), p. 739 (i).

134:27 **"Stand . . . Lord—"** The opening lines of 'Soldiers of the Cross' by George Duffield (1818–88), published in *The Psalmist* (1858) ('. . . soldiers of the Cross').

Red Trousers

136:3 **London dulness:** Cf. 'Why I don't Like Living in London' – entitled 'Dull London!' by the *Evening News* – DHL's previous article in that paper.

136:12 **Votes for Women,** The crusade, which began in the mid-nineteenth century, succeeded first when women of 30 or over were enfranchised in 1918, and again in May 1928 when the voting age was reduced to 21, thus placing women on the same footing as men.

136:19 **Votes for Women processions . . . policemen.** DHL witnessed at least one such procession, associated with the Croydon by-election of 29 March 1909 (see i. 122–4) . . . the most celebrated suffragettes were Emmeline Pankhurst (1858–1928), arrested and jailed three times in 1908–9, and twelve times in 1913, and her daughter Christabel (1880–1958) who was arrested for a technical assault on the police in 1905.

136:22 **Marching . . . Lifeline,** Isaac Watts's hymn, 'Come we that love the Lord', in his *Hymns and Spiritual Songs* (1707), has the chorus: 'We're marching to Zion, / Beautiful, beautiful, Zion: / We're marching upward to Zion, / The beautiful city of God.' In some hymnals the title derived from the chorus . . . 'Throw out the Life-Line a-cross the dark wave, / There is a brother whom some one should save', a hymn by Edward S. Thomas, in Ira David Sankey's *Gospel Hymns No. 6* (1891). On one occasion DHL sang this hymn and dramatised the opening line (see Nehls iii. 216–17).

137:10 **free Cecho-Slovakia** The Republic of Czechoslovakia (incorporating Bohemia, Moravia and Slovakia) was declared in October 1918.

137:40 **Eton crop,** This close-cropped hair style for women had been introduced relatively recently: the earliest reference in *OED* is 1926.

138:25 **Strand and Piccadilly . . . begun.** In 'The Diary of A Man About Town' alongside his *Evening News* article 'Master in his Own House!', on 2 August 1928, DHL may have noticed the description of a man in Piccadilly 'who had on the queerest coloured trousers I have seen outside a minstrel show . . . They were heliotrope and white and brown; something like the multi-coloured braces that used to be seen in old-fashioned country hosiers' shop windows . . . [they] seem to have been designed by a man who sought novelty in colour'.

138:27 **Captain Nobile** Umberto Nobile (1885–1978), Italian pioneer in Arctic aviation. With Roald Amundsen in 1926 he flew over the North Pole; with others he flew over the Pole in the airship *Italia* on 24 May 1928 and was reported missing on the 28th, being rescued the following month. The failure of the expedition became a journalistic *cause célèbre* during July and August, and would be fresh in the minds of *Evening News* readers in September.

Is England Still a Man's Country

141:2 **"When . . . me up."** Psalm xxvii. 10 (Authorised Version).

141:28 **There's the rub.** *Hamlet*, III. i. 64.

141:39 **dog-gone** US slang: 'God damn'.

142:8 **realise** Substituted by DHL in *TS* for 'lose' (in *MS*).

142:9 **enslavement,** *MS* has 'economic freedom'; DHL inserted 'enslavement' in *TS* when he recognised that *TS* had omitted 'freedom'. Though the insertion and the previous alteration both resulted from this error in *TS*, they have been adopted as having DHL's final authority.

142:24 **sure as eggs.** Proverbial: 'sure as eggs is eggs' (i.e. without doubt).

Sex Appeal

145:39 **Lilian Gish, . . . Valentino.** Lilian Gish (1896–1993), American stage and film actress; her reputation was built on her early portrayal of fragile and vulnerable heroines . . . Rudolph Valentino (1895–1926), film actor idolised in the 1920s as the 'Great Lover'; took the lead in *The Sheik* (1921) and *The Son of the Sheik* (1926) (cf. v. 574 n. 4).

146:8 **Charlie Chaplin's** (Sir) Charles Spencer Chaplin (1889–1977), famous English film actor and director; in 1929, his most recent major production was *The Gold Rush* (1925).

147:18 **Diane de Poictiers . . . Langtry** Diane de Poitiers (1499–1566), Duchess of Valentinois, mistress of Francis I and Henry II of France . . . Lillie Langtry (1853–1929), famous English beauty and actress, mistress of Edward VII; nicknamed 'Jersey Lily' (after her place of birth).

147:31 **delapidated** Obsolete form of 'dilapidated'.

148:13 **Balzac** Honoré de Balzac (1799–1850), French novelist whose works DHL – in his youth – considered 'magnificent and supreme' (i. 92).

Do Women Change

151:15 **Cleopatras . . . Eves,** Cleopatra (68–30 BC), eldest daughter of Ptolemy, king of Egypt, a woman of great beauty and fascination, the lover of Caesar and Antony . . . Zenobia, queen of the Roman colony of Palmyra, 267–72, wife of Odaenathus, Roman client ruler of Palmyra . . . Semiramis, mythical queen of Assyria . . . Judith, heroine of the book of the Apocrypha which bears her name, who killed Nebuchadnezzar's general, Holofernes . . . Ruth, eponymous character in the Old Testament book, who married Boaz thus becoming ancestress of King David . . . Genesis iii. 20: 'And Adam called his wife's name Eve; because she was the mother of all living.'

151:27 **logan-berry** The fruit was first cultivated by J. H. Logan (1841–1928), American horticulturist.

152:10 **Tiberias . . . Campanian** Tiberius (42BC–AD37), second Roman emperor. In AD 27 he left Rome en route for southern Italy, paused to visit Capri and never thereafter left the island . . . Campania, ancient geographical name for the district south-east of the Tiber containing such towns as Herculaneum and Pompeii.

152:35 **Blank-eye!** I.e. complete absence of any interest or emotion.

152:39 **I can't . . . Baby!** The title of a very recent popular song (1928) by Jimmy McHugh and Dorothy Fields.

153:5 **brass tacks,** I.e. the details of practical living.

153:16 **mills . . . grind on,** 'Though the mills of God grind slowly, yet they grind exceeding small', Henry Wadsworth Longfellow (1807–92), 'Retribution' ll. 1–2, in 'Poetic Aphorisms'. Cf. vii. 234.

153:21 **A lead-pencil** From this point to the end, the text is taken from DHL's handwritten extension to *TS*. At the head of the page on which this extension begins is written, in an unknown hand: 'D. H. Lawrence. Addition to "Do Women Change".'

154:35 **and life.** The typed transcript of DHL's autograph extension omitted these two words. *E1* repeated the error.

Enslaved by Civilisation

156:7 **young . . . maids,** A woman was disqualified by marriage from being a teacher in a state school.

158:21 **Miss Hight,** 'Arthur [Lawrence] had some infant schooling from Miss Eyte of Brinsley', *Early Years* 10.

158:26 **rackapelted** I.e. became high-spirited and riotous.

158:30 **Board . . . British . . . national schools,** See Explanatory note to '[Autobiographical Fragment]' 50:26 . . . a British School was a public elementary school on the non-denominational basis of the British and Foreign School Society . . . a National School was conducted and supported to some extent by the state.

159:4 **excellent . . . beard.** William Whitehead, Headmaster of Beauvale Board School.

159:7 **"David . . . man.** I.e. the biblical King David.

159:14 **Davy . . . safety lamp.** Sir Humphry Davy (1778–1829), the distinguished chemist who invented the miner's safety lamp in 1815.

159:32 **The last . . . strike.** See Explanatory note to '[Return to Bestwood]' 16:17.

Give Her a Pattern

162:13 **"Caesar's . . . suspicion."** Based on Caesar's justification of his divorce from Pompeia (reported by Plutarch in *Life of Caesar*): 'Because I would have the chastity of my wife clear even of suspicion.'

162:22 **Agnes.** The faithful, self-effacing Agnes Wickfield who becomes David Copperfield's wife after the death of the pretty but empty-headed Dora Spenlow (in Dickens's novel, 1849–50).

163:26 **Eton-boy girl** See Explanatory note to 'Red Trousers' 137:40.

164:4 *filles de joie.* Prostitutes (French).

164:15 **bead flap,** A loose cover for the pubic region, ornamented with beads.

Introduction to Pictures

168:2 **Man** In *MS* there are two opening paragraphs deleted by DHL:

> <<What is art? said serious Simon, and he's waiting still for an answer. He'll wait till Doomsday, before he gets a satisfactory one. Because, before you can say what art is, you've got to say what man is. And that, thank heaven, is impossible. Look at him, just look at him, and tell me what he is! I would defy even the Lord that made him, to define him.
>
> Nevertheless we *must*, now and then, take a pot shot at it. While man lives, he'll have to keep taking pot shots at himself and at art and at all the other <bag o' tricks,> ⌐troubles, Aunt Sallies, puzzles¬ to define them. It's fun, like anything else.>>

168:2 **forked radish** Shakespeare, *2 Henry IV*, III. ii. 331.

168:6 **American judge** Judge John Ford (1862–1941) of the New York Supreme Court was horrified to discover his daughter reading *Women in Love*; as a result, DHL's publisher, Thomas Seltzer, was indicted on 18 July 1923 for publishing 'unclean' books, but *Women In Love* was exempted from the case by the Grand Jury.

169:22 **Don Juan.** The aristocratic libertine most famously presented in Mozart's opera *Don Giovanni* (1787), Byron's poem *Don Juan* (1819–24) and Shaw's play *Man and Superman* (1903).

169:33 **Plato . . . spirit,** Plato (*c*.428–348/7 BC) declared in the *Phaedo* that the soul should be freed from dependence on the body, whose appetites and passions frustrate the pursuit of wisdom and goodness.

170:16 **corpuscules,** Obsolete form of 'corpuscles'.

171:24 **tree . . . nakedness":** God commanded Adam: 'of the tree of the knowledge of good and evil, thou shalt not eat . . . [Eve] took of the fruit thereof . . . and gave also unto her husband . . . And the eyes of them both were opened, and they knew that they were naked' (Genesis ii. 17, iii. 6–7).

171:38 **Sermon on the Mount** A collection of Christ's religious teachings, in Matthew v–vii.

173:14 **pale Galilean** Jesus Christ. Cf. Swinburne, 'Hymn to Proserpine', l. 35, in *Poems and Ballads*, First Series (1866): 'Thou hast conquered, pale Galilean'.

174:27 **volta face** Normally 'volte face' – a complete change of attitude – but DHL adapted the Italian form, 'volta faccia'.

174:28 *Life of Christ* Perhaps Ernest Renan's *Vie de Jésus* (1863) which DHL read (probably in the English translation, 1864) in his youth (i. 37 n. 1).

174:31 **excrementa** Obsolete form of 'excrements' (plural of Latin form, 'excrementum').

Myself Revealed

177:7 **mighty works,** A phrase commonly used in the New Testament, e.g. Matthew, xi. 20–1, xii. 54, 58; Mark, vi. 2.

177:10 **fell . . . chance** Cf. W. E. Henley (1849–1903), 'Invictus', ll. 5–8: 'In the fell clutch of circumstance, / I have not winced nor cried aloud: / Under the bludgeonings of chance / My head is bloody, but unbowed.'

177:21 **stall . . . butty,** A butty was a senior workman directing a team of miners who would extract coal from a length of seam (or 'stall') allocated to him.

177:34 **"Diana . . . Lynne."** Cf. 'Which Class I Belong To', 36:26 . . . Mrs Henry Wood, *East Lynne* (1861).

178:15 **"normal" . . . University.** Cf. 'Which Class . . . To', 37:13.

178:20 **girl** Jessie Chambers.

178:24 **Hueffer.** See Explanatory note to 'Getting On' 31:15.

178:27 **The girl . . . ship.** This sentence provided the motto on the title page of the memoir of Jessie Chambers by DHL's fellow-teacher in the Croydon years, and prototype for Helena in *The Trespasser*, Helen Corke (1882–1978): *D. H. Lawrence's 'Princess': A Memory of Jessie Chambers* (Thames Ditton, 1951).

179:10 **alter . . . smile.** At p. 230 of the *MS* of *The White Peacock* DHL's text read:

> God!—we were a passionate couple—and she would have me in her bedroom while she drew Greek statues of me—her Croton, her Hecules! I never saw her drawings.

DHL substituted the following for the Heinemann edition:

> Lord!—we were an infatuated couple—and she would choose to view me in an aesthetic light. I was Greek statues for her, bless you: Croton. Hercules, I don't know what!

See *The White Peacock*, ed. Andrew Robertson (Cambridge, 1983), pp. xxxiv–xxxv, 150:22–4.

179:31 **all sorts . . . conditions,** Cf. 'all sorts and conditions of men', prayer for 'All Conditions of Men' in *The Book of Common Prayer*.

180:32 ***padrone . . . ambiente*,** Cf. 'Which Class . . . To', 39:36.

181:2 **Barrie . . . Wells,** Cf. 'Which Class . . . To', 38:38.

Introduction to These Paintings

185:1 **Paintings** An undated manuscript reproduced in facsimile in Frieda Lawrence, *"Not I, But The Wind . . . "* (Santa Fe, 1934), p. 206, appears to consist of notes towards this essay. It reads:

> Instinct
> Sanity Intuition
> Spirit
>
> The English have never painted from intuition or instinct
> Man has two selves: one unknown, vital, living from roots: the other the known self, like a picture in a mirror or the objects on a tray. People live from this latter. And this

latter can only feel *known* feelings: and its only experience of liberation or freedom is in the experience of novelty, which is the clash of sensation and a katabolic process.

185:22 **Aretino** Pietro Aretino (1492–1556), Italian satirist.

185:28 **"mortal coil"** *Hamlet* III. i. 67. DHL also entitled a short story, 'The Mortal Coil', which he described as 'one of my purest creations' (ii. 669).

186:1 **Orestes** Son of Agamemnon and Clytemnestra; his father was murdered by his mother and her lover, Aegisthus, both of whom Orestes later assassinated. In *Twilight in Italy* DHL had explored the contrast between Orestes and Hamlet insisting on the latter's 'loathing of his own flesh. [*Hamlet*] is the statement of the most significant philosophic position of the Renaissance . . . the tragedy of the convulsed reaction of the mind from the flesh, of the spirit from the self' (ed. Paul Eggert, Cambridge, 1994, p. 144).

186:16 **"—Drink to me . . . honour more,"** Ben Jonson (1573?–1637), 'To Celia' (1616), l. 1 . . . Richard Lovelace (1618–58), 'To Lucasta, Going to the Wars' (1649), ll. 12–14 ('. . . so much, / Lov'd . . . ').

186:31 **Swinburne's "white thighs"** Swinburne frequently used 'white' to describe parts of the body but seemingly never the thighs.

187:12 **Darnley . . . St. Andrews** The syphilitic Henry Stuart, Lord Darnley (1546–67), m. Mary, Queen of Scots, in 1565. (Cf. vii. 168.) Their son, James VI of Scotland and I of England (1566–1625), was baptised on 15 December 1566 by John Hamilton (1511?–71), Archbishop of St Andrews, described by Mary as 'a pocky priest'; Mary insisted that Hamilton should not spit into her son's mouth (Gordon Donaldson, *Mary Queen of Scots*, 1974, p. 99).

187:17 **wisest . . . Christendom,** A remark attributed to Henri IV of France.

188:38 **casual reading.** DHL's interest in the effects of syphilis may be connected with his proposal (see vii. 564–5) that Orioli's projected 'Lungarno Series' of Italian Renaissance texts in translation should include an edition by Richard Aldington of Girolamo Fracastoro's *Syphilis, Sive Morbus Gallicus* (Verona, 1530). The term 'syphilis' originated in this work, deriving from the name of a shepherd Syphilus, the first sufferer from the disease.

190:25 **Shaw's creatures.** This sentence was added to MS in revision. As long ago as 1913 DHL had complained of 'the rather bony, bloodless drama' of George Bernard Shaw (1856–1950) among others (i. 509).

190:33 **Baedeker . . . pictures,** DHL may have been familiar with *Northern Italy . . . Handbook for Travellers* (in its 14th edn in 1913) by Karl Baedeker (1801–59); it included Florence and paid special attention to pictures in the Uffizi Gallery. Stars were attached to *Portrait of a Knight of Malta* and *Moses when a Child undergoes the Ordeal of Fire* by Giorgio Giorgione (1475–1510), and *Calumny*, *Birth of Venus*, *Adoration of the Magi* and *Madonna with Angels* by Alessandro Botticelli (1445–1510) (pp. 580–1).

190:40 **But [190:27] . . . aesthetic response.** This passage replaced the following (with revisions shown) in *MS* (p. 6):

> <<<Now by intuition alone can man *really* be aware of beauty, or really bring forth beauty. When people say they think Botticelli or Giorgione beautiful, all they

> mean is that they think Botticelli and Giorgione look nice. Real <beauty is a thing> ⌐pictures are living images¬ you feel in your arms and legs, <it is a> <<like>> ⌐as you feel¬ sensual, physical experience. You don't merely *see* beauty. It is like fire in your <bowels>, ⌐imagination¬ and it knocks at your bones.>>>

191:2 **Americans . . . whole imagination.** This was not the first time that DHL had been disparaging about the response of Americans to European art. See the Foreword to *Studies in Classic American Literature* (1923); vi. 79, where he recounts the experience, in June 1927, of trying to introduce Christine Hughes and her daughter Mary Christine to Florentine art: 'They're stone blind culturally'; and the short story 'Things' (1928), based on the American painters Earl and Achsah Brewster.

191:22 ***Ils . . . quoi,*** They don't have the wherewithal (French).

191:30 **English Tommy** From Tommy Atkins, a generic term for a private soldier in the British army, used in official regulations from 1815.

192:25 ***Dames de France*** A chain of French department stores.

193:1 **Maria Edgeworth's tales,** Maria Edgeworth (1767–1849) published such collections as *The Parent's Assistant* (1796–1800), *Moral Tales* (1801) and *Popular Tales* (1804).

193:6 **Milton . . . Satan.** Cf. William Blake (1757–1827) in 'The Marriage of Heaven and Hell' (1793): 'in the Book of Job Milton's Messiah is call'd Satan . . . [Milton was] of the Devil's party without knowing it'.

193:33 **Watteau . . . Gainsborough,** Jean-Antoine Watteau (1684–1721), a key figure in French Rococo art; Jean-Auguste-Dominique Ingres (1780–1867), the most generally admired French painter of his day; Nicolas Poussin (1593/4–1665), exceedingly influential in the classical tradition of French painting; Jean-Baptiste-Siméon Chardin (1699–1779), distinguished French painter of still life; William Hogarth (1697–1764), portraitist, and satirist through his anecdotal series of pictures; Sir Joshua Reynolds (1723–92), first President of the Royal Academy and the leading portrait painter of his day; Thomas Gainsborough (1727–88), portraitist and major landscape artist.

193:34 **The [193:16] . . . bourgeois.** This passage replaced the following deleted in *MS* (p. 9):

> <bodies, this reality once perceived, giving us the strange experience of beauty. If the intuitional faculty must be suppressed, and substantial bodies are *per se* immoral – just because they are substantial, where will painting and sculpture be? They will be just where we find them. The eighteenth century not being entirely moralised and ruined, we find a Watteau and an Ingres and much duller, a Reynolds and a Lawrence or a Raeburn. In Watteau and Ingres there is still some of the old gleam and splendour and innocence of the great days of man before he became despicable with his fear and hate obsessions. But Reynolds, Gainsborough etc. are already bourgeois.>

193:40 **Sargent's** John Singer Sargent (1856–1925), expatriate American painter, the outstanding society portraitist of his time; painted Lady Cynthia Asquith (1887–1960), the then Prime Minister's daughter-in-law, but DHL thought his own 'sketch of [her], in words', in 'The Thimble', superior to Sargent's portrait (ii. 419). His judgement of Sargent in 1909 had been of 'a man of startling vigor and brilliance – and cold heart' (i. 113).

194:4 **Titian . . . Rembrandt** The greatest painters of their several Schools: Titian (1477–1576), of the Venetian; Diego Velasquez (1599–1660), of the Spanish; and Rembrandt Harmensz van Rijn (1660–9), of the Dutch.

194:10 **Lawrence . . . Raeburn,** Sir Thomas Lawrence (1769–1830), leading portraitist; he succeeded Reynolds as Royal Painter in Ordinary; President of the Royal Academy, 1820 . . . Sir Henry Raeburn (1756–1823), foremost Scottish portrait painter of his day; George IV's Limner for Scotland.

194:15 **Pre-Raphaelites . . . Watts** The Pre-Raphaelite Brotherhood was founded in 1848 by (Sir) John Everett Millais (1829–96), William Holman Hunt (1827–1910) and Dante Gabriel Rossetti (1828–82) in rebellion against artificiality and sentimentality (though, now, they are widely regarded as escapist themselves) . . . George Frederic Watts (1817–1904), painter and sculptor whose work is marked by high moral purpose and often with abstruse allegory. DHL considered 'some of Watts pictures . . . commonplace, and a trifle vulgar'; he made an exception of *Love and Death* (1875) (i. 107), but particularly detested *Mammon* (1885) calling it 'hideous and hateful' ('Art and the Individual' in *Study of Thomas Hardy*, ed. Steele, 142:6). See also *Mr Noon* (ed. Lindeth Vasey, Cambridge, 1984) 22:2.

194:18 **Blake . . . produced.** DHL encouraged Lady Ottoline Morrell (1873–1938), his friend since 1914, to visit the exhibition of his own paintings, with the remark: 'Do go and look at the pictures . . . there is a suggestion of Blake sometimes' (vii. 235).

194:28 **Etty's . . . Leightons,** William Etty (1787–1849) specialised almost exclusively in painting nudes; the best collection of his work is in the City Art Gallery, York (his native city) . . . Frederic, Baron Leighton (1830–96), one of the dominant figures of late Victorian art; President of the Royal Academy 1878. DHL had considered his *Garden of the Hesperides*, shown in the Academy Winter Exhibition of 1909, 'magnificent' (i. 113), but thought his popular painting, *Wedded* (1881–2), 'beautiful' technically, though emotionally 'weak and shallow' ('Art and the Individual', *Study of Thomas Hardy*, ed. Steele, 141: 35–9).

195:13 **Wilson . . . Turner** Richard Wilson (1713/14–82), the first major British artist to specialise in landscape . . . John Crome (1768–1821), a leading member of the Norwich School; together with Wilson he represented the shift from eighteenth-century picturesque to the Romantic conception of landscape . . . John Constable (1776–1837) and Joseph Mallard William Turner (1775–1851), the two greatest British landscape artists. DHL's admiration for the luminosity and insubstantiality in Turner's pictures is strikingly present in *Study of Thomas Hardy*, ed. Steele, 86:17–87:7.

195:16 **Van Gogh's . . . Cézanne's** Vincent van Gogh (1853–90) and Paul Cézanne (1839–1906): with Gaugin, the greatest of the Post-Impressionists and key figures in twentieth-century art. Cézanne's work was introduced to England through the Post-Impressionist exhibitions of 1910 and 1912 organised by the art critic Roger Fry (1866–1934), to whom DHL devotes critical attention below. On Fry see also vi. 506.

195:36 **Hetty Sorrell's . . . burnt out.** In George Eliot's *Adam Bede* (1859) Hetty Sorrell is seduced by the young squire, Arthur Donnithorne, and is subsequently responsible for the death of their illegitimate child . . . Rochester, the hero of Charlotte Brontë's *Jane Eyre* (1847), is blinded in the fire at Thornfield Hall.

196:5 **Holbein.** Hans Holbein (1497–1543) was born in Germany but came to England in 1526 and was appointed court painter to Henry VIII in 1534.

196:20 *Ça . . . corps*! It's good for the body! (French).

196:30 **Puvis de Chavannes . . . Renoir** Pierre Puvis de Chavannes (1824–98), the leading French mural painter of the late nineteenth century . . . Pierre-Auguste Renoir (1841–1919), distinguished French Impressionist painter; he delighted in painting beautiful women. His alleged remark that he painted 'with [his] penis' may be a corruption of 'It's with my brush that I make love' (Albert André, *Renoir*, 1919, p. 10).

196:38 **Courbet . . . Dégas,** Gustave Courbet (1819–77), a leader of the French Realist School; DHL may have had in mind such pictures as *The Peasants at Flagey* (1850) or *The Stone Breakers* (1850) . . . Honoré Daumier (1808–79), French caricaturist, political and social satirist associated with Courbet's realists . . . Edgar Degas (1834–1917), French Impressionist.

197:18 *plein air . . . plein soleil*: Open air . . . full sun (French).

197:32 **blighters** A slang term (originating in the late nineteenth century) as an extravagant substitute for 'fellows'.

197:38 **Matisse . . . Braque** French painters: Henri Matisse (1869–1954), Impressionist; Paul Gauguin (1848–1903), Post-Impressionist; André Derain (1880–1954) and Maurice de Vlaminck (1876–1958) were, with Matisse, exponents of Fauvism in their use of non-naturalistic colour; Georges Braque (1882–1963) was, with Picasso, the creator of Cubism.

198:37 **Claude Lorraine,** Extremely influential French painter (1600–82) of idealised landscapes evoking the pastoral serenity of a Golden Age.

199:6 **We are . . . body we** From the hymn 'Onward, Christian soldiers' by S. Baring-Gould (1834–1924), ll. 29–30.

199:13 **Primitive Methodists,** See Explanatory note to 'Hymns in a Man's Life' 133:14.

199:17 **cry . . . wilderness.** Cf. Isaiah xl. 3, Matthew iii. 3, Mark i. 3, etc.

199:19 **æsthetic . . . ecstasy . . . the elect,** These terms and assertions recur frequently in Clive Bell's *Art* (1914), e.g. 'Before the grandeur of those Sumerian figures in the Louvre [the perfect lover] is carried on the same flood of emotion to the same aesthetic ecstasy as, more than four thousand years ago, the Chaldean lover was carried . . . The forms of art are inexhaustible; but all lead by the same road of aesthetic emotion to the same world of aesthetic ecstasy' (ed. J. B. Bullen, Oxford, 1987, pp. 36–7) . . . Cf. Bell: 'Probably it will always be difficult for the mass of men to consider pictures as works of art' and 'the mass of mankind will never be capable of making delicate aesthetic judgments' (pp. 227, 261).

199:20 **Ruskin . . . art.** John Ruskin (1819–1900), the dominant art and social critic of Victorian times, insisted on the direct relation between moral and artistic value: e.g. 'there is no other definition of the beautiful, nor of any subject of delight to the aesthetic faculty, than that it is what one noble spirit has created, seen and felt by another of similar or equal nobility' ('Aratra Pentelici', in *The Works of John Ruskin*, ed. E. T. Cook and Alexander Wedderburn, 1905, xx. 208–9) . . . echoing *The Merchant of Venice*, IV. i. 223, 'a Daniel come to judgment', DHL refers to the doctrine of election expounded by John Calvin (1509–64) in his *Institutes of the Christian Religion* (Basel, 1535), a doctrine which had probably influenced DHL's early religious beliefs (cf. i. 39).

199:24 **went whoring** Cf. Judges ii. 17: 'they went a whoring after other gods'.

199:34 **flesh-pots [199:25] . . . Significant Form.** Using language reminiscent of the Bible (e.g. Exodus, xvi. 3: 'the flesh pots when we did eat bread to the full'; Numbers, xxxi. 19: 'purify both yourselves and your captives'; John xiv. 6: 'I am the way . . . '; Revelation i. 1: 'The Revelation of Jesus Christ'; Jeremiah xlv. 26: 'saith the Lord, that my name shall no more be named . . . '), DHL mounts his ironic attack on the doctrine of 'Significant Form' promulgated by Bell in *Art*. Answering his own question, 'What quality is shared by all objects that provoke our aesthetic emotions?', Bell defined Significant Form: 'In each, lines and colours combined in a particular way, certain forms and relations of forms stir our aesthetic emotions. These relations and combinations of lines and colours, these aesthetically moving forms I call "Significant Form"' (p. 8). DHL also alludes to such remarks by Bell as 'the superb peaks of aesthetic exaltation' (p. 32) and the 'thrilling raptures of those who have climbed the cold, white peaks of art' (p. 33).

199:36 **jargon . . . are.** Revivalism was associated with heightened, emotive language coupled with the emphasis, especially in Puritanism and Methodism, on personal religious experience and holy living. DHL may have had in mind the revivalist preaching-tour of Great Britain, 1875–1915, by the Americans, Dwight. L. Moody (1837–99) and Ira D. Sankey (1840–1908), and their supporters.

200:5 **language of salvation.** The young DHL confessed the same inability in a letter to Revd Robert Reid, 1907; see i. 39–41. Cf. also 'Hymns in a Man's Life', 132:27: 'I never did understand how I could "save" [my soul]'.

200:8 **safe in . . . into glory:** 'Safe in the arms of Jesus' is the title of a hymn (1868) by Frances Jane Van Alstyne (1820–1915) . . . for 'Abraham's bosom', see Luke xvi. 22 . . . 'seeing the great light', see Isaiah ix. 2 and Matthew iv. 6 . . . for 'entering into glory' see Luke xxiv. 26.

200:18 **Rudolf Valentino.** See Explanatory note to 'Sex Appeal' 145:39.

200:31 **The ego . . . in heaven.** Unidentified.

200:33 **lamb of God!** John i. 29.

200:40 **Washed . . . Lamb!** Revelation vii. 14. Cf. also the hymn 'Have you been to Jesus?' (popularly known as 'Twelve Hundred'), in *Sacred Songs and Solos*, ed. Ira D. Sankey (n.d.), No. 379; its chorus is: 'Are you washed in the blood – In the soul-cleansing blood of the Lamb? Are your garments spotless? Are they white as snow? Are you washed in the blood of the Lamb?' In *Apocalypse* DHL quotes from a comparable Salvation Army hymn, 'Blessed be the fountains of blood' (1899): see *Apocalypse*, ed. Mara Kalnins (Cambridge, 1980), 99:37 and n.

201:2 **Jerome . . . wash again!** St Jerome (*c.* 340–420); DHL's quotation has not been identified. The reference might be to Jesus' reply to Peter at the footwashing

(John xiii. 10), or the remark may derive from one of the many writings wrongly attributed to Jerome.

201:22 **Cézanne's apples** In *Cézanne: A Study of his Development* (1927; ed. Richard Shiff, Chicago, 1989), pp. 43–9, Roger Fry pays particular analytic attention to Cézanne's picture *Le Compotier* (1877).

202:9 **one critic . . . humble.** Cf. Fry: 'every artist . . . requires an exceptional humility'; Cézanne 'learned thoroughly the lesson of humility' (*Cézanne*, pp. 28–9).

202:19 **the stone . . . tomb.** Cf. Mark xvi. 3–4; Luke xxiv. 2.

202:28 **fig-leaf nonsense.** Genesis iii. 7: after the 'Fall', Adam and Eve 'knew that they were naked; and they sewed fig-leaves together, and made themselves aprons'.

203:2 **Plato's Idea.** Plato (428–347 BC), affirming the existence of a world of ideas, divine types or forms of material objects, asserted that those ideas are real and permanent while individual material things are merely their imperfect and ephemeral imitations or shadows.

203:5 **rolled the stone . . . died,** DHL was probably recalling Fry's account of Cézanne's *Lazarus*, and alluding to the biblical story of Christ's raising of Lazarus after he had been dead four days and 'stinketh' (203:15) (see *Cézanne*, pp. 13–15 and Plate 1, and John xi. 39–44).

203:12 **spear through . . . crucified body,** Cf. John xix. 34.

204:6 **dead . . . dead.** Cf. Matthew viii. 22; Luke ix. 60.

204:16 **Friesz** Othon Friescz (1879–1949), French Fauvist, associated with Braque.

204:25 **Laurencin.** Marie Laurencin (1885–1956), French painter, costume designer for the Comédie Française and book illustrator.

205:11 **Veronese and Tintoretto,** Paolo Veronese (1525–88), with Tintoretto (1518–94), the dominant figures in Venetian painting after Titian.

205:18 **"With all . . . commercial art—"** Fry, *Cézanne*, p. 10.

205:29 **portrait of . . . so famous.** On the *Portrait of M. Geffroy* (1895), see Fry, *Cézanne*, pp. 66–8, 75, and Plate 35. (The 'cant phrases' were not Fry's.)

206:14 **his "willed . . . bad phrase.** Fry wrote of Cezanne's 'insatiable ambition' his 'soaring ambitions' and his 'wilful nature' (*Cézanne*, pp. 26, 32, 20), but seemingly not of his 'willed ambition'. On 'humility' see note on 202:9.

206:31 **hitch . . . star,** Ralph Waldo Emerson (1803–82), American essayist, in 'Civilization', in *Society and Solitude* (*Works*, New York, 1904 edn, vi. 28).

210:11 ***Pasha . . . Femme*.** Cf. Fry, *Cézanne*, pp. 16, 80, and Plates 3 and 49.

211:40 **sheltering behind . . . revolutionary.** See Fry, *Cézanne*, p. 36n.

212:12 *connu! connu!* known! known! (French).

212:29 **appleyness [212:20] . . . appearance.** With DHL's reflections on the 'appleyness' of an apple, cf. his remarks on 'the horsiness of a horse' in *Sketches of Etruscan Places* (ed. Simonetta de Filippis, Cambridge, 1992, p. 127).

212:34 **Madame Cézanne . . . with four.** See Fry, *Cézanne*, Plates 21 (*Mme Cézanne in a Red Armchair*, *c*. 1877), 34 (*Mme Cézanne in a Red Dress*, 1888–90), 36 (*The Cardplayers*, 1890–2, with four figures) and 37 (*The Cardplayers*, 1893–6, with two).

215:19 **I who . . . life."** Cf. Fry, *Cézanne*, pp. 16, 36n.

216:23 **Windsor and Newton . . . Lefranc:** Perfecters of modern water-colours and producers of the finest artists' materials, founded in 1832 by the artists and chemists, William Windsor (1804–65) and Henry Charles Newton (1805–82) . . . the leading French producer of artists' materials.

216:30 **turps,** I.e. oil of turpentine.

216:40 **Lyall's perfect medium:** Ephemeral trade-name given to a type of (probably oil) paint.

217:6 **become . . . children:** Matthew xviii. 3.

217:9 **born again,** Cf. 'Except a man be born again . . .', John iii. 3.

217:26 ***ne plus ultra.*** A final state (Latin).

The State of Funk

223:32 **if I . . . reel.** Cf. letter to Lady Ottoline Morrell, 28 December 1928: 'About *Lady C.* – you mustn't think I advocate perpetual sex. Far from it. Nothing nauseates me more than promiscuous sex in and out of season' (vii. 106).

224:13 **Restore . . . natural flow.** 'one of the reasons why the common people often keep – or kept the good *natural glow* of life, just warm life . . . was because it was still possible for them to say shit! or fuck without either a shudder or a sensation' (vii. 106).

Making Pictures

227:7 **Paris . . . grace,** DHL visited Paris from 12 March to 7 April 1929 (staying with his friends, the novelist Aldous Huxley and his wife Maria, at Suresnes, 18–25 March) principally to negotiate the publication of 'a cheap *Lady C*' by Edward Titus (vii. 242).

227:8 **Dufys . . . Ito** Raoul Dufy (1877–1953), French painter who, in the 1920s, produced calligraphic drawings, especially of Mediterranean scenes, in sparkling colours . . . Georgio de Chirico (1888–1978), Italian painter who worked in Paris, 1924–31; a precursor of the Surrealists, he originated 'Metaphysical painting' which presented ordinary objects in mysterious, disturbing relationships . . . Ito, the Japanese artist popular in Paris, whose name DHL could not remember and who has not been confidently identified even now (vii. 251).

227:12 **Friescz . . . Laurencin** Othon Friesz . . . . Marie Laurencin. See Explanatory notes to 'Introduction to These Paintings' 204:16, 204:25.

227:19 **Maria . . . canvases,** DHL told Dorothy Brett, 24 November 1926, that Maria Huxley had brought to the Villa Mirenda 'some canvases that her brother had daubed on: surely the worst beginnings that man ever made' (v. 585).

228:12 ***A Holy Family.*** DHL wrote to the Huxleys on 11 November 1926: 'I've already painted a picture on one of the canvases . . . I call it the "Unholy Family"; because the *bambino* – with a *nimbus* – is just watching anxiously to see the young man give the semi-nude young woman *un grand baiser. Molto moderno!*' (*'a big kiss. Very modern!*') (French and Italian) (v. 574).

229:4 **Minerva** Roman goddess of wisdom and patron of the arts.

229:33 **"Blessed . . . heaven."** Matthew v. 3 ('. . . the poor in . . . ').

230:3 **Ramblas** I.e. boulevards (Spanish).

230:17 **Leader's . . . water-colours.** English painters whose work DHL first encountered in *English Water-Colour*, ed. Charles Holme (1848–1923), published in eight parts by *Studio* (1902), six parts of which were given to him by the Chambers family on his 21st birthday, 11 September 1906. The painters were: Benjamin Williams Leader (1831–1923); Frank William Brangwyn (1867–1956); Peter de Wint (1784–1849); and Thomas Girtin (1775–1802). See C. E. Baron, 'D. H. Lawrence's Early Paintings', in *Young Bert* (Nottingham Castle Museum, 1972), pp. 32–40.

230:26 **Sandby** Paul Sandby (1730–1809), topographical painter and graphic artist.

230:27 **Brabazon,** Hercules Brabazon (1821–1906), whose sensitive presentation of natural scenes was 'impressionist', not in the sense of French Impressionism but in a style of English painting contrasting with Pre-Raphaelitism and suggesting a rapid statement avoiding minute details.

230:40 **Ten Commandment business,** For an account of the Mosaic law, see Deuteronomy v. 6–21.

231:12 **Fra . . . Venice.** DHL's copy of *Flight into Egypt* by the Italian painter Fra Angelico (*c.* 1400–55) was remembered, in 1928, by Dorothy Warren, as hanging 'over the mantelpiece in Byron Villas' (Nehls, iii. 222) where the Lawrences lived August–December 1925 . . . on 16 November 1920 DHL told Rosalind Baynes: 'I am copying a *very* amusing picture – Lorenzettis – *Anacoreti nelle Tebaidi* – thousands of amusing little monks doing things in the *Thebaid*' (iii. 622); the picture, attributed to Pietro Lorenzetti (1280?–1348?), is now associated with the Florentine School of the early fifteenth century (see iii. 622 n. 2) . . . Vittore Carpaccio (*c.* 1450/60–1525/6), leading Venetian painter.

231:19 **Rembrandt . . . tried,** Rembrandt, see Explanatory note to 'Introduction to These Paintings' 194:4 . . . Peter Paul Rubens (1577–1640), Flemish, the leading European Baroque painter.

231:21 **Peter . . . Vandyck,** Peter de Hooch (1629–84) Dutch genre painter . . . Sir Anthony van Dyck (1599–1641), Flemish, became painter to Charles I.

231:23 ***Death of Procris*** In March 1917, when DHL copied this picture by the Florentine painter, Piero di Cosimo (*c.* 1462–1521?), he was filled 'with great delight' (iii. 103). His copy is the object of harsh criticism ('very amateurish . . . colour muddy') from his painter-friend, Knud Merrild (1894–1954) in *A Poet and Two Painters* (1938), pp. 209–13.

231:24 ***Wedding* . . . Padua.** It is possible that DHL confused some painting in the Uffizi, Florence, with Raphael's famous *Marriage of the Virgin* (1504), in the Brera, Milan, in which one of the Virgin's suitors is prominently shown wearing red tights . . . Giotto di Bondone (*c.* 1267–1337), the famous Florentine painter believed to have created the fresco cycle in the Arena Chapel in Padua.

232:4 **Piero . . . Goya** Piero della Francesca (*c.* 1410/20–92), one of the supreme Italian artists of the *quattrocento* . . . Giovanni Antonio Bazzi Sodoma (1477–1549), Italian painter chiefly associated with Siena . . . Francisco de

Goya (1746–1828), Spanish painter whose mature work conveys a powerful sense of menace and morbidity.

232:8 **Greco.** El Greco (1541–1614), Cretan-born but worked chiefly in Spain; famous for the intense religious feeling of his later paintings.

Pornography and Obscenity

236:5 **pornography . . . harlot.** The word is derived from the Greek: *pornê*, a whore; *graphein*, to write or draw.

236:13 ***obscene*** **. . . means.** The word is adapted from Latin, *obscenus*, but its etymology is doubtful.

236:21 **Aristophanes** Greek comic and satiric dramatist (450?–380? BC).

236:32 **Vox . . . vulgum.** 'Vox populi, vox Dei' ('The voice of the people is the voice of God') is ascribed to Alcuin (735–804) . . . 'Odi profanum vulgus' ('I hate the uninitiated crowd'), Horace, *Odes*, III. i. 1 (Latin). In *MS* DHL wrote 'Odio'.

237:16 **steer . . . contaminated.** Cf. Mark vii. 1–5; Luke xviii. 10–12.

237:21 ***Deus ex machina*****,** A god brought on stage by a mechanical device (Latin); here, a contrivance to catch the popular attention.

237:34 **corn-pone . . . shew-bread . . . Graham . . . Bretzeln, Kringeln . . . damper, matsen—** Coarse maize bread (USA) . . . The twelve loaves offered weekly in the sanctuary of a Jewish synagogue . . . Bread made from unbolted wheaten flour . . . bretzel is a US synonym for a pretzel, kringel is a fancy biscuit (German) . . . .a kind of unfermented bread (Australian), matzo is unleavened bread eaten during the Jewish Passover (from Yiddish *matse*).

239:10 **Rabelais . . . Aretino . . . Boccaccio** François Rabelais (1494?–1553), French humorist and satirist . . . Pietro Aretino (1492–1556), Italian satirist . . . Giovanni Boccaccio (1313–75), renowned Italian writer, author of the *Decameron* (1353).

240:1 **Titian . . . Renoir . . . Song of Solomon . . .** ***Jane Eyre*****, Mozart . . .** ***Annie Laurie*****,** Tiziano Vecelli Titian (1477–1576), chief master of the Venetian School of painting . . . Pierre Auguste Renoir, see Explanatory note to 'Introduction to These Paintings' 196:30 . . . the 'Song of Solomon' is an alternative title for 'The Song of Songs' in the Old Testament . . . the novel by Charlotte Brontë; Wolfgang Amadeus Mozart (1756–91), DHL's 'favourite composer' (v. 570) . . . popular song composed by Charles Macpherson (1870–1927).

240:2 **Michael Angelo,** Michelangelo Buonarroti (1475–1564), poet, painter, architect and sculptor of the High Renaissance.

240:14 ***Pamela*** **or** ***Clarissa Harlowe*** Novels (1740 and 1747–8) by Samuel Richardson (1689–1761).

240:16 **Wagner's . . .** ***Tristan und Isolde*****,** Opera by Richard Wagner (1813–83) first performed in 1865.

240:22 **authoress . . .** ***Sheik*** The bestseller and *succès de scandale* in 1919 was written by Edith Maude Hull.

240:26 **Home Secretary,** Sir William Joynson Hicks (1865–1932) known as 'Jix', DHL's *bête noir*; resigned as Home Secretary in June 1929 and was then ennobled as Viscount Brentford. See introduction to *Pornography and Obscenity*.

243:2 ***Mill . . . Karenin.*** Novel (1860) by George Eliot (1819–80) was "adored' by DHL (i. 88 n. 3) . . . novel (1875–7) by Count Leo Tolstoy (1828–1910).

243:18 **Lasca** Anton Francesco ('Lasca') Grazzini (1503–84). DHL's translation of his *Story of Doctor Manente being the Tenth and Last Story from the Suppers of A. F. Grazzini* was published in November 1929.

243:21 At this point in *MS* DHL wrote: 'Continuation of the article *Obscenity and Pornography* contained in *This Quarter* – D. H. Lawrence'.

246:15 **Victoria's reign.** In pencil, in an unknown hand – presumably someone in the office of Curtis Brown or Faber's – in the margin of *TSI*, the printer was instructed to substitute 'the nineteenth century' for DHL's words. The same instruction occurs at 249:31.

246:30 **One . . . story.—** In his review of *Pansies*, in the *Sunday Times*, 11 August 1929, p. 6, Desmond MacCarthy (1887–1952) asserted that DHL's attitude to sex was misunderstood: 'He has attempted to express the Lucretian poetry of lust. If he did convert the world two things would disappear from it: the love lyric and the smoking-room story.' (MacCarthy repeated the remark in 'Notes on D. H. Lawrence', *Life and Letters*, 1930, iv. 394.)

246:31 **Who . . . she?—** The opening of the song – 'Who is Silvia? what is she / That all our swains commend her?' – in Shakespeare's *Two Gentlemen of Verona*, IV. ii. 38–9. DHL may have had in mind Schubert's setting, 'Was ist Silvia?' (1828).

246:34 ***Du*** **. . . Jawohl!** The opening line of the poem (1825) by Heinrich Heine (1797–1856) ('Oh, you are like a flower! Yes, indeed!') Cf. *Kangaroo*, ed. Bruce Steele (Cambridge, 1993), 44:31.

247:10 **"My . . . rose—!"** 'A red red Rose' (1794), l. 1, by Robert Burns (1759–96) ('O my Luve's like . . . —').

247:12 **lilies . . . festering,** Cf. Shakespeare, sonnet 94: 'Lilies that fester smell far worse than weeds' (l. 14).

247:37 **Marie Stopes:** Marie Carmichael Stopes (d. 1958), founder of the first birth-control clinic in the world; famous for publications such as *Married Love* (1918).

249:10 **mealy-mouthed lie,** 'Mealy-mouthed' was DHL's favourite description for Joynson Hicks (vii. 582, 584).

250:3 **Narcissus,** In Greek mythology, a beautiful youth captivated by his own reflection in a fountain.

250:12 **Marcel Proust,** French novelist (1871–1922) whom DHL regarded as 'too much water-jelly – I can't read him' (vi. 100); he was included in a list of the 'grand perverts' which DHL gave to Aldous Huxley (vi. 342).

252:6 **Benvenuto . . .** ***Nights*** *The Memoirs of Benvenuto Cellini* was a 'book that absorbed him [DHL]', *D. H. Lawrence: A Personal Record by E. T.* [Jessie Chambers] (1935), p. 112 . . . *The Arabian Nights' Entertainments* (1885), trans. Richard Burton (1821–90).

252:10 **article [251:36] . . . support."** Brentford's article, '"Censorship" of Books' appeared in *Nineteenth Century and After*, cvi. (August 1929), 207–11. His general theme was that 'there is in England no censorship of books' (p. 207). He claimed that, when he was Home Secretary, he was sent a copy of *The Well of Loneliness* by the publisher after an 'outcry in a section of the Press', and asked for his opinion: he declared that 'the publication of the book constituted an infringement of the law' (p. 209). (See Explanatory note on 252:15.) He therefore argued that he did not 'discriminate' against the book. He concluded with the two passages quoted by DHL.

252:15 ***The Well of Loneliness.*** The Home Office under Joynson Hicks banned the distribution of the novel (1928) by Marguerite Radclyffe Hall (1886–1943).

252:20 ***in propria persona?*** In person (Latin).

252:38 **You . . . time,** The remark by Abraham Lincoln (1809–65) in a speech on 8 September 1858.

252:40 **Sir James . . . Galsworthy . . . mass of** Barrie, see Explanatory note to 'Which Class I Belong To' 38:38 . . . Galsworthy, see Explanatory note to 'Getting On' 32:14. DHL held neither man in high esteem (see i. 509, iii. 184–5, 547, v. 94). Faber & Faber objected to the remarks and DHL agreed that they could be omitted; they were replaced in all published texts by: 'many contemporary writers, both big and' (see vii. 503 n. 2). A marginal instruction in *TS1* reads: 'omit names'. Cf. Explanatory note on 246:15 above. *TS2* also had a typed marginal note: 'omit names'.

253:5 **Thou . . . quietness** Keats, *Ode on a Grecian Urn* (1820), l. 1.

253:15 **police . . . show,** The police raided the exhibition of DHL's paintings in the Warren Gallery on 5 July 1929 (see vii. 361 n. 1).

253:27 **even . . . Secretaries,** Marginal instruction in *TS1* reads: 'omit'. Cf. 252:40n. above. At this point *MS* has a pencilled marginal note in an unknown hand and *TS2* a typed note: '(Grey HS a little overdone. Present regime has done no harm yet – why worry Clynes?)'. John Robert Clynes (1869–1949), succeeded Hicks as Home Secretary in June 1929.

Pictures on the Wall

258:14 **photogravures,** Photogravure is a method of engraving with the aid of photography by which the design is sunk into the surface of the metal (i.e. is not in relief).

258:16 **Baxter** George Baxter (1804–67), English printmaker who in 1835 patented a method of producing coloured illustrations. Initially he specialised in book illustrations but later produced large prints of royal occasions which were highly sought after.

258:32 **Raphael . . . Michael Angelo** Leading Italian painter, Raphael (1483–1520) . . . See Explanatory note to *Pornography and Obscenity* 240:2.

258:37 **Landseer . . . Alma Tadema,** Sir Edwin Landseer (1802–73), English animal painter and one of the most popular artists of the nineteenth century; he sentimentalised his animal subjects as with the dogs in *Dignity and Impudence* (1839) . . . Sir Lawrence Alma-Tadema (1836–1912), Dutch painter who settled in London; he painted scenes of Greek and Roman life.

258:38 **Dukes of Devonshire** William Cavendish (1640–1707), created 1st Duke of Devonshire in 1694, began the building of Chatsworth, his palatial residence in Derbyshire; it was enlarged by successive dukes until the early nineteenth century; they accumulated a large collection of paintings and drawings of varied quality.

259:8 **Millais'** ***Bubbles*****,** Sir John Everett Millais (1829–96), a member of the Pre-Raphaelite Brotherhood; he was capable of brilliant and minute accuracy of representation but, later, of superficial and sentimental portraiture as in *Bubbles* (1886); it was used in an advertisement for Pears's soap. Cf. Aldous Huxley, 'Farcical History of Richard Greenow' in *Limbo, Six Stories and a Play* (1920; 1946), p. 66: Greenow recalls 'an image of himself as a child, dressed in green velvet and lace, a perfect Bubbles boy'.

259:11 **Whistler's Portrait of his Mother** James McNeill Whistler (1834–1903), American-born painter who settled in London; his painting, *Arrangement in Grey and Black No. 1: Portrait of the Painter's Mother* (1872), continues to be used by greetings-card manufacturers.

259:24 **Giorgione** Major Italian High Renaissance Painter (*c.* 1477–1510).

260:31 **Renoir . . . Friesz . . . Brabazon** See Explanatory notes to 'Introduction to These Paintings' 196:30, . . . 204:16 and 'Making Pictures' 230:27.

260:34 **Titian** ***Adam and Eve*****,** Titian's painting entitled *The Fall of Man* (*c.* 1570) is in the Prado, Madrid.

260:40 **Picassos, . . . Braque . . . Romney** Pablo Picasso (1881–1973), Spanish artist, the dominant influence on the development of the visual arts in the twentieth century . . . Braque, see Explanatory note to 'Introduction to These Paintings' 197:38 . . . George Romney (1734–1802), English portrait painter; his work was over-valued and extremely highly priced in the period 1914–39.

261:17 **"pictuary",** DHL's coinage; no other use of the word is known.

262:4 **Matisse** See Explanatory note to 'Introduction to These Paintings' 197:38.

262:6 **Joyce . . . Proust?** James Joyce (1882–1941), whose writings DHL found neither congenial nor intelligible: see, e.g., vi. 507–8, 548 . . . Proust: see Explanatory note to *Pornography and Obscenity* 250:12.

262:30 **"Doughty's** ***Arabia Deserta*** Charles Montagu Doughty (1843–1926), whose *Travels in Arabia Deserta* (1888; reissued in 1921, intro. by T. E. Lawrence) DHL read in 1925 and clearly found rather tedious (see v. 246).

264:17 At the end of the text given here, the *Architectural Review* printed the following three paragraphs (annotation for these paragraphs follows):

> Instead of which we get these elaborate and expensive exhibitions of old masters, as in the present Italian exhibition,* which are simply museum-stuff to the great public. The great public goes to see these old masters out of mere snobbery, because, principally, the ship-load was insured for fourteen million pounds. Fourteen million pounds! just imagine it! And that is what the great public sees in the wonderful Italian exhibition.
>
> It is what the Italians themselves see in their old "masterpieces." Go through the Uffizi with an ordinary Italian from Rome or Milan, and he is bored stiff. All he will be able to say is: But they are worth millions!

It is perfectly natural. We don't ask the man in the street to sit down and read Milton or Ben Jonson or even Shakespeare. He can't – he is too bored. The whole point of view is utterly changed, and he can't "get it." In the same way, how many people will get anything at all out of Piero della Francesca's *Virgin and Child*, or Mantegna's, or Bellini's,* except a sense of acute boredom, amounting to repugnance. These pictures, nowadays, are just for a few specially educated people. To the vast mass they are merely odious. And the vast mass only troops through the exhibition out of pure snobbery. It is really quite ridiculous to provide marvellous exhibitions of Luca Signorelli and Mantegna and Paolo Uccello* for Cockney crowds.

the present Italian exhibition, The *Architectural Review* in January 1930 declared that 'the most exciting event this month is the opening of the Italian Exhibition at Burlington House' (lxvii. 30). The exhibition, entitled 'Italian Art 1200–1900', ran from 1 January to 8 March 1930.
Francesca's *Virgin and Child* . . . Mantegna's . . . Bellini's, Italian painters – Piero della Francesca (*c.* 1415–92), Andrea Mantegna (1430/1–1506) and Giovanni Bellini (1431/6–1516). Two paintings of the Christ child and His mother by each painter were included in the Exhibition.
Signorelli . . . Uccello Luca Signorelli (*c.* 1450–1523), the leading painter in central Italy in his day, principally of frescoes, altarpieces and smaller paintings (repeatedly copied by Cézanne); seven of his paintings were included in the Exhibition . . . Paolo Uccello (*c.* 1397–1475), Italian imaginative and decorative painter, and remarkable naturalist; one of his paintings was exhibited.

The Risen Lord

267:5 **"The . . . nesh,"** DHL here quotes the opening stanza of his own poem, 'The Risen Lord', first published in *Pansies* in July 1929. 'Nesh', a dialect word meaning 'tender'.

267:10 **The Creed . . . body . . . "** DHL wrote a note to Nancy Pearn on the MS (p. 1) of this essay: 'Dear Nancy Pearn – Do correct these if they are not right – so long since I went to church.' He was referring to the quotations from the Apostles' Creed, the first of which he initially (and rightly) attributed to the Creed but then, uncertain, wrongly changed to 'Litany'. In view of his clear request to Nancy Pearn, the corrections made in the typescript are accepted here. The manuscript readings are recorded in the Textual Apparatus.

269:1 ***Consummatum . . . finished*!** See Explanatory note to '[Return to Bestwood]' 19:21.

269:13 **Calvary** The name given to the place of Christ's crucifixion.

270:1 **Adonis.** The beautiful youth, beloved by Venus, whose death while hunting and his supposed resurrection were commemorated in midsummer.

270:19 **hands . . . certain:** A reference to the apostle ('Doubting') Thomas who, having declared that he must see the physical evidence of Christ's pierced hands and side before he would be convinced of His resurrection, was presented with it. See John xx. 24–9.

270:29 **Gethsemane,** Jesus prayed in agony in the Garden of Gethsemane on the night of his arrest and presentation before Caiaphas. See Matthew xxvi. 36.

271:25 **man friend . . . breast,** Presumably a reference to St John, 'the beloved disciple', who – in paintings of the Last Supper – was traditionally portrayed as affectionately close to Jesus.

271:37 **This time . . . wilderness,** St Matthew iv. 1–11 tells the story of Christ's being led 'into the wilderness' and, for forty days, being tempted by Satan with offers of physical satisfaction and earthly power.

272:1 **Mammon?** The god of this world, identified with the evils of wealth and greed.

272:6 **The earth . . . thereof,** Psalm xxiv. 1.

272:33 **mealy-mouthed . . . song.** The phrasing recalls the extension of *Pornography and Obscenity* written within weeks of this article. Cf. Explanatory note to *Pornography and Obscenity* 249:10.

Men Must Work and Women as Well

276:13 **Mr. Ford.** Henry Ford (1863–1947), American industrialist who revolutionised factory production with his assembly-line methods; the Ford Motor Co. was founded in 1903, the first mass-produced car, the Model T, appeared in 1913.

277:14 *hey presto!* A conjuror's command when, to general astonishment, he brandishes a hidden object.

277:40 **tabloid** The term was invented by a drug company in 1884 to denote a small tablet of a compressed drug or other medical substance.

279:12 **board-schools** See Explanatory note to '[Autobiographical Fragment]' 50:26.

281:10 **Which, given [280:39] . . . affect this?** This passage was substituted for the following deleted in *MS* (pp. 8–9):

> <This means not only a change of mind but a change of feeling, a change of the whole stream of feeling which carries our "civilisation" along. This is a revolution in the deepest sense of the word and may or may not be too much to hope for.
>
> But such being the condition pertaining between the social classes – made up of men and women, after all – ; what about the more immediate problem of private life, which is based on the relationship between man and woman? How is this affected by the "labour compulsion?>

Nottingham and the Mining Countryside

287:15 **B.W.& Co.** Barber, Walker & Company, owners of the Brinsley and other collieries developed in the Eastwood area from the 1840s.

287:20 **foot-rill mines** I.e. open-cast mines.

287:23 **my father** Arthur Lawrence began work at the pit when 7 years old. See *Early Years* 8–12.

287:27 **my grandfather,** John Lawrence (1815–1901).

289:14 **twitchells,** Narrow passages between houses or hedges (dialect).

289:21 **sheep were dipped:** Sheep were washed ('dipped') with vermin-killing disinfectant before being sheared. The scene is described in similar detail in *Sons and Lovers* 30:14–22.

289:30 **Fielding . . . Eliot.** The English novelists Henry Fielding (1707–54) and George Eliot.

289:36 **butty system . . . pit "stall",** See Explanatory note to 'Myself Revealed' 177:21. Cf. *Sons and Lovers* 26:5–13.

290:5 **moved . . . being.** Cf. Acts xvii. 28: 'in him [the Lord] we live, and move, and have our being'.

292:8 ***The Maiden's Prayer*,** Piano piece by the Polish composer Tekla Badarzewska-Baranowska (1838–61), published under the French title 'La Prière d'une vierge'. Cf. 'A Collier's Friday Night', II. 22 and n., *D. H. Lawrence: The Plays*, ed. Hans-Wilhelm Schwarze and John Worthen (Cambridge, 1999), p. 615.

293:3 **Siena . . . million,** Relatively small (in 1900 Siena's population was about 25,000), the Tuscan city had kept its intimate mediaeval character to a remarkable degree . . . according to *The Statesman's Year-Book* Nottingham's population had grown from 239,703 in 1901 to 266, 800 in 1929.

293:33 **promoter** Spelt 'promotor' in *MS* here and two lines below.

We Need One Another

296:1 **We . . . Another** In *MS* DHL deleted his original title: 'Human Relationship'.

The text of the essay in *Scribner's Magazine* was preceded by the following statement:

> The death of D. H. Lawrence brings to an end the career of a great writer whose works have been a source of contention for many years. Because they were so largely concerned with sex, his writings met with violent opposition from the official censors and from a large body of sincere readers. His supporters contend that Lawrence's attitude, far from being erotic and sensationally minded, is the effort of a sensitive man to make sex a vital and honest thing. The article we are publishing, which came to the magazine a month before his death, assumes the importance of a last statement. It seems to bear out the contention of Lawrence's friends that he was a profoundly moral and sympathetic man who used up his strength in trying to bring sanity and honesty to a sadly muddled discussion.

296:2 Two opening paragraphs were deleted in *MS*; DHL's first version read:

> <"For God's sake, let's get away from the women!" – says a man to his friend, in a low, intense voice. And a woman, ⌐to her woman-friend,¬ in a secret voice vibrating with indignation: "But you know, men *are* awful – they're horrible. They're such despicable egoists –"
>
> And it's perfectly true, men have a great need to get away from their women, at least for a time. And it's quite true, from a woman's point of view the peculiar

egoism of the modern male is despicable and horrible. Yet see the men scuttling back to these women they wanted so badly to get away from! And see the women darting home to the men whose egoism is so despicable!>

296:3 **kicking ... the pricks,** Cf. Acts ix. 5 (Authorised Version).

296:29 **In heaven ... marriage.** Cf. Matthew xxii. 30.

297:32 **Napoleon [297:26] ... Mary Queen of Scots ... hole.** Napoleon (1769–1821) was exiled on the island of St Helena from October 1815 until his death ... For Mary, Queen of Scots, see Explanatory note to 'Matriarchy' 104:1; she was executed in Fotheringay Castle, near Peterborough.

297:40 **St. Simeon ... pillar,** St Simeon Stylites (*c.* 390–459), a shepherd who became a hermit and ascetic; he lived atop a pillar from *c.* 420 until his death.

298:10 **Immanuel Kant,** Immanuel Kant (1724–1804), German metaphysician and philosopher.

298:14 **bhô-tree** The holy tree under which Buddha found enlightenment. On Nirvana see Explanatory note to 'The Real Thing' 308:15.

298:19 **"And I ... unto me."** John xii. 32 (' ... lifted up from the earth, will draw ... ').

298:28 **So that [298:21] ... and from** Replaced the following in *MS* (p. 5): <<From which we learn that we live and move and have our being *in connection*, in vital connection with <some> other human beings. Napoleon was the great Napoleon in connection with his soldiers, his men, with the whole French nation. Then there streamed forth from him a great power, and from>>

298:38 **move ... being.** See Explanatory note to 'Nottingham and the Mining Countryside' 290:5.

299:4 **bladders [298:40] ... real individuality.** Replaced the following in *MS* (p. 6): <<cyphers. We are like a great tree, an oak, reduced to a mere acorn, a seed, which in itself is ⌐next to¬nothing, <unless> ⌐until¬ it is put back into relationship with the moving elements, in the damp earth. Otherwise it is just pig-food.>>

299:11 **and through [299:10] ... nonentities.** Replaced the following in *MS* (p. 6): <we live and move and have our being, and it is time we began to realise it, and behave ourselves accordingly.>

299:15 **But [299:12] ... for killing** Replaced the following in *MS* (p. 6): <As a matter of fact, in the words of one of the earliest philosophers everything flows. A man is a flow, and a woman is another flow. A woman is not a plaster-cast bust stuck on a pedestal: nor a walking and talking machine: nor even a>

299:35 **Or else [299:29] ... let** Replaced the following in *MS* (p. 7): <<So this is a human relation, something we don't understand, and something we can't do much about. The only thing we can do with a human relation, deliberately, is to smash it. That is <rarely> ⌐never¬ difficult. On the positive side, we can only let it be, let>>

300:5 **The conquering ... Hindenburg,** DHL had told the American poet Harold Witter Bynner (1881–1968), on 13 March 1928: 'On the whole, I think you're right. The hero is obsolete, and the leader of man is a back number' (vi. 321). Thomas Morell (1703–84) supplied the line 'See the conquering hero comes' for Handel's oratorio, *Joshua* (1748) . . . Paul von Hindenburg (1847–1934), German Field Marshal during the First World War, became second President of the Weimar Republic in 1925.

300:20 **I AM** God would not reveal His name but instructed Moses to refer to Him as 'I AM' (Exodus iii. 13–14). See also 'The Crown' in *Reflections on the Death of a Porcupine and Other Essays*, ed. Michael Herbert (Cambridge, 1988), p. 268:5–32.

300:27 **flowing life [300:23] . . . life.** For another use of the river image see 'The Reality of Peace' in *Reflections*, ed. Herbert, pp. 28–9.

300:28 **all [300:18] . . . And** Replaced the following in *MS* (p. 8):

> <apart from his relation to his fellow men, and to woman particularly, he doesn't amount to a hill o' beans, let him be all the heroes of conquest or martyrdom he likes. It is in our relationships to one another that we really have our being, and even – really, have our soul. A man who has never had any vital relationship to any other human being doesn't really *have* a soul. A soul, it seems to me, is something you cant have all by yourself. My very soul is made up of the people I have loved, or hated, or truly *known*.
>
> And by my soul I only mean my own wholeness. What>

302:33 **For sex [302:19] . . . manifestation.** The whole of this final paragraph appears to have been a late addition; it is compressed at the foot of the last page in *MS* and written in – for DHL – an unusually small script.

The Real Thing

304:10 **soviet.** Following the 1917 revolution Russia was governed both locally and nationally by councils ('soviets') of workers.

305:16 **Anthony . . . killed himself.** Consequent on his defeat at the battle of Actium, Mark Antony (followed by Cleopatra) committed suicide, 30 BC.

306:40 **Nemesis . . . Furies,** The Greek goddess personifying divine retribution . . . in Roman mythology the Furies (in Greek, Erinyes) are the three avengers of wrong.

307:20 **Hector . . . chariot.** In the *Iliad*, Homer tells how Hector, eldest son of Priam, is killed by Achilles who then ties the corpse to his chariot and drags it three times round the walls of Troy.

308:15 **Nirvana . . . all understanding.** The state of bliss, to which a Buddhist aspires, when the soul is finally delivered from transmigration . . . Epistle to the Philippians iv. 7 ('the peace of God, which passeth . . . ').

309:8 **winged messenger,** In classical myth Mercury is the winged messenger; DHL may have had in mind an angelic messenger such as Gabriel at the Annunciation.

309:15 **The Bridge . . . Picasso,** Novel (1927) by Thornton Wilder (1897–1975); DHL regarded it as 'a dull dough-nut with artificial jam in it' (vi. 315) . . . Picasso, see Explanatory note to 'Pictures on the Wall' 260:40.

310:1 **Ah, there's the rub.** See Explanatory note to 'Is England Still a Man's Country' 141:28.

310:29 **even [310:6] . . . women too.** In *MS* (p. 9) a deleted passage reads:

<<I am at peace and at one with the onward flow of life itself, even if I have to fight like a wildcat against society. What makes me happy is to be at peace, in a peaceful flow, with some other human being. What gives me joy is to know that there is somebody who will never really break the peace with me. Little squalls, little outbursts, but the flow of peace only ruffled on the surface. Then shall the peace be as a river that is what life means. A great deal of life is taken up in battle. But the strength and the true energy and the beauty and the delight of life is in the river of peace, the flow, the flow between me and the universe, me and the spirit of man – me and a few friends, friends in the flow of peace, not in the skirmish of contest, and finally, the river of peace between me and a woman. The fight is for a day, maybe a long day. But the river of peace is forever.

And life is for delight. Try as I may, I can see no other <goal> ⌐meaning¬ of life but real delight. All this salvation and redemption and remission of sin, all this sacrifice and death and the grand mission of tragedy, I can see nothing in it but part of the process of the delight of life. I can see nothing in the blackness of Good Friday but the shadow before the lovely brilliance of Easter Sunday, when everything the sun in heaven and the sun in a man's breast, comes up new and splendid, for a summer of delight.>>

Nobody Loves Me

313:12 **New England . . . calm.** Transcendentalism was a nineteenth-century movement, in New England, of writers and philosophers who shared a belief in the essential unity of all creation, the innate goodness of man and the supremacy of insight over logic and experience. Walt Whitman (1819–92) was associated with them.

313:20 ***en masse*** Cf. Whitman, 'One's-Self I Sing', in *Leaves of Grass* (1855): 'One's-Self I sing, a simple separate person, / Yet utter the word Democratic, the word En-Masse –'.

314:17 **one flesh.** The words connect with a persistent theme in DHL's writings, deriving ultimately from Genesis ii. 23–4 and Matthew xix. 5–6 and associated for him with sexual, particularly married, love. E.g. *The White Peacock*, ed. Andrew Robertson, p. 196:33; 'Odour of Chrysanthemums' in *The Prussian Officer and Other Stories*, ed. John Worthen (Cambridge, 1983), p. 197:38; 'The Theatre' in *Twilight in Italy*, ed. Paul Eggert, p. 135:30. See also Michael Black, *D. H. Lawrence: The Early Fiction* (1986) and *The Early Philosophical Works* (1991).

314:34 **good Lord deliver us!** The petition in the Litany, *Book of Common Prayer.*

316:11 **poor suffering . . . negroes** DHL was presumably thinking of Ireland's generally impoverished economy and the consequences of the great potato famine of 1846–7. Nevertheless – despite his sympathy for the Irish people whose political life was 'so torn' (ii. 604) – he considered the Irish leaders of the 1916 Easter Rising against British rule, as 'mostly windbags and nothings who happen to have become tragically significant in death' (ii. 611) . . . Large numbers of Christian Armenians, subjects of the Ottoman empire, had been massacred by Muslim Turks in 1894–6, and more, with even greater brutality, during the First World War . . . The Congo (now Zaire) was ruled by Belgium, 1908–60. Extensive rubber, coffee and cotton plantations were developed under the paternalistic though severe régime; a rebellion against the government was harshly suppressed, 1919–23.

316:26 **father eats . . . on edge.** Cf. Jeremiah xviii. 2: 'The fathers have eaten sour grapes, and the children's teeth are set on edge.'

317:30 **a wild . . . service.** DHL probably had in mind the controversy resulting from attempts, rejected by Parliament, to revise the *Book of Common Prayer*, 1927–8.

TEXTUAL APPARATUS

TEXTUAL APPARATUS

The following symbols are used to distinguish states of the texts:

MS = Manuscript
TS = Typescript
TCC = Typescript carbon copy
Per = Periodical
A1 = First American book publication
E1 = First English book publication

The Note on the Texts, pp. 3–5, specifies which symbols are used for each essay or article and indicates which state is the base-text. It also gives details of the policy on silent emendations.

Whenever the base-text reading is adopted, it appears within the square bracket, with no symbol unless the base-text and a later state with the same reading need to be indicated. When a reading from a source other than the base-text has been preferred, it appears with its source-symbol within the bracket. Rejected readings follow the bracket, in chronological sequence, with their first source denoted. In the absence of information to the contrary, the reader should assume that a particular variant recurs in all subsequent states. All variants in the given states subsequent to the base-text are recorded, as well as adopted readings from any states previous to it.

The following symbols are used editorially:

Ed. = Editor
~ = Substitution for a word in recording a punctuation or capitalisation variant
Om. = Omitted
P = Paragraph
/ = Line break in verse or prose
R = Autograph correction by DHL to a state of the text later than MS
[ ] = Editorial emendation or addition
< > = Deletions from a manuscript or typescript
⌐ ¬ = Additions to a manuscript or typescript

Mercury

The chronological sequence is *MS*, *TS*, *Per*, *A1*.

8:1 **Mercury** *Ed.*] <Merkur> ⌐Mercury¬/ by D. H. Lawrence *MS* MERCURY. *TS* MERCURY/ BY D. L. LAWRENCE*Per* MERCURY*A1*

8:2 holiday-makers *MS*, *A1*] holiday makers *Per*

8:3 two-thousand] two thousand *TS*

8:6 its *MS*, *Per*] the *TS*, *A1*

8:7 that towards *MS*, *A1*] which toward *Per*
8:8 pine-trees *MS*, *A1*] pine trees *Per*
8:10 towards *MS*, *A1*] toward *Per*
8:13 cone, *MS*, *Per*] ~; *TS*, *A1*
8:13 tree-trunks *MS*, *A1*] tree trunks *Per*
8:15 river-plain *MS*, *A1*] river plain *Per*
8:16 westwards *MS*, *A1*] westward *Per*
8:16 southwards *MS*, *A1*] southward *Per*
8:17 east] ~, *TS*, *A1* last *Per*
8:19 north *MS*, *Per*] ~, *TS*, *A1*
8:20 castle-ruins] castle ruins *TS*
8:23 beer-garden *MS*, *A1*] beer garden *Per*
8:25 rock-garden *MS*, *A1*] rock garden *Per*
8:25 wilderness,] ~ *TS*
8:28 beer-garden *MS*, *A1*] beer garden *Per*
8:30 vapours *MS*, *A1*] vapors *Per*
8:33 Lying . . . at *MS*, *A1*] As you lay and looked upward at *Per*
8:34 middle-world *MS*, *A1*] middle world *Per*
8:34 pine-trees *MS*, *A1*] pine trees *Per*
9:1 pure *MS*, *A1*] ~, *Per*
9:2 downwards *MS*, *A1*] downward *Per*
9:3 earth-world *MS*, *A1*] earth world *Per*
9:4 tree-trunks *MS*, *A1*] tree trunks *Per*
9:5 watched, *MS*, *A1*] ~ *Per*
9:8 world, *MS*, *A1*] ~ *Per*
9:10 —there] There *Per*
9:11 matter! *MS*, *Per*] ~? *TS*, *A1*
9:13 fat, blue, *MS*, *A1*] ~ ~ *Per*
9:14 tree-trunks *MS*, *A1*] tree trunks *Per*
9:16 by, *MS*, *Per*] ~: *TS*, *A1*
9:16 re-appear] reappear *Per*
9:18 drink: *MS*, *A1*] ~; *Per*
9:18 tables: *MS*, *A1*] ~; *Per*
9:20 pine-trees] pine trees *Per*
9:22 tree-trunks *MS*, *A1*] tree trunks *Per*
9:24 outlook *MS*, *A1*] obsolete *TS*
9:24 tablet-stone *MS*, *A1*] tablet stone *Per*
9:25 Mercury, *MS*, *A1*] ~ *Per*
9:27 this *MS*, *Per*] the *TS*, *A1*
9:28 sun-head *MS*, *A1*] sun head *Per*
9:28 purplish red *MS*, *Per*] purplish-red *TS*, *A1*
9:29 no-one] no one *TS*
9:33 pine-trees *MS*, *A1*] pine trees *Per*
9:33 benches, *MS*, *Per*] ~; *TS*, *A1*
9:34 hot, *MS*, *A1*] ~ *Per*
9:35 pine-trees *MS*, *A1*] pine trees *Per*
9:36 semi-consciousness *MS*, *A1*] semiconsciousness *Per*
9:39 breast-feathers *MS*, *A1*] breast feathers *Per*
10:1 pine-trees, *MS*, *A1*] pine trees *Per*
10:3 down, *MS*, *Per*] ~; *TS*, *A1*
10:3 want *MS*, *A1*] wants *Per*
10:4 Mercury, *MS*, *A1*] ~ *Per*
10:4 this *MS*, *Per*] the *TS*, *A1*
10:5 towards *MS*, *A1*] toward *Per*
10:6 towards *MS*, *A1*] toward *Per*
10:6 station, *MS*, *A1*] ~ *Per*
10:8 movement, *MS*, *A1*] ~ *Per*
10:9 verandah] veranda *A1*
10:14 verandah, *MS*, *Per*] ~ *TS*, veranda *A1*
10:23 fire *MS*, *A1*] ~, *Per*
10:24 verandah] veranda *A1*
10:26 thunder,] ~*TS*
10:26 disappears, the *MS*, *Per*] ~. The *TS*, *A1*
10:30 again,] ~; *TS*
10:31 tree-trunks *MS*, *A1*] tree trunks *Per*
10:36 ground: *MS*, *A1*] ~; *Per*

11:3 pine-trees] pine trees *Per*

11:5 is *MS*, *A1*] are *Per*

11:7 threshing *MS*, *A1*] thrashing *Per*

11:10 ice-fall *MS*, *A1*] ice fall *Per*

11:10 sounds *MS*, *A1*] sound *Per*

11:13 débris] debris *A1*

11:15 ice-balls *MS*, *A1*] ice balls *Per*

11:20 hail-stones] hailstones *TS*

11:24 no-one] no one *TS*

11:28 dark blue *MS*, *Per*] dark-blue *TS*, *A1*

11:28 uniforms *MS*, *A1*] uniform *Per*

11:32 blonde] blond *A1*

11:34 downwards *MS*, *A1*] downward *Per*

11:35 gazed *MS*, *A1*] gaped *Per*

11:39 sloppy *MS*, *A1*] slippery *Per*

11:40 pine boughs *MS*, *Per*] pine-boughs *TS*

12:5 pine-branches *MS*, *A1*] pine branches *Per*

[Return to Bestwood]

The chronological sequence is *MS*, *E1*.

15:1 **[Return to Bestwood]** *E1*] *Om. MS*

15:13 Partly,] ~ *E1*

15:14 Co-op—] ~. *E1*

15:16 lugging] hugging *E1*

15:21 up,] ~. *E1*

15:23 though —] ~ *E1*

16:14 vapourousness] vaporousness *E1*

16:20 countryside] country-side *E1*

16:40 police-sergeant] police sergeant *E1*

17:9 Hafton] Hufton *E1*

17:11 day's *E1*] days *MS*

18:29 carriage!"] ~" *E1*

18:37 *did*] did *E1*

18:40 Austin] Justin *E1*

19:29 moustache lifter] moustache-lifter *E1*

20:8 black slate] black-slate *E1*

20:12 spring] Spring *E1*

20:25 Hardwick *E1*] Hardwich *MS*

20:37 ride] still ride *E1*

20:39 poaching,] ~ *E1*

21:1 lane-end] lane end *E1*

21:2 blue-bottles] "blue-bottles" *E1*

21:16 blue-bottles] "blue-bottles" *E1*

21:19 there] here *E1*

21:27 ones,] ~ *E1*

21:36 pit-bottles] pit bottles *E1*

22:10 football] foot-ball *E1*

22:12 football] foot-ball *E1*

22:21 think] ~, *E1*

Getting On

The essay is previously unpublished. *MS* changes are recorded.

27:1 **Getting On** *Ed.*] <My Career> Getting On/ by D. H. Lawrence *MS*

27:11 at a corner] <a corner house> ⌐at a corner¬

28:8 went . . . shillings]<diminished a little> ⌐went . . . shillings¬

28:10 his hired] <a> ⌐his hired¬

28:12 quick] <ground> ⌐quick¬

28:39 glow] <certain> glow

29:7 forty,] <fifty,> ⌐forty,¬

29:7 ⌐and he . . . more,¬

29:10 ⌐though this . . . unfortunately.¬

29:33 ⌐also¬

29:39 without . . . with] <but disconnected from> ⌐without . . . with¬

30:1 so . . . might] <so I never tried to deceive myself> ⌐so . . . might¬
30:5 Her people] <They> ⌐Her people¬
30:13 pushed . . . . the shelf] <she would read when I> ⌐pushed . . . the shelf¬
30:15 to me] t<oo> me
30:15 ⌐ Nor . . . her.¬
30:21 ⌐And if . . . alive.¬
30:27 re-written the] <written again> ⌐re-written the¬
30:34 ⌐nay, . . . presumptuousness.¬
30:36 ⌐Which . . . father.¬
30:37 presume] <dare>
30:39 me] <such a brat> ⌐me¬
30:40 So] <Well,> ⌐So¬
30:41 ⌐I hated . . . teacher.¬
31:4 sceptical] <*superior*> ⌐sceptical¬
31:5 annoyed] <merely>
31:13 was a . . . me] <meant nothing to me> ⌐was a . . . me¬
31:21 hewed] <?hewd> ⌐hewed¬
31:38 ⌐wrote to her¬
31:40 ⌐to be forty!¬
31:41 ⌐I might . . . live.—¬
32:3 ⌐But vitality . . . up.¬
32:4 forty-one . . . have I] <forty, and I have not> ⌐forty-one . . . have I¬
32:8 And what] <What> ⌐And what¬
32:15 couldn't] <cant>

Which Class I Belong To

The essay is previously unpublished. *MS* changes are recorded.

35:1 **Which Class I Belong To** *Ed.*] Which <Class> ⌐Class¬ I Belong To / D. H. Lawrence *MS*
35:4 consciousness] <culture> ⌐consciousness¬
35:6 conscious] <cultured> ⌐conscious¬
35:6 One . . . not] <One cannot> ⌐One . . . not¬
35:13 are] <is>
35:13 middle-class] <educated> ⌐middle class¬
35:26 now] <are>
37:4 ⌐ordinarily¬
37:16 gulf] gu<f> ⌐l¬f
39:8 among] <with> ⌐among¬
39:9 as] <and> ⌐as¬
39:9 among] <with> ⌐among¬

Making Love to Music

The chronological sequence is *MS*, *TS*, *A1*.

42:1 **Making Love to Music** *Ed.*] Making Love to Music/ by D. H. Lawrence *MS* MAKING LOVE TO MUSIC *TS*
42:4 individualist —] individual. *TS*
42:7 and] ~, *TS*
42:16 were] are *TS*
42:19 wished and] *Om. TS*
42:29 grandmothers *TS*] grandmother's *MS*
43:2 copulation] capitulation *TS*
43:2 no Sir] ~, sir *TS*
43:26 there] ~, *TS*
43:32 all-embracing,] ~ *TS*
43:34 off *TS*] of *MS*
43:36 sublimation: *TS*] ~ *MS*
44:11 actuality —] ~. *TS*
44:13 —We] ~ *TS*
44:18 it—] ~. *TS*
44:27 bodies. —] ~. *TS*

44:29 Grandmothers' *Ed.*] Grandmother's *MS* grandmothers' *TS*
44:32 music] ~, *TS*
44:36 country dances] country-dances *TS*
44:38 Lo] lo *TS*
44:40 one,] ~ *TS*
45:2 forever] for ever *A1*
45:18 herself:] ~, *TS*
45:21 woman,] ~ *TS*
45:28 content,] ~; *TS*
45:37 men] ~, *TS*
45:39 her:] ~, *TS*
46:11 lady?—] ~? *A1*
46:34 peculiar-large] peculiar large *TS*
46:39 out.—] ~. *A1*
47:5 strongly-dancing] strongly dancing *A1*
47:17 pet dogs] pet-dogs *TS*
47:18 then] ~, *TS*
47:19 stark naked] stark-naked *TS*
47:20 three parts] three-parts *TS*
47:21 it,] ~; *TS*
47:38 two-thousand five hundred] two-thousand-five-hundred *TS*
48:7 music-stunned] music-shunned *TS*

[Autobiographical Fragment]

The chronological sequence is *MS*, *TS*, *A1*.

50:1 **[Autobiographical Fragment]** *Ed.*] Untitled *MS* [AUTOBIOGRAPHICAL FRAGMENT] *A1*
50:6 buses *MS*, *A1*] 'buses *TS*
50:8 picture palaces] picture-palaces *TS*
50:8 palais de danse] Palais de Danse *TS*
50:19 roaring,] ~ *TS*
50:25 board school] board-school *TS*
50:26 Sunday school] Sunday-school *TS*
50:26 and] ~, *A1*
51:6 thin] then *TS*
51:10 fathers *TS*] fathers' *MS*
51:15 dumb,] ~: *TS*
51:20 grandmothers *TS*] grandmother's *MS*
51:30 pub.] ~ *TS*
52:4 m] *m TS*
52:18 eye,] ~; *TS*
52:20 grandmothers *TS*] grandmothers' *MS*
52:28 are . . . less] ~, . . . ~, *TS*
52:34 this] the *TS*
53:2 t':] t', *TS*
53:7 —This] ~ *TS*
53:18 Oh] ~, *TS*
53:20 many] any *A1*
53:25 family!] ~? *TS*
53:25 up,] ~ *TS*
54:14 have still] still have *TS*
54:22 But] And *TS*
54:28 true —] ~. — *TS* ~, *A1*
54:30 dragon,] ~ *TS*
54:33 impossible] Impossible *TS*
54:37 Pally",] ~" *TS*
55:2 her] *Om. TS*
55:15 It is] It's *TS*
55:21 half time] half-time *TS*
55:23 screens;] ~, *TS*
56:9 favorite] favourite *TS*
56:12 built-up] built up *TS*
56:28 no-one] no one *TS*
56:39 petrified," *MS*, *A1*] ~". *TS*
57:16 slantingly-upright] slantingly upright *A1*
57:24 spar,] ~ *A1*
57:36 — I] ~ *TS*
58:6 wonder-struck] wonderstruck *TS*
58:15 consciousness] ~, *TS*
59:29 stark naked . . . stark naked] stark-naked . . . stark-naked *A1*

59:38 woollen *TS*] wolen *MS*

60:2 not-rusted] not rusted *A1*

60:2 waist-coat] waistcoat *A1*

60:9 said] one said *A1*

60:23 harsh,] ~ *TS*

60:30 park land] park-land *TS*

60:33 tools,] ~ *TS*

60:38 walked] ~, *TS*

61:14 turned,] ~ *TS*

61:15 oxen,] ~ *TS*

62:15 yellow] golden *TS*

62:20 woollen *TS*] woolen *MS*

62:27 cord-fringe] cord fringe *A1*

62:31 no-one] no one *TS*

63:3 rampart-walls] rampart walls *TS*

63:24 Why] ~, *TS*

63:28 porticoes *TS*] porticos *MS*

63:37 woollen *TS*] woolen *MS*

64:30 crocus blue] crocus-blue *TS*

64:31 lilac] *Om. TS*

65:13 Some-one] Some one *TS*

65:33 lust] lusty

65:34 big,] ~ *TS*

65:39 liquid-butter] liquid butter *TS*

66:19 room.] ~? *A1*

66:26 still. The] ~. *P* The *TS*

66:32 softly lighted] softly-lighted *TS*

66:32 porticoes *TS*] porticos *MS*

66:36 softly-lighted] softly lighted *A1*

66:36 porticoes *TS*] porticos *MS*

66:39 congregational] Congregational *TS*

67:21 he] He *TS*

68:15 eat —] ~. *TS*

The "Jeune Fille" Wants to Know

The sequence is *E1*, *Per1*, *Per2*.

71:1 **The "Jeune Fille" Wants to Know** *Ed.*] THE "JEUNE FILLE" WANTS TO KNOW *E1* When She Asks "Why?"/ A Study of the "Jeune Fille" of To-day / by D. H. LAWRENCE, the novelist. *Per1* THE BOGEY BETWEEN THE / GENERATIONS / BY D. H. LAWRENCE *Per2*

71:9 "My] ~ *Per2*

71:10 suppressed!"] ~! *Per2*

71:10 "How] ~ *Per2*

71:11 her?"] ~? *Per2*

71:13 instant,] ~ *Per2*

71:19 crudely,] ~ *Per1* ~: *Per2*

71:20 see,] ~ *Per2*

71:21 him" — or] ~." Or *Per2*

71:21 out,] ~ *Per1* ~: *Per2*

71:26 two;] ~: *Per2*

71:27 sternly,] ~: *Per2*

71:27 daddy] Daddy *Per1*

71:31 prisms,] ~; *Per2*

72:1 daddy] Daddy *Per1*

72:2 ask.] ~. — *Per2*

72:3 its] his *Per2*

72:6 answer?] ~? — *Per2*

72:7 says;] ~. *Per2*

72:7 men] Men *Per2*

72:12 it] ~, *Per1*

72:13 Whys?] "~?" *Per2*

72:14 — and] ~ *Per2*

72:15 inquiring] enquiring *Per2*

72:15 says] ~: *Per2*

72:16 Now,] ~ *Per2*

72:17 daddy] Daddy *Per1*

72:22 timorously,] ~ *Per1* ~: *Per2*

72:22 "Why . . . woman?"] ~ . . . ~? *Per2*

72:23 whisper "He isn't!"] ~: ~ ~! *Per2*

72:24 up. "Why] ~: Why *Per2*

72:25 right?"] ~? *Per2*

72:27 anæmic;] ~ — *Per2*

72:27 anæmic] ~, *Per1*

72:27 ago;] ~ — *Per2*

72:30 Why?] "~?" *Per2*

72:30 Wherefore? —] ~? *Per1* "~ ?" — *Per2*

72:32 daddy] Daddy *Per1*
72:32 upon] about *Per2*
72:33 mother] Mother *Per2*
72:36 Why?] "~?" *Per2*
72:36 sweet-and-twenty] sweet and twenty *Per2*
72:37 celluloid!] ~ *Per2*
72:37 important!] ~: *Per2*
72:37 Really] really *Per2*
72:37 *why* . . . ?] ~ — ? *Per2*
72:38 bogey!] Bogey! *Per1*
72:38 elderly] ~, *Per1*
73:3 be,] ~ *Per2*
73:6 and] ~: *Per2*
73:6 daddy] Daddy *Per1*
73:7 bogey] Bogey *Per1*
73:10 "Ah] — ~ *Per2*
73:11 you!"] ~! *Per2*
73:11 As] — ~ *Per2*
73:21 old,] ~ *Per2*
73:22 ask] ~: *Per2*
73:22 bogey] Bogey *Per1*
73:23 And] — ~ *Per2*
73:23 reply,] ~: *Per1*
73:24 . . . !] —! *Per2*
73:26 bogey] Bogey *Per1*
73:28 it,] ~; *Per1*
73:29 crimes,] ~; *Per1*
73:29 bogey] Bogey *Per2*
73:31 "Of] — ~ *Per2*
73:31 course,] ~ *Per1*
73:32 mother . . . daddy] Mother . . . Daddy *Per1*
73:33 infants,"] ~, *Per2*
73:33 reiterates,] ~ *Per1* ~: *Per2*
73:37 bogey] Bogey *Per1*
73:38 importance] ~, *Per1*
74:6 The danger [74:1] . . . rid of.] *Om. Per1*

Laura Philippine

The chronological sequence is *TS*, *Per*, *E1*.

77:1 **Laura Philippine** *Ed.*] Laura - Philippine. *TS* By D. H. Lawrence / LAURA PHILIPPINE / A Complete Story *Per* LAURA PHILIPPINE *E1*
77:3 twins,] ~ *Per*
77:3 Philippine,] ~ *Per*
77:5 Joseph,] ~ *Per*
77:8 dancing] ~, *E1*
77:8 car] ~, *Per*
77:15 leg,] ~ *Per*
77:17 Hello] ~, *Per*
77:30 Well] ~, *Per*
78:8 had] has *Per*
78:8 parlour-maid] parlourmaid *E1*
78:12 parlour-maid] parlourmaid *E1*
78:13 galantine *Per*] galatine *TS*
78:14 galantine *Per*] galatine *TS*
78:21 afternoon,] ~ *Per*
78:35 dark-blue] dark blue *E1*
78:36 — Oh] ~, *Per*
78:37 buffaloes! —] ~ ! *Per*
78:38 cigarette-ash] cigarette ash *E1*
78:39 Philippine! — *TS*, *E1*] ~ ! *Per*
78:40 'em! — *TS*, *E1*] ~ ! *Per*
78:40 car,] ~ *Per*
79:1 shore. —] ~. *Per*
79:2 least. —] ~. *Per*
79:2 Why] ~, *E1*
79:3 it! — *TS*, *E1*] ~! *Per*
79:5 itself. —] ~. *Per*
79:6 Philippine? — *TS*, *E1*] ~? *Per*
79:6 anywhere! — *TS*, *E1*] ~! *Per*
79:6 Caesars? — *TS*, *E1*] ~? *Per*
79:7 right! —*TS*, *E1*] ~! *Per*
79:11 Hotel *TS*, *E1*] Hôtel *Per*
79:15 along! —] ~! *Per*
79:16 dark-blue] dark blue *E1*
79:18 wiggling] wriggling *Per*
79:20 wiggling] wriggling *Per*
79:20 there, *TS*, *E1*] ~; *Per*
79:22 lunch time] lunch-time, *Per*

79:25 four! —] ~. *Per* ~! *E1*
79:25 Yes!—] ~! *Per*
79:28 Show] "~ *E1*
79:29 fool.] ~." *E1*
79:32 wistful — you] ~. You *Per*
79:34 replied.] ~ *Per*
79:34 It!] it! *Per*
79:34 said she] she said *Per*
79:36 jazz.] ~ *Per*
79:36 Exactly!] ~. *Per*
79:40 I] ~, *Per*
79:40 ninety?] ~? — *Per*
80:3 mother *TS*, *E1*] Mother *Per*
80:3 show] *Show Per*

That Women Know Best

The chronological sequence is *MS*, *Per*, *A1*. Variants between *MS* and *A1* are few and trivial; with one exception the collation below is confined to *MS* and *Per*.

83:1 **That Women Know Best** *Ed.*] That Women know best. / By D. H. Lawrence *MS* WOMEN ALWAYS KNOW BEST. / *By* / *D. H. Lawrence. Per* D. H. LAWRENCE / THAT WOMEN KNOW BEST *A1*
83:2 boy,] ~ *Per*
83:3 footstep! — To] ~!" *P* To *Per*
83:4 *still*] still *Per*
83:4 legitimate] ~, *Per*
83:8 But] ~, *Per*
83:8 My] my *Per*
83:9 peculiar] ~, *Per*
83:9 laughs] ~, *Per*
83:12 — Away] ~ *Per*
83:13 shoes! or] ~, ~, *Per*
83:18 age,] ~ *Per*
83:18 *that*] that *Per*
83:19 more; and] ~. And *Per*
83:19 because] Because *Per*
83:21 women] woman *Per*
83:21 stick. From] ~. *P* From *Per*
83:22 parents:] ~. *Per*
83:24 — For] ~ *Per*
83:25 School] school, *Per*
83:26 — What] ~ *Per*
83:29 Which perhaps] ~, ~, *Per*
83:30 — If,] ~ *Per*
84:2 — That] ~ *Per*
84:4 round] around *Per*
84:6 Latin] ~, *Per*
84:8 But] ~, *Per*
84:8 mother. — My] ~. *P* "My *Per*
84:10 it.—But] ~." *P* "But, *Per*
84:10 she?—I] ~?" *P* "I *Per*
84:11 enquire] inquire *Per*
84:11 —And] ~ *Per*
84:11 fact] ~, *Per*
84:12 a] A *Per*
84:13 — Is] "~ *Per*
84:13 please?—No] ~?" *P* "No *Per*
84:14 out.—Er] ~" *P* "Er *Per*
84:14 meant the . . . William] meant Mr. William *Per*
84:15 William.—My] ~." *P* "My *Per*
84:15 home. —The] ~ ." *P* The *Per*
84:17 huzzy! —To] ~!" ~ *Per*
84:17 *why*] why *Per*
84:18 nice.—That's] ~." *P* "That's *Per*
84:22 fact] ~, *Per*
84:22 woman. Clergymen] ~. *P* Clergymen *Per*
84:23 be . . . administers] minister and administer *Per*
84:24 No,] ~; *Per*
84:26 brother] ~, *Per*
84:28 course] ~, *Per*
84:29 materially,] ~ *Per*
84:30 *vitally*] vitally *Per*
84:36 of] *Om. Per*
84:37 Alas,] ~! *Per*
84:37 out:] ~ — *Per*
84:37 don't] didn't *Per*
85:1 admit,] ~ *Per*

85:5 hams] chairs *Per*
85:7 sad,] ~ *Per*
85:7 all,] ~ *Per*
85:7 good] ~, *Per*
85:8 herself!] ~. *Per*
85:8 *absolute*] absolute *Per*
85:11 terrible. Perhaps] ~. *P* Perhaps *Per*
85:13 wrong,] ~ *Per*
85:13 example.] ~! *Per*

All There

The chronological sequence is *MS*, *TS*, *A1*.

87:1 **All There** *Ed.*] All There / by D. H. Lawrence *MS* ALL THERE. *TS* ALL THERE *A1*
87:16 myself,] ~ *TS*
87:17 Why] ~, *TS*
87:20 astonishment *TS*] astonisment *MS*
87:21 bus *MS*, *A1*] 'bus *TS*
87:24 Times] *Times A1*
87:24 extra-cheerfully] extra cheerfully *A1*
88:10 which] what *TS*
88:11 Which?—] ~? *A1*
88:17 I.—] ~. *A1*
88:19 jazz—] ~, *TS*
88:20 Well] ~, *TS*
89:2 Oh] O *TS*
89:4 yourself:] ~, *TS*
89:9 Alas,] ~ *TS*

Thinking about Oneself

The chronological sequence is *MS*, *TS1*, *TS2*, *A1*.

91:1 **Thinking about Oneself** *Ed.*] Thinking about Oneself /D. H. Lawrence *MS* THINKING ABOUT ONESELF. *TS1* THINKING ABOUT ONESELF *A1*
91:9 muse] ~, *A1*
91:14 cinema] cinemas *A1*
91:16 this] the *TS2*
91:18 Well] ~, *TS1*
91:21 girls *MS*, *TS2*] girl *TS1*
91:21 jazz *MS*, *TS2*] ~. *TS1*
91:23 cinema *MS*, *TS2*] cinemas *TS1*
91:25 cotton-wool] cotton wool *A1*
91:29 millstone] mill-stone *A1*
92:3 of? —] ~? *TS1*
92:4 Which] ~, *TS2*
92:4 course] ~, *TS2*
92:6 good solid *MS*, *TS2*] ~, ~, *TS1*
92:6 do *MS*, *TS2*] be *TS1*
92:7 No] ~, *TS1*
92:9 ourselves,] ~ *TS2*
92:10 Jove] jove *A1*
92:10 — And] ~ *TS1*
92:10 bolt. —] ~. *TS2*
92:10 Oh] ~, *TS1*
92:13 underground *MS*, *TS2*] Underground *TS1*
92:17 — As] ~ *TS1*
92:17 with a tiger] *Om. TS2*
92:18 alter ego *MS*, *TS2*] *alter ego TS1*, *A1*
92:18 me *MS*, *TS2*] *me TS1*
92:20 man *MS*, *TS2*] ~, *TS1*
92:27 wofully:] ~. *TS2* woefully. *A1*
92:33 it." *MS*, *A1*] ~. *TS2*
92:34 tigers *MS*, *TS2*] ~, *TS1*
93:1 life-time *MS*, *A1*] lifetime *TS2*

Insouciance

The chronological sequence is *MS*, *TS*, *Per*, *E1*. (The capitalisation of 'Fascism' in *Per* and *E1* has not been noted.)

95:1 **Insouciance** *Ed.*] Insouciance/ by D. H. Lawrence *MS* INSOUCIANCE. *TS* Over-Earnest Ladies. */By D. H. LAWRENCE. Per* INSOUCIANCE *E1*
95:3 wife,] ~ *TS*
95:5 another. When] ~. *P* When *Per*
95:6 wrapper] ~, *E1*
95:16 chaises longues] *chaises longues Per*
95:18 scythes] ~, *Per*
95:18 down-hill] downhill *Per*
95:19 near,] ~: *Per*
95:19 slush! slush!] *slush! slush! Per*
95:20 little] two little *TS*
95:20 become *MS*, *Per*] became *TS*
95:21 in *TS*] *Om. MS*
95:22 steamer-rugs] steamer rugs *Per*
95:22 chaises longues] *chaises longues Per*
95:24 disappears:] ~; *E1*
95:27 —A] ~*TS*
95:27 cooler!] ~*Per*
95:27 aimiability] amiability *TS*
95:28 mowing:] ~; *E1*
95:29 scythes! — By] ~! *P* By *Per*
95:29 now,] ~ *Per*
95:29 tête-à-tête] *tête-à-tête E1*
95:31 and the] and to *Per*
95:32 little white *MS*, *E1*] little-white *Per*
95:34 cherry-trees] cherry trees *E1*
96:6 effort. I] ~. *P* I *Per*
96:8 young *MS*, *E1*] ~, *Per*
96:9 stubby] shabby *TS*
96:13 cherry-trees] cherry trees *E1*
96:14 *there*] there *TS*
96:26 at *TS*] a *MS*
96:29 cherry-trees] cherry trees *E1*
96:36 her,] ~ *TS*
96:37 invisible] ~, *Per*
96:37 hypothetical *MS*, *Per*] hypoethetical *TS*
96:38 the] one *TS*
96:39 hear] ~, *E1*
97:1 Cher . . . noirs?] "*Cher . . . noirs? Per*
97:2 Why oh why] ~,~ ~, *TS* ~,~,~ *Per*
97:2 trousers?] ~?" *Per*
97:3 lady!— *MS*, *E1*] ~! *Per*
97:4 International] international *Per*
97:4 tiresome,] ~ *E1*
97:7 League] Leagues *TS*
97:7 right, *MS*] ~ *E1*
97:10 wrong] ~,*Per*
97:12 x] *x Per*
97:16 cherry-trees] cherry trees *E1*
97:18 word,] ~ *Per*
97:20 space —] ~ *TS*
97:23 ladies,] ~; *Per*
97:24 lime-blossom] lime blossom *E1*
97:27 young *MS*, *Per*] you young *TS*
97:27 bright-blue] bright blue *E1*
97:28 his scythe] the scythe *TS*
97:29 scythe-stroke] scythe strokes *TS* scythe-strokes *Per*

Master in his Own House

The chronological sequence is *MS*, *TS*, *Per1*, *Per2*, *E1*. (The italicisation of *The Rosebud* in *Per2* has not been noted.)

99:1 **Master in his Own House** Ed.] Men Must Rule /by D. H. Lawrence *MS* <MEN MUST RULE.> ⌐Master in his Own House¬ *TS* Master in His Own House! / by D. H. LAWRENCE, /the novelist. *Per 1* Deserted Battlefields / *A Polemic Against Mass Thinking and Men's Modern Indifference to the Ancient Rewards* / D. H. LAWRENCE *Per 2* MASTER IN HIS OWN HOUSE *E1*
99:2 Take] ~, *E1*
99:3 A *MS*, *Per2*] a *Per 1*
99:3 maxim, *MS*, *Per2*] ~; *Per 1*, *E1*
99:5 So *MS*, *Per2*] ~, *Per 1*
99:6 which] as *Per1*
99:8 These *MS*, *Per2*] these *Per 1*
99:8 women, *MS*, *Per2*] ~; *Per 1*
99:12 en bloc] *en bloc TS*
99:13 wool. In *MS*, *E1*] ~. *P* In *Per2*
99:14 fact] ~, *TS*
99:14 ideas, *MS*, *Per2*] ~ *Per 1*
99:16 cloud, *MS*, *Per2*] ~ *Per1*
99:16 mass-ideas, *MS*, *Per2*] ~ *Per1*
99:17 further. A *MS*, *Per2*] ~. *P* A *Per 1*
99:20 a *MS*, *E1*] the *Per 2*
99:21 Yes] ~, *TS*
99:21 husband: — *MS*, *Per2*] ~ — *Per 1* ~; *E1*
99:23 man, *MS*, *Per2*] ~ *Per1*
99:23 woman, *MS*, *Per2*] ~ *Per1*
99:25 Now *MS*, *E1*] NOW *Per 2*
99:27 say: *MS*, *Per1*] ~, *TS*
99:28 The Doves' Nest, *MS*, *E1*] *The Doves' Nest*, *Per 2*
99:29 Julia. — *MS*, *E1*] ~. *Per 1*
99:29 personal, *MS*, *E1*] ~ *Per 2*
99:30 it. You *MS*, *E1*] ~. *P* You *Per2*
100:2 make *MS*, *E1*] end by making *Per2*
100:4 eye —] ~, *TS*
100:7 coffee, *MS*, *Per2*] ~. *Per1*
100:11 A Man . . . house. *MS*, *E1*] *Om. Per2*
100:15 day, *MS*, *Per2*] ~ *Per1*
100:16 him. *MS*, *Per2*] ~ *Per1*
100:16 — That *MS*, *E1*] — that *Per1* That *Per2*
100:17 ordinary *MS*, *E1*] ~ and representative *Per2*
100:21 a man . . . house *MS*, *E1*] mastery in a house *Per2*
100:22 helplessly *MS*, *E1*] hopelessly *Per2*
100:23 idea, *MS*, *Per2*] ~ *Per1*
100:25 granted, *MS*, *E1*] ~ *Per1*
100:25 show, *MS*, *Per2*] ~ *Per1*
100:28 Wherever *MS*, *E1*] Whenever *Per2*
100:28 women. Men *MS*, *E1*] ~. *P* Men *Per2*
100:32 vacuum] vacuums *TS*
100:33 Commons filled *MS*, *E1*] Commons or a Congress filled *Per2*
100:34 indifferent,] ~; *TS*
100:35 Members *MS*, *E1*] Congressmen or Members *Per2*
100:38 Parliament — *MS*, *E1*] government — *Per2*
100:38 and *MS*, *E1*] ~, *Per1*
100:39 Parliament *MS*, *E1*] it *Per2*
100:40 own: and *MS*, *E1*] ~: ~, *Per1*
101:3 Indifference . . . [101:6] nearly *MS*, *Per2*] The indifference, inability to care, is nearly *Per1*
101:8 They . . . insouciance. *MS*, *Per2*] *Om. Per1*
101:8 women] woman *TS*
101:9 time they *MS*, *E1*] time, by a kind of infantile perversity, they *Per2*
101:9 women's *MS*, *E1*] woman's *Per2*
101:11 bossiness, *MS*, *E1*] ~ *Per1*
101:13 is always *MS*, *E1*] is of its nature that it be always *Per2*
101:17 politics. If *MS*, *E1*] ~. *P* If *Per 2*
101:20 homes, *MS*, *E1*] ~; *Per2*
101:25 battle. *MS*, *Per2*] ~. *P Per1*
101:25 They . . . drop. *MS*, *Per2*] *Om. Per1*

101:26 men,] ~ *TS*
101:26 let *MS*, *E1*] have let *Per2*
101:28 re-iterating] reiterating *TS*

Matriarchy

The chronological sequence is *MS*, *TS1*, *TS2*, *Per*, *E1*.

103:1 **Matriarchy** *Ed.*] <Rule of Women> ⌐Matriarchy¬ / D. H. Lawrence *MS* MATRIARCHY. *TS1* —And If Women *Were* Supreme . . . *Per* MATRIARCHY *E1*
103:2 a little] *Om. TS2*
103:6 war-path] warpath *E1*
103:9 silky *MS*, *E1*] silk *Per*
103:13 Elsie. But] ~, but *E1*
103:16 again! — *MS*, *E1*] ~! *TS2*
103:21 petticoat-rule *MS*] petticoat rule *TS1*
103:22 silky *MS*, *E1*] *Om. Per*
103:31 energy. He *MS*, *E1*] ~. *P* He *Per*
103:32 regimen *MS*, *TS2*] regiment *TS1*, *E1*
103:33 man *MS*, *E1*] men *TS2*
104:1 regimen *MS*, *TS2*] regiment *TS1*, *E1*
104:5 accord, *MS*, *E1*] ~ — *Per*
104:11 rule, the *MS*, *Per*] ~. The *TS1*, *E1*
104:15 husband swears *MS*, *E1*] husbands swear *Per*
104:15 spouse. — *MS*, *E1*] ~. *Per*
104:16 is: *MS*, *E1*] ~, *Per*
104:20 tide. Woman *MS*, *E1*] ~; it *Per*
104:24 actuality? — *MS*, *E1*] ~? *TS2*
104:25 took *MS*, *E1*] bore *TS2*
104:26 to the *MS*, *E1*] to their *TS2*
104:30 cocky, *MS*, *E1*] ~ *Per*
104:30 matriarchal *MS*, *E1*] *Om. TS2*
104:33 Abraham, *MS*, *TS2*] ~ *TS1*, *Per*
104:34 drudging *MS*, *TS2*] drudgery *TS1*, *E1*
105:1 weary *MS*, *E1*] every *TS2*
105:2 pueblo] Pueblo *TS2*
105:4 corn supply *MS*, *E1*] corn-supply *Per*
105:15 Daddy] daddy *E1*
105:18 house *MS*, *E1*] ~, *Per*
105:18 practices *TS1*] practises *MS*
105:31 thirteen, *MS*, *E1*] ~ *TS2*
105:34 in *MS*, *TS2*] on *TS1*, *E1*
105:35 house *MS*, *E1*] place *Per*
105:36 house. But] ~, but *E1*
106:1 man,] ~ *TS2*
106:1 in the *MS*, *E1*] at *TS2*
106:2 men, *MS*, *E1*] ~ *Per*
106:6 another *MS*, *TS2*] ~, *TS1*, *E1*
106:13 thwarted, *MS*, *E1*] ~: *Per*
106:17 it's . . . father. *MS*, *E1*] *Om. Per*
106:24 it, *MS*, *E1*] ~ *Per*
106:27 name, *MS*, *E1*] ~ *Per*

Ownership

The chronological sequence is *MS*, *TS1*, *TS2*, *E1*.

108:1 **Ownership** *Ed.*] <Property.> ⌐Ownership¬/ by D. H. Lawrence. *MS* OWNERSHIP. *TS1* OWNERSHIP *E1*
108:9 consider, *MS*, *E1*] ~ *TS2*
108:18 all, *MS*, *E1*] ~ *TS2*
108:22 house] houses *E1*
108:24 leavings:] ~; *TS1*
108:25 thrill:] ~; *TS1*
109:3 spend:] ~; *E1*
109:20 Why— *MS*, *TS2*] ~ . . . *TS1*, *E1*
109:29 the Times *MS*, *TS2*] the *Times TS1 The Times E1*

110:7 it *MS*, *TS2*] ~, *TS1*
110:18 women? to *MS*, *TS2*] ~? To *TS1*, *E1*
110:23 Which] ~, *TS1*
110:23 all] ~, *TS1*

Autobiography

The chronological sequence is *MS*, *TS*, *A1*. *A1* is faithful to *MS*; all variants listed are in *TS*. (The titles of DHL's publications are capitalised and placed in double quotation marks in *TS*; the practice is not noted below.)

112:2 11] 11th *TS*
112:4 or] and *TS*
112:9 miners'] miner's *TS*
112:30 she] *Om. TS*
112:34 step. —] ~. *TS*
113:4 miners] mines *TS*
113:5 Miriam's *TS*] Miriams *MS*
113:11 college] College *TS*
113:15 to,] ~ *TS*
113:16 affectation. —] ~. *TS*
113:20 the] *Om. TS*
113:27 hand —] ~. *TS*
113:35 supporter,] ~ *TS*
113:37 Friedrich] Freidrich *TS*
114:19 he] *Om. TS*
114:23 *Chatterley's*] CHATTERLING'S *TS*

Women Are So Cocksure

The chronological sequence is *MS*, *TS*, *A1*.

116:1 **Women Are So Cocksure** *Ed.*] Women Are So Cocksure. / D. H. Lawrence. *MS* WOMEN ARE SO COCKSURE. *TS* WOMEN ARE SO COCKSURE *A1*
116:5 woe-betide] woe betide *A1*
116:6 It] I *A1*
116:28 But] ~, *A1*
116:32 bogey] bogy *A1*
116:33 evil. —] ~. *A1*
117:2 harsher] harder *A1*
117:27 dangerous,] ~ *A1*
117:31 then —] ~ *A1*
117:32 driving-force] driving force *A1*

Why I don't Like Living in London

The chronological sequence is *MS*, *TS*, *Per*, *E1*.

120:1 **Why I don't Like Living in London** *Ed.*] Why I don't Like Living in London. / D. H. Lawrence *MS* <WHY I DON'T LIKE LIVING IN LONDON> Dull London *TS* DULL LONDON! / Everyone Is So Nice, and / Everything Is So Easy. / *By* D. H. LAWRENCE, / *the well-known novelist. Per* DULL LONDON *E1*
120:3 vaguely] ~, *TS*
120:5 sank. You *MS*, *E1*] ~. *P* You *Per*
120:5 policemen] policeman *E1*
120:10 nice,] ~ *E1*
120:17 overwhelming. Of *MS*, *E1*] ~. *P* Of *Per*
120:20 uneasy] uncanny *TS*
120:22 dull . . . dulled] ~! . . . ~! *E1*
120:29 arousing,] ~; *TS*
120:29 death,] ~; *TS*

120:30 Good-byes! *MS*, *E1*] good-byes! *Per*
120:30 Goodbye! Goodbye! . . . Goodbye! *MS*, *E1*] Good-bye! Good-bye! . . . Good-bye! *TS* Good-bye! Good-bye! . . . good-bye *Per*
121:7 all. But *MS*, *E1*] ~. *P* But *Per*
121:9 anaesthetic, *MS*, *E1*] ~ *Per*
121:18 ago,] ~ *Per*
121:25 heavy.] ~! *E1*
121:25 somewhere, *MS*, *E1*] ~ *Per*
121:26 and *TS*} and and *MS*
121:27 *going*. There *MS*, *E1*] ~. *P* There *Per*
121:28 buses' *MS*, *Per*] 'buses' *TS*, *E1*
121:28 bus *MS*, *Per*] 'bus *TS*, *E1*
121:32 monotony *TS*] monoty *MS*
121:36 friends, *MS*, *E1*] ~ *Per*
121:38 abroad] ~, *TS*
121:40 somebody, *MS*, *E1*] ~ *Per*
122:4 me, *MS*, *E1*] ~ *Per*
122:7 Russians *TS*] Russian's *MS*
122:8 inaction,] ~ *Per*

Cocksure Women and Hen-sure Men

The chronological sequence is *MS*, *TS*, *Per*, *E1*.

125:1 **Cocksure Women and Hen-sure Men** *Ed.*] Cocksure Women and Hen-sure Men / D. H. Lawrence *MS* COCKSURE WOMEN AND HEN-SURE MEN. *TS* Cocksure WOMEN /and Hensure MEN /*Forum Table Talk /by* D. H. LAWRENCE *Per* COCKSURE WOMEN AND HENSURE MEN *E1*
125:2 is *MS*, *E1*] are *Per*
125:2 demure, *MS*] ~ *Per*
125:4 Oh yes] ~, ~, *TS* , *E1* "~, ~, *Per*
125:4 sir! *MS*, *E1*] ~!" *Per*
125:6 mistresses *MS*, *E1*] ~, *Per*
125:7 not.] ~. And they don't pretend to be. *E1*
125:8 demure, *MS*, *E1*] ~; *Per*
125:9 members] Members *TS*
125:10 Oh yes] ~,~ *TS* "~, ~, *Per* ~, ~, *E1*
125:10 sir! *MS*, *E1*] ~!" *Per*
125:10 Though *MS*, *E1*] though *Per*
125:11 kidney. — *MS*, *E1*] ~. *Per*
125:11 telephone girl *MS*, *E1*] telephone-girl *TS*
125:12 or] Or *Per*
125:13 becoming, *MS*, *E1*] ~; *Per*
125:15 has got to *MS*, *E1*] must *Per*
125:15 pretty] ~, *TS*
125:18 cocksure, *MS*, *E1*] ~ *Per*
125:19 nor *MS*, *E1*] or *Per*
125:21 sure, *MS*, *E1*] ~ — *Per*
125:22 her . . . her] the . . . the *TS*
125:30 hen-house *MS*, *E1*] hen house *Per*
125:30 *Ah-ha!* [in italics] . . . *said*! — And] *Ah ha!* [in italics] . . . *said*! — and *TS* "Aha! Daylight . . . said!" — and *Per* *Ah ha! daylight, of course*, [in italics] . . . *said*! — and *E1*
125:31 chicken-ladder] chicken ladder *Per*
125:32 towards *MS*, *E1*] toward *Per*
125:34 *Ha-ha! here we are! — MS*, *E1*] "Ha-ha! Here we are!" *Per*
126:1 towards *MS*, *E1*] toward *Per*
126:4 doorway, *MS*, *E1*] ~ *Per*
126:8 tit-bit,] titbit *Per* tit-bit *E1*
126:9 surety, *MS*, *E1*] ~ *Per*
126:9 tit-bit *MS*, *E1*] titbit *Per*
126:10 hen-sure] hensure *Per*
126:15 confidence, *MS*, *E1*] ~ *Per*
126:16 hen-sure] hensure *Per*
126:19 hen-sure . . . hen-sure] hensure . . . hensure *Per*

126:19 cock-sure] cocksure *Per*
126:20 chicken-hawk *MS*, *E1*] chicken hawk *Per*
126:22 verandah *MS*, *E1*] veranda *Per*
126:23 fear, *MS*, *E1*] ~; *Per*
126:23 Alas, . . . bold!] "Alas, . . . bold!" *Per* Alas, . . . bold! — *E1*
126:24 huddle] ~, *E1*
126:25 hen-surety] hensurety *Per*
126:27 hen-bird] hen bird *E1*
126:27 more-or-less] more or less *TS*
126:28 yet,] ~ *E1*
126:29 hen-sure] hensure *Per*
126:29 Cocksure she is] ~, ~ ~ *TS*, *E1* She is *Per*
126:29 cocksure, *MS*, *E1*] ~ *Per*
126:29 Hensure, *MS*, *Per*] Hen-sure *TS*
126:29 trembles, *MS*, *E1*] ~ *Per*
126:35 hen-like] henlike *Per*
126:40 afterward *MS*, *Per*] afterwards *TS*, *E1*
127:1 dares] dare *E1*
127:1 defiance:] ~, *TS*
127:2 danger *MS*, *E1*] ~, *Per*
127:3 air:]~ — *Per* ~; *E1*
127:3 thereof. *P* But *MS*, *E1*] ~. But *Per*
127:5 *do*! *MS*, *E1*] *do*, *Per*
127:5 then it *MS*, *E1*] it *Per*
127:7 and *MS*, *E1*] And *Per*
127:12 ink-bottle *MS*, *E1*] ink bottle *Per*
127:12 object, *MS*, *E1*] ~ *Per*
127:16 assertion, *MS*, *E1*] ~ *Per*
127:17 Frightened *MS*, *E1*] Afraid *Per*
127:19 business, she] ~. She *Per* ~: she *E1*
127:19 marvellous *MS*, *E1*] marvelous *Per*
127:22 laid, *MS*, *E1*] ~ — *Per*
127:23 type-writing] typewriting *TS*
127:23 business-efficiency,] business efficiency, *TS* business efficiency — *Per*
127:26 hen-sureness] hensureness *Per*
127:27 her,] ~; *Per* ~: *E1*
127:27 has] had *E1*

Hymns in a Man's Life

The chonological sequence is *MS*, *Per*, *E1*. (Not recorded is the use of capitals or lower-case for 'Christian' names or denominational titles.)

130:1 **Hymns in a Man's Life** *Ed.*] Hymns in a Man's Life / D. H. Lawrence *MS* Hymns in a Man's Life */ By / D. H. Lawrence. Per* HYMNS IN A MAN'S LIFE *E1*
130:2 in and] ~,~ *Per*
130:4 forget] forgot *Per*
130:6 other. It] ~. *P* It *Per*
130:8 Keats' *MS*, *E1*] Keats's *Per*
130:9 lyrics] ~, *Per*
130:10 "Über . . . Ruh," *MS*, *E1*] "*Uber* [in italics] . . . *Ruh*," *Per*
130:10 Verlaine] Verlaine's *Per*
130:10 "Ayant . . . chancelle" *MS*, *E1*] "*Ayant* [in italics] . . . *chancelle*" *Per*
130:12 poems,] ~ *E1*
130:22 It draws] *To draw Per* To draw *E1*
130:23 Galilee. —] *Galilee*. *Per* Galilee. *E1*
130:24 sweet Galilee] *sweet Galilee*, *Per* sweet Galilee, *E1*
130:26 sweet Galilee] *sweet Galilee*, *Per* sweet Galilee, *E1*
130:28 me,] ~ *Per*
130:29 Palestine:] ~. *Per*
130:30 lovely] ~, *Per*
131:6 automatically,] ~ *Per*

131:8 — And] ~, *Per*
131:12 *wonder*:] ~; *Per*
131:13 increases,] ~ *Per*
131:14 again: *MS*, *E1*] ~; *Per*
131:16 — But] ~ *Per*
131:19 contempt,] ~: *Per*
131:20 says:] ~, *Per*
131:20 orb, *Per*] ~. *MS*
131:29 man,] ~ *Per*
131:35 life,] ~ *Per*
131:38 willy nilly] willy-nilly *Per*
131:39 straw,] ~; *Per*
131:39 grass. They] ~. *P* They *Per*
131:40 also,] ~ *Per*
132:21 dogma. It] ~. *P* It *Per*
132:21 me,] ~; *Per*
132:22 forbears] forebears *Per*
132:23 virgin] Virgin *Per*
132:26 about,] ~; *Per*
132:36 dear *MS*, *E1*] *dear*, *Per*
132:37 thou] *Thou Per* Thou *E1*
132:37 near —" / That] ~ — " *P* That *Per*
132:38 Board School] board school *Per*
132:39 dogma,] ~ *Per*
132:39 words] ~, *Per*
133:1 wonder,] ~ *Per*
133:2 was: / "Fair *Per*] ~: "~ *MS*
133:15 "saved." And] "~," and *Per*
133:17 oldest *MS*, *E1*] oddest *Per*
133:20 Methodists,] ~ *Per*
133:21 still:] ~; *E1*
133:22 colourwashed] colour-washed *Per*
133:23 Organ-loft:] organ-loft, *E1*
133:23 Holiness] holiness *Per*
133:25 hymn] ~, *Per*
133:25 too.] ~: *Per*
133:26 Worship] *worship Per* worship *E1*
133:26 holiness. *MS*, *E1*] *holiness*, *Per*
133:27 him, his] *Him, His Per* Him, His *E1*
133:27 proclaim] *proclaim*; *Per* proclaim; *E1*
133:29 him . . . his] *Him . . . His Per* Him . . . His *E1*
133:29 name—] *name*. *Per* name. *E1*
133:31 it,—] ~ — *Per*
133:33 really:] ~, *E1*
133:37 Lead] ~, *Per*
133:37 with me] With Me *Per*
133:38 hymns. / "At *Per*] ~." ~ *MS*
134:1 set] ~, *Per*
134:2 sick oh] *sick, O Per* sick, O *E1*
134:2 thee] *Thee Per* Thee *E1*
134:3 Oh] *Oh*, *Per* Oh, *E1*
134:4 Oh] *Oh*, *Per* Oh, *E1*
134:5 And *MS*, *E1*] ~, *Per*
134:5 had:] ~ *E1*
134:6 School *MS*, *E1*] school *Per*
134:6 Remington] ~, *Per*
134:8 hymns.] ~: *Per*
134:9 battle-cry] *battle-cry*, *Per* battle-cry, *E1*
134:10 See] *See*, *Per* See, *E1*
134:10 nigh] *nigh*. *Per* nigh. *E1*
134:12 Lord —] *Lord*. *Per* Lord. *E1*
134:14 II *MS*, *E1*] ~. *Per*
134:15 School *MS*, *E1*] school *Per*
134:15 woman-teacher] woman teacher *Per*
134:19 — And] ~ *Per*
134:20 crucifixion] Crucifixion *Per*
134:22 ago,] ~ *Per*
134:22 Sunday-school] Sunday school *Per* Sunday School *E1*
134:23 life,] ~ *Per*
134:23 coming —] ~. *Per*
134:26 Jesus] *Jesus*, *Per* Jesus, *E1*
134:27 Lord —" / Here] *Lord*." *P* Here *Per* Lord." *P* Here *E1*

Red Trousers

The chronological sequence is *MS*, *TS*, *Per*, *E1*. The spelling of 'dullness' in *Per* is not recorded.

136:1 **Red Trousers** *Ed.*] Red Trousers / by D. H. Lawrence *MS* RED TROUSERS. *TS* Oh! for a New Crusade/ *By* / D. H. LAWRENCE, *the novelist*. *Per* RED TROUSERS *E1*
136:3 Dear Sir,]"~ ~,—*Per*
136:5 civilisation.—] ~:—*TS* ~ —" *Per* ~." *E1*
136:9 march. Which] ~, which *TS*
136:11 But] ~, *TS*
136:11 dull:] ~, *E1*
136:15 Or] ~, *TS*
136:18 suffragettes *MS*, *E1*] Suffragettes *Per*
136:19 policemen *MS*, *E1*] policeman *Per*
136:21 Marching to Zion,] "~ ~ ~" *Per*
136:21 Throw Out the Lifeline,] "~ ~ ~ ~" *Per* "~ ~ ~ ~," *E1*
136:22 crusade, of . . . spunk! *MS*, *E1*] crusade! *Per*
136:24 correspondent,] ~ *TS*
136:25 But the . . . [136:31] interesting. *MS*, *E1*] *Om. Per*
136:30 Anyhow] ~, *E1*
136:34 crusade, *MS*, *E1*] ~; *Per*
137:2 infidel, *MS*, *E1*] ~ *Per*
137:9 Poland, *MS*, *E1*] ~ *Per*
137:10 Now,] ~ *TS*
137:10 Cecho-Slovakia] Czecho-Slovakia *TS*
137:14 hairs-breadth *MS*, *E1*] hair's-breadth *Per*
137:15 hairs-breadth *MS*, *E1*] hair's-breadth *Per*
137:15 though *MS*, *E1*] ~, *Per*
137:16 course *MS*, *E1*] ~, *Per*
137:16 is *MS*, *E1*] are *Per*
137:24 love,] ~ *TS*
137:32 Yet] ~, *TS*
137:35 money, *MS*, *E1*] ~; *Per*
138:1 see-you-damned-first,] see you damned first: *TS* see you blowed first: *Per* see you damned first; *E1*
138:2 women:] ~, *E1*
138:20 velvet,] ~ *E1*
138:27 Captain *MS*, *E1*] General *Per*
138:27 arctic *MS*, *E1*] Arctic *Per*
138:29 gaily, *MS*, *E1*] ~ *Per*

Is England Still a Man's Country

The chronological sequence is *MS*, *TS*, *Per*, *E1*. There are two authorial interventions, at 142:8 and 142:9, in the two identical copies of *TS* (here treated as one); both have been accepted; they are recorded in Explanatory notes.

140:1 **Is England Still a Man's Country** *Ed.*] Is England Still a Man's Country/ by D. H. Lawrence *MS* IS ENGLAND STILL A MAN'S COUNTRY? /By D. H. Lawrence *TS* Is England Still / *A Man's* Country?/ BY D. H. LAWRENCE, *Famous Novelist, Poet and Critic*. *Per* IS ENGLAND STILL A MAN'S COUNTRY? *E1*
140:4 landscape, *MS*, *Per*] ~ *TS*, *E1*
140:5 pubs, . . . wages, *MS*, *Per*] ~ . . . ~ *TS*, *E1*
140:5 boots? Is *MS*, *E1*] ~? *P* Is *Per*
140:6 lord?—] ~? *TS*
140:7 not very] not *TS*
140:8 what . . . name *MS*, *E1*] ~, . . . ~, *Per*
140:11 *don't MS*, *E1*] don't *Per*
140:11 England! The *MS*, *E1*] ~! *P* The *Per*
140:13 Not half! *MS*, *Per*] *Not half! TS*, *E1*
140:15 country — my . . . And *MS*, *E1*] ~. *P* And *Per*

140:16 Old *MS*, *E1*] old *Per*
140:17 exist? — *MS*, *E1*] ~? *Per*
140:20 If . . . [140:23] voices. *MS*, *E1*] *If* [in italics] . . . *voices. Per*
140:23 voices. Women *MS*, *E1*] *voices. P* Women *Per*
140:23 up. And] ~; and *TS*
140:26 don't. They *MS*, *E1*] do not. *P* They *Per*
140:28 chiffon] artificial silk *TS*
140:29 cigarettes. What *MS*, *E1*] ~. *P* What *Per*
140:32 chiffon] silk *TS*
141:10 England.— *MS*, *E1*] ~. *Per*
141:10 *could*] could *TS*
141:11 comfortable?—And *MS*, *E1*] ~? *P* And *Per*
141:13 England . . . [141:16] and bullied. *MS*, *E1*] *England* [in italics] . . . *and bullied. Per*
141:17 boss him] boss *TS*
141:17 up] *Om. TS* up and *Per*
141:18 plant] place *TS*
141:22 He's got *MS*, *E1*] He has *Per*
141:24 it. He *MS*, *E1*] ~. *P* He *Per*
141:25 He's *MS*, *E1*] He has *Per*
141:26 it. Which] ~, which *TS* ~; which *E1*
141:27 He's got . . . [141:31] job. *MS*, *E1*] *He's got* [in italics] . . . *job. Per*
141:28 it's] *it is Per* it *E1*
141:30 don't *MS*, *E1*] *do not do so Per*
141:34 it. Very *MS*, *E1*] ~. *P* Very *Per*
141:35 job! — that] ~! — That *TS*
141:36 job! Men *MS*, *E1*] ~! *P* Men *Per*
141:39 ask,] ~: *TS*
142:1 plum-tree, he] plum tree he *Per* plum tree, he *E1*
142:3 it:] ~, *Per* ~; *E1*
142:6 plum-trees] plum trees *Per* plums *E1*
142:7 men:] ~, *Per*
142:11 is . . . thing. *MS*, *E1*] is supremely valuable. *Per*
142:13 men do. *MS*, *E1*] men. *Per*
142:14 It . . . [142:17] them. *MS*, *E1*] *It* [in italics] . . . *them. Per*
142:16 problem] ~, *TS*
142:17 them. The *MS*, *E1*] *them. P* The *Per*
142:18 Slavery! *MS*, *E1*] ~? *Per*
142:20 again. Now *MS*, *E1*] ~. *P* Now *Per*
142:23 sure as eggs] *Om. Per*

Sex Appeal

The chronological sequence is *MS*, *Per1*, *Per2*, *E1*. A second manuscript exists (*MS2* UT) which contains no more than an opening sentence: 'It is all very well asking what sex appeal is, when we know so exceedingly little about sex.' It is ignored in the collation. (The unhyphenated spelling of 'peahen' in *E1* is not recorded.)

144:1 **Sex Appeal** *Ed.*] Sex Appeal / by D. H. Lawrence *MS* SEX LOCKED OUT. / *By* D. H. LAWRENCE. *Per1* Sex Appeal / An Enlightening Essay Concerning a Phrase Which Everybody Knows and Nobody Understands / By D. H. LAWRENCE *Per2* SEX *VERSUS* LOVELINESS *E1*
144:4 it, *MS*, *Per2*] ~ *Per1*, *E1*
144:5 instinct:] ~; *E1*
144:9 formed. Again *MS*, *Per2*] ~. *P* Again *Per1*, *E1*
144:9 An appetite:] ~ ~; *E1*
144:12 satisfy his appetite *MS*, *E1*] yearn *Per2*
144:15 has. We *MS*, *Per2*] ~. *P* We *Per1*

144:17 all. As *MS*, *Per2*] ~. *P* As *Per1*, *E1*
144:18 believe . . . moment *MS*, *E1*] ~, . . . ~, *Per2*
144:20 green. If *MS*, *Per2*] ~. *P* If *Per1*, *E1*
144:21 flamboyancy, *MS*, *Per2*] ~ *Per1*
144:27 naïve *MS*, *Per2*] naive *Per1*, *E1*
144:28 highly-aesthetic] highly aesthetic *Per1*
144:31 over, *MS*, *Per2*] ~ *Per1*, *E1*
144:32 her] the *Per1*
144:32 young.—] ~. *Per1*
144:33 Well *MS*, *Per2*] ~, *Per1*, *E1*
144:33 her, or] ~ and *Per1*
145:1 naïve *MS*, *Per2*] naive *Per1*, *E1*
145:1 are.] ~! *Per1*
145:3 strangely enough, *MS*, *Per2*] *Om. Per1*, *E1*
145:4 beauty. Because *MS*, *Per2*] ~. *P* Because *Per1*, *E1*
145:5 it.—] ~. *Per1*
145:5 Well *MS*, *Per2*] ~, *Per*, *E1*
145:6 naïve *MS*, *Per2*] naive *Per*, *E1*
145:8 where then *MS*, *Per2*] ~, ~, *Per1*, *E1*
145:8 trick.] ~? *Per1*
145:13 propagation-appetite] propagation appetite *E1*
145:16 old *MS*, *Per2*] ~, *Per1*, *E1*
145:21 —what] What *Per1*
145:24 self. The *MS*, *Per2*] ~. *P* The *Per1*, *E1*
145:25 diseased . . . intuitive] ~, atrophied condition of the intuitive *Per1*
145:30 is the flower] the flower *Per1*
145:34 But] ~, *Per1*
145:36 uneducated, *MS*, *Per2*] ~ *Per1*, *E1*
145:39 *think*. In *MS*, *Per2*] ~. *P* In *Per1*, *E1*
145:40 She's] "~ *Per1*, *E1* she's *Per2*
146:1 her.—] ~." *Per1*, *E1* ~. *Per2*
146:2 She] "She *Per1*, *E1* she *Per2*
146:3 me.] ~." *Per1*, *E1 me Per2*
146:5 glow, *MS*, *Per2*] ~ *Per1*, *E1*
146:7 blunted, *MS*, *Per2*] ~ *Per1*
146:7 best. But *MS*, *Per2*] ~. *P* But *Per1*, *E1*
146:7 film] films *Per1*
146:8 face,] ~ *Per1*
146:10 pure. But *MS*, *Per2*] ~. *P* But *Per1*, *E1*
146:13 Rudolf] Rudolph *Per1*
146:13 pleases . . . satisfies *MS*, *E1*] pleased . . . satisfied *Per2*
146:16 delicately, *MS*, *Per2*] ~ *Per1*, *E1*
146:17 beauty. And *MS*, *Per2*] ~. *P* And *Per1*, *E1*
146:18 no-one] no one *Per1*
146:18 repellant] repellent *Per1*
146:20 no-one] no one *Per1*
146:22 all] and all *Per1*
146:24 this] the *Per1*
146:25 shine, *MS*, *Per2*] ~ *Per1*
146:26 But . . . sex appeal. *MS*, *E1*] *Om. Per2*
146:27 of sex] ~ ~, *E1*
146:29 unfortunately are] are unfortunately *Per1*
146:30 world. Nothing *MS*, *Per2*] ~. *P* Nothing *Per1*, *E1*
146:33 alive, *MS*, *Per2*] ~ *Per1*
146:34 shines, *MS*, *Per2*] ~; *Per1*, *E1*
146:36 it. While *MS*, *Per2*] ~. *P* While *Per1*, *E1*
147:1 Luckily *MS*, *Per2*] ~, *Per1*, *E1*
147:4 Or . . . rouse *MS*, *Per2*] ~ ~ *Per1*, *E1*
147:5 flame: *MS*, *Per2*] ~; *Per1*, *E1*
147:6 sex fire] sex-fire *Per1*
147:6 through, *MS*, *Per2*] ~ *Per1*
147:8 I *MS*, *Per2*] "I *Per1*, *E1*
147:8 girl, *MS*, *Per2*] ~; *Per1*, *E1*
147:8 sort. It] ~." *P* It *Per1* ~. *P* It *Per2* ~." ~ *E1*
147:8 glow,] ~ *Per1*
147:10 She's *MS*, *Per2*] "~ *Per1*, *E1*

147:10 woman, . . . I] ~. ~ *Per1*, *E1* ~; . . . ~ *Per2*
147:10 her—. Or] ~." *P* Or *Per1*, *E1* ~. ~ *Per2*
147:12 She's *MS*, *Per2*] "~ *Per1*, *E1*
147:12 me . . . more— *P* It] me." *P* It *Per1*, *E1* me. *P* Let's say no more. *P* It *Per2*
147:14 rather] *Om. Per1*
147:17 Poictiers *MS*, *Per2*] Poitiers *Per1*, *E1*
147:18 Langtry *MS*, *Per2*] ~, *Per1*, *E1*
147:19 But oh, how *MS*, *E1*] But how *Per2*
147:19 *lovely*] lovely *Per1*
147:21 sex-appeal] sex appeal *Per1*
147:22 only] *Om. Per1*
147:23 her, *MS*, *Per2*] ~ *Per1*, *E1*
147:23 me. *Then*] ~. *P* Then *Per1*, *E1* our hearts. Then *Per2*
147:24 to me *MS*, *E1*] *Om. Per2*
147:24 is . . . flesh *MS*, *E1*] ~, . . . ~, *Per2*
147:25 lovely,] ~ *Per1*
147:26 But alas,] ~, ~! *Per1*
147:26 rare, *MS*, *Per2*] ~ *Per1*, *E1*
147:27 women.] ~! *Per1*
147:31 delapidated *MS*, *Per2*] dilapidated *Per1*, *E1*
147:32 appeal!— *MS*, *Per2*] ~ *Per1*, *E1*
147:32 Poictiers!— *MS*, *Per2*] Poitiers, *Per1*, *E1*
147:33 own wife!] wife— *Per1*, *E1* wife! *Per2*
147:33 Why *MS*, *Per2*] why, *Per1*, *E1*
147:33 it is *MS*, *E1*] is it *Per2*
147:34 itself. *P* Nowadays] ~. Nowadays *E1*
147:35 Nowadays . . . [148:7] flourishes. *MS*, *E1*] *Om. Per2*
147:35 loveliness] ~, *Per1*
147:36 levels. The] ~. *P* The *Per1*
147:37 business-man's] business man's *Per1*
147:39 slightest. Even] ~. *P* Even *Per1*
147:40 man,] ~ *Per1*
148:2 heat. Still] ~. *P* Still *Per1*, *E1*
148:3 business-man's] business man's *E1*
148:4 business-man] business man *E1*
148:5 her,] ~ *Per1*
148:6 flourishes. That . . . *P* There] ~. *P* There *Per1*, *E1*
148:8 sex-appeal — it *MS*, *Per2*] sex appeal. It *Per1*, *E1*
148:9 sex-appeal] sex appeal *Per1*
148:10 for her] to her *Per1*
148:12 was. The *MS*, *Per2*] ~. *P* The *Per1*, *E1*
148:13 Balzac *MS*, *E1*] Balsae *Per1* Balzac's novels *Per2*
148:14 They . . . vamp. *MS*, *E1*] *Om. Per2*
148:15 touch *MS*, *E1*] a-little-too-obvious touch *Per2*
148:16 today] to-day *Per1*, *E1* *Om. Per2*
148:18 successfully, *MS*, *Per2*] ~ *Per1*, *E1*
148:19 housework *MS*, *E1*] work at home *Per2*
148:20 of course, *MS*, *Per2*] *Om. Per1*, *E1*
148:21 years,] ~ *E1*
148:21 it. If *MS*, Per2] ~. *P* If *Per1*, *E1*
148:25 might *MS*, *Per2*] ~, *Per1*, *E1*
148:25 us *MS*, *Per2*] ~, *Per1*, *E1*
148:25 means kindled *MS*, *Per2*] means we should be kindled *Per1*, *E1*
148:26 zest, *MS*, *Per2*] ~ *Per1*, *E1*
148:26 things. Whereas *MS*, *Per2*] ~ . . . .*P* Whereas, *Per1*, *E1*
148:27 to life now!] in life now. *Per1*, *E1* in our lives at present! *Per2*

Do Women Change

The chronological sequence is *MS*, *TS*, *TSR*, *E1*.

151:1 **Do Women Change** *Ed.*] Do Women Change. / by D.H.Lawrence *MS* DO WOMEN CHANGE. / by/ D.H.LAWRENCE *TS* DO WOMEN CHANGE? *E1*
151:3 bottles] bottle *TS*
151:11 same:] ~ — *TS*
151:12 human; but *TSR*] ~. But *MS* ~. but *TS*
151:14 Ruths] ~, *E1*
151:19 And sophisticated people . . . all alike. *TSR*] *Om. MS*
151:21 unmodern *TSR*] elderly *MS*
151:22 And *TSR*] But *MS*
151:22 probably very little *TSR*] no *MS*
151:23 all *TSR*] *Om. MS*
151:29 today *TSR*] *Om. MS* to-day *E1*
151:30 sure] ~, *E1*
151:31 like ours *TSR*] *Om. MS*
151:31 and . . . been *TSR*] whom, if you were *MS*
151:32 one of *TSR*] *Om. MS*
151:32 wouldn't *TSR*] couldn't *MS*
151:32 have found her *TSR*] find *MS*
152:1 bobbed-haired] bob-haired *TS*
152:3 inspire,] ~ *TS*
152:5 hotel-balcony] ~ ~ *TS*
152:5 sea:] ~. *E1*
152:6 See . . . ocean—!] "~ . . . ~!" *E1*
152:6 Cut . . . 32!—] "Cut . . . 32!" *E1*
152:9 said:] ~ *TS*
152:9 *Cut it out!*] 'Cut it out' *TSR* "*Cut it out*" *E1*
152:12 round,] ~ *TS*
152:15 True,] ~ *TS*
152:16 Modernity,] ~ *TS*
152:16 modernness] modernism *TS*
152:20 chic] *chic E1*
152:22 money:] ~; *E1*
152:28 full stop] full-stop *TS*
152:30 full stops] full-stops *TS*
152:31 one-thousand] one thousand *E1*
152:32 plain,] ~ *TS*
152:36 Oh] ~, *E1*
152:39 Baby] ~! *TS*
153:1 from a] ~ the *TS*
153:2 from a *TSR*] ~ the *MS*
153:3 past. *P* And] ~. And *E1*
153:5 lie down *TSR*] sleep *MS*
153:6 Oh] ~, *E1*
153:8 lo!] ~ *TS* ~, *E1*
153:9 Victorian *TSR*] *Om. MS*
153:12 slave: . . . helpmeet: . . . spouse: . . . matron:] ~; . . . ~; . . . ~; . . . ~; *E1*
153:14 citizen,] ~; *E1*
153:14 female,] ~; *E1*
153:15 Oh] oh *TS*
153:20 — Oh] ~ *TS*
153:24 where . . . where] Where . . . Where *E1*
153:36 softly-flowing] softly flowing *E1*
153:40 pleasure —] ~, *E1*
154:1 pointed,] ~ *E1*
154:6 pad] part *E1*
154:9 it!—] ~! *E1*
154:17 disappears,] ~ — *E1*
154:27 intermingling:] ~; *E1*
154:33 flowers. And] ~ and *E1*
154:34 matters:] ~; *E1*
154:35 and life.] *Om. E1*

Enslaved by Civilisation

The chronological sequence is *MS*, *TS*, *Per*, *E1*.

156:1 **Enslaved by Civilisation** *Ed.*] Enslaved by Civilisation / by D. H. Lawrence *MS* ENSLAVED BY CIVILISATION. *TS* The Manufacture of Good Little Boys / How Modern Men Become Enslaved by the Pernicious Dictates of the Schoolmarms /By D. H. LAWRENCE *Per* ENSLAVED BY CIVILISATION *E1*
156:6 schoolmistresses *MS*, *E1*] school-mistresses *TS*
156:11 give] Give *Per*
156:12 life.— *MS*, *E1*] ~. *TS*
156:14 about, but they *MS*, *E1*] ~. They *Per*
156:19 exam. *MS*, *E1*] ~ *Per*
156:24 Manhood . . . unpleasant *MS*, *E1*] *Om. Per*
156:27 Haven't . . . same? *MS*, *E1*] *Om. Per*
156:34 infants] ~' *TS*
157:1 Gospel] gospel *TS*
157:4 Teachem] Teacher *TS*
157:5 voices. —] ~. *TS*
157:6 Teachem] Teacher *TS*
157:8 Poor Johnny *MS*, *E1*] Johnny *Per*
157:8 Now] ~, *Per*
157:10 Oh] ~, *Per*
157:12 they dear] ~,~ *TS*
157:14 then] *Om. TS*
157:15 little *MS*, *Per*] ~, *TS*
157:19 Teacher] teacher *E1*
157:22 railway-system] railway system *E1*
157:23 good lines *MS*, *E1*] tracks *Per*
157:23 shunted *MS*, *E1*] finally shunted *Per*
157:23 life, *MS*, *E1*] ~. *Per*
157:23 at the . . . on-lines *MS*, *E1*] And by then the running-on-tracks *Per*
157:24 is] it *E1*
157:26 rails,] ~; *TS*, *E1* ~. *Per*
157:26 he . . . boy! *MS*, *E1*] *Om. Per*
157:29 It . . . [157:32] boys. *MS*, *E1*] *Om. Per*
157:37 peep *MS*, *E1*] trace *Per*
157:37 maid's fingers . . . into *MS*, *E1*] maid at training a growing boy into *Per*
157:40 It is . . . [158:2] husband. *MS*, *E1*] *Om. Per*
158:1 boy!" —] ~!" *TS*
158:24 entirely: *MS*, *E1*] ~, *Per*
158:26 days,] ~ *E1*
158:30 Board schools] Board-schools *TS*
158:30 national *MS*, *E1*] National *Per*
158:31 dear!] ~ *E1*
158:32 bears] bear *TS*
158:33 Board school] Board-school *TS*
158:40 s'll] I'll *TS*
158:40 That . . . [159:2] school. *MS*, *E1*] To escape into the wild warrens of the pit, to get off the narrow lines of school was what they waited for. *Per*
159:3 school-master] schoolmaster *TS*
159:3 excellent] ~, *Per*
159:7 David!] ~? *TS*
159:8 David!"—] ~!" *TS*
159:15 school-master] schoolmaster *TS*
159:18 in *MS*, E1] *Om. Per*
159:25 lines . . . lines . . . lines *MS*, *E1*] tracks . . . tracks . . . tracks *Per*
159:29 difficult] ~, *TS*
159:29 so there . . . [159:36] rust there. *MS*, *E1*] *Om. Per*
159:31 coal strike *MS*, *E1*] coal-strike *TS*
159:36 in:] ~; *E1*
159:37 schoolmasters,] ~ *E1*
159:38 for England, *MS*, *E1*] *Om. Per*

Give Her a Pattern

The chronological sequence is *MS*, *TS*, *Per1*, *Per2*, *E1*. The title is adopted from *TS* where it was introduced by DHL; he made no other changes.

162:1 **Give Her a Pattern** *Ed.*] Oh these Women! / by D. H. Lawrence *MS* <*OH THESE WOMEN*!> ⌐Give Her a Pattern¬ / by / *D. H. Lawrence*. *TS* Woman in Man's Image / Concerning the Modern Male's Motives in Creating a Satisfactory Rôle for Womankind / By D. H. LAWRENCE *Per1* *Excuse D. H. LAWRENCE, but he wishes to write about* / WOMEN—Once More *Per2* GIVE HER A PATTERN *E1*
162:3 done. When *MS*, *E1*] ~. *P* When *Per2*
162:4 herself *MS*, *Per2*] ~, *TS1*, *E1*
162:6 be, *MS*, *Per2*] ~ — *Per1*
162:8 For] ~, *Per1*
162:8 For . . . [162:11] woman *MS*, *E1*] *For* [in italics] . . . *woman Per2*
162:11 woman. Those *MS*, *E1*] ~. *P* Those *Per2*
162:11 theory,] ~ *E1*
162:12 ideal *MS*, *E1*] ~, *Per2*
162:12 property lust *MS*, *E1*] lust for property *Per2*
162:13 suspicion."— *MS*, *E1*] ~." *Per2*
162:15 fell. Later *MS*, *E1*] ~. *P* Later *Per1*
162:16 fast *MS*, *E1*] "fast" *Per2*
162:16 anybody *MS*] everybody *Per1*
162:18 centuries. The *MS*, *E1*] ~. *P* The *Per2*
162:20 prose. Dickens *MS*, *E1*] ~. *P* Dickens *Per2*
162:22 Agnes *MS*, *E1*] *Agnes Per1*
162:23 confirmed. The *MS*, *E1*] ~. *P* The *Per2*
162:25 poor *MS*, *E1*] *Om. Per2*
162:25 sort. So *MS*, *E1*] ~. *P* So *Per2*
162:29 She's *MS*, *E1*] She is *Per2*
162:30 David's Dora *MS*, *Per2*] *David's Dora Per1*
162:30 Dora. No *MS*, *E1*] ~. *P* No *Per2*
162:30 thing, *MS*, *E1*] ~ — *Per2*
162:32 are of course] ~,~ ~, *Per1*
163:33 Doctors *TS*] Doctors' *MS*
163:2 women, *MS*, *E1*] ~ *Per2*
163:3 There . . . [163:4] to. *MS*, *E1*] *Om. Per1*
163:5 And . . . [163:7] pattern. *MS*, *E1*] *And* [in italics] . . . *pattern. Per2*
163:5 isn't *MS*, *E1*] is not *Per2*
163:6 she has. *MS*, *Per2*] ~ ~ — *Per1*
163:6 She's . . . has. *MS*, *E1*] *Om. Per1*
163:6 The . . . that *MS*, *Per2*] only *Per1*
163:7 Give . . . [163:11] her. *MS*, *E1*] *Om. Per2*
163:8 follow!—] ~! *Per1*, *E1*
163:13 not, even, *MS*, *E1*] not *Per2*
163:14 patterns, *MS*, *E1*] ~ — *Per1*
163:15 women . . . [163:23] being *MS*, *E1*] ~, or even that men will not accept them as real human beings *Per2*
163:17 the men: *MS*, *E1*] men: *Per1*
163:19 being. Man *MS*, *E1*] ~. *P* Man *Per1*
163:20 machine *TS*] machino *MS*
163:21 a womb, *MS*, *E1*] *Om. Per1*
163:21 encyclopedia *MS*] encyclopaedia *TS* encyclopædia *Per1*, *E1*
163:22 obscenity:] ~; *E1*
163:24 And of course] ~,~ ~, *Per1*, *E1*
163:24 And . . . [163:34] it. *MS*, *E1*] *Om. Per2*
163:24 patterns,] ~ — *E1*
163:27 And for *MS*, *E1*] ~, because of *Per1*

163:29 take it on *MS*, *E1*] adopt it *Per1*
163:32 chaste-untouched] chaste and untouched *TS*
163:33 cosy . . . kids *MS*, *E1*] wife and children *Per1*
163:36 among the boys, *MS*, *E1*] *Om. Per2*
163:38 public: *MS*, *Per2*] ~ — *Per1*, *E1*
163:38 thing—*MS*, *Per2*] ~! *Per1*
163:38 very *MS*, *E1*] same *Per1*
164:2 *type MS*, *E1*] type *Per2*
164:4 Agneses *MS*, *Per2*] *Agneses Per1*
164:4 clinging Doras *MS*, *Per2*] *Om. Per1*
164:4 Doras *MS*, *E1*] ~. *P* He *Per2*
164:4 and lurid . . . *joie MS*, *E1*] *Om. Per2*
164:6 he'll *MS*, *E1*] the man *Per1*
164:6 another. —] ~. *Per1*
164:8 Modern . . . [164:12] be. *MS*, *E1*] *Om. Per2*
164:8 a fool *MS*, *E1*] foolish *Per1*
164:10 a prize *MS*, *E1*] an exceptional *Per1*
164:13 furious, *MS*, *Per1*] ~*Per2*
164:14 hysterically don't *MS*, *E1*] ~ do not *Per1* do not *Per2*
164:14 want. Two *MS*, *E1*] ~. *P* Two *Per2*
164:15 — or . . . Africa — *MS*, *E1*] *Om. Per2*
164:17 Guards. *MS*, *Per2*] Guards or something equally different. *Per1*
164:17 They . . . want. *MS*, *E1*] *Om. Per1* They . . . men are hysterical and do not know . . . want *Per2*
164:19 The women *MS*, *E1*] Women *Per2*
164:19 *must MS*, *E1*] must *Per2*
164:20 *know* the men *MS*, *E1*] know men *Per2*
164:21 have, *MS*, *E1*] ~ *Per2*
164:22 are . . . They *MS*, *E1*] *Om. Per2*
164:24 complementary,] ~ *Per1*
164:24 the woman's *MS*, *E1*] woman's *Per2*
164:25 the man's *MS*, *E1*] man's *Per2*
164:27 the woman *MS*, *E1*] woman *Per2*
164:28 end, *MS*, *E1*] ~ *Per2*
164:30 satisfactory. This *MS*, *E1*] ~. *P* This *Per2*
164:32 child wives] child-wives *Per1*
164:32 on a sudden *MS*, *E1*] suddenly *Per1* all of a sudden *Per2*
164:32 bash! The *MS*, *Per2*] the *Per1*
164:33 roaring *MS*, *Per2*] *Om. Per1*
164:35 Whereas . . . They *MS*, *E1*] Men *Per1*
164:35 Whereas . . . [165:20] pattern. *MS*, *E1*] *Om. Per2*
164:38 till . . . her *MS*] until she is almost *Per1*
164:39 else. Oh *MS*,] ~. *P* Oh, *Per1*
165:3 Agnes *MS*, *E1*] *Agnes Per1*
165:4 business-woman] business woman *Per1*
165:4 on black silk sheets *MS*, *E1*] *Om. Per1*
165:6 reason! When *MS*, *E1*] ~. *P* When *Per1*
165:8 get . . . [165:10] bound *MS*, *E1*] get. It is a pity that women are bound *Per1*
165:11 And she *MS*, *E1*] Woman *Per2*
165:13 worn-out, *MS*, *Per2*] ~ *Per1*, *E1*
165:15 emotions! What] ~? ~ *Per1*, *E1* ~? *P* What *Per2*
165:16 What . . . idiot? *MS*, *Per2*} *Om Per1*
165:17 idiot?— And, *MS*, *E1*] ~? *P* And *Per2*
165:17 And, . . . pattern. *MS*, *E1*] *And*, [in italics] . . . *pattern*. *Per2*
165:18 she . . . her *MS*, *E1*] they . . . their *Per1*
165:19 Mother-dear! — *MS*] Mother dear! — *Per1* mother, thus *Per2* mother dear! — *E1*
165:20 changing his pattern. *MS*, *Per2*] causing him to change his pattern again. *Per1*

165:21 Bah! . . . fools *MS*, *E1*] *Om Per1*
165:21 they *MS*, *E1*] men *Per1*
165:21 anything *MS*, *Per2*] ~ real *Per1*
165:22 women *MS*, *E1*] her *Per2*
165:23 washed-out *MS*, *Per2*] vanished *Per1*

Introduction to Pictures

The chronological sequence is *MS*, *TS*, *A1*. (The practice of *A1* to hyphenate 'self-aware-of-itself' throughout has not been recorded.)

168:1 **Introduction to Pictures** *Ed.*] Introd. to Pictures *MS* INTRODUCTION TO PICTURES. / By / D. H. LAWRENCE. *TS* INTRODUCTION TO PICTURES *A1*
168:6 judge] ~, *A1*
168:14 too.—] ~. *A1*
168:17 repellant] repellent *TS*
168:20 food. *MS*, *A1*] ~? *TS*
168:23 over-loaded] overloaded *A1*
168:25 — But] ~ *A1*
168:33 licence *A1*] license *MS*
169:1 it, but] ~. But *TS*
169:6 consciousness,] ~ *TS*
169:11 *may*] may *TS*
169:30 it. —] ~. *A1*
169:38 then] thus *TS*
170:10 Our feelings are self-conscious.] *Om. TS*
170:11 clock-work] clockwork *TS*
170:12 brain!] ~, *A1*
170:12 still,] ~ *A1*
170:12 clock-work] clockwork *TS*
170:16 corpuscules] corpuscles *TS*
170:27 switch-board] switchboard *TS*
170:31 of —] ~, *TS*
171:2 corpuscules] corpuscles *TS*
171:16 flash-light] flashlight *TS*
171:31 conscious flow] consciousness *TS*
171:36 *always*] always *TS*
172:15 *bad*] bad *TS*
172:17 battle] ~, *TS*
172:21 2000 *MS*, *A1*] 2,000 *TS*
172:24 competition] ~, *TS*
172:31 Old] old *TS*
172:33 Old] old *TS*
172:36 on to] onto *A1*
172:36 affective *MS*, *A1*] effective *TS*
172:38 shameful!] ~. *TS*
172:39 Ah-ha!] A-ha! *A1*
173:7 Anyhow] ~, *A1*
173:14 Galilean *TS*] Gallilean *MS*
173:15 simulacrum] *simulacrum A1*
173:20 thousand-year *MS*, *A1*] thousand year *TS*
173:39 say:] ~ *A1*
174:20 bohemians] Bohemians *A1*
174:21 Old] old *TS*
174:22 take] *Om. TS*
174:27 volta face] *volte face TS* *volte-face A1*
174:31 excrementa] excrements *TS*
174:32 horror! —] ~! *TS*

Myself Revealed

The chronological sequence is *Per*, *E1*.

177:1 **Myself Revealed** *Ed.*] MYSELF REVEALED. / *By D. H. LAWRENCE: The Most-Discussed Novelist of the Day. Per* AUTOBIOGRAPHICAL SKETCH *E1*
178:6 delicate,] ~ *E1*
178:13 teacher] ~, *E1*
178:23 "English Review,"] *English Review*, *E1*
179:4 days,] ~ *E1*

179:13 "English Review,"] *English Review*, *E1*
179:21 17] seventeen *E1*
179:24 school-teacher] school teacher *E1*
179:34 friends] friendly *E1*
180:16 working-class] working class *E1*
180:16 middle-class] middle class *E1*
180:22 middle-class] middle class *E1*
180:25 working-class] working class *E1*
180:30 good-day] good day *E1*
180:36 mine. *P* I] ~. I *E1*
181:5 middle-class] middle class *E1*

Introduction to These Paintings

The chronological sequence is *MS*, *TS1*, *TS2*, *E1*, *A1*.

185:1 **Introduction to These Paintings** *Ed.*] Introd. to Painting / D. H. Lawrence *MS* INTRODUCTION TO PAINTING. *TS1* INTRODUCTION TO THESE PAINTINGS *E1*
185:3 though *MS*, *A1*] ~, *TS2*
185:12 what of, *MS*, *TS2*] of what, *TS1*, *A1*
185:15 arts: *MS*, *A1*] ~; *E1*
185:16 in to *MS*, *A1*] into *TS2*
185:21 Sixteenth] sixteenth *TS1*
185:26 Sixteenth] sixteenth *TS1*
185:32 itself: *MS*, *A1*] ~. *E1*
186:4 father] ~, *TS2*
186:12 love-poetry] love poetry *TS2*
186:16 thee dear] ~, ~, *TS2*
186:39 sixteenth, *MS*, *A1*] ~ *E1*
187:8 throne, *MS*, *A1*] ~ *E1*
187:19 royal *MS*, *A1*] Royal *TS2*
187:22 America,] ~; *TS1*
187:26 blood, *MS*, *A1*] ~ *E1*
187:29 also *MS*, *A1*] *Om.* *TS2*
187:32 Some-one] Someone *TS1*
187:34 Europe, *MS*, *A1*] ~ *E1*
187:38 pox] Pox *E1*
188:1 why . . . what's] Why . . . What's *TS1*
188:6 pox.] '~'. *TS1* "~." *E1*
186:7 syphilis.] '~'. *TS1* "~." *E1*
186:8 *clap*! *MS*, *A1*] ~, *E1*
186:10 "Why] "~, *TS1*
186:15 Now] ~, *TS1*
186:25 constituted,] ~ *TS1*
188:27 great,] ~ *E1*
188:38 Nevertheless *MS*, *A1*] ~, *E1*
189:2 formulated, *MS*, *A1*] ~ *E1*
189:20 unborn,] ~ *TS1*
189:39 syphilis, *MS*, *A1*] ~ *E1*
189:39 it, *MS*, *A1*] ~ *E1*
190:5 flesh and blood] flesh-and-blood *TS1*
190:18 kinship *E1*] oneness *MS*
190:39 bored, sometimes *MS*, *A1*] ~; sometimes *TS2*
191:7 monkey-musk] monkey-mush, *TS2* monkey-musk, *E1*
191:8 Oh,] "~, *TS2*
191:8 now . . . oh,] Now . . . Oh *TS1*
191:9 monkey-musk?] Monkey-musk? *TS1*, *E1* Monkey-mush? *TS2*
191:10 oh . . . oh] Oh . . . Oh *TS1*
191:11 is . . . velvetty,] Is . . . velvety, *TS1*
191:11 silky? — *MS*, *TS2*] ~? *TS1*
191:14 images] imagery *TS1*
191:20 get a little . . . thrill *MS*, *A1*] get little . . . thrills *TS2*
191:24 Ah] ~, *TS1*
191:24 high-brows *MS*, *A1*] highbrows *TS1*
191:31 'er *MS*, *TS2*] '~. *TS1*, *E1*
191:34 highbrow] high-brow *TS2*
191:38 ideas, *MS*, *A1*] ~. *E1*
192:5 in to] into *TS1*
192:6 skin-deep *MS*, *A1*] skin deep *E1*
192:18 though . . . building. *E1*] *Om.* *MS*
192:22 oh] Oh, *TS1*, *A1* oh, *TS2*
192:23 what! *MS*, *A1*] ~!— *E1*

192:26 crétin . . . crétin] *crétin . . . crétin* *TS2*
192:30 that. Modern] that modern *TS2*
192:34 pole] poles *E1*
193:8 it,] ~; *TS1*
193:23 physically *MS*, *A1*] ~, *TS2*
193:37 one *MS*, *A1*] you *TS2*
193:38 what really] What really *TS1*
194:10 Lawrence *MS*, *A1*] ~, *TS2*
194:11 cliché *MS*, *A1*] *cliché* *E1*
194:14 Pre-Raphaelites] pre-Raphaelites *TS1* pre-Raphælites *E1*
194:17 imaginative . . . landscape, *E1*] the first order *MS*
194:20 Nevertheless] ~, *E1*
194:22 human . . . imagination. *E1*] living, sensual human body: a thing which no other Englishman has dared to do. *MS*, living, sensuous human . . . do. *TS2*
194:25 beyond *E1*] below *MS*
194:26 failure, though . . . [194:31] optical. *E1*] failure: and the others don't bear mention. They illustrate ideas with clichés in paint. *MS*
194:34 me] be *TS1*
195:8 procreative] procreated *TS2*
195:13 landscape painters] landscape-painters *TS1*
195:15 among *E1*] *Om. MS*
195:23 But of course] ~, ~ ~, *E1*
195:28 And] ~, *TS2*
195:36 is] ~, *TS2*
195:38 couldn't] cannot *TS2*
196:2 painters,] ~ *TS1*
196:3 wash-out.] washout *E1* wash-out *A1*
196:18 copulation *MS*, *TS2*] capitulation *TS1*
196:19 you, just . . . *Ça*] you. *Ça* *TS2*
196:28 quarrelling *TS1*] quarreling *MS*
196:30 ça . . . corps] *Ça* [in italics] . . . *corps!* *TS1*
196:31 breasts, *MS*, *A1*] ~ *E1*
196:32 Ça . . . corps] *Ça* [in italics] . . . *corps!* *TS1*
196:36 Ça . . . corps!] *Ça* [in italics] . . . *corps!* *TS1*
196:36 —Yet] ~ *TS1*
197:13 it, *MS*, *A1*] ~*E1*
197:30 us *E1*] *Om. MS*
197:34 le grand néant] *le grand néant* *TS1*
198:16 whole, they *MS*, *A1*] ~ ~ *E1*
198:24 was, you] ~. You *TS1*, *A1* ~; you *TS2*
198:37 Landscape] ~, *TS1*
198:38 shadow *MS*, *A1*] shadows *TS2*
199:4 one-ness] oneness *E1*
199:4 holy *MS*, *A1*] Holy *TS2*
199:6 light! —] ~! *TS1*
199:10 chaos of course] ~, ~ ~, *TS1*
199:19 elect, among *TS2*] elect, the elect, among *MS*,
199:25 Oh purify . . . inspiration." *MS*,] *Om. TS1* ~, ~ . . . ~". *TS2*
199:33 behold] ~, *TS1*
199:39 told)] ~); *TS1*, *A1* ~): *TS2*
199:40 churches, Oh] ~, O *TS1*, *A1* ~, Oh, *TS2*
200:3 saved. —] ~. *E1*
200:11 experience,] ~ *TS1*
200:20 individual's] individual *TS1*
200:31 sky-blue,] sky blue, *E1* sky-blue *A1*
200:32 evangelist] evangelical *TS2*
200:34 woolly] ~, *TS1*
200:36 cross!] ~? *TS1*
200:37 a sort] A sort *TS1*
200:37 mistake?—] ~? *TS2*
200:40 blood] Blood *TS2*
201:8 breath: *MS*, *A1*] ~, *TS2*
201:9 Form!"—*MS*, *A1*] ~!" *E1*
201:14 vogue *TS2*] orgies *MS*
202:7 intuitive body *E1*] phallus *MS*
202:8 good,] ~; *TS1*
202:30 these he *wouldn't* paint *E1*] he *wouldn't* paint *them MS*
202:32 intuition,] ~; *TS1*
202:38 tooth and nail] tooth-and-nail *TS1*

202:39 and] ~, *TS1*
203:14 nineteenth *E1*] eighteenth *MS*, *A1*
203:16 corpses] ~, *TS2*
203:31 and piss] *Om. E1*
203:34 abstraction,] ~ *TS1*
203:39 ad infinitum] *ad infinitum TS1*
204:8 it] *it E1*
204:18 mental, mental, mental,] ~, ~, ~; *TS1*, ~, ~, *TS2*
204:22 minds *MS*, *A1*] ~, *TS2*
204:25 —As] ~ *TS2*
204:26 l'esprit] *l'esprit TS2*
204:26 fart *MS*, *A1*] fait *TS1*, fact *TS2* f— *E1*
204:30 that, . . . achievement,] ~ . . . ~ *TS2* ~, . . . ~ *A1*
204:34 imagination *MS*, *A1*] imaginative *TS2*
205:18 art —] ~. *TS1*
205:30 draw!] drww? *TS1* draw? *TS2*
206:18 re-incarnation] reincarnation *TS1*
206:23 rich] ~, *TS1*
206:30 Consciously] consciously *TS1*
206:32 are —!] ~! *TS1*, ~. *TS2*
206:35 honesty:] ~, *TS1*
206:36 gift or *MS*, *A1*] ~ of *TS2*
206:38 Tintoretto nor Veronese] ~, ~ ~, *E1*
207:16 are. —] ~. *TS1*
207:25 mental:] ~; *TS2*
207:26 concerned,] ~ *E1*
207:29 a] *Om. TS2* the *E1*
207:31 *appreciation*] appreciation *TS1*
208:2 bodies,] ~ *TS1*
208:5 circumstances] ~, *TS1*
208:9 —Of . . . believe it. *E1*] *Om. MS*
208:20 poppy-cock] poppycock *TS1*
209:3 respect!] ~? *TS1*
209:5 tooth and nail *MS*, *A1*] tooth-and-nail *TS2*
209:7 and *MS*, *A1*] or *TS2*
209:14 sensitive *MS*, *A1*] ~, *TS2*
209:23 them,] ~ *TS1*
209:33 Cézanne-clichés *MS*, *TS2*] Cézanne clichés *TS1*, *E1*
209:34 mostly] ~, *TS2*
209:34 baroque-clichés *MS*, *TS2*] baroque, clichés *TS1*, *E1*
210:4 re-appeared] reappeared *TS2*
210:7 cliché, *MS*, *A1*] ~ *E1*
210:21 life:] ~; *E1*
210:24 Then *MS*, *A1*] ~, *TS2*
210:33 long] ~, *TS2*
210:33 two-fold] twofold *E1*
210:33 activity: he] ~. He *TS2*
210:34 it,] ~ *E1*
210:39 chinese] Chinese *TS1*
210:39 dress-maker] dressmaker *TS1*
210:40 dress-maker] dressmaker *TS1*
211:3 explosions,] ~ *E1*
211:8 this] them *TS2*
211:19 mechanical] ~, *TS1*
211:20 socialism: *MS*, *A1*] ~, *TS2*
211:30 mental-visual *MS*, *A1*] mental visual *TS2*
211:32 past,] ~ *E1*
211:35 consciousness—] ~, *E1*
211:40 Be . . . apple! —] "~ . . . ~!" *E1*
212:17 her.—] ~. *TS2*
212:19 soul] personality *E1*
212:20 apple! —] ~! *E1*
212:26 only fronts *E1*] all fronts *MS*
212:31 than *TS1*] that *MS*
212:32 Geffroy *MS*, *A1*] Geoffroy *E1*
212:39 fully,] ~ *E1*
212:40 domination] denominator *TS2*
213:5 conceptual] concepted *TS2* concept *E1*
213:8 Geffroy *MS*, *A1*] Geoffroy. *E1*
213:13 colour] ~, *TS1*
213:14 colour] ~, *TS2*
213:19 me,] ~ *E1*
213:29 Cézanne, *MS*, *A1*] ~ *E1*
213:31 appleyness,] ~ *E1*
213:35 time,] ~ *E1*
214:3 cliché,] ~ *E1*
214:6 landscapes,] ~ *E1*
214:7 eyes,] ~; *TS1*
214:18 fashion —] ~; *TS1*, ~, *TS2*
214:23 art,] ~ *E1*
214:29 cliché!] ~. *TS1*, ~? *TS2*
214:30 Still . . . that] ~, . . . ~, *TS1*

214:38 re-construct] reconstruct *E1*
215:13 apple —] ~. *TS1*
215:15 terms, *MS*, *A1*] ~ *E1*
215:19 life." But] ~". But *TS1* ~" — but *TS2*
215:21 it — not] ~. Not *TS1*
215:27 man] ~, *TS2*
215:27 But] "~ *E1*
215:30 painting?—] ~? *TS1* ~?" *E1*
215:32 pictures, *MS*, *TS2*] ~ *TS1*, *E1*
216:9 flies, as the cow walks, *TS1*, *A1*] flies, as cow walks, *MS* flies, *TS2*
216:15 to, *MS*, *A1*] ~ *E1*
216:15 sex-appeal *MS*, *A1*] sex appeal *E1*
216:40 its *MS*, *A1*] the *TS2*
217:2 London: — All] ~. — ~ *TS2* ~ — all *E1*, *A1*
217:4 Now] ~, *E1*
217:14 again, *MS*, *TS2*] ~ *TS1*, *E1*
217:30 now] Now *TS2*
217:32 age! . . . up!] age! *Bandol, 1929.* D. H. LAWRENCE *E1* age! *A1*

The State of Funk

The chronological sequence is *MS*, *TS*, *E1*. (Two incomplete typescripts – 4 pp. (UCB) and 1 p. (UNM) – play no part in the collation.)

219:1 **The State of Funk** *Ed.*] The State of Funk /D. H. Lawrence *MS* THE STATE OF FUNK / by D.H.LAWRENCE. *TS* THE STATE OF FUNK *E1*
219:10 sometime] some time *E1*
219:25 fell into] feel into *TS* feel in *E1*
219:34 pangs.—] ~. *E1*
220:9 steam-engine] steam engine *E1*
220:21 adaptations] adaptation *TS*
220:34 men. *MS*, *E1*] ~, *TS*
220:40 mass-bullying] mass bullying *E1*
221:3 change. You] ~, you *TS*
221:11 tadpole:] ~; *E1*
221:34 good-nature] good nature *E1*
221:36 feelings:] ~; *TS*
222:6 rage,] ~ *TS*
222:6 morning,] ~ *E1*
222:12 social,] ~ *TS*
222:14 himself:] ~; *TS*
222:15 herself:] ~; *E1*
222:15 itself:] ~; *E1*
222:21 it.—] ~. *E1*
222:22 remember,] ~ *TS*
222:33 man,] ~ *TS*
222:33 enraged,] ~ *TS*
223:8 men and men] ~ ~ ~, *E1*
223:14 lurid",] ~"; *TS*
223:23 of] *Om. TS*
223:32 love-affairs . . . love-affairs] love affairs . . . love affairs *E1*
224:1 animal:] ~; *E1*
224:10 cut-off] cut off *E1*

Making Pictures

The chronological sequence is *MS*, *TS*, *Per1*, *Per2*, *E1*. (*Creative Art*, July 1929, reproduced the *Studio* text in every detail and does not appear in the collation. Tedlock states that in *TS* 'some correction in ink and pencil [is] apparently in Lawrence's hand' (234). The claim, relating to minor spelling changes, is dubious and plays no part in the collation.)

227:1 **Making Pictures** *Ed*] Making Pictures. by D. H. Lawrence *MS* MAKING PICTURES. / by D. H. Lawrence. *TS* D. H. LAWRENCE ON / "MAKING PICTURES" *Per1* Making Pictures / An English Novelist, Turned Painter, Discovers That Creative Art Is a Thing of the Spirit / By D. H. LAWRENCE *Per2* MAKING PICTURES *E1*
227:3 Everything *MS*, *Per2*] "~ *Per1*
227:5 end.— *MS*, *Per2*] ~. *TS* ~." *Per1*
227:7 picture-shops] picture shops *E1*
227:8 Dufys *MS*, *Per1*] Dufrys *E1*
227:8 Chiricos etc,] ~, etc., *Per1*
227:9 the . . . one. *MS*, *E1*] one feels the same weariness. *Per2*
227:11 them,] ~ *TS*
227:11 Friescz] Friesz *Per1* Friday *Per2* Friscz *E1*
227:12 Laurencin *MS*, *Per1*] Laurençin *E1*
227:13 *natural MS*, *Per2*] fresh *Per1*
227:13 paint: trivial] ~. Trivial *TS*
227:13 to *MS*, *Per2*] with *Per1*
227:14 real *MS*, *Per2*] pictorial *Per1*
227:15 then?] ~! *TS*
227:16 expression:] ~; *E1*
227:18 and *MS*, *E1*] and then *Per2*
227:22 life. But *MS*, *E1*] ~. *P* But *Per2*
227:24 turps,] ~ *E1*
227:25 drogheria *MS*, *E1*] *drogheria Per2*
227:30 concerned; *MS*, *Per1*] ~, *TS*, *Per2*
228:2 canvas. It *MS*, *E1*] ~. *P* It *Per2*
228:4 then *MS*, *E1*] there *TS*
228:4 swim. As *MS*, *E1*] ~, so *TS* ~. So *Per1* ~; so *Per2*
228:7 needle:] ~; *Per1*
228:8 intuition,] ~ *TS*
228:9 get *MS*, *Per2*] gets *TS* , *E1*
228:9 *happens*, *MS*, *Per1*, *E1*] ~ *TS*, *Per2*
228:19 enough *MS*, *E1*] long enough *Per2*
228:21 brass tacks *MS*, *Per1*, *E1*] brass-tacks *TS*, *Per2*
228:27 theses,] these, *TS* these *Per1*, *E1* these: *Per2*
228:27 expositions *MS*, *Per2*] demonstrations *Per1*
228:29 Dufy] Dufry *E1*
228:30 Theorise, theorise *MS*, *Per1*, *E1*] Theorise, theories *TS* Theorize theories *Per2*
228:33 Myself, I *MS*, *E1*] I *Per2*
228:34 art-school *MS*, *Per2*] art school *Per1*, *E1*
228:35 But . . . course *MS*, *Per2*] ~, . . . ~, *Per1*
228:39 Plaster casts] Plaster-casts *TS*
228:40 draw." I *MS*, *E1*] ~." *P* I *Per2*
229:2 potatoes] ~, *TS*
229:3 Nature *MS*, *Per2*] nature *Per1*
229:3 plaster cast] plaster-cast *TS*
229:4 Dying Gladiators *MS*, *Per2*] dying gladiators *Per1*
229:6 it, to *MS*, *E1*] ~ ~ *Per2*
229:7 So . . . course] ~, . . . ~, *TS*
229:14 copying] Copying *Per1*
229:14 scene . . . reproduction *MS*, *Per2*] scene reproduction *TS* reproduction *Per1*
229:17 square-inch . . . square-inch *MS*, *Per2*] square inch . . . square-inch *Per1*
229:21 managed, *MS*, *Per2*] ~ *Per1*
229:24 exaltation *MS*, *Per2*] passion *Per1*
229:26 is *MS*, *Per1*] if *TS*
229:32 School . . . Art *MS*, *Per2*] school . . . art *Per1*

229:34 and] ~, *TS*
229:35 can paint *MS*, *E1*] has painted *Per2*
229:36 was *MS*, *Per2*] is *Per1*
229:37 was *MS*, *Per2*] is *Per1*
229:38 musical: *MS*, *Per2*] ~; *Per1*
230:1 objects:] ~; *E1*
230:2 little *MS*, *E1*] *Om. Per2*
230:3 Ramblas *MS*, *Per2*] Rambla *Per1*
230:6 in to *MS*, *Per1*, *E1*] into *TS*, *Per2*
230:6 nature *MS*, *E1*] Nature *Per2*
230:8 only. *MS*, *Per1*] ~, *TS*
230:9 Cézanne. *MS*, *Per1*] ~, *TS*, *Per2* ~; *E1*
230:9 Staring] staring *TS*, *Per2* But staring *Per1* but staring *E1*
230:10 draw,] ~ *TS*
230:15 ambitious, *MS*, *Per2*] ~ *Per1*
230:17 I can . . . [230:23] study. *MS*, *E1*] *Om*, *Per2*
230:18 Water-Colour Painters] water-colour Painters *TS* water-colour painters *Per1*
230:18 the Studio] THE STUDIO *Per1* the *Studio E1*
230:26 Sandby *MS*, *Per1*, *E1*] Sandley *TS*, *Per2*
230:26 Girtin] ~, *TS*
230:29 develop *TS*] develope *MS*
230:31 really,] ~ *Per2*
230:34 art-schools *MS*, *Per2*] art schools *Per1*, *E1*
230:35 This *MS*, *E1*] this *Per2*
230:36 Isn't *MS*, *E1*] isn't *Per2*
230:38 —But *MS*, *E1*] ~ *TS*
231:2 object. *MS*, *E1*] ~ *Per1* ~; *Per2*
231:2 Art] But *TS*, *E1* but *Per1*
231:2 delight— *MS*, *Per2*] ~, *Per1* ~?— *E1*
231:4 life,] ~ *E1*
231:6 deeper,] ~ *TS*
231:8 water *MS*, *Per1*] waters *TS*, *Per2*
231:10 Thebaïd] *Thebaïd Per2* "Thebaïd" *E1*
231:11 [a] *Ed.*] *Om. MS*
231:11 photograph] photographs *TS*
231:11 colour: *MS*, *Per2*] ~; *Per1*, *E1*
231:12 more,] ~ *TS*
231:15 comes] ~. *Per1*, *E1* ~! *Per2*
231:15 back . . . Italian.] *Om. TS*
231:17 flemings] Flemings *TS*
231:17 shallow—] ~. *TS*
231:19 now:] ~; *Per1*
231:20 much.] ~, *TS*
231:20 Only] only *TS*
231:21 Hooch, *MS*, *Per2*] ~ *Per1*
231:21 Vandyck, *MS*, *E1*] ~ *TS*
231:22 lovely *MS*, *E1*] *Om. Per2*
231:23 in *MS*, *Per2*] by Piero di Cosimo, in *Per1*
231:31 Sometimes *MS*, *E1*] Some times *Per2*
231:32 always *MS*, *Per2*] nearly always *Per1*
231:33 made: *MS*, *Per2*] ~; *Per1*, *E1*
231:37 inside *MS*, *Per2*] ~, *TS*, *E1*
231:39 vision *MS*, *Per2*] bird *Per1*
232:4 Goya] ~, *Per1*, *E1* Goza, *Per2*
232:9 No . . . making. *MS*, *E1*] *Om. Per2*
232:10 making. *MS*, *E1*] making for his strongest impulse. *Per1*

Pornography and Obscenity

The chronological sequence is *MS*, *TS1*, *TS2*, *Per*, *E1*, *E2*.

236:1 **Pornography and Obscenity** *Ed.*] <What is> Pornography and Obscenity/ by D. H. Lawrence *MS* PORNOGRAPHY / AND / OBSCENITY. / by / D. H. Lawrence. *TS1* PORNOGRAPHY AND OBSCENITY by / D. H. Lawrence. *TS2* PORNOGRAPHY / AND OBSCENITY / by / D. H. Lawrence *Per* PORNOGRAPHY / AND / OBSCENITY / D. H. LAWRENCE *E1* PORNOGRAPHY AND/ OBSCENITY *E2*
236:4 harlots"— *MS*, *Per*] ~" *TS2*
236:13 *obscene MS*, *Per*] obscene *TS2*
236:14 *obscena MS*, *Per*] obscena *TS2*
236:15 stage,—] ~; *TS1* ~: *E2*
236:19 hundred:] ~; *TS1*
236:19 hence, *MS*, *TS2*] ~ *TS1*, *E1*
236:20 majority *MS*, *Per*] the majority *TS2*
236:20 Puritans, *MS*, *Per*] ~ *TS2*
236:21 some] some of *TS1*
236:31 Odi *TS1*] Odio *MS*
236:31 vulgum. Profanum vulgum!] vulgus! Profanum vulgus. *TS1*, *E1* volgus! Profanum volgus. *TS2* vulgum! Profanum vulgum. *Per*
236:32 profanum vulgum.] *Om. TS1*
237:2 —Quite] ~ *TS1*
237:6 obscenity, *MS*, *Per*] ~ *TS2*
237:8 *Vox* [in italics] . . . *Dei*] Vox . . . Dei *TS1*
237:9 —At] ~ *TS1*
237:10 *vox Dei*] vox Dei *TS1*
237:10 movie-pictures] moving-pictures *TS1*
237:14 *Vox* [in italics] . . . *Dei*] Vox . . . Dei *TS1* Vox . . . Dei, *E1*
237:19 *Vox* [in italics] . . . *Dei*] Vox . . . Dei *TS1*
237:21 *Deus ex machina*] Deus ex machina *TS1*
237:26 forever . . . mob-meaning, *MS*, *Per*] *Om. TS2*
237:27 *bread MS*, *Per*] bread *TS2*
237:28 loaves,] ~ *TS1*
237:28 —But] ~ *TS1*
237:29 *bread*] bread *TS1*
237:31 unleavened *MS*, *Per*] unleaved *TS2*
237:34 *bread*] bread *TS1*
237:36 *bread*] bread *TS1*
237:38 imaginative *MS*, *E1*] imagination *Per*
238:2 *almost MS*, *Per*] almost *TS2*
238:4 meaning] ~, *TS1*
238:9 mob self] mob-self *TS1*
238:15 feeble-minded *MS*, *Per*] feeble minded *TS2*
238:23 individual-meanings *MS*, *TS2*] individual meanings *TS1*, *E1*
238:23 vulgar, *MS*, *Per*] ~ *TS2*
238:32 mob self?—] mob-self? *TSI*, *Per* mob-self. *TS2*
238:36 thoughts,] ~ *TS1*
238:37 Am *MS*, *Per*] am *TS1*, *E1*
238:37 *really MS*, *Per*] really *TS1*, *E1*
238:37 *really MS*, *Per*] really *TS2*
238:37 indignant? —] ~? *TS1*
238:38 And . . . [238:40] nor indignant. *MS*, *Per*] *Om. TS2*
238:38 who has . . . sincerely,] *Om. TS1*
239:1 molehill] mole-hill *TS1*
239:2 world.—] ~. *TS1*
239:5 word-prudery] word prudery *TS1*
239:10 pornographic: *MS*, *Per*] ~; *TS2*
239:12 Pornography] pornography *TS1*
239:15 *intended MS*, *Per*] intended *TS2*
239:22 However —!] ~! *TS1*
239:22 *pornography MS*, *Per*] pornography *TS2*
239:29 — And] ~ *TS1*
239:31 stirring] stirrings *TS1*
239:31 perverts,] ~ *TS1*
239:37 ipso facto] *ipso facto E1*

239:40 Song of Solomon *MS*, *TS2*] *Song of Solomon TS1*, *Per*
240:9 hallucinations!] ~? *TS1*
240:21 so,] ~ *TS1*
240:22 *not MS*, *Per*] not *TS2*
240:26 British *MS*, *Per*] late British *TS1*, *E1*
240:26 who *MS*, *Per*] whose *TS2*
240:30 together — !!!!" —] ~!!!" *TS1*
240:30 *One* [in italics] . . . *them! MS*, *Per*] One . . . them! *TS2*
240:40 it,] ~ *TS1*
241:9 instances] instance *TS1*
241:9 post-cards] post-card *TS1*
241:10 underhand *MS*, *E1*] under hand *TS1*
241:20 smoke-room *MS*, *Per*] smokeroom *TS2*
241:21 ugly,] ~ *TS1*
241:21 repellant] repellent *E2*
241:24 too often] just *TS1*
241:28 squalid,] ~ *TS1*
241:30 Heaven] heaven *E2*
241:33 be sneaking] to sneak *TS1*
241:35 a] and a *TS1*
241:36 ordinary] ~, *TS1*
241:38 carriages] ~, *TS1*
241:40 to] toward *TS1*
242:2 to] toward *TS1*
242:11 a neuter *MS*, *Per*] neuter *TS2*
242:12 washed-out *MS*, *Per*] whashed-out *TS2*
242:14 nude] *Om. TS1*
242:17 dirt-lust *MS*, *Per*] dirt lust *TS2*, *E1*
242:17 sex . . . in *MS*, *Per*] ~ functions in *TS2*
242:25 *This MS, Per*] This *TS2*
242:26 vulgar . . . pornography] vulgar and of pornographical people *TS1*
242:32 *Vox* [in italics] . . . *Dei*] Vox populi, vox Dei *TS1*
242:36 Bronte *MS*, *E1*] Brontë *Per*, *E2*
242:38 Rochester's *MS*, *Per*] Rochester' *TS2*
242:39 burnt] burned *TS1*
242:39 disfigured,] ~ *TS1*
243:6 nineteenth-century *MS*, *E1*] nineteenth century *TS1*
243:7 them, and *MS*, *Per*] them, never was the pornographical side to them and *TS2*
243:9 disease is . . . [243:11] come] ~ ~ to come *TS1*
243:16 us] *Om. TS1*
243:26 Home Secretaries] guardians *E1*
243:28 secret. —] ~. *TS1*, *E1* ~: *TS2*
243:31 scratched, *MS*, *E1*] ~ *TS2*
243:37 secretive, *MS*, *E1]* ~ *TS2*
243:37 furtive *MS*, *E1*] *Om. TS2*
243:38 sex *MS*, *TS2*] *Om. TS1*, *E1*
244:1 sneaking, *MS*, *E1*] ~ *TS2*
244:6 grey . . . other] *Om. E1*
244:15 rubber-goods *MS*, *E1*] rubber goods *TS2*
244:16 film, *MS*, *TS2*] ~ *TS1*, *E1*
244:17 self abuse] self-abuse *E2*
245:2 — If] ~ *TS1*
245:3 then *MS*, *E1*] there *TS2*
245:13 humiliation, *MS*, *TS2*] ~ *TS1*, *E1*
245:21 civilisation. *P* Instead *MS*, *TS2*] ~. Instead *TS1*, *E1*
245:24 with, *MS*, *E1*] ~ *TS2*
245:29 where *MS*, *E1*] whose *TS2*
245:40 way . . . criticism, *MS*, *E1*] *Om. TS2*
246:2 sentimentalism *MS*, *TS2*] sentimentalities *TS1*, *E1*
246:3 self-analysis, *MS*, *E1*] ~ *TS2*
246:14 The . . . reign. *MS*, *TS2*] (The . . . reign.) *TS1* the nineteenth century *E1*
246:16 emptying *MS*, *E1*] emphasizing *TS2*
246:20 self-pre-occupied] self-preoccupied *E1*
246:23 nullus *MS*, *E1*] nullos *TS2*
246:28 If *MS*, *TS2*] '~ *TS1*, *E1*
246:29 then *MS*, *E1*] these *TS2*
246:30 smoking room] smoking-room *E1*
246:30 story.—] ~.' *TS1*, *E1* ~ — *TS2*
246:30 it *MS*, *E1*] is *TS2*

246:30 depends *MS*, *TS2*] ~ on *TS1*, *E1*
246:31 Who . . . she? *MS*, *TS2] Who* [in italics] . . . *she? TS1*, *E1*
246:31 — then *MS*, *E1*] ~ *TS2*
246:34 *Blume*! *MS*, *E1*] ~? *TS2*
246:36 tickling *MS*, *E1*] Tickling *TS2*
246:38 — in *MS*, *E1*] ~ *TS2*
246:40 or *MS*, *TS2*] and *TS1*, *E1*
247:4 glad, *MS*, *TS2*] ~ *E1*
247:5 — But *MS*, E1*]* ~ *TS2*
247:6 — Away *MS*, *E1*] ~ *TS2*
247:9 love-lyric *MS*, *E1*] love-lyrics *TS2*
247:9 — "My] "~ *TS1*
247:9 My . . . rose *MS*, *TS2*] *My* [in italics] . . . *rose E1*
247:10 ground. *MS*, *E1*] ~ *TS2*
247:14 other. *Du MS*, *E1*] ~. *P Du TS2*
247:16 — But *MS*, *TS2*] ~ *TS1*, *E1*
247:18 rose? *MS*, *TS2*] ~. *TS1*, *E1*
247:23 friends — *MS*, *E1*] ~, *TS2*
247:24 time, *MS*, *E1*] ~ *E2*
247:26 circle! *MS*, *E1*] ~. *TS2*
247:32 My . . . begetting you *MS*, *TS2*] "my . . . you" *TS1* 'My . . . you' *E1*
247:35 rid *MS*, *TS2*] out *TS1*, *E1*
247:38 hypocritical *MS*, *TS2*] hypothetical *TS1*
247:39 serious *MS*, *E1*] *Om*. *TS2*
248:2 it *MS*, *E1*] ~, *TS2*
248:14 bohemia] Bohemia *E1*
248:21 bohemia] Bohemia *E1*
248:23 killed, *MS*, *E1*] ~ *TS2*
248:29 its *MS*, *E1*] ~, *TS2*
248:31 everywhere *MS*, *E1*] ~, *TS2*
248:40 She can't! . . . triumphs. *MS*, *E1*] *Om*. *TS2*
249:2 encloses *E1*] enclose *MS*
249:7 — But *MS*, *E1*] ~ *TS2*
249:8 under *MS*, *E1*] *Om*. *TS2*
249:10 of the *MS*, *TS2*] of *TS1*
249:11 Nineteenth Century] nineteenth century *TS1*
249:16 ones *MS*, *E1*] one *TS2*
249:16 It doesn't . . . is. *MS*, *E1*] *Om*, *TS2*
249:17 They are all grey ones, *MS*, *E1*] *Om*. *TS2*
249:19 young:] ~; *E2*
249:24 feebleness, *MS*, *E1*] ~ *TS2*
249:28 in *MS*, *TS2*] of *TS1*, *E1*
249:30 generations;] ~, *TS1*
249:31 19th century] nineteenth century *E1*
250:3 Narcissus . . . Narcissus] narcissus . . . narcissus *E1*
250:4 audience. *P* The *MS*, *TS2*] ~. The *TS1*, *E1*
250:6 re-appears] reappears *E1*
250:19 wherever *MS*, *TS2*] whenever *TS1*, *E1*
250:20 self-enclosure. *MS*, *E1*] ~, *TS2*
250:21 And wherever . . . self-enclosure, *MS*,*E1*] *Om*. *TS2*
250:21 wherever] whenever *TS1*, *E1*
250:25 it, *MS*, *E1*] ~. *TS2*
250:31 self-consciousness: *MS*, *E1*] ~. *TS2*
250:37 outside world *MS*, *TS2*] world outside *TS1*, *E1*
250:37 19th Century] nineteenth century *TS2*
251:9 reality. *MS*, *E1*] ~, *TS2*
251:10 It is . . . to myself *MS*, *TS2*] from the lie of myself, from the lie of my all-importance, even to myself; it is freedom. It is first freedom from myself *TS1*
251:11 all-importance *MS*, *E1*] all importance *TS2*
251:17 defenseless *MS*, *TS2*] defenceless *TS1*, *E1*
251:26 Century] century *TS1*
251:36 '*censorship*'] "*censorship*" *TS1* *censorship TS2* 'Censorship *E1*
251:36 *Books*] *books TS1* Books' *E1*
251:37 the new] *Om*. *TS2*
251:37 late] the late *E1*
252:12 roll. —] ~. *TS1*, *E1* ~: — *TS2*
252:14 He discriminates . . . *Loneliness?*] *Om*. *E1*

252:16 How do . . . [252:24] *Loneliness?*] *Om. E1*
252:24 What] Yet what *E1*
252:29 themselves. *P* But] ~. But *TS1*
252:31 smash the *MS*, *E1*] smash a *TS2*
252:32 19th century] nineteenth century *TS2*
252:39 Sir James . . . mass of] many contemporary writers, both big and *E1*
253:1 in the] in *The E1*
253:4 Thou . . . quietness] *Thou* [in italics] . . . *quietness E1*
253:14 bewildered,] ~ *TS1*
253:17 organs *MS*, *TS2*] organ *TS1*, *E1*
253:17 or *MS*. *E1*] of *TS2*
253:20 *pudenda MS*, *E1*] pudenda *TS2*
253:27 of *MS*, *E1*] if *TS2*
253:27 even . . . Secretaries] (even . . . Secretaries) *TS2 Om. E1*
253:28 a dirty *MS*, *TS2*] dirty *TS1*, *E1*
253:29 secret] secrets *E1*
253:29 masturbation *MS*, *E1*] ~. *TS2*
253:31 Perhaps,] ~ *TS1*
253:32 us! *MS*, *TS2*] ~. *TS1*, *E1*

Pictures on the Wall

The chronological sequence is *TS*, *Per1*, *Per2*, *E1*.

257:1 **Pictures on the Wall** *Ed.*] PICTURES ON THE WALLS. *TS* dead pictures on the walls/ BY D. H. LAWRENCE *Per1* Pictures on the Walls. / *By* D. H. Lawrence. *Per2* PICTURES ON THE WALLS *E1*
257:2 wall-pictures] wall pictures *E1*
257:3 Yet *TS*, *E1*] ~, *Per2*
257:7 alike, *TS*, *E1*] ~; *Per1* ~ — *Per2*
257:9 room, *TS*, *E1*] ~ *Per2*
257:10 rule,] ~ *E1*
257:11 past, *TS*, *E1*] ~ *Per2*
257:15 say, *TS*, *E1*] ~: *Per1*
257:15 Now . . . [257:18] keeping? *TS*, *Per2*] *Now* [in italics] . . . *keeping? Per1*
257:16 oil-painting,] ~ *E1*
257:18 keeping? — *TS*, *E1*] ~? *Per2*
257:19 be *TS*, *E1*] ~, *Per2*
257:19 No *TS*, *E1*] *No Per1*
257:19 say, *TS*, *E1*] ~: *Per1*
257:19 Oh, . . . them!— *TS*, *E1*] *Oh*, [in italics] . . . *them!— Per1* Oh, . . . them! *Per2*
257:22 I've . . . years. — *TS*, *E1*] *I've*[in italics] . . . *years.— Per1* I've . . . years. *Per2*
257:25 Spring-cleaning] Spring cleaning *Per2*
257:27 change, *TS*, *E1*] ~ *Per2*
257:27 imagine *TS*, *Per2*] try to imagine *Per1*
257:32 close *TS*, *Per2*] closely *Per1*
258:1 room: *TS*, *E1*] ~ — *Per2*
258:1 cushions; *TS*, *E1*] ~, *Per1* ~ — *Per2*
258:2 life-time] lifetime *Per2*
258:3 is,] ~ *Per2*
258:6 especially *TS*, *Per2*] ~, *Per1*
258:6 we live *TS*, *Per2*] one lives *Per1*
258:6 our *TS*, *Per2*] the *Per1*
258:9 in us *TS*, *Per2*] *Om. Per1*
258:16 charm, *TS*, *E1*] ~; *Per1*
258:19 brown,] ~ *E1*
258:21 change: *TS*, *E1*] ~, *Per2*
258:25 two, *TS*, *E1*] ~ *Per2*
258:26 life-time] lifetime *Per2*
258:27 life-times] lifetimes *Per2*
258:28 sort,] ~ *Per2*
258:29 remains, *TS*, *Per2*] ~: *Per1* ~ *E1*
258:32 us, *TS*, *E1*] ~ *Per2*
258:32 Michael Angelo *TS*, *E1*] Michaelangelo *Per2*
258:34 Michael Angelo *TS*, *E1*] Michaelangelo *Per2*

258:34 keep *TS*, *Per2*] kept *Per1*
258:37 Landseer, *TS*, *E1*] ~ *Per2*
259:1 dogs:] ~, *Per2*
259:1 the *TS*, *Per2*] a *Per1*
259:2 immensely *TS*, *Per2*] ~, *Per1*
259:3 years,] ~ *Per2*
259:6 are, . . . taste. *TS*, *Per2*] are. *Per1*
259:9 which *TS*, *Per2*] ~ are pictures that *Per1*
259:10 none. *TS*, *E1*] ~? *Per2*
259:11 Portrait . . . Mother] portrait . . . mother *Per1*, *E1* *Portrait* [in italics] . . . *Mother* *Per2*
259:11 advertisement *TS*, *Per2*] an advertisement *Per1*
259:12 appeal, *TS*, *E1*] ~ *Per2* become *TS*, *Per2*] becomes *Per1*
259:14 forever] for ever *Per2*
259:17 bride,] ~ *Per2*
259:21 that *TS*, *Per2*] a *Per1*
259:25 interest — *TS*, *E1*] ~ *Per2*
259:25 lovely, *TS*, *E1*] ~ *Per2*
259:29 doornails *TS*, *E1*] doornail *Per2*
259:33 another.— *TS*, *E1*] ~. *Per1*
259:33 Which we do *TS*, *Per2*] This is done *Per1*
259:34 manufacture *TS*, *E1*] produce *Per2*
259:36 regarded, *TS*, *Per2*] ~ *Per1*
259:39 ten shillings *TS*, *Per2*] two or three dollars *Per1*
259:40 ten shillings *TS*, *Per2*] our dollars *Per1*
259:40 two guineas *TS*, *Per2*] twenty dollars *Per1*
260:2 two guineas *TS*, *Per2*] the money *Per1*
260:4 embroidery.— *TS*, *E1*] ~. *Per1*
260:5 two pounds *TS*, *E1*] ten dollars *Per1* £2 *Per2*
260:8 real *TS*, *Per2*] ~, *Per1*
260:9 In . . . [260:12]flower. *TS*, *Per2*] *Om. Per1*
260:9 school,] ~ *Per2*
260:10 away!— *TS*, *E1*] ~! *Per2*
260:13 dead *TS*, *Per2*] once dead *Per1*
260:15 room, *TS*, *E1*] ~ *Per1*
260:18 course] ~, *E1*
260:20 decoration, *TS*, *E1*] ~ *Per1*
260:24 be done in *TS*, *Per2*] indeed be unfortunate *Per1*
260:26 half-an-hour *TS*, *Per2*] half an hour *Per1*, *E1*
260:29 half-an-hour *TS*, *Per2*] half an hour *Per1*, *E1*
260:31 nude . . . colour, *TS*, *Per2*] *Om. Per1*
260:31 Friesz] Fricsz *E1*
260:32 two, *TS*, *E1*] ~ *Per2*
260:34 the Titian *TS*, *Per2*] Titian's *Per1*
260:35 at: *TS*, *E1*] ~; *Per2*
260:36 life, *TS*, *E1*] ~. *Per1* ~ *Per2*
260:36 and . . . delightful *TS*, *Per2*] *Om. Per1*
260:37 Picassos,] ~ *E1*
260:38 Braque *TS*, *Per2*] Braques *Per1*
260:39 year: *TS*, *E1*] ~; *Per2*
260:39 probably *TS*, *Per2*] possibly *Per1*
260:40 Romney *TS*, *Per2*] ~, *Per1*
261:1 individual *TS*, *Per2*] ~, *Per1*
261:2 present,] ~ *E1*
261:4 *property* *TS*, *E1*] "property" *Per2*
261:5 But . . . [261:8]clearance. *TS*, *Per2*] *Om. Per1*
261:8 all, *TS*, *E1*] ~ — *Per2*
261:9 Harrod's *TS*, *Per2*] the department store *Per1* Harrods *E1*
261:9 sake,] ~ *Per2*
261:10 twenty guineas *TS*, *Per2*] a hunded dollars *Per1*
261:11 time *TS*, *Per2*] ~, *Per1*
261:11 twenty guineas *TS*, *Per2*] a hundred dollars *Per1*
261:12 Harrod's *TS*, *Per2*] the department store *Per1* Harrods *E1*
261:12 Picture scheme *TS*, *Per2*] Pictures *Per1*

261:13 circulating library *TS*, *Per2*] Circulating Library *Per1*
261:13 circulating libraries *TS*, *Per2*] Circulating Libraries *Per1*
261:14 content *TS*, *Per2*] contents *Per1*
261:16 Harrod's *TS*, *Per2*] the stores *Per1* Harrods *E1*
261:20 us: *TS*, *Per2*] ~, *Per1*
261:20 wish: *TS*, *E1*] ~; *Per2*
261:24 art, *TS*, *E1*] ~ *Per2* artists, *TS*, *Per2*] artist *Per1*
261:24 paintings:] ~; *Per1*
261:26 buy:] ~; *Per1*
261:27 joy,] ~ *Per2*
261:29 There . . . [261:35] them. *TS*, *E1*] *Om. Per2*
261:32 They . . . [261:35] them. *TS*, *E1*] *Om. Per1*
261:33 great":] ~"; *E1*
261:34 years:] ~; *E1*
261:36 Now *TS*, *Per2*] *Om. Per1*
262:1 life, *TS*, *E1*] ~ *Per2*
262:5 horrific *TS*, *Per2*] *Om. Per1*
262:15 just *TS*, *Per2*] merely *Per1*
262:16 dare never *TS*, *Per2*] never dare *Per1*
262:19 five-guinea . . . days *TS*, *Per2*] days *Per1*
262:21 squire *TS*, *Per2*] cultivated *Per1*
262:21 reading-public] reading public *Per1*
262:27 books, *TS*, *Per2*] ~ *Per1*
262:27 till *TS*, *Per2*] until *Per1*
262:28 estate, *TS*, *Per2*] ~ *Per1*
262:32 —he] He *Per2* he *E1*
262:32 say: *TS*, *E1*] ~ *Per2*
262:32 eighteenth century *TS*, *Per2*] Eighteenth Century *Per1*
262:33 example *in folio TS*, *Per2*] ~, *in folio*, *Per1*
262:34 — and] ~ *Per1*
262:39 When . . . [263:2] personally. *P* There *TS*, *E1*] *P* There *Per1* When . . . personally. There *Per2*
263:5 hopelessly *TS*, *E1*] ~, *Per2*
263:6 them,] ~; *Per2* ~, *E1*
263:7 few, *TS*, *E1*] ~ *Per2*
263:8 time, *TS*, *E1*] ~ *Per2*
263:9 want *TS*, *E1*] ~, *Per2*
263:9 things *TS*, *E1*] ~, *Per2*
263:10 we *TS*, *E1*] I *Per2*
263:12 them, *TS*, *E1*] ~ *Per2*
263:16 are: *TS*, *Per2*] ~ — *Per1* ~, *E1*
263:17 silks, *TS*, *Per2*] ~; *Per1*
263:17 beyond . . . time:] *Om. Per1* ~ . . . ~; *Per2*
263:18 now . . . days *TS*, *Per2*] means hours *Per1*
263:22 simple *TS*, *Per2*] a simple *Per1*
263:23 for . . . and *TS*, *Per2*] is the opportunity for the department stores and *Per1*
263:25 or purchase *TS*, *Per2*] *Om. Per1*
263:25 Today . . . [264:17] books. *TS*, *Per2*] *Om. Per1*
263:30 entertaining, *TS*, *E1*] ~; *Per2*
263:32 entertained *TS*, *E1*] ~, *Per2*
263:32 and, *TS*, *E1*] ~ *Per2*
263:32 sometimes, *TS*, *E1*] ~ *Per2*
263:37 studios, *TS*, *E1*] ~ *Per2*
263:38 stale:] ~, *Per2* ~; *E1*
264:2 pictures, *TS*, *E1*] ~ *Per2*
264:7 twenty pounds . . . ten pounds . . . five pounds *TS*, *E1*] £20 . . . £10 . . . £5 *Per2*
264:9 shy, *TS*, *E1*] ~; *Per2*

The Risen Lord

The chronological sequence is *MS*, *TS*, *Per*, *E1*. (In *TS*, *Per* and *E1*, pronouns relating to Jesus Christ are capitalised; in *Per*, 'Heaven' is capitalised; none of these is recorded below.)

267:1 **The Risen Lord** *Ed.*] The Risen Lord. / by D. H. Lawrence. *MS* THE RISEN LORD. *TS* THE RISEN LORD /By D. H. LAWRENCE *Per* THE RISEN LORD *E1*

267:2 "The . . . nesh"] "~ . . . ~." *TS*, *E1* ~ . . . ~. *Per*

267:2 lord . . . lord *MS*, *E1*] Lord . . . Lord *Per*

267:3 has *MS*, *E1*] Has *Per*

267:4 and *MS*, *E1*] And *Per*

267:5 though *MS*, *E1*] Though *Per*

267:6 churches] Churches *TS*

267:6 crucified! — *MS*, *E1*] Crucified! *Per*

267:7 doing, *MS*, *E1*] ~ *Per*

267:7 passion,] ~ *Per* Passion, *E1*

267:8 Creed *TS*] ⌐Litany¬ <Creed> *MS*

267:8 "Was *TS*] Was *MS*

267:8 . . . the third . . . dead." *TS*] and rose again on the third day *MS*

267:8 And, again, . . . body . . ." *TS*] and the Creed says: I believe in the resurrection of the flesh —. *MS* And, again: "I . . . body . . . " *Per*

267:12 Christmas —;] ~; *Per*

267:12 crucified, *MS*, *E1*] Crucified *Per*

267:13 Risen, *MS*, *E1*] ~ — *Per*

267:19 Christ Child] Christ-Child *Per* Christ-child *E1*

267:21 preparatory, *MS*, *E1*] ~; *Per*

267:22 Christ Child] Christ-Child *Per* Christ-child *E1*

267:26 experience] experiences *E1*

267:27 Countries] countries *TS*

267:28 Christ Child] Christ-Child *TS*

267:29 war *MS*, *E1*] War *Per*

267:31 *Oh MS*, *Per*] ~, *TS*, *E1*

267:31 — The *MS*, *E1*] ~ *Per*

267:33 the child] a child *TS*

267:33 saviour-child,] ~ *TS*

268:3 war, *MS*, *E1*] War *Per*

268:4 war, *MS*, *E1*] War *Per*

268:6 nor wife] no wife *E1*

268:8 Christ-child *MS*, *E1*] Christ-Child *Per*

268:9 crucified *MS*, *E1*] Crucified *Per*

268:12 Christ-child *MS*, *E1*] Christ-Child *Per*

268:14 significance; *MS*, *E1*] ~ *Per*

268:16 man *MS*, *Per*] men *TS* , *E1*

268:16 war *MS*, *TS*, *E1*] War *Per*

268:16 him] them *E1*

268:17 Christ Child] Christ-child *TS*, *E1* Christ-Child *Per*

268:21 men, *MS*, *E1*] ~ *Per*

268:21 war *MS*, *E1*] War *Per*

268:22 Woman *MS*, *E1*] woman *Per*

268:24 it, *MS*, *E1*] ~ *Per*

268:24 Christ Child] Christ-child *TS*, *E1* Christ-Child *Per*

268:25 war,] War, *Per* war *E1*

268:28 war *MS*, *E1*] War *Per*

268:29 Christ-child *MS*, *E1*] Christ-Child *Per*

268:36 Christ-child *MS*, *E1*] Christ-Child *Per*

268:37 safe-guard] safeguard *Per*

268:40 crucified] Crucified *TS*

269:1 as] — ~ *TS*

269:2 Thirdly] ~, *TS*

269:13 stage, *MS*, *E1*] ~ *Per*

269:14 Christ-child *MS*, *E1*] Christ-Child *Per*

269:14 saviour] Saviour *Per* savour *E1*

269:17 life, *MS*, *E1*] ~ *Per*

269:19 women] woman *TS*

269:22 The] the *Per*

269:23 Christ Child] Christ-Child *TS* Christ-child *E1*

269:23 crucified] Crucified *TS*

269:25 vision *MS*, *E1*] visions *Per*

269:26 Christ Child] Christ-Child *Per* Christ-child *E1*

269:26 crucified] Crucified *TS*

269:29 young, *MS*, *E1*] ~ *Per*

269:29 Christ Child] Christ-Child *Per* Christ-child *E1*

269:33 onwards, *MS*, *E1*] ~ *Per*

270:5 plum-blossoms] plum blossoms *E1*
270:9 passion *MS*, *E1*] Passion *Per*
270:10 in *MS*, *E1*] of *Per*
270:10 sacrifice] ~, *TS*
270:15 we] We *Per*
270:31 inward-experience] inward experience *TS*
270:32 flesh and blood *MS*, *Per*] flesh-and-blood *TS*
270:35 earth, *MS*, *Per*] ~ *TS*
270:37 flesh and blood *MS*, *Per*] flesh-and-blood *TS*, *E1*
270:37 rose *MS*, *E1*] ~, *Per*
271:2 state,] ~ *Per*
271:16 way. If *MS*, *E1*] ~. *P* If *Per*
271:19 two-ness] twoness *Per*
271:24 them. If *MS*, *E1*] ~. *P* If *Per*
271:25 man friend] man-friend *TS*
271:28 flesh] ~, *TS*
271:31 shavings. If *MS*, *E1*] ~. *P* If *Per*
271:39 Luckily] ~, *TS*
271:40 conceit. But *MS*, *E1*] ~. *P* But *Per*
272:1 and] And *E1*
272:2 Well . . . here] ~, . . . ~, *TS*
272:4 Satan *MS*, *E1*] ~, *Per*
272:5 them. The *MS*, *E1*] ~. *P* The *Per*
272:11 nothing. Whom *MS*, *E1*] ~. *P* Whom *Per*
272:13 Lord's,] ~ *E1*
272:16 your *Per*] you *MS*
272:21 possession. For *MS*, *E1*] ~. *P* For *Per*
272:23 me . . . my *MS*, *E1*] Me . . . My *Per*
272:26 Mammon:] ~; *E1*
272:27 values, *MS*, *E1*] ~. *Per*
272:29 tree:]~; *E1*
272:31 song] ~, *E1*
272:34 Oh] O *TS*
272:36 him—*MS*, *E1*] ~, *TS*
273:8 men —] ~. *E1*

Men Must Work and Women as Well

The chronological sequence is *MS*, *TS*, *Per*, *E1*.

275:1 **Men Must Work and Women as Well** *Ed.*] Men and Women / D. H. Lawrence *MS* <MEN AND WOMEN> ⌐Men Must Work and Women as Well¬ *TS* Men and Women. / BY D. H. LAWRENCE *Per* MEN MUST WORK AND / WOMEN AS WELL *E1*
275:10 railway train *MS*, *E1*] railway-train *TS*
275:21 handbags *MS*, *E1*] hand-bags *TS*
275:23 that] ~, *TS*
276:3 The great . . . yourself.] *Om.* *TS*
276:14 but] '~' *TS*
276:21 every one] everyone *TS*
276:24 woman —] ~, *TS*
276:27 over:] ~; *E1*
276:28 scrubbing:] ~; *E1*
276:33 *Is*] Is *TS*
276:36 pittance,] ~ *E1*
277:1 work — like] ~ ~ *TS*
277:14 tea-cups] teacups *Per*
277:19 beefsteak] beef-steak *TS*
277:21 potatoes] ~, *TS*
277:31 repellant] repellent *TS*
277:32 repellant] repellent *TS*
277:36 dinner things] dinner-things *TS*
277:39 What then] ~, ~, *TS*
278:6 house-wife] housewife *TS*
278:7 it —] ~, *TS*
278:28 Why] ~, *TS*
278:30 beefsteaks . . . beefsteaks] beef-steaks . . . beef-steaks *TS*
278:32 continues] ~, *TS*
278:34 super-factories –] ~. *TS*

278:36 did;] ~, *E1*
278:39 coal seam] coal-seam *TS*
279:10 working-classes] working classes *E1*
279:12 schools however] ~, ~, *TS*
279:15 school-teacher] school teacher *E1*
279:15 collier. —] ~. *TS*
279:20 mining-district] mining district *TS*
279:20 ninety] 90 *E1*
279:20 percent] per cent *TS*, *E1* per cent. *Per*
279:21 ninety] 90 *E1*
279:21 per cent *MS*, *E1*] per cent. *Per*
279:22 malcontents:] ~, *E1*
279:27 ninety] 90 *E1*
279:27 per-cent] per cent *TS* per cent. *Per*
279:28 school-teachers] school teachers *E1*
279:37 malcontent. *P* Now] ~. Now *TS*
280:1 levers. And] ~, and, *TS*
280:4 where *MS*, *E1*] when *Per*
280:5 smelted,] ~ *E1*
280:6 Ford] Ford's *E1*
280:13 laborer] labourer *TS*
280:17 intensely. — *MS*, *E1*] ~. *Per* time] ~, *TS*
280:18 board] Board *E1*
280:20 conditions,] ~ *TS*
280:22 do do] do *TS*
280:24 themselves." Which] ~", which *TS*
280:25 abandoned:] ~, *E1*
280:28 laborers] labourers *TS*
280:37 then] ~, *TS*
280:39 it. Which] ~: which *E1*
280:39 sounds] ~, *E1*
280:40 is] ~, *E1* fatuous:] ~. *TS*
281:4 work. —] ~. *E1*
281:5 work. *P* But *MS*, *E1*] ~. But *TS*
281:12 home life] home-life *TS*
281:14 house-work] housework *E1*
281:14 house-keeping] housekeeping *E1*
281:21 house-wives] housewives *E1*
281:33 own —] ~, *TS*
282:13 woman] women *TS*
282:14 husbands-and-wives] husbands and wives *TS*
283:10 long run] ~, ~ *TS*
283:11 of our . . . "spirituality",] *Om.* *TS*
283:13 refinement:] ~; *E1*
283:13 fastidiousness:] ~; *E1*
283:14 feeling:] ~; *E1*
283:14 flat thin] ~, ~, *TS*
283:16 caricature: what] ~. What *E1*
283:25 flesh-and-blood] flesh and blood *E1*
283:30 working man *MS*, *E1*] working-man *TS*
283:34 the beer] beer *TS*
283:35 women,] ~, — *TS* ~ — *E1*
283:35 showy] *Om.* *TS*
283:36 the] an *TS*
284:8 social *MS*, *E1*] *Om.* *Per*
284:9 spirituality",] ~" *E1*
284:11 insanity. We] ~: we *TS*
284:13 fact] ~, *TS*
284:17 even] *Om.* *E1*
284:19 materialised,] ~ *TS*
284:21 it] ~, *TS*
284:24 and] ~, *TS*

Nottingham and the Mining Countryside

The chronological sequence is *MS*, *TS*, *Per1*, *Per2*, *A1*. (In *MS* 'Company' is capitalised, elsewhere it is not; the variants are not listed.)

287:1 **Nottingham and the Mining Countryside** *Ed.*] Nottingham and the Mining Countryside/ by D. H. Lawrence *MS* *NOTTINGHAM AND THE MINING COUNTRYSIDE.* *TS* NOTTINGHAM AND THE /MINING COUNTRYSIDE / *By* D. H. Lawrence *Per1* Then Disaster Looms Ahead / Mining-Camp Civilization. / The English Contribution to Progress. / *By* D. H. Lawrence. *Per2* NOTTINGHAM AND THE MINING / COUNTRYSIDE *A1*
287:26 machinery,] ~ *TS*
287:30 mole-skin] moleskin *TS*
288:3 in in *MS*, *Per1*] in *TS*, *A1*
288:9 it *MS*, *Per1*] *Om. TS*
288:16 side,] ~ *TS*
288:20 grim] ~, *TS*
288:21 W.C.] w.c. *TS*
288:23 back yards *MS*, *A1*] backyards *Per2*
288:24 desert *MS*, *A1*] deserted *Per2*
288:28 The] the *TS*
288:35 Wesleyan *MS*, *Per1*] Wesleyans *TS* Wesleyans' *A1*
288:36 square] Square *TS*
288:37 big] ~, *TS*
288:37 Chapel] chapel *TS*
288:40 Sun Inn *MS*, *A1*] "~ ~" *Per2*
289:1 pestle-and-mortar *MS*, *A1*] pestle and mortar *Per2*
289:6 red-brick] ~, *TS*
289:9 Squares . . . Squares] squares . . . squares *TS*
289:12 Then *MS*, *A1*] ~, *Per2*
289:16 on,] ~ *TS*
289:20 trees:] ~, *TS*
289:21 dipped:] ~, *TS*
289:31 instinct, *MS*, *A1*] ~; *Per2*
289:33 system, *MS*, *A1*] ~ *Per2*
289:37 instinctive] ~, *A1*
290:1 Nevertheless] ~, *TS*
290:2 above-ground] above ground *A1*
290:3 contact, *MS*, *A1*] ~; *Per2*
290:10 colliers' *TS*] colliers *MS*
290:17 daylight,] ~ — *TS*
290:17 all,] ~ *TS*
290:18 weeks:] ~ — *TS*
290:18 herself,] ~ *TS*
290:23 drank,] ~ *TS*
290:27 pub:] ~, *TS*
290:30 women, *MS*, *Per1*] ~ *TS*, *A1*
290:31 it!—] ~! *TS*
290:32 that *MS*, *A1*] ~, *Per2*
290:32 from?—] ~? *TS*
290:34 countryside,] ~ *Per2*
290:38 Very often, *MS*, *A1*] ~ ~ *Per2*
290:39 often,] ~ *TS*
290:40 and often, *MS*, *A1*] ~ ~ *Per2*
291:5 —And] ~ *TS*
291:20 him] ~, *TS*
291:20 sense,] ~ *TS*
291:21 it,] ~; *TS*
291:25 generation, *MS*, *A1*] ~ *Per2*
291:35 Now *MS*, *A1*] ~, *Per2*
292:12 Squares] squares *Per2*
292:15 space:] ~, *TS*
292:17 If *MS*, *A1*] ~, *Per2*
292:28 castle] ~, *TS*
292:28 etc. — *MS*, *Per2*] ~. *TS*
292:30 square,] ~ *TS*
292:31 W. C.] w.c. *Per1*
292:33 Anyhow] ~, *TS*
293:12 castle" —] ~" *TS*
293:16 farm-laborer] farm-labourer *TS*, *A1* farm labourer, *Per2*
293:20 pseudo-cottagey] pseudo-cottagy *A1*
293:27 betrayed:] ~. *TS*
293:36 like *MS*, *Per1*] liked *TS*
294:10 as *TS*] as /as *MS*
294:11 nag all *MS*, *A1*] ~, ~ *Per2*
294:11 time *MS*, *A1*] ~, *Per2*

We Need One Another

The chronological sequence is *MS*, *Per*, *A1*.

296:1 **We Need One Another** *Ed.*] <Human Relationship> ⌐We Need One Another¬ / D. H. Lawrence *MS* We Need One Another / BY D. H. LAWRENCE *Per* WE NEED ONE ANOTHER *A1*
296:12 mine!",] ~" *Per*
296:13 woman:] ~, *Per*
296:16 rôle] role *A1*
296:20 is! —] ~. *Per*
297:1 Heaven,] heaven, *Per* heaven *A1*
297:4 Now] ~, *Per*
297:8 High?" —] ~?" *A1*
297:8 then] Then *A1*
297:9 answer,] ~ *A1*
297:14 Yes."] yes." *Per*
297:26 she? . . . he?] he? . . . she? *A1*
297:27 he?] ~?— *Per*
297:27 fellow *MS*, *A1*] flow *Per*
297:34 feathers,] ~ *Per*
298:2 trashy] ~, *Per*
298:2 silly] ~, *Per*
298:5 fine] fair *Per*
298:7 remains,] ~ *Per*
298:9 fag end] fag-end *Per*
298:16 wouldn't] would *Per*
298:17 much:] ~; *Per*
298:18 saving;] ~, *Per*
298:22 eighteenth century] eighteenth-century *Per*
298:28 nation,] ~; *Per*
298:30 greatness,] ~ *Per*
298:36 people] ~, *Per*
299:10 *become*] become *Per*
299:10 individuals, *MS*, *A1*] ~; *Per*
299:12 But] ~, *Per*
299:13 it. —] ~ — *Per*
299:14 That] that *A1*
299:24 — Or] Or *Per*
299:25 everyone *MS*, *A1*] every one *Per*
299:25 A man] ~ ~, *Per*
299:27 towards *MS*, *A1*] toward *Per*
299:27 some-one] some one *Per* someone *A1*
299:30 everyone *MS*, *A1*] every one *Per*
299:33 unconsciously — we]~. We *Per*
299:35 side,] ~ *Per*
299:37 labouring *MS*, *A1*] laboring *Per*
300:1 clamour *MS*, *A1*] clamor *Per*
300:3 rubbish heap]rubbish-heap *Per*
300:5 Marshal *Per*] Marshall *MS*
300:10 it:] ~, *Per*
300:17 dud] dead *Per*
300:27 fellow-men *MS*, *A1*] fellow men *Per*
300:27 myself,] ~ *Per*
300:33 clue *MS*, *A1*] clew *Per*
300:33 — And] ~ *Per*
301:7 time] ~, *Per*
301:13 And] ~, *Per*
301:16 sneeringly:] ~, *Per*
301:17 —I] ~ *Per*
301:18 — He] ~ *Per*
301:20 a hollow] hollow *Per* hollow, *A1*
301:22 But] And *Per*
301:26 so is] as to *Per*
301:35 — But] ~ *Per*
301:40 divorce,] ~ — *Per*
302:2 man.] ~? *Per*
302:3 itself,] ~; *Per*
302:4 Why oh] ~, ~, *Per*
302:5 menu-card *MS*, *A1*] menu card *Per*
302:5 changed.] ~? *Per*
302:11 forthcoming] ~, *Per*
302:21 forms,]~ *Per*
302:21 sweet-heart] sweetheart *Per*
302:22 rôle] role *A1*
302:23 sweet-heart] sweetheart *Per*
302:24 womanhood] woman *Per*
302:25 life] ~, *Per*
302:29 life-long . . . life-long *MS*, *A1*] lifelong . . . lifelong *Per*
302:32 life-time,] lifetime, *Per* life-time *A1*
302:33 most-vivid] most vivid, *Per*

The Real Thing

The chronological sequence is *MS*, *TS*, *Per*, *A1*.

304:1 **The Real Thing** *Ed.*] The Real Thing / D. H. Lawrence *MS* *THE REAL THING. TS* The Real Thing /BY D. H. LAWRENCE *Per* THE REAL THING *A1*
304:12 women: *MS*, *Per*] ~; *TS*, *A1*
304:14 bitter: *MS*, *Per*] ~, *TS*, *A1*
304:20 home. The *MS*, *Per*] ~. *P* The *TS*, *A1*
304:25 it: *MS*, *Per*] ~; *TS* , *A1*
305:22 himself,] ~; *TS*
305:23 began: *MS*, *Per*] ~, *TS*, *A1*
305:24 freedom. Which *MS*, *Per*] ~. *P* Which *TS*
305:28 another. Today] ~. *P* To-day *TS* ~. To-day *Per* ~. *P* Today *A1*
305:29 strung up] strung-up *TS*
305:35 have formed] have been formed *TS*
306:4 forever] for ever *A1*
306:7 vapour *MS*, *A1*] vapor *Per*
306:15 great-grandmothers: *MS*, *Per*]~; *TS*, *A1*
306:16 grandmothers:] ~; *TS*
306:19 children. We *MS*, *Per*] ~. *P* We *TS* , *A1*
306:20 now, the] ~ this *TS*
306:23 and therefore] that therefore *TS*, *A1* therefore *Per*
306:24 doomed. *P* We] ~. We *A1*
306:25 children: *MS*, *Per*] ~, *TS*, *A1*
306:27 phemonenal. And *MS*, *Per*] ~. *P* And *TS*
306:30 itself. And *MS*, *Per*] ~, and *TS*, *A1*
306:33 instinctively] ~, *TS*
307:8 her?] ~ *TS*
307:8 fraud)] ~)? *TS*
307:9 all—] ~. *TS*
307:13 inexorable. Why *MS*, *Per*] ~. *P* Why *TS*, *A1*
307:28 even] when *TS*
307:37 — do] Do *A1*
307:40 —It] ~ *TS*
308:2 creature: *MS*, *Per*] ~, *TS*, *A1*
308:5 is] Is *TS*
308:12 there, *MS*, *Per*] ~ *TS*, *A1*
308:14 liberation, the] ~, this *TS*
308:15 *is*] is *TS*
308:23 on other individuals *MS*, *Per*] or another individual *TS* , *A1*
308:23 man,] ~ *TS*
308:26 — delicately] ~ *TS*
308:27 egoism: *MS*, *A1*] ~ — *TS*
308:28 ones: *MS*, *A1*] ~ — *Per*
308:37 pieces:] ~, *TS*, *A1* ~; *Per*
308:39 behaviour *MS*, *A1*] behavior *Per*
309:1 rarified] rarefied *TS*
309:9 Cologne] cologne *TS*
309:11 banality: *MS*, *A1*] ~, *TS*
309:14 The . . . Rey,]"~ . . . ~," *Per The* [in italics] . . . *Rey A1*
309:15 film star] film-star *TS*
309:17 and] ~, *TS*
309:30 Fifth] fifth *TS*
309:30 they *MS*, *A1*] *Om. Per*
309:31 forlornness] ~, *TS*
309:32 new] other *TS*
309:32 that,] ~ *TS*
309:33 bus *MS*, *Per*] 'bus *TS*
309:35 bus *MS*, *Per*] 'bus *TS*
309:35 slang!] ~. *Per*
310:7 touch, *MS*, *Per*] ~ *TS*, *A1*
310:9 "World." . . . World] "world." . . . world *TS*
310:10 strength,] ~ *TS*
310:12 forever,] ~ *TS* for ever *A1*
310:17 avoided,] ~; *TS*
310:18 inwardly] outwardly *TS*
310:18 is once] ~. Once *TS*
310:19 sustenance. She] ~, she *TS*
310:23 for ever *MS*, *A1*] forever *Per*
310:28 re-born] reborn *Per*
310:28 re-vivified: that] revivified? That *TS*

Nobody Loves Me

The chronological sequence is *MS*, *TS*, *Per1*, *Per2*, *A1*.

313:1 **Nobody Loves Me** *Ed.*] Nobody Loves Me / D. H. Lawrence *MS* *NOBODY LOVES ME.* *TS* D. H. LAWRENCE NOBODY LOVES ME *Per1* NOBODY LOVES ME / By D. H. LAWRENCE *Per2* NOBODY LOVES ME *A1*
313:2 year] ~, *TS*
313:4 — "And] "~ *TS*
313:6 — "Well *MS*, *Per2*] '~ *Per1*, *A1*
313:8 opposite. —] ~, *TS*
313:9 well! — *MS*,*Per2*] Well! — *TS* well — *Per1*
313:10 of] *of TS*, *for A1*
313:10 *humanity* —] ~. *TS*
313:24 friends:] ~, *TS*
313:24 felt] felt that *A1*
314:3 spirit] ~, *TS*
314:3 fellow men] fellow-men *TS*
314:6 generalisation] generalisations *TS*, *Per2* generalizations *Per1*, *A1*
314:8 course] ~, *TS*
314:14 be *MS*, *Per2*] ~, *Per1*
314:16 cotton workers,] cotton-workers, *TS*, *A1* cotton-workers *Per2*
314:18 cotton workers] cotton-workers *TS*
314:19 rice-growers] rice growers *Per2*
314:19 China] ~, *TS*
314:19 me *MS*, *Per2*] ~, *Per1*
314:21 are all more] are more *A1*
314:31 mankind, *MS*, *Per2*] ~ *TS*
314:39 naïve *MS*, *Per2*] naive *TS*
315:9 brightly coloured *MS*, *A1*] brightly-coloured *TS*
315:17 benevolent] malevolent *TS*
315:24 Because *MS*, *Per2*] ~, *Per1*
315:25 time, *MS*, *Per2*] ~ *Per1*, *A1*
315:35 *Keep smiling*!] "Keep Smiling!" *Per2*
316:4 say: *MS*, *Per1*] ~, *TS*, *Per2*
316:4 *devoted*] devoted *TS*
316:7 —And] ~ *TS*
316:10 that *MS*, *Per2*] ~, *Per1*
316:11 Armenians *MS*, *Per2*] ~, *Per1*
316:11 Rubber negroes]~ ~, *Per1* rubber negroes *Per2* rubber Negroes *A1*
316:15 negroes] Negroes *A1*
316:16 English *MS*, *Per2*] ~, *Per1*
316:16 Turks *MS*, *Per2*] ~, *Per1*
316:17 severely —] ~. *TS*
316:20 No . . . me! *MS*, *Per2*] '~ . . . ~!'. *Per1*
316:23 cotton workers] cotton-workers *TS*
316:25 —And] ~ *TS*
316:31 forbears *MS*, *Per1*] forebears *TS*, *A1*
317:4 dear!—] ~! *TS*
317:5 light!"—] ~!" *TS*
317:12 music box] music-box *TS*
317:15 example. *MS*, *Per2*] ~: *Per1*
317:17 —At] ~*TS*
317:19 enquire *MS*, *Per2*] inquire *Per1*, *A1*
317:20 —they] ~ *TS*
317:20 fervently: *MS*, *Per2*] ~, *Per1*
317:21 Which] which *TS*
317:24 marriage bed] marriage-bed *TS*
317:30 burial service *MS*, *Per2*] Burial Service *Per1*
317:34 For *MS*, *Per2*] ~, *Per1*
317:34 young, *MS*, *Per2*] ~ *Per1*
317:36 emptiness,] ~; *TS*
317:38 Now *MS*, *Per2*] ~, *Per1*
317:38 young *MS*, *Per2*] ~, *Per1*
318:1 amusement *MS*, *Per1*] Amusement *TS*, *Per2*
318:2 course *MS*, *Per2*] ~, *Per1*
318:4 angel face] angel-face *TS*
318:4 game,] ~; *TS*
318:5 man's] men's *TS*
318:8 pet! —] ~! *TS*
318:14 horse hair] horsehair *TS*

318:18 Peters *MS*, *Per2*] ~, *Per1*
318:19 on *MS*, *Per2*] ~, *Per1*
318:20 the young *Per1*] young *MS*
318:21 cocktail-shaker *MS*, *Per2*] ~, *Per1*
318:28 something *MS*, *Per2*] ~, *Per1*
318:33 something is *MS*, *Per2*] ~, ~ *Per1*
318:35 emphatically:] ~; *TS*
319:34 women] woman *TS*

APPENDIX II

Do Women Change?

The *Vanity Fair* text appears within the brackets, the *Sunday Dispatch* outside.

329:4 But it] It
329:4 bosh. We] ~. *P* We
329:5 But don't we] We
329:5 ourselves?] ~.
329:7 distinction. But] ~. *P* But
329:8 any, from] any, it seems to me, from
329:9 Jordan,] ~
329:14 Ruths] ~,
329:15 as there were] the same as
329:15 yesterdays. Circumstances] ~. *P* Circumstances
329:19 Atlantis. And] ~, and
329:20 alike. All] ~. *P* All
329:22 And they] They
329:26 apart] in the void
329:29 themselves. They] ~. *P* They
329:32 them,] ~
329:32 different] very different
329:33 wife. Women] ~. *P* Women
330:2 our] the
330:4 I saw . . . [330:9] But] When the young woman of to-day tells her romantically inclined lover to "cut it out" when he talks to her about the stars, the moonlight, and the restless ocean, that is supposed to be very, very modern. *P* But
330:10 Capri] ~,
330:10 Tiberius] Tiberias
330:10 Never mind that nonsense!] *Cut it out!*
330:11 lovers,] ~
330:12 time. Certain] ~. *P* Certain
330:16 never . . . nonsense] *cut-it-out*
330:17 Only . . . differently.] *Om.*
330:22 never . . . nonsense] cut-it-out
330:22 pretty . . . they] as they jolly well
330:25 money:] ~;
330:25 her,] ~
330:26 never mind . . . minds the] cut it out, boy!" — So the boy cuts it out — all the
330:28 stuff. — [330:39] No,] stuff — till there's nothing left to cut out. *P* Then the thoroughly modern girl begins to moan: "Oh, boy, do put back the romance!" *P* No,
330:40 slave: . . . helpmeet: . . . spouse: . . . matron: . . . citizen: . . . female:] ~; . . . ~; . . . ~; . . . ~; . . . ~; . . . ~;
331:2 never-mind-it girl.] modern girl (Oh, cut-it-out, boy!)
331:3 her . . . God] the boy has cut it all out, the mills of the gods
331:4 having . . . [331:9] And the] the whole cycle starts afresh, till in the course of a thousand years or two we come once more to a really "modern" girl. *P* The
331:13 business. So] ~. *P* So
331:15 continues,] ~
331:16 solitude] ~,
331:16 bouquet] bunch
331:16 flowers] violets
331:17 and dwindles] *Om.*
331:17 feelings,] ~

331:18 nothing. And not] ~. *P* Not
331:19 (except . . . irritant)] *Om.*
331:21 out, completely. For] out. *P* For,
331:25 consciousness,] ~
331:26 be. She] ~. *P* She
331:29 complete . . . she] ~. She
331:30 For the] The
331:33 time,] ~
331:34 nothing; or] ~. *P* Or
331:37 her. And this] ~. *P* This
331:37 time,] ~
331:40 bouquet of flowers] bunch of violets
332:1 For after] After
332:4 flattery. A] ~. *P* A
332:10 him. The] ~. *P* The
332:12 hold.] hold over that man, and the more real she becomes to her self.
332:13 lesson,] ~
332:15 ocean,] ~
332:15 boy,] ~, just because she did not think the stars and ocean near enough to her own precious person,
332:15 ocean,] ~
332:17 nonentity.] ~. *P* By forcing immediate attention on herself, by forcing the man to come to the point — the point being *herself*, of course, she has just brought about her own nonentity.
332:18 the cycle . . . again] to go back on her traces

Line-end hyphenation

Of the compound words which are hyphenated at the end of a line in this edition, only the following hyphenated forms should be retained in quotation:

9:20	116:3	223:32
10:31	120:7	227:33
30:26	125:31	228:35
35:29	134:24	230:24
36:20	146:13	237:31
38:4	148:17	238:22
39:3	164:12	238:30
39:15	180:3	242:8
39:33	183:27	247:20
44:17	186:7	250:20
47:5	189:26	250:27
48:7	191:20	252:31
51:24	191:25	253:24
57:8	194:14	262:8
62:20	195:12	268:12
71:17	198:15	271:39
77:33	200:20	288:38
79:18	209:38	289:6
87:24	211:6	293:16
96:13	212:36	306:15
105:17	214:9	308:21
108:14	214:34	314:13
113:20	221:31	

A note on pounds, shillings and pence

Before decimalisation in 1971, the pound sterling (£) was the equivalent of 20 shillings (20/– or 20s). The shilling was the equivalent of 12 pence (12d). A price could therefore have three elements: pounds, shillings and pence (£, s, d). (The apparently anomalous 'd' is an abbreviation of the Latin *denarius*, but the other two terms were also originally Latin: the pound was *libra*; the shilling *solidus*.) Such a price might be written as £1 2s 6d or £1/2/6; this was spoken as 'one pound, two shillings and sixpence', or 'one pound two-and-six', or 'twenty-two and six'.

Prices below a pound were written (for example) as 19s 6d, or 19/6, and spoken as 'nineteen shillings and sixpence' or 'nineteen and six'. Prices up to £5 were sometimes spoken in terms of shillings: so 'ninety-nine and six' was £4/19/6.

The penny was divided into two half-pence (pronounced 'ha'pence') and further divided into four farthings, but the farthing had minimal value and was mainly a tradesman's device for indicating a price fractionally below a shilling or pound. So 19/11$\frac{3}{4}$ (nineteen and elevenpence three farthings) produced a farthing's change from a pound, this change sometimes given as a tiny item of trade, such as a packet of pins.

The guinea was £1/1/- (one pound, one shilling) and was a professional man's unit for fees. A doctor would charge in guineas (so £5/5/-= 5 gns). Half a guinea was 10s 6d or 10/6 (ten and six).

The coins used were originally of silver (later cupro-nickel) and copper, though gold coins for £1 (a sovereign) and 10s (half-sovereign) were still in use in Lawrence's time. The largest 'silver' coin in common use was the half-crown (two shillings and sixpence, or 2/6). A two-shilling piece was called a florin. Shillings, sixpences and threepences were the smaller sizes. The copper coins were pennies, half-pence and farthings.

Common everyday terms for money were 'quid' for a pound 'half a crown', 'two bob' for a florin, 'bob' for a shilling (or shilling piece), 'tanner' for a sixpence (or sixpenny piece), 'threepenny-bit' (pronounced 'thripenny-bit'), and 'coppers' for pennies, half-pence or farthings.